EARLY MODERN PRINT MEDIA AND THE ART OF OBSERVATION

Early modern printmakers trained observers to scan the heavens above as well as faces in their midst. Peter Apian printed the *Cosmographicus Liber* (1524) to teach lay astronomers their place in the cosmos, while also printing practical manuals that translated principles of spherical astronomy into useful data for weather watchers, farmers, and astrologers. Physiognomy, a genre related to cosmography, taught observers how to scrutinize profiles in order to sum up people's characters. Neither Albrecht Dürer nor Leonardo da Vinci escaped the tenacious grasp of such widely circulating manuals called *Practica*. Few have heard of these genres today, but the kinship of their pictorial programs suggests that printers shaped these texts for readers who privileged knowledge retrieval. Cultivated by images to become visual learners, these readers were then taught to hone their skills as observers. This book unpacks these and other visual strategies that aimed to develop both the literate eye of the reader and the sovereignty of images in the early modern world.

A specialist of early modern printmaking, Stephanie Leitch received a collaborative research fellowship from the ACLS for a new project about the role of copied images in early modern travel narratives. Her book *Mapping Ethnography in Early Modern Germany* (2010) won the Roland Bainton Book Prize in Art History.

EARLY MODERN PRINT MEDIA AND THE ART OF OBSERVATION

TRAINING THE LITERATE EYE

STEPHANIE A. LEITCH
Florida State University

CAMBRIDGE
UNIVERSITY PRESS

CAMBRIDGE
UNIVERSITY PRESS

Shaftesbury Road, Cambridge CB2 8EA, United Kingdom

One Liberty Plaza, 20th Floor, New York, NY 10006, USA

477 Williamstown Road, Port Melbourne, VIC 3207, Australia

314–321, 3rd Floor, Plot 3, Splendor Forum, Jasola District Centre, New Delhi – 110025, India

103 Penang Road, #05–06/07, Visioncrest Commercial, Singapore 238467

Cambridge University Press is part of Cambridge University Press & Assessment, a department of the University of Cambridge.

We share the University's mission to contribute to society through the pursuit of education, learning and research at the highest international levels of excellence.

www.cambridge.org
Information on this title: www.cambridge.org/9781009444521

DOI: 10.1017/9781009444491

First published 2024

Printed in the United Kingdom by CPI Group Ltd, Croydon CR0 4YY

A catalogue record for this publication is available from the British Library

A Cataloging-in-Publication data record for this book is available from the Library of Congress

ISBN 978-1-009-44452-1 Hardback

For Astrid, may the stars hold ample secrets for you

CONTENTS

The plates will be found between pages 258 and 259.

ACKNOWLEDGMENTS

One February evening during the passing of the evasive "green comet," my child tells me that this is the day that no one is born. Deep into my project about the connection between the stars and printed books, it was heartening to hear echoes of the early moderns alive and well in my kitchen. While few of us scan the heavens on a daily basis, the moment a lurid comet sweeps across the sky, the amateur observers come out in force. Unfamiliarity with the stars today perhaps arises from not knowing what to look *for* when we look up. After all, the constellations never appear quite the way the cartographers of the heavens have pictured them. And light pollution today is complicit in knocking out most of the stars that early moderns used to connect the dots of Leo.

Peter Apian, a printer at the heart of this study, keenly sensed that celestial uncertainty was what prevented most people of his day from scanning the sky. So he produced the *Cosmographicus Liber*, a book that could teach audiences to read the starry vault from the sublunar world. While he was shaping this into a book of printed instruments the amateur stargazer could use, he dispensed this same knowledge in the form of shorter pamphlets that made general predictions for astronomical events of the year. These so-called *Practica* had practical applications and were very much like the *Old Farmer's Almanacs* that now gather dust at the checkout at Lowe's. In a manual and a related publication on the comet of 1532, Apian used the word "observation" to describe his sightings and he encouraged his readers to look for themselves. For quarter-moon viewings, a group of local astronomers assembles in Tallahassee's Cascades Park with telescopes, rushing in after the skies have cleared, hoping to catch a glimpse of the moon, the stars, or other bodies on the ecliptic. Without them and their venerable ancestors whom Apian addressed in his book, this knowledge would remain locked away in university or monastery libraries.

Still, without these libraries, I could not have written this book. Chicago's Newberry Library has been my giving tree, a trove of not just primary sources but also rich resources of homegrown professionals in the scholars Suzanne Karr Schmidt, Lia Markey, and Paul Gehl. I am grateful for the many platforms where I have admired the panache and brilliance of my colleagues Walter Melion, Lee Palmer Wandel, Tom Conley, Claire Farago, Bronwen Wilson,

Dana Katz, Sachiko Kusukawa, Alexander Marr, Daniela Bleichmar, and Pamela Smith. Jeffrey Chipps Smith, Larry Silver, Tom DaCosta Kauffmann, and Hans-Jörg Künast have all given me very large shoes to fill. For a wonderful semester in 2014 when I was able to work in the sunken garden and villa of the Max Planck Institute for the History of Science (MPIWG) in Berlin, I owe wholehearted thanks to Sven Dupré and Lorraine Daston. For a memorable introduction to Krakow, I am grateful to Michał Kurzej; for help at the Jagiellonian Library, my thanks to Izabela Korczyńska.

For the many seasons I have been able to call the Herzog August Bibliothek in Wolfenbüttel my summer home, I am thankful to Jill Bepler, Elizabeth Harding, Volker Bauer, Gerlinde Strauss, and Peter Burschel. I'm nostalgic for the time when the guest houses of the Friends of the Herzog August Bibliothek were still available to researchers. In those halcyon days, my regular companions were Mara Wade, Gerhild Scholz Williams, Cornelia Niekus Moore, Bob and Pauline Kolb, Peter Hess, Ulrich and Birgit Kopp, Britta-Juliane Kruse, Valentina Sebastiani, Andreas Uhr, and Beth Plummer. I'm grateful for the affable assistance of Heike Kirschstein and the staff at the Zeughaus. For making Wolfenbüttel home, I'm grateful to Shirin Zangeneh, Mimi and Uwe Mohrmann, Monika and Andreas Müller, Yvonne and Jens Kalweit, and all their wonderful kids, as well as for the cooperation of the staff and teachers at the Grundschule Karlstrasse and the Gymnasium im Schloss. I'm grateful to my colleagues who have been ready with offers to peruse drafts and answer questions; chief among them are Lisa Voigt, Joost Depuydt, Lieven Verbrugge, Thomas Schauerte, Karin Leonhard, Barbara Tramelli, Volker Remmert, Livia Cárdenas, Michael S. Korey, Stephanie Porras, Ruth Noyes, Evelyn Lincoln, Ashley West, Christopher Wood, Surekha Davies, Elio Brancaforte, and the formidable Charlotte Lang Brancaforte. I'm very grateful to the staff of the University Library in Erlangen, especially for the prompt offers of help from Tamara Lust. Michele Ferrari was gracious enough to let me trot out some ideas at a conference in Erlangen in the summer of 2022, "Die Welt im Bild. Bildenzyklopädien um 1500." Manuel Teget-Weltz, Johanna Wittstatt, and my fellow participants at the conference provided an insightful audience for some of these ideas.

My colleagues in the Department of Art History at Florida State University keep me on my toes and frequently raise my spirits; I'm grateful for the guidance and support of Adam Jolles and Lorenzo Pericolo. Thanks for the cheerful assistance of Sheri Patton, Jean Hudson, Emily Johnson, Thomas Jones, and Pavel Protsyuk. Indispensable colleagues across the campus are François Dupuigrenet-Desrousilles, Gary Taylor, Anne E. B. Coldiron, Dana Weber, Christian Weber, Maximilian Scholz, Aimee Boutin, Peggy Wright-Cleveland, and Jennifer Buchanan. I have deep gratitude for the students and young scholars with whom I have crossed paths and who continue to nourish me with their expertise and provoke me with new challenges, especially Carolina Alarcón, Britt Boler Hunter, Taylor Clement, Jennifer Baez, Chase van Tilburg, Alexandra Challenger, Lacy Gillette, Rachel Carlisle, Nina Gozalbez, Emily White, Allison Marino, and Raigen Sumrall.

I am grateful for the guidance of my editor at Cambridge University Press, Beatrice Rehl, as well as Edgar Mendez, and I offer warm thanks for the generous feedback from the press's external readers. They helped shape this text into a vastly better book. I am grateful to my copy-editor Judith Forshaw for her sharp eyes and prudent suggestions. This book has received the Weiss-Brown Publication Subvention Award from the Newberry Library. This award, which commemorates the career of Howard Mayer Brown, supports the publication of outstanding works of scholarship that cover European civilization before 1700 in the areas of music, theatre, French or Italian literature, or cultural studies.

Funding for images and license fees was graciously provided by Dean James Frazier and the College of Fine Arts at Florida State University. I am grateful for the speedy assistance of Sally McRorie and Shelby Heitmueller and their help in the push to the endzone. For promptly answering summons to help me prepare images for this text, I am thankful for the help of Jean Hudson and Carlos Ortiz Burgos. Raigen Sumrall provided text, image, and sanity checks. DeWayne Carver of the Tallahassee Astronomical Society has generously and patiently schooled me in the stars. In addition to revising my view of the starry vault, DeWayne also plotted corrections on the page; I am fortunate to benefit from his prodigious editorial chops.

I am thankful for my family: Roswitha, Art, and Erik Leitch. Their support over the years has been tremendous and unstinting, notwithstanding the occasional eye-rolling. My circle of supporters, who have cheerfully tolerated sudden appearances and research-induced absences, is larger than I deserve: Ria and Heinz Leute, Hans and Corma Vandermark, Paul Vandermark, Karin Prent, Onno Vandermark, and especially my big-hearted family in Berlin – Erik and Claartje Vandermark, Joris, Lieke, and Femke. For everything else stateside, I'm grateful to Antonio Terraciano, Gina Sutin, Beth Alexander, Jane McAdams, Mary Lincer, Lena McLane, Denise Bookwalter, Volker Crede, Eric Bouchard, Bettina Teson, Tim Lynch, and Régine Maligne. Jim, Heather, and Anna Wilgenbusch provided unmatched hospitality and cheer during a cold month and succor during indexing. Chief among my supporters is Astrid, to whom I dedicate this book. For tacitly understanding why I need to chase footnotes wherever they need tracking down, thank you. I'm grateful for your high spirits during Lessing Haus stays, involuntary immersion in German, *Krambuden* charades, desserts at dawn, and sketching expeditions. Thank you for these and for so many other adventures. Your observations will always enrich my own.

ONE

INTRODUCTION

Learning to Look with Books for the Literate Eye

In the early sixteenth century, images in printed books began to target a new intelligence agent: the literate eye. This eye became the focus of repeated encounters with images that aspired to a range of purposes, including cognitive prompts, memory devices, and instructions for performing specific tasks. The way these pictures began to confront the viewer sparks a reconsideration of the genres in which they were embedded, such as popular astrology or cosmology, as examples of popular science in which eyewitness authority was often constituted by texts but cemented by images. Images in books crystallized knowledge domains; one of the ways in which they did so was by demanding visual attention. This project inspects how sixteenth-century viewing practices were organized around pictures.

The eye was both magnetized by images and also appears in them, especially those in which thinking and seeing came together. The eye that the Ingolstadt mathematician Peter Apian planted at the base of the tandem terrestrial and celestial spheres (Figure 1.1) in his *Cosmographicus Liber* (1524) performs a physically impossible act: it must see "through" the earth to the celestial realm. The eye summoned by sixteenth-century prints was sometimes a literal eye and sometimes a thinking eye. Apian's eye is both: it sees past the earth and makes visual judgments about the heavens. Apian aimed to show viewers what they saw, but he also wanted to illustrate the theoretical principles that undergirded what the observer was seeing. This "literate" eye both observed and performed other cognitive acts. The stagings of such relationships in

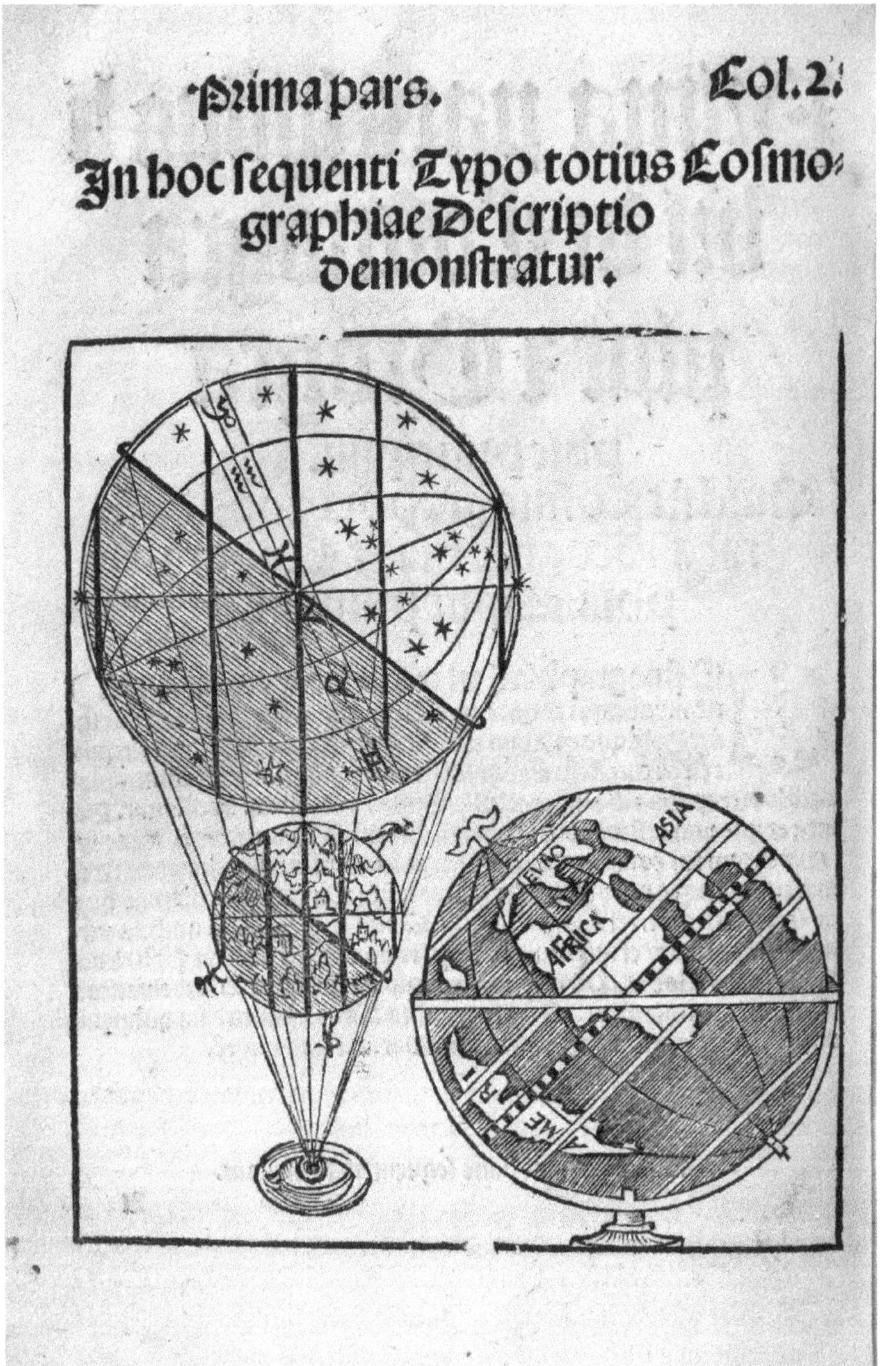

1.1. Peter Apian, *Cosmographicus Liber* (Landshut: Weyssenburger, 1524), fol. 2. *Source:* Zentralbibliothek Zürich, NR 870. Courtesy of ETH-Bibliothek Zürich.

complex multilevel diagrams became integral to his developing scientific program, but the existing print infrastructure was inadequate to the task of producing these diagrams. Apian set out to build his own printing press to accommodate the pictorial complexities he envisioned for future volumes.

Firmly committed to the didactic properties of images, Peter Apian mobilized different types of pictures throughout a cosmographic text he published in 1524 to promote the merits of visualized thinking. Apian set out to instruct the reader that cognition must be routed through the visual field. Providing a cheat sheet for harder to grasp abstractions of cosmography, Apian chose a method of visual knowing with which he assumed his readers would be more familiar. With a diagram of an ear and an eye, Apian ingeniously linked the concept of cosmography to a genre already constituted as visually knowable: portraiture. This diagram helped viewers recall which mental images to conjure when contemplating complex concepts. The equation of a face with the representation of the terrestrial sphere that Apian announces with this image (Figure 1.2) shows cosmography to be a visual pursuit that can be likened to portraiture and explains them as kindred epistemic pursuits. Although each image reflected distinct modes of knowing the world, they were similar in that they could best be communicated by pictures. This book breaks down this metaphor into its component parts and asks how the subject matter of cosmography and faces, as well as other popular genres aimed at knowledge acquisition, began to shape the visual aptitude of vernacular viewers.

Illustrated books alerted the eye to a new consciousness in the early sixteenth century. Self-confident agents of learning, these heuristic tools aimed to help navigate the viewer's visual horizons. While expectations of viewers' visual sophistication are clear from Renaissance paintings, we tend not to think of books of the period as having a well-developed visual language.[1] But among the earliest printed books were ones in which illustrations were so integral that they were carved into the same block as the text. The first generation of books printed in northern Europe included just such instructional block books, which taught readers how to preach, how to live well, and how to die honorably, as well as warning about the perils of the apocalypse.[2] Advice for achieving salvation was delivered by pictorialized self-help books in which illustrations were the driving force. Even though these xylographic books (books with words and images cut into the same block) may seem unlikely ancestors of the technical books that are the subject of this study, they were similar in that their illustrations presume the reader as a user. In focusing on the visual epistemology of early printed books, this book argues that such manuals were usable tools that prompted empirical investigations. While manuscripts had delivered elements of the classical tradition through ancient texts, the how-to manuals of the sixteenth century marketed themselves as concise agents of visual data delivery.

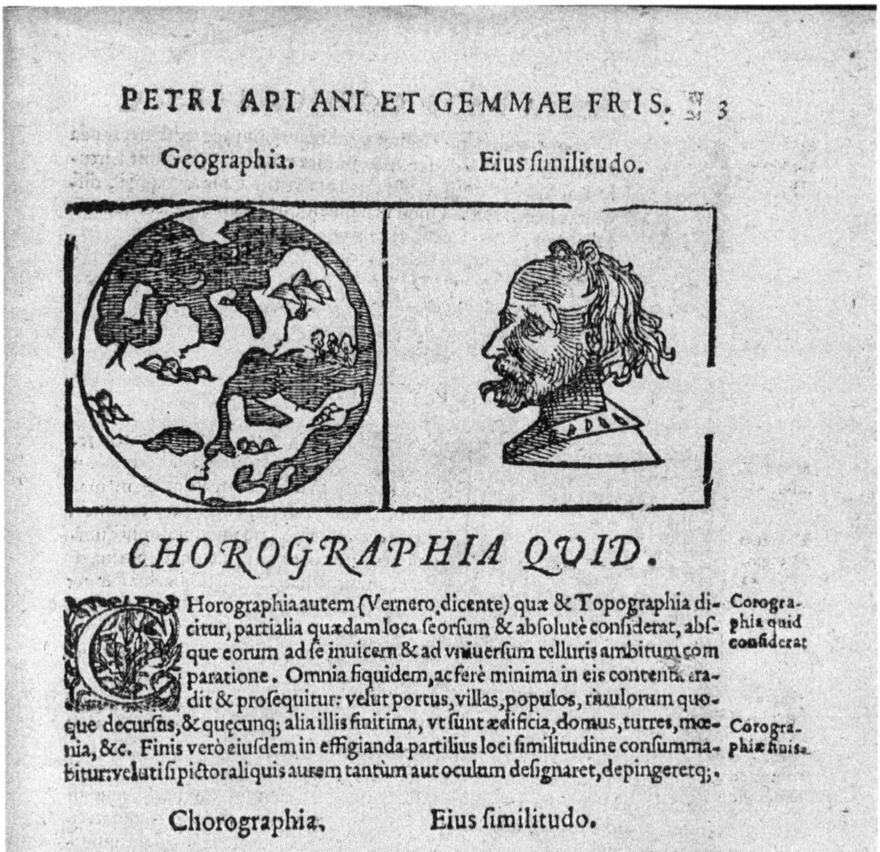

1.2. Peter Apian and Rainer Gemma Frisius, *Cosmographia, siue Descriptio vniuersi orbis* (Antwerp: Withagen, 1584). *Source:* Vault GA6.A55. Florida State University Special Collections and Archives.

Theories of representation emerged from these new printed books and their images became the locus around which practical knowledge collected. The history of early printed books largely neglected images, instead narrating their technical achievement in terms of how many lines of movable type a page could offer (forty-two lines, in the case of the *Gutenberg Bible*).[3] While this bibliographic focus on text reminds us that many first-generation technical books were not illustrated, in a very short time, from 1510 to the 1540s, the pamphlets printed in German-speaking lands gave way to graphic layouts that were designed around illustrations. These books still accommodated text but their pedagogical intent was delivered with visual formatting in mind. If, in the past, text had chaperoned the images, images now became the codicological units *par excellence* and were the eyecatchers around which books were organized. In a mad rush to illustrate, publishers of complexion books, shepherds' calendars, and farmers' almanacs included arguably many more illustrations than their contents actually required. Calendars and almanacs were record keepers for wide usage and often covered a range of materials; they were mostly compilations of how-to knowledge, extending from *The Art of a Good Life and a Good Death* to collections of helpful shepherds' lore or instructions for farmers (*Bauern Practica*), from descriptions of purgatory to mnemonics to help the reader remember the Ten Commandments.[4] Calendar books printed with blank fields encouraged readers to pencil in activities as to-do lists.[5] Consultation of such visualized books, I argue, armed the viewer with new epistemic potential. Such books equipped vernacular viewers with skills to scan and scrutinize.

Early modern readers consulted printed schedules for lunar conjunctions before planting crops and cued the changing of bed linens to the stars' alignment; meanwhile, amateur observers were scrutinizing the firmament to figure out the time at night. Books taught merchants to gauge volumes of solids via instructive diagrams and formulas that could help them assess values in foreign markets. Another book tried to help readers identify potential scoundrels based on their profiles. Books featuring the palm of the hand engraved with lines (chiromancies) tried to help an employer assess the potential loyalty of an itinerant worker. Some of the information was culled from a number of older genres, such as Pliny's *Natural History*, Konrad von Megenberg's *Buch der Natur*, and the pseudo-Aristotelian *Secretum Secretorum*, but, in their new formats, this information was presented as visual data. Savvy printers such as Johannes Schott in Strasbourg, Sigmund Feyerabend in Frankfurt, and Walter Ryff and Levinus Hulsius in Nuremberg saw the value of repackaging information into pamphlets that were easier to consult. Publishers marketing these diverse genres as handbooks presented a united front that encouraged new audiences to engage interactively with their surroundings. The key to that engagement was the faculty of sight.

This book argues that the visual program of certain early printed books mandated a systematic visual engagement with the world. We might think of the manuals and pamphlets under review here as the root genealogy of books available today for purchase in hardware and drug stores: astronomy manuals, astrology charts, travel guides, and how-to manuals on a host of esoteric topics. They all share a desire to instruct and most of them place a premium on delivering and organizing that information visually. Some books advocated memorization, others delivered information about the care of horses and the types of bit a blacksmith could forge to control them, or they collected motifs for fancy headdresses and furniture designs. Other books offered sections of map gores, which, when cut along dotted lines, could be assembled into personal globes. Music amateurs could purchase instructional volumes that showed the correct finger placements for playing a recorder.

We cannot assume transparency or ease in the process of teaching the average early modern amateur scientific practitioner new skills: the lack of proper instructions on how to operate a rudimentary telescope sent by Galileo to his brother at the Wittelsbach court in 1611 left at least one hapless viewer very confused.[6] In a letter describing the event to Galileo, his brother ridiculed the observer's ineptitude as he peered through the wrong end of this hastily assembled telescope. While this clumsy observer was called out in the letter, those of us who hang our heads before complex online instructional tutorials might have more sympathy for the unfortunate chap. We tend to assume that knowing how to properly observe was an endowment of nature, not nurture. But according to the productions of the early modern corner presses, pinpointing where and how to look was indeed a learnable, and marketable, skill.

Of the many genres that were emerging in that market, two were especially insistent about their function as heuristics on the path to making visual judgments: physiognomy and cosmography. Indeed, these two genres were already related through their common origin in judicial astrology. Predictive astrology was the practical outcome of the training of physicians and mathematicians, whose skill sets merged theories of humoral balances with the complex mathematics required to draw horoscopes. The outcomes of astrological observations were made manifest in the many pamphlets marketed as usable knowledge called *Practica*, calendars, and horoscopes. The planets were thought to exert influence on a person's complexion, and if their trajectories were properly tracked, their positions could also render predictions and useful assessments about patients' health. The mathematical foundations of astrology turned planetary positions into complex problem sets that aided physicians and geomancers in determining humoral diagnoses. The printing environment for predictive astrology was served by trained mathematicians who simultaneously drafted horoscopes for courtly patrons and churned out pulp astrology for wider audiences. Eventually, an ecology of urban printers channeled academic astrology into printed manuals for new publics of cosmographic practitioners whose eyes were schooled by cosmographies, geomancies, physiognomies, and complexion books.[7]

Cosmography and physiognomy find their common inspiration in predictive astrology. Unlike the modern tendency to separate the aims of astronomy from astrology, the array of publications about data drawn from the stars indicates that neither publishers nor readers found those two fields at cross purposes; on the contrary, they functioned symbiotically. In fact, Apian's day job printing prognostications under the title *Practica* was perhaps the most lucrative arm of his press. Apian's understanding of the stars fed both his scholarly preoccupations, and there is nothing to suggest that he privileged one over the other. Both genres aimed to unpack and systematize the knowledge he was seeking in the heavens.

The authors of such *Practica* observed the stars in order to link planetary and lunar movements to vernacular practices in the form of seasonal recommendations. This updated the doctrine of signs from Aristotelian material into more practical concerns: such information circulated for the purposes of weather watching and scheduling seasonal activities. Scanning the heavens closely at night, the day job of most celestial observers was to predict and schedule the occurrence of lunar eclipses for the public and to turn their observations into predictions and prognostications.[8] While the modern reader tends to consider the purview of astronomy as discrete from astrology, most early modern astronomers were unapologetic about the predictive origins of their trade. Johannes Kepler acknowledged that the astronomy of his era rested on the shoulders of astrologers scanning the sky for practical advice.[9] The symbiotic nature of the relationship of the two genres was made manifest in their shared iconography. For example, the precise schedule of lunar eclipses provided in Regiomontanus's *Kalendaria* (1532) closely resembles that which appeared in Apian's *Cosmographicus Liber*, a cosmographic manual of the sort that was transitioning from theoretical material to more practical concerns. Eclipses and comets were important events in calendars and *Practica*, linked to omens and prognostications.[10] Calendars and almanacs charted activities of both universal and particular relevance, ranging from the predicting of collective disasters (such as floods and plagues) to the scheduling of personal hygiene and health practices.[11] A typical passage in such a publication recommends restricting bathing and cupping to specific intervals in the lunar cycle, when a waning moon appeared in particular star signs.[12] As early as the 1480s, printed almanacs and calendars promoted regimens for scheduling bloodletting and baths. Image programs that included content such as a practitioner setting cups on a patient served as mnemonics for what activities to undertake during that part of the month.[13]

Sometimes it was the printer who cemented the connection of one sphere of study (astronomy) to another sphere of influence (medicinal care of the body). Jacob Cammerlander, the printer of the *Kalendarius* of Johannes Müller von Königsberg (called Regiomontanus after 1534), specifically geared astronomical information toward readers who used calendars for scheduling health regimens; the preface tightens still further the connection between astronomy and medicine. Many such manuals were printed in Strasbourg, where presses producing books on field surgery provided medical information for a market not driven by the needs of an academic institutional presence – a university would not appear in the city until approximately 1621.[14] Until that time, Strasbourg printers (as well as those in other towns such as Augsburg and Nuremberg) supplied knowledge largely to a vernacular public, and this public played a significant role in shaping publishers' lists. Robin Barnes's *Astrology and Reformation* outlines the prodigious trade in printing astrological literature in the urban centers of the Holy Roman Empire.[15] Vernacular publications are among the best extant sources we have of how craft-based professions were organized; in fact, the publications themselves did prodigious structural work for certain trades. Field surgeons, for instance, were grouped into guilds with barbers by virtue of the common tools that they used. Their instructional manuals were organized according to practical concerns and they helped match battle-induced wounds to the specific tools required for their treatment. *Practica* also articulated relationships between related modes of empirical learning; publishers were often the ones to forge these ties.[16]

Astronomy's connection to medicine is cemented in the title page of Regiomontanus's *Kalendarius*: "a pleasant comparison of astronomy with medicine/ [which asserts that] a successful Doctor must also be a skilled Astronomer."[17] This particular section of *Kalendarius* linked health regimens to the movement of the stars. The tracking of stars was related to other types of systematic visual investigations performed by physicians, such as evaluating urine samples.[18] Both types of analysis called for the observation of specific details and even comparative cross-referencing. Such manuals placed expectations of daily observations on the shoulders of amateur observers and vernacular readers. Physicians were expected to keep their eyes trained on the movements of celestial bodies through the constellations as well as on patients' humoral complexion.[19]

Early modern astronomy and astrology were locked in a symbiotic bind. The day job of an astrologer required the rigorous training of astronomy. Horoscopes commissioned by powerful patrons depended on correct predictions; these show the related pursuits of astrology and its handmaiden, astronomy.[20] Astronomy's tracking of movements in the heavens was the basis of the very practical concerns of judicial astrology. Perhaps the already close connection between astronomy and practical astrology in this period grew tighter as astronomers and mathematicians took the helm of some early modern print shops.[21] Both astronomy and astrology were underwritten by firsthand practice, and printers parlayed related skill sets into a wide array of visually profuse genres that would guide future empirical activity.

In these new urban environments arose the twin genres of physiognomy and cosmography. Physiognomic texts can be thought of as guides to navigating a landscape of people, taking the generic data of faces and repackaging it into novel informational formats. Unlike the taxonomy of peoples that would manifest itself in costume books, the physiognomy book was for people watching, a manual that could help levy judgments about neighbors via the close inspection of their features. Physiognomy's collection of character heads presented tools for a practical science that developed around pictures. That many of these illustrated faces were shown in profile should not surprise us: Profiles best reflected the mountains and valleys of the face, the important data points of portraits. The heightened scrutiny that profiles received as a result of these manuals can be mapped onto the new forms of cosmography that likewise encouraged viewers to scan surfaces and volumes, such as the horizon or the heavens. Cosmography was a synthetic science that merged many individual observations. Apian's book tried to reconstruct that process by showing explicitly how to make those observations. In a study of the stimulus to cognition instigated by Apian, one group of book historians invoke these visualized genres in their description of the book itself. They describe the book's morphology as its "physiognomy," while their approach to it capaciousness as a whole work is presented as a measure of its "cosmography."[22] It is perhaps therefore auspicious that we consider here how the book constituted and facilitated physiognomic and cosmographic investigations.

TRAINING THE EYE

Prints made their readers look with rapt attention at things, some of which had always been fixtures on people's horizons, such as the stars, the moon, and rises and dips in the land's topography. But unique among illustrated books was the method they prescribed to take in that information via an appeal to the senses. Note, for example, Campanus of Novara's *Theorica Planetarum*'s goal of providing instructions for constructing rotating planetary models: "they may be able to see with their eyes by an instrument which is perceptible to the senses."[23] One thing that books suggested viewers do was to scrutinize in ways that other media did not. Prints of the sixteenth century invited new subjects for viewing as they solicited unfamiliar viewing practices. Some of these subjects were consonant with a newly activated viewer.

That the practice of sight was construed now as subject, rather than as object, can be seen clearly in the shift in visual interest in the eye. Gregor Reisch's *Margarita Philosophica* presented a diagram of the eye from a frontal view as well as a cross-section that showed it like an onion with the layers that comprised it.[24] The image of a passive eye included in Reisch's text is embedded in a discussion of light and the optical power of the organ of the sensing soul. A theoretical discussion of optics as a multiplication of species precedes the depicted eye; these discussions also sometimes pull in luminous bodies, such as the sun and moon, to explain light and shadow, and darkness as the absence of light.[25] Reisch's eye is a passive receptor, a theoretical model in the domain of natural philosophy.

By contrast, the eye presented in the *Cosmographicus Liber* was a sensing, judging, and literate eye. Apian's illustration at folio 11 marshaled the reader's eye to participate in an active proof: in order to infer the shape of the earth, an observer was compelled to track the change of the shadow of the earth on the moon's surface during an eclipse. Even readers familiar with basic astronomy had never been ordered to scrutinize the moon so closely, let alone made to believe that their observations could verify such proof. Apian insists that seeing is the key to understanding. We could say that a similar scrutiny of a full moon activated the viewer of the back of the Farnese Hercules, engraved by Hendrik Goltzius in 1595 (Figure 1.3). Walter Melion explores Goltzius's engraving at the intersection of observation, cognition, and *handelingh*, or rendering as an executive skill.[26] In the latter, Goltzius's technical virtuosity made advanced claims for how printmaking could visualize observable objects, not just in the pattern of overlain hatched lines, but also in the way in which he conceptualized the process of observation. The print's viewer joins the pictured audience as a fellow onlooker. After exploring the intricate cross-hatched netting of Hercules's gluteal muscles, the beholder is also encouraged to muse on the prospect enjoyed by the pictured observers. Multiplying the angles of eyewitnessing, Goltzius pushes the viewer into reluctant voyeurism. The fine *moiré* pattern that shapes Hercules's rear established a syntax for engraving that diverted attention from the subject matter to the technique itself as another site of optical interest. This graphic feast pointed back to the act of observation itself; for Melion, the fine lines of Goltzius's prints "represent the cognitive act of knowing the world through the agency of attentive sight."[27] It was the intense web of lines, the *handelingh* of these aesthetic threads as an extension of Goltzius's burin hand, that commanded the viewer's aroused stare. By the end of the sixteenth century, such self-aware viewing was increasingly in demand.

This book unpacks the journey of the kind of close looking that Goltzius both expected and exposed. The history of our seeing as a materialized act that can be represented takes as an arguable start date the moment when artists posited the picture plane as an extension of the viewer's space. This was ushered in by Florentine architectural theorist Alberti's suggestion to artists that they use a *velo* or a gridded-off perspective screen as a trick of the trade, a crutch with which they might capture the view beyond the screen in the same way that a prospect might appear to an observer. In this conceit, the artist

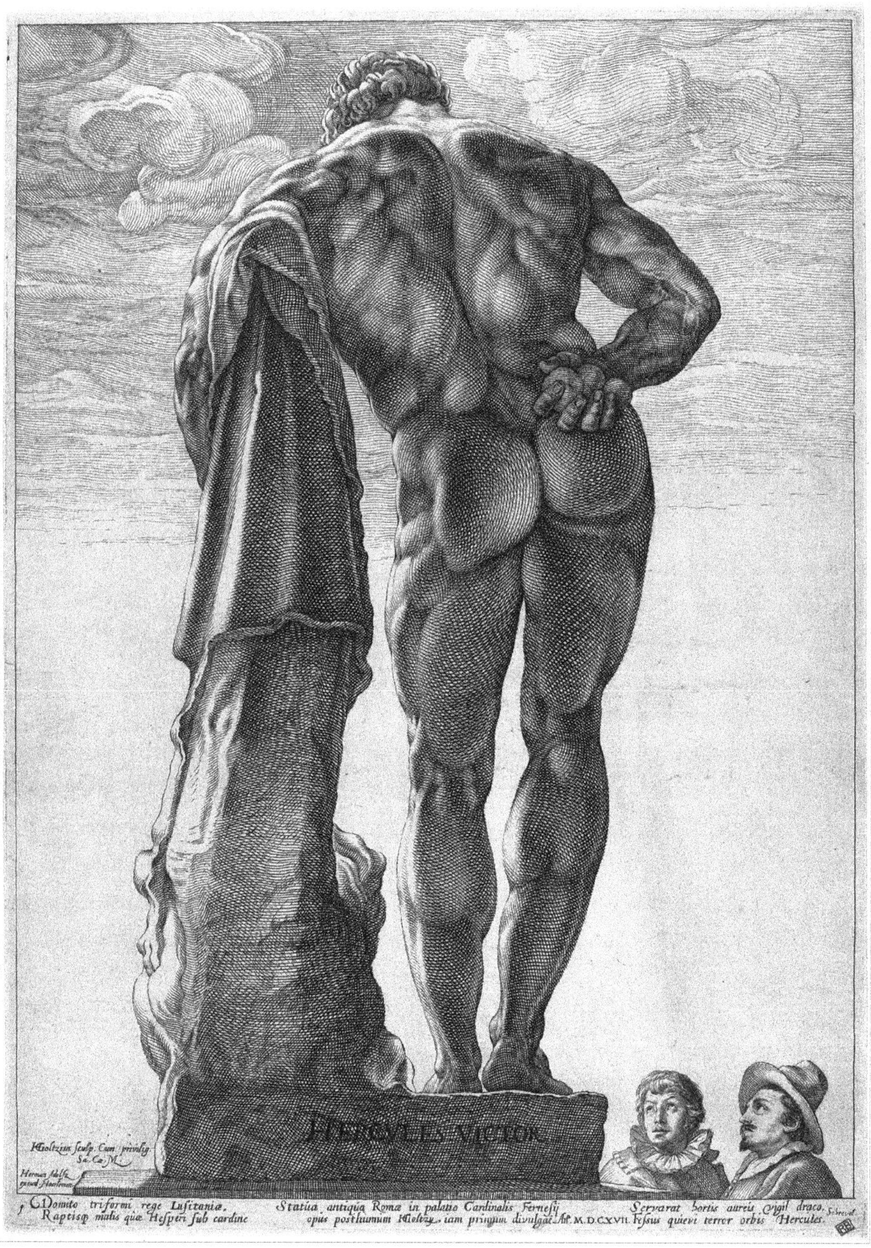

1.3. Hendrick Goltzius, *Farnese Hercules*, engraving, 1592. *Source:* Metropolitan Museum of Art.

posited himself as the director of that view. Painting in the centuries following the Renaissance represents a concretization of the format of the picture plane as a window, a historical model of spatialized vision that retained a stranglehold in the Western tradition until experiments in abstraction took over in the artistic experimentation of the early twentieth century. Privileging the exigencies of vision and optical art made Renaissance pictorial conceits seem naturalized to future generations. In an important article that exposes the nationalist and Europocentric historiography of vision, Claire Farago has argued that an art history that captures the reality of intellectual and cognitive exchanges in early modernity would be one that acknowledges the constructed nature of such visual experiments and doesn't presume Renaissance naturalism as normative.[28] Vision itself, she argues, deserves its own history. Efforts to expose the seedy underside of naturalized vision that were already afloat in early modernity also preoccupied Stuart Clark's scholarship about vision's cultural determinism versus its normativity.[29]

This book tells observation's backstory by way of a history of attentive looking. Bracketed between advances in naturalism and perspective, the discourse on early modern vision has sidelined the prints that helped to shape it. The metaphor of Alberti's window was ill-suited to the prerogatives of printmaking, whose concerns were not vested in illusion but in market forces and in the art of persuasion. This book attempts to answer the question of how illustrated books and prints mediated visual processes and coached the viewer to see. Where did early modern viewers go for advice about how to see the world around them, if indeed they sought such advice? Cosmographies and physiognomies make it possible to tell the history of visual searches and speculate about the ways in which viewers made sense of what they saw, how they arrived at visual decisions, how they calibrated their eyes for analysis, and finally how they schooled their eyes to take note, remember, and recognize. Printed books tried to serve just such a market of readers in search of sharpened visual skills. Short, portable, and richly illustrated editions were issued by humming presses in the sixteenth century that were straining rag pulp, inking movable type and custom-made woodblocks. Publishers used these same methods to produce large tomes and slim volumes. Many were printed in vernacular languages that invited large publics of first-time book buyers to consume their content. In essence, these were how-to manuals. They taught people how to distinguish thieves from trusted companions, measure distances between stars, and gauge the height of the sun. Ultimately, it was books such as these that taught viewers how to use optical instruments, a skill whose development is outside the purview of this current study.[30]

Such books and their attendant illustrations helped stabilize subjects for visual investigation. Two examples – one from physiognomy, one from cosmography – show how this worked. In the first (Figure 1.4), two faces stare at each other across the page, offering poles of consideration for a reader trying to decide which face has the more trustworthy profile. Their formal set-up was very different from the types of heads that were familiar from painted portraits. In print, heads were turned to profile view and reproduced along

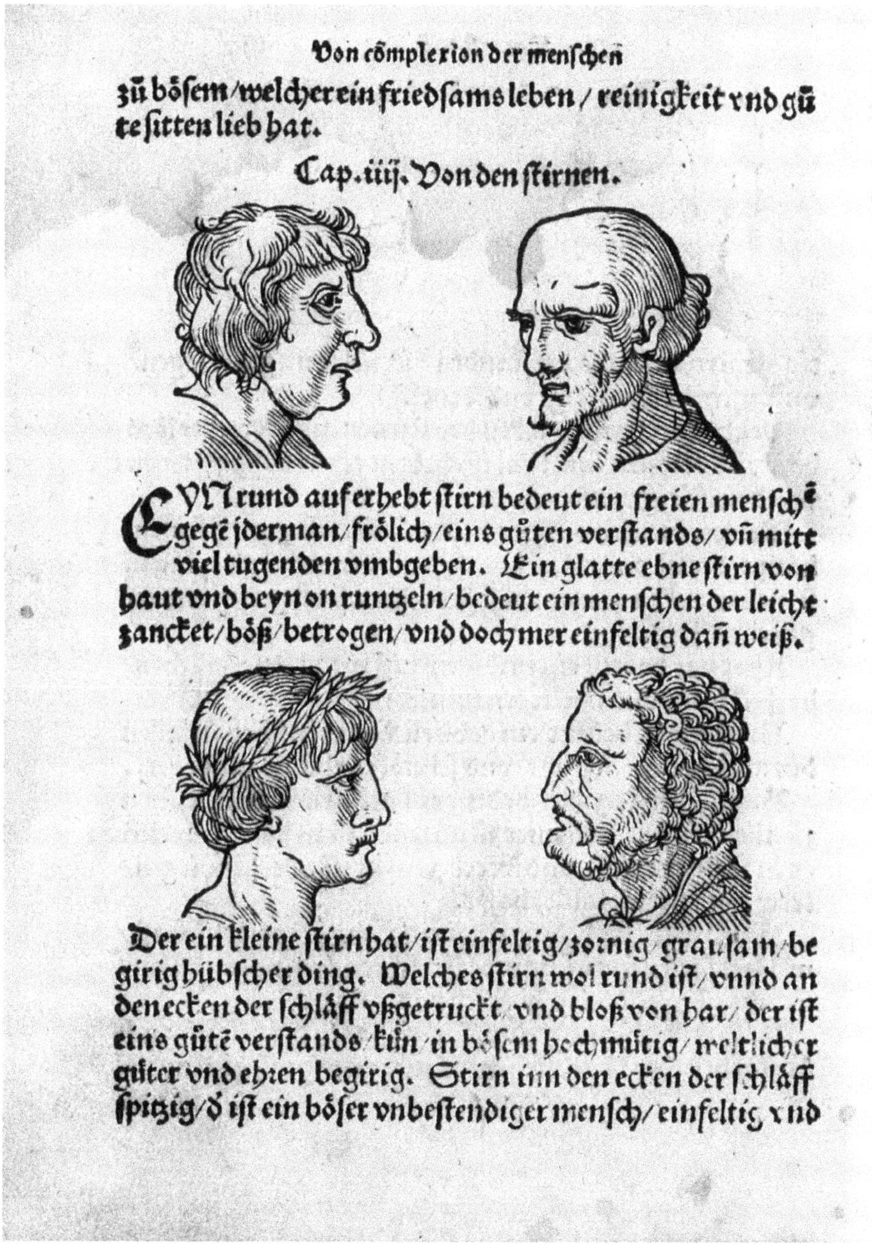
Von cõmplexion der menschen
zů bősem / welcher ein friedsams leben / reinigkeit vnd gů
te sitten lieb hat.
Cap. iiij. Von den stirnen.
EYn rund auferhebt stirn bedeut ein freien menschē
gegē jderman / frőlich / eins gůten verstands / vñ mitt
viel tugenden vmbgeben. Ein glatte ebne stirn von
haut vnd beyn on runtzeln / bedeut ein menschen der leicht
zancket / bőß / betrogen / vnd doch mer einfeltig dañ weiß.
Der ein kleine stirn hat / ist einfeltig / zornig / grausam / be
girig hübscher ding. Welches stirn wol rund ist / vnnd an
den ecken der schläff vßgetruckt / vnd bloß von har / der ist
eins gůtē verstands / kün / in bősem hochmütig / weltlicher
güter vnd ehren begirig. Stirn inn den ecken der schläff
spitzig / d ist ein böser vnbestendiger mensch / einfeltig / vnd

1.4. "Sets of foreheads," by an anonymous artist, in Bartolomeo Cocles, *Phisionomi und Chiromanci. Eyn newß Complexion Büchlein* (Strasbourg: Jacob Cammerlander, 1540), 3 volumes. *Source:* HAB N97.4 Helmst. 3. Courtesy of Herzog August Bibliothek Wolfenbüttel.

with directives to the observer to scrutinize them. A somewhat surprising feature of the accompanying instructions was that visual judgment was meant to be worked out on the page itself. A similar trend can be seen in a cosmographic text printed the same year, Peter Apian's *Cosmographicus Liber.*

In a woodcut that enacted visual comparisons at folio 11, the earth assumes a variety of geometric possibilities, presenting the reader with a demonstration of how the shape of the earth can be inferred by observing the surface of the moon during a lunar eclipse. Most of the knowledge of the heavens on offer at the time came from astronomy textbooks available only to academics; these were both outdated and printed in Latin. While the first edition of Apian's book was issued in Latin to attract audiences perhaps already exposed to the medieval textbooks, a better marketing ploy was launched by printers in Antwerp who pirated the text and released it in a series of vernacular editions. Instead of targeting academics, these texts were designed for educated laymen. These printers found that texts printed in Dutch, Spanish, and French provided more accessible companions than scholarly Latin for the visual demonstrations appearing in the book.[31] Rather than simply recycling ancient content, printers formulated these volumes for a new purpose: coaching visual decision-making in the book's users.

Is it possible to historicize such practices of observation? In so far as we can, this book aims to unpack the phenomenology of visual searches. This study examines how printers coached observers to look and to make sense of what they saw, helping them earn credibility as reliable eyewitnesses. The act of eyewitnessing has been trending as a popular mode of constituting early modern subjectivity, or as an investigative mode of historical evidence.[32] This book amplifies these studies by considering the concrete way in which the eyewitness was defined in these printed manuals; indeed, these were the first books that told anyone to look anywhere in a manner that could be widely understood. Efforts to historicize the act of eyewitnessing have sent scholars to mine textual passages in which self-conscious looking was both hailed and demanded. Among such professional eyewitnesses were sailors, spies, and travelers. Navigation reports and Sacrobosco's astronomy pamphlet *De Sphaera* staged proofs of the earth's sphericality from the crow's nest of a ship – and often from the perspective of pictured eyes. We might also look for clues to purposeful viewing in the reports of Venetian spies who were sent out and tasked with providing reconnaissance on things that they observed. "Views" were suggested and prompted by those seeking data, in many cases requiring written reports in response.[33]

This book argues that recommendations for visual practice resided in illustrated texts whose images not only hailed the eyewitness with insistent pleas, but also guided readers in seeing sights. It tracks the rise of illustrated texts designed to coach the autodidactic viewer. Some texts were newly endowed with the potential to render the results of eyewitness testimony, such as Breydenbach's *Peregrinatio in Terram Sanctam* (published in Mainz in 1486), for whose graphic program an artist was specifically commissioned to capture the look of people and sights collected during the journey described. Later,

Sebastian Münster's *Cosmographia* (1551) aimed to collect the reports of eyewitnesses.[34] The *Relaciones Geográficas* of the 1570s, produced for King Philip II as a survey of his holdings in New Spain, also depended on local observers in the field to report back reliable descriptions of landmarks and the contours of the territory.[35] But prior to these mid-century large-scale and ambitious efforts, short and informative vernacular texts encouraged their readers to see with their own eyes.

Cheap printed books afforded a wider spectrum of the population the ability to interpret texts and images themselves. Although appreciably different in appearance from the publications that emerged from developing scientific societies, they provide the critical start date for the launch of vernacular observations in northern Europe. These books not only provided the impetus for the formation of professional assemblies; they also armed their readers with recommendations about systematic viewing practices. Images appearing in short and inexpensive vernacular how-to publications accompanied the reader through the procedures of physiognomy, chiromancy, field surgery, and astronomy and assisted in the execution of tasks that were shaping new skill sets. This volume also builds on recent studies of prints' agency to demonstrate a coordinated effort by printers to raise the intellectual horizon of knowledgeable laypeople through image-based learning.[36]

MAKING OBSERVATIONS

Images generated from Galileo's telescope have long marked an inaugural attempt in the history of observation. Perhaps ironically, we have sought the origins of scientific scrutiny in the views produced by instruments because we now see in them objectivity that we mistake for naturalism.[37] Yet, for which observers could Galileo's published images have been considered naturalistic – or, stranger yet, objective? We have already learned of one befuddled observer who couldn't determine the viewing end of the telescope. Galileo's contributions to observation are indeed important, but more for solidifying the idea that the results of scientific inquiry could be recorded in print. Views from instruments became normative in their own right. Galileo's publishers contributed to this by suggesting that the look of a mechanical process of recording mirrored Galileo's own drawn "observations."[38] This idea would also color the subsequent productions of the Royal Society, which sought to collect the direct results of observations made with instruments.[39] But even before scientific societies began to archive such observations, there was a market demand for how-to books that coached the public in how to perform systematic observations.

We must also briefly historicize what was meant by the term *observation* when it was used in a text. Practices defined by this rubric shifted in early modernity from a connotation of following rules and procedures to eventually refer to experimentation and, ultimately, to the coordinated efforts to share information that would later underwrite scientific inquiry.[40] The idea of precise and careful observations evolved in the early sixteenth century alongside its definition, which came to represent acts of sustained looking that, in some cases, would ultimately be mediated by instrumentation. The activation of the term *observatio* in early modernity to mean regular scrutiny represents a significant departure from its medieval usage, which implied following a set of practices or dogma. Scholars have located this syntactical change in the title of editions sent to press by the Nuremberg astronomer and cosmographer Johannes Schöner, whose designation of the term *observationes* refers to astronomic data collected from Regiomontanus, along with more recent weather observations.[41] But the idea of observation was also alive and well in Apian's *Practica* and related publications, such as those that tracked the path of a comet across the sky between the months of October and December in 1532.[42]

"Observations" could also refer to the descriptions, specimens, and images by naturalists such as Aldrovandi, Conrad Gessner, and Carolus Clusius. The collectivization of authored observations was a critical link to what eventually would become scholarly consensus.[43] Collections of pictures preserved in paper museums and printed "laboratories" were as much acts of visual common-placing as they were natural history per se. The methods of examination and classification staged by the artists and naturalists of the Accademia de Lincei would prefigure Cartesian eyewitnessing.[44] Living things seen under these intense practices of scrutiny were surrounded by the rhetoric of observation on the printed page. When Pierre Belon's research into zoological and natural historical material emerged with the title *Observationes* in its Paris printings (*c.* 1550), this guarantee prioritized the "things seen" over any particular traveler who might have generated those observations. The title pages of other such books with roughly similar content often featured the traveler's name or the travel itinerary itself. Publishing a book like Belon's as a record of observations, however, brought the author to the stand as an eyewitness and proposed the visual accompaniments of the book as a type of storage solution for the presentation of natural knowledge.

To this venerable lineup of observers, we can now add the amateur practitioners of cosmography, physiognomy, and other practical genres. The artisans of the book trade supplied their reading publics with a steady stream of images against which readers could check their own observations. In part, this was also a result of the claims advanced by the printmaker for the sovereignty of images. This project provides the prehistory of seeing, organizing, and observing through images, an approach whose privileging eventually earned Galileo his invitation to the faculty at Padua, before the market for empiricism became saturated with images of "observations" made by instruments.

METHODS

This book about how practical knowledge was visualized is perched at the intersection of an interdisciplinary rapprochement between art history, the history of science, book history, and the history of knowledge. Some new methodologies current in these fields have assisted me. A productive symbiosis of art history with the history of science has been underway in German approaches to *Bildwissenschaft,* essentially a science of images. The questions I pursue here about the use and methods of printed media to convey documentary observation and visual skills bring two scholarly avenues of inquiry into dialogue: the practice of scientific observation currently treated by historians of science, and the role of print media in circulating new knowledge as explored by historians of the book. The importance of images in codifying what became systematic studies of botany and anatomy already looms large in scientific observation's past; this book expands the investigation of the use of illustration to the realm of cosmographic, physiognomic, and related texts.

My evidence requires a decentering of standard art historical paradigms that value artistic originality. It likewise challenges mainstream approaches to illusionistic representation, especially art history's tenacious bias toward optical naturalism and mimesis. As we will see, the road to practical knowledge was strewn with non-naturalistic, optically and mentally challenging images that frequently coaxed users' participation and demanded their involvement. Because the viewer was directly implicated, we must also reshuffle the standard agents of art history: this story is about, in part, the printmakers who educated new publics through strategies of visualization.

The German branch of the study of visual culture, *Bildwissenschaft,* or the science of images, permits a look not only at the interstitial space between naturalism and didactics, but also at the dynamics between maker and receiver. The address to reader/viewers enunciated in the books' front matter evolved into a commonplace of marketing printed volumes. The strategy of hailing readers was in part advertising, but it was also a rhetorical spur to arouse the reader's epistemic potential. The polymath printer Walter Ryff summoned the attention of the *Hausvater,* a class of literate, but not necessarily learned, urban citizens.[45] In the early 1500s, readers in Strasbourg found themselves addressed as an aspirational how-to audience of *gestreifte Laien,* or "striped laymen," identified by the striped clothing they sported in the accompanying woodcuts.[46] Other Strasbourg printers entreated these laypeople to rehearse the diagnostics and procedures of specialists via the book's images. Single-sheet flap prints of female and male anatomical dolls printed by the Strasbourg physician Heinrich Vogtherr in 1539 also enticed the common man, or *gemeiner Mann,* to simulate surgery by lifting the layers of printed viewing fields as though they were virtually removing them with a surgeon's knife.[47]

With the intention of targeting non-professional audiences, some impressions of these prints were fortified on canvas supports that could withstand the repeated lifting of flaps to reveal interior organs by lay viewers interested in anatomy; these prints might have been mounted in public places, such as in bathhouses, or at church festivals. These types of publication constituted a subject whom I like to call a vernacular viewer: a non-specialist schooled by vernacular texts.

Printers cultivated empirical engagement with the world and argued that the purchase of their books could make readers visually astute by providing ersatz empirical experience that rivaled the firsthand experience that came with travel. The Antwerp printer of Apian's *Cosmographia* (1553) had such confidence that books could deliver this that he entreated readers not to swap hard-earned income for the uncertainties of travel, but to buy his books instead. Fatigued and cash-strapped artists burdened with family obligations could find themselves consoled by the efforts of Heinrich Vogtherr's *Ein frembds und wunderbars Kunstbüchlin ... hochnutzlich zu gebrauchen* (printed in Strasbourg in 1537), which provided a model book and copy manual for artists that cribbed designs from other artworks and was meant to be used in furniture making, armor design, painting, and presumably also printmaking.[48] Vogtherr advocated that the book's purchase could spare the journeyman the expenses and stress of traveling during his *Wanderjahr*.

Such ersatz acts of "eyewitnessing" were cultivated by a range of books that recommended readers' engagement with the world. Sometimes their images took the shape of things to observe, methods of measuring, or profiles to assess. Readers of these texts were invested with new eyewitness authority, which, in fact, had been an important rhetorical claim intimately tied to the history of printmaking. This guarantee of "being there" was frequently rehearsed by authors in travel literature. When travel literature became a mainstay of the early press, these eyewitness claims transferred to print. This may have spurred some printmakers to fortify their authors' claims through images surprisingly equipped to do just that – often imbuing special status through a variety of rhetorical tropes (such as *ad vivum*, *naer het leven*, or *contrafacere*) that suggested the presence of an observer with the guarantee that the image had been taken "from life," or at least from observation.[49] Images in the cosmographic and physiognomic literature reprised the strategies of these images and gave viewers the tools to make informed eyewitness assessments.

My study builds on scholarship that argues for the cultural determinism of vision, with an emphasis on how the eye was conditioned for scrutiny in order to develop a knowledge base. It builds on Claire Farago's charge to reposition Renaissance paradigms in *Reframing the Renaissance* by exposing the relativism of vision as a cultural practice; this thread is picked up by Dana Leibsohn and Jeanette Favrot Peterson's *Seeing across Cultures in the Early Modern World*.[50]

Jeffrey Chipps Smith's investigation into how visual and sensory communication in early modern Germany contributes to the discourse on the phenomenology of the senses in the art of early German modernity is likewise critical.[51] This type of investigation also characterizes some recent studies by historians of science and of craft practice, as well as historians of the book, and the history of technology. The relationship of epistemology to craft practice as explored by Pamela H. Smith previews artisanal practice that would later be codified in book form.[52] Instruments provide another way in which to measure the content around which observations, optics, and the physiology of sight were directed; the investigations by Sven Dupré and Samuel Gessner have broadened the scope of agents and practitioners.[53] The proceedings of a research group at the Max Planck Institute for the History of Science on the history of observation and scientific practice led by Lorraine Daston and Elizabeth Lunbeck provided fertile ground for new research in this area.[54] Studies of the book and the history of printing by Jonathan Sawday and Neil Rhodes, A. E. B. Coldiron, Elizabeth Spiller, Adrian Johns, and Tom Conley have all made great strides in showing how print shaped cultures of knowledge.[55] Peter Dear, Steven Shapin, and Matteo Valleriani have presented work on the transmission of knowledge as a technical revolution instigated by books.[56] These studies provide the spine of my investigation into epistemology and the working mechanism of the print.

To the paradigms of evidence in early modernity, I add and unpack the patterns and the paradoxes of printed images. How reproductive technology mediated the ontology of artifacts is the focus of study of *Forgery, Replica, Fiction*, in which Christopher Wood illuminates the role of print in constructing notions of historical time, as well as marking distinctions between the disciplines of archaeology and historical fiction.[57] We might also examine the hermeneutics internal to print by querying what functions as fact or fiction within the printed image and what constitutes evidence for those claims. For instance, while "*ad vivum*" was a rhetorical guarantee frequently elided with verisimilitude in other media, what special claims adhere to its use in the printed medium, one hopelessly inept at taking on illusionistic concerns? Was the look of truth vetted in the printed image itself, or in the paratexts on the print's surface? In the sixteenth century, prints began in earnest to organize subjects of investigation at the ontological level. Among other things, this study asks how such media called methods of inquiry into being.

SHAPING COGNITIVE PRACTICES

The community of visual literates that early modern prints sponsored has not been addressed by the substantial field that has developed around visual literacy.[58] The idea of collective interpreters of images in the field of art history has been largely restricted to nineteenth-century developments in photography and the decoding of technical images (radiography, LiDAR), yet the pervasiveness of the idea of visual literacy can be seen in the assumption of it as a competency that many art historians regularly proclaim their syllabi will develop. James Elkin's edited volume on *Visual Literacy* acknowledges the historicity of the form and function of images, mostly modern.[59] For the social art historian Michael Baxandall, visual literacy was a paradigm for considering the public's conversance with contemporary iconography and historical modes of visual address; his study produced the idea of a socially determined visual fluency that he called the "period eye."[60] But while the idea of image-literacy particular to historical periods seems still current in art history, scant attention has been given to the modalities of observing that printmaking engendered.

Studies of the history of the book suggest that the shifting layouts of text and paratexts and experiments with the typographic book birthed new cognitive experiences with the text.[61] It was indeed between the covers of books that images began a particularly close association with text. W. J. T. Mitchell's "Visual Literacy or Literary Visualcy?" showed how the image is inextricable from the textual matrix in which it is embedded, and indeed it is inseparable from words themselves.[62] Like Mitchell's premise, this book also argues that the pictorial component of early printed books was critical to the apparatus itself. Paratextual elements such as title pages, tables of content, glosses, and illustrations (both didactic and narrative) allowed readers to search for specific questions, and thus exposed them to new horizons of inquiry.[63]

The tightrope that these books trod between theoretical and practical knowledge was just one of the new cognitive balancing acts that the reader would learn to manage. The new organization of books reveals a tension between theory and practice – this plumped the trading zones between theoreticians and practitioners. Newly implicated as a practitioner, the reader/viewer braced for new empirical interfaces with the world.

The experiential horizon of the reader of printed pamphlets was broadened by information that was repackaged into guide books and manuals that attempted to structure experience. The stakes of this interface between the reader and the world brought about new cognitive approaches to understanding. Attempts to historicize such experiences gave rise to a methodology we can think of as historical phenomenology. Bruce Smith has tried to establish the period eye for the phenomenon of color.[64] Early modern experience could also be assessed by the ways in which images hailed their audiences. Suzanne Karr Schmidt shows how prints, in transforming the reader into a "user," assumed the work that physical tools previously did and distributed that knowledge to wider audiences. Autodidacts were developed through the agency of three-dimensional, or sculptural, prints that could be spun and lifted by users, and Schmidt counts the woodcuts of the fifteenth and sixteenth century as early examples of the mutual synergy between image and viewer that we today label interactivity.[65] Early modern prints functioned as substitutions (for the Eucharist, for example), re-enactments (of surgical dissections), or as *memento mori* (as reprimands for engagement with worldly concerns).

This activation of the reader/viewer is an important heuristic that goes beyond the development of interiority to actual do-it-yourself sleuthing. Directing highly personal empirical experiences can be considered one of the primary goals of volvelles, or moving paper dials. Peter Apian's *Cosmographicus Liber* includes instructional tools whose didactic and dynamic interface to teach the principles of astronomy and measurement to users superseded their ability to render accurate readings.[66] Apian's example shows well the detente between studies of theoretical models and practical skills, a dichotomy that Matteo Valleriani sees as on the mend in recent studies of practical knowledge.[67] The materiality of the print – i.e., its tactility and its simultaneous visuality, and in some cases its prompt to handmade autodidactic DIY construction – is the topic of *Prints in Translation*, as authors Suzanne Karr Schmidt and Edward Wouk invite the reader to consider the range of cultural practices that developed around the print.[68] Of critical importance to these authors is how prints became agents of social epistemic transformations – redirecting experiences typically reserved for more elevated art forms designed for higher classes, and catapulting them instead toward a broader public. Prints' growing ubiquity occasioned reflexive commentary from within: Printmakers began to offer critiques on the medium itself. Producers invited reflections on their prints' self-referential quality, often mobilizing the idea of an "impression" as central to the print's agency.[69]

EPISTEMIC IMAGES

Increasingly, such tools were designed for helping viewers to size up their surroundings, to make knowledgeable inferences about the world, and to do this primarily through visual means. Printed images circulated widely and cultivated practical uses; the intersection of these aims with growing disciplinary investigations forms the content of *Prints in the Pursuit of Knowledge in Early Modern Europe*, an important scholarly intervention in the field.[70] The role of images in shaping new fields of knowledge generally is the subject of Alexander Marr's work on epistemic images, research that recognizes the novelty of these images' visual strategies.[71] Images were certainly being deployed for new purposes.

How prints mediated humanity's interface with the natural world, especially in the fields of anatomy and botany, has been explored in Sachiko Kusukawa's standard-bearer, *Picturing the Book of Nature*.[72] Sustained investigations of plants and the human body gave rise to new fields of optical interest and visual preoccupation. Changes in the organizational arrangement of printed botanicals from curative properties to a system ordered by visual morphology was a result of the degree to which prints shifted the science's emphasis to pictorial arrangements and inspired the future of visually driven, or phytographic, investigation.[73] Thus, images received new agency and sometimes assumed sovereignty over the texts into which they had once been embedded as supplemental information.

Recent scholarship has treated volumes of experimental science produced by the press as technical or knowledge-based publications. As a result, we can now review the complicity of their accompanying images. A consideration of images' epistemological work, per Renzo Baldasso, might provide a corrective to the artificial dichotomies in the study of Renaissance art and nature. His essay, "The Role of Visual Representation in the Scientific Revolution," outlined the roadblocks to an integrated study that could treat many aspects of images in science's service: aesthetics, naturalism, perspective, technology, didactics, and the ersatz "means available for the study of nature," as they were considered by members of the Lincean Academy.[74] The nomenclature of these images as epistemic images has opened up a productive mechanism for considering a range of disparate images united by their common objectives, but scholars have also offered caveats that the broad and anachronistic use of this term could bankrupt its usefulness.[75] A review of new heuristic and technical practices that expand the remit of epistemic images is the subject of a recent publication edited by Ruth Noyes, *Reassessing Epistemic Images in the Early Modern World*.[76]

Epistemic is a term that evolved to cover experimental and scientific images that contributed to a body of systematic inquiry. It also served to repair a divide between images with self-consciously technical functions and images of the artifacts of such inquiry. The anachronistic separation of technical concerns from aesthetic ones in Anglophone art history, per Renzo Baldasso, is an artificial gap that belies efforts of early modern publishers to endow books with the latest technical advances in the medium of printmaking, such as experiments in chiaroscuro and new printing forms for geometrical designs.[77] While some scholarship asserts a need to attend to the distinction between technical images and representations of technology in weighing the value of the term "epistemic," images themselves have invited this tension. *Bildwissenschaft*, a form of image-inquiry mobilized in German-language studies of visual culture, unites the purpose of technical images with their stylistic properties.

Under the umbrella of a "science of images," we can consider the images' agency in producing both knowledge and the structure of knowledge. How do images rise to the level of knowledge generators? The sheer organizing force of observers in search of collective knowledge, per Lorraine Daston, had the power to stabilize subjects for investigation.[78] Images that accompanied the results of these pursuits can be seen as capturing scholarly consensus. Alternatively, some empirical pursuits were organized around images; Daniela Bleichmar has explored the footprint of this directive in the visual attachments of travel undertaken in the name of science.[79] Other images strategically advanced particular scientific positions; Volker Remmert has shown how the controversies of the Copernican revolution were mediated by the printed title pages of these treatises, shaping the sovereignty and argumentative thrust of a certain kind of image.[80]

Bildwissenschaft, as pioneered by Horst Bredekamp's research group, argues for the autonomy of images through the notion of style.[81] Under the rubric of technical images, this group interrogates potential stylistic commonalities that might unite diverse content under common epistemological origins. Analyses of images in *Das Technische Bild* straddle those that are diagrammatic and aesthetic, as well as those that are produced by instruments.[82] To bridge these anachronistic divides between useful, artistic, and technical images, Alexander Marr has proposed considering them as *knowing images*, thus welcoming a broader range of content and foregrounding instead how images signal the idea of knowledge and gesture at epistemology.[83] My book picks up the tracks of these investigations, examining images that incited epistemic inquiry. Those images sometimes coopted the sovereignty of their own visual searches and they themselves provoked organized inquiry into a host of experimental sciences.

CHAPTER PRÉCIS

The book is divided into two sections. The first two chapters reclaim images' role in standardizing methods of empirical investigation. Cosmography and physiognomy were both major initiatives in instructing laypeople to observe the world and make visual assessments about it. Images articulated these fields of study as visual ones – and breathed life, systematization, and longevity into modes of analysis that were critical for the future development of the disciplines of astronomy, natural history and the study of morphology. As such, images activated firsthand investigations of the world.

Chapter 2, "Don't Forget Your Apian: A DIY Guide to the Cosmos," discusses the achievements of Peter Apian, a sixteenth-century mathematician and printer of cosmographic texts, who successfully translated classical works into updated and pictorially enhanced editions that brought arcane scholarly astronomy and cosmography to a wider audience. Abstract principles of mathematized geography, per Apian, were better explained via mechanical pictures, diagrams that centered humans at the nexus of a world to be experienced firsthand and observed. Handy editions of the *Cosmographicus Liber* (1524) simplified musty academic astronomic knowledge and attracted a broader reading public with the explanatory clarity of its diagrams. Using visual and interactive volvelles with moving parts, Apian demonstrated principles of astronomy and mathematized geography in ways that could help the reader situate the local environment within the solar system. This chapter provides an art historical treatment of Apian's key mechanical images. It argues that Apian converted academic astronomy into prescriptions for observational practices designed to school the user in making visual judgments. Featuring visual tools and demonstrations that animated both the celestial and the terrestrial spheres, Apian's cosmography became a guide for the vernacular viewer. Early modern empirical encounters with the moon, sun, and stars were reconceptualized by cosmography's sponsorship of a lay observer with new cognitive potential. By presenting such phenomena relative to an earth-bound observer, Apian's *Cosmographicus Liber* brought the heavens to earth.

Chapter 3, "Facial Profiling: Physiognomy and the Art of Inspection," treats printed physiognomies as visualized books for people watching. These were shot through with generalized images of character heads that served to cue the viewer's experience in the field. With these images, publishers promoted interest in facial content among audiences; this resulted in new forms of visual stereotypes and a new form of how-to pedagogy. The introduction of such printed profiles in sixteenth-century editions of physiognomies, a genre with a long unillustrated tradition, revised its concerns. Printed heads challenged the text's diagnosis of moral character by shifting the emphasis to the realm of developing visual acuity. Paired profiles showing the difference between a variety of forehead types encouraged the reader to make visual comparisons. A similar comparative framework drove Mark Zuckerberg's pre-Facebook search engine *FaceMash*, a platform on which he asked users to make quick (and sexist) visual assessments of female undergraduates at Harvard that hinged on a simple essentialism: hot or not? This type of judgment was already enshrined in the early physiognomies, and our use of the word *profile* today to describe social media users' portfolios retains some of physiognomy's formal characteristics. Significantly, physiognomies were also among the earliest genres to utilize the term *observations* to characterize the searches they recommended and to provide illustrations to help organize their readers' viewing practices.

Many early modern printed portraits did not make rigorous claims to the positive identification of any particular subject; rather, they floated in the fluid in-between of type and identity. Instead of providing verisimilitude, generic character heads in physiognomies were intended to help streamline the practice of observation. This chapter argues for the contribution of physiognomic portraits to the development of skills such as visual acuity, and it shows how the aim of representing particularity as a guide for personal observations took precedence over mimetic claims. The reuse of many of these generic profiles is surprisingly vast in publications across the continent; we see the same content appearing in cosmographies, for example, and we see their formal properties at work in sources as diverse as model books and costume books. Exploring common aspects shared by printed physiognomies in the epistemic tradition, this chapter looks at their organizational aptitude, the middle ground they formed between mimesis and idealization, and their role in shaping disciplinary activity related to empirical experience.

The following two chapters consider some of the outcomes of this enhanced visual acuity: the collecting and cognitive practices stimulated by these emergent how-to genres – namely, picture atlases and trick images. Picture atlases crystallized these genres as visually sovereign and contributed to their stability. The premise of fixity was interrogated by a special form of visual rhetoric that developed in tandem with the content of cosmography and physiognomy: trick images. With growing visual fluency among an audience that they themselves developed, printmakers also began to propose interpretative models alongside their pictures' content. This content took a back seat to the manner in which it was conveyed. As images increasingly assumed didactic roles in print media, other images volunteered to complicate their methods of delivering knowledge. Viewers with observational skills finely tuned by collected knowledge now found that visual acuity in the crosshairs of tricky images that destabilized their conclusions.

Chapter 4, "Visualized Data and Searchable Science: the *Liber Quodlibetarius* (*c.* 1524)," argues that the rising status of print media can be seen in the way in which prints were organized and collected in the period. Early modern cognitive practices can be tracked by the manner in which printed images deputized empirical searches. The novelty of these cognitive leaps can be seen in the way these newly sovereign images were collected together, and also in the manner in which they challenged their viewers. Presenting diverse material from chronicles, cosmographies, physiognomies, and model books, the *Liber Quodlibetarius*, an unusual manuscript compiled in the second decade of the sixteenth century and furnished with many designs copied from printed sources, leaves us with little doubt that prints were sought and collected for their capacity to intersect with observational practice. The compiler of this unpublished manuscript lifted images already enshrined in print culture and repackaged material from several epistemic sources, including cosmographies, physiognomies, chiromancies, artists manuals, and manuals of field surgery. Far from direct copying, however, the illustrator recomposed and reconfigured the prints' motifs on the manuscript's pages to feature their informational claims and enhance their didactic strategies. Extrapolations from texts such as Apian's cosmography and Cocles's physiognomy were supported by the vocabulary surrounding them, some of which was also derived from familiar print sources.

The *Liber Quodlibetarius* presents images of instrumentation and practical information on how to use quadrants, horologia, and astrolabes. These images were derived from printed guides for investigating the terrestrial and celestial world via these instruments.[84] Throughout the manuscript, we see familiar images from how-to texts and artists' model books, abridged here by using their illustrations alone. What connects the images in this miscellany of diverse data is the manuscript's endorsement of their practical use for empirical activity. The way in which these prints were appropriated, cataloged, and intended for mixed use suggests a function for them grounded in knowledge acquisition. For us, it serves as an excellent case study of the parameters of sixteenth-century visual and searchable knowledge. In transposing only the images from these printed books, the compiler deputized that data to speak for those genres in the shape of searchable and consultable formats. In the manuscript, the images populate visual fields of a new type of storage solution that enabled collecting, collating, and cross-referencing.

Chapter 5, "Vexed Viewing: Anamorphosis and the Visual Argumentation of Labored Looking," positions visual tricks as the outgrowth of empirical practices taught by contemporary prints. Given the claims of observational authority that my argument suggests were accruing to printed images, it is not surprising that prints also became the locus of optical tricks. Tension between pictorial surfaces arose in anamorphic or "deformed" images, whose distortions commented on strategies of recording by deconstructing representation. By sacrificing fixed content to the process of skewing viewpoints, the pictorial tension of anamorphic images thematized their ambivalence about the practice of recording "sights."

By foregrounding the spatial conflict produced by perspective, anamorphic images thematized the process of viewing. Assuming both representational and phenomenological space, like many of the images treated in the previous chapters, anamorphic images inhabit a realm between directing the embodied practice of vision and representation. By exposing the construction of vision, anamorphosis presented a challenge to naturalism like the one that print posed to illusionism. Anamorphic prints pushed the viewer to question the range of optical exercises that they could handle precisely around the subject matter of portraiture and geography, seen here as an outgrowth of cosmography.

Images that took anamorphosis as a visual premise commented on the ambivalence of recording observations generally; but, in the medium of printmaking, this critique also took aim at print's authority to convey such observations. Anamorphic images rendered in print take the content of epistemic pursuits such as likeness and cosmography and place it on the ontological level of art. It is at this point that we find painting occupying itself with kindred concerns. It was the intersecting claims of knowledge and portraiture that brought the three portraits of Holbein's *The Ambassadors* into alignment, just like planetary conjunctions. Such reflections on the stability of the image surely overworked the observer, but they seem to have occasioned a new species of trick images in which portrait and topography were conjoined. Observation was never well compensated – not in the sense of empirical scrutiny, nor in the sense of surveying an image. Images became increasingly demanding. Visual acuity honed in the world turned into an arduous journey of visual attention to the images themselves.

NOTES

1 An important exception is the primer in social history by Michael Baxandall, which delved into the way in which accounting and mathematic texts taught Florentine merchants of the Quattrocento to recognize those same volumes and ratios in the visual vocabulary of paintings and frescos. See Michael Baxandall, *Painting and Experience in Fifteenth Century Italy: A Primer in the Social History of Pictorial Style*, 2nd edition (New York: Oxford University Press, 1988).

2 Peter Parshall and Rainer Schoch, *Origins of European Printmaking: Fifteenth-Century Woodcuts and Their Public* (New Haven, CT: Yale University Press, 2005).

3 David Price, *In the Beginning Was the Image: Art and the Reformation Bible* (New York: Oxford University Press, 2021). Price's book aims to repair the bibliographic focus on text by staging the Renaissance Bible as a visual field.

4 Phillipa Hardman and Nicola Bradbury, *Medieval and Early Modern Miscellanies and Anthologies*, Yearbook of English Studies 33 (Leeds: Maney Publishing for the Modern Humanities Research Association, 2003), 200.

5 For these almanacs designed for annotations, or *Schreibkalendar*, see the project at the Friedrich-Alexander-Universität Erlangen-Nürnberg (FAU) led by Klaus-Dieter Herbst and Daniel Bellingradt on manuscript entries in these printed calendars: *Der frühneuzeitliche Schreibkalendar und seine handschriftlichen Einträge*, https://schreibkalender.wisski.data.fau.de/about. Many thanks to Richard Kremer for pointing out this initiative to me.

6 Eileen Reeves, *Painting the Heavens: Art and Science in the Age of Galileo* (Princeton, NJ: Princeton University Press, 1999), 3.

7 Steven Vanden Broecke, *The Limits of Influence: Pico, Louvain and the Crisis of Renaissance Astrology* (Leiden and Boston, MA: Brill, 2003). Vanden Broecke shows how Gemma Frisius was the first to officially direct his mathematical training into the service of a discipline constituted as cosmography versus astrology. Peter Apian is also part of this tradition.

8 Jonathan Green, *Printing and Prophecy: Prognostication and Media Change 1450–1550* (Ann Arbor: University of Michigan Press, 2012).

9 Anthony Grafton, *Commerce with the Classics: Ancient Books and Renaissance Readers* (Ann Arbor: University of Michigan Press, 1997), 215ff.

10 Anthony Grafton, "Some Uses of Eclipses in Early Modern Chronology," *Journal of the History of Ideas* 64, no. 2 (2003), 213–29.

11 Green, *Printing and Prophecy*.

12 "*Wann mann baden oder schrepffen will/ sol der Mon im abnemen sein und im Stier/ Zwilling/ Krebs/ Wag/ Scorpion und Fisch*," in Johannes Regiomontanus, *Kalendarius: News Und Volmon* (Strasbourg: Cammerlander, 1532), HAB HN97.4 Helmst. 2, 29r.

13 For an image of the application of cups, see *Kalendar: Iatromathematisches Hausbuch* (Augsburg: Blaubierer, 1481), http://daten.digitale-sammlungen.de/~db/0002/bsb00029544/images/index.html?seite=136&fip=193.174.98.30.

14 A Protestant secondary school, or gymnasium, founded by Johannes Sturm in 1538 would ultimately become the university in Strasbourg. Malcolm Walsby and Graeme Kemp, *The Book Triumphant: Print in Transition in the Sixteenth and Seventeenth Centuries* (Leiden and

Boston, MA: Brill, 2011). For the similar situation in Venice and Augsburg, see essays in the same volume by Neil Harris and Hans-Jörg Künast. For the Strasbourg press, see Miriam Usher Chrisman, *Lay Culture, Learned Culture: Books and Social Change in Strasbourg, 1480–1599* (New Haven, CT: Yale University Press, 1982). The university founded in Altdorf in 1578 would become the academic center of Nuremberg.

15 Robin Bruce Barnes, *Astrology and Reformation* (New York: Oxford University Press, 2016), 18–47.

16 Pamela H. Smith, "Making as Knowing: Craft as Natural Philosophy," in Pamela H Smith et al., *Ways of Making and Knowing: The Material Culture of Empirical Knowledge* (New York: Bard Graduate Center, 2017), 18. Schott, for example, brought together Otto Brunfels and Hans Weiditz for an important herbal; Panse also indicates that Gersdorff brokered the relationship between field surgeons and physicians, possibly an idea that also originated with Schott. See Melanie Panse, *Hans von Gersdorffs "Feldbuch der Wundarznei"* (Wiesbaden: Reichert, 2012), 33–5.

17 Or *Eyn Schön vergleichung der Astronomi mit der Artznei/ das ein berümbter Artzt auch muß eyn Astronomus sein.* See Regiomontanus, *Kalendarius*, HAB HN97.4 Helmst. 2.

18 Regiomontanus, *Kalendarius*, 36r. For example, in a passage that suggests judgment of quality: "*Alle harn seint dreierhandt. Eins ist weiß on drusen/ mit eim kleynen nebelin/ der ist böß. Das ander ist weiß on nebelin/ mit eim kleinen genist/ das ist vast ser böß. Das drit ist weiß/ dick/ und durchschinet/ und mann mag es doch nit durch sehen/ das ist gar todtlich.*"

19 This is made plain in the couplets above the venesection man.

20 Franz Machilek, "Astronomie und Astrologie: Sternforschung und Sternglaube im Verständnis von Johannes Regiomontanus und Benedikt Ellwanger," *Astronomie und Astrologie in der Frühen Neuzeit: Akten des Interdisziplinären Symposions* 21, no. 22 (1990), 12.

21 Matteo Valleriani, ed., *The Structures of Practical Knowledge* (Cham: Springer, 2017), 345.

22 K. A. E. Enenkel and Wolfgang Neuber, eds., *Cognition and the Book: Typologies of Formal Organisation of Knowledge in the Printed Book of the Early Modern Period* (Leiden and Boston, MA: Brill, 2005).

23 See Richard L. Kremer, "Incunable Almanacs and *Practica* as Practical Knowledge Produced in Trading Zones," in Valleriani, ed., *The Structures of Practical Knowledge*, 333–69, especially 344.

24 Gregorius Reisch, *Margarita Philosophica* (Strasbourg: Johannes Schott, 1504), Liber X, Tract. II, *De Potentiis Animae Sensitivae*. See fol. 238 of the copy at the Herzog August Bibliothek (M:Li5881). See Andrew Cunningham and Sachiko Kusukawa, eds., *Natural Philosophy Epitomised: A Translation of Books 8–11 of Gregor Reisch's Philosophical Pearl (1503)* (Farnham, VT: Ashgate, 2010).

25 Cunningham and Kusukawa, *Natural Philosophy Epitomised*, 174–6.

26 Susanne Küchler and Walter S. Melion, *Images of Memory: On Remembering and Representation* (Washington, DC: Smithsonian Institution Press, 1991), 8–9, 18–19.

27 Küchler and Melion, *Images of Memory*, 17.

28 See "Even Vision Has a History," in Claire J. Farago, *Reframing the Renaissance: Visual Culture in Europe and Latin America, 1450–1650* (New Haven, CT: Yale University Press, 1995), 67–88.

29 Stuart Clark, *Vanities of the Eye: Vision in Early Modern European Culture* (Oxford: Oxford University Press, 2007).

30 See Heinz Herbert Mann, "Optische Instrumente," in Hans Holländer, ed., *Erkenntnis, Erfindung, Konstruktion: Studien zur Bildgeschichte von Naturwissenschaften und Technik von 16. bis zum 19. Jahrhundert* (Berlin: Gebr. Mann, 2000), 357–409.

31 "*Den welcken dit teghenwoordich boeck der Cosmographien Apiani/ uiten latÿne in duytsche nu eerst getranslateert zeer behulpich sal wesen*" (fol. 2r) in Peter Apian, *Cosmographie, Oft Beschrijvinghe Der Geheelder Werelt van Petrus Apianus. 3. Werk, Nu Ghecorrigeert van Gemma Frisio. Metten Zeecompasse Ende Anderen Boecxkens Byden Selven Gemma Daer Toegedaen*, ed. Rainer Gemma Frisius (Antwerp: de Bonte, 1553).

32 Peter Burke, *Eyewitnessing: The Uses of Images as Historical Evidence* (Ithaca, NY: Cornell Paperbacks, 2008).
33 Lorraine Daston and Elizabeth Lunbeck, *Histories of Scientific Observation* (Chicago: University of Chicago Press, 2011), 89. I thank Lorraine Daston for pointing this out to me. For instructions to Venetian ambassadors for recording what they saw, see Giovanni Comisso, ed., *Gli ambasciatori veneti, 1525–1792. Relazion di viaggio e di missione* (Milan: Longanesi, 1985). On views gathered by travelers, see also Joan-Pau Rubiés, "Instructions for Travellers: Teaching the Eye to See," in Rubiés, *Travellers and Cosmographers: Studies in the History of Early Modern Travel and Ethnology* (Aldershot: Ashgate, 2007), 139–90.
34 Jasper Van Putten, *Networked Nation: Mapping German Cities in Sebastian Münster's "Cosmographia"* (Leiden: Brill, 2018).
35 Barbara E. Mundy, *The Mapping of New Spain: Indigenous Cartography and the Maps of the Relaciones Geográficas* (Chicago: University of Chicago Press, 1996); Daston and Lunbeck, *Histories of Scientific Observation*, 87.
36 The history of knowledge-based aspirations in print was launched in an important exhibition and catalog *Prints and the Pursuit of Knowledge* that addressed the work that prints performed in a host of related genres. See Susan Dackerman, et al., *Prints and the Pursuit of Knowledge in Early Modern Europe* (Cambridge and New Haven, CT: Harvard Art Museums, 2011). Suzanne Karr Schmidt's *Interactive and Sculptural Printmaking in the Renaissance* (Leiden: Brill, 2018) unpacks the user's interface as a heuristic endemic to early printmaking.
37 Lorraine Daston and Peter Galison, *Objectivity* (New York: Zone Books, 2007).
38 Ruth S. Noyes, "Mattheus Greuter's Sunspot Etchings for Galileo Galilei's Macchie Solari (1613)," *Art Bulletin* 98, no. 4 (2016), 473. Because he could not look through the scope at the sun, Galileo describes exposing the lens to a sheet of paper which would capture the impression of the spots. Noyes argues that the special quiddity of sunspots that Mattheus Greuter referenced in his etchings of Galileo's observations matched the indexical reflexivity that prints of the Vera Icon asserted with the relic of the Holy Face.
39 Such as the images made by van Leeuwenhoek's draftsmen, who recorded the views produced by his microscope, in Sietske Fransen, "Antoni van Leeuwenhoek, His Images and Draughtsmen," *Perspectives on Science* 27, no. 3 (2019), 485–544.
40 Daston and Lunbeck, *Histories of Scientific Observation*, 45–80, especially 50. For Gianna Pomata, observation would eventually come to represent "collective empiricism."
41 See Gianna Pomata, "Observation Rising: Birth of an Epistemic Genre, 1500–1650," in Daston and Lunbeck, *Histories of Scientific Observation*, 49. Regiomontanus's own efforts on behalf of observational practice can also be seen in his teaching of optics at Vienna, and his production of scientific instruments that supported the technical observations that underwrote his general predictions.
42 Peter Apian, *Practica auff das 1532 Jar . . . Auch wird nachvolgenden von dem naeschst erschinen Cometen / wie und in was gestalt in gemelter Apianus observiert hat und welhe biß her dero vil sindt in irem schreiben irrig gefunden bewerlich angezaygt* (Landshut: Georg Apian, 1532).
43 Daston and Lunbeck, *Histories of Scientific Observation*, 87.
44 David Freedberg, *The Eye of the Lynx: Galileo, His Friends, and the Beginnings of Modern Natural History* (Chicago: University of Chicago Press, 2002). Freedberg asserts that these methods acted as an impetus to visualized natural history.
45 William Eamon, *Science and the Secrets of Nature: Books of Secrets in Medieval and Early Modern Culture* (Princeton, NJ: Princeton University Press, 1996), 100–1. Eamon identifies this person as an industrious householder, an urban citizen, a member of the village community, with an established position in the middle ranks of society. These would include citizens, non-noble landowners, and householders. The prerequisites of being *gemein* included having legal rights in a municipality or village corporation (*Gemeinde*); this status increasingly included women.
46 See Tillmann Taape, "Common Medicine for the Common Man: Picturing the 'Striped Layman' in Early Vernacular Print," *Renaissance Quarterly* 74 (2021), 1–58.

47 See *Außlegung und beschreybung der Anatomi* (Strasbourg: Vogtherr, 1539) in Schmidt, *Interactive and Sculptural Printmaking in the Renaissance*, 2, 122.

48 Heinrich Vogtherr, *Ein frembds und wunderbars Kunstbüchlin allen Molern, Bildschnitzern, Goldschmiden, Steinmetzen, Schreinern, Platnern, Waffen und Messerschmiden hochnutzlich zu gebrauchen* (Strasbourg: Vogtherr, 1537); see also "Heinrich Vogtherr: Heinrich Vogtherr: Ein frembds und wunderbars Kunstbüchlin allen Molern/ Bildschnitzern/ Goldschmiden/ Steinmetzen/ Schreinern/ Platnern/ Waffen und Messerschmiden hochnutzlich zu gebrauchen (Straßburg 1538/1572) herausgegeben und kommentiert von Maria Heilmann," ed. Maria Heilmann, *FONTES* 61 (2011).

49 For scholarship that unpacks these terms, see Thomas Balfe, Joanna Woodall, and Claus Zittel, *Ad Vivum?: Visual Materials and the Vocabulary of Life-Likeness in Europe before 1800* (Leiden: Brill, 2019); Peter Parshall, "Imago Contrafacta: Images and Facts in the Northern Renaissance," *Art History* 16, no. 4 (1993), 554–79.

50 Farago, *Reframing the Renaissance*; Dana Leibsohn and Jeanette Favrot Peterson, eds., *Seeing across Cultures in the Early Modern World* (Burlington, VT: Ashgate, 2012).

51 Jeffrey Chipps Smith, ed., *Visual Acuity and the Arts of Communication in Early Modern Germany* (Abingdon: Routledge, 2018).

52 See, for example, Pamela H. Smith, *The Body of the Artisan: Art and Experience in the Scientific Revolution* (Chicago: University of Chicago Press, 2004); Smith et al., *Ways of Making and Knowing*.

53 Sven Dupré investigates how the circulation through merchant networks of materials such as glass has shaped early modern cultural capital, while Gessner studies the intersection of tools and technical processes. See Sven Dupré, "Trading Luxury Glass, Picturing Collections and Consuming Objects of Knowledge in Early Seventeenth-Century Antwerp," *Intellectual History Review* 20, no. 1 (2010), 53–78; Sven Dupré and Christoph Lüthy, eds., *Silent Messengers: The Circulation of Material Objects of Knowledge in the Early Modern Low Countries* (Berlin: Lit Verlag, 2012); Samuel Gessner, "The Use of Printed Images for Instrument-Making at the Arsenius Workshop," in Nicholas Jardine and Isla Fay, eds., *Observing the World through Images: Diagrams and Figures in the Early-Modern Arts and Sciences* (Leiden and Boston, MA: Brill, 2014), 124–52.

54 Daston and Lunbeck, *Histories of Scientific Observation*, 1–9.

55 Neil Rhodes and Jonathan Sawday, *The Renaissance Computer: Knowledge Technology in the First Age of Print* (London and New York: Routledge, 2000); A. E. B. Coldiron, *Printers without Borders: Translation and Textuality in the Renaissance* (Cambridge: Cambridge University Press, 2015); Jonathan Sawday, *The Machine Mind: Technology and Culture in the European Renaissance* (London: Routledge, 2007); Elizabeth Spiller, *Science, Reading, and Renaissance Literature: The Art of Making Knowledge, 1580–1670* (Cambridge: Cambridge University Press, 2007); Adrian Johns, *The Nature of the Book: Print and Knowledge in the Making* (Chicago: University of Chicago Press, 2009); Adrian Johns, "The Uses of Print in the History of Science," *Papers of the Bibliographical Society of America* 107, no. 4 (2013), 393–420. Tom Conley has also written prolifically on Peter Apian; see, for example, Tom Conley, *An Errant Eye: Poetry and Topography in Early Modern France* (Minneapolis: University of Minnesota Press, 2011); Tom Conley, "A Topographer's Eye: From Gilles Corrozet to Pieter Apian," in Walter S. Melion and Lee Palmer Wandel, eds., *Early Modern Eyes* (Leiden: Brill, 2010), 55–79.

56 Peter Robert Dear, *Revolutionizing the Sciences: European Knowledge in Transition, 1500–1700* (Oxford and London: Macmillan International Higher Education and Red Globe Press, 2019); Steven Shapin, *Scientific Revolution* (Chicago: University of Chicago Press, 2019); Valleriani, ed., *The Structures of Practical Knowledge*.

57 Christopher S. Wood, *Forgery, Replica, Fiction: Temporalities of German Renaissance Art* (Chicago: University of Chicago Press, 2008), especially 95–107.

58 Indeed, these efforts concern much later periods. For an intriguing account of deploying photography to develop visual skills, see Josh Ellenbogen and Adam Jolles, "Visual Literacy

and 1960s Photography," *Critical Inquiry Critical Inquiry* 47, no. 3 (2021), 565–91. On visual learning more generally, see Barbara Maria Stafford, *Artful Science: Enlightenment, Entertainment, and the Eclipse of Visual Education* (Cambridge, MA: MIT Press, 1994); Barbara Maria Stafford, *Body Criticism: Imaging the Unseen in Enlightenment Art and Medicine* (Cambridge MA and London: MIT Press, 1997).

59 James Elkins, *Visual Literacy* (New York: Routledge, 2008).

60 Baxandall, *Painting and Experience in Fifteenth Century Italy*; Michael Baxandall, *The Limewood Sculptors of Renaissance Germany* (New Haven, CT: Yale University Press, 1980).

61 A. E. B. Coldiron, "Translation and Transformission; Or, Early Modernity in Motion," *Canadian Review of Comparative Literature/Revue Canadienne de Littérature Comparée* 46, no. 2 (2019), 205–16.

62 W. J. Thomas Mitchell, *Picture Theory: Essays on Verbal and Visual Representation* (Chicago: University of Chicago Press, 2014); Elkins, *Visual Literacy*.

63 Enenkel and Neuber, *Cognition and the Book*, 3.

64 Bruce R. Smith, *The Key of Green: Passion and Perception in Renaissance Culture* (Chicago: University of Chicago Press, 2009).

65 Schmidt, *Interactive and Sculptural Printmaking in the Renaissance*, 10.

66 Margaret Gaida, "Reading Cosmographia: Peter Apian's Book-Instrument Hybrid and the Rise of the Mathematical Amateur in the Sixteenth Century," *Early Science and Medicine* 21, no. 4 (2016), 297.

67 Valleriani, ed., *The Structures of Practical Knowledge*, 2.

68 Suzanne Kathleen Karr Schmidt and Edward H. Wouk, *Prints in Translation, 1450–1750: Image, Materiality, Space* (Abingdon: Routledge, 2017), 3.

69 Schmidt and Wouk, *Prints in Translation*, 10.

70 Dackerman, *Prints and the Pursuit of Knowledge*.

71 Alexander Marr and Christopher Heuer, "Introduction: The Uncertainty of Epistemic Images," *21: Inquiries into Art, History, and the Visual* 1, no. 2 (2020), 251–5; Alexander Marr, "Knowing Images: A Review Essay," *Renaissance Quarterly* 69, no. 3 (2016).

72 Sachiko Kusukawa, *Picturing the Book of Nature: Image, Text, and Argument in Sixteenth-Century Human Anatomy and Medical Botany* (Chicago: University of Chicago Press, 2011).

73 Brian W. Ogilvie, *The Science of Describing: Natural History in Renaissance Europe* (Chicago: University of Chicago Press, 2006). Peter Parshall stops short of claiming that images drove later taxonomic models but stresses the importance of how morphology emerged from the woodcut illustrations that accompanied mid-sixteenth-century printed herbals; Peter Parshall and David Landau, *The Renaissance Print 1470–1550* (New Haven, CT: Yale University Press, 1994), 245–59.

74 Renzo Baldasso, "The Role of Visual Representation in the Scientific Revolution: A Historiographic Inquiry," *Centaurus* 48 (2006), 83.

75 Marr, "Knowing Images," 1005.

76 Ruth S. Noyes, ed., *Reassessing Epistemic Images in the Early Modern World* (Amsterdam: Amsterdam University Press, 2022), especially 43–8.

77 Baldasso, "The Role of Visual Representation in the Scientific Revolution."

78 Daston and Lunbeck, *Histories of Scientific Observation*, 81–113, especially 87ff.

79 Daniela Bleichmar, *Visible Empire: Botanical Expeditions and Visual Culture in the Hispanic Enlightenment* (Chicago: University of Chicago Press, 2012).

80 Volker R. Remmert, *Picturing the Scientific Revolution* (Philadelphia: Saint Joseph's University Press, 2011).

81 Horst Bredekamp, Vera Dünkel, and Birgit Schneider, *The Technical Image: A History of Styles in Scientific Imagery* (Chicago: University of Chicago Press, 2015), 18ff.

82 Horst Bredekamp, Vera Dünkel, and Birgit Schneider, *Das Technische Bild: Kompendium zu einer Stilgeschichte wissenschaftlicher Bilder* (Berlin: Akademie Verlag, 2012).

83 Marr, "Knowing Images," 1000–13.

84 Apian himself published succinct manuals on these topics after 1524.

PART I

COACHING THE EYEWITNESS

TWO

DON'T FORGET YOUR APIAN

A DIY Guide to the Cosmos

Peter Apian, a student of prominent astrologers at the University of Vienna, put practical astronomy on the map in a book he published in 1524, the *Cosmographicus Liber*. Before he attained a university position as a mathematician at the University of Ingolstadt in 1527, Apian earned his credentials as a printer of materials intended to chaperone stargazers as a type of field guide.[1] To do this, he translated Ptolemaic cosmography into an observer-based pedagogy that he packaged into printed books. Academic cosmography was delivered via lectures to audiences of armchair astronomers who occasionally used visual aids in their classes. These took the form of metal and paper instruments meant for demonstration purposes and were largely theoretical in nature. By contrast, Apian's update and visualization of the arcane genre into pictorially enhanced editions resurrected cosmography's use for lay stargazers, whom he expected to make their own observations. Apian explained the rather abstract principles of mathematized geography via mechanical pictures, creating diagrams that centered individual viewers at the nexus of a world to be experienced firsthand and observed. Apian's *Cosmographicus Liber*, printed by the cleric Johannes Weyssenburger in Landshut, simplified musty academic astronomy and attracted a broader public with the explanatory clarity of his diagrams.[2] By way of visual and interactive volvelles with moving parts, Apian demonstrated principles of astronomy and mathematized geography to readers in a manner that could help them navigate the world. This chapter provides an art historical treatment of Apian's work by way of his key mechanical images. It argues that

Apian converted academic astronomy into prescriptions for viewing practices designed to school the user in making visual judgments. With visual tools that literally pop out of the book, Apian animated both the celestial and the terrestrial spheres. Apian's *Cosmographicus Liber*, a book for learning to look at the heavens, strove to sharpen the eye of the literate stargazer.

This chapter treats observations as practices recommended for early modern night-sky exploration. According to Apian, the vault of the heavens was legible if one understood what one saw there. The author made self-conscious pitches to the reader about how to use vision to confirm the precepts of positional astronomy. This visual knowing, according to Apian, was an analytical category mediated by book illustrations. Objects on the canvas of the sky appear in Apian's texts to be confirmed by observations, using pictures to visually verify phenomena on the horizon. By suggesting prompts for visual reasoning, this chapter argues, Apian instrumentalized observation as the tool for unlocking knowledge of the heavens.

In a dedication to the reader in a French translation of Peter Apian's *Cosmographie* published in Paris in 1553, the editor alludes to the cosmography's usefulness by specifically invoking its ability to present information to the reader's eye:

> My friend, dear reader, Apian . . .
> describes and portrays in this book
> The perfect heavens, earth and planets,
> The movements, powers of nature,
> And he shows to the naked eye,
> In diagrams and figures,
> The regions of the habitable earth:
> To whose end the human creature
> Contemplates in itself what brings profit.[3]

Invoking the "naked eye" as the target of this cosmography's design was not just a publisher's idle pitch; it was a theme that had been developed by Peter Apian in the *princeps* of the *Cosmographicus Liber* and one that would be reprised in Apian's other publications directed to a lay public. In fact, twenty years after the *Cosmographicus Liber*'s first edition, printers still advertised this as the book's most marketable asset. Already from the date of its first printing in 1524 in the Bavarian town of Landshut, Apian appealed to the eye's authority by picturing it frequently in the text. In so doing, Apian acknowledges it as an important agent for whose edification his book strives. The content Apian presented was hardly new; it was cribbed from multiple sources, some of which had been in circulation for centuries.[4] Entirely novel, however, was Apian's presentation of that data as visual templates for discoveries that readers in the field could make for themselves. This update amounted to a popular science for lay observers.

Apian's *Cosmographicus Liber* is a manual of mathematical and astronomical geography that treats the basics of both astronomy and geography, breaking the discipline down into sections.[5] Invoking Ptolemy in the headlining use of the word "cosmography," Apian upheld the tradition of labeling Ptolemy's geographic work as his fifteenth-century Florentine translator Jacopo d'Angelo had also done, recognizing the importance of Ptolemy's work as one that mediated between geographic coordinates and the astronomical data from which those terrestrial coordinates were derived.[6] Sixteenth-century editors of Ptolemaic data such as Apian referred to their efforts as cosmographic ones.[7]

To illustrate the aims of cosmography, Apian included a visual simile that sought to distinguish between geographic and chorographic levels of description active in cosmography by visualizing an analogy that most epitomizers of Ptolemy's *Geographia* had overlooked, and possibly misinterpreted (Figures 2.1 and 2.2).[8] Ptolemy had invoked the juggling act performed by the portraitist to explain this distinction between modes of describing. When rendering an entire head, the portraitist borrows the cognitive framework of the geographer when he contemplates the globe. The production of individual features, on the other hand, is analogous to the task of chorographic, or local, description.

Apian was the first editor of Ptolemy's work to pictorialize this conceit. With this image, Apian announced his book's campaign to visualize the pedagogy of cosmography. In a woodcut consisting of four visual fields, Apian invoked these products of the portraitist: the rendering of the entire head compares favorably to geography's pursuit to capture the macrocosm, whereas topographic description, or chorography, embodies the level of particular features.[9] The illustration demonstrates these two ways to think about the terrestrial sphere, linking a globe to a head and a townscape to an ear and an *eye*. These images enshrined what might otherwise have been a couple of throwaway conclusions. The first point that Apian drove home was that the description of the earth could be translated into inherently visual terms; the second is that distinctions between incipient disciplines could be cultivated by informed observation. Apian was not only the first to recognize the visual potential of Ptolemy's model, but also the first to formalize these principles of visual description as the modus operandi of his campaign to pictorialize cosmography.

The opening images of the eye and the ear in the *Cosmographicus Liber* have been frequently mobilized in the secondary literature; they are usually employed to showcase a dawning self-consciousness in early modern visual practice and the range of description suitable to rendering by a draftsman.[10] But these images, significantly, are also the opening gambit of a text that goes beyond lip service to the eye's role in knowing and describing. Rather than presenting just a handy mnemonic, Apian uses the visual analogy to pitch a claim with larger stakes, one with significant implications for the role of images in early modern scientific pursuits in general. The image provides the rationalization for understanding cosmography through picturing and, thus, underwrites the visual practices active in the book. The *Cosmographicus Liber*'s

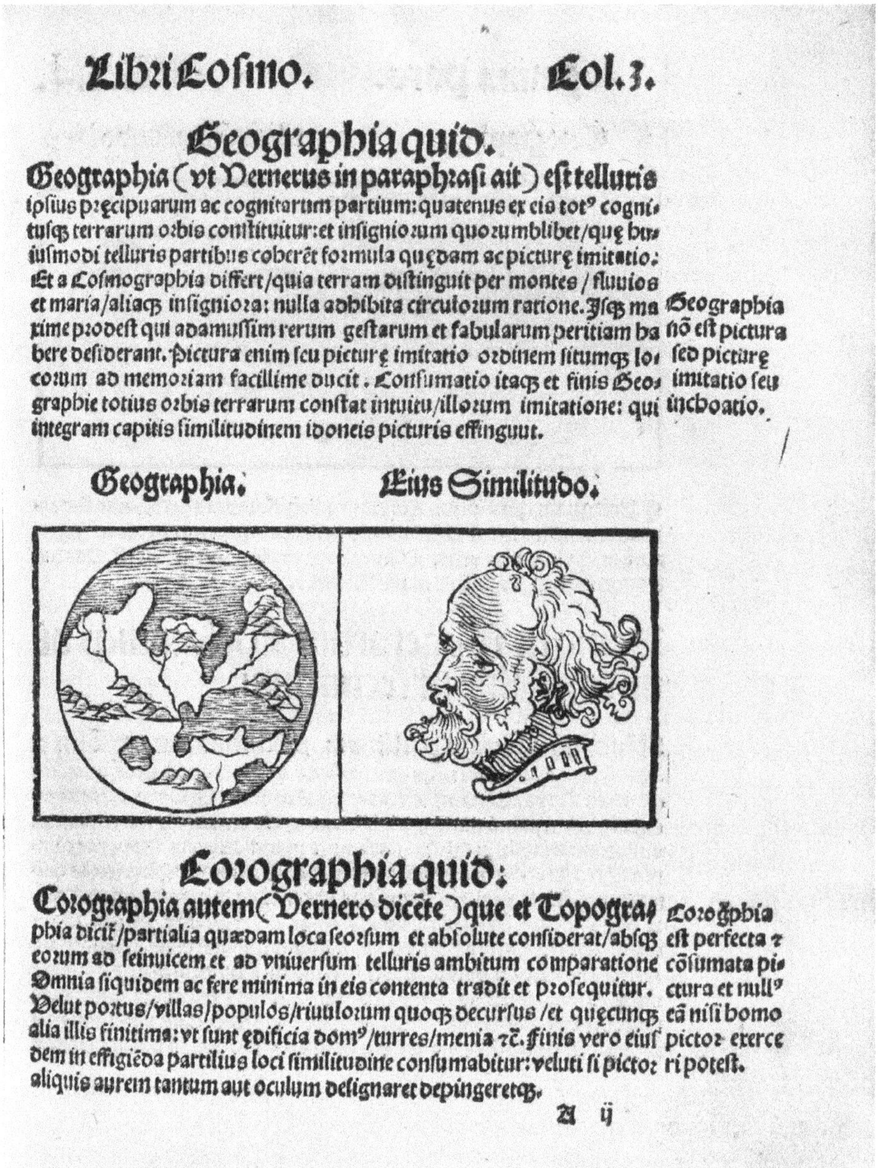

Libri Cosmo. Col. 3.

Geographia quid.

Geographia (ut Vernerus in paraphrasi ait) est telluris ipsius precipuarum ac cognitarum partium: quatenus ex eis totus cognitusque terrarum orbis constituitur: et insigniorum quorumlibet/que huiusmodi telluris partibus coherent formula quedam ac picture imitatio: Et a Cosmographia differt/quia terram distinguit per montes / fluuios et maria/aliaque insigniora: nulla adhibita circulorum ratione. Isque maxime prodest qui adamussim rerum gestarum et fabularum peritiam habere desiderant. Pictura enim seu picture imitatio ordinem situmque locorum ad memoriam facillime ducit. Consumatio itaque et finis Geographie totius orbis terrarum constat intuitu/illorum imitatione: qui integram capitis similitudinem idoneis picturis effinguut.

Geographia non est pictura sed picture imitatio seu inchoatio.

Geographia. Eius Similitudo.

Corographia quid:

Corographia autem (Vernero dicente) que et Topographia dicitur/partialia quædam loca seorsum et absolute considerat/absque eorum ad seinuicem et ad vniuersum telluris ambitum comparatione. Omnia siquidem ac fere minima in eis contenta tradit et prosequitur. Velut portus/villas/populos/riuulorum quoque decursus /et quecunque alia illis finitima: vt sunt edificia domus/turres/menia &c. Finis vero eiusdem in effigienda partilius loci similitudine consumabitur: veluti si pictor aliquis aurem tantum aut oculum designaret depingeretque.

Corographia est perfecta et cosumata pictura et nullus eam nisi homo pictor exercere potest.

A ij

2.1. Peter Apian, *Cosmographicus Liber* (Landshut: Weyssenburger, 1524), fol. 3. *Source:* Zentralbibliothek Zürich, NR 870. Courtesy of ETH-Bibliothek Zürich.

strategy for observing the world through visual means potentially revises the matrix in which the relationship between images and the development of popular science has been considered historically. Instead of simply supplementing understanding, images could also activate the observer's eyes.

Apian studied in Leipzig and Vienna. After a brief sojourn in Landshut, he was summoned to Ingolstadt for a university post in mathematics in 1527, and

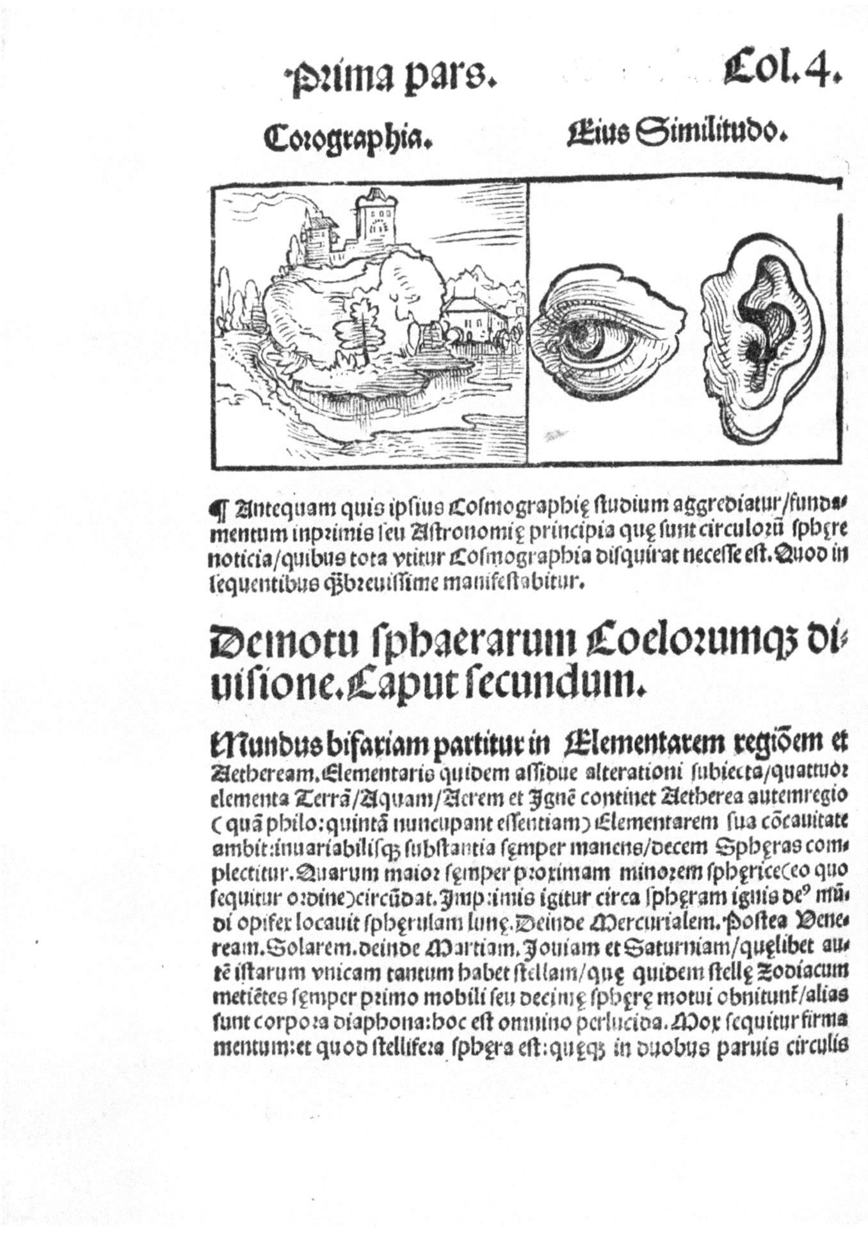

Prima pars. Fol. 4.

Corographia. Eius Similitudo.

¶ Antequam quis ipsius Cosmographie studium aggrediatur/fundamentum inprimis seu Astronomie principia que sunt circulorū sphere noticia/quibus tota vtitur Cosmographia disquirat necesse est. Quod in sequentibus q̄ breuissime manifestabitur.

De motu sphaerarum Coelorumq; diuisione. Caput secundum.

Mundus bifariam partitur in Elementarem regiōem et Aetheream. Elementaris quidem assidue alterationi subiecta/quattuor elementa Terrā/Aquam/Aerem et Ignē continet Aetherea autem regio (quā philo: quintā nuncupant essentiam) Elementarem sua cōcauitate ambit: inuariabilisq; substantia semper manens/decem Spheras complectitur. Quarum maior semper proximam minorem sphericè (eo quo sequitur ordine) circūdat. Imprimis igitur circa spheram ignis de⁹ mūdi opifex locauit spherulam lune. Deinde Mercurialem. Postea Veneream. Solarem. deinde Martiam. Iouiam et Saturniam/quelibet autē istarum vnicam tantum habet stellam/que quidem stelle Zodiacum metiētes semper primo mobili seu decime sphere motui obnituntur/alias sunt corpora diaphona: hoc est omnino perlucida. Mox sequitur firmamentum: et quod stellifera sphera est: queq; in duobus paruis circulis

2.2. Peter Apian, *Cosmographicus Liber* (Landshut: Weyssenburger, 1524), fol. 4. *Source:* Zentralbibliothek Zürich, NR 870. Courtesy of ETH-Bibliothek Zürich.

it was here that he would establish his own print shop around 1525.[11] As a printer, Apian speculated that privileging visual knowledge was a prerogative that the publishing market was uniquely capable of meeting. He guessed right. The *Cosmographicus Liber* was printed in Latin and in several vernacular tongues from 1524 until the seventeenth century, and the text even withstood Copernicus's reconceptualization of the universe from a geocentric to a heliocentric model. An updated edition was released in Antwerp in 1529 with corrections by the Louvain mathematician and cartographer Rainer Gemma Frisius (1508–55).[12] New additions by Gemma prompted another printing in 1533. Dutch and French vernaculars appeared shortly thereafter (Dutch in 1537; French in 1544). An almost continuous stream of Latin editions accompanied these new vernaculars. Before the end of the sixteenth century, there were at least forty-three editions in four languages.[13] The vernacular editions must have seemed relatively risk-free transpositions of the original Latin to the printers, who surely based the logic of these wider offerings on the strength of Apian's visual apparatus in conveying the book's themes. Indeed, such synthetic astronomical content had never before circulated in vernaculars – as the subjects of astronomy and geography were restricted to university audiences and learned circles. To be sure, many contemporary books repackaged material already in circulation, but the manner in which Apian reconfigured his sources makes this book scarcely resemble any of its direct forebears.[14] It was indebted to material from a number of significant sources of wide-ranging chronology: Ptolemy and Pliny as antique sources; Sacrobosco as medieval; more contemporary practitioners such as Regiomontanus and Martin Waldseemüller; and, later, Gemma Frisius. In fact, as Steven Vanden Broecke argues, it was only with Gemma's enhancements to Apian's *Cosmographicus Liber* that the book's content elevated the status of cosmography in academic settings.[15] Out of this admixture of old and new sources, Apian invented a popular science for lay observers. This chapter shows how Apian reformatted his major sources to configure the eye as the central agent of a pictorial guide to the heavens and the earth's geography.

IMAGES AND VISUAL LITERACY

Apian's illustrations and instruments offer visual evidence that impacts two major scholarly trajectories: first, the development of scientific images; and second, the structuring of visual literacy. The historiography of scientific images has primarily been the province of the history of science, perhaps predictably, but more recently it has generated substantial interest from art history. Apian's diagrams offer a productive reconciliation of these two fields. On the role of scientific images, this chapter proposes Apian's instruments as consequential in shaping empirical practices that would themselves come to define new disciplinary approaches. On the topic of visual literacy, it aims to suggest that Apian's program readied new audiences for the exercise of this skill.

Recent treatments of early modern epistemic, or knowledge-making, images track their role in the scientific revolution, and in a related area, the development of new disciplines of scholarly inquiry. These lines of academic investigation intersect with the history of printmaking at the juncture of the circulation and standardization of pictorial motifs.[16] For both of these concerns, scholars have been particularly attentive to the fields of botany and anatomy.[17] The emphasis on naturalism, along with its ahistorical accomplice "accuracy," in early scholarship on the illustrated natural sciences skewed the attention toward the aesthetic accomplishments of illustrations in a few select fields. This emphasis had the further effect of alienating the treatment of images in the physical sciences whose illustrations were not naturalistically driven. This privileging of mimetic images by select fields, according to Renzo Baldasso, also bankrupted potentially more productive investigations of images' epistemological functions.[18] Mimetic concerns have been tempered in more recent studies, driving considerations toward the rhetorical claims of their media.[19] Examinations of images' conventions and non-unique qualities are also being offered over teleological celebrations of naturalism.[20] More nuanced and historical applications of aesthetics in epistemic images have been tracked in astrological charts and horoscopes.[21] Other efforts have tracked the role of images in guiding scientific practice, especially images considered to be operative in establishing new epistemologies.[22] An important recent intervention has gone some distance to repair this void, considering a heterogeneous range of printed visual media to investigate their role in the formation of disciplinary sciences.[23]

Analyses of the historical reception of images has enabled more nuanced social histories of literacy. The work of images in shaping visual literacy has shifted from considering printed images as mere accompaniments to texts that were otherwise inscrutable to nonreaders to showing how they enlivened popular lay practices, such as devotion.[24] Visual literacy has also been pursued by investigations of images to both reflect and shape a cognitive understanding of collective cultural values, a concept to which an influential study gave the term *period eye*.[25] Studies of the synergy of words and images have emphasized scientific images' efforts to serve as technical support where words failed.[26] Images could also clarify for the reader opaque passages in the text.[27] Some recent inquiries also foreground images' functionality, such as those of technical images;[28] or they have argued for them as a vital component of text technologies.[29] Important work by Suzanne Karr Schmidt that features the reception of prints by early modern publics has given agency to these viewers as *users* – a claim that is backed by a surprising array of genres (including anatomical flap prints, devotional art, and movable dials) that stimulated interactivity.[30] In a concurrent development, the rubric of epistemic images has been invoked to characterize the images' internal pursuit of knowledge itself and explores the degree to which they toggle between representing and showing.[31]

This chapter bridges the themes of epistemic images and visual literacy by arguing that Apian's cosmographic images raised new epistemological concerns for the reading public. The illustrations conspired to shape the visual literacy of a particular stratum of educated readership; Apian's *Cosmographicus Liber* represents a coordinated effort to enhance readers' ability to make visual decisions and sharpen their capacity to observe. Apian relied on popular knowledge as diverse as astrology, amateur navigation, and instructional manuals for scientific instruments, as well as more scholarly sources in astronomy and cosmography. Apian's instruments embedded these forms of lay and learned knowledge into a pictorial program that aimed to facilitate new observational skills. The extent to which these images turned texts into a user's guide can be measured in the next generation of printed books that adopted these images to prompt eyewitness investigations. Epistemic images mediated visual learning, enunciated new fields of inquiry, accompanied technical manuals, and thus helped establish new practices.[32] My inquiry aims to contribute new scholarship on these knowledge-generating images and the investigation of the role of printed images in establishing new competencies in visual practices.[33] Printed media directed the collaborative inquiry that underwrote new scientific disciplines, especially in their capacity to recommend and coordinate visual searches.

UPDATING THE ANCIENTS

In light of the proven strength of Apian's visual program in the course of the long printing history of sixteenth-century cosmographic material, it is highly significant that the first visual analogy in the *editio princeps* already foreshadows the role that visual explanations will play in the illustrations that follow. Apian's first step in transforming Ptolemaic content into empirical principles was to invite the viewer to make visual judgments. Instructed to use the book's illustrations as a template for examining the stars, the viewer is asked by Apian to parse concepts such as cosmography and geography, marking these pursuits as distinct levels of epistemic engagement with the world.

Apian forecasts the guiding principle of his book as one of visual lessons, explicitly announced in the introduction, in which he says, "In these pictures, I will tell you what is meant by cosmography."[34] The isolated eye, as pictured here, is the sense organ with which Apian is most intently engaged, insofar as the eye is directly referenced by many of his diagrams, but, more importantly, by the extent to which the experience of cosmography is presented to a receptive ocular agent. The eye has literal agency for Apian. The book considers cosmography an art to be apprehended sensorily, as Tom Conley has convincingly shown, noting how Apian empowers the limbs of the vernacular reader, presenting body parts as "organs of locative perception."[35] Although he activates the observer's anatomy in the spirit of do-it-yourself investigations, Apian positions the eye as the layperson's antenna to unlocking material previously available only to those initiated in classical astronomical literature via the university. Destined for a broader lay public, which he attracted with the explanatory force of his visual diagrams, Apian's text coached the layperson to access this information with his senses using his eye to measure, to gauge, and to observe. The extent to which Apian overhauls his source material by interactive demonstrations enabled by moving dials makes this text's graphic conception and formatting a milestone in textual illustration and in the history of the book.[36] The *Cosmographicus Liber* positioned illustrations to provide visual tools (both actual and conceptual) as the groundwork for empirical knowledge about the universe. Apian also made special claims for the role of the artist in capturing that empirical knowledge, evoking the artist in his explanation of chorography or topographic description: "Chorography is a complete and useful picture and no one other than a painter is able to do it."[37]

Ptolemy's *Geographia* circulated throughout the manuscript tradition in the form of instructions for making visual projections of the coordinates he treated, but its content throughout its manuscript career was transmitted by text alone. Apian capitalized on this paradox, charging himself with the task of visualizing Ptolemy's principles. A set of images after the title page provides a conceptual introduction to cosmography, using an image of the eye at the base to tie the celestial and terrestrial spheres to each other (Figure 2.3). The adjacent illustration of a globe, a "detail" or fleshing out of the terrestrial sphere (including a continent labeled America), announces the interdisciplinary aims of the book and the ambitious plan to unite mathematical astronomy with geography. The lines that connect this pair of spheres show how information from the celestial sphere provides a basis for data for the terrestrial sphere.[38] Apian sets the conceptual model into dialogue with representations of objects that have analogues in scientific tools, the world globe, and the armillary sphere. Apian's image on the left can be seen as a type of exploded armillary sphere; perhaps more importantly, it is also a projection connected to a hypothetical viewer.

The apex of a set of rays resolves on the surface of a pictured eye. This image of an eye has been discussed as the source of omniscient vision belonging to God, a medieval view of God's place as prime mover in a theologically formatted universe.[39] This conceit depends on the framework of linear perspective to impart coherence to the visual model. Arguments for the tenacity of perspective in modeling the infinite, such as Erwin Panofsky's, could logically underwrite readings of Apian's eye as representing God's point of view.[40] Because the eye includes both the earth and the celestial sphere in its purview, as the perspectivist argument would go, it cannot belong to man.

But I would argue that this eye *must* belong to man, by virtue of another model of mathematized space also dependent on perspective: the projection.[41] This type of perspective is not the kind that we detect in Renaissance panel painting, but it did govern certain types of scientific images. That Apian's

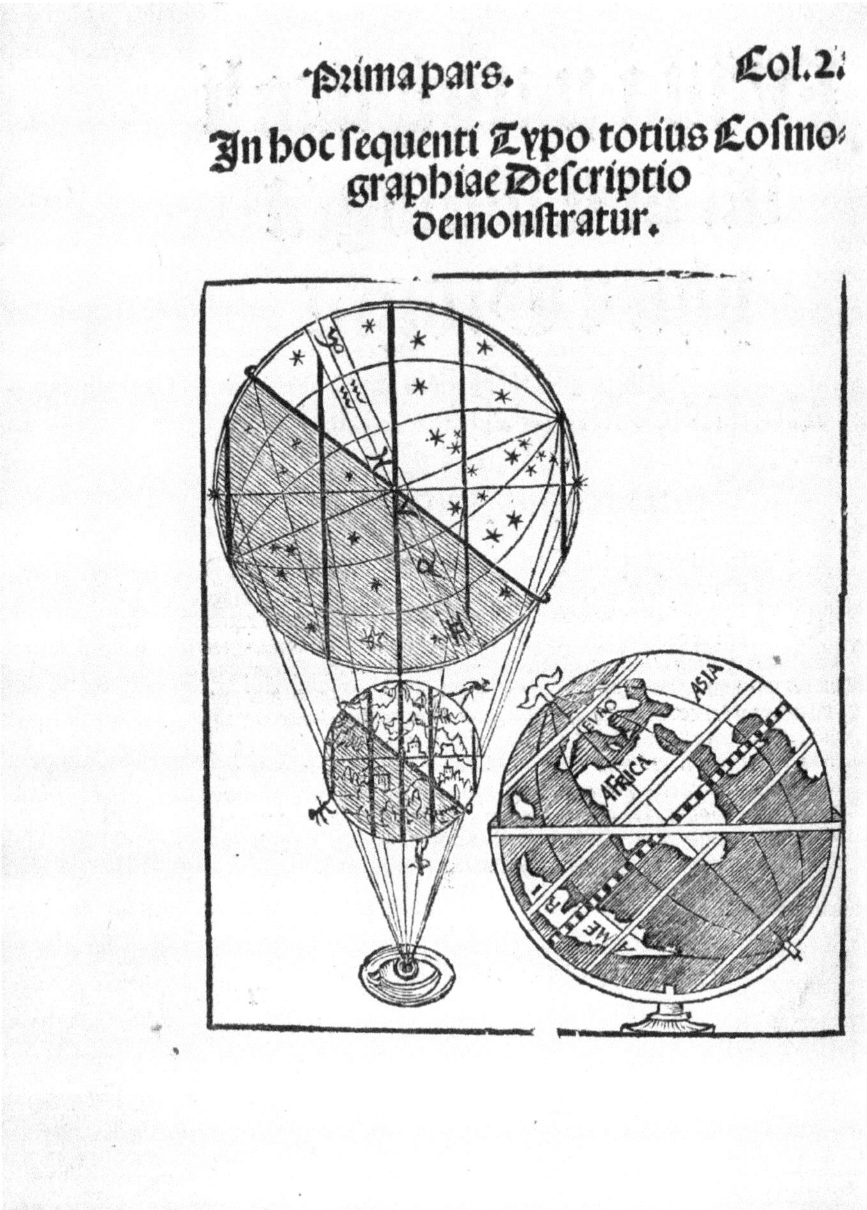

2.3. Peter Apian, *Cosmographicus Liber* (Landshut: Weyssenburger, 1524), fol. 2. *Source:* Zentralbibliothek Zürich, NR 870. Courtesy of ETH-Bibliothek Zürich.

cosmographic model is imagining a planispheric projection (that situates man at the base) makes sense given the reciprocity cartographic projections are assumed to have had with linear perspective.[42] Another visual mode from which Renaissance perspectival models might have taken their cues was architectural projection developed by engineers and theorists, whose designs may have facilitated the visualization of Ptolemy's ideas into cartographic projections.[43]

Most theories of perspective's origins agree on the importance of Ptolemy as a catalyst in the transition to perspectival projections. Ptolemy's projection methods were intended to help readers conceptualize his observations.

Whether these prescriptions originated in cartographic or astronomic materials (which, as this chapter will show, were intimately related), Ptolemy serves as a linchpin for scholarly speculation on the origin of visual projections. Rather than in Ptolemy's geographic works, however, other scholars find this origin in his theorizations of astronomic projections.[44] The construction of a planisphere, according to Ptolemy, requires one to imagine the eye at the south pole; he envisions the equator as the picture plane for the planisphere. Onto this, he projects the tropics of Cancer and Capricorn and the ecliptic.[45] Ptolemy's strategy for planispheric projection, according to Kim Veltman, encompassed all the basic elements for linear perspective (an eye at a fixed point, a picture plane, and an object) and suggests itself as a compelling precedent for the type of abstractions on which linear perspective is built.[46]

Rather than representing the vision of God, it is more likely that Apian means to hail the human eye in this conceptualization of one's visual cone. The resemblance these lines bear to rays depicted in optical models, as Steven Vanden Broecke asserts, also supports a reading of this as a human eye. The eye, for Apian, "centralizes perception as such."[47] Apian's emphasis on the agency of human vision forges a new link in the realm of what was visually possible. Apian's efforts to empower visual knowledge leave no doubt that it is our visual acuity that this book attempts to hone. A similar human eye also anchors the diagram on folio 110r, which shows the various phases of the waxing and waning moon (Figure 2.4). These moons surround the pictured eye like spokes on a wheel that align the sun's light to what the eye takes in; the degrees of shading indicate portions of reflected light. The centralized eye tracks the face of the moon as it waxes and wanes through its cycle. Apian's visualization of these perceptual complexities even extends to what the observer *cannot* see but should understand: the dark side of the moon. In this respect, the human eye can also function as an omniscient eye.

Inserting man's eye as the primary receptor of cosmographic knowledge that connects both the heavenly and the earthly spheres pictured, Apian's text represents an updating and visualizing of the data in Ptolemy's *Geographia*. Apian's aim is to make Ptolemy's principles practical. He sizes Ptolemaic knowledge for the reader's local coordinates. In so doing, Apian engages with his sources in a forthright way; his volume does not disguise his predecessors, but reconfigures their contributions in a way that is useful to the reader.[48] Ptolemy as such had never been considered particularly useful to the academic curriculum; even when Ptolemy did make it into university syllabi, the *Geographia* did not lend itself to the structural commentary that was the modus operandi of university textbooks.[49] The discipline of cosmography in the

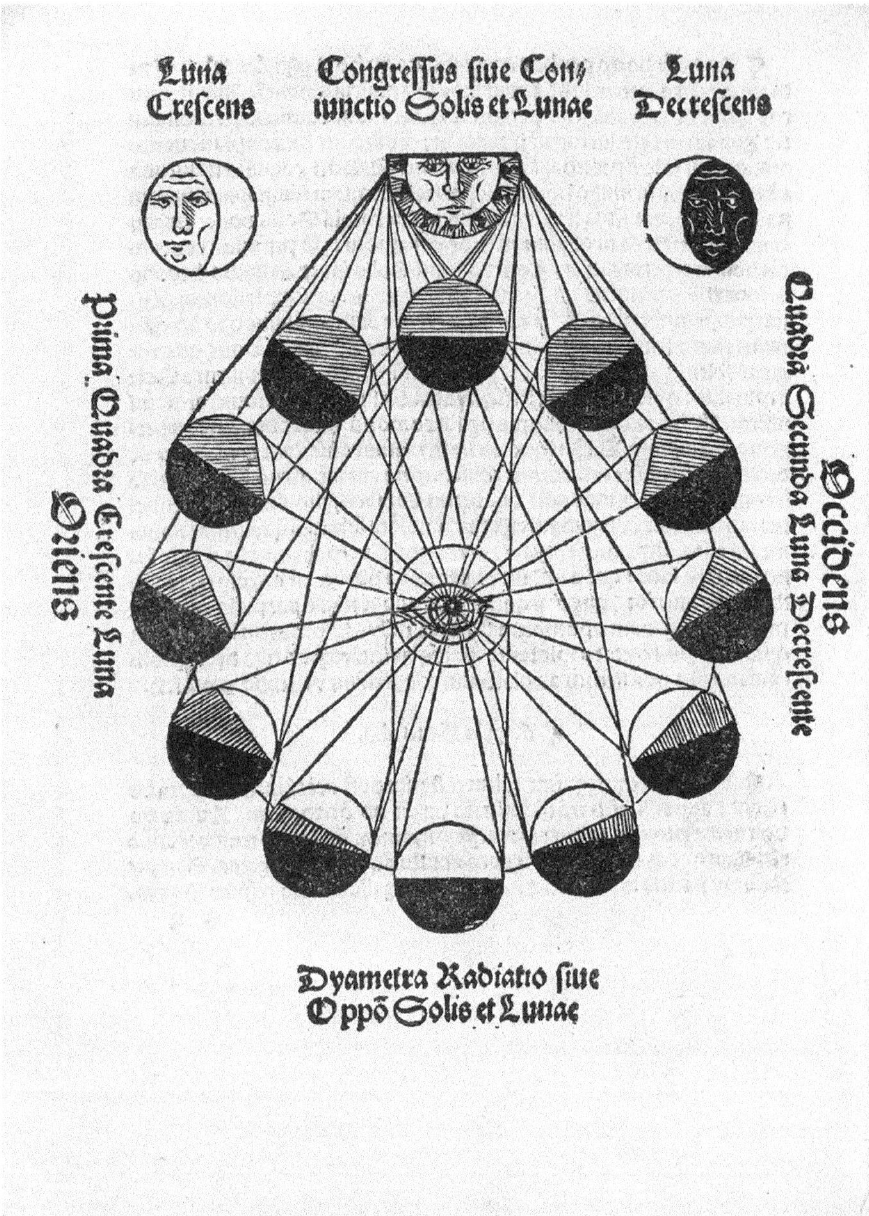

2.4. Moon phases, Peter Apian, *Cosmographicus Liber* (Landshut: Weyssenburger, 1524), fol. 110. *Source:* Zentralbibliothek Zürich, NR 870. Courtesy of ETH-Bibliothek Zürich.

sixteenth century, therefore, seems to have developed outside the university and through the back door via the popular press and works such as the *Cosmographicus Liber.*[50] More critical seemed to be the practical summaries of Ptolemaic learning in which astronomers trafficked in the medieval period. One of these was Sacrobosco's *De Sphaera* – incidentally, one of the texts for which Apian was also plotting an overhaul.[51]

Although the demand for a synthetic text such as the *Cosmographicus Liber* seems like it should have been secure for a readership of amateur astronomers who recognized the advantage of illustrated and interactive editions, the market for popular astronomy was just getting off the ground.[52] The bulk of information on astronomy proper had been tucked away in the realm of university learning for centuries.[53] As a professional mathematician with a side job printing astrological pamphlets, or *Practica*, Apian must have gauged the spectrum of competencies in and appetites for digesting astronomical literature. This audience likely ranged from stargazers and geographers to monastics in charge of scheduling, or even physicians who were naturally linked to mathematicians through their common interest in astrology.[54] For this diverse reading public, Apian clearly saw a market for crossover works like the *Cosmographicus Liber*, which might have been issued to supplement and clarify existing university texts, but he also updated older, more classical examples of the genre.[55] At the time of the cosmography's printing, Apian was also preoccupied with retooling the substance of one such manual, Sacrobosco's *De Sphaera*. Our evidence for this is twofold: in the first place, the *Cosmographicus Liber* relies heavily on Sacrobosco as source material; and second, Apian would himself publish a new edition of *De Sphaera* in 1526, two years after the first printing of the *Cosmographicus Liber*. It is reasonable to assume that Apian developed the pictorial accompaniments for both his *De Sphaera* and *Cosmographicus Liber* in tandem. It is also therefore not surprising that for his own edition of Sacrobosco, Apian was primarily concerned with updating the visual apparatus of the text, given his sustained translation of astronomical and cosmographic thinking into pictorial formulae in the cosmography.

From the continuous popularity of Sacrobosco's *De Sphaera* from 1220 through the sixteenth century, we can infer that many savvy fifteenth- and sixteenth-century printers saw the rewards of offering popular and vernacular editions.[56] Repackaging information from Ptolemy's *Almagest* and its Arabic commentaries, *De Sphaera* was one of the major sources of Ptolemaic cosmographic knowledge in late medieval and early modern Europe that explained the shape and apparent motion of heavenly bodies.[57] It epitomized the portions of the *Almagest* that referred to earthly coordinates and incorporated the Arabic commentary on Ptolemy.[58] *De Sphaera* was the most popular text on positional astronomy for use in academic instruction throughout the Middle Ages, but its circulation ballooned in the age of print, when it remained a popular manual for teaching astronomy in the university *quadrivium*.[59] Illustrations aided the text's many proofs about the relationship of the terrestrial to the celestial spheres and gave readers a conceptual model of cosmography.[60] Sacrobosco, unlike Ptolemy himself, proved an excellent foundation on which to hang astronomical commentary.[61] The *editio princeps* of *De Sphaera* appeared in either Ferrara or Venice in 1472 or 1473, and the text enjoyed a heavy traffic in reprints until the mid-seventeenth century.[62]

The advent of heliocentrism did little to disturb the useful nature of Sacrobosco's text for practical navigation or instrument learning; it remained a vital source for astronomical knowledge even after Copernicus's revised model of the solar system.[63]

Important developments in the pictorialization of astronomy texts that would influence Apian occurred in Erhard Ratdolt's graphic laboratory. A *Kalendario* in which Regiomontanus's corrected data met novel experiments in design was printed in Venice in 1476 by Ratdolt, followed by a color printing of Sacrobosco in 1482.[64] These moves to streamline the graphic interface and to use color to help the reader discern differences in celestial phenomena show Ratdolt's investment in visualization for the teaching of astronomy.[65] Indeed, these experiments in color inaugurate a new emphasis on visualization in the history of printmaking: Ratdolt's bicolor images of eclipses shown in black and yellow are generally considered to be the first woodcuts printed in color; he expanded such experiments in color printing several years later in Augsburg.[66] Another important chapter in the pictorialization of Sacrobosco was begun by vernacular German editions printed from 1516 onwards, when *De Sphaera* received ample illustrations in recensions by the Nuremberg humanist Conrad Heinfogel.

Apian's *Cosmographicus Liber* follows a tradition of visualization already gaining traction in the printed Sacrobosco editions, capitalizing on a major shift in the relationship between observation and scientific inquiry already being promulgated by these sources. Peter Barker and Kathleen Crowther have explored how this shift was mediated by images in their article "Training the Intelligent Eye," which also provides a useful historiography of the role of images in natural knowledge in general. Even in the tradition of Sacrobosco's tenacious models of spherical astronomy, empirical inquiry had been the prerequisite for the conceptualization of these abstract principles.[67] Observation had always been a necessary component to conceptualization; it was reliance on observables such as the precession of certain planets that held the Ptolemaic model of epicycles and deferents together. Theoretical models were cooked up to explain what stargazers were seeing. Yet with these theories of planetary motion in place, there was little need for most students to leave their warm studies for chilly examinations of the heavens. With Sacrobosco and Peurbach, as the authors argue, the images grapple with explaining old theories.[68] Images are prerequisites for users to form their mental conceptualizations.

While some early sixteenth-century designers of images for Sacrobosco's *De Sphaera* considered the agency of the reader's eye, it was not the focus of visual programs per se. Rather than commandeering the eye's agency to certify a proof, celestial events were presented to the eye in terms of something an observer might have happened to notice. A typical example of the eye's peripheral role can be found in Sacrobosco's explanation of the spherical shape of the earth; the corollary he provides is of the sphericity of water on the earth's surface. According to Sacrobosco, the shape of the earth's surrounding layer of water can be inferred from the spherical shape of dew drops: from the homogenous properties of these drops, we can infer that bodies of water are also round.[69] A supporting proof about the earth's shape confirms this: when at sea, sailors atop a ship's mast can spy a light on land not visible to those on deck. The visual impediment of the deck hands demonstrates the earth's curvature.[70] Some early printed editions tried to convey this parallax with woodcuts showing a square cutaway image of the water and a ship with lines drawn to shore (Figure 2.5).[71] Although the idea of observation is implied by the proof, the accompanying illustration did not necessarily reinforce its demonstration as an empirical act. In Apian's version of the *De Sphaera*, however, he positions observers at the ends of these projected lines, clarifying the proof via an outsized ship sailing on a sphere – literally a round earth that takes account of both ship and shore, picturing observers on the deck and atop the mast (Figure 2.6).[72] Apian's image reprises designs for editions of Sacrobosco printed in Venice in the late fifteenth century that feature the sightlines of the observers in the diagram, marking what they see as "visual rays" (Figure 2.7).[73] The sightings modeled by the pictured observers were critical to the proof at hand – Crowther and Barker explain that such hybrids of diagrammatic and narrative images could be found in manuals designed explicitly for beginners.[74] Deferring to visual strategies like these that attempted to clarify principles, Apian sought to foreground the aspect of the proof that was based on observational practice and pictorialized actual observers. Not far from Apian's illustration appears another optical proof of the heaven's corresponding roundness, and it describes the situation observed as analogous to how rays appear to bend in an atmosphere thicker than air. The illustration provides an example of the magnification of a coin through an aqueous medium (Figure 2.8) – at the receiving end is a disembodied eye that sees through the diffuse light. Eye guides such as this that taught the position of the eye in a diagram about observation have a precedent in sections of astronomical manuscripts devoted to measuring and gauging.[75]

Apian stages his demonstration of the earth's curvature through a visual exercise (Figure 2.9). The image provides the reader with a menu of shapes against which to compare their observations of the moon's surface during a lunar eclipse. By matching the geometry of the shape that appears on the lunar surface with options provided in his diagram, the reader can eliminate erroneous options. The earth's projection of a sphere-shaped shadow confirms to an astute observer that the earth must be a sphere. This proof demonstrates how a finely tuned eye can visually verify evidence. To execute this proof visually, Apian indulged in a lengthy digression of pictorial counterproofs with redundancy built in. Apian's full-page illustration enumerates a variety of other

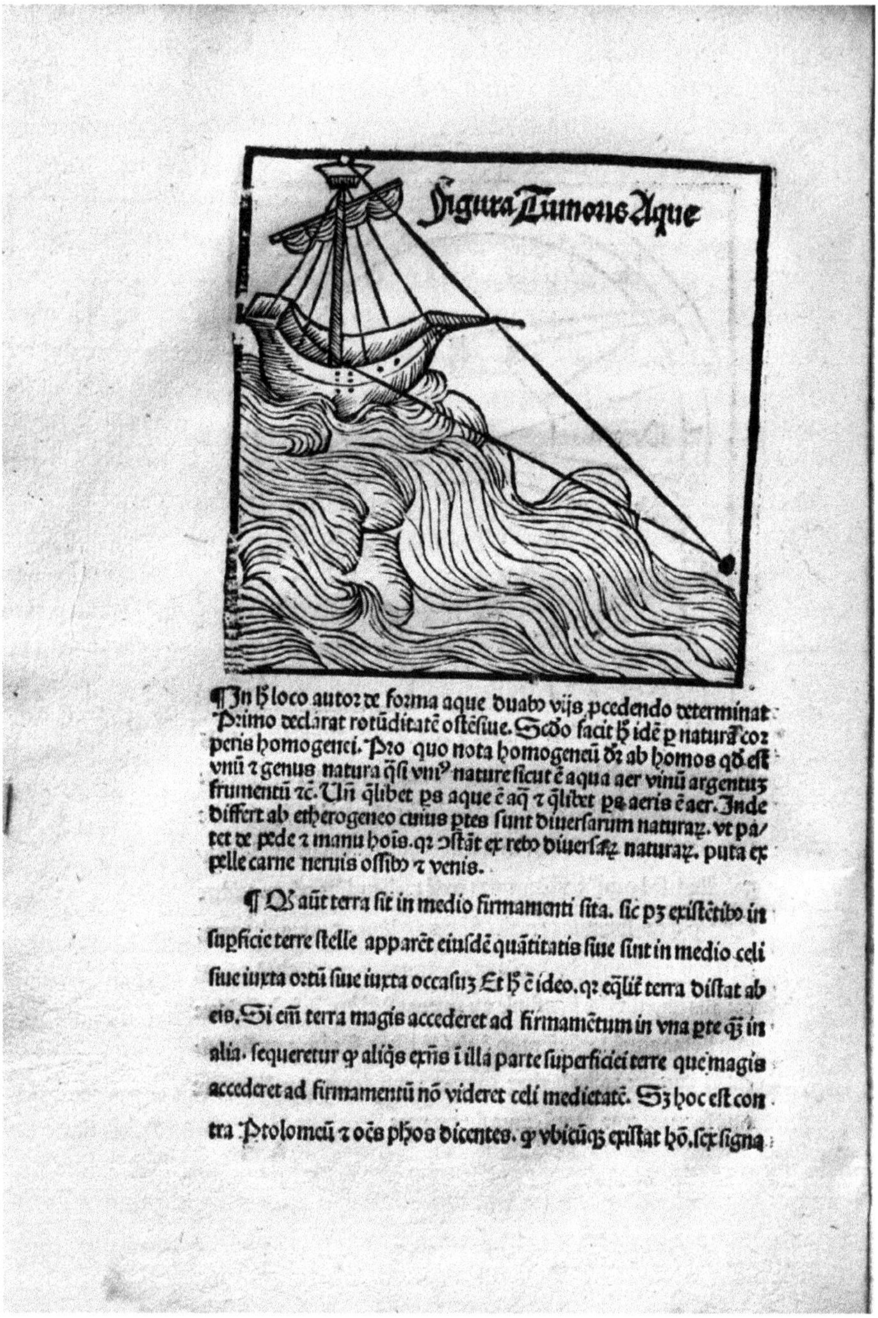

¶ In h loco autor de forma aque duab vijs pcedendo determinat: Primo declarat rotũditatẽ ostẽsiue. Scd̃o facit h idẽ p naturã cor peris homogenei. Pro quo nota homogeneũ dr̃ ab homos qd̃ est vnũ ⁊ genus natura q̃si vni⁹ nature sicut ẽ aqua aer vinũ argentuz frumentũ ⁊c̃. Vñ q̃libet ps aque ẽ aq̃ ⁊ q̃libet ps aeris ẽ aer. Inde differt ab etherogeneo cuius ptes sunt diuersarum naturaz. vt pa/tet de pede ⁊ manu hoĩs. q2 ↄstãt ex reb diuersaz naturaz. puta ex pelle carne neruis ossib ⁊ venis.

¶ Q2 aũt terra sit in medio firmamenti sita. sic pz existẽtib in supficie terre stelle apparẽt eiusdẽ quãtitatis siue sint in medio celi siue iuxta ortũ siue iuxta occasuz Et h ẽ ideo. q2 eq̃lĩt terra distat ab eis. Si eñ terra magis accederet ad firmamẽtum in vna pte q̃z in alia. sequeretur q̃ aliq̃s exñs ĩ illã parte superficiei terre que magis accederet ad firmamentũ nõ videret celi medietatẽ. Sz hoc est contra Ptolomeũ ⁊ oẽs phos dicentes. q̃ vbicũqz existat hõ. sex signa

2.5. Sacrobosco and Wenceslaus Fabri, *Opus sphericum Johannis de sacro busto: figuris et p[er]utili co [m]mento illustratu[m]* (Cologne: Quentell, 1501), 10r. *Source:* Augsburg, Staats- und Stadtbibliothek 4 Math 491. Courtesy of Augsburg, Staats- und Stadtbibliothek.

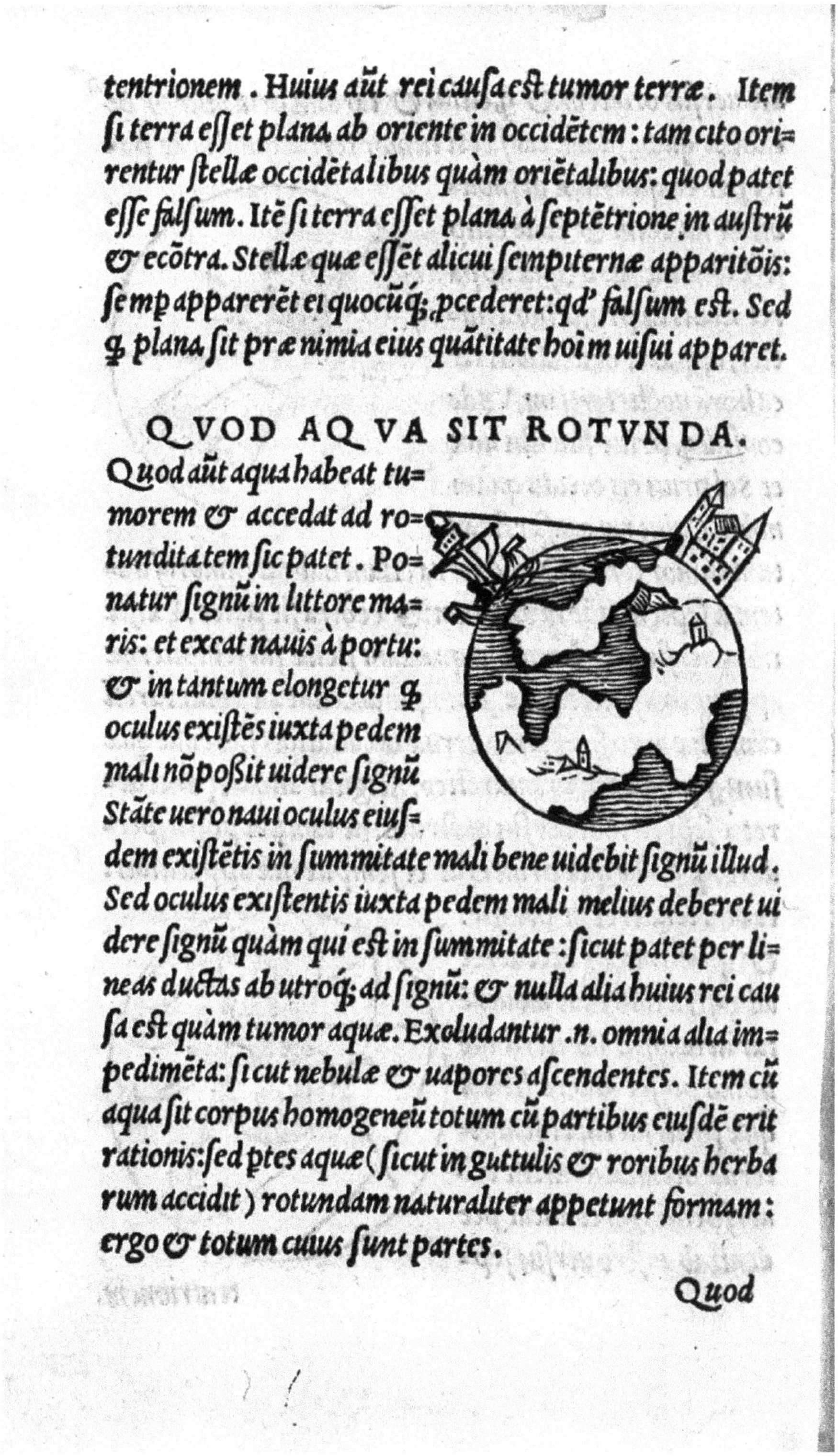
tentrionem. Huius aũt rei cauſa eſt tumor terræ. Item
ſi terra eſſet plana ab oriente in occidẽtem: tam cito ori=
rentur ſtellæ occidẽtalibus quàm oriẽtalibus: quod patet
eſſe falſum. Itẽ ſi terra eſſet plana à ſeptẽtrione in auſtrũ
& ecõtra. Stellæ quæ eſſẽt alicui ſempiternæ apparitõis:
ſemꝑ apparerẽt ei quocũq; ꝓcederet: qđ falſum eſt. Sed
ꝙ plana ſit præ nimia eius quãtitate hoĩm uiſui apparet.

QVOD AQVA SIT ROTVNDA.

Quod aũt aqua habeat tu=
morem & accedat ad ro=
tunditatem ſic patet. Po=
natur ſignũ in littore ma=
ris: et exeat nauis à portu:
& in tantum elongetur ꝙ
oculus exiſtẽs iuxta pedem
mali nõ poſſit uidere ſignũ
Stãte uero naui oculus eiuſ=
dem exiſtẽtis in ſummitate mali bene uidebit ſignũ illud.
Sed oculus exiſtentis iuxta pedem mali melius deberet ui
dere ſignũ quàm qui eſt in ſummitate: ſicut patet per li=
neas ductas ab utroq; ad ſignũ: & nulla alia huius rei cau
ſa eſt quàm tumor aquæ. Excludantur .n. omnia alia im=
pedimẽta: ſicut nebulæ & uapores aſcendentes. Item cũ
aqua ſit corpus homogeneũ totum cũ partibus eiuſdẽ erit
rationis: ſed ꝑtes aquæ (ſicut in guttulis & roribus herba
rum accidit) rotundam naturaliter appetunt formam:
ergo & totum cuius ſunt partes.

Quod

2.6. Sacrobosco, *Sphaera Iani de Sacrobusto* (Ingolstadt: Apian, 1526), 6v. *Source:* BSB Astr.u.151. Courtesy of Bayerische Staatsbibliothek, Munich.

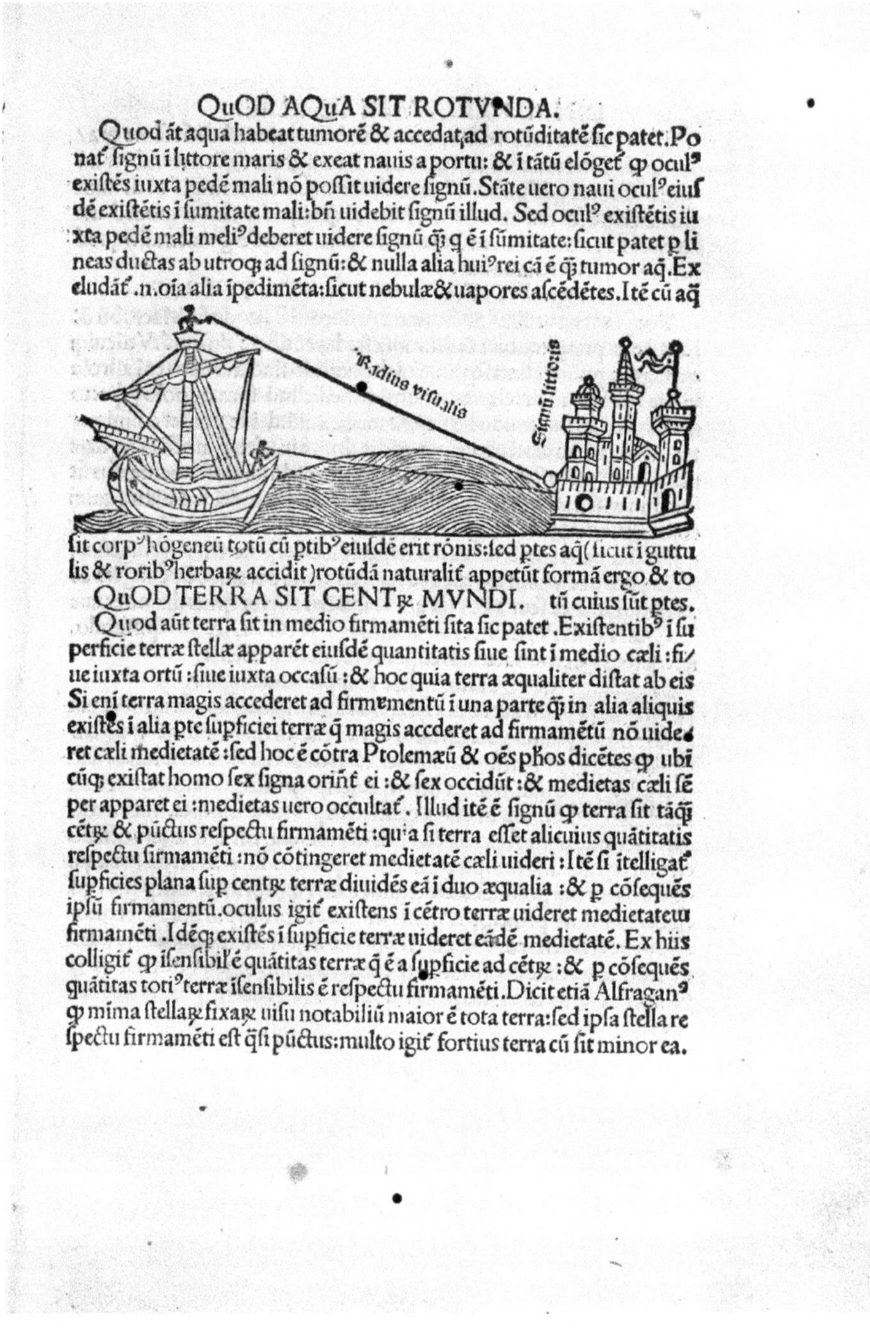

QuOD AQuA SIT ROTVNDA.

Quod ãt aqua habeat tumorẽ & accedat ad rotũditatẽ ſic patet. Ponat̃ ſignũ i littore maris & exeat nauis a portu: & i tãtũ elõget̃ ꝙ ocul⁹ exiſtẽs iuxta pedẽ mali nõ poſſit uidere ſignũ. Stãte uero naui ocul⁹ eiuſdẽ exiſtẽtis i ſumitate mali: bñ uidebit ſignũ illud. Sed ocul⁹ exiſtẽtis iuxta pedẽ mali meli⁹ deberet uidere ſignũ q̃ȝ q ẽ i ſũmitate: ſicut patet p lineas ductas ab utroqȝ ad ſignũ: & nulla alia hui⁹ rei cã ẽ q̃ȝ tumor aq̃. Excludãt̃ .n. oĩa alia ĩpedimẽta: ſicut nebulæ & uapores aſcẽdẽtes. Itẽ cũ aq̃ ſit corp⁹ hõgeneũ totũ cũ ptib⁹ eiuſdẽ erit rõnis: ſed ptes aq̃ (ſicut i guttulis & rorib⁹ herbaꝝ accidit) rotũdã naturalit̃ appetũt formã ergo & totũ cuius ſũt ptes.

QuOD TERRA SIT CENTꝜ MVNDI.

Quod aũt terra ſit in medio firmamẽti ſita ſic patet. Exiſtentib⁹ ĩ ſuperficie terræ ſtellæ apparẽt eiuſdẽ quantitatis ſiue ſint ĩ medio cæli: ſiue iuxta ortũ: ſiue iuxta occaſũ: & hoc quia terra æqualiter diſtat ab eis Si enĩ terra magis accederet ad firmamentũ ĩ una parte q̃ȝ in alia aliquis exiſtẽs ĩ alia pte ſupficiei terræ q̃ magis accderet ad firmamẽtũ nõ uideret cæli medietatẽ: ſed hoc ẽ cõtra Ptolemæũ & oẽs pħos dicẽtes ꝙ ubicũqȝ exiſtat homo ſex ſigna orĩũt̃ ei: & ſex occidũt: & medietas cæli ſẽper apparet ei: medietas uero occultat̃. Illud itẽ ẽ ſignũ ꝙ terra ſit tãq̃ȝ cẽtꝜ & pũctus reſpectu firmamẽti: quia ſi terra eſſet alicuius quãtitatis reſpectu firmamẽti: nõ cõtingeret medietatẽ cæli uideri: Itẽ ſi ĩtelligat̃ ſupficies plana ſup centꝜ terræ diuidẽs eã ĩ duo æqualia: & p cõſequẽs ipſũ firmamentũ. oculus igit̃ exiſtens ĩ cẽtro terræ uideret medietatem firmamẽti. Idẽqȝ exiſtẽs ĩ ſupficie terræ uideret eãdẽ medietatẽ. Ex hiis colligit̃ ꝙ ĩſenſibil' ẽ quãtitas terræ q̃ ẽ a ſupficie ad cẽtꝜ: & p cõſequẽs quãtitas toti⁹ terræ ĩſenſibilis ẽ reſpectu firmamẽti. Dicit etiã Alfragan⁹ ꝙ mĩma ſtellaꝝ fixaꝝ uiſu notabiliũ maior ẽ tota terra: ſed ipſa ſtella reſpectu firmamẽti eſt q̃ſi pũctus: multo igit̃ fortius terra cũ ſit minor ea.

2.7. Sacrobosco, *Sphaerae Mvndi Compendium Foeliciter Inchoat. … Iohannis de sacro busto sphæricum opusculum* (Venice: Sanctis & Santritter, 1488), fol. 77. *Source:* Zentralbibliothek Zürich, Ink. K 294. Courtesy of ETH-Bibliothek Zürich.

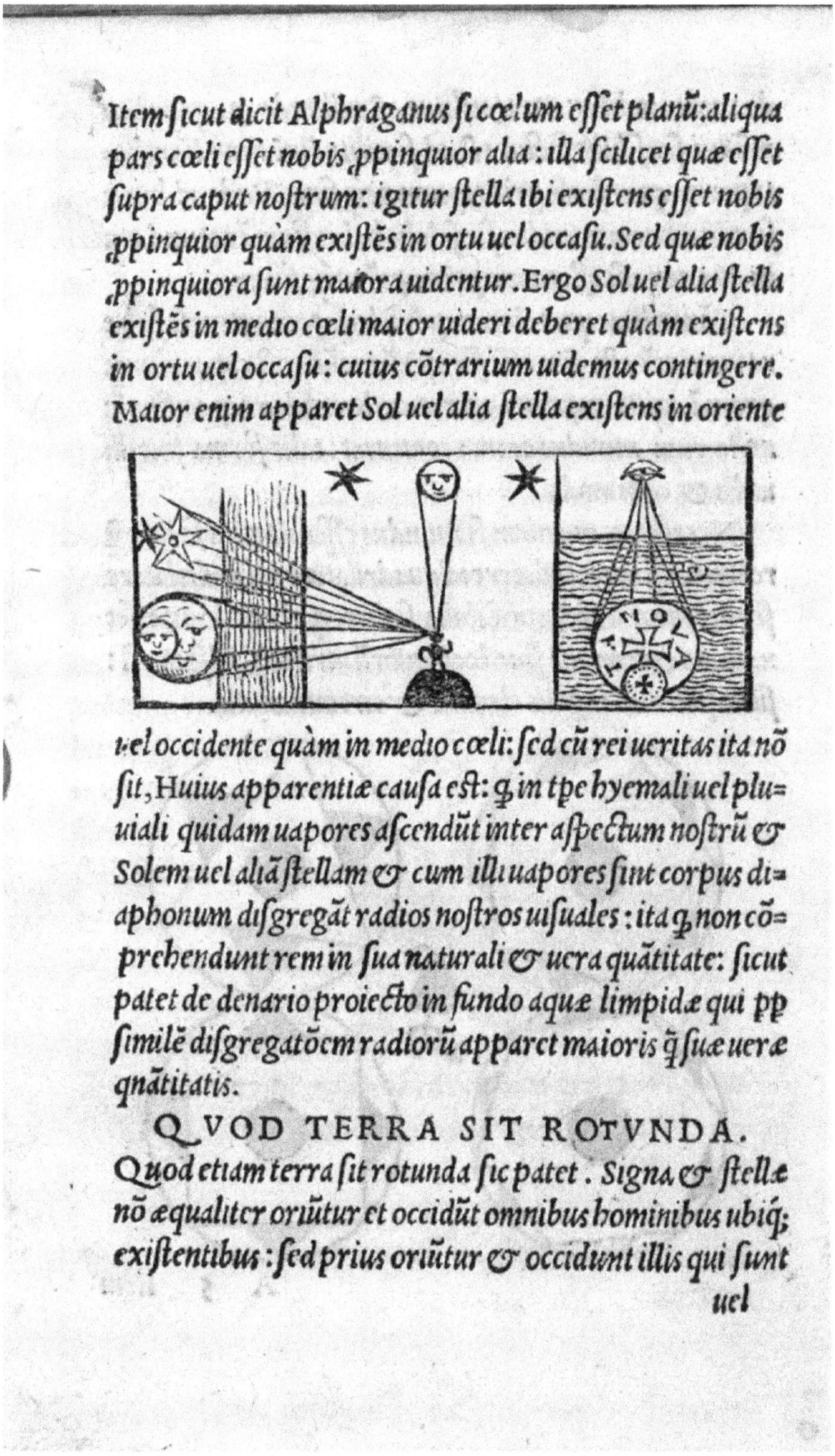

Item sicut dicit Alphraganus si cœlum esset planū: aliqua pars cœli esset nobis ꝓpinquior alia: illa scilicet quæ esset supra caput nostrum: igitur stella ibi existens esset nobis ꝓpinquior quàm existēs in ortu uel occasu. Sed quæ nobis ꝓpinquiora sunt maiora uidentur. Ergo Sol uel alia stella existēs in medio cœli maior uideri deberet quàm existens in ortu uel occasu: cuius cōtrarium uidemus contingere. Maior enim apparet Sol uel alia stella existens in oriente uel occidente quàm in medio cœli: sed cū rei ueritas ita nō sit, Huius apparentiæ causa est: ꝙ in tpe hyemali uel pluuiali quidam uapores ascendūt inter aspectum nostrū & Solem uel aliā stellam & cum illi uapores sint corpus diaphonum disgregāt radios nostros uisuales: ita ꝙ non cōprehendunt rem in sua naturali & uera quātitate: sicut patet de denario proiecto in fundo aquæ limpidæ qui ꝓp similē disgregatōem radiorū apparet maioris q̄ suæ ueræ qnātitatis.

QVOD TERRA SIT ROTVNDA.

Quod etiam terra sit rotunda sic patet. Signa & stellæ nō æqualiter oriūtur et occidūt omnibus hominibus ubiq; existentibus: sed prius oriūtur & occidunt illis qui sunt uel

2.8. Sacrobosco, *Sphaera Iani de Sacrobusto* (Ingolstadt: Apian, 1526), 5v. *Source:* BSB Astr.u.151. Courtesy of Bayerische Staatsbibliothek, Munich.

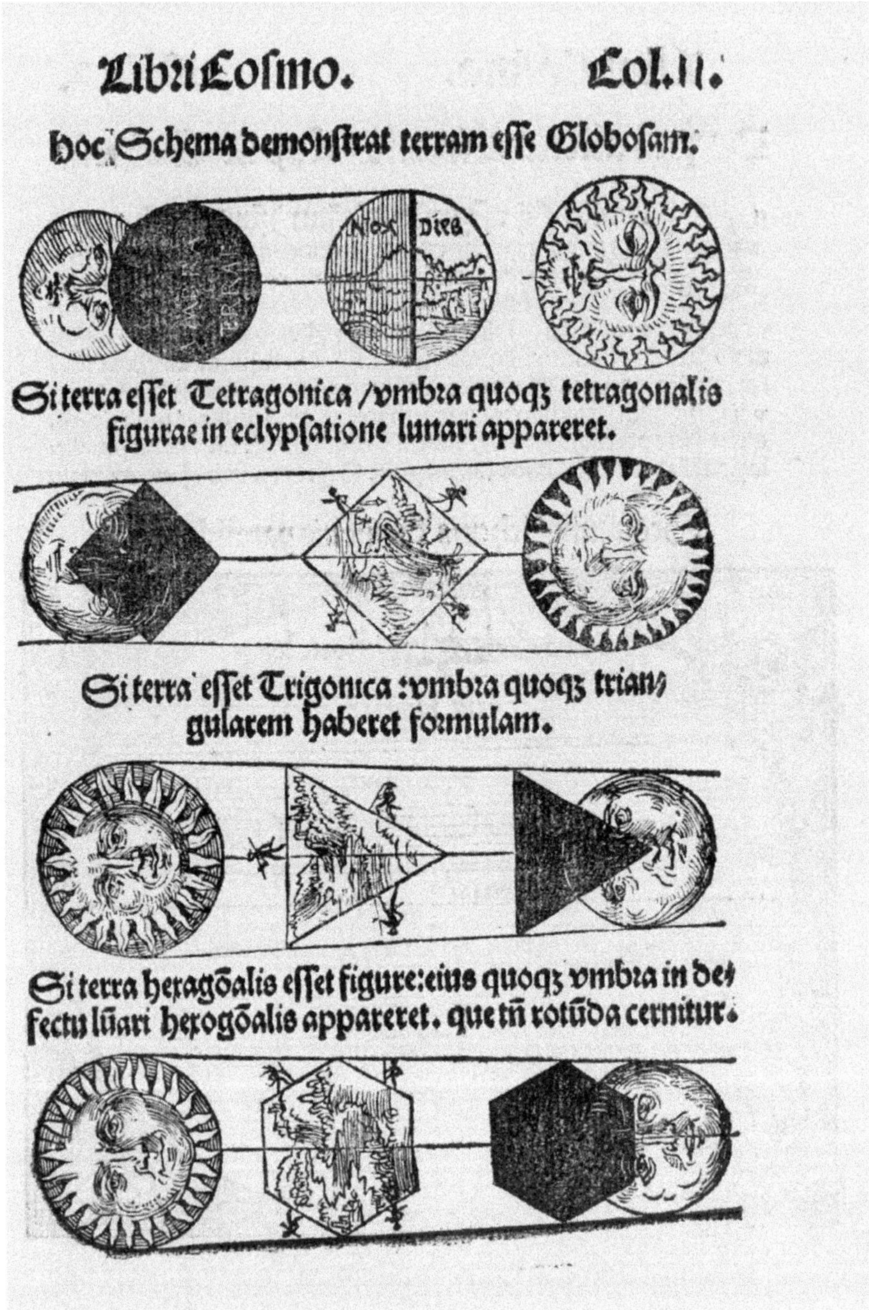

2.9. Peter Apian, *Cosmographicus Liber* (Landshut: Weyssenburger, 1524), fol. 11. *Source:* Smithsonian. Image in the public domain.

shapes that the earth's shadow might assume when projected onto the lunar surface; these include a triangle, a square, and a hexagon.[76] Apian used these differently shaped earths to caution his reader to rule out conditions that were not empirically verifiable. This explanation assumes good evidence to be observations that can or cannot be confirmed by the naked eye during eclipses, explicitly coaching the making of visual judgments. The sphericality of the earth enjoys incontrovertible proof when based on the empirical experience of an actual observer.[77] This image records eyewitness observations, accompanied by caveats to rule out options that cannot be empirically supported.

Apian's experiments with explanatory diagrams and such visual reiterations suggest that he developed the cosmography for readers for whom such proofs based on empirical experience seemed persuasive. Instead of the recursive bundles of resemblances and conveniences that characterized Michel Foucault's explanations of causality in the premodern episteme, Apian's empirically activated reader was empowered by books to settle for nothing less than visually verifiable truths.[78] Illustrated guides to the heavens were proving increasingly useful to a broader stratum of the lay population in search of manuals to accompany their firsthand searches.

MECHANICAL PICTURES FOR OBSERVER-CENTERED PEDAGOGY

University lectures presented the basics of positional astronomy and frequently relied on various tools for their pedagogy. Apian trained in mathematical astrology in Leipzig and Vienna under Georg Tannstetter, whose own pedigree included Regiomontanus, Peurbach, and Andreas Stiborius – all of whose tenures were financed by imperial projects. The wall calendars and almanacs that resulted from these efforts expressed abstract designs and theories primarily intended for a group of university and court professionals. While many of his teachers' efforts were in the service of explaining universals and updating tables, Apian instead envisioned a market that could unpack these trade secrets for the layperson.[79] As a major strategy for popularizing basic astronomy for lay audiences, Apian converted narrative academic proofs into mechanical pictures, or volvelles, that centered observers by positing them as users. The earliest volvelles in printed literature appeared in the 1474 Nuremberg edition of Regiomontanus's *Calendarium* and Erhard Ratdolt's editions printed in Venice in 1476; these were also tools for gauging the movement of heavenly bodies.[80] Printed volvelles embodied the premise of spherical astronomy and likely were intended to recall tools like armillary spheres that were a cornerstone of classroom instruction. Engagement with moving tools such as these spawned printed volvelles in works including Johannes Schöner's *Aequatorium Astronomicum* (printed in Bamberg in 1521 and in Nuremberg in 1534), a work with which Apian was certainly in dialogue, and one that Suzanne Karr

Schmidt cites as a precedent for Apian's later horoscopic opus, the *Astronomicum Caesareum* (published in Ingolstadt in 1540).[81] Apian likewise implemented complex moving paper dials and tools assembled from a variety of printed parts that translated the theoretical teachings of Sacrobosco into more practical information.[82] With these, Apian could simplify his explanation of cosmographic principles. Placing man himself literally within the picture, Apian redirected astronomy away from principles and toward observer-centered pedagogy. For the spherical astronomy that Sacrobosco's text served, little math was actually required – so it was the perfect text into which to insert observer-centered focus.[83] Apian tweaks Sacrobosco to privilege the visual study of the viewer's surroundings by articulating the observer as a recipient of sensory stimulus.

The relationship between the horizon and the zenith formed a major pillar of lay astronomy: the intersection of these lines centered the human observer. The zenith–horizon volvelle (Figure 2.10) anchored celestial circles to an earth-bound perspective. It encouraged the reader to envision the zenith as the extension of their head into space. Apian's diagram teaches that the zenith is the pole of *any* observer's horizon; the observer's zenith is expressed in terms of the point it describes on the celestial meridian. The dial also aimed to show the relationship of the observer's position to both their horizon and to their pole; and how the angular relationship between any observer's zenith and their respective horizon is always preserved.[84] Apian's horizon volvelle incorporates the salient points of Sacrobosco's textual proof, cuing the landmarks of spherical astronomy (such as the poles and the celestial circles) to adjustable earthly positions.[85]

The imaginary lines of the horizon and the zenith were important values for the amateur student of astronomy because they explained cosmographic truths in terms that could be confirmed visually. Circumscribed by the practitioner's empirical experience, the horizon describes the portion of the globe that one can see. Apian's dial consequently blocks from view the portion of the sphere that sinks beneath the horizon. The dial spins by way of a pointer fashioned as an earth-bound observer. By setting the figural index at the observer's latitude, the dial reveals the horizon formed by that terrestrial circle. Thus, no matter what the latitude, the observer's head remains at the center of a hemisphere articulated by what he is able to observe. The observer can also infer from this tool that their latitude is also equal to the altitude of the celestial pole. The fact that the hemisphere beneath the horizon remains hidden beneath the decorated space reinforces the idea of it as "that [line] which limits [one's] vision."[86]

The horizon also served as an important pedagogical benchmark for deriving latitude. Apian's interactive dial converts Sacrobosco's similes into coordinates of latitude that can help the user find geographic bearings in the world picture, providing an explanation that is easier to grasp than Sacrobosco's original proposition.[87] Apian's reader is taught to convert the abstract lines of

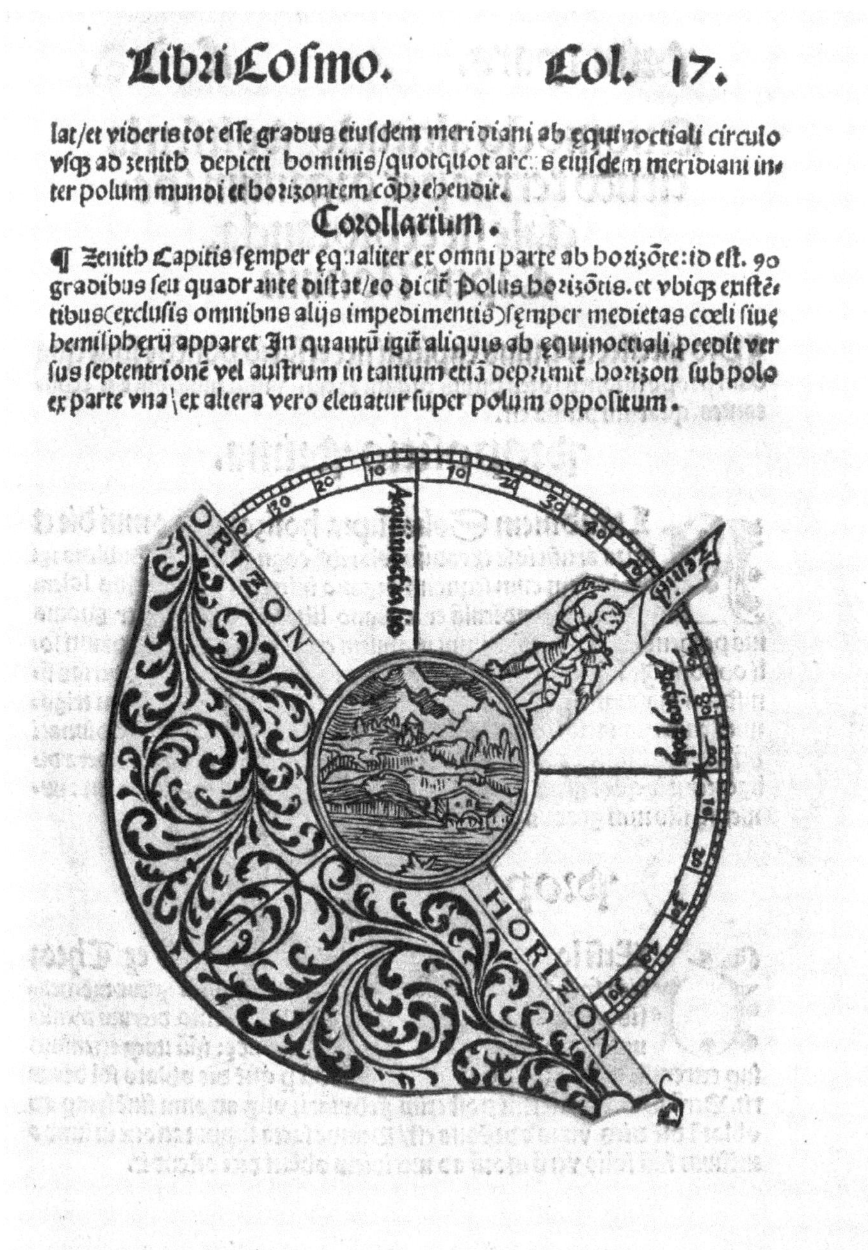

Libri Cosmo. Col. 17.

lat/et videris tot esse gradus eiusdem meridiani ab equinoctiali circulo vsqꝫ ad zenith depicti hominis/quotquot arc:: s eiusdem meridiani inter polum mundi et horizontem cōprehendit.

Corollarium.

¶ Zenith Capitis semper eq:aliter ex omni parte ab horizōte: id est. 90 gradibus seu quadrante distat/eo dicit Polus horizōtis. et vbiqꝫ existētibus(exclusis omnibus alijs impedimentis)semper medietas cœli siue hemispherū apparet In quantū igit aliquis ab equinoctiali pcedit versus septentrionē vel austrum in tantum etiā deprimit horizon sub polo ex parte vna\ex altera vero eleuatur super polum oppositum.

2.10. Peter Apian, *Cosmographicus Liber* (Landshut: Weyssenburger, 1524), fol. 17. *Source:* Zentralbibliothek Zürich, NR 870. Courtesy of ETH-Bibliothek Zürich.

zenith and horizon into the practical value of latitude. The volvelle's index, a figure of a man indicating his zenith, provides a stand-in for the user, to show how an observer's latitude can be measured against the horizon and zenith. Apian's dial extrapolates from Sacrobosco's text practical knowledge useful to an amateur stargazer. Apian's staging of this point through a demonstrative model follows what Steven Vanden Broecke claims marks an important shift to non-verbal visual thinking in the explanation of astronomy.[88] The eye, whose intelligence Kathleen Crowther and Peter Barker argue was conditioned by the visual programs of astronomic texts that helped steer readers' corporeal vision into inner mental visions of the cosmos's order, becomes truly animated in Apian.[89] The illustrations of the *Cosmographicus Liber* prioritized what the viewer could observe and assisted the mental visualizations necessary to grasp celestial motions within an observer-centered universe.

APIAN'S UPDATE OF SACROBOSCO'S *DE SPHAERA*

Sacrobosco's text had weathered the generations fairly intact until its collision with Apian's emphasis on pictorial learning. Recognizing the significance of his recent visual re-evaluations of Sacrobosco within the cosmography, Apian printed his own edition of *De Sphaera* in 1526, two years after the *Cosmographicus Liber*'s first printing.[90] Apian, also the father of the portable "in octavo" editions of *De Sphaera,* significantly improved on the visual didactics found in most printed editions of Sacrobosco up to that date.[91] As we have already seen in the example of the ship and the light on land (see Figure 2.6), for instance, Apian amplifies the triangular diagrams found in earlier editions of Sacrobosco to feature the more salient point that the water's bulge must show the round earth that lay beneath it. Whereas Sacrobosco tells the entire story of astronomy through Euclidean geometry of spheres and intersecting lines, Apian's repackaging imagines what these laws and propositions would look like to a roving agent.[92] As with his *Cosmographicus Liber,* Apian's update of Sacrobosco expanded on the existing cosmographic literature, hoping to clarify it through visual, and frequently interactive, demonstrations.

Apian's volvelles and diagrams were popularized in his own *Cosmographicus Liber* as well as in editions of Sacrobosco that he printed for academic communities. Sacrobosco continued to be printed throughout the century, with many publications issuing from university towns such as Wittenberg. Aware of their didactic advantages, printers pirated Apian's volvelles for their own mid-sixteenth-century editions of Sacrobosco's *De Sphaera.*[93] New volvelles were adapted from Apian's *Cosmographicus Liber,* such as the one found in a *Sphaera* printed in 1538 in Wittenberg by Joseph Clug (Figure 2.11).[94] Later editions, such as one printed in 1540, combined the teachings of volvelles that appeared separately in the source material.[95] Integrating Apian's zenith–horizon dial and

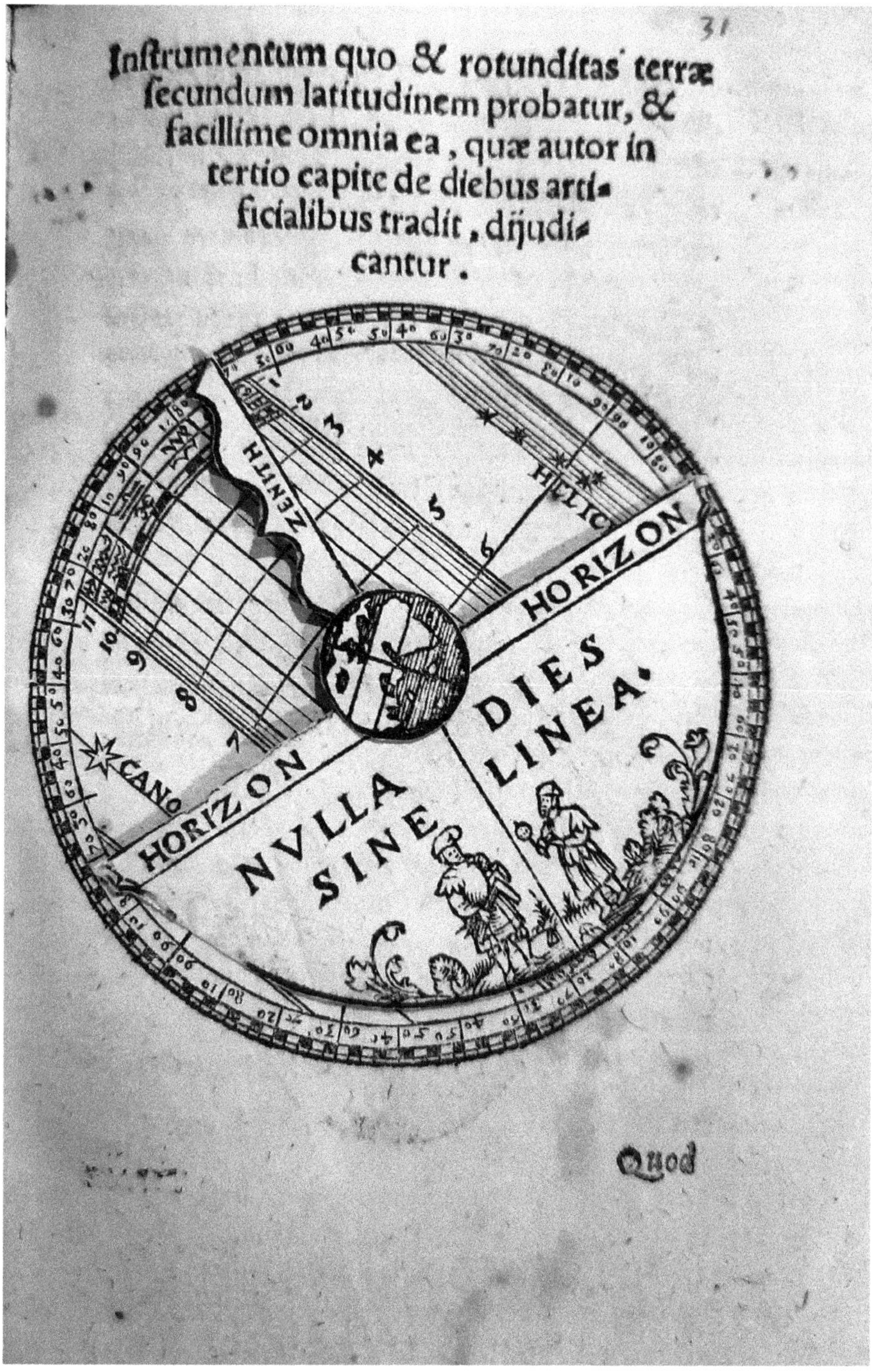

2.11. Sacrobosco and Melanchthon, *Ioannis De Sacrobusto Libellus, De Sphaera* . . . (Wittenberg: Joseph Clug, 1538), fol. 31. *Source:* HAB N62.8 Helmst. Courtesy of Herzog August Bibliothek Wolfenbüttel.

the *Organum Ptolomei*, the user of Clug's volvelle could set the horizon hemisphere to their latitude on top of a disc marked with lines of the sun's declinations. The caption on the dial reads: "With this instrument, the roundness of the earth can be tested, followed by latitude. And it will be easier to judge all things which the author teaches about the artificial day in the third chapter."[96] Such declarations prompted the readers' interaction with the dials.

New objectives could be mapped onto these paper instruments, endorsing practices by printers eager to lend them an imprimatur of usefulness that served their own brand. "*Nulla Dies Sine Linea*," or "No day without its line," pleads the inscription on a volvelle in an edition of Sacrobosco printed in Wittenberg. With this motto, the printer advertised the celestial decoding that users could perform with the tool.[97] This adage about daily routines popularized by Erasmus originated in Pliny's commentary about the artist Apelles's practice of daily drawing. It is mobilized here by the printer Joseph Clug to incite his readers to observe the daily linear path of the sun.[98] The word *linea* frequently appears in Apian's volvelles as demarcations of regions – on the *Organum Ptolomei* dial, for example – and perhaps that term also carried references to the threads themselves that accompanied dials as indicators throughout Apian's oeuvre. Clug surely reprises the adage here not just to refer to the notional lines of the celestial sphere or planetary paths, but as an exhortation to readers to engage in artisanal operations – in other words, a note to the self about self-help. Clug's semantic shift from the idea of "lines" from daily observances or routines to the "lines" of the sun's path was received in a context where a concomitant change was occurring in the meaning of the word *observation* itself. Katherine Park and Gianna Pomata have pointed out how *observationes* transitioned in early modernity from connotations of regimens followed into a term explicitly signaling empirical practice.[99] It seems that observation in both senses of the word converge in Clug's volvelle: the dial's motto inspires the user to make celestial observations a regular routine.[100] The recycling of this hybrid volvelle throughout the century seems to confirm the growing popularity of the firsthand tracking of the sun's path as a daily pastime for do-it-yourself observers.[101]

The transformation of academic astronomy into the subject of amateur investigation for "vernacular" viewers was achieved through the visualization of its principles. I would argue that the resurgence that the *De Sphaera* enjoyed in the sixteenth century came in large part from the potential that Apian saw in the visualization of spherical astronomy. We can say that Apian boosted future printings of Sacrobosco's text on the strength of the popularity of their visual devices, which were borrowed from his cosmography. Vernacular editions of Sacrobosco's material both laicized and energized observational practice. The vernacular *Sphera Materialis* edited and translated by Conrad Heinfogel in Nuremberg in 1516, already emphasized visual pedagogy.[102] A reader's annotations in the 1533 German edition of Sacrobosco's *Sphera Materialis: Eyn Anfang und Fundament der Astronomi* suggest that this emphasis made an impact. That reader's own drawings, which follow the foregoing Sacrobosco edition bound with other volumes at the Herzog August Bibliothek in Wolfenbüttel, include a featured eye.[103] The illustrations on added manuscript pages indicate that the author tried to supplement textual content derived from Sacrobosco with images that expand the principles of spherical astronomy by mapping them onto the plates of a torquetum, an astronomical instrument that simulates the celestial sphere by featuring different coordinate systems on several movable plates. This reader's pictorial supplement materializes the "material sphere" of Sacrobosco: an attempt to familiarize abstract principles by applying them to an actual instrument. While instruments such as the torquetum were designed to help the user envision the abstractions of spherical astronomy, this particular user seems to have been trying to facilitate comprehension of Sacrobosco's principles by thinking them through with an instrument.

The vernacular *Sphera Materialis* edited and printed by Johannes Dryander in 1539 derived illustrations from Apian.[104] While Dryander's edition was an important contribution to the vernacularization of spherical and theoretical astronomy, such as in Waldseemüller's *Der Welt Kugel* (printed by Grüninger in Strasbourg in 1509) and the Sacrobosco *Sphaerae* edited by Conrad Heinfogel, his was not prolifically illustrated. It was likely destined for a university audience, probably at Marburg, where Dryander occupied the chair in mathematics.[105] But illustrations were becoming a priority for the popular editions of Sacrobosco, especially after Apian's publication; Isabelle Pantin, for instance, notes the impact of Apian's visual program on astronomy's waxing pedagogical clarity.[106] Whereas the marketing of Conrad Heinfogel's German *Sphaera Mundi* in 1516 rested in part on the new vernacular translation from Latin, the title pages of the 1533 and 1539 editions explicitly advertised their contents as easier to understand because of the accompanying illustrations.[107] These many recensions owe a debt to *De Sphaera*'s open design, a format that Matteo Valleriani claims was critical to Sacrobosco's reception in the sixteenth century as a commentary useful for presenting practical mathematics for a number of fields.[108]

Perhaps this new enthusiasm for vernacular editions of *De Sphaera* can be attributed to astrology's popularity in Wittenberg, where academic reforms by Lutherans were also afoot.[109] Sacrobosco's circulation within the local faculty was probably fed by intense interest in astrology and spurred by the reformer Philip Melanchthon's own advocacy for popular astronomy.[110] Just a few years after Apian's edition, Melancthon penned an introduction for an edition of the *De Sphaera* (1531). Here, he articulated a reciprocal relationship between the observer's eye and the practice of scanning the heavens for stars, suggesting that vision was particularly well suited to, if not explicitly designed for, astronomy.[111] If the relevance of this thirteenth-century text was waning, sentiments like these reinvigorated Sacrobosco's work and publishers attempted to boost sales with such hyperbole that linked the function of vision itself to the pursuit of amateur stargazing.[112] Melanchthon's suturing of the eyes to the stars was no doubt intended to elevate the importance of astronomy, but perhaps his comments were also prompted by the new publics of lay observers educated by the *Cosmographicus Liber*. Volvelles and diagrams derived from Apian's cosmography came increasingly to define the profile and format of Ptolemaic recensions (such as Sacrobosco) produced in the wake of it.[113] Diagrams derived from Apian also became a hallmark for many subsequent printings from the 1530s onward.[114] Owen Gingerich notes that the moving dials became features adopted in most printing sites (including Paris, Antwerp, Cologne, and Venice) and the *sine qua non* of printed Sacroboscos from the 1540s onwards.[115] Thus, the sixteenth-century reception of Ptolemy was greatly indebted to Apian's visual apparatus for the *Cosmographicus Liber*.

Apian's mechanical pictures as filtered through vernacular editions of *De Sphaera* ultimately made Sacrobosco a new locus for popular knowledge about the heavens. It is precisely in these updates to Sacrobosco that Matteo Valleriani locates a general trend of unifying diverse strains of study into early modern books that would become the sites of codified practical knowledge.[116] That Sacrobosco would continue to be a mainstay in astronomic literature is clear from the many later publications, as well as the fact that significant debates about geocentrism would revolve around this publication as an authoritative source, including the 1611 commentary by the Jesuit Christopher Clavius, who would spearhead the Catholic Church's resistance to Galileo.[117] Printed beginning in 1570, the eight versions of the Clavius edition of Sacrobosco were no longer useful as practical guides to the heavens, as they were weighty and printed in larger formats. In place of Apian's market-ready volvelles, they instead made room for propagandistic commentary in service of Jesuit science.[118]

Almost exactly contemporary with the vernacularization of Sacrobosco's *De Sphaera* and its retrofitting with visual tools was the appearance of Apian's *Cosmographicus Liber* in a number of vernacular editions, particularly Dutch and French volumes produced in Antwerp and Paris.[119] It is perplexing, in light of these other versions, that Peter Apian seems never to have offered a German translation of the *Cosmographicus Liber*. Explanations for this could include the inability of Middle High German to handle scientific vocabulary, but many vernacular neologisms for spherical astronomy had been introduced by Conrad Heinfogel's vernacular *Sphera Materialis* in 1516.[120] Apian's own trade in printed vernacular editions of instrument manuals for a wide readership may have also diverted the need for a German-language *Cosmographicus Liber*.[121] I suspect that Apian never sensed a specialized market for a German vernacular edition of the

Cosmographicus Liber in regions where the Latin version was already circulating – so confident was he that the pictures could carry his argument. He might have judged that amateur stargazers in academic and humanist circles were equally well served by the Latin, or any of the number of vernaculars circulating post-1537. Perhaps Apian's preoccupation with other projects that likewise promoted the role of tools in the visualization of complex astronomic principles kept him too busy. Or he might have considered that a new vernacular *Cosmographicus Liber* would be a duplication of visualization efforts already underway in *De Sphaera* (1526) or the *Cosmographiae Introductio* (1529), and especially in his anticipated *Instrument-Buch*.

In any event, it is significant that Apian's *Instrument-Buch* of 1533 delivered a synopsis of cosmographic principles formatted as a very visual how-to book.[122] Apian explicitly designed this book with vernacular audiences in mind. The *Instrument-Buch*'s pictorial demonstrations would have served amateur astronomers and surveyors in an even more practical way than the *Cosmographicus Liber* itself.[123] That Apian was cited in vernacular contexts provides evidence that his content was available among the burgeoning audience hungry for ways to develop their empirical experience of the world. Evidence of Apian's role as a popularizer of astronomy can be seen in the contemporary manuals that introduced instruments such as the cross-staff and celestial globe and that invoked his name as an authority.[124] Authors of printed practical mathematics still referred back to Apian's *Cosmographicus Liber* for instructions on how to calibrate the eye in the night sky.

This last section has examined the dialogue between the *Cosmographicus Liber* and vernacular circulating astronomical texts in order to show how the theoretical content of spherical astronomy ceded its authority in the printed press to a growing visualized practice. Historians of science agree that not until the sixteenth century did Sacrobosco editions attempt to activate the hands and eyes of the astronomer; I would argue that much of this impetus to shape Sacrobosco into a useful text in the mid-1530s came from Apian's visual engagement with those principles in the *Cosmographicus Liber.*[125] While Apian was thoroughly steeped in updating Sacrobosco's teachings for the 1526 Latin reprint he designed for university audiences, he simultaneously imagined the ways in which he could reshape the content for a learned but lay readership. Mechanical pictures not only helped locate a new audience for fusty academic knowledge, but these audiences also prompted a novel demand for spherical astronomy to be explained via interactive how-to volumes.

EXERCISING OBSERVATIONS

In tracking the premium placed by epistemic genres on the direct interface of observers with their environment, a milestone is marked by their self-conscious use of the term *observation* to characterize their searches. Such a turning point has been located in the appearance of the term (or some variation of the Latin verb *observare* or *observatio*) in the mid-sixteenth-century publication of astronomic material in Nuremberg. The rubric of *Nachlass Observationes* (1544) was invoked in the title of a volume that included a variety of visual samplings: the collected notes and coordinates of the astronomer George Peurbach, Regiomontanus's treatise on astronomical instruments, and the weather observations of Bernard Walther and Johannes Werner. Historians of scientific observation hail Johannes Schöner's use of *Observationes* in the title of his *Scripta Clarissimi Mathematici M. Ionnis Regiomontani … Observationes XXX annorum a I. Regiomontano et B. Walthero Norimbergae habitae*, a book that included treatises on astronomical instruments such as the astrolabe, torquetum, Ptolemaic regulum, and the cross-staff by Regiomontanus and George Peurbach.[126] With the term *observationes*, Schöner, functioning as an editor here, indicated the idea of collective observing practices.[127] While this term had previously signaled individual case studies, we might say that the shift in its use around the mid-sixteenth century to promote "collective empiricism" might have been the result of individual agency in practicing observations as pictorially developed by Apian's *Cosmographicus Liber.*[128] In fact, Apian was already using the term *observatio* in a pamphlet announcing the comet of 1532 as well as in the related *Practica* for that year.[129] The degree to which both Schöner and Apian attended to the publication of their works with interactive diagrams and volvelles, and the fact that both of them resorted to self-publishing in order to more precisely supervise a printing process increasingly reliant on visual props, suggests a dialogue between them that went beyond the formal similarities of some of their astronomical publications.[130] Their labors cultivated audiences for empirical experiences customized by the practice of observation.

At least one of the practical applications of systematic celestial observations arose at the point at which academic astronomy and astrology came together. Apian's list of publications reflects the interpenetration of the two pursuits in early modernity and illuminates how their concerns were brought together within the publishing industry. In the age of print, it was inevitable that academic astronomy would meet the visual platform that was active in genres that *did* present useful information derived from celestial knowledge: astrology.

Celestial knowledge was the basis of astrology, a lay genre related to astronomy that traced the sun's path through the zodiac in order to cue those movements to quotidian labor, health, hygiene, and aspirations for matrimonial bliss.[131] Published data on the movements of celestial bodies circulated on a popular level in the form of almanacs, prognostications, and short pamphlets, typically of eight to ten leaves, called *Practica.*[132] In addition to other topics, these books suggested propitious times for daily activities based on knowledge of the heavens. Many seasonal practices such as bathing, cupping, and venesection were scheduled by astrological observations; the published recommendations for these routines were generated by mathematicians.[133] Apian's publishing activity spanned lay genres such as astrology and more academic astronomy, and thus promoted cross-fertilization between the pictorialized cosmographic publications and the vernacular literature on prophecies and prognostications.

Apian's own roots in practical mathematics served his busy program of printing vernacular astrological pamphlets. The annual lunar calendars and predictions that Apian printed beginning in 1523 as *Practica* financed his more scholarly ventures.[134] Seasonal almanacs that predicted weather, *Practica* also speculated on the outcomes of wars, public health hazards, and the success of harvests. Eclipse schedules in Apian's *Practica* followed the design of those found in contemporary calendars.[135] Perhaps it was Apian's attention to the needs of local astrologers, physicians, and weather watchers that fed his conviction that Ptolemy need not be the first and last word in astronomical texts. Instead, Apian emphasized in these publications how observations obtained with modern instrumentation could serve useful ends.[136] Such pragmatic needs were also serviced by the wide array of *Practica* (including almanacs and "weather books") marketed to a growing audience of practitioners. In both their address to readers and their title page illustrations featuring farmers and peasants, these books were among the first that hailed a broad cross-section of social classes as reading publics of lay learners.[137]

Ambitions to serve markets for both academic and popular literature in Apian's press probably guided his fashioning of the *Cosmographicus Liber* into a perfect text to reach crossover audiences – it borrowed images from academic astronomy texts, but it was also clearly indebted to the practical demands of astrological publications.[138] Schedules of lunar phases and eclipses inspired by Regiomontanus's *Calendaria* also appeared in the *Cosmographicus Liber.* Apian's version of such a calendar showed an approximately fifty-year schedule of eclipses relating to specific coordinates on the globe (in this case, the coordinates of Apian's hometown of Leisnig in Saxony). Such data mimicked that found in local astrological publications. While academic texts on spherical astronomy did publish images of lunar phases, how, one might ask, was such data pertaining to local coordinates such as Leisnig actually useful to readers of theoretical astronomy? The cosmography's lunar calendar took a middle ground: this schedule was a theoretical model with practical applications. In the context of the *Cosmographicus Liber*, it was one of two methods Apian presented to help determine one's location. The eclipse times shown for Leisnig provided the prospective observer with a reference meridian and time. If observers could time the eclipse at their local coordinates, they could then calculate the time difference between Leisnig and their own locations. Converting this to an angular measure would produce a longitude reading.

A more practical way of deriving longitude involved tracking the motion of the moon relative to a fixed star, a technique employed by mariners in celestial navigation. This strategy elaborated on the lunar distance method publicized by the Nuremberg mathematician and astronomer Johannes Werner in an edition of the *Geography* printed in 1514. Apian's text coupled instructions on how to obtain these values through the use of a simple instrument, a section introduced on folio 30 as the *Use of the Cross-Staff* (Figure 2.12), and followed by an illustration that explained how to make and deploy such an instrument. With it, one could determine the elevation of an object above the horizon, or measure the angles between two celestial features.[139]

Apian's cross-staff illustration can be seen as a hybrid model with both narrative and diagrammatic components. This tripartite woodcut shows principles that governed the cross-staff's production, including the angular scale by which it should be calibrated, a depiction of an actual observer using it to measure the angle between the moon and a star, and, lastly, a demonstration of its application on earth by a user.[140] The pedagogical value of Apian's three images together clearly outstrips the narrative explanation offered by the text itself.[141]

One of the challenges facing the non-specialist researching the secondary literature of early modern scientific instruments is that their use, calibration, and purpose are never presented in a predictable or pedagogically clear order. Furthermore, explanations are typically vague about which quantities are already known or required in order to use them. This stands in stark contrast to some relatively complete early modern explanations. Apian's illustration aims to clearly deliver instructions for the proper calibration and use of the cross-staff as related aspects. For this reason, his illustrations are vastly more informative than many later ones. They pictorialize the purpose and use of instruments and often show methods and results of observations made using them.

As the illustration at the base of the image shows, the staff was supported just under the eye to sight both the moon and a nearby star. The user then slid a movable cross-piece until it spanned the distance between two points; the reading taken from the staff would show the angle of separation. The device should be calibrated via a scale shown in the left-hand woodcut.[142] Instead of showing how to hold the staff itself, the illustration in Apian's *princeps* simply floats the staff before a pictured eye.[143] Lack of instructions was perceived as a shortcoming that was rectified in Apian's later editions, as he increasingly came to see the job of images to be to assist the user in the field. Apian retooled his images around the needs of a prospective user: in many practical publications that would follow the *Cosmographicus Liber*, he would feature practitioners in the field using the instruments he recommended in the text. Apian would continue to publish pamphlets for amateur observers of the heavens, sometimes in the context of *Practica*, and sometimes in pamphlets devoted to a particular celestial event. In *Ein kurtzer bericht der Observation unnd urtels des*

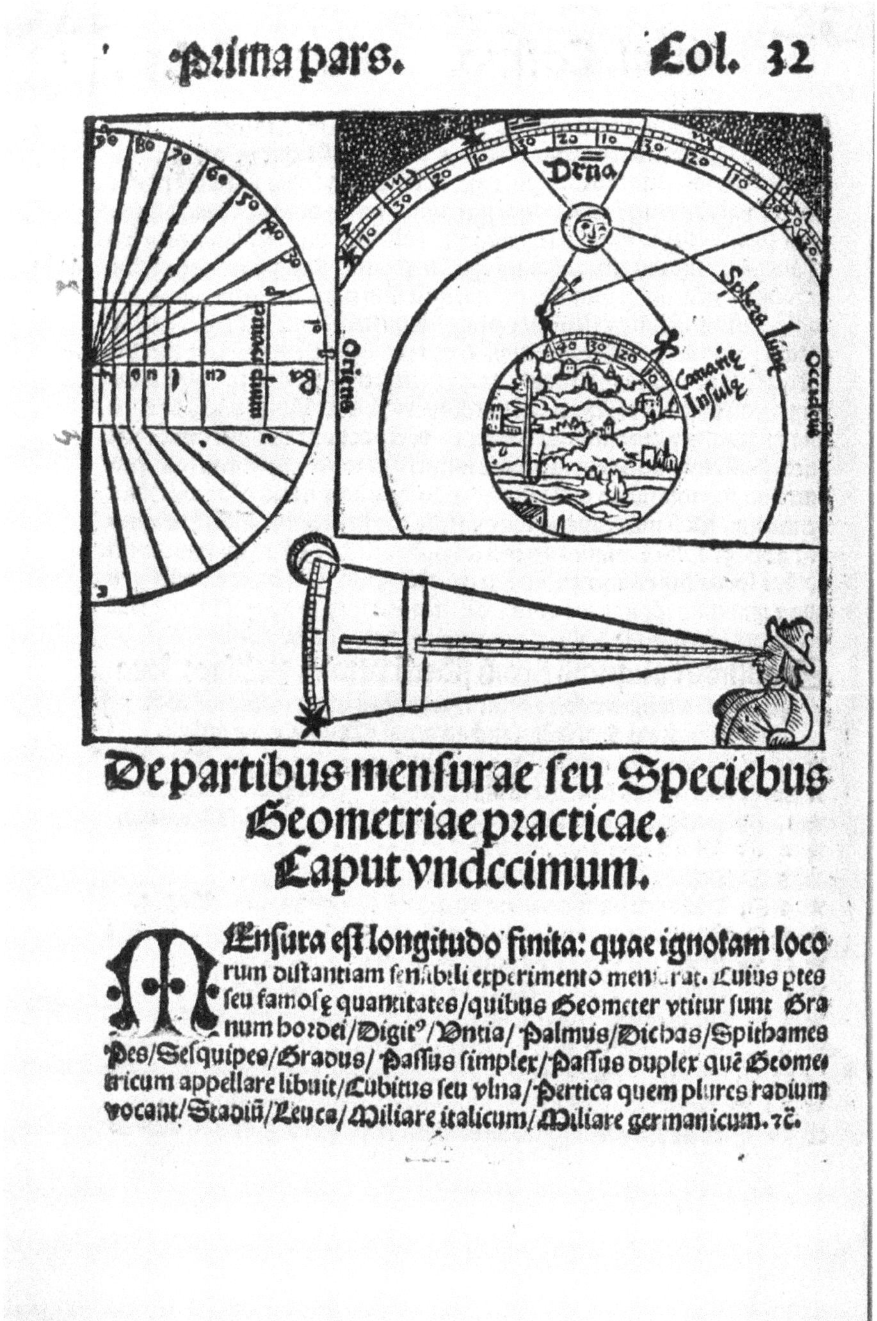

2.12. Peter Apian, *Cosmographicus Liber* (Landshut: Weyssenburger, 1524), fol. 32. *Source:* Zentralbibliothek Zürich, NR 870. Courtesy of ETH-Bibliothek Zürich.

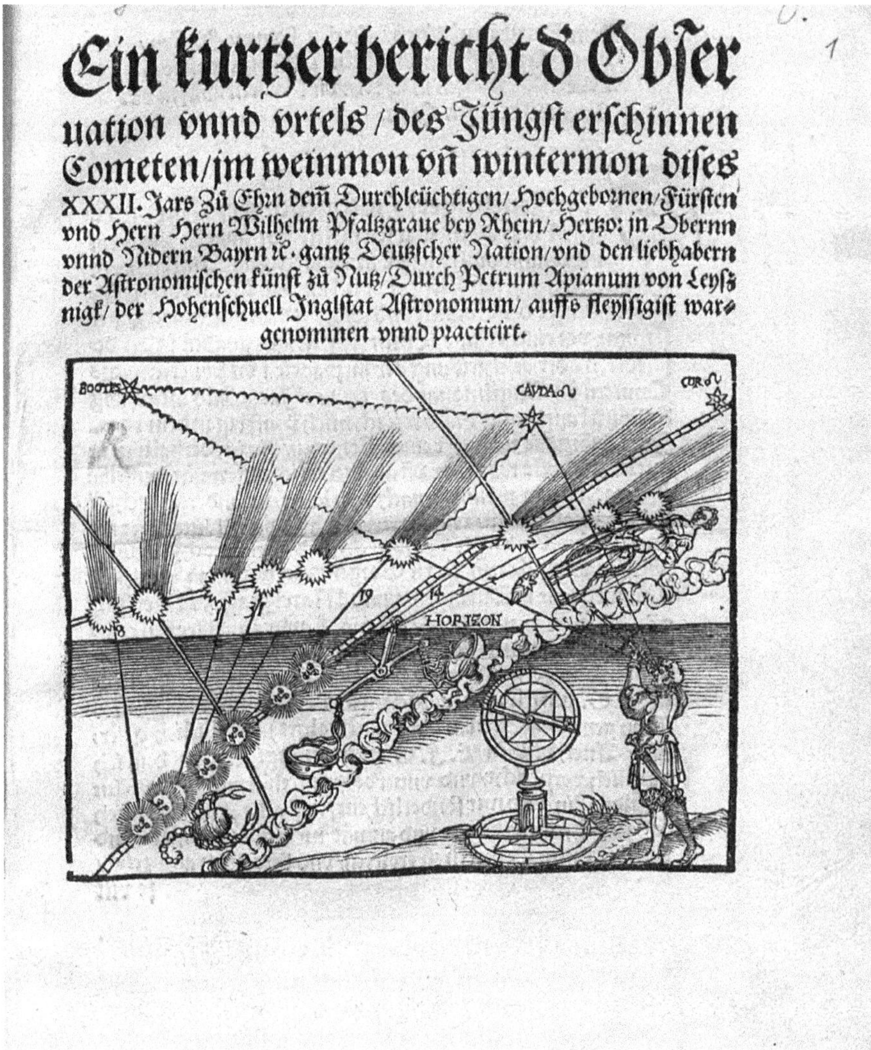

2.13. Peter Apian, *Ein kurtzer bericht der Observation unnd urtels des jüngst erschinnen Cometen jm Weinmon vnd Wintermon dises XXXII. Jars* (Ingolstadt: Apian, 1532). *Source:* BSB Res/4 Astr. p. 511.30. Courtesy of Bayerische Staatsbibliothek, Munich.

jüngst erschinnen Cometen... dises XXXII. Jars (printed in 1532), a title page image shows a comet blazing across the sky viewed by a pictured observer who tracks its position against reference stars with a cross-staff (Figure 2.13).[144] Illustrations of the path of the sun against a backdrop of the zodiac band, as well as dates of his observations, appear in both this publication and an almanac Apian printed that same year, *Practica auff das 1532. Jar.* In these two publications, we see echoes of both the methodology and the pictorial apparatus of the *Cosmographicus Liber* constructing the foundation for Apian's future visual programs for his vernacular spinoffs. Significantly, we also see the term *observation* creeping into these titles and providing the justification for the publication.

In both of these works on the comet, Apian clamors repeatedly for observational acuity that underwrites the rigorous training of the astronomer. Even in the more astrologically oriented text of the *Practica auff das 1532. Jar*, Apian announces himself as an astronomer whose assiduous observations ensure the precision of his predictions. Such visual explanations of instruments for amateur stargazers would reach an apogee in a publication designed around the use of instruments, *Instrument-Buch* (1533). These works conspired to turn the products of university astronomers into more practical field guides.

Period advancements in determining longitude through both the eclipse and the lunar distance method have not been properly credited to Apian's relatively clear diagrams, according to Uta Lindgren, who also believes that these illustrations' alleged purposes are masked by captions that dilute their true contributions.[145] The chapter of the *Cosmographicus Liber* preceding the diagram announces the *Usus Baculi* or the "use of the cross-staff" (fol. 30). According to Lindgren, this title does not go far enough to highlight the device's more significant contribution as a means of calculating longitude – a purpose that is unequivocally announced in the text that follows the subject heading. The image of observers placed at some distance from one another serves as an explanation of longitude; the difference between their respective angles of vision is equivalent to their difference in longitude.[146] The word *differentia* found in later printings of the woodcut, according to Lindgren, indicates the difference in degree between the moon and the fixed star at the observer's locations. Apian's pedagogy not only coached readers to make their own observations, but it also taught the principle that observations were relative to their observers.

This lesson was adopted by later publications that extrapolated from these principles. The Louvain mathematician Gemma Frisius has often been considered a student of Apian's because of his long engagement with Apian's texts as his editor. Gemma spurred the printing of the *Cosmographicus Liber* in the Antwerp press, frequently padding those editions with his own notes and amendments. One popular addition were charts that would enable longitude to be found via the lunar distance method. This entailed providing data of the relative positions of moon and stars. To find longitude via the lunar distance method, data points obtained must be read against a table of relative positions of the moon to the stars, such as those enumerated in Regiomontanus's *Ephemeridies*.[147] Later editions of the *Cosmographicus Liber* also include a chart inserted by Gemma that details the positions of fourteen stars near the ecliptic that can be used to calculate the moon's position. Such data had already been presented in novel visualized formats in contemporary print productions. Johannes Stabius's wall chart *Astrolabium imperatorium* (1515) offered an aesthetic presentation of the diurnal location of the sun and also the position of ten bright stars.[148] A compelling graphic presentation of the stellar positions, according to Richard Kremer, was Stabius's most important contribution to mathematical astronomy.[149] Kremer argues that the coordinates rendered by this device, a geometrical tool without moving parts, were explicitly conceived so that the viewer could simply consult the device as a visual model, rather than as a conceptual one. It cleverly displayed, rather than proved, and thus encouraged new types of cognition. Apian embedded demonstrations of celestial data collecting in short sections labeled with explanatory chapter titles and images that illustrated how to perform these tasks, balancing practical application with more theoretical objectives.

Although the first textual mention of the cross-staff surfaced *c.* 1342 in the context of surveying and astronomy, its use in the sixteenth century by mariners and navigators was surely expedited by Apian's clear explanations. Apian geared his tools toward the amateur who could now attempt personal celestial observations. Graphically embedding visual demonstrations within the explanatory text, Apian designed the *Cosmographicus Liber* to instruct amateur astronomers to gather observations. With this objective, Apian's work inspired a generation of practical publications, primarily spearheaded by Gemma Frisius. With this practical agenda, Frisius's works differed from those of his French counterpart Oronce Fine, whose emphasis was on theoretical practical mathematics.[150] Gemma Frisius's corrections and additions to editions after 1529 made Apian's cosmography even more versatile for a class of professional observers such as surveyors. Sections on surveying added by Gemma came with diagrams and appeared as an appendix entitled *Libellus de Locorum describendorum ratione* in the editions printed in Antwerp beginning in 1533, with a reprint by Arnold Birckman and Johannes Graepheus.[151] In later Antwerp editions, these sections are accompanied by woodcuts of surveyors armed with the cross-staff measuring angles they could see but not reach. That readers were developing a new useful position vis-à-vis the text can be seen in a copy preserved at the Museum Plantin-Moretus into which the owner directed the book binder to insert periodic gatherings of blank pages. Clearly, this patron added extra pages to enable commentary on the text. The comments by the owner here include marginal synopses of the text's discussion, principles of geography distilled into a list of twenty-two points, observations about eclipses, and a drawing of a hand whose fingers form a didactic model of the climate zones.[152] Gemma's amendments to Apian would go on to serve a community of non-academics such as surveyors, architects, and builders who needed to make use of such angular measurements for their calculations.[153] Vernacular editions from 1561 feature Gemma's tools, such as the sea-compass, in their titles.[154] Practical knowledge about how a compass might have been used for navigation would certainly have been of interest for the reader/viewers Apian developed: a community of mathematical amateurs.[155]

ENABLING EMPIRICISM

Another form of data collection Apian popularized was finding the time at night. That Apian's cosmography was being sought for these practical aspects is suggested by a brief table of contents in the 1561 Dutch edition that lists finding the "hour of the night via the stars" to be the third most noteworthy feature of the book. The nocturnal dial needed for this was used principally by mariners whose time readings enabled them to stay on course in their latitudes and to predict the tides.[156] Other segments of the populace who could profit from readings of nocturnal time were astrologers producing horoscopes, or monastic communities in charge of scheduling prayers, chants, and other rituals.[157] A nocturnal dial determines the time at night, just as sundials mark the hour during the day. The last few pages of Apian's 1524 edition were devoted to the explanation of the nocturnal (Figure 2.14), explaining the principles, theory, and use of the dial. One page even provided a model of the instrument itself.[158]

Apian both illustrates the theoretical model of the nocturnal dial and provides one that could be used to find the time by sighting Polaris through the center and then aligning the arm to the reference stars (Figure 2.15). Over successive pages, he illustrates a user employing the tool to find the angle between the pole star and the reference star; lastly, he includes a page that contains a model of the dial and a pointer arm, presumably to be cut out and attached to firm backing and a stick. Most of these seem to have been printed on or glued to sturdier parchment and tipped into the manual.[159] Once the instrument was detached from the book, it either could have been used in the field in a rudimentary way or could be manipulated alongside the book for better comprehension of the actual tool's workings.[160] These explanations showed how to make use of local coordinates for telling the time and to help stargazers orient themselves. Tools like these would form the focus of Apian's guides to a variety of instruments (such as ones on quadrants and dials) published in the 1530s, including the *Instrument-Buch* that established the foundation for the observations of Tycho Brahe, for instance, whose attention to description and use of instrumentation were key in formulating a working model of the universe.[161]

A lunar instrument, the *Instrumentum Noctis* (Figure 2.16), was more of a theoretical volvelle than the nocturnal dial, but one whose elegance was predicated on stunning design. It appears in the appendix to the *Cosmographicus Liber* along with Apian's disclaimer that it was designed at the behest of his brother Georg. Using two moving plates, to each of which a pointer is attached, one should be able to derive the time at night. A lower plate carries a design made from an algorithmic projection that simulates the moon's changing phases through an opening in the circular plate. Apian's text

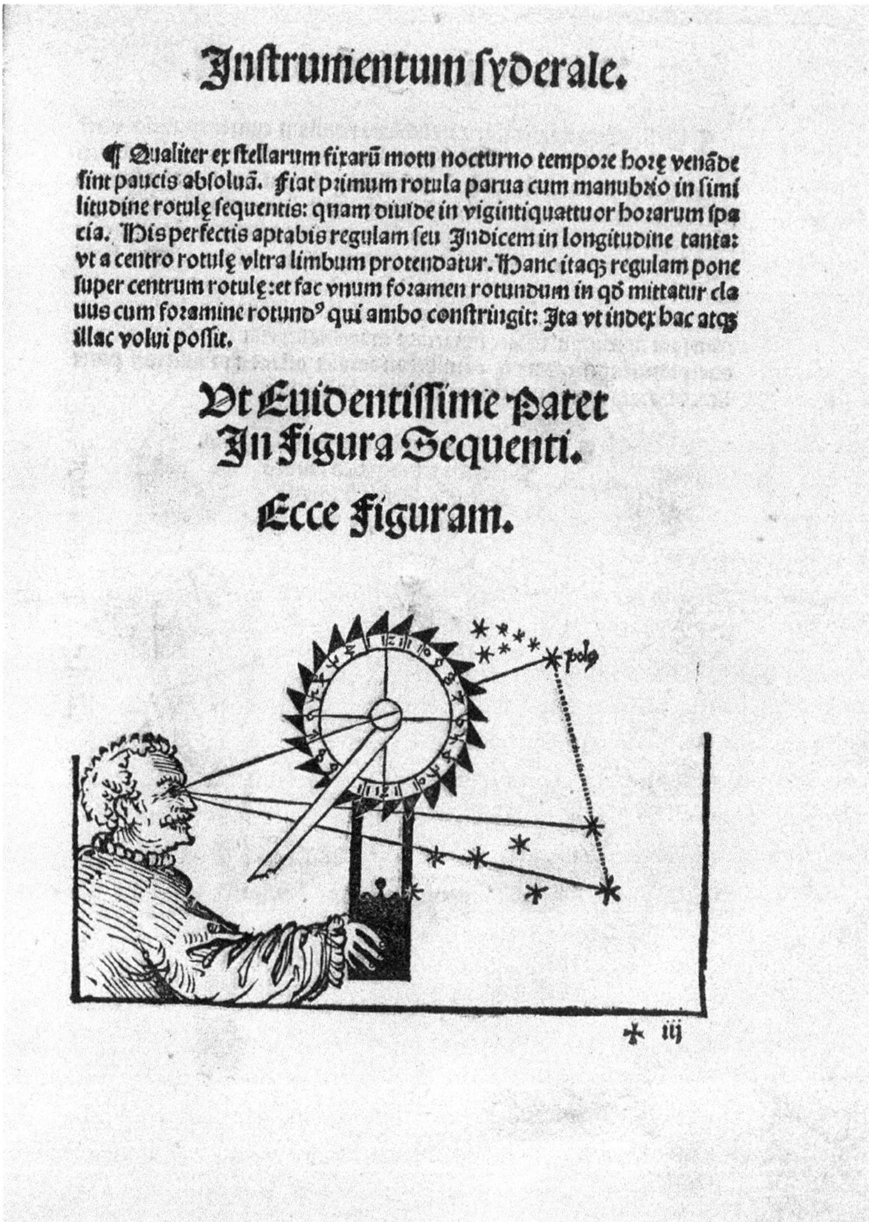

Instrumentum syderale.

¶ Qualiter ex stellarum fixarū motu nocturno tempore horę venāde sint paucis absoluā. Fiat primum rotula parua cum manubrio in simi litudine rotulę sequentis: quam diuide in vigintiquattuor horarum spa cia. His perfectis aptabis regulam seu Indicem in longitudine tanta: vt a centro rotulę vltra limbum protendatur. Hanc itaqz regulam pone super centrum rotulę: et fac vnum foramen rotundum in qd mittatur cla uus cum foramine rotundo qui ambo constringit: Ita vt inde hac atqz illac volui possit.

Vt Euidentissime Patet In Figura Sequenti.

Ecce Figuram.

iij

2.14. Peter Apian, *Cosmographicus Liber* (Landshut: Weyssenburger, 1524), appendix, fol. 109. *Source:* Zentralbibliothek Zürich, NR 870. Courtesy of ETH-Bibliothek Zürich.

explains that the pointer of one dial is set to the altitude of the moon; the other dial, with the circular window, should be squared to the moon's phase. Together, these two dials point to a number that renders the time at night. The dial derives useful data from the observation of the moon's phase: the reflected light seen on the lunar surface is a measurement of the relative angle between the moon and the sun. Coupling this with a measurement of the

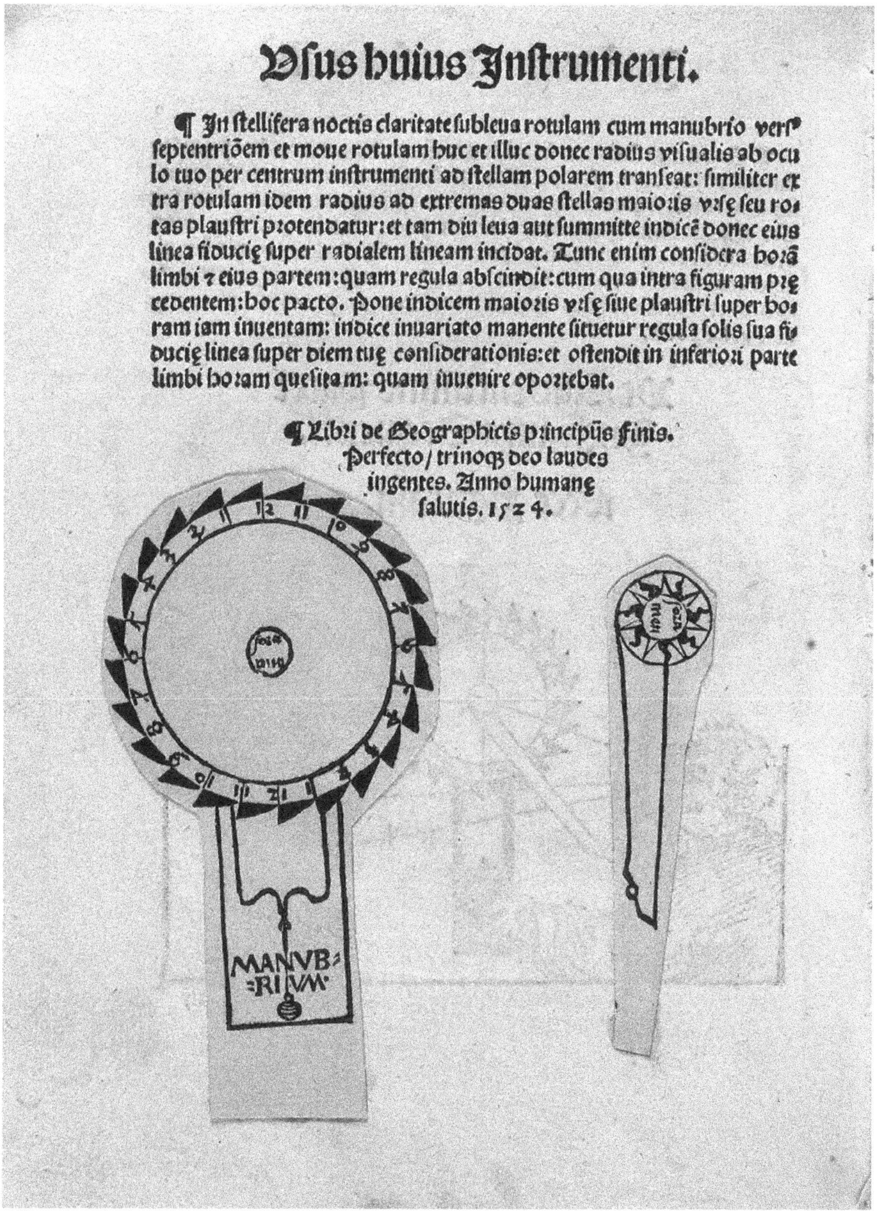

2.15. Peter Apian, nocturnal parts in *Cosmographicus Liber* (Landshut: Weyssenburger, 1524), appendix, fol. 110. *Source:* Burndy Library. Image in the public domain.

moon's altitude provides the location of the sun. The time at night can thus be inferred by triangulating the position of the sun beneath the horizon.[162] This data point renders a value more useful to the viewer: the time at night. This value could be used for scheduling events, predicting eclipses, making horoscopes, or simply estimating the number of daylight hours. Apian's stargazers would also have found the lunar volvelle admirable for its elegance in design

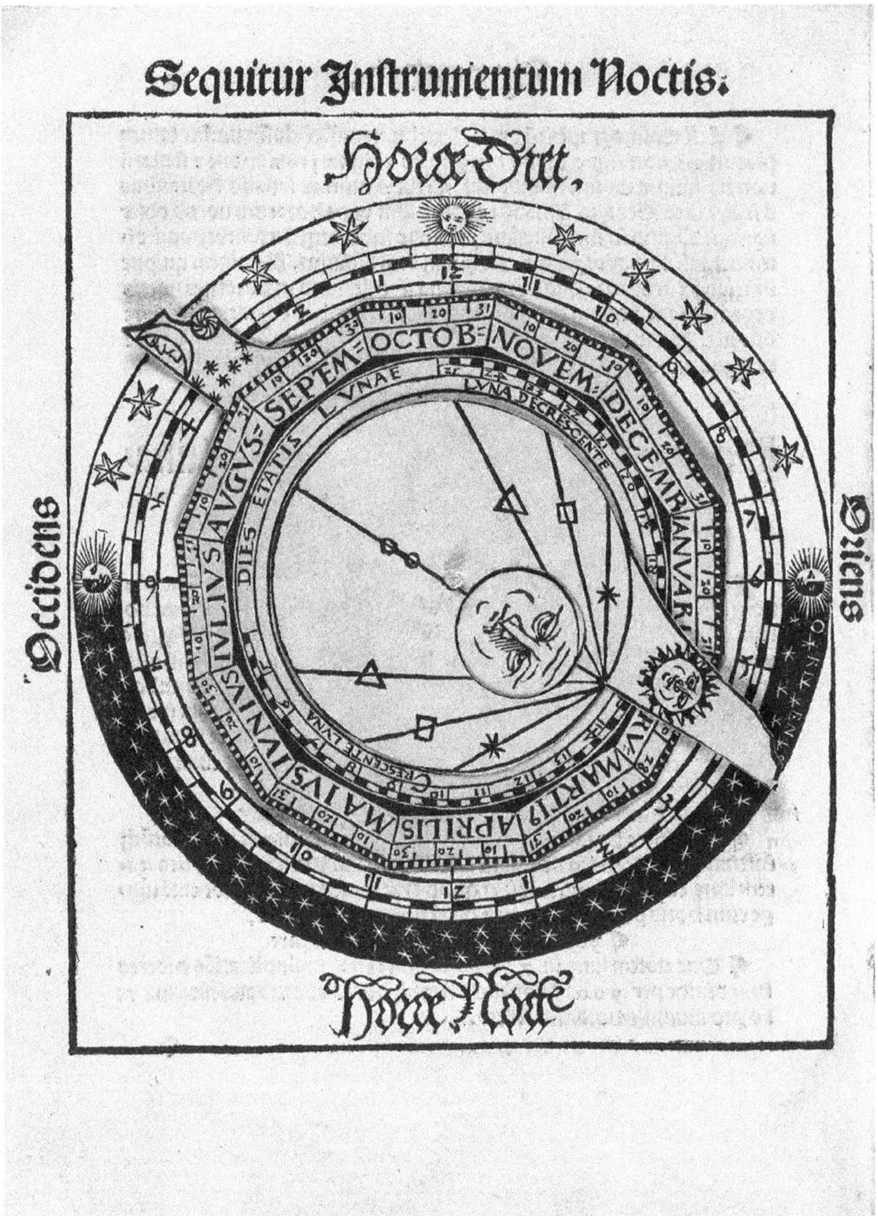

2.16. Peter Apian, nocturnal instrument in *Cosmographicus Liber* (Landshut: Weyssenburger, 1524), appendix, fol. 106. *Source:* Zentralbibliothek Zürich, NR 870. Courtesy of ETH-Bibliothek Zürich.

and the way it synthesized the clockwork of the heavens with just a few moving parts.

Paper instruments could also pictorially synthesize theoretical astronomic propositions. With another moving paper volvelle, readers could derive practical values from complex Ptolemaic concepts. This dial found on folio

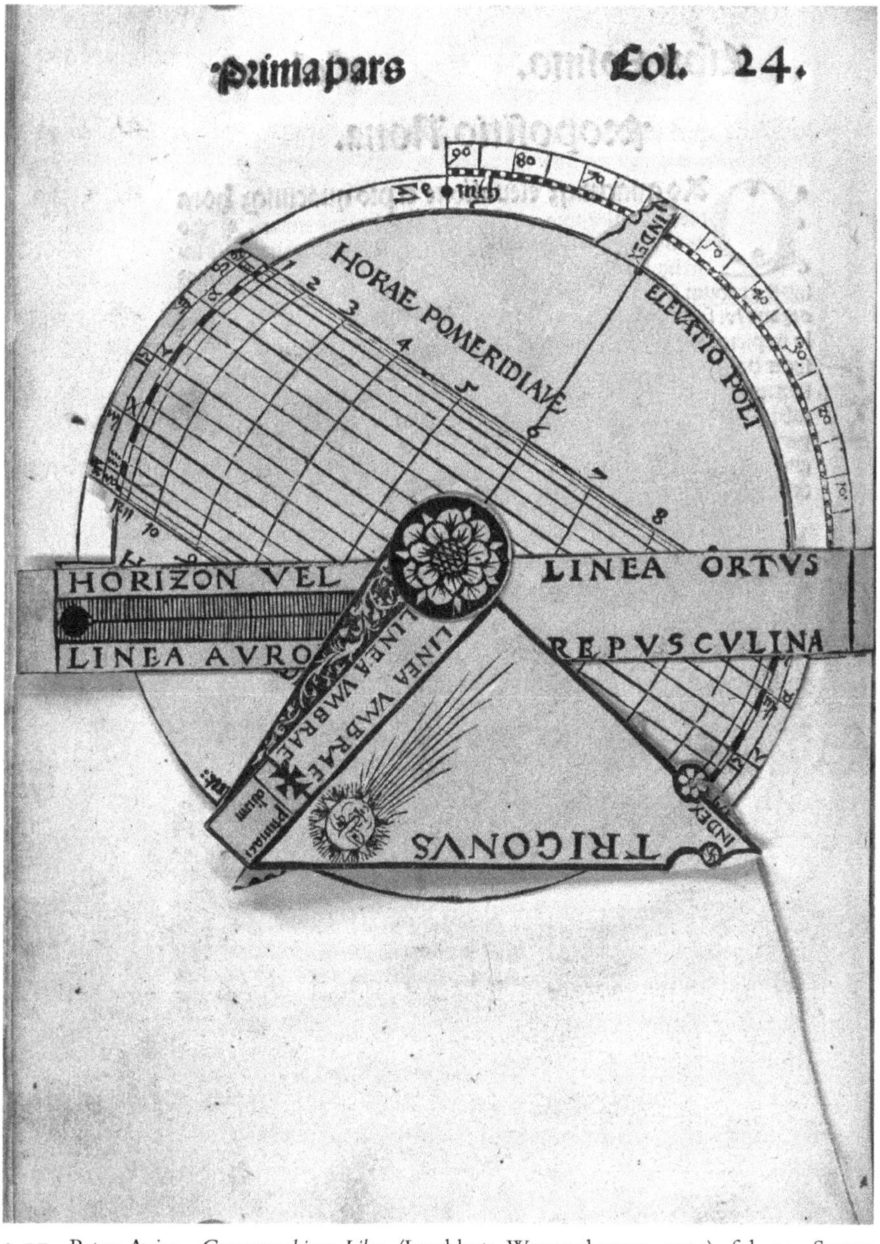

2.17. Peter Apian, *Cosmographicus Liber* (Landshut: Weyssenburger, 1524), fol. 24. *Source:* Zentralbibliothek Zürich, NR 870. Courtesy of ETH-Bibliothek Zürich.

24 revives the *Organum Ptolemei* (Figure 2.17), a disc with a projection of the sun's declination and the hours. It was a tool that astronomers over the centuries had tried to reconstruct from Ptolemy's prescriptions.[163] While reports about the *Organum Ptolemei* proliferate in manuscript sources, Apian's might actually be an early attempt to create one in paper.[164]

Apian's version of the Ptolemaic instrument is comprised of three movable parts mounted atop a disc with latitude markings. The components include a rectangle representing the horizon; a rotating triangle called *Trigonus* marked with the line of shadow that would be cast by the sun; and a rotating disc with a grid of morning and afternoon hours bordered by the zodiac band. The cylindrical grid printed on this disc is an orthographic projection of the equinoctial (colure); it offers a schema that reconciled the parallels of the celestial sphere to the plane of the equator.[165]

The instrument's functionality was loosely explained by the ten propositions that precede it in the text. With the instrument, it is possible to calculate one's latitude and the position of the sun in the house of the zodiac, derive the height of the celestial pole from the altitude of the sun (via the triangle activated as a shadow vane), and also determine the height of the pole star. Furthermore, one could derive the time of day in the same way as one might employ a sundial; establish the time of sunrise and sunset; measure the length of unequal hours of days and nights; and lastly, determine the height of the sun on cloudy days.

Users are instructed by Apian how to set the dials. The user would align the horizon bar to the appropriate latitude and set the index pointer of the large disc in the marked quadrant to the height of the pole star. While the dials are meant primarily to demonstrate principles, at least two of the propositions suggest that the parts could work in concert to enable empirical investigations. Once the user's latitude was entered in the *Organum Ptolemei*, "the intersection of the triangle with the grid of parallel and hour lines on the rotating disc works like an equatorial sundial, while the intersection of the horizon line with this grid can easily be related to the set-up of a horizontal sundial."[166] While the tool mimics the principles of the sundial in this way, Apian expanded the dial's practical operations. He layered both practical ends and theoretical didactics onto the dial.[167]

A sundial was a purely practical tool designed to measure time from readings of the sun's altitude at specific locations, and it was tied to those specific locations. By contrast, Apian's instrument can be used for determining the length of daylight hours for a given latitude, enabling the user to calculate the length of the day or night at any location and at any time of year. From these values, the user could generate new data, such as measuring fluctuations in daylight hours over the seasons. While information about local daylight hours could also be found in almanacs and calendar pamphlets, this tool could help derive data that was handy for cuing regimens to the length of the day at specific times of the year.[168] From practical *calendaria*, the reader could schedule precise dates for activities such as planting, harvesting, healing, and distilling. But Apian's tool is in fact *more* useful than these purely practical aids, argues Vanden Broecke, because it clarifies the operation of a sundial by mapping astronomic data onto terrestrial coordinates that could be visualized.[169] By demonstrating principles of the empirical processes by which that data was derived, the *Organum Ptolemei* enabled the reader to translate theoretical knowledge into more practical applications.

By synthesizing data from observations gathered over time, this tool could demonstrate variance in the length of daylight hours over seasons. These were data points that amateur observers had little chance of grasping in the absence of regular and sustained investigations. In this way, we can think of the *Organum Ptolemei* as a calculator of real values for a series of variables, such as how to divide the day up into hours of daylight. It is thus a tool that replicated a phenomenon that could be observed, and it gave the reader a purchase on the observable world. It taught the reader how to turn observations into practical knowledge.

The tool could illuminate other astronomical phenomena that could be inferred from observations. On the movable triangle marked *Trigonus*, there is a boundary line marked *Linea Umbrae*; this refers to the line of shadow that would supposedly be cast by the instrument. But another function can be inferred from it beyond its function as a pop-up shadow vane: the *Terminus* could also have potentially suggested to the viewer the boundary between light and darkness. This line might also represent the threshold of light and darkness, that boundary, or terminator, that we witness in air travel today, but one that could only be inferred in Apian's day.[170] Apian's tool aims to help conceptualize a phenomenon that, at least in principle, should be observable. Imagined here as a visual exercise, this terminator between night and day was surely a theoretical notion in this period, but one derived from the data of collective observations.

While the experts still disagree about the precise practical applications of the complex *Organum Ptolemei*, most would concur that this volvelle had an enormously influential afterlife. The volvelle's capacity to direct do-it-yourself activity can be seen in subsequent printings of other astronomic material. Versions of the volvelle surface regularly in later editions of Sacrobosco's *De Sphaera*, in which, we will remember, it became a critical feature of the afterlife of that text in the sixteenth-century printed editions.[171] It should also be noted that, at this point, Apian's volvelles find their way back home into more academic contexts – indeed, Gingerich calls these Sacrobosco editions the first true ancestors of modern astronomy textbooks. Steven Vanden Broecke argues convincingly for how Apian's illustrations rewire the practice of cosmography by prioritizing visual learning; he argues that these tools "technologized" cosmography, making it mechanical and useful.[172] This knowledge also helped to make celestial events foreseeable. On the road to shaping a more predictable universe, Apian's instruments required users' input, incentivized empirical engagement with the world, helped sharpen their observational acuity, and created expectations of visual verifiability.

The goal of informed peerings into the heavens under the rubric of cosmography was to bring astronomy down to earth. Apian's cosmography ripened in the age of geographic discovery and paralleled empirical developments in that field. In addition to astronomy, the other discipline to which sixteenth-century cosmography was indebted was geography, a field whose practice was simultaneously being overhauled by empirical experience in cartography. New knowledge was made possible by firsthand reports of data confirmed by navigational techniques and data recording enabled by instrumentation. This synergy displaced old coordinates and plotted new ones. Apian established cosmography as a genre that bridged the disciplinary divides between astronomy and geography. To be sure, the second-century AD Alexandrian Ptolemy himself had envisioned cosmography in this way. Ptolemy's intention was to furnish the *Geography* with maps, but these were never transmitted along with the projection methods and the data. Despite Ptolemy's original vision, astronomy and geography had essentially remained discrete pursuits in the scribal tradition.

Travel accounts printed in Latin and in vernacular languages were profuse enough by the 1480s to be collected by publishers in anthology format in the early 1500s. Their rapid furnishing with visual accompaniment brought new credibility to the eyewitness when those claims were backed by empirical experience suggested by images. One of the first important syntheses of empirically derived data sourced from travelers occurred in a cartographic think-tank located in St. Dié in present-day Alsace. Chief among those amendments made to geography was the incorporation of the Americas into existing models of the globe. These developments in the visualization of these "discoveries" (as Europeans understood them) took place against the backdrop of the Ptolemaic world picture and were specifically registered in the St. Dié workshop as revisions made on empirical grounds. Ptolemaic cartography was challenged by new facts whose novelty was accompanied by a self-conscious embrace of instruments and technology. The geographical revisions made at St. Dié reached their widest audiences via the circulation of newly drawn maps – it can be argued that the strikingly visual impact of these revisions underwrote the success of their conclusions. Therefore, it is not surprising that Apian, whose graphic projects were already heavily invested in the display and use of instrumentation, purposefully cribbed the cartographic novelties from St. Dié as a foundation for the second half of the *Cosmographicus Liber*. This appropriation can be interpreted as Apian's kindred pursuit of evidence derived from instrumentation and empirical inquiry.

Apian's geographic pictures and Gemma Frisius's maps that would later accompany editions of *Cosmographicus Liber* are among those that helped broadcast the cartographic knowledge developed in the St. Dié workshop. As Apian illustrates at the beginning of the *Cosmographicus Liber*, geography and astronomy supported the intellectual weight of cosmography in equal measure. The text's entire second half aimed to incorporate geography's new developments, following the dictates of a slim volume from St. Dié that was also engaged with contemporary advancements in instrumentation and data collecting. Incidentally, this volume also bore the word "cosmography" in its title. Edited by Matthias Ringmann and including maps made by cartographer Martin Waldseemüller, the *Cosmographiae Introductio* (1507) was a pamphlet dedicated to the Emperor Maximilian that included Amerigo Vespucci's reports of travels to the Americas and was intended to provide commentary to an accompanying map.[173] In addition to this world map, the workshop also printed gores for a terrestrial globe that could be constructed by the reader.[174] Cartography was intimately tied to other cosmographic disciplines such as astronomy, navigation, and especially instrument making during the sixteenth century. Many advances in cartographic precision would emerge from the instrumentation produced in the workshop of Gemma, whom we have already met as the editor of Apian's *Cosmographicus Liber*.[175] This cross-pollination between cartography and instrument making, with their byproducts visible in cosmography, was also highlighted by Apian and Frisius.[176] Like astronomy, revisions to cartographic knowledge would keep pace with the production and use of tools. Printmakers involved in these innovations frequently found it expedient to construct their own presses for their customized publications: such was the case with Waldseemüller and Mercator, in addition to Apian, who established a press in Ingolstadt in 1525.

Waldseemüller and Ringmann's collaborative publications were among the earliest humanist productions to plot coordinates derived from recent travel accounts of merchants against the world picture established by Ptolemy.[177] Vespucci, after all, had also referred back to Ptolemy when accounting for his geographic findings.[178] Among the adjustments that Ringmann and Waldseemüller made to the world map was the clearing of space in the Atlantic for a new continent they had the temerity to name after the Florentine merchant who claimed it to be both recently discovered territory and the fourth part of the world.[179] Waldseemüller's map projection can be thought of as a major intervention in the visualization of early modern data, and it reflected a series of visual choices so powerful that it not only rearranged the world picture but also gave birth to one of the largest early modern maps. The size of the printed woodcuts (set together, they measure 4.5 × 8 feet or 1.37 × 2.44 meters), in addition to the effort extended to produce and assemble them, suggests that St. Dié mapmakers were prescient in finding a graphic format to match the size of the epistemic break that using the new name of America would forge. The Waldseemüller map, a document whose touting as the "birth certificate of America" aimed to justify the $10 million price tag that accompanied its sale to the US Library of Congress in 2003, also made a sizable splash at the time of its printing.[180]

The St. Dié workshop published their new work in productions that privileged pictorial formats and visual "tools" such as globes and maps, but texts still provided the explanatory mortar for the featured visual accompaniments. Ringmann and Waldseemüller's *Cosmographia Introductio*, a roughly fifty-page manual, was intended as a primer for this large map. The publication introduced the new territories presented on the map, but the text itself is disappointingly peremptory, disorganized, and visually bereft, especially considering the unambiguous visual impact of the map. It was without clear chapter markings, and the occasional diagrams of the globe with degree and axis markings brought the total number of included images to four. Short shrift is given to spherical astronomy, with a brief sketch of circles encountered on the globe, yet the book is flush with glosses that point to ancient commentators on the world picture, such as Virgil, Ovid, Ptolemy, and Caesar. Three diagrams of spheres try to model celestial astronomy for the reader, and one larger celestial map folds out of the quarto-sized volume. Rudimentary discussions of climate zones are given, followed by lists of placenames. Perhaps the most flamboyant novelty, Vespucci's discovery of America, is embedded in a discussion of zones and climates, winds, and sections of the world unknown to Ptolemy.

Like the lines dividing the earth into terrestrial circles, "places unknown to Ptolemy," or *extra Ptholomeum*, was a time-honored way of demarcating boundaries in early modern geography as a black and white divide, with little gray area. Early sixteenth-century cosmographers were quick to invoke the zonal episteme of *extra Ptholomeum* for the stark contrast it provided between ancient facts and novelties still struggling for reconciliation. It was a handy scrim on which new data could easily be projected, and a well-functioning model of the order of things. Taking the name *Cosmographia* from Ptolemy, Apian's own *Cosmographiae Introductio* of 1529 still opened summarily with the analogy from Ptolemy that laid out the principles for the notional divisions between geography, which, perhaps most importantly, provided the rhetorical justification for the practice of picturing to convey information.[181] Using a woodcut showing the observer's eye as a vertex for the terrestrial and celestial sphere, Apian borrows for his front matter of this text an image similar to the opening visual gambit of his *Cosmographicus Liber* in 1524. Despite deference paid to Ptolemy on the first page, Apian invokes Ptolemy later in the text for the purpose of correcting him. If Apian neglects to mention Waldseemüller as a source in the text, he alludes to him in the book's title and spirit; they shared a kinship in their projects to revise Ptolemy.

Apian's *Cosmographiae Introductio* initiated a dialogue with the printed products of the St. Dié workshop. His streamlining of Waldseemüller's content around graphic design was critical to its production, a characteristic of Apian's publications post-1524. Apian designed the *Cosmographiae Introductio* to be a more useful guidebook to the cosmos than was Waldseemüller's original publication.[182] It was divided into clear chapters inspired by Waldseemüller, but then expanded and organized around diagrams that served to explain their principles. Following twelve years on the heels of Waldseemüller's text, Apian filtered Waldseemüller's content through the thoroughly visual programs of recent cosmographic publications of his own. He used Ptolemy strategically, placing emphasis on his data – i.e., coordinates – and reinforced his advocacy of visual aids.[183] In a text of approximately eighty pages in length, Apian's choice to include twenty-five images made the visual component substantial. Like his reissue of Sacrobosco's *De Sphaera* in octavo format in 1526, Apian's updating of Waldseemüller was crafted into a handy and portable edition. That it also appeared in Latin perhaps also testified to Apian's desired crossover appeal to both lay and academic audiences. Printed first in Ingolstadt in 1529, Apian's *Cosmographiae Introductio* then went into sixteen later editions in Paris, Cologne, and Venice, including some vernacular printings.[184]

Apian was forthright about the aspect of Waldseemüller's *Cosmographiae Introductio* that he found most important. He privileged the map that expressed the relationship between the astronomical and terrestrial coordinates in a systematic and technological manner. Waldseemüller's map cast the new data in light of the instrumentation used to obtain it: here, instruments pose as attributes of the protagonists at the map's top, where Ptolemy holds a quadrant and Vespucci holds dividers, a tool used by mariners and mapmakers. Waldseemüller's unequivocal emphasis on the visual material contrasts with evidence buried in the text's ramblings and disorganized quotations from ancient sources.

Apian's visualization zeroed in on the cartographic advances made in the think-tank of St. Dié in the early 1520s; it was probably exactly these geographic entanglements that partly inspired the production of the book at this chapter's center, the *Cosmographicus Liber*. Apian's terrestrial globe in the graphic description of cosmography on folio 2 was positioned to feature America. But Apian cribbed from Waldseemüller most assiduously in the projection of the terrestrial globe in the *Speculum Cosmographicae*, a unique instrument in the cosmography to be discussed below.

Several of Apian's publications prior to the *Cosmographicus Liber* also took the new world map as their subject, albeit in a slightly altered format. Apian repurposed Waldseemüller's data in a scaled-down woodblock version of a world map (Figure 2.18), considerably reducing the size of the 1507 original.[185] A cordiform projection derived from Waldseemüller, it even borrowed the design of the northern wind head Septentrio, from whose mouth not only gusts but also longitude lines seem to emerge. Designed by Apian for Camertius's commentary on Solinus, *Solini Polyistoria Enarrationes*, published in Vienna in 1520, the map appears as a single-sheet foldout tipped into the text near the beginning.[186] The map can also be found in some editions of

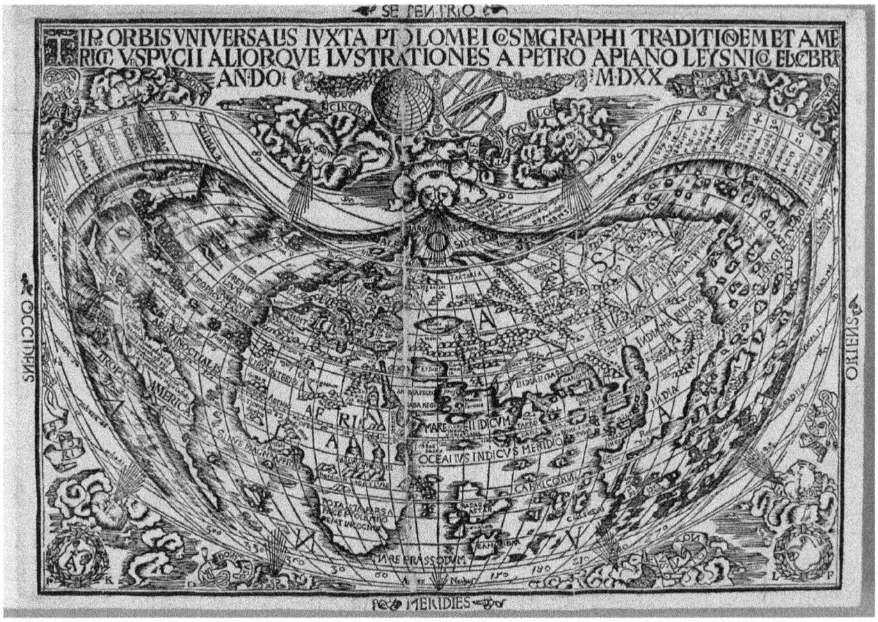

2.18. Peter Apian, world map in *Joannis Camertis ... in C Julii Solini Polyistora enarrationes. Additus eiusdem Camertis Index* (Vienna: Sigrenius and Alantse, 1520), 28.5 cm × 42 cm. *Source:* Courtesy of John Carter Brown Library. CC by 4.0; cf. https://jcblibrary.org/permissions.

Pomponius Mela's *De Situ Orbis*, such as the one that appeared in Basel in 1522. Another publication of Apian's, the 1521 *Isagoge*, a short pamphlet of cosmographic propositions, discussed strategies for picturing the earth's surface, included an explanation of Waldseemüller's map, and forecasted the author's plans for a cosmography.[187] The announced cosmography is widely believed to have become Apian's *Cosmographicus Liber* of 1524. In 1522, Apian provided the text for a pamphlet, *Declaratio et Usus Typi Cosmographici* (published by Paul Khol in Regensburg), with illustrations by Michael Ostendorfer, including a title page with a south-oriented oval-shaped map that shows a tiny, though assertive, America marked with the initials AM.[188] Lastly, twelve globe gores were printed *c.* 1520 and also are likely from Apian's press – these certainly appear to be designed to function on the level of a tool, a purpose that the later *Speculum Cosmographicae* would also serve.[189] Apian published the results of Waldseemüller's findings in these various repackagings, so we should not be surprised that the initial credit for Waldseemüller's original wall map was in fact usurped by him in the early secondary scholarship. Before the wall map's rediscovery in the Waldburg-Wolfegg collection in Swabia in 1901, most scholars assumed Apian to have been the first printer to place America's name on the globe, so avid a promoter was he of Waldseemüller's findings.[190]

While it is unclear whether Apian's cosmography announced in his 1521 *Isagoge* eventually became the *Cosmographicus Liber*, it is certainly true that the

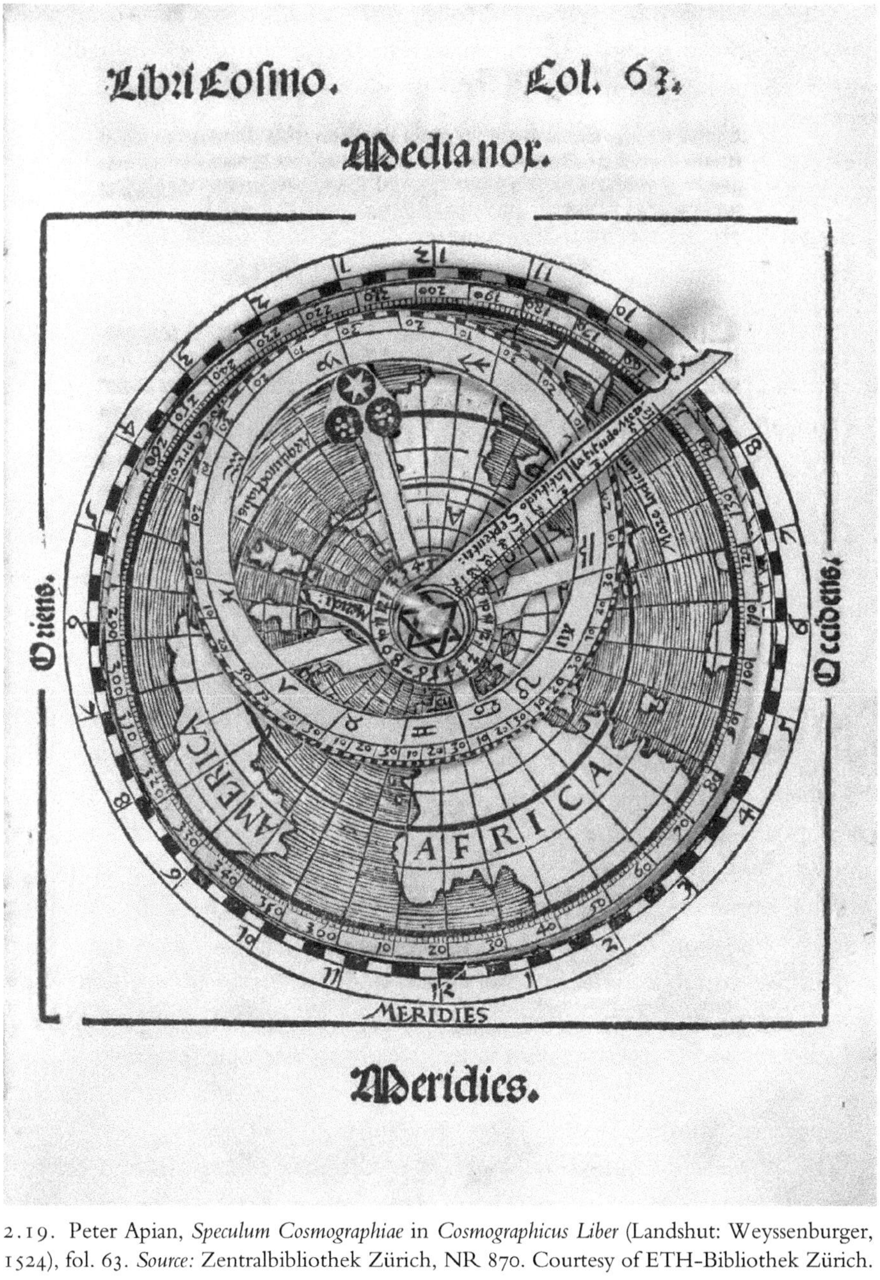

2.19. Peter Apian, *Speculum Cosmographiae* in *Cosmographicus Liber* (Landshut: Weyssenburger, 1524), fol. 63. *Source:* Zentralbibliothek Zürich, NR 870. Courtesy of ETH-Bibliothek Zürich.

cosmography was his synthesis of geographic advancements made in St. Dié. Privileging usable information, Apian presented these adjustments to the world map in the unique form of a coordinate dial in the *Cosmographicus Liber*, an instrument he dubbed the *Speculum Cosmographicae* (Figure 2.19). This was a geographically oriented astrolabe, in which Waldseemüller's projection of the earth forms the backdrop of the device. While the astrolabe proper schematized the heavens in order to show what the sky looks like at a given latitude and how celestial bodies move in relation to each other, Apian's *Speculum* provided instead information about terrestrial coordinates. On a traditional astrolabe, the bottom-most plate, or *mater*, shows the stereometric projection of the celestial sphere that maps stars onto the interior of the vault of the heavens. But the *mater* of Apian's device carries a projection of the earth seen from the north pole; the dial attempts to set the celestial coordinates into dialogue with their terrestrial analogues.[191] Placed at the conclusion of the astronomical part of the *Cosmographicus Liber* on folio 63, the tool introduces the book's second half on geography.

To construct the *Speculum*'s series of rotating parts, Apian borrowed the design and nomenclature from astrolabes.[192] Apian preserves the equator, tropics, and the ecliptic but projects these on top of a terrestrial map, instead of a celestial one. A movable disc carried the ecliptic and zodiac markers. Insofar as it represented a projection of the celestial circle, it mimicked the traditional astrolabe's star map, or *rete*, a circle that typically carries the zenith–horizon coordinate system for a particular latitude. Atop this moved the *rule* that serves as an index or pointer for the front; it is usually marked with a scale of declinations.

Physical astrolabes were outfitted with a number of removable discs that could be set to the local latitude; then, with the aid of a sighting device, or *alidade*, with which most were equipped on their rear surfaces, sightings could be taken to determine the altitude of sun or stars to find the time in order to appropriately position the discs.[193] Modern scholars agree that most astrolabes, until the weighty mariner's astrolabe that could be stabilized on board a ship became common, were primarily didactic tools for showing the stars and circles in relation to each other. Contemporary readers might have been familiar with publications such as Johann Copp's *Erklärung unnd gründtliche Underweysung alles nutzes, so in dem edlen Instrument, Astrolabium genannt* . . ., which appeared in 1525. This included a ready-to-assemble instrument, along with many images that set store by measurements made by the eye and observers in action.[194]

The astrolabe permitted investigation of the major terrestrial and celestial lines and attempted to provide knowledge of the celestial system as a whole. But Apian's instrument rehabilitated cosmography's intention to combine positional astronomy with *geography* – by using it to visualize earth-bound observations. Apian's text preceding the placement of this disc was a summation of five propositions that explained the purpose of this "mirror of cosmography," among which was to help the user understand the earth in the way one encounters one's face in the mirror: in other words, to develop visual intimacy with the earth as one knows oneself.[195] Again, Apian invokes the epistemic bite of portraiture: just as peering into a mirror would reveal self-knowledge, to observe one's coordinates was to understand one's place in the universe.

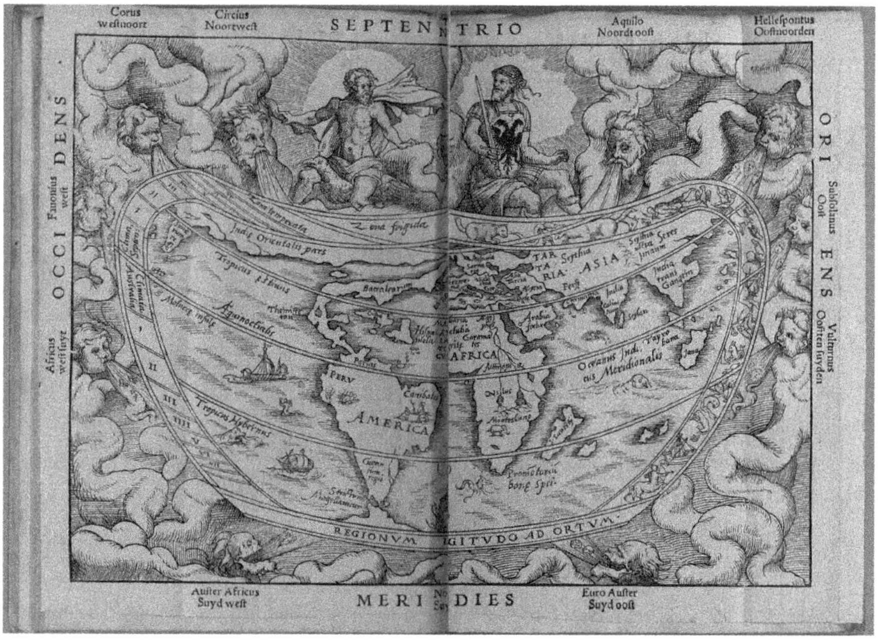

2.20. Peter Apian and Gemma Frisius, world map in *La Cosmographie de Pierre Apian,... nouuelleme[n]t traduict de latin en francois* (Antwerp: de Bonte, 1544). *Source:* Courtesy of John Carter Brown Library. CC by 4.0; cf. https://jcblibrary.org/permissions.

The dial was intended to help visualize abstract principles – showing readers the processes by which geographic coordinates operate and how to visualize their relationship to the cosmos. Retooling the projections of the traditional astrolabe, the celestial circles have been replaced by a projection of the continents from the north pole. This was a clear sign of Apian's intention to bring cosmography quite literally down to the study of the earth. After all, this was cosmography's guiding philosophy. This tool cast the net of celestial lines over a geographic representation of the earth befitting the book's section on geography. The *Speculum* volvelle precedes this narrative section and combines astronomical and geographic knowledge, placing it in the text at the threshold between astronomy and geography. The following narrative about continents and a list of coordinates for the world's cities presents the map as a system that links the celestial and terrestrial realms. The *Speculum* activates the Ptolemaic system by adding a user interface. The tool helps conceptualize geographic coordinates by having users capture the data themselves in the manner of professional cartographers.

Like the *Speculum*'s globus, a world map is also a tool. Editions of the cosmography printed after 1544 included a map of the world not present in Apian's *editio princeps* (Figure 2.20).[196] This was another addition made by Gemma, the instrument designer best known for his contributions to surveying and mapmaking and in whose workshop the future cartographer

Gerard Mercator worked.[197] Gemma's position on the faculty of medicine at the university in Louvain hardly alludes to his range of teaching or to the subject areas for which he was responsible, which included mathematics, astronomy, and geography. This map anchored Gemma's most heavily edited section of the *Cosmographicus Liber.* The map placed the new discoveries within the discursive context of geopolitical cartography which the image at the top announced: the Holy Roman Emperor Charles V in a Roman cuirass sits with Eolus, the wind, astride a dove.[198] The framing figures of this map echoed a trend in the updating of geography by agents already active in Waldseemüller's map of 1507, the document on which this map is based. Framing revisions to the world picture with portraits of the two empiricists who generated them, Waldseemüller had placed Ptolemy with a quadrant at the top, alongside the navigator Amerigo Vespucci, styled here as Ptolemy's early modern updater. Both earned their spots in the cartographic firmament on the strength of their reputations as observers, wielding tools of firsthand inquiry and presciently aware of the novelty of their data. By positioning the modern observer Vespucci at the top of his map, Waldseemüller tacitly argued for the agency of instrument users to reshape the world picture. This reference was surely not lost on Apian, who promised that the secrets of geography and spherical astronomy could be unlocked by his own printed tools.

The allegorical trappings of empire would dominate the shape of later cosmography, where portraits of sovereigns would edge out the representations of tool-laden empiricists. New discoveries in astronomy and geography would soon be mobilized in the service of geopolitical aims. The empirical basis for cosmography would later surrender to a genre that would feature narrative accounts of the world's spaces, providing the history of peoples and their conflicts, and a parceling out of what belonged to whom. In this period, we can already detect the slow creep of these empirical projects into the territory of imperial imaginings. Waldseemüller's edition was dedicated to the Emperor Maximilian, after all, and Apian's later projects reflect the involvement of Charles V, who commissioned a horoscope from him in the shape of a book with movable dials, the *Astronomicum Caesareum.*[199] Cosmography fell increasingly into the hands of operatives eager to win dominion over geographic territories.[200] Later cosmographies (such as those by Sebastian Münster and André Thevet) changed course and "wrote themselves back into medieval, encyclopedic tradition, bestiary, universal history, adding to these recent geographic encroachments."[201] But cosmography as Apian conceived it was still the appropriate genre for both mathematical geography and tools.

Thus, Apian's *Speculum Cosmographicae* visualized the main geographic contributions of Waldseemüller's publications and also raised the profile of empirical study of both the heavens and the world. The *Speculum* might be the first model to set the jewel of a geographically mapped earth into the setting of the starry vault, an instrument with which stargazers could orient themselves in the broader context of the universe. In short, this model reprises the principles of Apian's first linear diagram that connected the celestial and terrestrial spheres to the eye (see Figure 2.3). With the *Speculum*, Apian assembles into one interactive tool all the components of his opening diagram that explains cosmography: this volvelle completes the ambition to graphically depict the world system as a dialogue between astronomical and geographic spheres. At this juncture of the book, users themselves usurp the authority of the prime mover: observers activate the tools with their own hands, producing individually relevant data points.[202]

TOOLS AND THE "VERNACULAR" VIEWER

The *Cosmographicus Liber* fully endorsed the use of tools as a means for vernacular observers to discover things in their own environment and made explicit that the book's content was derived largely from firsthand study. Empirical observations not only helped fill in the mortar between the ancient bricks; in some cases, they repaired some of the crumbling patches as well. Karl Röttel has judged the complex visual lessons learned from Apian's mechanical pictures as a critical intermediary stage for the development, and especially the popularization, of instruments.[203] Apian's translation of mathematized astronomy into visual terms laid the groundwork for a spate of vernacular publications devoted to the use of instruments: sundials, quadrants, astrolabes, and nocturnal dials.[204] Apian popularized tools and brought knowledge of them to a much broader swath of the general public. The collection of tools in the *Cosmographicus Liber*, per the argument of Margaret Gaida, fashioned Apian's text into a toolkit.[205] This amounted to no less than the birth of a new reading public: mathematical autodidacts ready to brave a cosmos that could be unlocked by do-it-yourself tools.

In fact, Apian's *Cosmographicus Liber* identified so much as a book about tools that Gemma Frisius commandeered the 1539 edition as a vehicle to publicize his new scientific instrument: the astronomical rings, later called Gemma's rings. Gemma's first edits to Apian's text appeared in Antwerp in 1529; these emboldened him to use Apian's text as a malleable palimpsest for his own cosmographic musings. Soon after the first edition, in which his corrections appeared in an appendix, Gemma relocated some of Apian's volvelles into a separate section, likely sensing this as a space that he could later amplify with copy written around his own tools.[206] The Antwerp edition printed by Arnold Birkman in 1539 bundled a number of spinoff publications with Apian's text.[207] Birkman's printing attached Gemma's appendix on surveying and trigonometry, the *Libellus de Locorum describendorum ratione, & de eorum distantijs inueniendis, numquam antehac visus, per Gemmam Frisium*, to the cosmography. This text was followed by a thirteen-page discourse on Gemma's astronomical rings, the *Usus Annuli Astronomici, Gemma Frisio Mathematico Auctore*, a text that Gemma had printed as an independent short pamphlet in 1534 under the title *L'usage de l'anneau astronomique*. This practical text featured a number of pictured observers making trigonometric calculations of the altitudes of fortresses and steeples through ringed instruments that Gemma had designed.[208] Gemma's how-to treatise on the rings essentially hijacked Apian's text in order to publicize his instruments in the appendices. Gemma rewired the cosmography into a manual that would provide the foundation for the use – and, importantly, the sale – of his instruments. This marketing initiative broadened the scope of empirical knowledge that could be processed with the book.

Gemma Frisius became an ardent proponent of the practice of observation. Gemma's son Cornelius reported in 1561 that his father kept two journals of his own observations. Apparently expecting that perusal of his printed texts would mobilize similar types of data recording, Gemma chastised stargazers for simply following Ptolemy and not using their own observations to update the Alfonsine Tables. The empirical approach that united the interdisciplinary activity of Gemma and Cornelius in the collection of astronomic, weather, and medical data, according to Gianna Pomata, reveals a new method afoot in empirical explorations of the period.[209] This type of visual investigation of the world was spearheaded by Apian, but it was endorsed and perfected by Gemma. The move away from doctrine – even when the older sources were still invoked in the contemporary literature – is what united the multiple categories of empirical inquiry that coalesced into a *modus operandi* for exploring the world. Both Apian and Gemma knew that this user-based interface could best be achieved by images that would chaperone these visual searches in the world picture. These images and tools centered the agency of a literate eye schooled by books.

Images in astronomical texts, mechanical and otherwise, brought lofty principles to earth and sometimes functioned together with words in new pedagogical combinations: images and even verse appear in these books to facilitate understanding for the reader and to encourage personal observation in these pursuits.[210] Apian himself capitalized on the content of texts such as Conrad Heinfogel's vernacular translation of Sacrobosco's *De Sphaera* that provided helpful hints about the progression of lunar phases in language that only a layman could love. In the 1516 edition, verses accompany two diagrams that set the sun and moon in relation to each other to explain reflected light from the sun. In the 1533 edition, an unrelated diagram of a lunar eclipse accompanies versions of the original verses:

> Note what I diligently teach you:
> The way the moon ignites
> when the sun bathes it,
> you should understand it to be half-lit
>
> Although the moon is at all times
> rather more than half-illuminated
> One never sees its full shine
> only sometimes large, then small again.[211]

This was a far cry from their lofty cosmographic precedents; sixteenth-century pointers about astronomy were rendered in doggerel for the practical purpose of serving the reader's memory. Heinfogel's use of a jaunty imperative mood was intended to stimulate memory, not unlike lessons learned today by amateur stargazers who need to distinguish between waning and waxing moons with mnemonics such as "when the light is on the right, the moon is getting bright." Delivery of such wisdom by speaking images was another tactic to engrave those precepts in the mind. The subtitle of this volume – "the path of the heavens together with all of the stars, much easier to learn with the accompanying pictures" – foregrounds its attempt to cultivate a new public of amateur astronomers by way of helpful images.[212]

A clue to the efficacy of popular astronomy's visual pedagogy is embedded in one reader's response to the material. A hand-drawn sheet of astronomic principles that appears in a codex gathering of a book preserved in the Herzog August Bibliothek in Wolfenbüttel cribs from a variety of sources.[213] This sheet collates diagrams from Sacrobosco's *Sphera Materialis: Eyn Anfang* (the 1533 edition from Cammerlander) and other works of popular cosmography, probably including Apian's *Cosmographicus Liber.* A rare example of likely contemporary reception of this material, here we see a reader working out principles of observation derived from the images. One drawing rehearses Sacrobosco's familiar proof of the ocean's sphericality demonstrated by the contrasting views of two shipboard observers, one on deck and one at the mast. To clarify the proof, this scribe added another image in which he replaced the actual observers with two eyes, each labeled "*Aug[e]*," in order to situate the eye at the receiving end of the observation (Figure 2.21).[214] With this, he substantiated the agent also at the heart of Apian's concerns: the eye of the user. Apian frequently animated eyes, ears, hands, and feet in his illustrations. Small, black, thickened stick figures dot his schematic models to provide human receptors for the observations his demonstrations taught. Human actors served as surrogate reference points for the users' own observations. When the reader of the Wolfenbüttel Sacrobosco saw an unanchored eye in a cosmographic text, it was clear that they did not mistake it for the eye of God; rather, they saw it as their own. With the aid of Apian's tools, this earth-bound eye peered through the earth into the heavens for the purpose of drawing up a practical data set. This perspective was increasingly

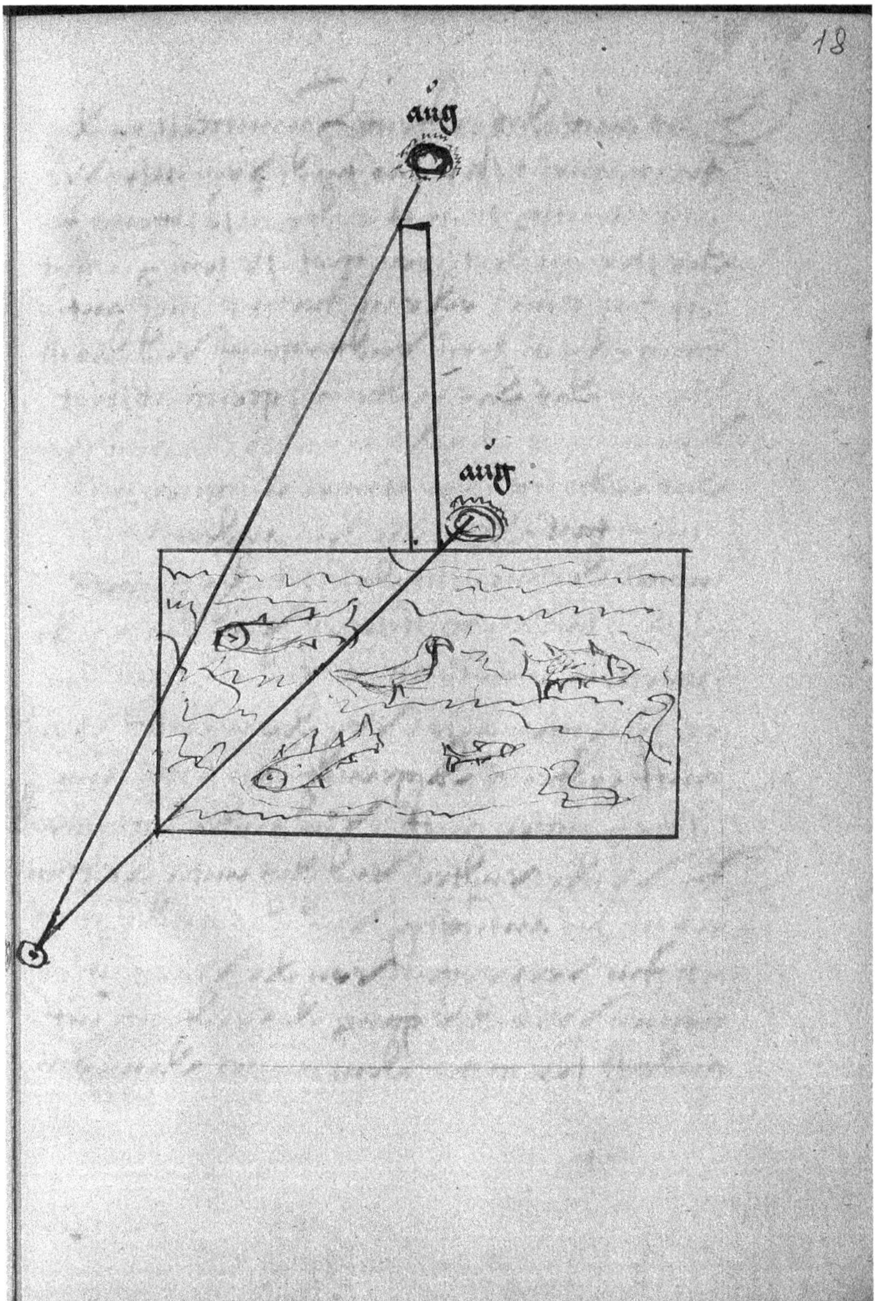

2.21. Drawing included with Heinfogel and Sacrobosco, "*Aug[e]*" in *Sphera Materialis: Eyn Anfang* (Strasbourg: Cammerlander, 1533). *Source:* HAB A17.4 Astron. 18r. Courtesy of Herzog August Bibliothek Wolfenbüttel.

conditioned by the visual acuity taught by these manuals and reiterated their promotion of visual knowledge.

Apian himself called on such visual vigilance in his practical publications. He argued vociferously for his own expertise as an observer, a claim that was designed to activate the intended reader to follow in his footsteps. This confidence rested on the premise of the expanse of the heavens over Ingolstadt as a visual horizon he shared with an imagined community of fellow observers whom he hoped to goad into becoming a group of collective empirics: "We see the sky everywhere before our eyes because it spins day and night around the earth, and we would like to easily observe and describe it."[215] In the prologue of his *Practica auff das 1532. Jar*, Apian distinguishes the empirical knowability of the heavens from that of the earth. Because the earth stretches beyond the visual field of the observer, it presents a greater challenge to description because it cannot be encompassed without costly travel. On the strength of his visual acuity, Apian intones, the reader should summon the services of an astronomer who has been observing and recording the effects of the stars on weather and storms (the topic of this almanac), because he has trained his eye to track these conditions.

Peter Apian led the era of publishing cosmographic texts framed as methods to train the visual aptitude of amateur observers. Packaged for new readerships, this foray into new territory and its fallout can be tracked in new vernacular manuals that capitalized on the gathering of empirical knowledge. The age of Apian's publications was firmly dedicated to serving up usable manuals to new devotees of astronomy. Apian situates his reader locally (important to cosmographical accuracy) and provides demonstrations of things that can be observed on earth. Never asked to take phenomena on faith alone, Apian's readers were provided with a theoretical armature to accompany their search for events in a visually constituted field. We need only remember Apian's pictorial demonstration of how the shape of the earth can be visually verified during observations of lunar eclipses: we see the roundness of the earth projected onto the eclipsed moon. Apian reminds his readers that if the earth took the shape of a square or triangular or hexagon, they would instead see these shapes reflected on the lunar surface. As a direct and easy appeal to the eye, the point is shored up by a rhetorical directive to the viewer: compare and contrast. What the naked eye sees can unpack larger principles. How-to tools that helped activate and contextualize both astronomical and geographical observations centered them no longer around a theoretical "eye," but around an actual earth-bound "*Aug[e]*."

NOTES

1 For Apian's activities as a printer and mathematician in Ingolstadt, see Peter Meurer, "Cartography in the German Lands, 1450–1650," in David Woodward, ed., *The History*

of Cartography. Volume 3: Cartography in the European Renaissance (Chicago and London: University of Chicago Press, 2007), 1198–201.

2 The colophon announces that Apian had the work printed at his expense but using the infrastructure of the Weyssenburger press: "*Excusum Landshutae Typis ac formulis D. Joannis Weyssenburgers: impensis Petri Apiani* [Printed in Landshut with the typographic material of Joannes Weyssenburger, at the expense of Petrus Apianus]." Many thanks to Joost Depuydt and Paul Gehl for help with the translation of printing terms. For Apian's printer, Johannes Weyssenburger, see K. Steiff, "Weyssenburger, Johannes," *Allgemeine Deutsche Biographie* 42 (1897), 290–1; see also Karl Schottenloher, *Die Landshuter Buchdrucker des 16. Jahrhunderts* (Nieuwkoop: B. de Graaf, 1967), 39f., no. 117.

3 Peter Apian, *La Cosmographie de Pierre Apian Docteur et Mathematicien Tres Excellent: Traictant de Toutes les Regions Pais Villes & Citez du Monde* (Paris: Gualtherot, 1553), fol. 1r. I use Tom Conley's translation in Tom Conley, *An Errant Eye: Poetry and Topography in Early Modern France* (Minneapolis: University of Minnesota Press, 2011), 58.

4 The content includes Ptolemy's *Geographia*, a medieval astronomy textbook of Sacrobosco's *De Sphaera*, as well as a much more contemporary source, Martin Waldseemüller's *Cosmographia Introductio*.

5 For a complete list of Apian's publications, along with their current locations, see Karl Röttel, *Peter Apian: Astronomie, Kosmographie und Mathematik am Beginn der Neuzeit: Mit Ausstellungskatalog* (Buxheim: Polygon-Verlag, 1995), 259–76.

6 For the reception of Ptolemy in the early modern period, see Zur Shalev and Charles Burnett, eds., *Ptolemy's Geography in the Renaissance*, Warburg Institute Colloquia (London: Warburg Institute, 2011), 8ff.

7 Later editions of Ptolemy's work would restore the title of *Geographia*. For the translation history of the vocabulary *geographia* and *cosmographia*, see especially Dario Tessicini, "Definitions of 'Cosmography' and 'Geography' in the Wake of 15th and 16th Century Translations and Editions of Ptolemy's *Geography*," in Shalev and Burnett, eds., *Ptolemy's Geography in the Renaissance*, 31–49; see also Adam Mosley, "The Cosmographer's Role in the Sixteenth Century: A Preliminary Study," *Archives Internationales d'Histoire des Sciences* 59 (2009), 424–39.

8 Denis E. Cosgrove, ed., *Mappings* (London: Reaktion Books, 1999); see also Lucia Nuti, "Mapping Places: Chorography and Vision in the Renaissance," in Cosgrove, ed., *Mappings*, 90–108. According to Nuti, Apian misread Jacopo d'Angelo in his transcription.

9 Contrasting the mathematical modeling of geography (or world cartography) with the descriptive aims of chorography (regional cartography), Ptolemy says: "World cartography is an imitation through drawing of the entire known part of the world. Regional cartography sets out individual localities . . . the goal of regional cartography is an impression of a part, as when one makes an image of just an ear or an eye; but [the goal] of world cartography is a general view, analogous to making a portrait of the whole head." Claudius Ptolemaeus, *Ptolemy's Geography: An Annotated Translation of the Theoretical Chapters*, ed. John L. Berggren and Alexander Jones (Princeton, NJ: Princeton University Press, 2000). Here, I have used the editors' translation (at 57).

10 Jessica Maier, *Rome Measured and Imagined: Early Modern Maps of the Eternal City* (Chicago: University of Chicago Press, 2015), 5; Bronwen Wilson, *The World in Venice: Print, the City and Early Modern Identity* (Toronto: University of Toronto Press, 2005), 191ff.; Svetlana Alpers, *The Art of Describing: Dutch Art in the Seventeenth Century* (Chicago: University of Chicago Press, 1983), 119ff.

11 For Apian's press in Ingolstadt, see Christoph Schöner, *Mathematik und Astronomie an der Universität Ingolstadt im 15. und 16. Jahrhundert* (Berlin: Duncker & Humblot, 1994), 361–3.

12 For Gemma, see Samuel Gessner, "The Use of Printed Images for Instrument-Making at the Arsenius Workshop," in Nicolas Jardine and Isla Fay, eds., *Observing the World through Images: Diagrams and Figures in the Early-Modern Arts and Sciences* (Leiden and Boston, MA: Brill, 2014), 129ff.; see also Gessner, "The Perspective of the Instrument Maker: The

Planispheric Projection with Gemma Frisius and the Arsenius Workshop at Louvain," in Sven Dupré, ed., *Perspective as Practice: Renaissance Cultures of Optics* (Turnhout: Brepols, 2019).

13 Fernand van Ortroy, *Bibliographie de l'oeuvre de Pierre Apian* (Amsterdam: Meridian, 1963); Shalev and Burnett, eds., *Ptolemy's Geography in the Renaissance*, 94.

14 As much as Apian relied on earlier sources for his content, his own content was also repackaged in later publications roughly bearing the title *Cosmographia* in fifty-eight editions in four languages between 1524 and 1609.

15 Mosley, "The Cosmographer's Role," 424–39, especially 435; Steven Vanden Broecke, *The Limits of Influence: Pico, Louvain and the Crisis of Renaissance Astrology* (Leiden and Boston, MA: Brill, 2003), 113–36.

16 William Mills Ivins, *Prints and Visual Communication* (New York: Da Capo Press, 1969); Elizabeth L. Eisenstein, *The Printing Press as an Agent of Change: Communications and Cultural Transformations in Early-Modern Europe* (New York: Cambridge University Press, 1979).

17 George Sarton, *The Appreciation of Ancient and Medieval Science during the Renaissance (1450–1600)* (Philadelphia: University of Pennsylvania Press, 1955); John W. Shirley and F. David Hoeniger, eds., *Science and the Arts in the Renaissance* (Washington, DC and London: Folger Shakespeare Library and Associated University Presses, 1985).

18 This edged out considerations of images' roles in astronomy, mathematics, and physics, for example. See Renzo Baldasso, "The Role of Visual Representation in the Scientific Revolution: A Historiographic Inquiry," *Centaurus* 48 (2006), 69–88, especially 84.

19 See Martin Kemp, "Temples of the Body and Temples of the Cosmos: Vision and Visualization in the Vesalian and Copernican Revolutions," in Brian Scott Baigrie, ed., *Picturing Knowledge: Historical and Philosophical Problems Concerning the Use of Art in Science* (Toronto: University of Toronto Press, 1996); Sachiko Kusukawa, *Picturing the Book of Nature: Image, Text, and Argument in Sixteenth-Century Human Anatomy and Medical Botany* (Chicago: University of Chicago Press, 2011); Sachiko Kusukawa and Ian Maclean, *Transmitting Knowledge: Words, Images, and Instruments in Early Modern Europe* (Oxford and New York: Oxford University Press, 2006).

20 Stephanie Leitch, "Visual Acuity and the Physiognomer's Art of Observation," *Oxford Art Journal* 38, no. 2 (2015), 187–206; Lisa Voigt and Elio Brancaforte, "The Traveling Illustrations of Sixteenth-Century Travel Narratives," *PMLA* 129, no. 3 (2014), 365–98.

21 Alexander Marr, "Ingenuity in Nuremberg: Dürer and Stabius's Instrument Prints," *Art Bulletin* 100, no. 3 (2018), 48–79.

22 Jardine and Fay, eds., *Observing the World through Images.*

23 Susan Dackerman, *Prints and the Pursuit of Knowledge in Early Modern Europe* (Cambridge, MA and New Haven, CT: Harvard Art Museums, 2011).

24 Jörn Münkner, *Eingreifen und Begreifen: Handhabungen und Visualisierungen in Flugblättern der Frühen Neuzeit* (Berlin: Erich Schmidt, 2008); Lisa Pon, *A Printed Icon: Forlì's Madonna of the Fire* (New York: Cambridge University Press, 2015); David S. Areford, *The Viewer and the Printed Image in Late Medieval Europe* (Farnham and Burlington, VT: Ashgate, 2010).

25 Michael Baxandall, *Painting and Experience in Fifteenth Century Italy: A Primer in the Social History of Pictorial Style*, 2nd edition (New York: Oxford University Press, 1988).

26 Baldasso, "The Role of Visual Representation," 78; see also Marie Boas, *The Scientific Renaissance 1450–1630* (New York: Harper and Row, 1962), 53–4.

27 Richard J. Oosterhoff, "A Book, a Pen, and the *Sphere*: Reading Sacrobosco in the Renaissance," *History of Universities* 28, no. 2 (2015), 1–54.

28 Renzo Baldasso, "Illustrating the Book of Nature in the Renaissance: Drawing, Painting, and Printing Geometric Diagrams and Scientific Figures," PhD dissertation, Columbia University, 2007; Horst Bredekamp and Pablo Schneider, *Visuelle Argumentationen: Die Mysterien der Reprasentation und die Berechenbarkeit der Welt* (Munich: Wilhelm Fink, 2006); Horst Bredekamp, Vera Dünkel, and Birgit Schneider, *The Technical Image: A History of Styles in Scientific Imagery* (Chicago: University of Chicago Press, 2015).

29 Stephanie Leitch, *Mapping Ethnography in Early Modern Germany: New Worlds in Print Culture* (Basingstoke: Palgrave Macmillan, 2010).

30 Suzanne Karr Schmidt, *Interactive and Sculptural Printmaking in the Renaissance* (Leiden and Boston, MA: Brill, 2018); see also Suzanne Kathleen Karr Schmidt, "Art – A User's Guide: Interactive and Sculptural Printmaking in the Renaissance," PhD dissertation, Yale University, 2006; Suzanne Karr Schmidt and Kimberly Nichols, *Altered and Adorned: Using Renaissance Prints in Daily Life* (Chicago and New Haven, CT: Art Institute of Chicago, distributed by Yale University Press, 2011); see also Suzanne Karr Schmidt and Edward Wouk, *Prints in Translation, 1450–1750: Image, Materiality, Space* (Abingdon: Routledge, 2017).

31 See Lorraine Daston, "Epistemic Images," in Alina Alexandra Payne, ed., *Vision and Its Instruments: Art, Science, and Technology in Early Modern Europe* (University Park: Pennsylvania State University Press, 2015), 13–35.

32 Alexander Marr, "Knowing Images: A Review Essay," *Renaissance Quarterly* 69, no. 3 (2016), 1000–13; Bredekamp, Dünkel, and Schneider, *The Technical Image*.

33 Lorraine Daston and Elizabeth Lunbeck, *Histories of Scientific Observation* (Chicago: University of Chicago Press, 2011), 81–113.

34 Peter Apian and Gemma Frisius, *Cosmographie, oft Beschrijinghe der geheelder werelt* (Antwerp: Gregorius de Bonte, 1553), fol. 3r.

35 Conley, *An Errant Eye*, 69. Conley suggests that the disembodied body parts that appear in the text might be related to the tradition of bodily blazons; to this I add that the isolated features might also be in dialogue with the focus on the same body parts in contemporary physiognomies.

36 For Apian's engagement with the Ptolemaic curriculum in general, see Benjamin Weiss, "The Geography in Print: 1475–1530," in Shalev and Burnett, eds., *Ptolemy's Geography in the Renaissance*, 93–6.

37 "*Corographia est perfecta (et) consumata pictura et nulla eam nisi homo pictor exerce ripotest.*" Many thanks to Barbara Tramelli for help with the translation.

38 Michael J. Sauter, *The Spatial Reformation: Euclid between Man, Cosmos, and God* (Philadelphia: University of Pennsylvania Press, 2019); for globe pairing, see 55ff. Johannes Schöner was the first to produce a paired set of terrestrial and celestial globes in 1515. See also Karr Schmidt, *Interactive and Sculptural Printmaking*, 265.

39 Tom Conley, "A Topographer's Eye: From Gilles Corrozet to Pieter Apian," in Walter S. Melion and Lee Palmer Wandel, eds., *Early Modern Eyes* (Leiden: Brill, 2010), 70. Tom Conley shows the agency active in man's eye.

40 Erwin Panofsky, *Perspective as Symbolic Form*, trans. Christopher S. Wood (New York: Zone Books, 1991).

41 Sauter, *The Spatial Reformation*. Sauter would also claim this eye for man's eye. Excluding God from this space, Sauter argues, Apian's image credits humanity with this mode of projection (pp. 56–7).

42 Samuel Y. Edgerton, *The Renaissance Discovery of Linear Perspective* (NY: Basic Books, 1975), 91ff. Edgerton argues that Ptolemaic projection contributed to geometric abstraction that preceded the embrace of linear perspective by Florentine artists and theorists in the fifteenth century.

43 See Angelo Catteneo, "Map Projections and Perspective in the Renaissance," in Shalev and Burnett, eds., *Ptolemy's Geography in the Renaissance*, 54.

44 Kim H. Veltman, "Ptolemy and the Origins of Linear Perspective," *Atti del Convegno Internazionale di Studi Tenutosi al Castello Sforzesco, Civiche Raccolte d'Arte di Milano, dall'11 al 15 Ottobre del 1977* (Florence: Centro Di, 1980), 403.

45 The astrolabe incorporates a few more projections: latitudes (in the form of almucanthars) and longitudes (or azimuths) relative to a viewer's position. Veltman, "Ptolemy and the Origins of Linear Perspective,"403.

46 Veltman, "Ptolemy and the Origins of Linear Perspective," 404.

47 Steven Vanden Broecke, "The Use of Visual Media in Renaissance Cosmography: The Cosmography of Peter Apian and Gemma Frisius," *Paedagogica Historica* 36, no. 1 (2000), 130–52, here 137.
48 Anthony Grafton, *Commerce with the Classics: Ancient Books and Renaissance Readers* (Ann Arbor: University of Michigan Press, 1997), 220–1.
49 Shalev and Burnett, eds., *Ptolemy's Geography in the Renaissance*, 116. The holograph Ptolemy texts themselves do not appear in the university curricula until the mid-sixteenth century.
50 Vanden Broecke, "The Use of Visual Media in Renaissance Cosmography," 142.
51 Shalev and Burnett, eds., *Ptolemy's Geography in the Renaissance*, 107.
52 Vanden Broecke, "The Use of Visual Media in Renaissance Cosmography," 133.
53 Darin Hayton, *The Crown and the Cosmos. Astrology and the Politics of Maximilian I* (Pittsburgh: University of Pittsburgh, 2015); for the academic context for astrology, see 68–97.
54 On the relationship between mathematicians and physicians, see Robert S. Westman, "The Astronomer's Role in the Sixteenth Century: A Preliminary Study," *History of Science* 18 (1980), 118. Apian's teacher George Tannstetter was also primarily employed as a physician; see Hayton, *The Crown and the Cosmos*, 96–7.
55 Shalev and Burnett, eds., *Ptolemy's Geography in the Renaissance*, 94.
56 Johannes Sacrobosco, an astronomer likely originally from England, taught at the University of Paris in the thirteenth century, where the first copies of the *De Sphaera* appeared around 1220. See Lynn Thorndike, ed., *The* Sphere *of Sacrobosco and Its Commentators. Corpus of Mediaeval Scientific Texts: Volume 2* (Chicago: University of Chicago Press, 1949). Thorndike's English translation of Sacrobosco is available online at www.esotericarchives.com/solomon/sphere.htm. Another useful online resource is the collection of astronomical images in the University of Cambridge Digital Library.
57 Jürgen Hamel, *Studien zur "Sphaera" des Johannes de Sacrobosco* (Leipzig: Akademische Verlagsanstalt, 2014). Michael Scot's commentary on it appeared in 1230–5.
58 Charles Coulston Gillispie, *Dictionary of Scientific Biography. Volume 12* (New York: Scribner, 1975).
59 For the use of Sacrobosco in university settings, see "Sacrobosco, Johannes De (or John of Holywood)," in *Complete Dictionary of Scientific Biography* (Detroit: Charles Scribner's Sons, 2008); available online at www.encyclopedia.com/doc/1G2-2830903812.html.
60 The bulk of Sacrobosco's medieval commentators, according to Richard Oosterhoff, foregrounded the theoretical underpinnings of the cosmos rather than providing a practical guide to it. See Oosterhoff, "A Book, a Pen, and the *Sphere*," 6–7. Commentary by these readers were still surrounded by the matrix of older notions of resemblances and conveniences based on received knowledge rather than observed practice. For the extent to which patterns of resemblance characterized the Renaissance episteme, see Michel Foucault, *The Order of Things: An Archaeology of the Human Sciences* (New York: Vintage Books, 1994), especially 17–25.
61 For the early modern commentaries, see Matteo Valleriani, ed., *De Sphaera of Johannes de Sacrobosco in the Early Modern Period: The Authors of the Commentaries* (Berlin: Springer, 2020).
62 Owen Gingerich, "Sacrobosco as a Textbook," *Journal for the History of Astronomy* 19, no. 4 (1988), 272–3. See also Kathleen M. Crowther and Peter Barker, "Training the Intelligent Eye: Understanding Illustrations in Early Modern Astronomy Texts," *Isis* 104, no. 3 (2013), 429–70, here 430–1.
63 The Jesuit Christopher Clavius provided commentaries for a new edition of Sacrobosco in 1611, despite its strictly geocentric emphasis. See James M. Lattis, "Christopher Clavius and the 'Sphere' of Sacrobosco: The Roots of Jesuit Astronomy on the Eve of the Copernican Revolution," PhD dissertation, University of Wisconsin-Madison, 1989. For various editions of Sacrobosco online, consult astronomical images in the Cambridge Digital Library. See also Matteo Valleriani, ed., *The Structures of Practical Knowledge* (Cham:

Springer, 2017), 438; Volker Remmert, "Catholic Biblical Exegesis and the Origins of the Galileo Affair: The Engraved Title Page of Clavius's *Opera Mathematica* (1612)," in Volker R. Remmert, *Picturing the Scientific Revolution* (Philadelphia: Saint Joseph's University Press, 2011), especially 31–6.

64 Baldasso, "Illustrating the Book of Nature in the Renaissance," 207, 209ff., 221–3. Printers of Sacrobosco's text also inherited the idea of a visual apparatus from a tradition of printing technical astronomic diagrams active in Nuremberg *c.* 1473–5, where Regiomontanus was the first to update ancient astronomic data by purposefully transmitting it into print.

65 Melanie Grimm, Claudia Kleine-Tebbe, and Ad Stijnman, *Lichtspiel und Farbenpracht: Entwicklungen des Farbdrucks 1500–1800: Aus den Beständen der Herzog-August-Bibliothek* (Wiesbaden: Harrassowitz, 2011), 70. The hand-coloring of the eclipse diagrams in the early Ratdolt edition from 1482 attempts to distinguish among various spheres. The moons are executed in brown wash, while the earth and suns are rendered in yellow. By 1490, the Venetian printer Scotus prints the moons in orange and the suns in gold. The 1490 Venice imprint is one of the first to be illustrated in detail and also included demonstrations. See also Ad Stijnman and Elizabeth Savage, *Printing Colour 1400–1700: History, Techniques, Functions and Receptions* (Boston, MA: Brill, 2015).

66 Stijnman and Savage, *Printing Colour 1400–1700*, 29ff.

67 Crowther and Barker, "Training the Intelligent Eye," 429–70.

68 Crowther and Barker caution contemporary readers about our own post-Copernican biases to see orbits in the two-dimensional cross-sections of Peurbach's planetary models. Instead, these nesting circles were meant to represent conceptualizations of epicycles.

69 See Sacrobosco on the spherical nature of drops of water: "Also, since water is a homogeneous body, the whole will act the same as its parts. But parts of water, as happens in the case of little drops and dew on herbs, naturally seek a round shape. Therefore, the whole, of which they are parts, will do so." Thorndike, ed., *The* Sphere *of Sacrobosco and Its commentators*.

70 "Let a signal be set up on the seacoast and a ship leave port and sail away so far that the eye of a person standing at the foot of the mast can no longer discern the signal. Yet if the ship is stopped, the eye of the same person, if he has climbed to the top of the mast, will see the signal clearly. Yet the eye of a person at the bottom of the mast ought to see the signal better than he who is at the top, as is shown by drawing straight lines from both to the signal. And there is no other explanation of this thing than the bulge of the water. For all other impediments are excluded, such as clouds and rising vapors" (Sacrobosco, book I).

71 Johannes and Wenceslaus Fabri, *Opus sphericum Johannis de sacro busto: figuris et p[er]utili co [m]mento illustratu[m]* (Agrippine: Per Henricum Quentell, 1501).

72 Johannes de Sacrobosco and Peter Apian, *Sphaera Iani de Sacrobusto astronomiae ac cosmographiae candidatis scitu apprime necessaria* (Ingolstadt: Peter and Georg Apian, 1526).

73 Sacrobosco, Johannes Regiomontanus, and Georg von Peuerbach, *Spaerae Mvndi Co[m]pendiu[m] Foeliciter Inchoat.: Daran: Regiomontanus, Johannes: Disputationes contra Cremonensia in planetarum theoricas deliramenta. Mit Widmungsvorrede des Autors an die Gelehrten. – Peuerbach, Georg: Theoricae novae planetarum. Mit Gedicht auf die Drucker'Uranie quantum quantum* ... (Venice: Johannes Lucilius Santritter and Hieronymus de Sanctis, 1488).

74 Crowther and Barker, "Training the Intelligent Eye," 453.

75 See, for example, the astronomical miscellany Garrett MS. 99 in Princeton University Special Collections: Anon., *Tractatus Astronomici*, *c.* 1275–1325, Parisian. Gift of Garrett, Robert, acquired through Wilfred Michael Voynich.

76 "This schema demonstrates that the earth is a sphere. If the earth were square, during a lunar eclipse, its shadow would appear to be a square; if a triangle, the shadow would appear as a triangle; if a hexagon, a hexagon."

77 Cf. the 1553 Antwerp edition, in which layout and images make knowledge comprehensible to audiences.

78 Foucault, *The Order of Things*.

79 Hayton, *The Crown and the Cosmos*, 68–97.

80 Karr Schmidt, *Interactive and Sculptural Printmaking in the Renaissance*, 241; Johannes Regiomontanus, *Calendarium ... Dvctv Ioannis De Monteregio* (Nuremberg: Johannes Regiomontanus, 1474), www.loc.gov/resource/rbc0001.2013rosen0051/?sp=2&st=gallery. Regiomontanus's models for his volvelles and instructions for constructing the diagrams in this work are found in the *Ars generalis and Ars brevis* of the fourteenth-century Catalan philosopher Ramón Lull. Regiomontanus owned manuscript copies of these works. See www.prphbooks.com/blog/2019/9/3/volvelles-what-a-passion.

81 For an extensive discussion of the *Astronomicum Caesareum*, see Karr Schmidt, *Interactive and Sculptural Printmaking*, 3ff., chapters 8 and 10; for Schöner, see 261, 244, sections 10.1, 10.3–10.5; for Apian's involvement with Schöner's work and principles, see 295ff.

82 Vanden Broecke, "The Use of Visual Media in Renaissance Cosmography," 132. Vanden Broecke's article provides the most ambitious English-language overview of the working of the instrumentation in Apian's *Cosmographicus Liber*.

83 Vanden Broecke, "The Use of Visual Media in Renaissance Cosmography," 133.

84 Sacrobosco's text renders it thus, in terms of a three-dimensional image of the world: "the sphere is divided into the sphere right and the sphere oblique. For those are said to have the sphere right who dwell at the equator, if anyone can live there. And it is called 'right' because neither pole is elevated more for them than the other, or because their horizon intersects the equinoctial circle and is intersected by it at spherical right angles. Those are said to have the sphere oblique who live this side of the equator or beyond it. For to them one pole is always raised above the horizon, and the other is always depressed below it. Or it is because their artificial horizon intersects the equinoctial at oblique and unequal angles." See Thorndike, ed., *The* Sphere *of Sacrobosco and Its commentators*, chapter 1.

85 "The zenith of the head is always equidistant from the horizon on every side (that is, by 90 degrees or a quadrant); and therefore it is called the pole of the horizon, and (in the absence of other impediments) it always appears to people in any location as the middle point of the sky or hemisphere. Therefore, to the extent that someone proceeds from the equator to the north or south, to the same extent the horizon is pushed down under the pole on one side, but raised above the opposite pole on the other side. This can be seen more plainly from the instrument."

86 "*Unde appellatur horizon.i. terminator visius.*"

87 The proof in *De Sphaera*, book II, demonstrates this concept via similar triangles. Sacrobosco explains that the angle between the elevation of the pole and the horizon is equal to the angle between the zenith and the celestial equator. Apian's proof, by contrast, demonstrates this relationship to his reader in terms of latitude (the measurement of the height of the pole star, or Polaris, above the horizon renders terrestrial latitude). When the user spins the dial, one obtains the numeric value of Sacrobosco's angles as a latitude reading. Apian shows the relationship between terrestrial latitude and the celestial pole, expressed by Apian as the "height of the world."

88 Vanden Broecke, "The Use of Visual Media in Renaissance Cosmography," 140.

89 Such as editions of Sacrobosco and Georg von Peuerbach's *Theorica Planetarum*; see Crowther and Barker, "Training the Intelligent Eye," 438.

90 Sacrobosco and Apian, *Sphaera Iani de Sacrobusto astronomiae ac cosmographiae candidatis scitu apprime necessaria* (Ingolstadt: Peter and Georg Apian, 1526).

91 Apian followed on the heels of pedagogical illustrations presented in a vernacular text edited by Heinfogel in Nuremberg in 1516. On the practical aspects of Apian's *Sphaera*, as well as its resonance for the next generation of printed editions of *Sphaera*, see Isabelle Pantin, "Borrowers and Innovators in the History of Printing Sacrobosco: The Case of the In-Octavo Tradition," in Valleriani, ed., *De Sphaera of Johannes de Sacrobosco in the Early Modern Period*, 273–282.

92 Baigrie, ed., *Picturing Knowledge*. We might say that this style contributes to what Martin Kemp calls "rhetoric of irrefutable precision" (p. 444).

93 Apian's 1526 update of Sacrobosco's *De Sphaera* did not include volvelles.

94 Johannes de Sacrobosco, *Ioannis De Sacrobusto Libellus, De Sphaera: Eiusdem Autoris Libellus, Cuius Titulus Est Computus, Eruditißimam Anni & Mensium Descriptionem Continens*, ed. Philipp Melanchthon (Wittenberg: Jospeh Clug, 1538). The digital copy in Staatsbibliothek Berlin (HAB HN62.8Helmst) is missing the top dial.

95 Sacrobosco, *Ioannis de Sacrobusto Libellus, De Sphaera* (Wittenberg: Clug, 1540), 38. The copy at the Bayerische Staatsbibliothek shows a volvelle with the *Organum Ptolomei* at the base, but without the (likely) top hemisphere dial.

96 *Instrumentum quo & rotunditas terrae secundam latitudinem probatur, & facillime Omnia ea, quae autor in tertio capite de diebus artificialibus tradit, dijudicantur.* An image of the dial appears in Gingerich, "Sacrobosco as a Textbook," 271.

97 These appeared in later editions printed in Wittenberg and Paris as well.

98 Gingerich, "Sacrobosco as a Textbook," 271. Erasmus's *Adage* about the importance of observing daily regimens is reinterpreted here to refer to the daily path of the sun.

99 Katherine Park treats the continuity and distinctions between *experimentia* and *observatio* in "Observation in the Margins, 500–1500," while Gianna Pomata's essay "Observation Rising: Birth of an Epistemic Genre" tracks the high incidence of *observationes* between 1530 and the 1570s in astronomy and medical texts specifically. Both essays appear in Daston and Lunbeck, *Histories of Scientific Observation*, 21ff., 49ff.

100 I thank DeWayne Carter for his insight into this and other astronomical problems.

101 Owen Gingerich, "Astronomical Paper Instruments with Moving Parts," in R. G. W. Anderson, J. A. Bennett, and W. F. Ryan, eds., *Making Instruments Count: Essays on Historical Scientific Instruments Presented to Gerard L'Estrange Turner* (Aldershot: Variorum, 1993), 63–6.

102 Sacrobosco and Conrad Heinfogel, *Sphera Materialis* (Nuremberg: Gutknecht, 1516); see http://dx.doi.org/10.3931/e-rara-2230, ETH-Bibliothek Zürich, Rar 4468; VD16 J739. The preface of this volume claims for Germans' proprietary interest in this art, a point reinforced in the colophon that mentions its translation for German audiences.

103 Johannes de Sacrobosco, *Sphera Materialis: Eyn Anfang und Fundanment der Astronomi*, ed. Jakob Cammerlander and Conrad Heinfogel (Strasbourg: Cammerlander, 1533), HAB A17.4 Astron. For instance, see the eyes drawn in manuscript hand on 18r. The author of this manuscript is clearly consulting images derived from related sources. The German-language text of the accompanying 1533 Sacrobosco emphasizes the word "eye" where the observer is concerned and this emphasis is also taken up by the illustrator. Some of these images likely come from Apian's edition of the *Sphera* of 1526. Among these are the eyes in the diagram of the eye seeing the coin underwater on fol. 4v; cf. Ms. 29v with the cutaways in Apian 1526, fol. 9r; Ms. fol. 68r with Apain's diagrams on fol. 24r.

104 Johann Dryander, *SPHERA MATERIALIS| Siue globi coelestis. <Das ist>|| Des Hymels lauff gründtliche außle=||gung/ so vil zur anleytung der Astro||nomie dienet/ mit vilen nützlichen regeln verfast/|| durch IOHAN DRYANDERN/ genent || Eychman/ ordinarien Medicum, der löblichen Vni=||uersiteten Marpurg/ von newem ver=||deütscht vnnd ann tag bracht.||* (Marburg: Johannis Dryander and Christian Egenolff d.Ä., 1539). Dryander was a mathematician and a high-ranking official in the administration at the University of Marburg. As he was the sub-rector of the University of Marburg at the time of the 1539 printing, Dryander very likely introduced material from Sacrobosco into the classroom.

105 Westman, "The Astronomer's Role in the Sixteenth Century," 119.

106 Valleriani, ed., *De Sphaera of Johannes de Sacrobosco in the Early Modern Period*, especially 273.

107 Johannes de Sacrobosco, *Sphaera Mundi: Eyn Anfang und Fundament der Astronomi/ Aus den Alten Astronomis dur Johannem de Sacro Busto ins Latin Zusamen Gesetzt und Nachmals Durch M. Cunrad Heynfogel von Nuremberg Verteutscht/ Unnd in Vier Teyl Getylt/ Deß Himmels Lauff Sampt Allem Gestirn/ Leichtlicher auß den bei Gesatzten Figuren Zuerlernen*, ed. Conrad Heinfogel (Strasbourg: Cammerlander, 1539), http://digital.onb.ac.at/OnbViewer/viewer.faces?doc=ABO_%2BZ178846106.

108 Valleriani, ed., *The Structures of Practical Knowledge*, 427–38. Valleriani maintains that authors who were involved in the production of knowledge around *De Sphaera* likely numbered over 150; most of these were natural philosophers and mathematicians, including humanists, experts in mechanics, and those preparing for military careers. Among the knowledge traditions to which the book contributed were navigation, nautical astronomy, geography, cartography, and meteorology.

109 For Melanchthon, see Jennifer Nelson, *Disharmony of the Spheres. The Europe of Holbein's Ambassadors* (University Park: Pennsylvania State University Press, 2019), especially 23–49; Sachiko Kusukawa, *The Transformation of Natural Philosophy: The Case of Philip Melanchthon* (Cambridge and New York: Cambridge University Press, 1995); Wolf Dieter Müller-Jahncke, "Melanchton und die Astrologie: Theoretisches und Mantisches," in Frank Günter and Stefan Rhein, eds., *Melanchthon und die Naturwissenschaften Seiner Zeit* (Sigmaringen: Jan Thorbecke, 1998), 105–36.

110 For astrology and astronomy in Wittenberg, see Claudia Brosseder, *Im Bann der Sterne: Caspar Peucer, Philipp Melanchthon und andere Wittenberger Astrologen* (Berlin: Akademie Verlag, 2004); Claudia Brosseder, "The Writing in the Wittenberg Sky: Astrology in Sixteenth-Century Germany," *Journal of the History of Ideas* 66 (2005), 557–76.

111 Gingerich, "Sacrobosco as a Textbook," 269. "Plato has very admirably written that eyes were given to men for the sake of astronomy . . . for he wished to point out that nothing is more beautiful in all of nature than those celestial lights and that nature compels mankind to this enjoyment of beauty; and to me the eyes themselves would seem to bear a very important affinity with the stars."

112 Crowther and Barker, "Training the Intelligent Eye"; on the early modern distinctions between corporeal and spiritual vision, see 441–2.

113 Dryander's 1539 vernacular volume is sparsely illustrated, but the frontispiece aims to show the functioning (and labeled) parts of an armillary sphere, with meridian line and ecliptic band shown ready for assembly. Dryander says of the sphere (a demonstration sphere), "on certain globes you find a band for the zodiac, day and month." The accompanying image on fol. 12r appears to be derived from the *Cosmographicus Liber*, complete with graphic representation of a thread marked "filum."

114 See, for example, the 1537 edition of Sacrobosco from Venice that borrows the globe and cosmos diagram from Apian, as does the 1538 Wittenberg edition; see also https://cudl.lib.cam.ac.uk/collections/astronomicalimages/1.

115 Gingerich, "Sacrobosco as a Textbook," 270.

116 Valleriani, ed., *The Structures of Practical Knowledge*, 4, chapter 16.

117 Remmert, *Picturing the Scientific Revolution*; Lattis, "Christopher Clavius and the 'Sphere' of Sacrobosco."

118 I often wonder why Apian's *Cosmographicus Liber* did not overhaul the demand for new Sacrobosco textbooks. Although Apian's contributions to lay astronomy were substantial, perhaps the *Cosmographicus Liber* was simply too summarily synopsized, empirically driven, and therefore too popular for the more established market of university professors and students. As university audiences had provided a secure readership for Sacrobosco for centuries, Peter and Georg Apian may have been wise to cover all potential markets by re-releasing an edition of Sacrobosco's *De Sphaera* in 1526.

119 For a list of editions, see the virtual exhibition "Cosmographia: A Close Encounter," hosted at the Museum of the History of Science at Oxford, at www.mhs.ox.ac.uk/students/98to99/.

120 Kathleen Crowther et al., "The Book Everybody Read: Vernacular Translations of Sacrobosco's Sphaera in the Sixteenth Century," *Journal for the History of Astronomy* 46, no. 1 (2015), 8.

121 Karr Schmidt, *Interactive and Sculptural Printmaking in the Renaissance*, 301.

122 Peter Apian, *Instrument-Buch Durch Petrum Apianum erst von new beschriben. Zum Ersten ist darinne begriffen ein newer Quadrant, dardurch Tag vnd Nacht, bey der Sonnen, Mon vnnd andern*

Planeten, auch durch ettliche Gestirn die Stunden vnd ander nutzung Gefunden werden. Zum Andern, wie man die höch der Thuern vnd anderer gebew . . . messen soll. Zum Dritten wie man das wasser absehen oder abwegen soll . . . vnd wie man die Bruenne suchen soll. . . . (Ingolstadt: Apian, 1533). For a cogent description of the *Instrument-Buch*'s merits, see Alexandra Challenger, "Printing the Cosmos: Images, Readers, and Mathematics in Peter Apian's Instrumental Texts," PhD dissertation, Florida State University, 2022, 52–76.

123 Karr Schmidt, *Interactive and Sculptural Printmaking*, 240.

124 As we see in Johannes Dryander's German vernacular edition of *Sphaera materialis sive globi coelestis, Das ist des hymels lauff gründtliche außlegung* . . . (1539?), 8r, www.e-rara.ch/zut/content/zoom/12598857. The text's author referred his readers back to Apian to clear up any confusion about how to gauge the elevation of the pole star: "note here what Peter Apian has to say: look for the back wheels of the *Heer-Wagon* [Ursa Major, which contains the Big Dipper], find a line directly over your face, and the closest star that you will find in this line will be the pole star; then measure its height from the earth with a quadrant" (10r).

125 Oosterhoff, "A Book, a Pen, and the *Sphere*," 6–7. Oosterhoff maintains that these textbook editions teach "students how to manipulate the tools of the astronomer."

126 Johannes Regiomontanus and Johannes Schöner, *Scripta clarissimi mathematici M. Ioannis Regiomontani, de torqueto, astrolabio armillari, regula magna ptolemaica, baculo[que] astronomico, & observationibus cometarum, aucta necessariis, Ioannis Schoneri . . . additionibus. Item observationes motuum solis, ac stellarum tam fixarum [qua . . .] erraticarum. Item libellus M. Georgii Purbachii de quadrato geometrico* (Nuremberg: Joannis Montanus and Ulricus Neuber, 1544), www.e-rara.ch/doi/10.3931/e-rara-18965.

127 Daston and Lunbeck, *Histories of Scientific Observation*. See Pomata, "Observation Rising," 45–80, especially 49; see also Vanden Broecke, *The Limits of Influence*, 204–5.

128 Daston and Lunbeck, *Histories of Scientific Observation*, 50.

129 Peter Apian, *Practica Auff Das 1532 Jar . . . auch wird nachvolgenden von dem naeschst erschinen Cometen/ wie unnd in was Gestalt in gemelter Apianus Observiert hat und welhe biß her dero vil sindt in irem Schreiben irrig gefunden bewerlich angezaygt* (Landshut: Georg Apian, 1532); Peter Apian, *Ein kurtzer bericht der Observation und urtels des jüngst erschienenen Cometen jm Weinmon vnd Wintermon dises XXXII. Jars* (Ingolstadt: Apian, 1532).

130 Karr Schmidt, *Interactive and Sculptural Printmaking*, 295.

131 A horoscope is the measure of the sun's entry into a particular zodiac sign as determined by the position of the moon at night when directly overhead.

132 The term "to practice," or *practicieren*, emerged in German printshops *c.* 1470; the term *Practica* evolved into the name of printed practical literature. On *Practica* and their printers, see Richard L. Kremer, "Incunable Almanacs and *Practica* as Practical Knowledge Produced in Trading Zones," in Valleriani, ed., *The Structures of Practical Knowledge*, 333–69, especially 345ff.

133 The earliest appearance of the term in a title accompanied a work by Johannes Engel, a mathematics and astronomy professor at Ingolstadt, for a work printed in Nuremberg in 1488: *Die dewtsch practick* . . . See Valleriani, ed., *The Structures of Practical Knowledge*, 339.

134 Apian says he printed such publications to pay the bills and ceased this activity later. Röttel, *Peter Apian*, 135–7.

135 These included the *Kalendarium* (Nuremberg: Regiomontanus, 1474); see Baldasso, "Illustrating the Book of Nature in the Renaissance," 202–3. Such visual motifs can also be seen in the 1496 *Shepherd's Calendar*; see Max Engammare, *Calendrier des bergers* (Paris: Presses Universitaires de France, 2008).

136 Grafton, *Commerce with the Classics*, 185. While Apian and Copernicus had not forged a break with Ptolemy, Kepler broke with traditional cosmology here in his first major cosmographical work, the *Mysterium cosmographicum* (1596). Basing his work on Tycho Brahe's data gathered using measuring instruments in the Uraniborg, Kepler rejected the notion that Ptolemy necessarily provided a single point of origin for astronomical study.

137 Sky Michael Johnston, "Printing the Weather: Knowledge, Nature, and Popular Culture in Two Sixteenth-Century German Weather Books," *Renaissance Quarterly* 73, no. 2 (2020), 395.

138 Apian later imported some of the information from the *Cosmographicus Liber* into his more popular vernacular publications. Apian builds a bridge from the autodidactic cosmographic texts to small pamphlets that were eminently more readable, condensed, and directed toward an audience of laypeople to whom he broadcast lunar and solar eclipses for what they could tell their readers about the weather. Apian's practical pamphlet *Practica auff das MDXXXXI Jar/ durch Petrum Apianum von Leyßnick auß dem lauff der gestirn/ Zu Ingolstat Practicirt/ und in vier Capiteln auffs kürzest begriffen* (1541) imports lunar and solar diagrams from his more cosmographical texts. Here, Apian shows both lunar and solar eclipses for the coming year in diagrams that show the trajectories of each in their path through the constellations. The frontispiece provides the dates of the coming celestial conjunctions: 12 March and 21 August (for the local area). In the text, Apian discusses these happenings as ones that are clearly visible and take place before the backdrop of the night sky, indicating where in the constellation they can be seen and also when they disappear. This is a practical prediction that can serve as a guide to the night sky during lunar conjunctions that were likewise important for cosmography.

139 Bruce Stephenson, Marvin Bolt, and Anna Felicity Friedman, *The Universe Unveiled: Instruments and Images through History* (New York: Cambridge University Press, 2000), 40.

140 An explanation of this scale is also included in the 1514 publication of Johannes Werner's translation of Ptolemy, *In hoc opera haec continentur Noua translation primi libri geographiae Cl. Ptolemaei.*

141 Vanden Broecke, "The Use of Visual Media in Renaissance Cosmography," 139.

142 Röttel, *Peter Apian*, 160.

143 The scale necessary to clarify this point would have required an extraordinarily long arm to move the cross-piece.

144 Apian, *Ein kurtzer bericht der Observation und urtels des jüngst erschienenen Cometen jm Weinmon vnd Wintermon dises XXXII. Jars* (Ingolstadt: Apian, 1532).

145 Röttel, *Peter Apian*, 158–60.

146 Vanden Broecke, "The Use of Visual Media in Renaissance Cosmography," 139.

147 Röttel, *Peter Apian*, 159–60.

148 For the value of aesthetics in scientific instrument prints, see Marr, "Ingenuity in Nuremberg."

149 Richard L. Kremer, "Playing with Geometrical Tools: Johannes Stabius's Astrolabium Imperatorium (1515) and Its Successors," *CNT Centaurus* 58, no. 1–2 (2016), 116.

150 Adam Mosley positions Fine's spherical astronomy, such as his *Sphaera Mundi*, between a theoretical model of the universe and natural philosophy's search for causation. Fine's geometry set an agenda for publications that used scientific instruments to unpack a theoretical image of the cosmos. See Adam Mosley, "Early Modern Cosmography: Fine's *Sphaera Mundi* in Content and Context," in Alexander Marr, ed., *The Worlds of Oronce Fine: Mathematics, Instruments, and Print in Renaissance France* (Donington: Shaun Tyas, 2009), 122–3.

151 See http://kvk.bibliothek.kit.edu/view-title/index.php?katalog=ARCHIVE_ORG&url=http%3A%2F%2Farchive.org%2Fdetails%2Fcosmographicusli00apia&signature=AKO8P0Jk E0UuL8sbEecPUrBlNbaHEiW-yG7rMVlFJ2w&showCoverImg=1. An edition at the John Carter Brown Library includes at the rear manuscript tables that treat degrees and distances.

152 Apian and Frisius, *Cosmographia Petri Apiani, per Gemmam Frisium* ... (Antwerp: Plantin, 1574). See the blank pages and handwritten notes and diagrams throughout: MPM A27 at https://anet.be/digital/opacmpm/mpm/dg:mpm:474/N.

153 Woodward, ed., *The History of Cartography. Volume 3*, 477–508; see Uta Lindgren, "Land Surveys, Instruments, and Practitioners in the Renaissance," in Woodward, ed., *The*

History of Cartography. Lindgren argues for Gemma's instantiation of a practical treatment of triangulation, following in the tradition of Alberti and Regiomontanus. See also Conley, "A Topographer's Eye," 63ff.

154 Apian and Frisius, *Cosmographie, oft beschrievinghe der gheheelder werelt van Petrus Apianus / ... metten Zeecompasse ende anderen boecxkens byden selve Gemma daer toegdedaen* (Antwerp: Jan Verwithaghen (I), 1561), ETH-Bibliothek Zürich, MPM A 2049.

155 Margaret Gaida, "Reading Cosmographia: Peter Apian's Book-Instrument Hybrid and the Rise of the Mathematical Amateur in the Sixteenth Century," *Early Science and Medicine* 21, no. 4 (2016), 277–302.

156 I am indebted to discussions with Alexandra Challenger on this topic.

157 Michael Hoskin, ed., *The Cambridge Concise History of Astronomy* (Cambridge: Cambridge University Press, 1999), 79–81.

158 Stephenson, Bolt, and Friedman, *The Universe Unveiled*, 62–3. The nocturnal dial needed to be calibrated for the particular day by setting a tooth on the inner disk marked with hours to the date indicated on the outer disk. The other tooth is set for the reference star. The user orients it as he would a clock dial, holding its face parallel to him and sighting Polaris through the center hole. The movable arm is rotated to align with the reference star (generally the pointer stars in the Big Dipper, sometimes marked on the arm itself as alpha and beta). Once aligned to the reference star, the large arm should intersect with the hour of the night marked on the notched inner dial. In the darkness, one can count the number of notches from the longest tooth (midnight) and thus the user can find the time.

159 For volumes with the instruments tipped in, see the copy at the Morgan Library (PML 127688).

160 This is precisely the function of an app based on Apian's nocturnal developed by the Mathematisch-Physikalischer Salon at the Staatliche Kunstsammlungen Dresden. The free tablet/smartphone app "Behind the Stars" (in English or German versions, for iOS or Android) can be found at BehindTheStars@skd.museum.

161 Baigrie, ed., *Picturing Knowledge*, 71. On Tycho's repeated observations, see also Daston, "Empire of Observation," in Daston and Lunbeck, *Histories of Scientific Observation*, 93–5. Among these instrument books were the *Horoscope* (1531) and *Quadrant* (1532), which preceded his *Instrument-Buch* (1533).

162 I am grateful to the kind assistance of DeWayne Carver, Kevin Huffenberger, Chase van Tilburg, and Alexandra Challenger for making this complex tool come to life. Editions at the Museum Plantin-Moretus and the Morgan Library and Museum both have a missing top dial that allows us to see the algorithmic projection of the moon – inscribed with circles made by the compass used to figure it out. The traces of the compass markings print because they *de facto* engrave the wood. For this, see the Newberry Library's copy.

163 On sources for the *Organum Ptolomei*, as well as conventions for distinguishing between instruments and diagrams in manuscripts, see Catherine Eagleton, "Medieval Sundials and Manuscript Sources: The Transmission of Information about the *Navicula* and the *Organum Ptolomei* in Fifteenth-Century Europe," in Kusukawa and Maclean, eds., *Transmitting Knowledge*, 41–71, especially 67–9. Eagleton shows that most instruments known as the *organum* were ones that primarily shared a similar geometric method of construction. Ernst Zinner, *Deutsche und niederländische astronomische Instrumente des 11.–18. Jahrhunderts*, 2nd ed. (Munich: Beck, 1967), 131–4. According to Zinner, Apian creates an *Organum vel rota mobilis*, an invention of either Georg von Peuerbach or Regiomontanus, which is a device more useful than a sundial.

164 The incipit "*organum ptolomei ita sit*" describes dials in a variety of fifteenth- and sixteenth-century manuscripts linked to Vienna. Eagleton posits that these dials are of a *navicula* type that are medieval English in origin. See Catherine Eagleton, "Oronce Fine's Sundials: The Sources and Influences of *De solaribus horologiis*," in Marr, ed., *The Worlds of Oronce Fine*, 83–100.

165 James E. Morrison, *The Astrolabe* (Rehoboth Beach, DE: Janus, 2007), 37; see also note 3, p. 37. Here we see the "plane that passes through the solstices ... pulled back the center of

the projection to an infinitely distant point on the line passing through the equinoxes. It is thus properly described as an orthographic projection, and it is easily recognized, as the parallels of the celestial sphere become straight lines parallel to the equator." The Rojas astrolabe (*c.* 1550), introduced by Gemma's pupil, the Spanish astronomer Juan de Rojas, added an orthographic projection.

166 Vanden Broecke, "The Use of Visual Media in Renaissance Cosmography," 141.

167 Gingerich is likewise skeptical of its use as an actual sundial, citing the potential difficulties involved in stabilizing it. Gingerich, "Astronomical Paper Instruments with Moving Parts," 64.

168 Does the Nulla Dies dial in the Wittenberg Sacrobosco infer this?

169 Vanden Broecke, "The Use of Visual Media in Renaissance Cosmography," 140.

170 I acknowledge a debt to my brother Erik Leitch for helping to interpret both the workings and the novelty of this instrument.

171 Gingerich, "Astronomical Paper Instruments with Moving Parts," 64–6.

172 Vanden Broecke, "The Use of Visual Media in Renaissance Cosmography," 138ff.

173 Albert Ronsin, Pierre Monat, and Amerigo Vespucci, *La fortune d'un nom: America: le baptême du Nouveau Monde à Saint-Dié-des-Vosges* (Grenoble: J. Millon, 1991), 111–12. The Vespucci letter is omitted from the edition preserved in Wolfenbüttel (HAB HN94.4 Helmst. 6).

174 Anthony John Turner, *Early Scientific Instruments: Europe 1400–1800* (London: Sotheby's Publications, 1987), 47.

175 The cartographer Gerard Mercator also worked in Frisius's workshop.

176 See the website developed by the Museum of the History of Science in Oxford: www.mhs.ox.ac.uk/students/98to99/.

177 See also Waldseemüller, *Der Weltkugel* (1509). This might be the earliest Ptolemaic cosmographic text in vernacular.

178 Shalev and Burnett, eds., *Ptolemy's Geography in the Renaissance*, 11.

179 Christine R. Johnson, *The German Discovery of the World: Renaissance Encounters with the Strange and Marvelous* (Charlottesville: University of Virginia Press, 2008), 81.

180 *Universalis cosmographia secunda Ptholemei traditionem et Americi Vespucci aliorum que lustrationes* (A drawing of the whole earth following the tradition of Ptolemy and the travels of Amerigo Vespucci and others). See http://purl.oclc.org/coordinates/b4.htm.

181 Petrus Apian, *Cosmographiae Introductio: Cum Quibusdam Geo-Metriae ac Astronomiae Prin=||cipijs ad eam Rem Necessarijs.||* (Ingolstadt: Peter and Georg Apian, 1529).

182 Denis Cosgrove argues that Apian's work was fuller than Waldseemüller's because its instructions in spatial surveying were designed to clarify the world map; see Cosgrove, "Images of Renaissance Cosmography," in Woodward, ed., *The History of Cartography. Volume 3*, 67.

183 Apian, *Cosmographiae Introductio* (1529/1533). See chapter 14, which mentions "the whole world known to Ptolemy"; chapter 18 explains how to use the *Tabularum Ptolemei.*

184 Apian, *Cosmographiae Introductio.* For a digital edition, see http://daten.digitale-sammlungen.de/~db/0003/bsb00039825/images/. For the sixteen editions of this text, see Röttel, *Peter Apian*, 267–8.

185 Röttel, *Peter Apian*, 169–71. Map size 28.5 cm × 42 cm.

186 Caius Julius Solinus, Joannes Camers, and Johann Singriener, *Joannis Camertis ... in C Julii Solini Polyistora Enarrationes. Additus Eiusdem Camertis Index* (Vienna: Alantse, 1520).

187 Röttel, *Peter Apian*, 171.

188 Röttel, *Peter Apian*, 173. For the map, see the entry for Michael Ostendorfer in F. W. H. Hollstein et al., *Hollstein's German Engravings, Etchings and Woodcuts 1400–1700*, vol. 30 (Amsterdam: M. Hertzberger, 1991), no. 56. The pamphlet today is preserved in the Staats- und Stadtbibliothek Augsburg.

189 Röttel, *Peter Apian*, 173.

190 Röttel, *Peter Apian*; Rodney W. Shirley, *The Mapping of the World: Early Printed World Maps, 1472–1700* (Riverside: Early World Press, 2001), 45.

191 See John P. Snyder, "Map Projections in the Renaissance," in Woodward, ed., *The History of Cartography*, 367. Snyder classifies this as the polar stereographic projection.

192 Apian's *Speculum Cosmographiae* mimicked the moving components of an astrolabe and included many indicators related to astrolabes, including rotating parts for which Apian cribbed astrolabe nomenclature, calling these parts a limb, a rete, and an alidade. Conley, *An Errant Eye*, 73ff.

193 Turner, *Early Scientific Instruments*, 12. A traditional astrolabe features a number of rotating discs held together in a circular case called the *mater*. The first solid plate shows a projection of the world sphere on the two-dimensional plane of the equator, consisting of the circles of the equator, the tropics, the path that the sun describes on the celestial sphere (the ecliptic), and the fixed stars. A cutaway and movable circle, called a *rete*, revolves on top of this bottom plate; the *rete* usually carries the zenith–horizon coordinate system for a particular latitude (the ecliptic marked with the signs of the zodiac and certain prominent stars). Then there is the *rule* that serves as an index or pointer for the front; it is usually marked with a scale of declinations. The astrolabe permitted investigation of the major terrestrial and celestial lines and attempted to provide knowledge of the celestial system in toto. Actual astrolabes were outfitted with a number of removable discs with which actual latitude could be accounted for; then, with the aid of a sighting device with which most were equipped on their rear surfaces, sightings could be taken to determine the altitude of sun or stars to find the time in order to appropriately position the discs.

194 Johann Copp, *Erklärung unnd gründtliche Underweysung alles nutzes, so in dem edlen Instrument, Astrolabium genannt, begriffen, und erfunden würt/ denen so der lateinischen Sprach unverstendig/ doch liebhaber der Kunst/ erkannt trewlich verteütscht/ unnd durch den Truck außgegangen* (Augsburg: Otmar, 1525).

195 "Just as we look in a mirror . . . we can think about the entire world this way . . . Hereafter follows the ways you can use the Speculum of Cosmography." Apian, *Cosmographicus Liber*, chapter 19.

196 The world map's first appearance was in the French edition of 1544 printed in Antwerp: Peter Apian and Gemma Frisius, *La Cosmographie de Pierre Apian* (Antwerp: de Bonte, 1544).

197 The 1533 edition of Peter Apian's *Cosmographicus Liber* (Antwerp: Birckman, 1533) included Gemma's *Libellus de Locorum describendorum*, a tract that supplied the first image of triangulated surveying.

198 Röttel, *Peter Apian*, 181.

199 For Apian's plans for the book, see Schöner, *Mathematik und Astronomie*, 407. For the printing context of Apian's Astronomicum Caesareum (Ingolstadt: Apian, 1540), see Challenger, "Printing the Cosmos," 78–110.

200 In fact, it was in the context of courts that professional cosmographers came into being. Mosley, "The Cosmographer's Role," 430–5.

201 Denis E. Cosgrove, *Apollo's Eye: A Cartographic Genealogy of the Earth in the Western Imagination* (Baltimore: Johns Hopkins University Press, 2001), 96–9. By the mid-sixteenth century, the cosmographer's job became that of a data collector, processing incoming information from a variety of sources. Court cosmographers were responsible for processing the data that came into the realm and cosmography necessarily became a collective enterprise of explorers, navigators, writers, and engravers, a "center of calculation."

202 For the tension between the data that pertained to universals versus data relevant to individuals, see Nelson's discussion of the locative. Nelson, *Disharmony of the Spheres*, 51–88.

203 Röttel, *Peter Apian*, 160.

204 Schöner, *Mathematik und Astronomie an der Universität Ingolstadt*.

205 Gaida, "Reading Cosmographia," especially 279.

206 To be sure, Apian had already begun to print books devoted to the explanation of instruments, including vernacular treatises on the quadrant (1532) and the sundial/

horologium horoscope (1533), perhaps spurred on by these developments in the vernacular instrument books being published in Antwerp.

207 Petrus Apian, *Cosmographia, Additis de Eadem Re Libellis, ut Sequens Pagina Docet*, ed. Rainer Gemma Frisius (Antwerp: Birckman, 1539).

208 The *Usus Annuli* was nearly always included in Gemma's editions of Apian's cosmography printed after 1539.

209 See Pomata, "Observation Rising," 55, 61. Gemma kept two notebooks: one recorded data about the disposition of the stars, while a second recorded his experience as a physician.

210 One reader's customized response to Apian can be found in an Antwerp edition of *Cosmographia* printed by the Plantin press (Antwerp: Plantin and Verwithaghen, 1574); see MPM A27 at https://anet.be/digital/opacmpm/mpm/dg:mpm:474/N. This edition was bound with blank pages in periodic gatherings throughout to accept marginal notes. Some annotations enhance the text, such as in the sections on the principles of geography, and notes on eclipses.

211 The verses originate in the 1516 edition, where the diagrams show lunar phases: www.digitale-sammlungen.de/en/view/bsb00002755?page=56. In an annotated edition from 1533, an unrelated eclipse diagram accompanies those verses: cf. https://digital.slub-dresden.de/werkansicht/dlf/15207/65. Thanks to Britta-Juliane Kruse and Peter Hess for improving my translation.

Merck ich lerne dich fleissiglich
Wiewol der Mond entzundet sich
Allzeyt wie ihn die Son sicht an
Ist er halb liecht soltu verstan.

Wie wol der Mond zu aller frist
Vilmer dann halb erleuchtet ist
Doch siht man steets nit gantzen scheyn
Nur yetzund groß dann wider kleyn.

212 Sacrobosco, *Sphera Materialis*; "*deß himels lauff sampt allem gstirn/ leichtlicher auß den bei gesatzten figuren zuerlernen.*"

213 This *Sammelband* is preserved in the Herzog August Bibliothek in Wolfenbüttel (HAB A17.4 Astron.). The manuscript gathering begins with "*Thier hebt sich an Spera materialis* . . ."; in Heinfogel and Sacrobosco, *Sphera Materialis: Eyn Anfang* (Strasbourg: Cammerlander, 1533).

214 See HAB A17.A #2, fol. 18r. The manuscript hand borrows the idea of the "*Aug[e]*" from Sacrobosco's text that explains the shape of the water from the perspective of an eye.

215 Peter Apian, *Practica Auff Das 1532 Jar*, prologue, p. 3: "*wir sehen vor augen den hymel allenthalben/ die weyler tag und nacht gerings umb die Erde geet/ und mögen in auch leichtlich observieren unnd beschreiben. Die Erde aber mag so leicht nit beschreiben/ un(d) die natur on allen orten oder flecke(n) in achtgehalten werden/ die weyl der mensch dieselbigen on gro(ss)e unkost un(d) langes rayßen nicht shen oder umbziehen mag/ vil weniger die natur recht beschreyben.*" On collective empiricism, see Pomata, "Observation Rising," 50.

THREE

FACIAL PROFILING

Physiognomy and the Art of Inspection

When Martin Guerre returned after a long absence from his home near Toulouse in the mid-1550s, an extended lawsuit was required to solve what a background check might clear up today: how to distinguish his identity from that of a persistent impostor. Instead of assuming widespread misrecognition on behalf of Guerre's neighbors, knowing what early moderns looked for when they perused faces would give us a better sense of how their eyes were calibrated for scanning.[1] Martin Guerre's case coincided with new visual developments in physiognomy, a genre that encouraged facial literacy. Complexion books and physiognomies, little known today but wildly popular in the sixteenth century, guided the data embedded in the stars to the ground. More specifically, these books correlated astrological knowledge with the signatures they left on the body. Deciphering these external signs was among the first visual inferences that vernacular viewers were conditioned by books to make.

This chapter argues that the pictorial programs of sixteenth-century German physiognomies organized texts into visual menus of faces that would invite diverse types of empirical investigation. Among the epistemic objectives that they accomplished were inciting the potential in readers to compare, contrast, certify, prompt reflections, and remember, as well as inspire viewing practices that would be parsed into more precise modes of cognition. Broad audiences were schooled by complexion books; readers honed their visual acuity and ability to recognize images that they could later find elsewhere. The visual pedagogies of complexion books later influenced the making of books in a wide range of genres, including artists' manuals. Instructional manuals for artists also collected faces and were united with physiognomies by their prescriptions for dynamic looking. Diverse domains of knowledge in early modernity were served by common visual programs that would soon become the *sine qua non* of the new how-to genres they inspired. Even artistic productions by Leonardo and Dürer labored under their influence. Both artists were as informed by physiognomies' pictorial didactics as they were suspicious of their principles.

COMPLEXION BOOKS: FROM *SECRETS* TO DATA

Printed complexion books of the sixteenth century divide their origins between the manuscript tradition of the Books of Secrets and printed vernacular *Practica*. In an image of the kinds of knowledge that the latter could purvey, we see a group of stargazers actively discussing celestial influence on the title page of *Complexion/ Natur vnd eigenschafft eines yeden menschen zu erfahren* ... of 1534 (Figure 3.1). In addition to pictorializing the audience this book addressed, this title page also suggests that the acquisition of practical astrological skills is one of the book's benefits.[2] These lay astrologers making optical examinations of the natural world headline a type of popular science in the making that depends on two important struts. The first is that these practitioners would evolve into a reading public shaped by books such as these. Second, these skills would be accessed by active observation. Situating observers of signs in the local environment was a surprising new emphasis in the complexion literature printed between 1520 and 1540, as were these pictures' dedication to a new group of lay practitioners.

Deciphering complexions as an art that could be unlocked by books themselves was the aim of a mass-marketing directive to coach the reading of the signs that the stars left on the shapes of faces and in the lines on palms. Publishers would attempt to reclaim these skills from both the *Books of Secrets* and from a marketplace of quack practitioners, as suggested by the bare-breasted gypsy palm reader and children on the reverse page of Peter Jordan's edition (Figure 3.2). These publications empowered their lay audiences to understand and participate in a public discourse about lunar cycles, planetary conjunctions, the zodiac, and the influence of all three on human wellness and human nature. The locus of all of these interactions would eventually be impressed on the plane of the face. The visual programs that developed around lay astrology in print helped channel assessments into visualized and particularized content.[3]

When physiognomic literature first made the transition from pseudo-Aristotelian manuscripts to print in northern Italy around 1480, editions were

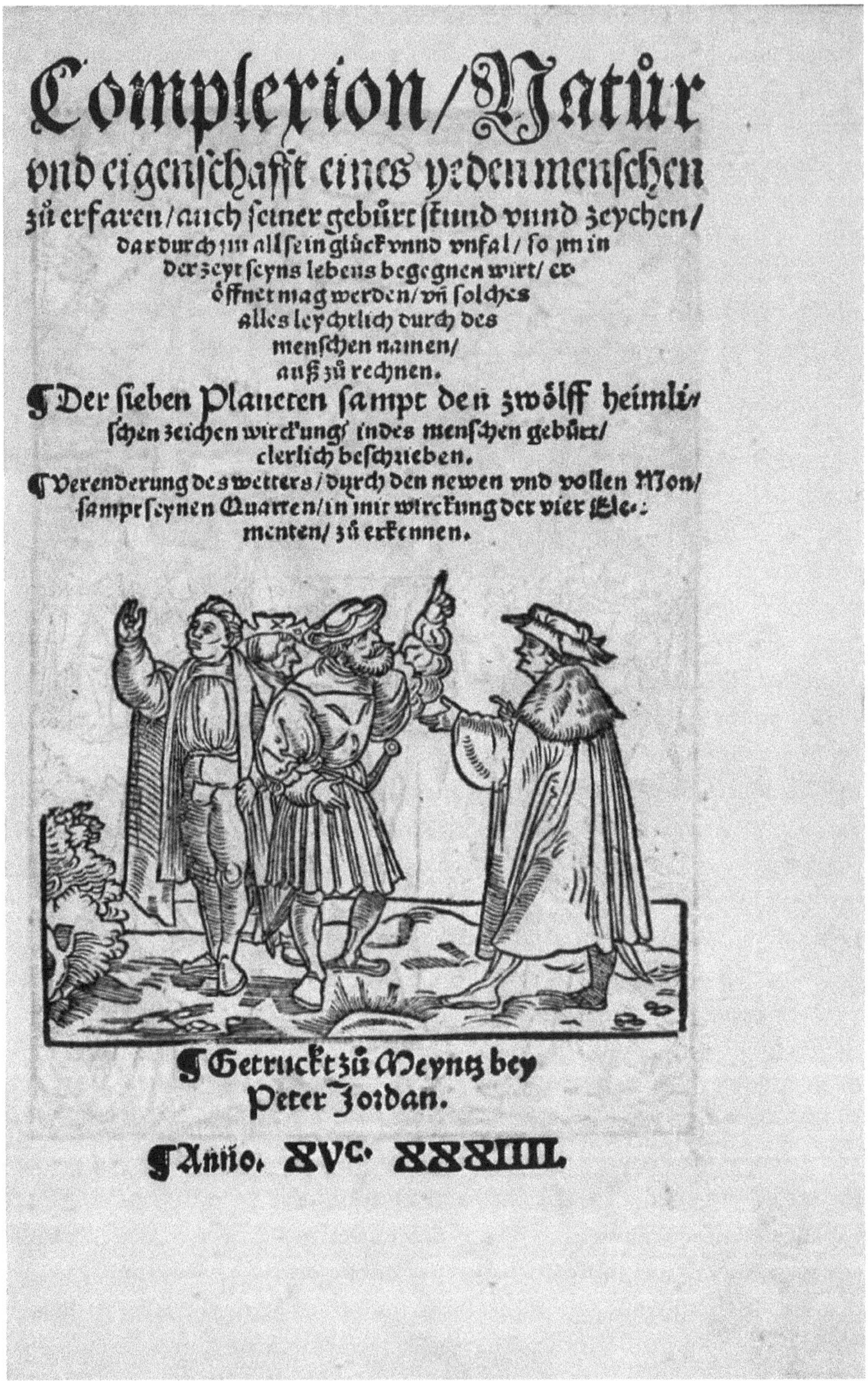

3.1. Cocles, *Complexion* (Mainz: Peter Jordan, 1534), 1r. *Source:* HAB HN97.4 Helmst. 3. Courtesy of Herzog August Bibliothek Wolfenbüttel.

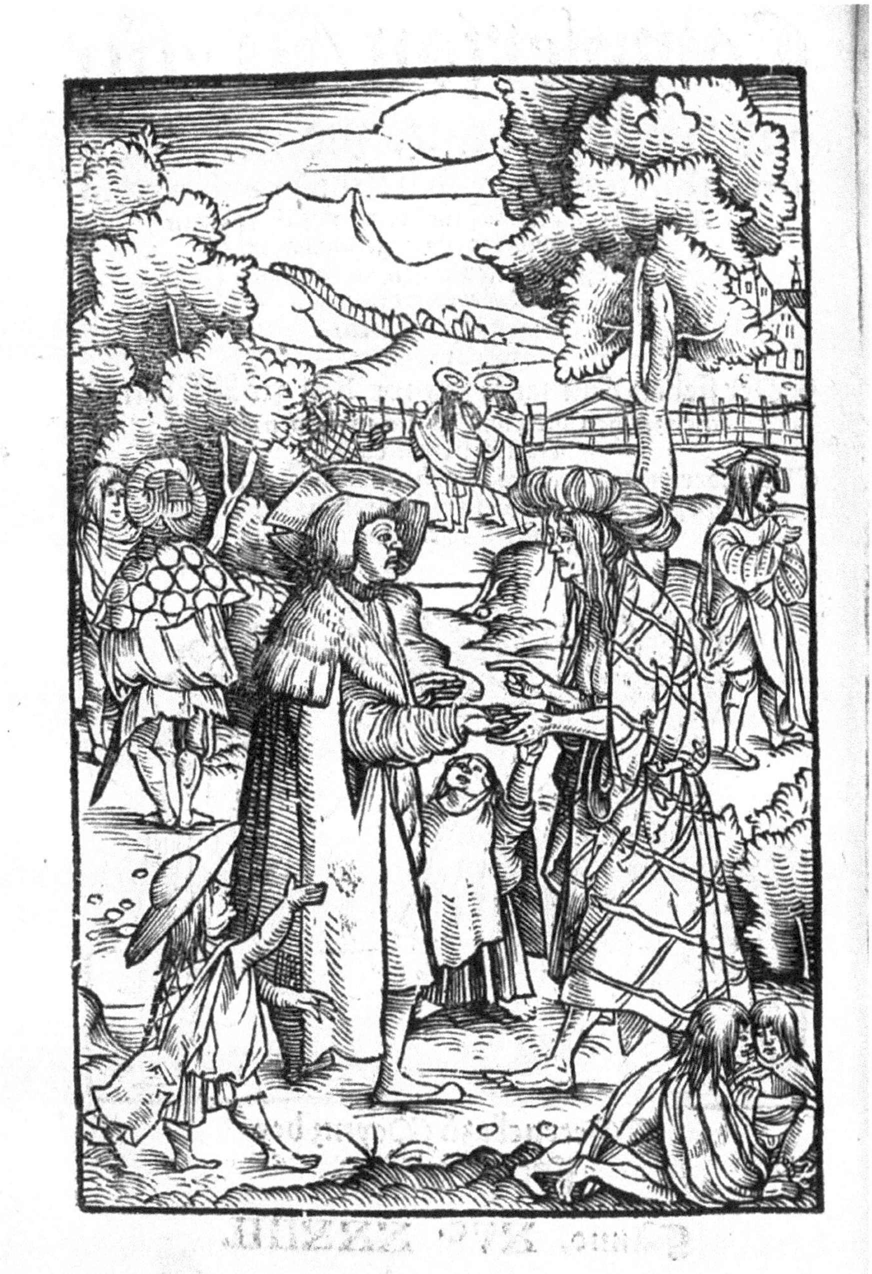

3.2. Cocles, *Complexion* (Mainz: Peter Jordan, 1534), IV. *Source:* HAB HN97.4 Helmst. 3. Courtesy of Herzog August Bibliothek, Wolfenbüttel.

issued in unillustrated printings of complexion material dense with textual but visually sparse predictions. These texts were primarily associated with ancient authors through which *Secreti* associated with Aristotle were disclosed. The art of deciphering a person's nature via the stars and signs on the body, and especially on the face, underwent a visualization in the printed literature, especially in publications from the German-language press. The pictorial material that printers in Strasbourg, Augsburg, and Mainz used to illustrate these texts bear traces of the look of short prognosticatory *Practica*. These images, which were frequently reused and readapted for complexion literature, gave rise to new pictorial formats onto which physiognomic information was mapped. An array of visual material was brought together in complexion literature; this visualization matched the growing pictorialization of kindred didactic genres that aimed to outline the methods of a vernacular science.[4]

This chapter argues that a new facial index came to characterize physiognomies, and, as it did so, emphasis shifted from humoral diagnoses to manuals about the discovery and articulation of human difference acquired through empirical investigation. Instead of allying themselves with precise moral judgments by linking features to specific conditions, these profiles unmoored themselves from the doctrine of signs and instead celebrated their epistemic properties. We can track the rise of observation alongside such books that asked readers to perform visual experiments in the outside world.

In the late fifteenth and early sixteenth century, human nature was understood to be a balance of humors believed to be governed by planetary influences.[5] Human complexions shaped by celestial bodies furnished common content for seemingly diverse genres such as chiromantia, metoscopia, and physiognomy – genres linked by celestial influence and their predictive tendencies. Chiromancy and physiognomy would split from the branch of the study of complexion to which they were previously sutured when they bonded with the visual tradition of *Practica* that sixteenth-century printers had spun into richly illustrated volumes. Printed physiognomies developed an emphasis on profile in early sixteenth-century Germany, and, by mid-century, their general discussions of human traits became increasingly organized around facial characteristics.

For example, in a Strasbourg edition of Cocles's *Physiognomiæ et Chiromantiæ Compendium* from 1536, we see that the text's discussion of humors, complexions, and facial features has been mapped onto a series of approximately thirty portraits (Figure 3.3).[6] These were probably designed and cut by the Strasbourg artist Hans Wechtlin.[7] This group of faces solidified into the physiognomic repertoire for some time to come – both continental and English physiognomies over the course of the next several decades borrowed their images from this group.[8] Although these woodcuts were among the most recognizable designs for the genre from the 1530s onwards, speculation about the origins of face-reading generally conjures other efforts in the mind of the modern reader.

The extent to which the profile came to constitute the most legible index of knowledge about human character has indelibly linked physiognomic

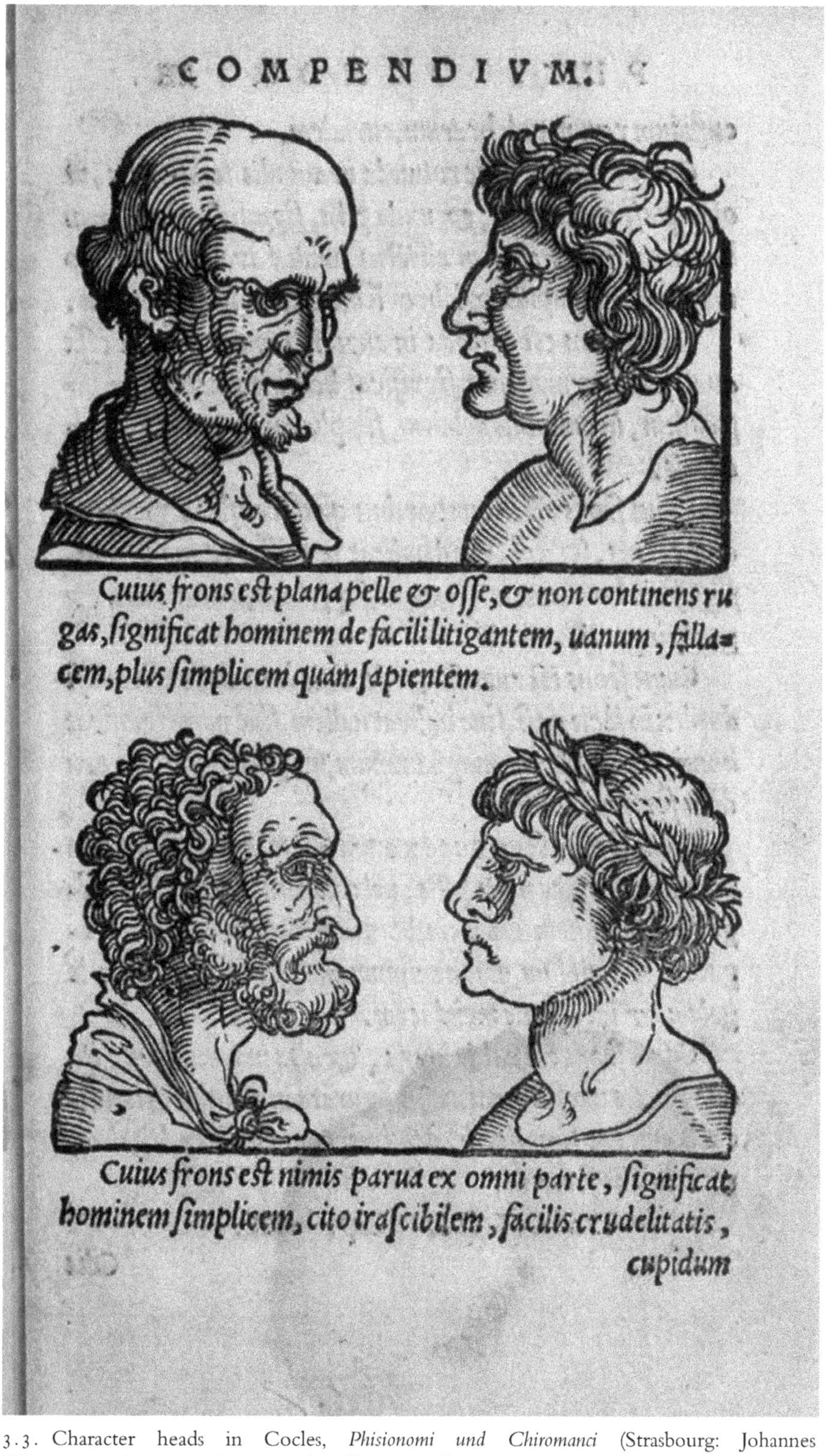
COMPENDIVM.

Cuius frons eſt plana pelle & oſſe, & non continens ru gas, ſignificat hominem de facili litigantem, uanum, falla= cem, plus ſimplicem quàm ſapientem.

Cuius frons eſt nimis parua ex omni parte, ſignificat hominem ſimplicem, cito iraſcibilem, facilis crudelitatis, cupidum

3.3. Character heads in Cocles, *Phisionomi und Chiromanci* (Strasbourg: Johannes Albertus, 1536). *Source:* Courtesy of Wellcome Collection.

investigation to the silhouette profiles of Swiss Zwinglian pastor Johann Caspar Lavater (1741–1801). Although Lavater's facial experiments share a locus of visual emphasis with these early physiognomies and make it tempting to map early physiognomic investigations onto later cranial inquiries of his own, there is little to suggest that they share a kinship in diagnoses of the human head. Lavater's investigation into the shapes of skulls aimed to uncover the original language in which God's intent for humankind was made manifest. While he believed that people's endowed form could yield clues about their inner nature, most assumptions about Lavater's theories miss the mark on the role of physiognomy in his doctrine of signs.[9] In fact, the early physiognomies' lack of coherence about the correlation of character traits to particular profiles, their reliance on generalized images, and lastly their publishers' own caveats about using them too literally make them poor indicators of moral determination.[10] A short summary of the printing history of physiognomies can help us see where their trajectory intersected with facial images.

Physiognomic knowledge had ancient roots in the *Book of Secrets* and was bound to the pseudo-Aristotelian tradition that served as advice and moral guidance for rulers, the so-called *Mirror of Princes*. This tradition built on the *Secretum Secretorum* that derived from fragments of the Arabic manuscript *Kitab-Sirr al-Asrar* (1209), which included letters on governing purported to be written to Alexander the Great by Aristotle. The premise of Aristotle advising Alexander on the suitability of candidates for his cabinet was propagated through the manuscript tradition, where the nature of his advice took different forms, mostly instructional. This counsel taught how to recognize moral rectitude in potential advisors and how to steer around devious types. Some pointed directly to identifying human character through physiognomy. Physiognomy and metoscopy must have been popular enough at Alexander's court for both of these modes of diagnosis to have made appearances in Pliny's account of Apelles, the famous artist in Alexander's entourage. Pliny's *Natural History* cites contemporary metoscopers (presumably also in Alexander's court) who could predict the moment of death of subjects drawn by Apelles's hand.[11] By the late fifteenth century, remnants of the *Mirror of Princes* had become institutionalized in the roles of court physicians, whose judicial astrology assisted in medical diagnoses and event planning.

Early modern physiognomies were popular iterations of a genre begun in antiquity that by the sixteenth century had picked up several medieval fragments, abridgments, and glosses. Most were derived from Arabic treatises, largely based on the pseudo-Aristotelian *Secretum Secretorum*, which became known to the Latin West in the mid-twelfth century.[12] Along with these *Secreti*, Renaissance physiognomies also incorporated glosses by natural philosophers, such as Albertus Magnus, as well as by Michael Scotus, the thirteenth-century mathematician and astrologer at Frederick II's court.[13]

Most sixteenth-century vernacular editions of the *Phisonomei* or *Complexionbuch*, under which titles portions of the *Secreti* were published, began with fragments from treatises by Galen on humors, the distribution of which in humans comprised their complexion.[14]

This tradition was updated as it transitioned to print, where it was advertised under the authorship of newer natural philosophers and physicians. Some of those advisors gained notoriety as more contemporary redactors of the physiognomic material. Although surely known locally, the broader reputations of some sixteenth-century physiognomic advisors were primarily made in print: notably, the Bolognese physician Bartolomeo della Rocca (1467–1504), known as Cocles; and Johannes Rosenbach (1467–1537), known as Johannes ab Indagine, a priest at Steinheim, the dean of St. Leonhardt in Frankfurt, and astrological advisor to Albrecht von Brandenburg.[15] While both were likely queried more frequently by their patrons about the advisability of actions and the scheduling of events, facial diagnoses proved the best way to preserve their erudition in book form.

Cocles, an astrologer and physician from Bologna, studied all the arts of divination, including astrology, chiromancy, physiognomy, and geomancy. Cocles began his text *Chiromantiae ac physionomiae Anastasis: cum approbatione magistri Alexandri Achillinis* in 1500. When drafting a horoscope for Ermes Bentivoglio, Cocles correctly predicted the demise of the *condottiero* in an upcoming battle. Unimpressed with such news, his patron ordered Cocles's own execution in 1504.[16] The Bentivoglios were expelled from Bologna in 1506 by the forces of Julius II, and Ermes died just as Cocles had foretold. In early modernity, physiognomic material could easily be sourced in books that treated astrological material generally, and certainly in the tradition of *Secreti* from which they originally came. But, after the 1480s, books of physiognomy and chiromancy printed in northern Italy began to carry the names of the authors such as Cocles who popularized them, reflecting their updates to the tradition of *Secreti* and positioning themselves as investigators of "chiromancy" or "physiognomy" versus secrets per se. As these were often practicing physicians who employed such astrological texts in their own diagnoses, we see a concomitant shift in which the diagnostic material rose to the top, or to the beginning, of the text. The most widely circulated physiognomy was associated with Cocles; the popularity of his redaction, and the focus on physiognomy rather than on humoral complexion, shuffled the order of the content in these publications.

Large unillustrated folio editions of the early 1500s combined Cocles's *Anastasis* with a manual written by his promoter Alessandro Achillini, the *Chyromantiae principiis et Physionomiae* (1503).[17] For this resulting text attributed to Cocles, *Chyromantie ac physionomie Anastasis: cum approbatio(n)e magistri Alexandri Achillinis*, the physician Achillini supplied a preface and a short letter of praise for his student.[18] Achillini lectured in medicine and philosophy at

Bologna, and is best remembered for having identified two bones in the middle ear.[19] But the dedication to Cocles expands his student's scholarly remit; it announces Cocles's expertise in medicine, distillation, geomancy, chiromancy, and physiognomy.[20] Although this printed text commences with the physiognomic material, these first-generation physiognomies printed in Bologna resembled their manuscript ancestors insofar as historiated initials were often their sole pictorial accompaniments.

Academic physicians such as Achillini and Cocles spurred the widespread popularization of physiognomic information through sixteenth-century repackagings. Material comprising Cocles's *Anastasis* was culled from several medieval sources, cribbing largely from the third part of Michael Scotus's *Liber Physiognomiae* and circulating this content in printed editions.[21] Cocles's premature death prevented the release of his announced publication of an abbreviated physiognomy; nevertheless, printers posthumously summarized his *Anastasis* and opportunistically published excerpts under his name as *Complexionsbüchlein*, *Compendium*, or *Chiromantiae*.[22] Although the printed Cocles editions originated in northern Italy (Bologna and Venice) and were later circulated all over Europe, the German-language editions are the most prolific, numbering around fifty-six in the sixteenth century alone, and set the standard for the illustrations.[23] German printers advertised the usefulness of the physiognomy manuals and added illustrations. The initial volumes printed in the German-speaking territories reveal a mixed bag of designs, including recycled profiles, coin portraits, palms for palm reading, zodiac emblems, surgical images, and even images of ancient cosmographers.

In their scantily illustrated printed editions derived from manuscript recensions, physiognomies could still be considered diagnostic insofar as they relayed textual summaries of humors and presented Aristotelian universals as the last word.[24] Physiognomy's place in the tradition of prognostic literature was reinforced by recycled illustrations that pointed to the divinatory arts and also to the received Aristotelian tradition. The robed philosophers appearing in those pamphlets were holdovers from the calendar and *Practica* literature.[25] The title page portraits of natural philosophers that were typical of the sparsely illustrated pamphlet-sized editions point back to the prognostic origins of the physiognomic literature.[26]

In sixteenth-century physiognomy, we witness these speculative universals succumbing to particulars gathered by eyewitnesses.[27] Cocles directly linked the science of physiognomy to other observation-based pursuits such as medicine and astrology, advocating these fields as proper training for the physiognomist.[28] Similar links are enunciated in contemporary how-to publications or *Practica*. Printed illustrations mediate the physiognomies' transition from the realm of deciphering external signs and into a genre that encouraged empirical engagement with particulars in order to discover causes.

PRACTICAL ASTROLOGY

We have already seen in Chapter 2 how cosmographic content had a symbiotic relationship with popular calendars and almanacs. In German print media, complexion books also joined with a tradition of printing calendars and *Practica*, with which they shared a visual kinship. Their common predictive origins likely prompted printers to reutilize imagery from their backlist relating to astrological and weather predictions. In almanacs and these how-to *Practica*, the lunar charts of Regiomontanus met bloodletting regimens long established by Abu Ali Ibn Sina's *Al-Qanun Fi Al-Tibb*, a canon of medicine with eleventh-century origins known in the West as the work of Avicenna.[29] For instance, a Strasbourg printing of Regiomontanus's *Kalendarius* from 1532 combined a calendar with a companion complexion book, whose title bills it as a chart of the "*New and Full Moon … (plus) An attractive comparison of Astrology with Medicine*."[30] In addition to updating ancient medical paradigms with more recently empirically derived cosmographic knowledge, this volume also gave that information a practical spin. While clearly derived from astrology, the content of this "complexion" book reorients its discourse around astral influences on humoral balance.

The planets were thought to exert considerable influence over a person's humoral complexion, and if properly tracked, their positions could also render diagnoses about illnesses or recommend cures. In this calendar, a zodiac man poses as a venesection doll (*Aderlassman*), an anatomical model that connected organs to the stars via strings that linked complexions and remedies to the heavens (Figure 3.4).[31] The packaging of this information into such a diagram reflects practitioners' dependence on astrological math to show the influence of the planets over people's innate nature.[32] For physicians, this included pinpointing the celestial coordinates of birthdays and gauging the auspiciousness of certain days for recalibrating humors through curative treatments such as bloodletting, cupping, and bathing.[33] Such mnemonic maps of planetary influence on hygiene and wellness from the calendar tradition connected *Practica* to complexion books.

The diverse data provided by the *Practica* came together in such a model. Here, the more recent data from the calendar tradition of Regiomontanus met health recommendations active in medical sources such as Avicenna's. The zodiac man inspired by this source took the form of an anatomical doll, whose interior was governed by signs of the constellations.[34] The Strasbourg *Kalendarius* is organized into short chapters designed to give information about the planets and their placement, the wind, the seasons, the balance of humors, regimens for diet, recommendations about the duration of sleep, and propitious times for bathing.[35] The *Kalendarius* included diagnoses by the medical authorities of antiquity, such as Hippocrates, Galen, and Pliny. But it also

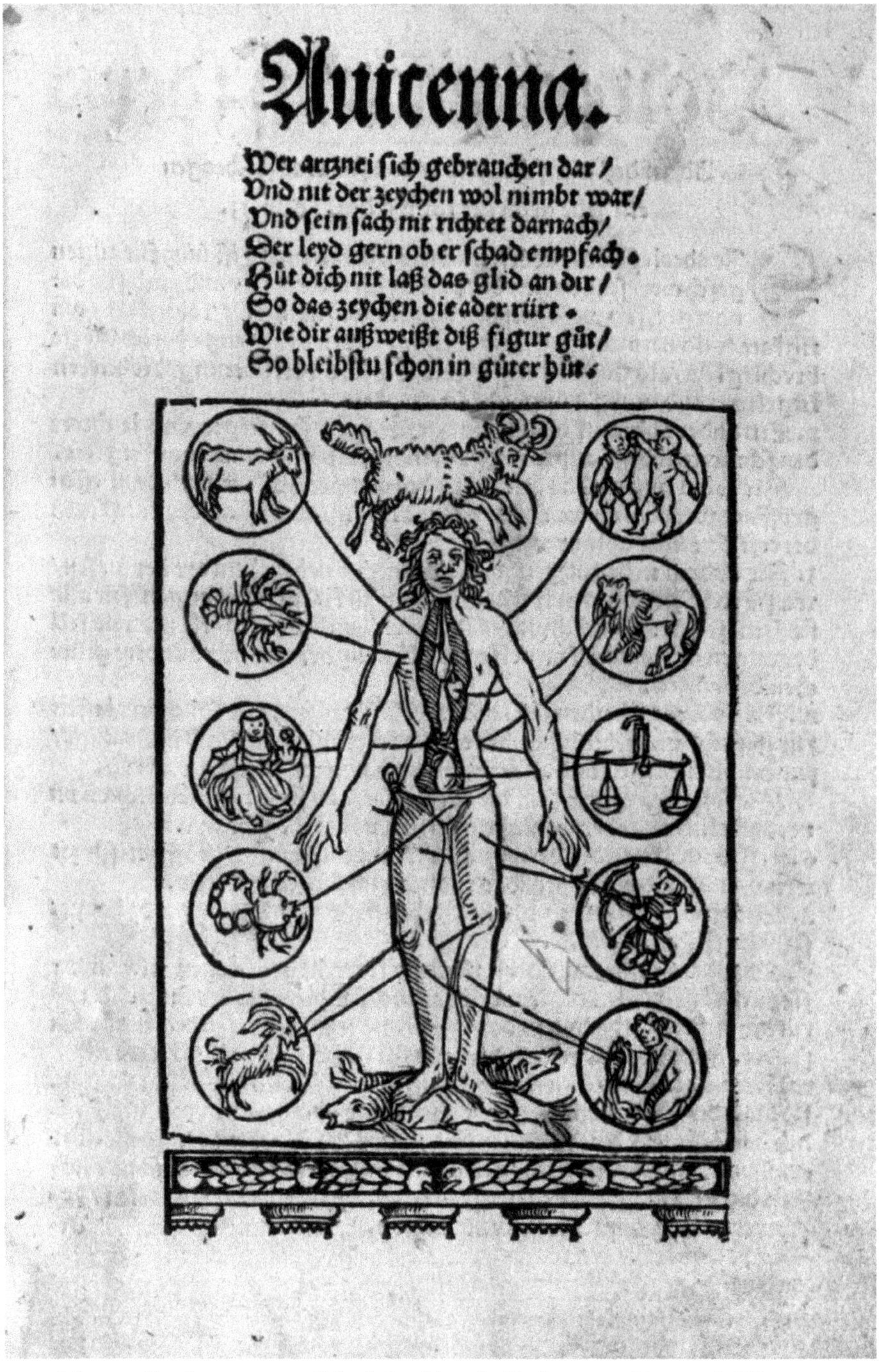

3.4. Johannes Regiomontanus, *Kalendarius Johannis Künigspergers: News und Volmon … eyn schön Vergleichung der Astronomi mit der Artznei* (Strasbourg: Cammerlander, 1532), 31r. *Source:* HAB HN97.4 Helmst. 2. Courtesy of Herzog August Bibliothek, Wolfenbüttel.

reported on how to use distilled waters for medical treatments and on the value of urine inspection, and counseled how to schedule bloodlettings.[36]

In short, publishers taught the calendar's readers to diagnose by observing symptoms. By suggesting readers scrutinize their complexion and even their urine for signs of celestial influence, vernacular texts such as calendars, almanacs, and *Practica* provided medicinal recommendations for physicians and lay practitioners.[37] According to these publications, correct diagnoses often hinged on the reader's precision in visual discernment. Cautionary notes against shoddy observations warned practitioners of diagnostic medicine to properly educate themselves in the related epistemic field of monitoring the arrangement of heavenly bodies before embarking on medical procedures.[38] The zodiac man cued organs to the astral bodies that influenced them, data that spurred the reader's memory about monthly and seasonal activity.[39] In the next generation of manuals for practical health, instead of the zodiac man, data collected about planetary influence would come to be organized around complexion types themselves.

A RIOT OF FACES

Diverse systems of epistemic inquiry congregated under the tent of complexion-related publications, including astronomy, medicine, and practical astrology. While the data from such systems coalesced in visual aids such as the zodiac man in early complexion publications, by 1510 the graphic design of these books would be dominated by a visual program engineered by images of faces. In hindsight, it was far from given that the visual components of these complexion books would ultimately land on the face's profile. In other forms of judicial astrology, such as geomancies, for example, the celestial map was used as a springboard for further calculations about human nature; this form of divination was essentially numerology. The math of star signs was also the thrust of the manual *Complexion/ Natur vnd eigenschafft eines yeden menschen zu erfahren/ auch seiner geburt stund vnnd zeychen*, which features computational exercises to unlock the nature of people born under the influence of a certain planet.[40] Such complexion books were based on astrological numerology and foregrounded astral and planetary influence instead of physiognomic information. But even this complexion book has adopted the imagery of the physiognomic profiles (Figure 3.5). In the section describing the purview of the seven planets, profiles now accompany brief character sketches of people born under particular star signs.[41] Flanking the personified embodiments of the planets are representations of character "types" shaped by the planet's influence. Facial features are indeed described in the text – such as round faces, pleasant eyes, wide foreheads – but without a close correspondence between the character described in the text and the accompanying images, which are

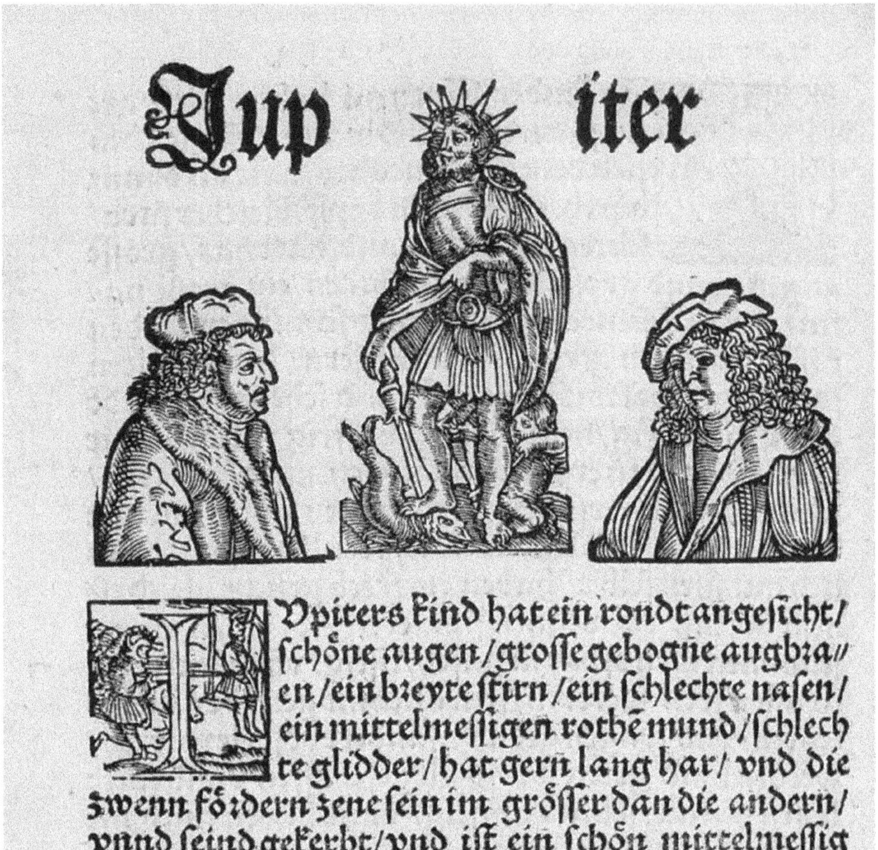

Jup iter

IVpiters kind hat ein rondt angesicht/ schöne augen/grosse gebogne augbra/en/ein breyte stirn/ein schlechte nasen/ ein mittelmessigen rothē mund/schlechte glidder/ hat gern lang har/ vnd die zwenn fördern zene sein im grösser dan die andern/ vnnd seind gekerbt/vnd ist ein schön mittelmessig mensch eins züchtigen freüntlichen angesichts/ vñ wandels/ Er liebet gerechtigkeit/vnd hat auch gerechte leüt/vñ sonderlch die weiber ser lieb/ist auch niemandt schedlich/vnd hasset böse leut/ist barmhertzig/vnnd von natür ein Sanguineus/er wirt reich oder ja nit gantz arm/darzü so ist er ein mitler aller gerechtigkeit/dünckt sich selber schön/ wie ers dann auch ist/vnd ist auch weyß/vernünfftig/ wol redent/ schimplich/mild/ vnd frölich/vnd lebt auch lang/vnd in Summa er ist von der aller besten natür.

Mars

3.5. Cocles, *Complexion/ Natur vnd eigenschafft* (Mainz: Peter Jordan, 1534), 3v. *Source:* HAB HN97.4 Helmst. 3. Courtesy of Herzog August Bibliothek, Wolfenbüttel.

most likely drawn from other sources. Nevertheless, the printer Peter Jordan specifically sought out physiognomic profiles to embellish the book.

Generic portraits adequately served the text's program to generalize about types. Allusions to appearances in the text that accompany the sign of Libra (*Waage*) might have invited the use of portraits: "The child born in Libra is a truthful person, has a thick nose, large eyebrows, and broad shoulders." The accompanying image had only to be specific enough not to contradict such a description.[42] Other horoscopes, such as Scorpio (*Crebs*), hardly required a portrait: the child born in Scorpio "will have luck with buying and selling, will travel through many lands, but will die alone, will outlive his father, but will have little use for his children. He who takes a wife in Aries will die in Taurus."[43] Yet character heads were good visual features in which to embed the idea of humans as humoral types with legible physical traits.

By the 1530s, the *Complexion* publications had adapted images from the pictorial desiderata of cosmography and physiognomy. With such practical information abounding in the complexion texts that had very little to do with humoral dispositions, it is surprising that profiles assume pride of place. Another genre of judicial astrology, geomancy, attempted to derive character profiles from complex numerical calculations based on names and star signs. While the text itself did not engage in the issue of physical appearances, the *Geomantia* printed by Peter Jordan in 1534 also used physiognomic illustrations. Jordan obviously saw physiognomy as a related form of divination – the language of *revelation* (*ausweisen*/to reveal) is increasingly accompanied by the idea of *experience*, in this case protracted observation.[44] Jordan's wide sweep of illustrations recycled from other publications provided the two portraits of Roman emperors who appear beneath a design for a volvelle that schedules the quarterly cycle of the moon and predicts the height of the sun and moon throughout the year (Figure 3.6). In addition to images like these from numismatic literature or antiquarian texts, Jordan's borrowing of the personification of the planets in the volume reveals his access to the work of Hans Burgkmair, who originated those designs.[45] Jordan's use of the antique roundels also suggests his familiarity with the tendency of some early physiognomies printed in Augsburg to headline their title pages with such numismatic profiles. These numismatic heads are stylistically close to those emperor heads designed by Burgkmair for the *Kaiserbuch*, Conrad Peutinger's intended chronicle of emperors, to be discussed shortly.[46] Because the content of this *Geomantia* ranges from nativities based on numerology to seasonal recommendations for the best time to purchase weapons, the use of portraits here is indeed unexpected.[47]

What, then, recommended the profile heads of two Caesars to conclude Jordan's *Geomantia*, a book that deciphered one's fortune from the stars and numerical puzzles? If Jordan used images of faces to connect geomancy's

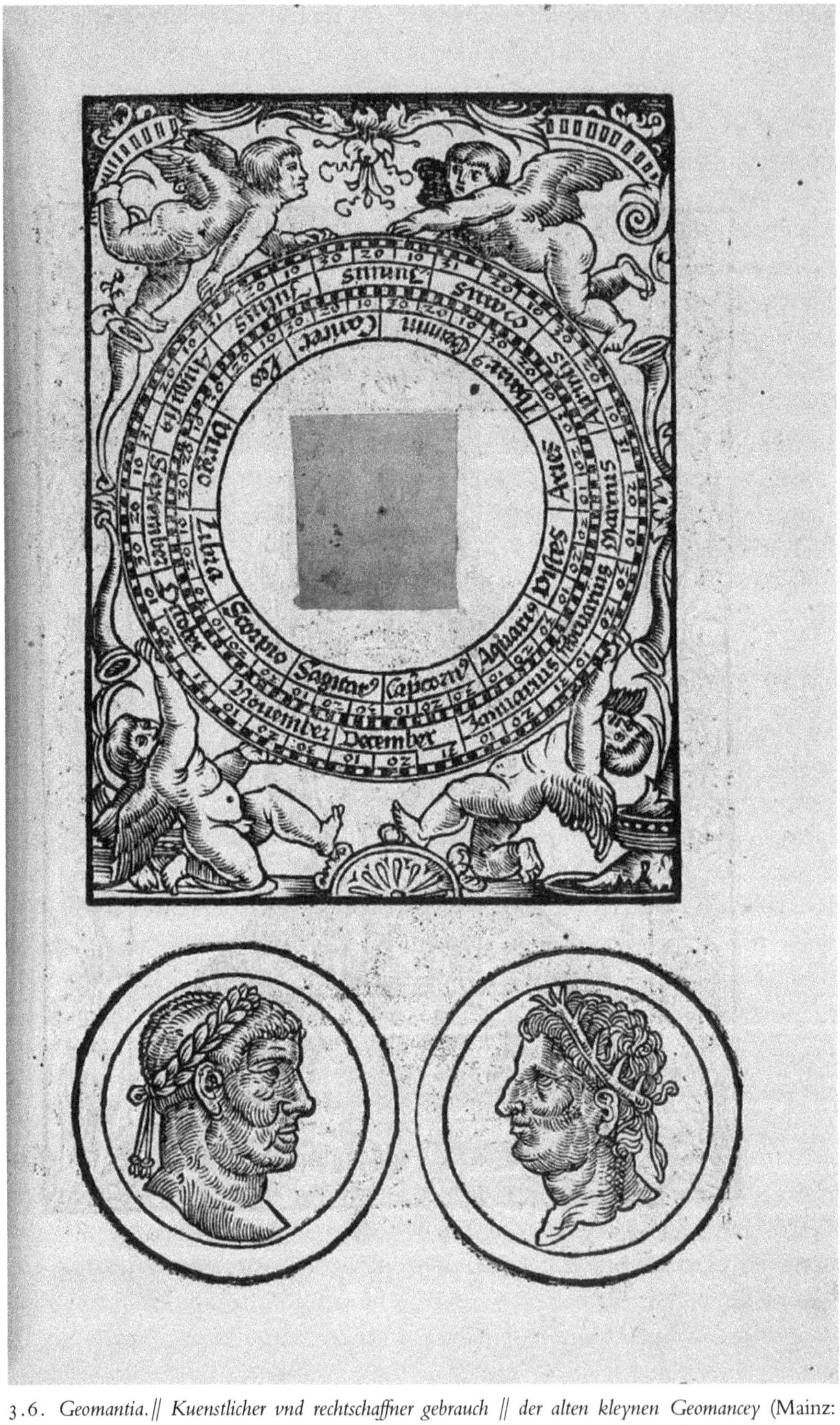

3.6. *Geomantia.|| Kuenstlicher vnd rechtschaffner gebrauch || der alten kleynen Geomancey* (Mainz: Peter Jordan, 1534), 22R. *Source:* HAB HN97.4 Helmst. 5. Courtesy of Herzog August Bibliothek, Wolfenbüttel.

numerical methods to physiognomy, he must have regarded it as a kindred epistemic genre. Similarly, he used facial types as convenient and appropriate vessels to hold empirically derived datasets. Images repeated and recycled between genres were sometime just accidents of hasty production, in addition to examples of sustainable practice. Jordan's complexion and geomancy volumes were both printed in 1534; the publisher's approaching deadlines might have suggested the expediency of using images already on hand. Typical of early sixteenth-century print practice, Jordan was culling from a field of related epistemic pursuits; it is likely that he saw geomancy as a type of empirical reckoning from the stars similar to the complexion genres from which he was cribbing his images. Profiles also crept into the astrological diagnostic literature, particularly as it became more popularly oriented around physiognomic analysis. Images of faces were an easy way to refer to astrological influence, specifically as it pertained to man's fortune. These diagnostic genres were becoming ever more closely aligned, at least in part as a result of printers who saw the benefits of marketing them as related by way of similar pictorial programs.

PRACTICING FACIALITY

As we have seen, printed literature about the external aspects of human complexions reached German-speaking audiences via a range of genres, but mostly in the form of handy octavo- and quarto-sized *Practica*, calendars, and physiognomies. By the 1520s, physiognomic literature became radically visualized around images of human faces, a change that accompanied a gradual transition in the idea of human complexion. Reflections on human nature as once determined by the interiority of humoral disposition, according to Valentin Groebner, shifted in early modernity toward externally searchable traits. This gave rise to a number of genres that dealt with identity politics, such as chiromancy and physiognomy.[48] This shift in emphasis of complexion books from humoral diagnoses based on astral information to documents that focused on external features can be tracked alongside publications that featured the face as the key to unlocking the interior of human nature. The following section considers the role of images in redirecting character diagnoses to searchable signs on the body's exterior.

The decision to illustrate a physiognomic manual with a profile anticipates the later trajectory of physiognomies' pictorial program, where images of faces would come to define the genre. The frequent reuse of existing woodblocks in many early illustrated books reflects a tendency for printers to match "appropriate" images to the existing text in lieu of fabricating custom designs. Take, for example, the particular profile fronting a complexion book printed in Augsburg in 1515 (Figure 3.7). Not specifically designed for the physiognomy,

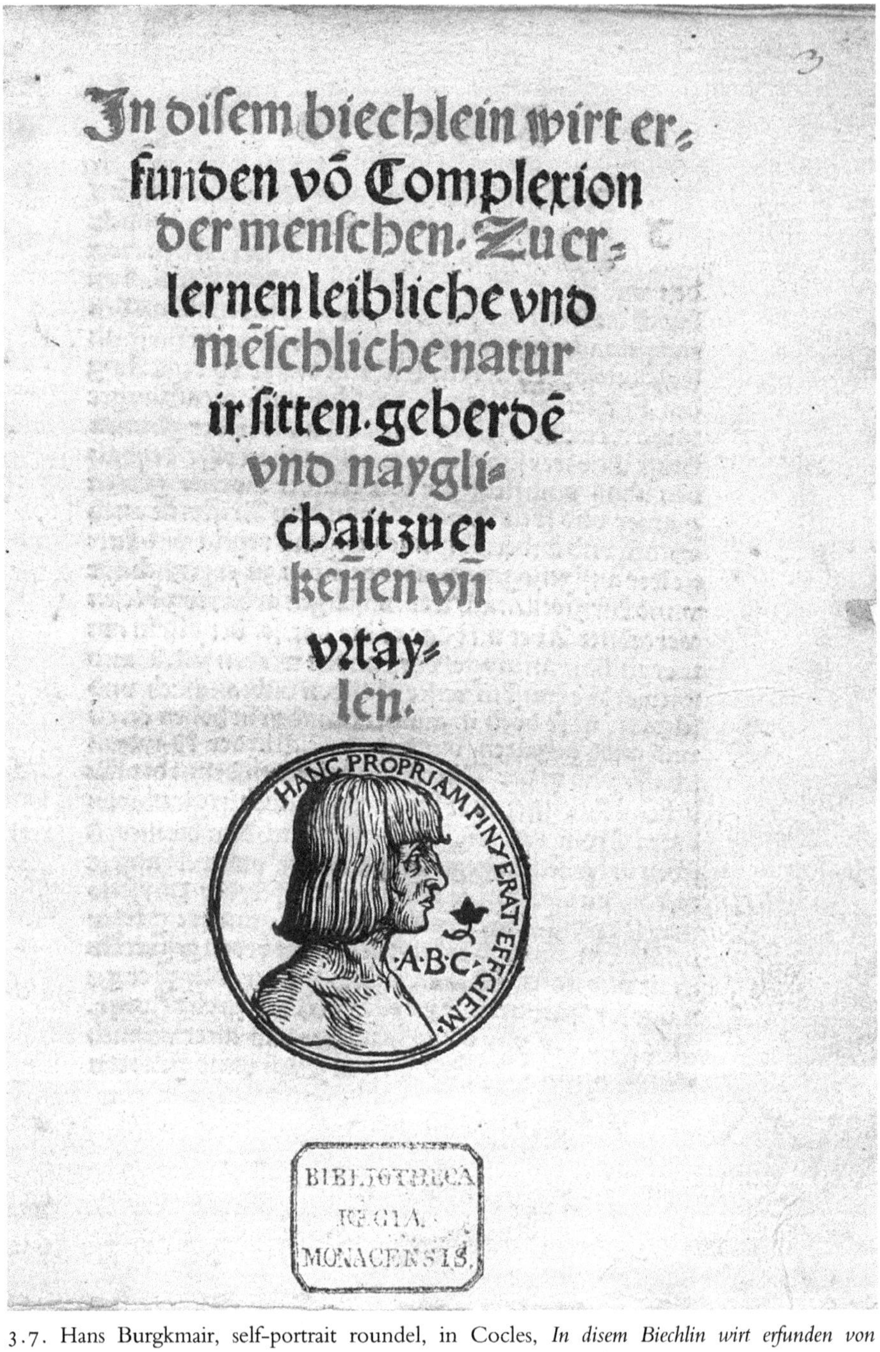

3.7. Hans Burgkmair, self-portrait roundel, in Cocles, *In disem Biechlin wirt erfunden von Complexion der Menschen* (Augsburg: Schönsperger, 1515), woodcut, sheet, 14 cm × 19 cm. *Source:* BSB Res/4 Anthr. 8. Courtesy of Bayerische Staatsbibliothek, Munich. CC BY-NC-SA 4.0.

this image likely responds to a local trend of collecting ancient coins and to styles of numismatic representation in Augsburg.[49] As such, aspects of the physiognomic literature can supplement investigations of faces in numismatic books, a topic already explored by Stephen Perkinson, who sees their intervention in the changing benchmarks of likeness.[50] Numismatic books began as records of artifacts but evolved into collections of "portraits" that traded on physiognomic likeness for guarantees of their authenticity.

The prefaces of small-sized editions of pseudo-Cocles from 1510 onwards forcefully articulated the more practical and contemporary uses of such manuals, even when they announced themselves to be in the tradition of *Secreti*. Their front matter advertised the physiognomer's art or skill (*Kunst*) as one "used in places (as I have seen, experienced, and read about in credible chronicles) where slaves are bought and sold."[51] The diagnostic skills to be gained from this manual also invoked the horse trader's art of judging the age and nature of a horse by inspection of its teeth and limbs. How did the shroud of arcane and princely knowledge associated with the Aristotelian tradition of *Secreti* lift to reveal the very practical concerns of assessing external features to assist in horse trading and human trafficking? Distributed in short vernacular pamphlets that announced such practicalities in the front matter, these physiognomies' concerns were closely aligned to those of printers wanting to drum up audiences for printed books.

DO YOU WANT TO BE A PHYSIOGNOMER?

The earliest illustrated physiognomies entreated their readers to practice visual acuity in order to detect specimens in the field. Portable and pithy, the early German vernacular editions of pseudo-Cocles physiognomies printed between 1510 and 1520 in Augsburg started to market themselves to practitioners of the art of physiognomy, or "physiognomers." Suggesting practical advice, some tips are given in which renowned practitioners of the ancient art are dropped in as exemplars. One preface told of a legendary encounter in which the profile of Hippocrates, the spiritual father of physiognomy, was misjudged by Philemon, a professional practitioner of the art. This cautionary tale served as a warning against the superficial and peremptory exercise of physiognomy, in which the consideration of traits in isolation could lead to misreadings and false conclusions. Per the preface, Aristotle recounts how Hippocrates's disciples brought a rendering of their master to Philemon, an experienced reader of physiognomy, and asked for his judgment.[52] On the basis of the "*abkunterfayt*" rendering, Philemon pronounce Hippocrates the Elder a scoundrel, a fraud, and a lover of all unchaste deeds.[53] Infuriated, Hippocrates's disciples inform Philemon that he has woefully misjudged the drawing.[54] The indignant students report this back to their master, who, to the disciples' great surprise, agrees with Philemon's diagnosis. According to Hippocrates, Philemon had read the true nature of his tendencies, ones that he spent a lifetime trying to surmount. The moral renders the book's self-help program to be attaining self-knowledge with the purpose of recognizing and overcoming one's natural evil proclivities in order to live a worthy life. Without the ability to detect and change these tendencies, the text intones, man is no better than an animal.[55]

A question posed at the end of *In disem Biechlin wirt erfunden von Complexion der Menschen* reinforces the practical purpose of the book in an unusually direct address to the reader in the epilogue: "Do you want to become a physiognomer? [If so] then you must learn and wisely observe everything noted in these chapters, so that you will be certain in your judgments."[56] The author then follows up with some short tips on how to use the information presented in the book: readers should peer into themselves, judge their own traits, and then weigh them together. It warns that the hasty practice of physiognomy can lead to the dead end of false readings. Perhaps it was these cautionary statements that spurred the first illustrations to assist in cataloguing many different traits. The colophon articulates the direct and practical benefit that would reward the buyer of this book: skill in the recognition of signs – in short, how to hone the skills to become a physiognomer.

How did amateur physiognomers use the book? The evidence suggests that they looked around and noted what they saw. We can see that one reader took seriously the physiognomy's entreaty to record visual judgments in a chiromancy compendium from 1540 preserved in the Herzog August Bibliothek in Wolfenbüttel (Figure 3.8).[57] That reader set himself the task of conducting minor visual experiments by cuing the traits observed to the names of people they knew, likely neighbors. In the section that discusses the shapes and pitches of foreheads, the reader labeled them with the names "Heinrich" and "Gerken." In a nearby section on inspecting the dimensions of arms, the fellow on the left with the large and crooked arms recalled "Heinrich," whereas the arms of the man on the right evoked the look of those of "Caspar."[58] This reader also either scribbled a mustache on or defined the frown of a subject on another page of this volume, perhaps to shore up fidelity to their actual likenesses. Even if these defacements by the doodler of the Wolfenbüttel physiognomy were simply an exercise to entertain that reader, such firsthand encounters with the visual material of early modern titles shows us that books' pictorial accompaniments did indeed provoke empirical engagement with the world around their readers. Faithfully following the book's advertised prescriptions, this reader was recording and organizing visual impressions of the world. Were not such observers the ideal members of the do-it-yourself audiences whom the writers of these books' prefaces envisioned?

These readers of texts became *de facto* readers of images that had corresponding signs in the real world. Physiognomy's later emphasis on the facial index

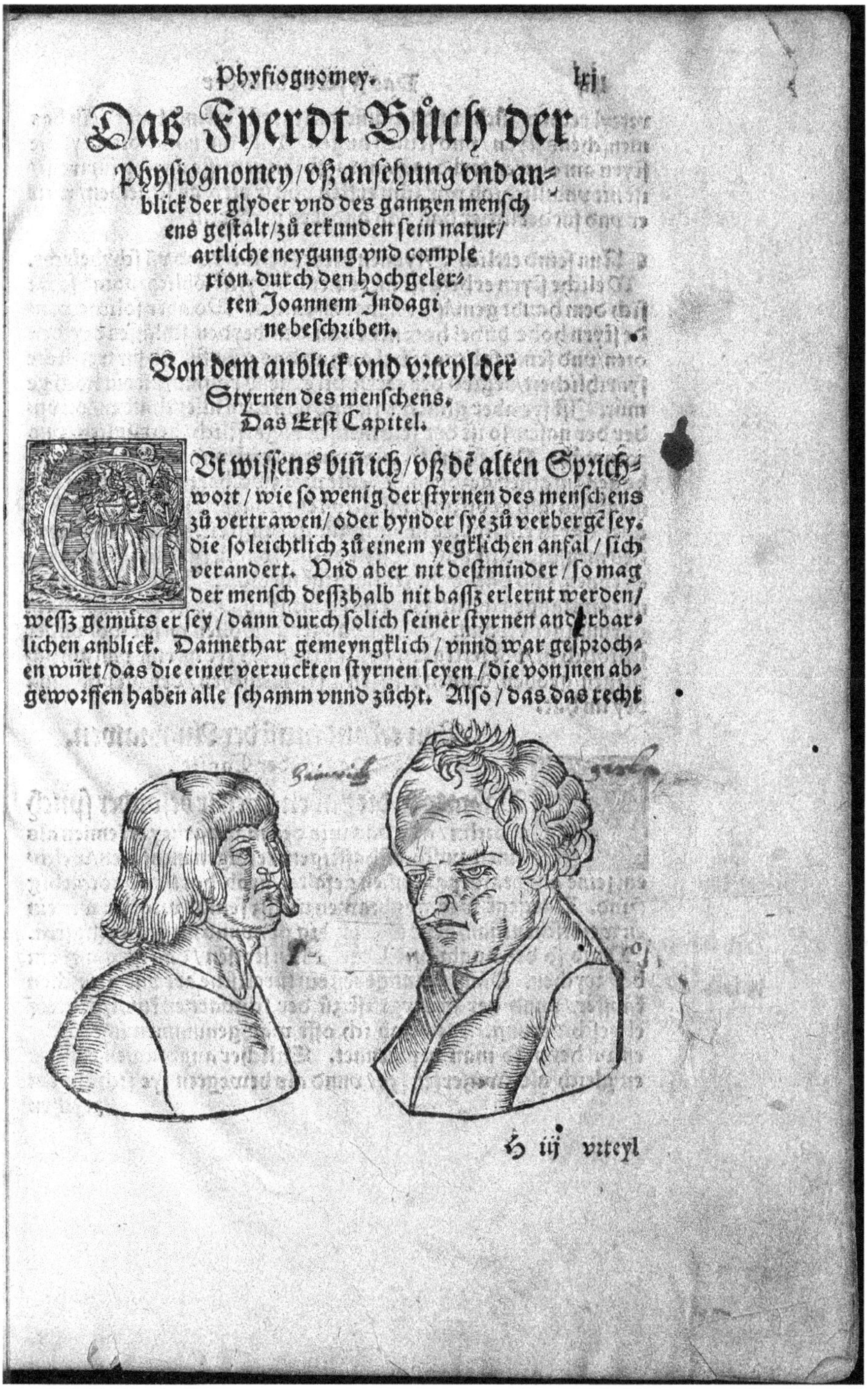
Physiognomey. lxj

Das Fyerdt Bůch der

Physiognomey/vß ansehung vnd anblick der glyder vnd des gantzen menschens gestalt/zů erkunden sein naturliche neygung vnd complexion. durch den hochgelerten Joannem Indagine beschriben.

Von dem anblick vnd vrteyl der Styrnen des menschens.
Das Erst Capitel.

Vt wissens bin ich/vß dē alten Sprichwort / wie so wenig der styrnen des menschens zů vertrawen/ oder hynder sye zů verbergē sey. die so leichtlich zů einem yegklichen anfal / sich verandert. Vnd aber nit destminder / so mag der mensch desszhalb nit basz erlernt werden/ weszz gemüts er sey / dann durch solich seiner styrnen andrbarlichen anblick. Dannethar gemeyngklich / vnnd war gesprochen würt/das die einer verruckten styrnen seyen / die von jnen abgeworffen haben alle schamm vnnd zůcht. Also / das das recht

H iij vrteyl

3.8. Hans Wechtlin's "Foreheads" in a chiromancy compendium. Hans von Gersdorff, *Feldtbůch der Wund-Artzney: sampt vilen Instrumenten der Chirurgey; vß dem Albucasi contrafayt* (Strasbourg: Schott, 1540), 61r. *Source:* HAB HQuH20.4. Courtesy of Herzog August Bibliothek, Wolfenbüttel.

was already anticipated by the title page images emerging in southern Germany between 1510 and 1520. At most, these smallish quarto-sized pamphlets feature a single woodcut on their title page, but, significantly, they became visualized in a way that would come to define the genre as an explicitly visual one.[59] The valence of the Books of Secrets shifted, according to Martin Porter, as they emerged from the classical tradition and merged with attempts to synthesize Christian precepts with Egyptian hermetics and Neoplatonism in the Renaissance. The Neoplatonists sought to inscribe text onto the pre-text world. As Porter argues, the "audio-visual *scientia* of physiognomy" was a result of these operations.[60] We can perhaps trace such visualization of physiognomic thinking to southern Germany, where, after two decades of unillustrated analysis of body parts and types published primarily in northern Italy, the locus of physiognomic diagnosis began to collect around the face – and we see a concomitant evaporation of the aura of the tradition of *Secreti* proper. We also see a graphic attempt on the part of the publisher to market the literature via a facial index that bridged the reader to the text's physiognomic content.

OBSERVATIONS

This direct command to the reader to execute a series of visual judgments runs parallel to approaches recommended by contemporary publications on the treatment of battle wounds. Recent research into the history of scientific observation has revealed communities of early modern observers who could analyze, vet, and confirm data. According to the outcomes of a working group at the Max Planck Institute for the History of Science in Berlin, these communities underwrote the development of disciplinary science. The term *observationes* transcended genres and signaled standardized practices of collecting, comparing, and systematizing knowledge across the disciplines. We see the term used to describe the recording of medical case studies, for example, or the investigation of the weather, or the movement of the stars.[61] Such collective observations ultimately came to represent best practices in these fields and have been interrogated for their role in developing the kind of consensus that became scientific knowledge. The systematic collection of results ultimately led to the establishment of associations of professional observers, such as the Academy of the Linceans and the Royal Society. The contributions of these organizations are typically discussed in terms of the recording of the "views" that they produced, debating whether or not they were "objective."[62] Indeed, firsthand engagement with books by lay readers portended new practices that would ultimately become regularized and standardized.

Complicit in encouraging these new observational skills were printers whose choices aimed to help guide readers through the world by first leading them through a text. While physiognomies would follow the lead of many how-to pamphlets that cross-pollinated images from *Kalendaria* and *Complexion* literature, the illustrations' function in the early stages was to organize the text into blocks of narrative divided into sections via pictorial prompts.

The printer Christian Egenolff, active in the 1520s in Strasbourg and later in Frankfurt, issued several physiognomic publications based on the Cocles material toward the end of the decade.[63] Egenolff's Cocles edition of 1529, *Phisonomei: Complexio und Art eins ieden Menschen, ausz Gestalt und Form des Angesichts, Glider unnd allen geberden zu erlernen* . . . reused a random assortment of images borrowed from older *Kalendaria* and also numismatic texts.[64] When printers recycled illustrations in the early physiognomies, it was typically to find a close match to the new text and rarely to illustrate a specific condition – in fact, the images frequently demonstrate only a loose connection to the text. For example, Egenolff's image of musicians that headlines a section on "voices" in the Strasbourg physiognomy (Figure 3.9) was similar to ones used earlier to illustrate phlegmatic natures in a practical publication, *Kalender: Iatromathematisches Hausbuch*, which appeared in Augsburgin 1481.[65] This kind of repurposing of the printer's idle woodblocks and setting them into new combinations was sanctioned practice in early printshops. Rarely did printers try to cover the tracks of their borrowings. Without even removing the planetary symbols from woodblocks likely developed for an earlier calendar, Egenolff recycled the blocks of zodiac signs in his *Phisonomei* to headline the sections on chins (with an image of Aquarius), eyebrows (with an image for Virgo), and shapes of heads (with an image of twins representing Gemini).[66] Later, in 1533, he retrofitted these symbols to accompany monthly schedules in a book composed by the Frankfurt city physician Eucharius Rößlin and Johannes Stöffler, *Kalender mit allen Astronomischen haltungen*, where they appeared in the introductory calendar pages that marked important birth-days.[67] Therefore, the pictorial attachments of the astrological *Kalendaria* also furnished the interior design of the early illustrated physiognomies. This formatting structured the loose collection of Aristotelian signs and symptoms into regular sections of searchable material. Along with indices and tables of contents, such paratextual elements enabled quick scanning, cross-referencing, and organized perusal of the text.

In addition to personifications of astrological symbols, Egenolff also used images of profiles to illustrate certain physiognomic traits in the book. These roundel-shaped profiles represent the variety of features discussed by the text, such as hair, foreheads, eyes, noses, and lips. The designs for the woodcuts have clearly been derived from medallions; they carry inscriptions that identify the sitters, but they are not directly relevant to the particular trait discussed in the section. The section on noses in Egenolff's 1530 edition of *Phisonomei: Eins jeden menschen Art* is headlined by a woodcut imitating a coin roundel with the

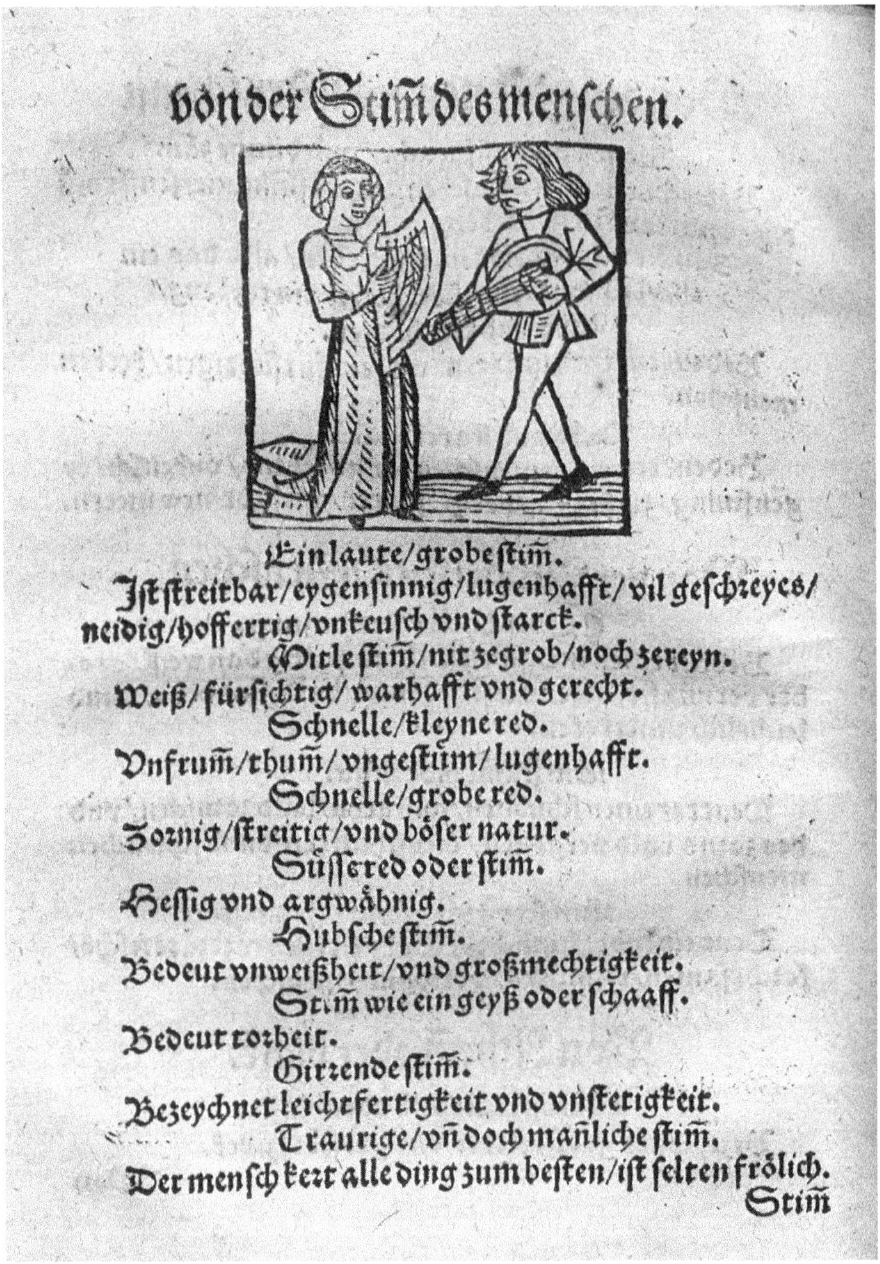

Von der Stim̃ des menschen.

Ein laute/grobe stim̃.
Ist streitbar/eygensinnig/lugenhafft/vil geschreyes/ neidig/hoffertig/vnkeusch vnd starck.
Mitle stim̃/nit zegrob/noch zereyn.
Weiß/fürsichtig/warhafft vnd gerecht.
Schnelle/kleyne red.
Vnfrum̃/thum̃/vngestüm/lugenhafft.
Schnelle/grobe red.
Zornig/streitig/vnd böser natur.
Süsse red oder stim̃.
Hessig vnd argwähnig.
Hubsche stim̃.
Bedeut vnweißheit/vnd großmechtigkeit.
Stim̃ wie ein geyß oder schaaff.
Bedeut torheit.
Girrende stim̃.
Bezeychnet leichtfertigkeit vnd vnstetigkeit.
Traurige/vñ doch mañliche stim̃.
Der mensch kert alle ding zum besten/ist selten frölich.
Stim̃

3.9. Figures illustrating voices in Cocles, *Phisonomei: Complexio und Art eins ieden Menschen, ausz Gestalt und Form des Angesichts, Glider unnd allen geberden zu erlernen* (Strasbourg: Egenolff, *c.* 1529). *Source:* NLM WZ 240 C666 pg 1550. Courtesy of US National Library of Medicine.

mature profile effigy of Guglielmo II Paleologo (1494–1518), of the northern Italian Margravate Monferrato (Figure 3.10).[68] The text does not provide details about the choice of the margrave's portrait for this section's headlining image, but the sitter's featured nose gestures toward the section's topic of subtle

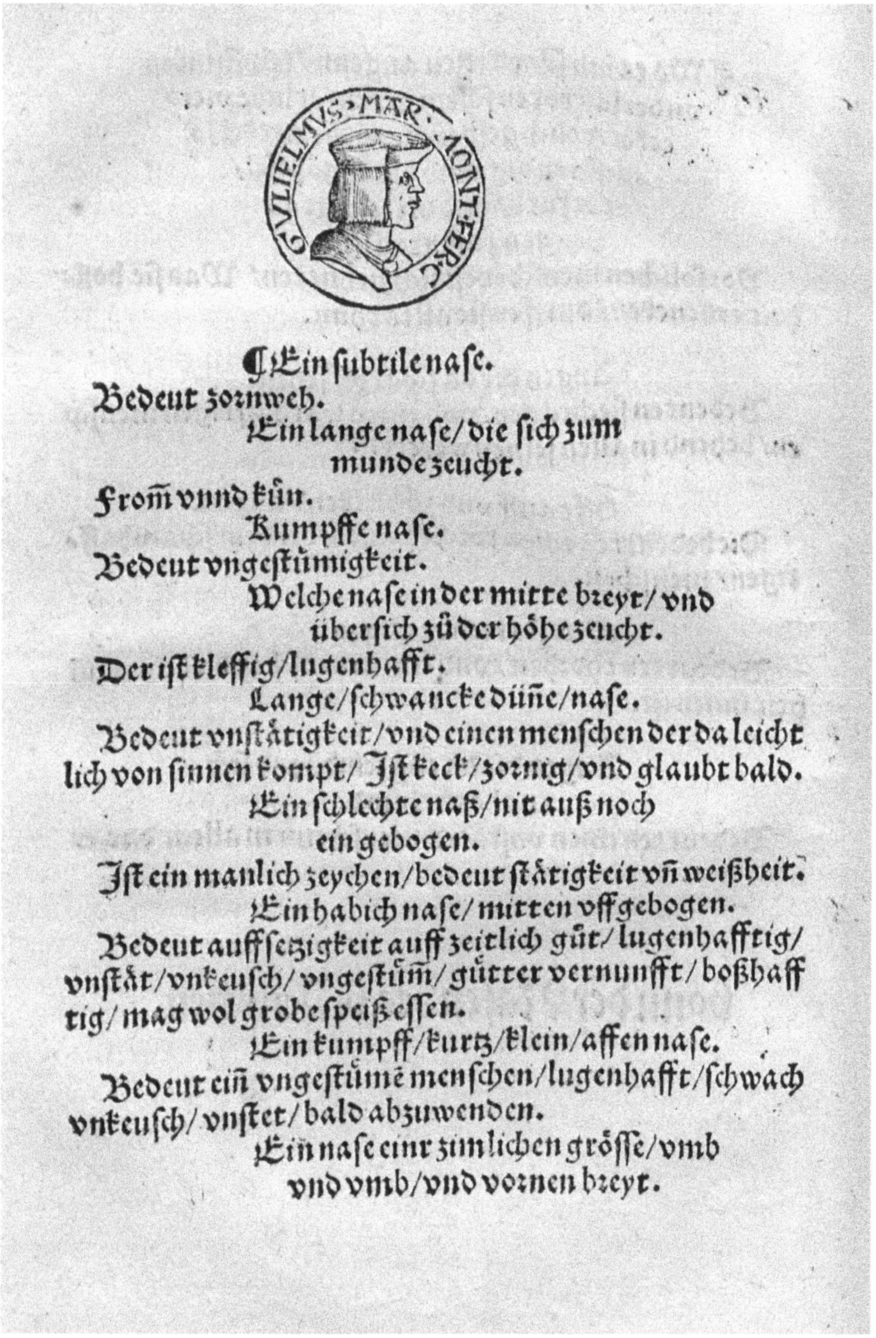

¶ Ein subtile nase.
Bedeut zornweh.
Ein lange nase/ die sich zum
munde zeucht.
From̄ vnnd kün.
Kumpffe nase.
Bedeut vngestümigkeit.
Welche nase in der mitte breyt/ vnd
übersich zů der höhe zeucht.
Der ist kleffig/lugenhafft.
Lange/schwancke dün̄e/nase.
Bedeut vnstätigkeit/vnd einen menschen der da leicht
lich von sinnen kompt/ Ist keck/zornig/vnd glaubt bald.
Ein schlechte naß/nit auß noch
eingebogen.
Ist ein manlich zeychen/bedeut stätigkeit vn̄ weißheit.
Ein habich nase/ mitten vffgebogen.
Bedeut auffsetzigkeit auff zeitlich gůt/ lugenhafftig/
vnstät/vnkeusch/ vngestüm̄/ gůtter vernunfft/ boßhaff
tig/ mag wol grobe speiß essen.
Ein kumpff/kurtz/klein/affen nase.
Bedeut ein̄ vngestůme menschen/lugenhafft/schwach
vnkeusch/ vnstet/ bald abzuwenden.
Ein nase einr zimlichen grösse/vmb
vnd vmb/vnd vornen breyt.

3.10. Roundel of Gulielmus Mar Mont-Ferc-C, in Cocles, *Phisonomei: Eins jeden menschen Art* (Egenolff: Strasbourg, 1530). *Source:* NLM WZ 240 C666 pg 1530. Courtesy of US National Library of Medicine.

noses. Thus, images were probably nominated by printers for the traits they loosely signaled. Egenolff's selection of portraits demonstrates his awareness of similar physiognomies printed in Augsburg whose title pages also featured medallion-like portraits.

Antiquarian interest in numismatics in early modern Germany collided with the medium of print in the first few decades of the sixteenth century. This was especially the case in Augsburg, where a group of local humanists began to collect coins and, importantly, commissioned artists to record their findings. In 1505, the city secretary Conrad Peutinger collaborated with the local printmaker Hans Burgkmair on portraits planned for Peutinger's *Kaiserbuch*, which he intended to publish with the title *Imperatorum Augustorum et tyrannorum quorundam Romani imperii brevis gestorum annotatio*, an edition to be loosely modeled on Suetonius's *Lives of the Caesars* (Figure 3.11).[69] Burgkmair fashioned over one hundred faithful likenesses of these emperors after models provided by Peutinger's coin collection.[70] This involvement with veristic portraiture in Augsburg may have inspired Burgkmair's own self-portrait roundel we find on the title page of a Cocles edition with the inscription ABC.[71] Interest in medallions and coin portraiture reached a fever pitch in Augsburg during the meeting of the imperial diet of 1518, where many such likenesses in profile with *all'antica* stylistic qualities were made of the attendees, as well as of members of the patriciate and the merchant community.[72] In southern Germany in the 1520s, the production of medals was closely aligned with the medium of print not only in their material production, as both types were produced by models first carved in wood, but also in their aspirations for circulation. A spiritual kinship with prints made medals appealing collectibles to both artists and humanists active in the printmaking trade. The same assurances embedded in medallion-like portraits in this period are often rehearsed on the surface of prints, providing the name, date, and age of the sitter, mimicking the text and even the typeface on the medallion, and sometimes using the guarantee of "*warhafftig abconterfeiung*," or true likeness.[73] In the mutual reinforcement of portraits and medals that we witness in early sixteenth-century examples, Larry Silver argues that the portrait print that developed at this time resembles the portrait medal.[74] The profusion of portraits that ensued, as well as portraits' accompanying guarantees of authenticity, catapulted a demand for them across a wide spectrum of professionals: artists, historians, and natural philosophers alike.[75] Later enthusiasts, such as the polymath Thomas Browne, would reiterate the idea of the face as a surface for signs: a space wherein one who could not read the alphabet might still find the face legible.[76] This legibility was also the objective of Johann Caspar Lavater, who hoped that facial expressions could recuperate a lost natural language. Faces bore the burden of evidentiary work in archaeology, history, natural philosophy, and physiognomy.

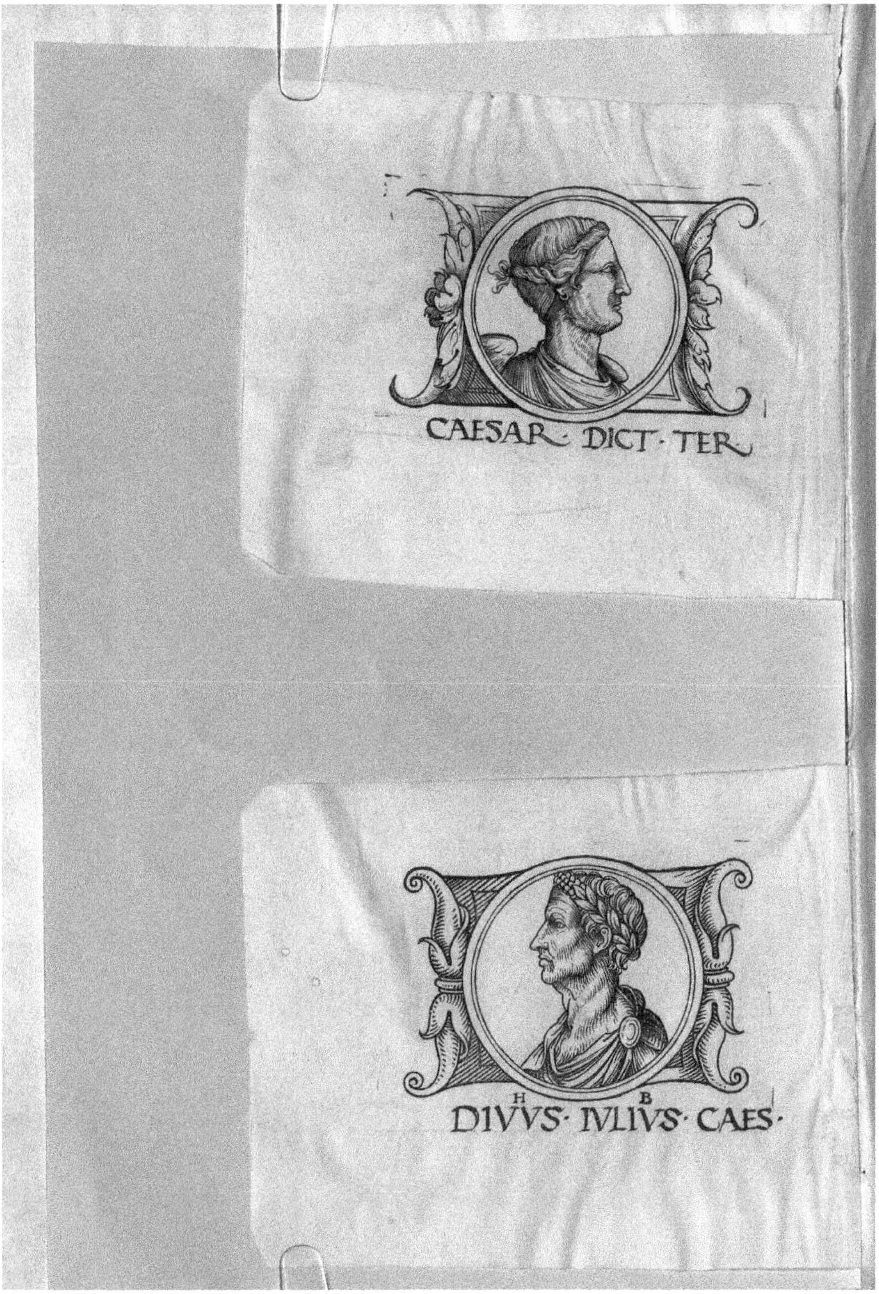

3.11. Hans Burgkmair, emperor heads for Conrad Peutinger, *Kaiserbuch*, bound in Filippo Beroaldo, *Commentationes in Suetoniam Tranquillum* (Paris: Hornken & Hittorp, 1512). *Source:* Mag/V 1462. Courtesy of Studienbibliothek Dillingen.

The connection of portraiture to imperial biographies, and the extent to which portraiture could deliver memorable information about character, likely informed the printer Egenolff's choice to promote his quarto-sized *Phisonomei* of 1529 with a title page roundel portrait of Trajan (Figure 3.12). This image

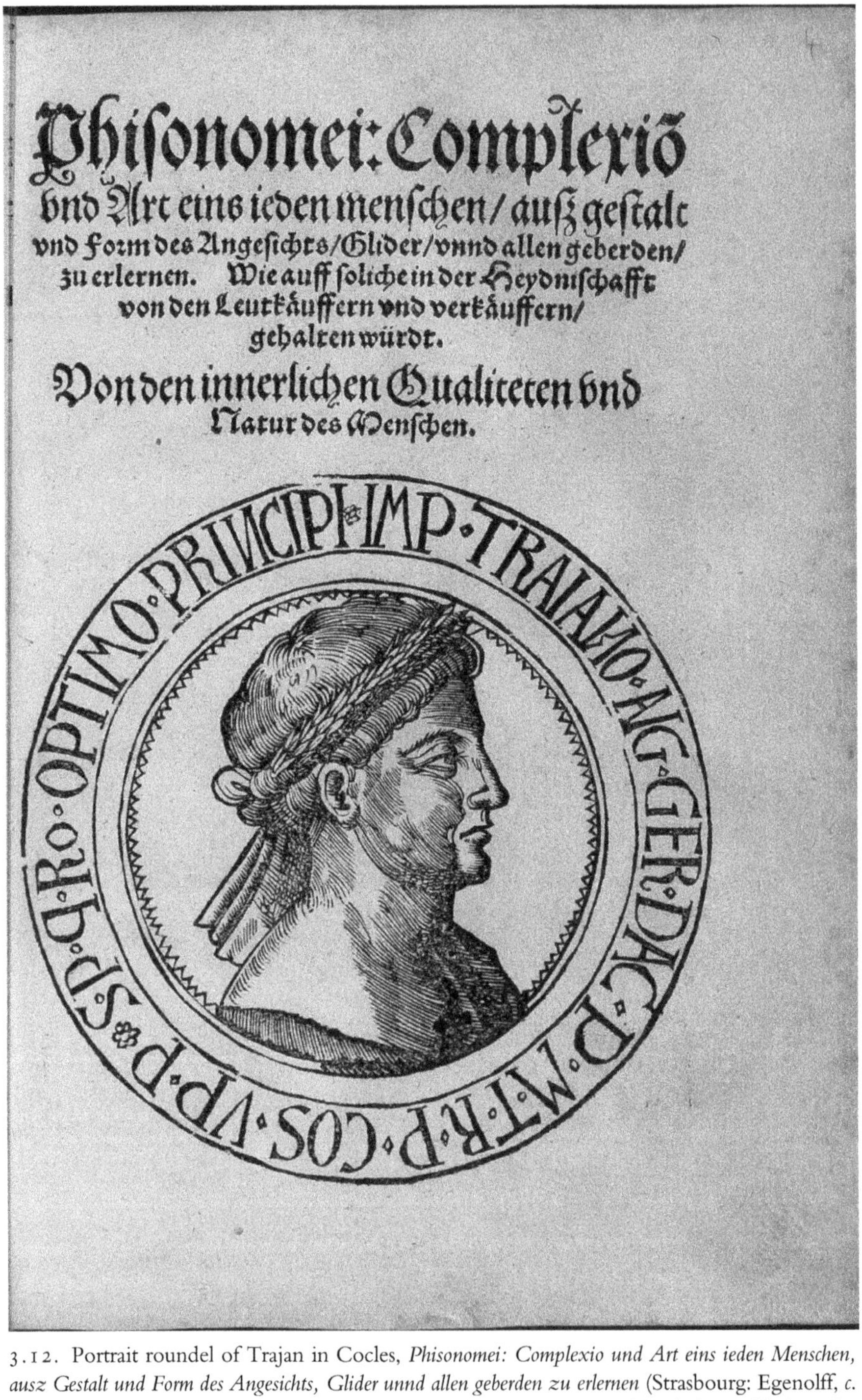

3.12. Portrait roundel of Trajan in Cocles, *Phisonomei: Complexio und Art eins ieden Menschen, ausz Gestalt und Form des Angesichts, Glider unnd allen geberden zu erlernen* (Strasbourg: Egenolff, *c.* 1529), 1r. *Source:* HAB A23.1 Med. 4. Courtesy of Herzog August Bibliothek, Wolfenbüttel.

included an inscription mimicking Roman epigraphy and noting the sitter's title as "best of princes."[77] Bestowed in Pliny the Younger's *Panegyricus*, Trajan's title was officially adopted in AD 115.[78] Conjuring character profiles of famous rulers, the images linked back to the rhetorical tradition out of which physiognomy initially emerged, the *Mirror for Princes* and the *Secretum Secretorum*. Testimonials of character were also presented in printed collections of coins and biographies, the *Bildnisvitienbücher*, whose printers entertained, according to Perkinson, a diversity of mimetic demands depending on their audiences.[79]

The prominence of faces on physiognomies' title pages also seemed a prudent choice for printers given the merging of this tradition with the books' purpose to detect moral character. Portraits of benevolent princes arguably made good headlining images for books about human nature. Or did they? Just a year later, Egenolff reissued his Cocles with the same image but removed the surrounding inscription that identified it as Trajan's profile (Figure 3.13).[80] Just at the time when the work of distinguishing character was being vetted by the printed profile, Egenolff decided against positive identification of his portrait. It appears that specific identities were simply too individualized to be truly useful for the genre's visual strategy. Removing the specific reference to Trajan made more room for text on the title page.[81] But perhaps Egenolff's choice to supply an anonymous identity for the title image was a decision to use a more generic image. The book's mandate to diagnose character might also have made the translation of Trajan into a "type" a more sensible marketing decision as well, since most readers were unlikely to find such a specimen in their midst.

THE PATH TO CHARACTER HEADS

Character heads have a venerable history in the visual tradition of the *Arma Christi*, where disembodied heads symbolized Christ's tormentors in Passion cycles. A variety of human types levitate on a flattened surface behind the altar in depictions of the Mass of St. Gregory, such as the one we see in Israhel van Meckenem's engraving of around 1480–5 (Figure 3.14). Those heads functioned as symbols or even mnemonic devices, images whose intention was to guide the devotee in contemplative but directed meditation on the torments suffered by Christ. Instead of conjuring specific identities, they were meant to be memorable; per Peter Parshall, they were purposely designed to make a striking impression on the viewer.[82] The vernacularization of physiognomy follows a larger trend in printed genres that were developed for the laity in early modernity, beginning with vernacular publications that advertised the sale of indulgences across a vast social spectrum. Such literacy was reinforced by devotional trends in the Lowlands, especially those associated with Geert Grote, whose populist religious movement, the *Devotio Moderna*, increased the

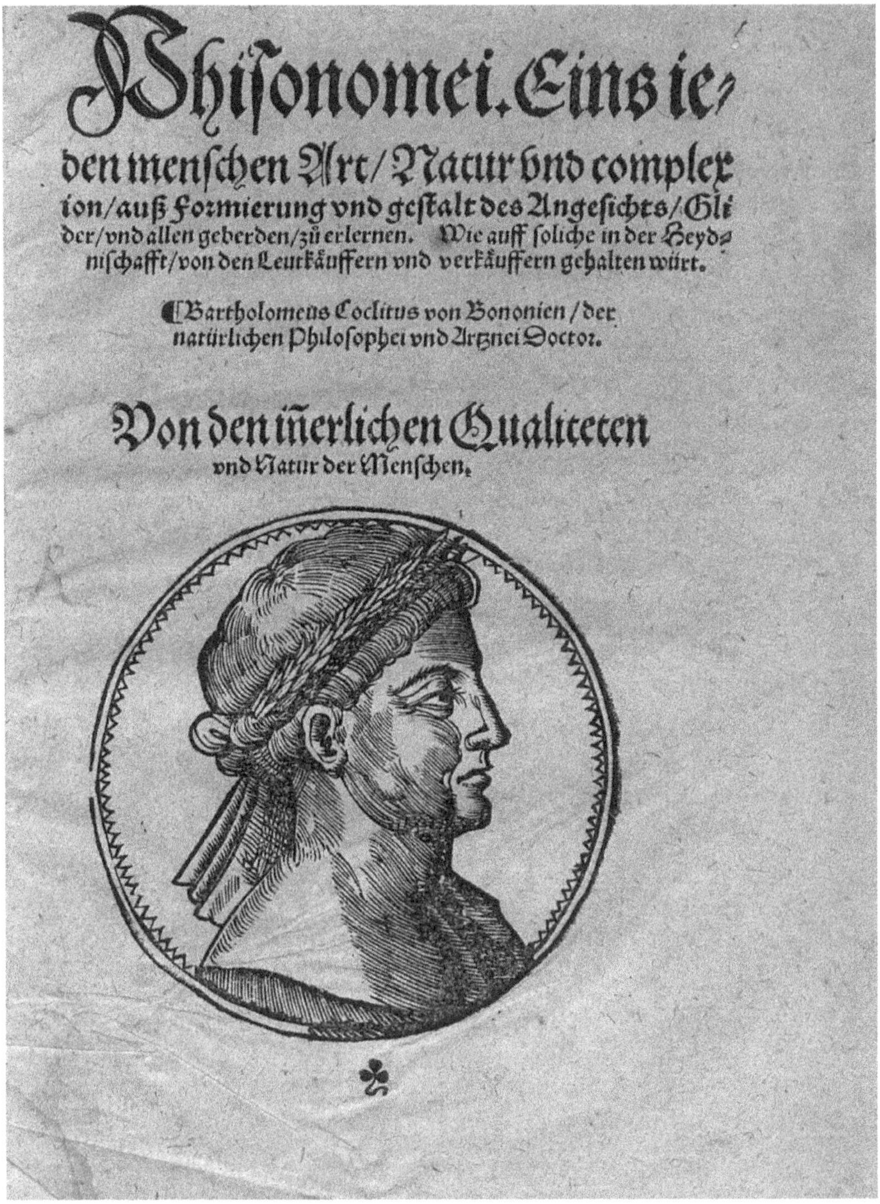
Phisonomei. Eins ie-
den menschen Art/Natur vnd complex-
ion/auß Formierung vnd gestalt des Angesichts/Gli-
der/vnd allen geberden/zů erlernen. Wie auff solche in der Heyd-
nischafft/von den Leutkäuffern vnd verkäuffern gehalten würt.

Bartholomeus Coclitus von Bononien/der
natürlichen Philosophei vnd Artznei Doctor.

Von den iñerlichen Qualiteten
vnd Natur der Menschen.

3.13. Portrait roundel, possibly of Trajan, in Cocles, *Phisonomei: Eins jeden menschen Art* (Strasbourg: Egenolff, 1530), 1r. *Source:* VD16 C4447. Courtesy of Bayerische Staatsbibliothek, Munich. CC BY-NC-SA 4.0.

supply of vernacular devotional texts.[83] In fact, some of the character head images that later graced the pages of physiognomies and *Kunstbücher* might have been suggested by popular devotional imagery, such as the mocking profiles that floated freely with the *Arma Christi* in spare visual stagings of Christ's torment. Such heads have a long history in painted panels and frescos devoted to Christ's Passion.[84] Van Meckenem's engraving reflects just these

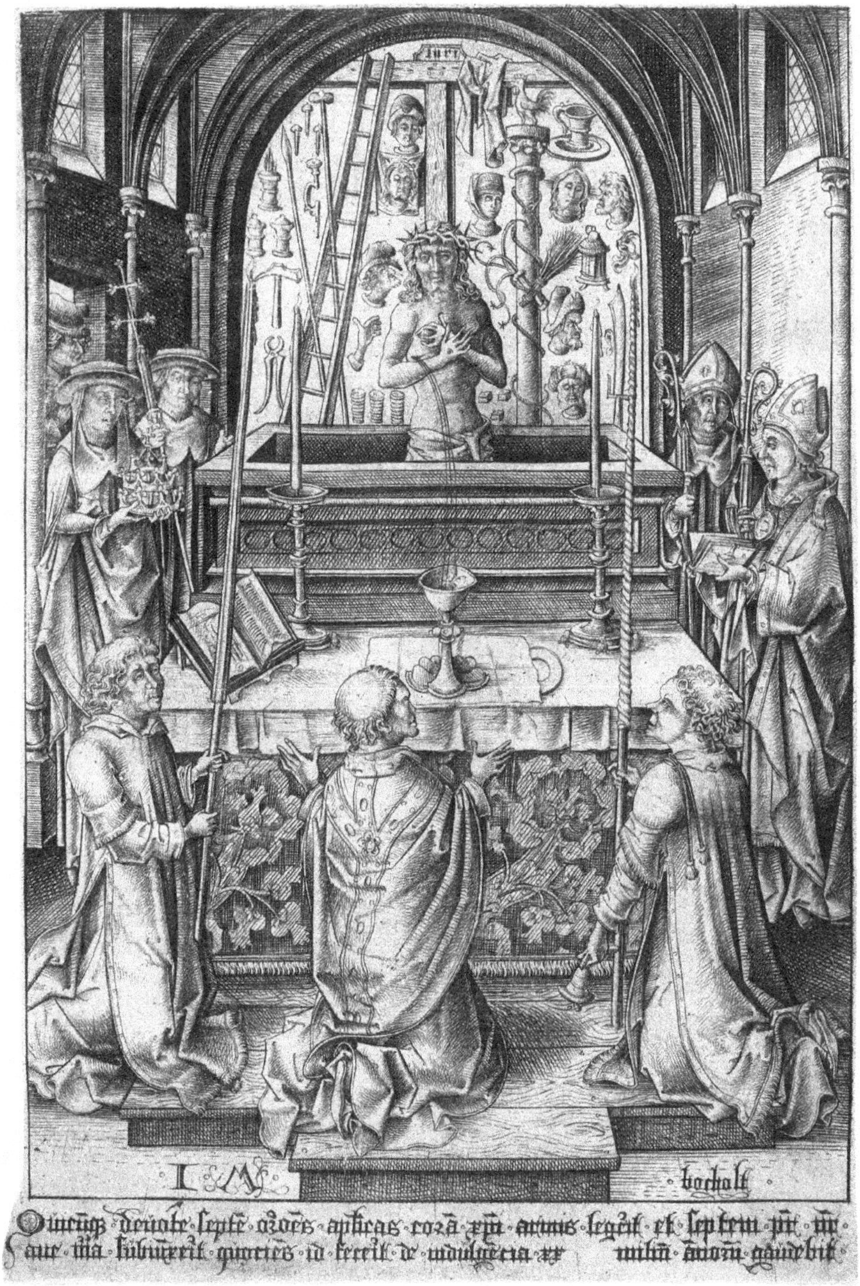

3.14. Israhel van Meckenem, *The Mass of Saint Gregory*, *c.* 1480/85, engraving. *Source:* Rosenwald Collection, 1949.5.75. Courtesy of National Gallery of Art, Washington, DC. Image in the public domain.

types of character heads, showing both secular and profane types across the spectrum of social classes.[85]

Character heads also had the virtue of being non-specific, a quality whose growing usefulness in early modern prints can be observed in other emergent genres, such as printed botanicals.[86] The evolution of images toward this generic quality seems surprising to the modern reader, unless we consider how the shift away from particularity permitted the phytographic searchability of plants in botanical literature. At first, a certain individuality and unswerving naturalism prevailed in printed botanicals, such as we see in the precise descriptions of plants made for Otto Brunfels's *Herbarum Vivae Icones* (printed in Strasbourg by Johannes Schott in 1530) by a protégé of Hans Burgkmair, Hans Weiditz.[87] In 1533, the printer Christian Egenolff, now relocated to Frankfurt, would be sued by his erstwhile Strasbourg colleague Schott for liberally copying a number of Weiditz's prints from the *Herbarum Vivae Icones* for Egenolff's Latin and German editions of *Kreuterbuch* printed between 1530 and 1536. Egenolff had commissioned the text of this *Kreuterbuch* from the naturalist Eucharius Rösslin, who had based his edition on an older text by the Frankfurt city physician Johannes von Cube.[88] Egenolff had in fact ordered new woodblocks to be made from Schott's prints – and while these designs are smaller and appear in reverse in the Rösslin edition, no further effort was made to distinguish them from their prototypes. Why should he tweak the prototypes, Egenolff argued, when Hans Weiditz's originals were perfectly serviceable representations of the plant? Here we see the increasing confidence of recognizable signs to represent the *sine qua non* of their referents. It was exactly this strategy that Egenolff employed when he argued in 1533 before the imperial court, the *Reichskammergericht*, that his "copies" merely represented the true likenesses of the plant and to alter them would be to compromise the truth.[89] We've already caught Egenolff in the act of recycling illustrations for his physiognomies, but this particular borrowing of the plant designs did not prove especially auspicious. Weiditz's illustrations ultimately proved too specific to the specimen to represent a distillation of the essence of the plant, and particularity quickly died out as a stylistic trend for botanicals. This adjustment toward the generic and idealized image would be an important milestone for botanical audiences.

As new parameters for subjects of the natural world rendered by prints were being established, one of the remarkable new developments was a tendency toward generalized representation. Scholars have raised the possibility that naturalistic detail potentially detracted from the perhaps more useful conventional aspects of an illustration – this was especially the case in genres that were honing their user-friendliness.[90] In a host of genres, generalization evolved at the expense of fidelity to a single sample. A botanical printed in 1542 in Basel proved this to be the case. Leonhart Fuchs's *Remarkable Commentaries on the History of Plants* concocted woodcuts of plants posing as "types" to counter a unique moment of excessive particularity in some earlier botanicals.[91] Those images' close attention to naturalism might have captured an authentic portrait of plants, but their particularities (such as Weiditz's withered blooms and worm-eaten leaves) compromised the book's usefulness for amateur scouts wishing to identify a flower in the field. Somewhat ironically, but perhaps more importantly, such specificity was of little use to developing a consensus about what the plant actually looked like. This was a matter of increasing importance to a group of practitioners of the "skill," or art, of botany as a visual, or phytographic, pursuit.[92]

A character head that embodied exactly those non-particular qualities was chosen by the printer and mathematician Peter Apian to set up the problem of understanding cosmography as an act of portraiture in his *Cosmographicus Liber* (see Figure 2.1). Apian might have derived just such a head from representations of the tormentors in the *Arma Christi* or in a physiognomic manual printed in southern Germany – cosmography was making similar claims to diagnoses and empirical experience, so a non-specific sample might have found favor here, following trends in other epistemic genres of the period. In fact, Apian shows in the next frame of his visual proof a particular ear and eye (see Figure 2.2). Apian's distinction between generalized heads and particularized features was a difference that the readers of such publications were increasingly able to spot from their growing familiarity with the physiognomic literature. The German-language physiognomies of the 1520s vet exactly these distinctions between features.

Similar to trends underway in cosmography (see Chapter 2), physiognomy sought to add new visual evidence to the ancient repertoire. Such modifications in the form of contemporary data accompanied a significant turn in the physiognomic literature, updating the old sources with new evidence. This shift in the physiognomic arts spurred actual observation and the inclusion of real-life data; this shift was accompanied by the most significant visual revision of the material into paired groupings of portrait heads, introduced by the early 1520 printed editions authored by the German cleric Johannes Rosenbach, who later took the name Indagine. In doing so, we can say that Indagine empowered his readers to comprehend principles from which further inferences can be drawn, rather than simply recycle ancient citations.[93] Perhaps to accommodate these new facts, Johannes Schott – that same printer who would later sue Egenolff for infringement of his images – framed Indagine's novelties with a new visual apparatus.

Instead of using images to suggest particular likenesses, printers of vernacular physiognomies in the 1520s organized the text into paired facing profiles that asked viewers to scrutinize them strategically. Images accompanying Johannes ab Indagine's *Introductiones Apotelesmaticae* and the German edition *Die Kunst der Chiromantzey* (Figure 3.15) show the stark profiling by way of paired character heads, a visual strategy that seems to have been developed for the purpose of organization. The practice of pairing such character heads, most of which are attributed to Hans Wechtlin, begins with the printings of Indagine's

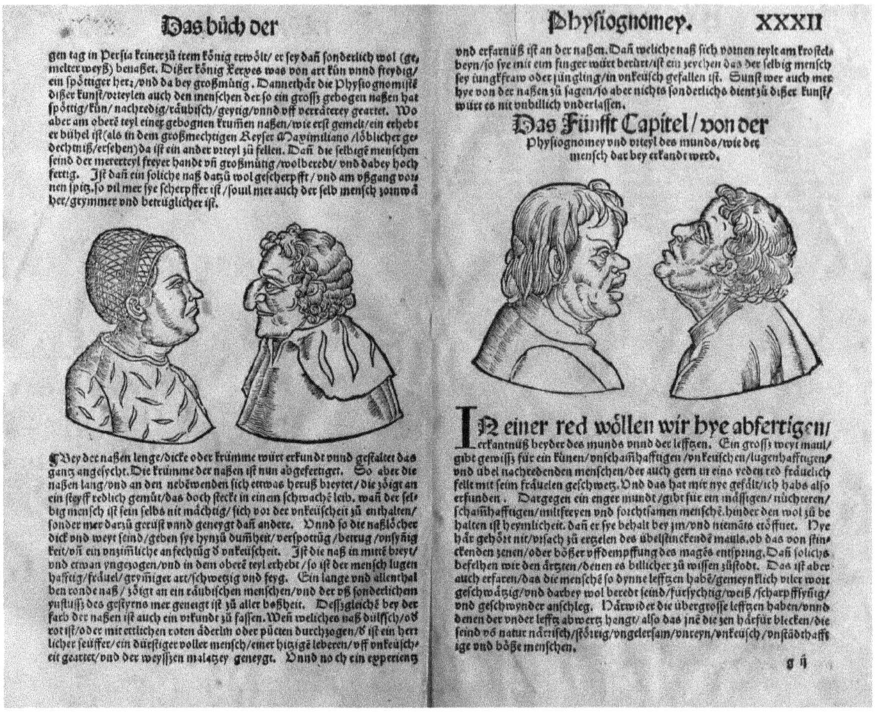

Das buch der

gen tag in Persia keiner zu irem könig erwölt/ er sey dan sonderlich wol (gemelter weyß) benaßet. Dißer könig Xerxes was von art kün vnnd freydig/ ein spöttiger herz/vnd da bey großmütig. Dannethär die Physiognomiste dißer kunst/vrteylen auch den menschen der so ein grossz gebogen naßen hat spöttig/kün/ nachredig/räubisch/geytig/vnnd vff verräterey geartet. Wo aber am oberē teyl einer gebognen krumen naßen/wie erst gemelt/ein erhebter bühel ist(als in dem großmechtigen Keyser Maximiliano /löblicher gedechtniß/ersehen)da ist ein ander vrteyl zü fellen. Dan die selbigē menschen seind der mererteyl freyer handt vn großmütig /wolberedt/ vnd dabey hochfertig. Ist dan ein soliche naß datzü wol gescherpfft / vnd am vßgang vornen spitz.so vil mer sye scherpffer ist /souil mer auch der selb mensch zornwäher/grymmer vnd betrüglicher ist.

¶Bey der naßen lenge/dicke oder krümme würt erkundt vnnd gestaltet das gantz angesycht.Die krümme der naßen ist nun abgefertiget. So aber die naßen lang/vnd an den nebēwenden sich etwas heruß breytet/die zöigt an ein steyff redlich gemüt/das doch steckt in einem schwachē leib. wan der selbig mensch ist sein selbs nit mächtig/ sich vor der vnkeüschent zü enthalten/ sonder mer darzü gerüst vnnd geneygt dan andere. Vnnd so die naßlöcher dick vnd weyt seind/geben sye hynzü dumheit/ verspottūg /betrug /vnsynnigkeit/vn ein vnzimliche anfechtūg d vnkeüscheit. Ist die naß in mittē breyt/ vnd etwan yngezogen/vnd in dem oberē teyl erhebt /so ist der mensch lugenhafftig/fräuel/grymiger art/schwetzig vnd feyg. Ein lange vnd allenthalben ronde naß / zöigt an ein räubischen menschen/vnd der vß sonderlichem ynflüssz des gestyrns mer geneigt ist zü aller boßheit. Desszgleichē bey der farb der naßen ist auch ein vrkundt zü fassen. Wen welicher naß dülfsch/od rot ist/oder mit ettlichen roten äderlin oder pücten durchzogen/d ist ein herrlicher seüffer/ein dürstiger voller mensch/einer hitzigē leberen/ vff vnkeüscheit geartet/vnd der weyssen malatzey geneygt. Vnnd noch ein experientz

Physiognomey. XXXII

vnd erfarnüß ist an der naßen. Dan weliche naß sich vornen teylt am krostelbeyn/so sye mit eim finger würt berürt/ist ein zeychen das der selbig mensch sey iungkfraw oder jüngling/in vnkeüsch gefallen ist. Sunst wer auch mer hye von der naßen zü sagen/so aber nichts sonderlichs dient zü dißer kunst/ würt es nit vnbillich vnderlassen.

Das Fünfft Capitel/von der Physiognomey vnd vrteyl des munds/wie der mensch dat bey erkandt werd.

IN einer red wöllen wir hye abfertigen/ erkantnüß beyder des munds vnnd der lefftzen. Ein grossz weyt maul/ gibt gewissz für ein künen/vnschamhafftigen /vnkeüschen/lugenhafftigen/ vnd übel nachredenden menschen/der auch gern in eins veden red fräuelich felle mit seim fräuelen geschwetz.Vnd das hat mir nye gefält/ich habs also erfunden. Dargegen ein enger mundt /gibt für ein mässigen/ nüchteren/ schamhafftigen/miltfreyen vnd forchtsamen menschē.hinder den wol zü behalten ist heymlicheit. dan er sye behalt bey jm/vnd niemāts eröffnet. Hye här gehört nit/vrsach zü ertzelen des übelstinckendē mauls.ob das von stinckenden zenen/oder bößer vffdempffung des magēs entspring.Dan solichs befelhen wir den ärtzten/denen es billicher zü wissen züstodt. Das ist aber auch erfaren/das die menschē so dynne lefftzen habē/gemeynklich viler wort geschwätzig/vnd darbey wol beredt seind/fürsychtig/weiß /scharpffsynnig/ vnd geschwynder anschleg. Härwider die übergrosse lefftzen haben/vnnd denen der vnder lefftz abwertz hengt/ also das jnē die zen härfür blecken/die seind vō natur närrisch/störrig/vngelersam/vnreyn/vnkeüsch /vnstädthafftige vnd bößē menschen.

g ij

3.15. Hans Wechtlin, pairs of noses and mouths, in Johannes Indagine, *Die Kunst der Chiromantzey … Physiognomey … Natürlichen Astrologey … Complexion eines yegklichen menschens …* (Strasbourg: Johannes Schott, 1523), fols. XXXIv–XXXIIr. *Source:* NLM WZ 240 I38G 152. Courtesy of US National Library of Medicine.

text, engineered by the Strasbourg printer Johannes Schott.[94] The woodcuts loosely follow the prescriptions discussed in the catalogue of features. Notably, these paired heads, with their distinguishing features, reinforce the idea of Indagine's manual as a type of catalogue or field guide, according to Ulrich Reisser, who sees this as the first physiognomy whose illustrations were intended to accompany the visual catalogue of traits described in the text.[95] Indeed, self-conscious reference to the text's images becomes typical in later editions. These generalized heads would come to articulate a *modus operandi* that would prompt readers to observe the images themselves in order to conduct investigations like comparisons.

We see the unequivocal force of such a strategy in a rare, but telling, exception to the rule. In the same way that overly specific illustrations would not survive in the scientific botanical literature, individualized portraits would also fail to do the work that physiognomies were being designed to do. One attempt to include "portraits" in physiognomy surfaced in Utrecht in 1536. Such particularity then immediately slipped quietly beneath the surface, never gaining traction in the physiognomical literature. The visual program of the Dutch-language edition of *Chyromantia* adds two portrait likenesses discussed in the text to the pairing structure.[96] The Utrecht printer Jan Berntsz interrupted the strict formatting by pairs of features to accommodate these specific portraits of Xerxes and Maximilian (Figure 3.16). Included for the purposes of parsing fine distinctions among types of noses, these illustrations endeavored to help differentiate between two examples of a type: the *Habichtsnase*. In cataloging this "hawk's nose," Indagine rehearses the qualities that accompanied it through the profiles of historical figures. For example, the proud, clever, yet blasphemous nature of the Persian king Xerxes was signaled by the hooked nose of his profile (on fol. 31r-v). Indagine's text then proceeds to exonerate the Holy Roman Emperor Maximilian from these same qualities on the grounds that the hook in his aquiline nose was a modified one, the hump being restricted to the upper part. This deviation from the standard *Habichtsnase* accounted for the difference in Maximilian's nature, which, according to Indagine's text, was valorous and generous (31v). This distinction, Berntsz was willing to wager, was one that the vernacular viewer was increasingly equipped to handle. Berntsz had taken readymade images for those two individual "portraits" from a Brabant chronicle printed by Jan van Doesborch in Antwerp in 1530, where they were cribbed from images representing King Louis the Stammerer and Maximilian respectively.[97] The exception to this formulaic structure in the Utrecht printing simply reinforces how standardized the pairing strategy of character heads had become.

Rather than privilege a unified visual program, the Utrecht printer Berntsz sacrificed the traditional formatting to accommodate other images that some complexion books included: profiles, coin portraits, palms for palm reading, zodiac emblems, surgical images, and even images of ancient cosmographers. This pictorial overload challenged the how-to function developing in the physiognomic literature; Berntsz's *Chyromantia* was more a venue for random common-placing of images rather than a collection of prompts for visual comparisons in the field. It was the paired heads of the Indagine and Cocles editions that came to characterize the analytical operation of the physiognomic literature in general, and, as such, they became the visual tools for the practice of physiognomy.

The printing of Indagine's editions represents an overhaul in the physiognomic literature, primarily in how it was updated, illustrated, and packaged. First of all, it was significant that the name of a contemporary authority such as Indagine superseded the old purveyors of diagnostic wisdom. Many physiognomic editions persisted in crediting their contents to Aristotle, Albertus Magnus, Scotus, and Regiomontanus. Indagine had garnered his credibility as a reader of signs by nailing an auspicious date for the imperial election of Charles V on behalf of his patron Albrecht von Brandenburg, then archbishop of Mainz.[98] Thereafter, he adopted the Latinized name *Indagine* (Latin for "investigation" or "sign") to invoke the idea of his book aiding in the

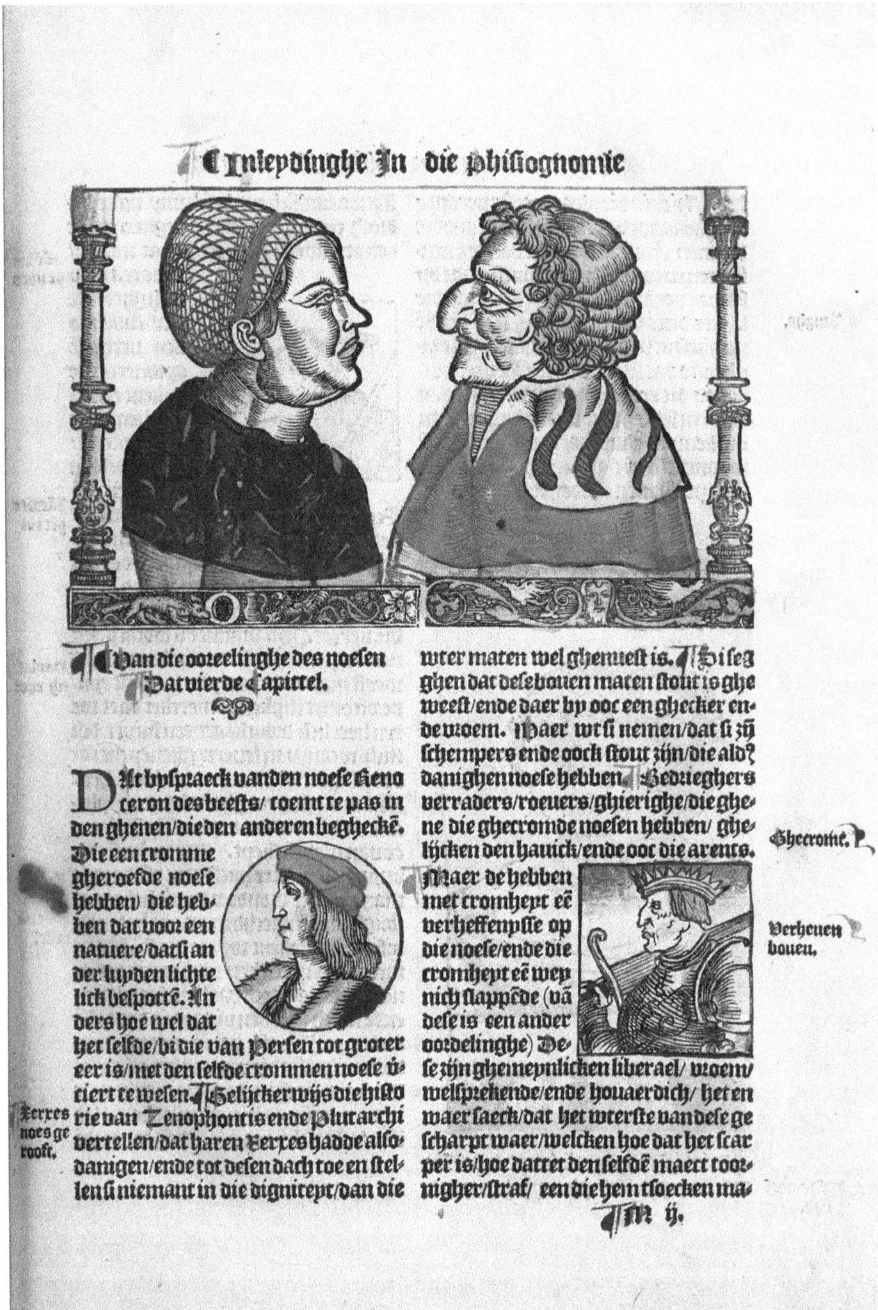

Inleydinghe In die phisiognomie

Van die oordeelinghe des noesen
Dat vierde Capittel.

DAt byspraeck vanden noese Kenoceron des beests/ coemt te pas in den ghenen/ die den anderen beghecke͂. Die een cromme gheroefde noese hebben/ die hebben dat voor een natuere/ dat si ander luyden lichtelick bespotte͂. Anders hoe wel dat het selfde/ bi die van Persen tot groter eer is/ met den selfde crommen noese v̈ciert te wesen. Gelijckerwijs die historie van Zenophontis ende Plutarchi vertellen/ dat haren Xerxes hadde alsodanigen/ ende tot desen dach toe en stellen si niemant in die digniteyt/ dan die

Xerxes noes ghe roost.

uter maten wel ghenuest is. Di segghen dat dese bouen maten stout is ghe weest/ ende daer by ooc een ghecker ende vroem. Maer wt si nemen/ dat si zijn schempers ende ooch stout zijn/ die ald? danighen noese hebben. Bedrieghers verraders/ roeuers/ ghierighe/ die ghene die ghecromde noesen hebben/ ghelijcken den hauick/ ende ooc die arents. Maer de hebben met cromheyt ee͂ verheffenysse op die noese/ ende die cromheyt ee͂ weynich slappe͂de (va͂ dese is een ander oordelinghe) Dese zijn ghemeynlicken liberael/ vroem/ welsprekende/ ende houaerdich/ het en waer saeck/ dat het wterste van dese ghescharpt waer/ welcken hoe dat het scarper is/ hoe datter den selfde͂ maect toornigher/ straf/ een die hem tsoecken ma-

Ghecromt.

Verheuen bouen.

M ij.

3.16. Profiles of Maximilian and Xerxes, in Johannes ab Indagine, *Chyromantia ... Enn dit boec leert van drie naturlike consten als phisiognomia, astrologia naturalis, chiromantia ...* (Utrecht: Jan Berntsz, 1536), 89r. *Source:* NLM ID 2255015R. Courtesy of US National Library of Medicine.

discovery of "signs."[99] Pride in this scheduling serendipity took the form of self-promotion in the front matter of the text: Indagine announced himself prominently on the title page as a priest in Steinheim and deacon of St. Leonhart in Frankfurt, and even commissioned from the local artist Hans Baldung a large portrait of himself clad in decorative damask and set under an arch, just like the author portraits of many contemporary humanists.[100]

Johannes Rosenbach (1467–1537), called Indagine, began his career as a priest in Steinheim near Frankfurt. In 1514, Indagine assisted in the embassy to Rome that would confer the pallium on Albrecht von Brandenburg in his role as archbishop of Magdeburg, who, from 1513, also presided over the bishopric of Halberstadt.[101] Indagine's chiromancy and physiognomy compendium was first published in Strasbourg in 1522 in a Latin large-format folio, *Introductiones Apotelesmaticae elegantes, in Chyromantiam, Physiognomiam, Astrologiam naturalem, Complexiones hominum, Naturas planetarum.*[102] *Apotelesmatiká*, or "effects," is the Greek name that the astrological treatises of Ptolemy carried before they were revised as *Tetrabiblos* in 1535 by Camerarius.[103] Schott printed the first vernacular edition of Indagine in the year following the *Introductiones* under the title *Die Kunst der Chiromantzey ... Physiognomye.*[104] The text received later treatments in Latin, French, and English. The chiromancy compendium consisted of discrete diagnostic texts, among which Indagine seeks to distinguish in the table of contents chiromancy, physiognomy, natural astrology, complexion book, planetary influence, the aspects (or *Angesychten*) of the zodiac signs, and canons by which to determine human illnesses.[105] Woodcuts attributed to Hans Wechtlin guide the reader throughout.[106]

While Indagine credits many of the classical sources he excerpted for his complexion books, such as Albertus Magnus and Scotus, he adds his own material, and, perhaps more importantly, he calls attention to his abridgments. He frequently curtailed discussion of features unproductive for sustained physiognomic assessment, such as the chin.[107] Contradicting Indagine's no-confidence vote in the diagnostic usefulness of the chin, however, the printer Schott overrode the author and developed two images for the chin section anyway. Such visual decisions seem even to challenge the caveat against placing too much emphasis on a single trait, as lodged by Aristotle, confirmed by Scotus, and by this point enshrined in the prefaces of most physiognomic material. This "sum of parts" doctrine is even contradicted by the organization of the text, which called attention to individual features.[108] In light of this, Schott's decision to pictorialize these characteristics suggests that a parallel purpose for the text is being engineered by its printer: to put the heterogeneous collection of aphorisms into a searchable order. Illustrations increased the user-friendliness of the text and encouraged new cognitive skills: they spurred the reader to search for specimens in the field, and pictures provided the tools to do this. These visual aids opened up new cognitive strategies for the practitioner.

FACIAL INDEX: VISUAL COMPARISONS OF FACES

Printers of physiognomies between 1530 and the 1550s followed Schott's and Wechtlin's format in organizing their material into paired profiles. Illustrated with twenty-two character heads disposed as pairs, Indagine's edition shows the transformation of the physiognomy from texts associated with complexion books that merely summed up moral characteristics into manuals shot through with "facial images." Some of these images attempt to show a contrast, others simply amplify negative characteristics established in the text. Without being able to detect a single unambiguous strategy, one could say that perhaps the most important development is that the text becomes searchable by images. The images index traits – importantly, mostly facial ones. Despite some lingering references in chapter 15 to non-facial features, such as "stomach, back, shins and feet," none of these are illustrated. Faces became the indexical mainstay of Wechtlin's physiognomic illustrations.

Without turning his woodcuts into likenesses of individuals, Hans Wechtlin paid close attention to facial features, taking care to mark distinctions between them. For instance, in the fourth chapter, which describes the shapes of noses (see Figure 3.15), two profiles face off toward each other. The left profile shows a slim and upturned nose (which loosely follows the text's linking of long noses to candid natures), while the right profile shows a bulbous and hooked nose, which corresponds to the description of a man with a "long and altogether round nose with a thieving nature ... if the nose is red in color, with red veins or pockmarked, this is the mark of an extreme drunkard with a hot liver, given to bouts of unchaste behavior and predisposed to leprosy" (31v). These are not portraits per se but instead do duty as generalized likenesses. Indeed, it is not exactly clear which characteristics can be pinned on the man with the cap and the thin nose. While the man with the bulbous nose can indeed be matched with several of the text's damning descriptions, in other cases there is no careful or close correlation between the images and the features described. The illustrations seek to suggest differences in profiles generally, rather than to tag them to specific traits. While Indagine's text sometimes expresses skepticism about physiognomy's capacity to determine character traits with any degree of reliability, the images clearly have their own visual agenda and *modus operandi*.

Although printed physiognomies are often believed to be the ancestors of volumes meant to diagnose morals, their more important contribution lies in supplying the means for viewers to make visual decisions about features of faces through their illustrations.[109] They also challenge the idea of the retreat of judicial astrology into the realm of private arcana.[110] As they entered the province of how-to literature, physiognomies promised to help sum up character by the inspection of appearances, and thus assisted in the development of visual acuity. From their front matter, we can detect these volumes' intention not only to instill confidence in the value of visual inspections, but also increasingly to hone visual acuity in those observations.

The insistent advertisement of such skills of discernment in later editions reflects efforts by printers to manage visual practices from their print shops. Specialized terminology developed to distinguish among modes of visual inquiry. For example, Schott's first vernacular edition of Indagine's *Die Kunst der Chiromanzey* (printed in Strasbourg in 1523) introduced the book on physiognomy thus: *Physiognomey, ußz anblick des menschens*, or "Physiognomy, from the appearance of a person."[111] In redactions of this material printed after 1523, Schott expanded the compendium of physiognomy, chiromancy, and natural astrology by bundling it with other related diagnostic texts, such as a manual of field surgery. On the strength of a kindred pictorial program he developed for them, we can say that Schott hoped to entice readers via the new modes of analysis that his illustrations offered.

Such pictures were analytical tools that increasingly shaped the knowledge conveyed. In the title page of such a diagnostic compendium he printed in 1540 of various how-to manuals in which physiognomy was included, Schott used both the words "*Anblick*" and "*Augenschein*" to try to distinguish between two distinct modes of visual inquiry: "The fifth Book: called *Physiognomia*, provides for 'investigation' of man's nature by both the '*Augenschein*, or scrutiny that carries evidentiary claims;' and the '*Anblick*, or sight or appearance' of a person."[112] Schott deployed images strategically and self-consciously to help readers hone the skill of performing visual assessments. *Anblick* and *Augenschein* signal two different modes of visual perception: *Anblick* to cue sight and *Augenschein*, detailed scrutiny that intensified the initial observation. The physiognomy reinforced this instruction by planting visual prompts in the text. Pairs of profiles set side by side provided two poles between which to capture sights, or *Anblicke*. Once captured, the viewer could perform the closer investigation implied by *Augenschein*.

Indagine occasionally invokes eyewitnessing as a practical skill, one already being vetted in his physiognomy via the illustrations. The text presents itself as a handbook to guide observations, so that other inferences can be made from deciphering appearances. It suggests tips by which the reader, specifically constituted as an observer, can, for example, detect cholerics by the appearance of their hair: "By contrast, we scrutinize with our eyes [*sehen wir augenschynlich*] that cholerics, because of their heat and burning moisture, have thick and coarse hair."[113] That deference to the development of useful skills can be seen throughout this physiognomy – it calls attention to the value of visual scrutiny. We have already encountered this term in the zodiac man labeled "*Augenschinliche Anatomie*," and it also appears in artists' manuals of the period. But *Augenschein* also refers to judicial inspection, *richtlicher Augenschein*, where it comes to assume the burden of proof in evidence. It is exactly at this moment, shortly after the establishment of the imperial court, the *Reichskammergericht*, in 1495, that the term *Augenschein* comes to refer to a particular mode of cartographic rendering that carried evidentiary claims before the judicial body; Daniel Kaune locates this mode of certification in hand-drawn maps, known as *Augenschein*, which assume unique representational guarantees in the settling of border disputes.[114]

Indagine's use of the term *Augenschein* also connects it to evidentiary knowledge, or knowledge gained by empirical investigation. The words that proliferate in these texts point us to visual distinctions that their users are growing adept at making; I would argue that this emerges as an outgrowth of the pictorial discernment that the repertoire of physiognomic images fostered. Physiognomy borrowed some of its precepts from the other diagnostic genres with which it was grouped. The examination of hands in chiromancy or foreheads in metoscopy were related forms of scrutiny that paved the foundation for newly honed visual judgments.

The physiognomer's art of observation, as constituted by Schott's images, prompted close examination of features and visual acuity. In this, the printer likely follows Indagine's assumptions about the degree of familiarity with the results of a hypothetical tactile experiment that is *visualized* and expects the reader to process that visually: "and further *experience* and *knowledge* can be derived from the [investigation of] the nose. The nose which divides in the front at the septum as if touched by a finger is a sign of a maiden or youth who has become unchaste."[115]

Indagine cites two modes of epistemic data gathering – experience and knowledge – as well as the resultant cognitive distinctions that would obtain from such an exercise in close looking.[116] For example, inspection of the nose offered both experience (*experientz*) and knowledge (*erfarnüß*).[117] Proceeding through Indagine's series of visualizations, the observer could achieve recognition and experience in sharpening visual skills. Rendered in German as *Experientz*, with its Latin root in *experientia*, this refers to practical demonstration. While this word surfaced in the *Practica* genre as well, here it also recalls the skill set of artisans, who would be able to parse such distinctions.[118] Such references to practical knowledge are reprised elsewhere in the text: "it is also experienced [*erfahren*] that people with thin lips are garrulous, cautious, wise, ingenious, and quicker."[119] Indagine also announces general knowledge that will obtain from the book – "Of the physiognomy and judgment of the mouth, how a person can be recognized [*erkannt*] by this" – employing the term *Kenntnis*, or knowledge. We also learn that its discussion will "dispatch knowledge [*erkantnüß*] of the mouth and the lips."[120]

The distinction between knowledge derived from experience and from tradition is made unequivocal in Indagine's omissions. Much of the cleric's true innovation lodges in what Indagine chooses to excise from his predecessors' analyses. For example, at the end of the judgment on noses, we read: "There would be more to say here on the topic of noses, but since none of it would particularly benefit this skill [of judging observed noses], it is omitted, not unreasonably."[121] What the author likely omitted was a catalogue of diagnoses collected from the older received tradition, for instance the type of data summaries that were common in natural histories and etymologies. Indagine decided not to print diagnoses that he likely found specious, or at the very least not supported by visually verifiable evidence. The point of Indagine's guidebook, after all, was not to rehearse a litany of facts from tradition, but to frame the material via his own experience to help readers develop practical visual skills.

PRACTICAL PHYSIOGNOMY

The expansion of a reading public for such diagnostic material, from primarily esoteric to more popular audiences, is part of a larger trend in the early modern press to cultivate new readers. Physiognomy's shift away from *Secreti* proper in the mid-sixteenth century and toward practical applications may have been anticipated in some of Schott's earlier publications. The artist of the *Chiromancy* compendium, Hans Wechtlin, had already been commissioned by Schott to illustrate a folio-sized edition of Hans von Gersdorff's *Manual of Field Surgery* in 1517. This book would remain a staple of Schott's list and underwent revisions over several decades.[122] By 1528, Schott decided to repackage Gersdorff's manual for field surgeons into a more overtly useful volume by issuing it in a quarto-sized edition. He drew attention to the field guide's usefulness in the preface of that edition, touting the volume as easily searchable, portable, handy, and one in which desired information appeared "right before the eyes."[123] The text went through a variety of smaller-sized printings before being reissued as a folio again in 1540.[124]

Schott recycled Gersdorff's work again when he introduced a reprint of the Indagine compendium along with the *Feldbuch* in 1540, this time as a folio-sized publication.[125] Perhaps the similarity of the two books' visual program was what inspired Schott to combine them. Both shared a common designer in Hans Wechtlin, but the two volumes were likely bundled on the strength of their kindred epistemic concerns. As a publisher, Schott sought to capture a corner of the market through the quality of his illustrations; for example, he also hired the painter and printmaker Hans Baldung to provide additional artwork for the Indagine edition, including the book's introductory author portrait.[126] Perhaps it was the publisher who instigated the cult of personality around his authors: Schott was instrumental in bringing together various humanists and important figures of the Protestant reform movement.[127]

Schott also articulated a new artistic level for his images: he was the first printer in Strasbourg to seek tonal woodcuts for his books.[128] The inks used in these books matched those used by both Baldung and Wechtlin in their color woodcuts, according to a technical analysis by Alice Klein; scholarship on Wechtlin asserts a pivotal role for the printer Schott in disseminating knowledge of this technology in Strasbourg.[129] Schott's promotion of these two artists might have inspired him to print Gersdorff and Indagine together in a single volume. The stylistic similarity of Wechtlin's images recommended such a decision, as well as the ways in which these two editions relied on images to carry the epistemological armature of the text.

The anthology was likely masterminded by Schott himself, who saw a benefit in printing together kindred types of how-to publications – indeed, two kinds of "field books." Gersdorff's practical volume had been designed to assist barber surgeons performing live battle wound operations. Because Schott had also designed Indagine's volume with similar experiential goals in mind, both books were already driven by their visual didactics and must have paired well together in the publisher's opinion. In this volume, the contributions are announced as: "Field guide to battle injuries together with many surgical instruments: rendered after Albucasi; Chiromancy of Johannes Indagine: this is the art of observing hands." In the German moniker *Handtbesehung* (hand inspection), the idea of observation is implicit. The table of contents continues with:

> Natural Astrology: [information derived] from the true path of the sun; Physiognomy: how to derive man's natural tendencies from an examination of the face and limbs; and Complexion Book: how to recognize man's nature from the planets and through the location of the constellations at the time of his birth; and lastly, Canons: or Rules to precisely ascertain each sickness, in addition to how and what medication to use.[130]

Chiefly uniting these pursuits was the texts' collective tendency toward pictorialization, bringing together the various forms of visual knowledge already assembled in earlier editions of both Hans von Gersdorff and Johannes Indagine. Indeed, the texts counsel in different disciplines: while the illustrations of surgical instruments and stagings of wound repairs were of a different order from the physiognomic faces, there is an important similarity in their approach to visual epistemology.

The kinship that Schott forged between these two texts was amplified by the book's organization by Wechlin's images. The new title developed for the compilation authorized the images: Schott announces the fact that the instruments depicted in Gersdorff practical manual were "conterfeyted" from, or produced after, images transmitted from the eleventh-century Andalusian surgeon Albucasi, or Al-Zahrawi.[131] Thus, the claim about the authoritative nature of certain images was already advertised in the book's title page, as was their recommended use as visual prompts to observation in the field.

ARTISTS' PHYSIOGNOMIES

Just as German physiognomies of the 1520s to 1550s began to collect representations of faces, physiognomy became a field of visual knowledge around which faces collected. Artists' interest in exploring facial variety seems to coincide with the proliferation of physiognomic texts on the book market. Draftsmen such as Leonardo da Vinci and Albrecht Dürer incorporated distinctions and characters discussed into their own physiognomic sketching. Leonardo was making physiognomic studies that were comparative in nature, frequently pairing contrasting profiles. His efforts were once interpreted as merely representing classical rhetorical tropes of opposition, such as studies in antithesis known in Latin as *contrapositum*.[132] But scholars are now convinced that his inspiration to make these came in equal measure from his familiarity with both physiognomic texts and artistic manuals.[133] Leonardo's drawing of physiognomic types *c.* 1493, *A Man Tricked by Gypsies (Five Grotesque Heads)*, has prompted readings from scholars who see humoral types embedded in the characters – based either on Leonardo's encounter with itinerant populations or on printed physiognomies, and possibly on both.[134]

Contemporary printings of physiognomies in Italy might have exerted a visual pull on Leonardo, even if he dismissed the merits of their textual analyses.[135] Leonardo went on record as extremely skeptical about physiognomy's value as a science, condemning the "chimeras . . . of false physiognomy and chiromancy."[136] Yet even as he condemned the misuse of these diagnostic arts, he was clearly mesmerized by the range of faces they suggested to an artist. Why else would he have collected several chiromantic texts from the early 1490s onward?[137] We know that a copy of Aldobrandino da Siena's unillustrated *Philosomia degli uomini* (with editions published in Florence in 1491 and Venice in 1500) sat on his shelf.[138] Leonardo might have also been familiar with a manual for sculptors that included a chapter on physiognomy, Pomponio Gaurico's *De Sculptura* (Florence, 1504).[139] Artistic manuals and physiognomy also seemed related to several Strasbourg printers, who, from 1603 on, routinely packaged Indagine's chiromancy together with Pomponio Gaurico's artistic treatises.[140] The two later physiognomies Leonardo acquired were likely illustrated.[141] Illustrated physiognomies probably shored up Leonardo's conviction about the contrastive potential of physiognomic analysis on which some of his drawings rely.

Leonardo's *A Man Tricked by Gypsies* explores facial variety and perhaps the spectrum of types discussed in chiromantic texts. Interestingly, some of

Leonardo's grotesque studies of the 1490s, as well as ones inspired by Leonardo but attributed to his pupil Francesco Melzi, seem to emphasize comparative groupings.[142] Leonardo's *Libro di pittura* included sketches of ten types of noses. Later recensions of the *Libro* included a passage on how to commit them to memory; this passage made it into the abridged *Trattato* (although the images did not).[143] In the context of the *Trattato*, Leonardo proposed to investigate physiognomies for the "movements of the mind" under the rubric of *moti mentali*.

Leonardo saw physiognomic scrutiny as critical to the artistic process, even if he discredited the idea of physiognomy as a systematic science. Leonardo's aim, according to Michael Kwakkelstein, was to limit his "theoretical concern with physiognomics to the particularization of facial types ... [as] an *aide-mémoire* for remembering the shapes of faces."[144] Leonardo may have been experimenting visually with material that he read about in physiognomic texts; they certainly would have given him fodder for considering facial extremes, a subject by which he was intrigued. Interestingly for our purposes, he entreats artists to "observe" when considering these elements in his instructional manuals.[145] In "On the Human Body," a treatise planned *c.* 1489, Leonardo proposed to describe a "fully grown man and woman, with their proportions, and the nature of their complexions, color, and physiognomy ... then, in four drawings, [to] represent four universal conditions of men."[146] Such willingness to explore the canon shows his engagement with the idea of prototypes in his formulations of human identity.[147]

Albrecht Dürer likewise made many sketches that explored physiognomic variety before formalizing some of these in *Four Books on Human Proportion*, a manual printed after his death in 1528. In 1513, he produced a view of four profiles in a drawing preserved today in the Nelson-Atkins Museum of Art in Kansas City, Missouri.[148] Such comparative ideas about human variety developed here would surface again later in his manual of proportion studies, in which he presented systematic studies of a variety of profiles in gridded boxes. In these grids, Dürer attempted to develop precise techniques for how proportions and ratios could control the expression of such differences.

Several of Dürer's drawings made between 1510 and 1515 show successive studies of heads, presented either individually or in sets of three, four, or ten; many appear on pages that include other studies, notably those of drapery.[149] These individual drawings can now be considered a group representing Dürer's technical and thematic interests from 1513 to 1520. Dürer frequently worked comparatively, sometimes juxtaposing opposites and often contemplating faces in relation to each other. Dürer enunciates comparatism as a mode of investigation in the Berlin drawing of *Ten Profiles and Drapery* (*c.* 1513) (Figure 3.17), where he again investigates facial variety. The head on the far right starts the progression; the remainder of the heads were sketched in at a

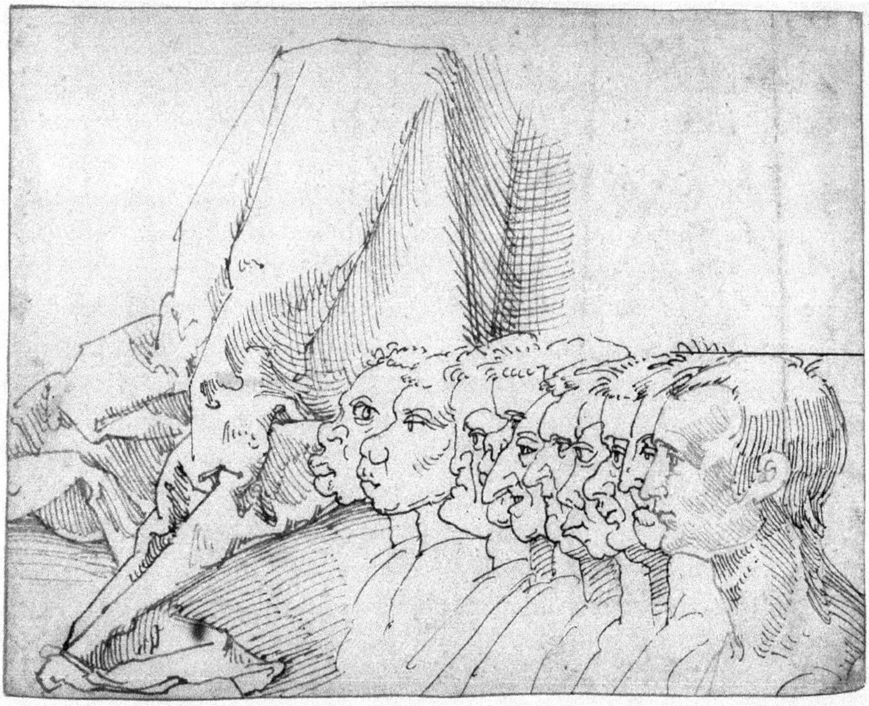

3.17. Albrecht Dürer, *Ten Profiles and Drapery*, c. 1513, brown ink on paper, 10.3 cm × 13.1 cm. *Source:* Inv. nr. 43. Courtesy of Staatliche Museen zu Berlin, Kupferstichkabinett / Jörg P. Anders. Image in the public domain.

later date and in a different medium. The nine remaining heads develop the theme of the first and express distortions from the baseline of the initial profile.[150] Dürer records how the shapes of noses vary in relation to the drape of the chins. We cannot imagine sitters for this sketch; the variety on display here emerges from Dürer's tweaks to the baseline of his starting profile. He pushes and pulls on the parameters established by the right-hand head. Dürer's imagination flourishes around the theme of the profile. As a finishing touch, the observant eye of the last figure's profile stares back to the beginning, or at us, the viewer. With this narrative accent and comment on observation, Dürer takes this study beyond a technical exercise and confirms his belief in the expressive potential of physiognomy, as well as its potential for intelligence – as the critical eye of the African man's profile suggests.[151] Such experiments probably ultimately led Dürer to abandon his pursuit of the ideal in favor of a variety of types; here, he celebrates the variety of the heads. Set together, they provide a reflection on the manifold types of human nature that comprise an ever-expanding society.

What was the purpose of such a drawing? Perhaps Dürer's profile sketches were studies made with the intent to formally instruct other artisans, a type of artists' manual.[152] Already around 1508, Dürer previewed plans for an artists' manual in a rough draft for a book he intended to call "*Die Speis der Malerknaben*." In 1513, Dürer was working on such a manual that could help artists create proportional studies and vary them. *Ein Unterricht alle Mass zu ändern* was never printed but its themes were reprised in his later proportion studies.[153] Changes in proportions were to be executed between the poles of *antithetische Begriffspaare*, or paired opposites. In the *Aesthetic Excursus*, Dürer calls paired opposites *Contraria, Variabeln*, or *Relationen* and labels them *klein/lang; kurz/breit; schmal/dick*.[154] During this period, Dürer developed a parallel interest in systematizing the study of faces for instruction. In 1514, he produces an unembellished physiognomic study of his mother, whose coolly objective nature Fedja Anzelewsky maintains ran like a concurrent strain next to his later attempts to classify the human visage.[155] Dürer's later thrust toward idealization and adjustments of proportion – one might even say taxonomy – would manifest itself in the *Vier Bücher von menschlicher Proportion*, the book in which he charted the ratio and proportion of all parts of the body.

Was Dürer simply processing the physiognomic variety on offer? Or do these early studies forecast his later, more instructional imagery? In 1512, he began the highly geometric studies of the body (of which the Dresden Sketchbook harbors the majority), whose resolution we ultimately see in his posthumous *Four Books on Human Proportion*.[156] Dürer's interest in technical manuals such as Pomponio Gaurico's *De Sculptura* is plain, as well as his curiosity about geometry, which can be seen in some of the volumes we know he owned, such as the edition of Euclid's *Elements* that he purchased in 1507 in Venice.[157] His acquisition of ten volumes "useful to the artists' trade" from the library of Willibald Pirckheimer and Regiomontanus in 1523 demonstrates Dürer's longstanding commitment to gathering theoretical and practical literature to inform his scholarly endeavors.[158]

No doubt Dürer sought out these geometry and sculpture manuals in preparation for his anticipated technical publications, as well as the ones that actually were published, including the *Four Books on Human Proportion* (*Vier Bücher von menschlicher Proportion*), in which he ultimately abandoned a search for the ideal human form in favor of a celebration of its diversity. Dürer's interest in the dialogue between human proportions and physiognomic variety on exhibit in this book seeks a systematization of types that Leonardo never sought to formalize. These types of noses and faces of varying proportions that he offered in gridded formats in the *Four Books* create a rational basis for this experimental science through a systematic visual apparatus.[159] The contrastive potential of his profile series of drawings anticipates this apparatus. The features of the profiles in the *Four Books* (Figure 3.18) vary with the height of the horizontal bars. Adjusting the bars stretches the shape of the nose, resulting in a systematic method of creating variety. These illustrations continue his earlier pursuit of the expressive potential of physiognomy begun in the *Ten Heads*, but

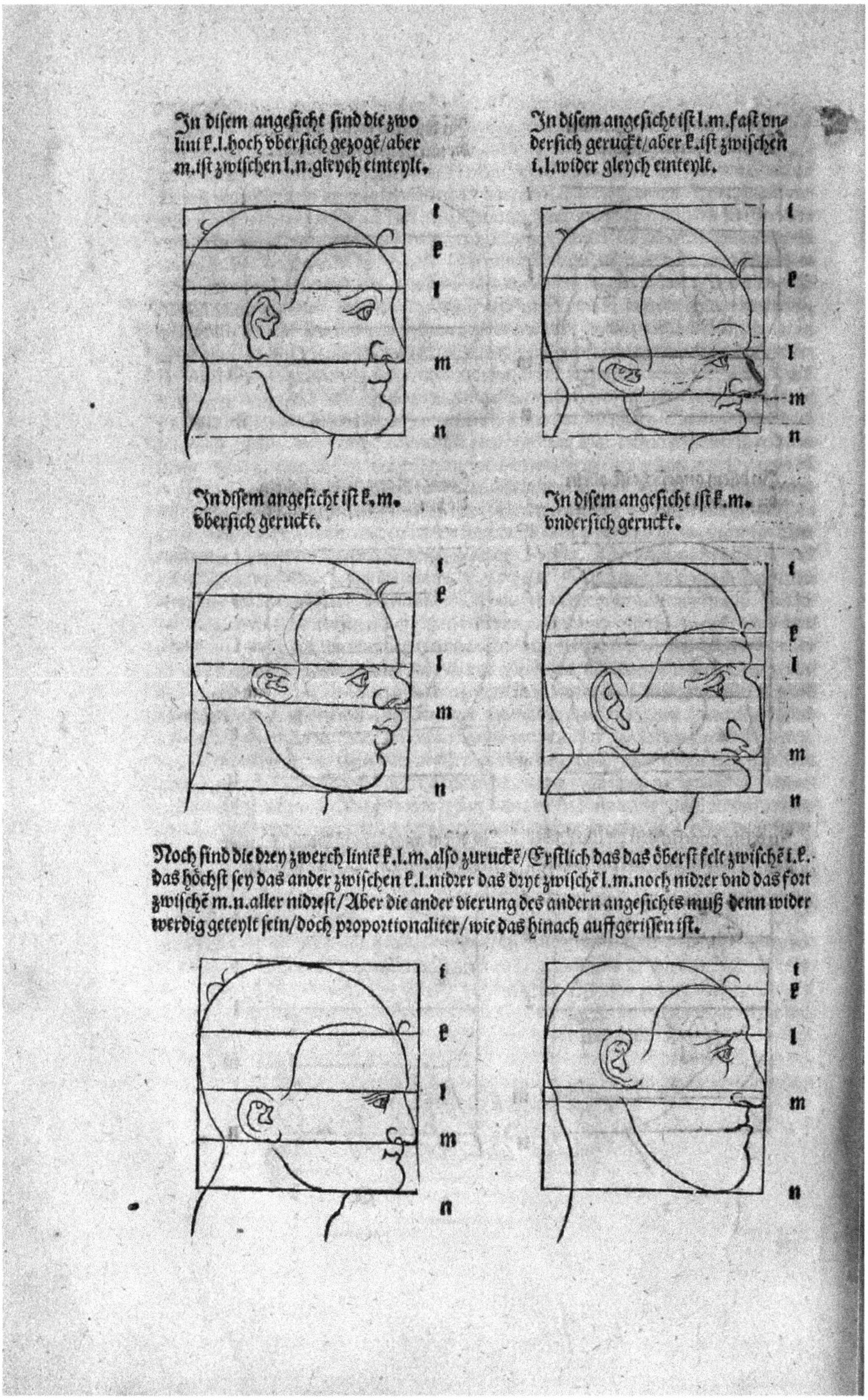

3.18. Albrecht Dürer, six physiognomic heads in *Vier Bücher von menschlicher Proportion* (Nuremberg: Hieronymus Andrea, 1528; Agnes Dürer, 1532 and 1534). *Source:* Courtesy of National Gallery of Art, Washington, DC.

here Dürer shows how to create this difference artificially. The physiognomic difference explored in Dürer's grids, or *Maßteilen*, even though they are bereft of a moral message, resonate with the types of variety presented in contemporary physiognomic publications. The formal layout of the illustrations in physiognomy manuals paralleled the look of Dürer's studies.

Dürer's studies of human proportion run parallel to contemporary thinking about differences in human nature. Character differences in early modernity were believed to have emerged from bodily fluids, or humors. Humoral theory, which guided medicinal practice, measured the fluids that determined human complexion. Dürer's creations engaged with humoral theory in a variety of ways in the early decades of the sixteenth century. The delicate balance of humors that Dürer might have suggested by way of the animals poised on the threshold between the pre- and the postlapsarian world in the *Fall of Man* (1504) is dismantled by the unleashed temperaments of his later study of complexion, *Melencolia I*, in an engraving from 1514 (Figure 3.19). According to Michael Roth, the ideas of perfection embodied in proportion that preoccupied Dürer in his renderings of Adam and Eve in the *Fall of Man* would later give way to considerations of variety and difference in types, temperaments, complexion, and character.[160] While Erwin Panofsky suspected that Dürer was informed by complexion literature in his composition of *Melencolia I*, we know less about whether Dürer's engraved *Melencolia* was received in this tradition.[161] Tracking *Melencolia*'s influence by and ripple through the complexion and calendar traditions might help us connect the dots between two distinct modes of visual knowledge that have rarely spoken to each other in the secondary literature: fine art and the vernacular press. Did Dürer's engraving have any meaningful connection to complexion literature?

Integrating older pictorial traditions of representations of complexions with new allegorical and narrative characterizations of abstract ideas was one of Dürer's particular skills, and some examples are on view in his *Meisterstiche*, a set of master engravings produced *c.* 1514. *Melencolia I* (Figure 3.19) merged several traditions related both to astrology (the influence of Saturn) and the liberal arts (geometry). A byproduct of these new threads was a more intimate and complex view of human interiority.

Elements of Dürer's *Melencolia* appear in a calendar and physiognomy edition printed by Ludwig Dietz in Rostock in 1523, *Der schapherders Kalender.*[162] The astronomer, or geometer, who appears on the title page shares the robe and dividers with Dürer's winged figure (Figure 3.20).[163] On folio 69, we again see echoes of Dürer's *Melencolia* in a despondent figure with a distaff at the left, pictured here with other stock manifestations of this complexion type (Figure 3.21). Evidently, the designer of this print scavenged Dürer's *Melencolia I* for a variety of types that could be relevant to the almanac literature.

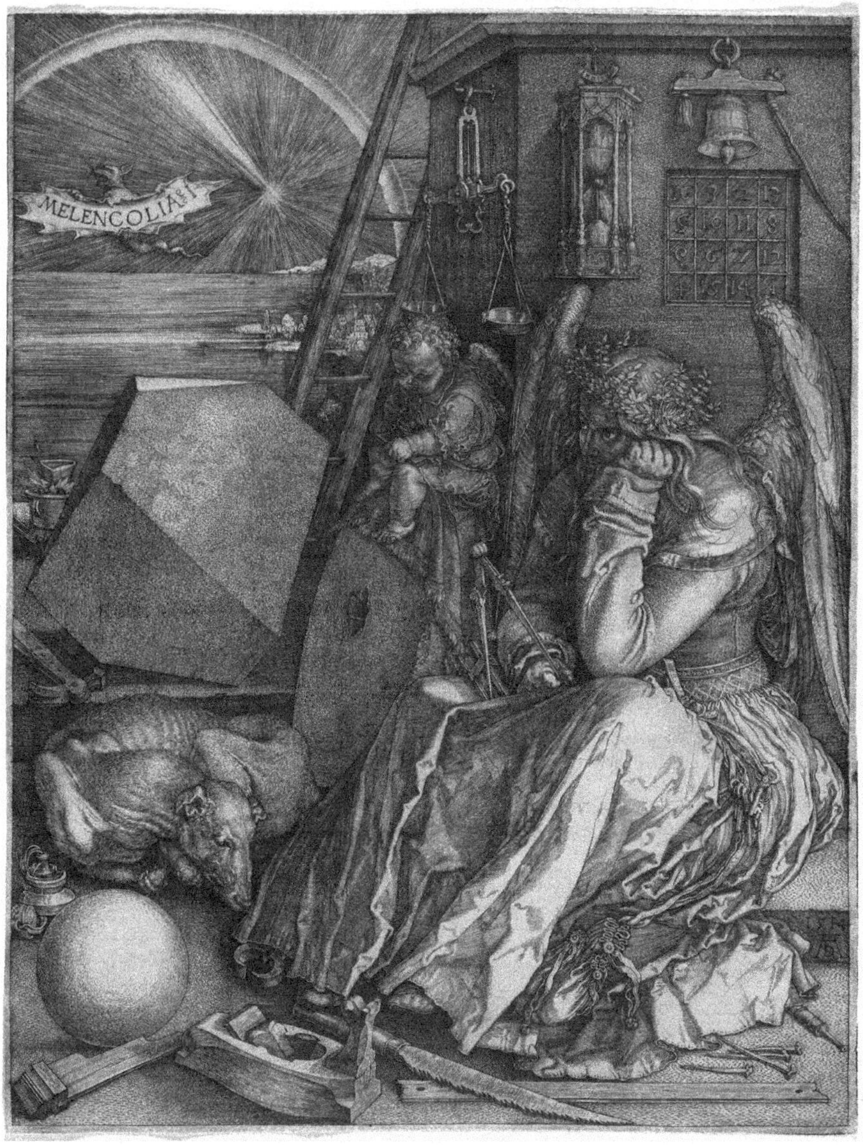

3.19. Albrecht Dürer, *Melencolia I*, 1514, engraving, 24 cm × 19.2 cm. *Source:* Acc. 1949.1.17. Courtesy of National Gallery of Art, Washington, DC.

But Dürer's *Melencolia* itself descends from image types that appeared in earlier printings of complexion and calendar literature. Images of stock types of sanguines and melancholics headline sections of physiognomy, complexion, and calendar publications. In such *Practica*, images of complexion types appeared in sections that organized monthly activities, often alongside guidelines about auspicious times to undertake ablutions, cupping, and venesection. The Rostock *Shepherd's Calendar* itself was issued with the Cocles edition, *Kleyne Physonomye*. These books provided related material. Calendars, as we

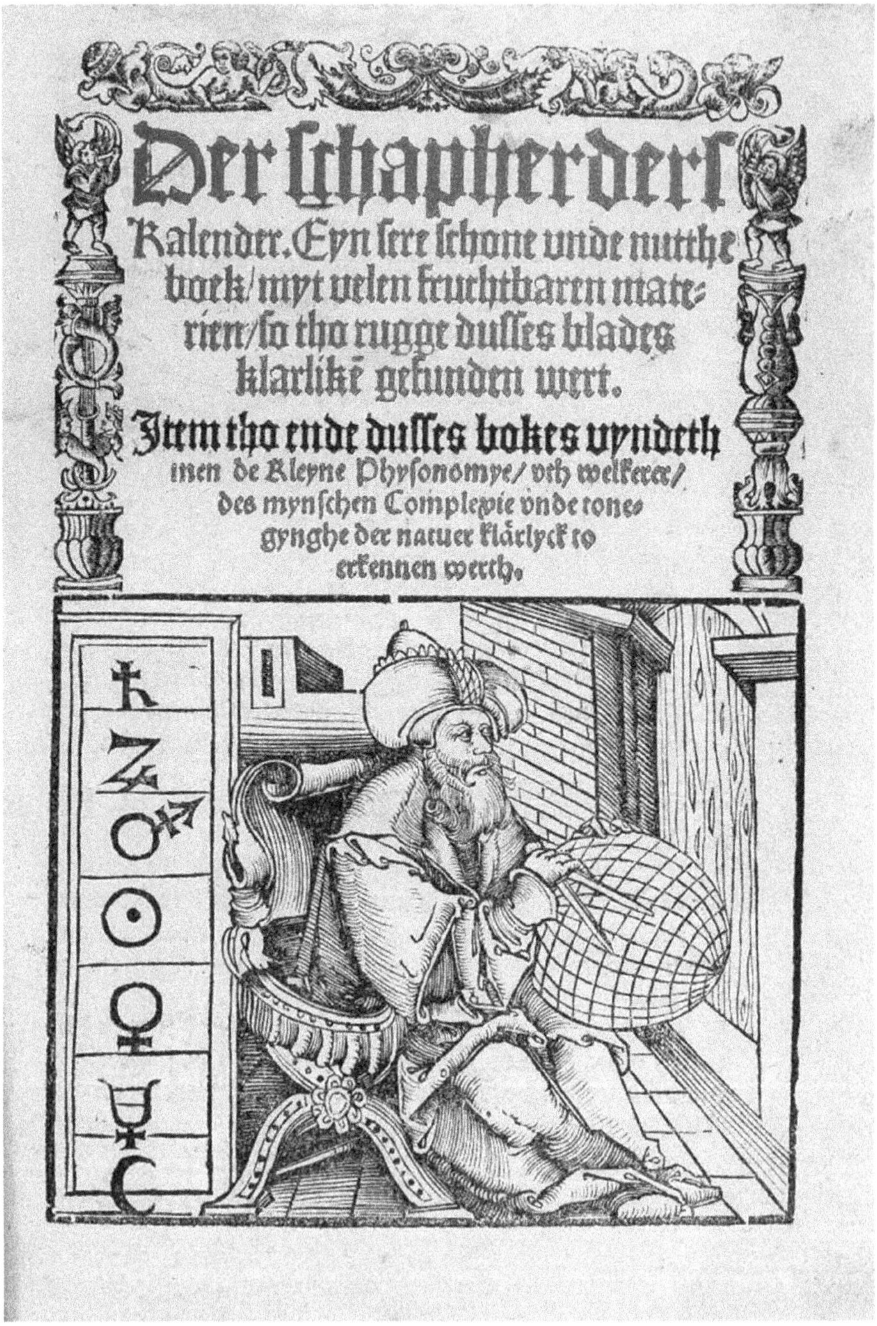

3.20. *Der schapherders || Kalender. Eyn sere schone vnde nutthe || boek* (Rostock: Ludwig Dietz, 1523), 1r. *Source:* HAB A36 Astron. Courtesy of Herzog August Bibliothek, Wolfenbüttel.

have seen, were flush with prescriptions about when and how to bathe depending on complexion.[164] Dürer's own depiction of bathers, *Das Männerbad*, a woodcut of 1496–7, may very likely have reflected on humoral types, and it may reveal Dürer's own perusal of calendar publications.

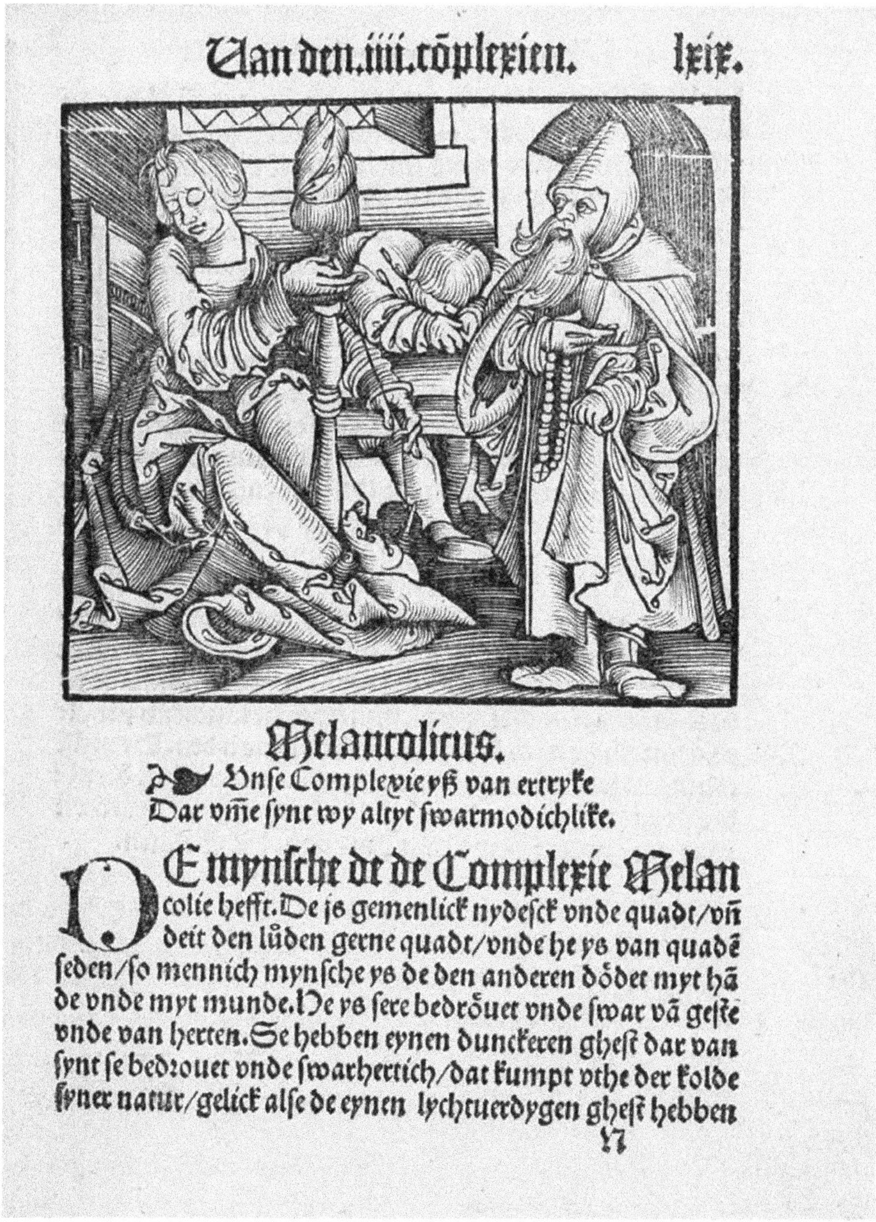

3.21. *Der schapherders || Kalender. Eyn sere schone vnde nutthe || boek* (Rostock: Ludwig Dietz, 1523), 69r. *Source:* HAB A36 Astron. Courtesy of Herzog August Bibliothek, Wolfenbüttel.

Such borrowings from Dürer that surface in the Rostock *Shepherd's Calendar* strengthen the idea that publishers of vernacular *Practica* literature saw their concerns reflected in his engraving and were eager to begin a dialogue with it. Dürer's visual thinking about character types and physiognomy is therefore exactly contemporary with the slate of complexion publications that instructed their buyers to detect signs of humoral balances in the faces of their neighbors.

Dürer's *Melencolia* sought to express more than just an exemplar of a humoral type with excess of black gall; she is an individual broken off from type, and a monumental exploration of complex human emotions that included frailty and fragility. Dürer's digression on melancholy pushes back against the oversimplified readings of human nature on offer in the physiognomic texts.[165] Still, this visual essay on the darker movements of the mind was at least in part in dialogue with the kinds of speculation about human nature that were active in the physiognomic literature. In the spirit of epistemic invention, Dürer routed his knowledge of the *Practica* literature through his own experience, turning a discourse on humors into a visual essay that broached the idea of human complexity and even possibly self-portraiture.

In the *Four Books on Human Proportion*, Dürer sought to distill active ideas about physiognomy into their proportional analogues – and, importantly, in the form of faces whose differences Dürer intended other artists to mine for their own constructions. It might also be worth exploring Dürer's own experience with the growing how-to literature, which we know he sought out and in whose lineage he certainly intended to publish his proportion studies, the treatise on measurement, and the *Four Books on Human Proportion.*[166] Perhaps it was his engagement with Leonardo as well as his knowledge of complexion literature that eroded his confidence in the ideal and "balanced" humoral complexions set forth in his 1504 engraving of the *Fall of Man.* After all, physiognomic variety as a subject of artistic investigation was celebrated in classical literature: Pliny's *Natural History* proclaimed Apelles as a great physiognomist.[167] Although the connection between the artists' shared gift for faces was not expressly drawn, the mantle of Apelles was bestowed on Dürer by Conrad Celtis as early as 1500.[168] Erasmus later repeated the compliment in *Dialogus de recta latini* ... in 1528, as would Philip Melanchthon.[169] Dürer was indeed refining skill sets in physiognomy that matched Apelles's renown. Dürer was also cognizant of making his mark in portraiture, shaping his self-portrait in the image of Christ at exactly this point in his career.[170] As he matured as an artist, Dürer would shift his interests away from the pursuit of the ideal and toward offering a range of bodily forms that would be more useful to the practical objectives of the artist's trade.[171] Perhaps the designation as a second Apelles spurred Dürer both to make contributions to the field of physiognomy and also to participate in the didactic aspects of practical how-to literature.

The extent to which Dürer would later aim to codify and taxonomize facial expressions and types (perhaps one a function of the other) *c.* 1525 is an opportunity to bring into focus yet another genre with which he was grappling: the how-to book. In his physiognomic grids, Dürer attempted to make sense of human diversity so that it could be reproduced by the next generation of artists. He did this in several ways. One task was to quantify diversity as a series of types, but he also saw in this a technical directive: how to measure that diversity and to prepare that data for transfer. For Dürer, donning the mantle of Apelles also meant preserving ancient know-how of proportions, perspectives, and ratios. At the same time, it also meant combining this traditional and theoretical approach with an emphasis on art's practical application.

In 1512, Dürer was already bemoaning the loss of skill that had animated the great artists of antiquity as exemplified by Phidias, Praxiteles, and Apelles. It was the destruction and suppression of their writings that barred the transfer of their achievements to posterity.[172] Dürer asserts himself as the conduit of their tradition to modern artists, borrowing the language of praxis and theory from Ghiberti, who in turn borrowed it from Vitruvius.[173] Mourning the collective loss of artistic knowledge of the past inspired him to write about technique. Based on the content of his own work and that of the technical manuals he planned to author, we can detect a motivation to school the autodidact. Acknowledging Dürer's contributions to how-to instruction, fellow Nuremberg publisher Walter Ryff would praise him for his vernacular contributions to the mathematical and mechanical arts.[174] Dürer was clearly adopting the procedural approach of technical texts; he combined theoretical precepts with the search for practical knowledge. His later theoretical treatises formalize lessons learned from publications that included calendar, complexion, geometry, and physiognomy.

In addition to the instructional use of facial images in print, another purpose that accrued to them was their function as a visual record of collected faces. This was especially true of artist-entrepreneurs such as Heinrich Vogtherr (1490–1556). A painter, printer, and amateur ophthalmologist active in Augsburg and Strasbourg, Vogtherr published one work that capitalized on the repertoire of facial images to which he had been exposed as an artist.

Inflected by Dürer's theoretical treatises, Vogtherr's artists' manual *Ein frembds und wunerbars Kunstbüchlin alln Molern, Bild/ schnitzern, Goldschmieden, Steinmetzen, Schreinern/ Platnern, Waffen und Messerschmiden hochnutzlich/ zu gebrauchen* ... of 1537–8 promoted the usefulness of his images, as well as their variety.[175] A "high degree of usefulness" was touted in the *Kunstbüchlin*'s title, a publisher's enticement to the buyer that followed the precepts of other how-to manuals in a printing ambient flush with them. The scholarly preface makes grand claims that pictures can substitute for experience – Vogtherr directly targets here an audience of artists whose responsibilities at home made travel impractical, also possibly alluding to the increasing difficulty of financing *Wanderjahre* in areas where waves of iconoclastic agitation were siphoning off commissions.[176] But the promises of utility from Vogtherr's preface were also guaranteed by his own experience printing practical publications. By the late 1530s, Vogtherr had issued a number of *Kunstbücher*, including ones on sundials, anatomy, and various curative *Practica*. In almost all his prefaces to these works, Vogtherr asserts their utility to the buyer of his publications.[177]

Surely overstated were such claims for all but the most intrepid of amateur eye doctors in Vogtherr's *Ein newes hochnutzlichs Büchlin von Erkantnüs der Kranckeyten der Augen sampt einer Figur oder Anothomia eines Augs*; appearing in Strasbourg in 1538, this was the first vernacular pamphlet on ophthalmology.[178] The making of this manual of optical diagrams and curative recipes, which included an image of an eye labeled *Anatomia Oculi*, no doubt sensitized Vogtherr to the idea of presenting visual processes.[179] Vogtherr's booklet calls attention to images of the eye as pedagogical tools for learning about the eye's illnesses. He reanimates this organ as a pedagogical tool when he focuses an image of himself around his own eye, portraying himself as an artful looker in a woodcut he used as a printer's colophon in several of his manuals. That same self-portrait appears again on the title page of Vogtherr's aforementioned artists' manual, *Ein frembds und wunderbars Kunstbüchlin*, where he is now accompanied by his son (Figure 3.22). On the title page, the two artists announce themselves with white-line portraits that identify them unequivocally as the book's producers. Such portraits of book printers are rare paratextual elements for publications of this period. The father, Heinrich the Elder, marked with the date and his age of forty-seven years, peers out of the frame. He addresses his audience with a look reminiscent of the close peering that his contemporary Hans Baldung also undertook in his portraits: for example, that of Indagine in the *Chyromantia*, Otto Brunfels, Caspar Hedio, and even a self-portrait. Enquiring eyes seem to pop out of portraits fashioned in Strasbourg in the same period as if to assert their sitters' credentials as observers.

In the artists' model book whose cover these peering eyes grace, Vogtherr suggests in as many words that close observation of his own motifs can substitute for empirical experience. This claim challenged the reader to see in the printer's images the potential for a new cognitive vista (Figure 3.23). What kinds of audience sought out the experiential horizon that such illustrations afforded? While clearly of interest to artists, Vogtherr pitched the *copia*, or variety, of his content broadly enough to attract any buyers interested in positioning themselves as observers. It was surely Vogtherr's promises of the virtual visual experience that propelled such volumes onto the shelves of humanists such as Beatus Rhenanus, who collected this volume as well as Vogtherr's ophthalmology manual, alongside cartographic publications related to Vespucci's discoveries in the Americas.[180] Other humanists, such as Willibald Pirckheimer, a close associate of Dürer's, had also scoured the Regiomontanus-Walther library for books pertaining to the artist's trade.[181] What these books had in common was their commitment to firsthand experience. Book owners such as Rhenanus and Pirckheimer were not aspiring artists, but they believed that artists' manuals could expand their experiential horizons. Artists' manuals offered visual variety and ersatz experience. Along with shin guards, headdresses, and designs for furniture, a sea of faces peered

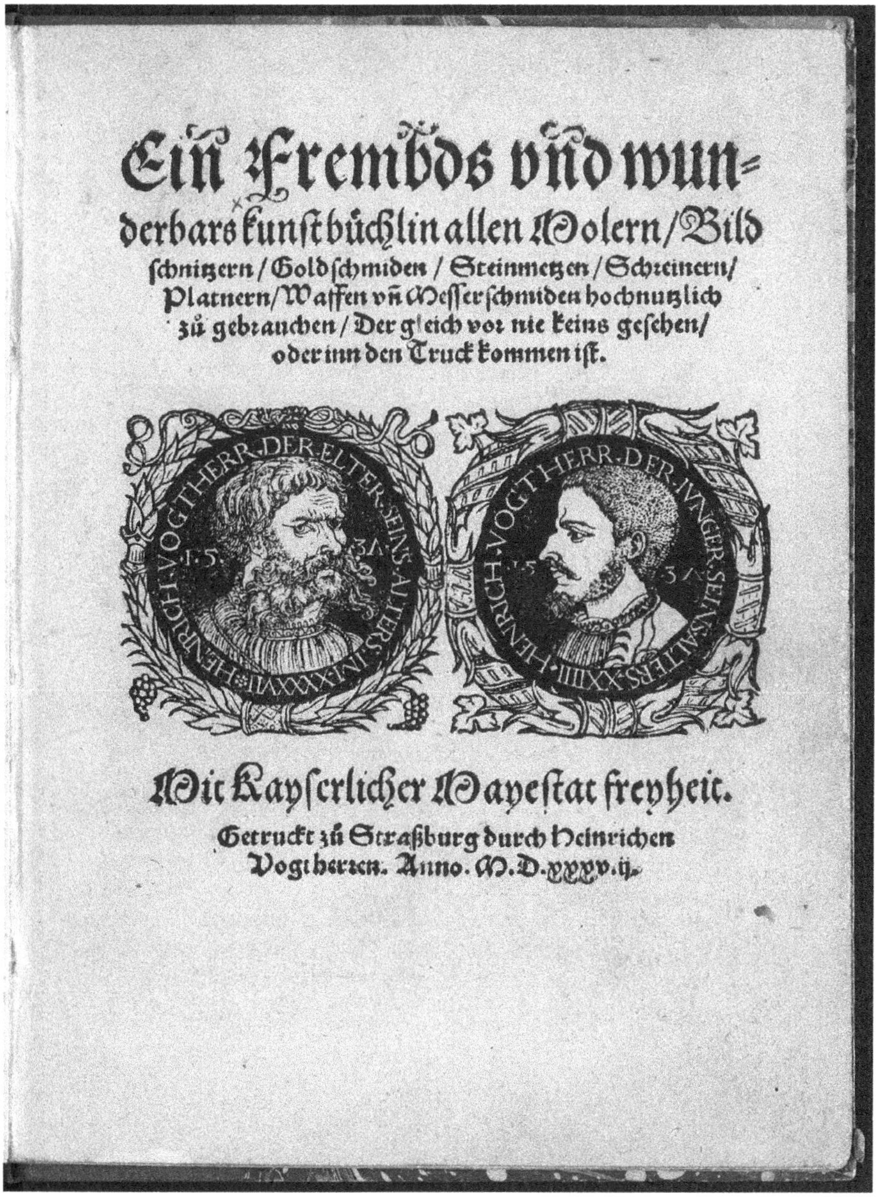

3.22. Portraits of the printers, Heinrich Vogtherr, *Ein frembds und wunderbars Kunstbüchlin allen Molern / Bildschnitzern / Goldschmiden / Steinmetzen / Schreinern / Platnern / Waffen un Messerschmiden hochnutzlich zu gebrauchen* (Strasbourg: Vogtherr, 1537), sig. 15/157. *Source:* Courtesy of Universitätsbibliothek Johann Christian Senckenberg, Frankfurt.

out of twelve pages of Vogtherr's volume. The facial variety on display here advertised the epistemic operation of the *Kunstbuch* generally. The diminishing relevance of text in such art primers, as we see in other *Kunstbücher* issued in the same period by Erhard Schön, Sebald Beham, and Jost Amman, serves as proof that the new cognitive skills being peddled by printers skewed toward the

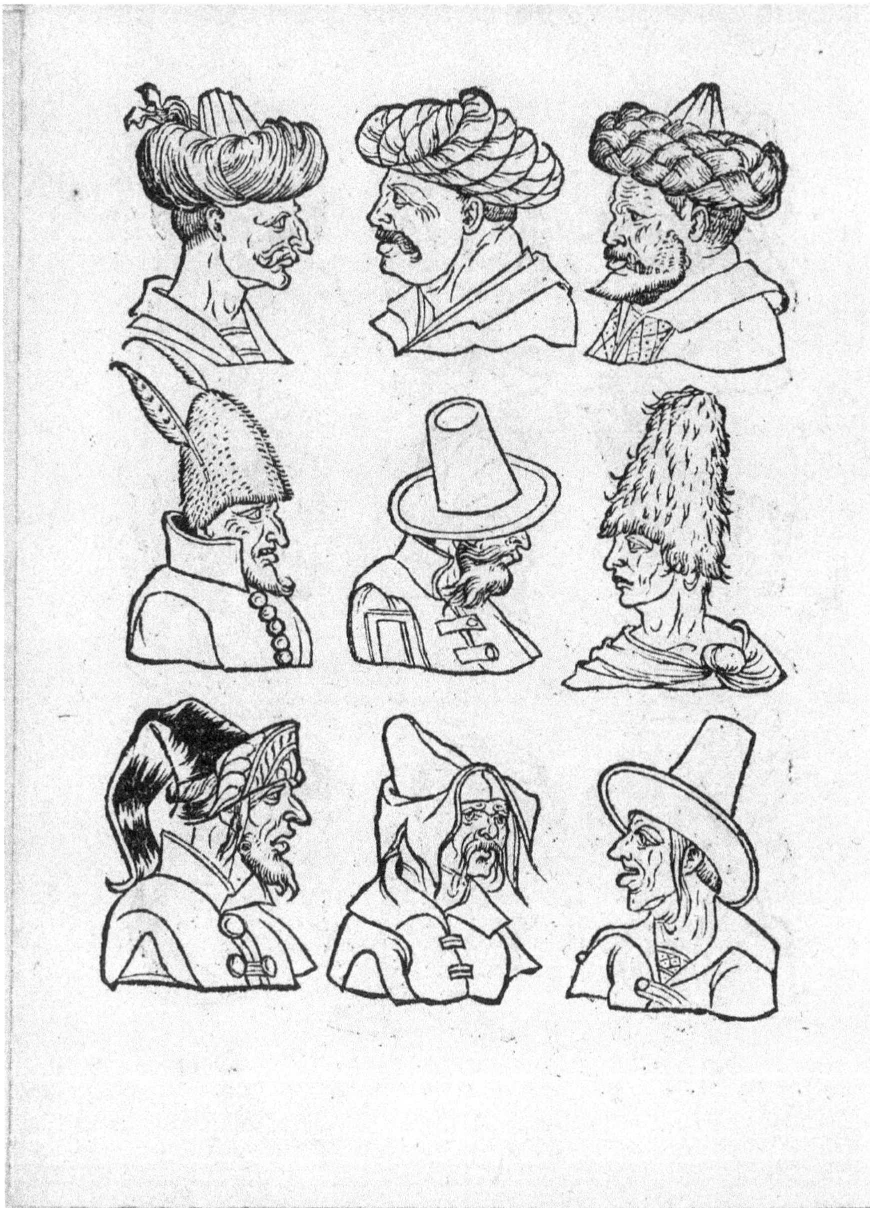

3.23. Male heads in Heinrich Vogtherr, *Ein frembds und wunderbars Kunstbüchlin allen Malern, Bild/ schnitzern, Goldschmieden, Steinmetzen, Schreinern/ Platnern, Waffen und Messerschmiden hochnutzlich/ zu gebrauchen* … (Strasbourg: H. Vogtherr, 1538), sig. 15/157. *Source:* Courtesy of Universitätsbibliothek Johann Christian Senckenberg, Frankfurt.

visual. Foremost in these books' interpretive epistemologies was the charge to the reader to make sense of the content through dynamic looking.[182]

That Vogtherr's profusion of heads intersects with the public's growing visual acuity with physiognomy was not simply coincidental. An array of male heads appears with distinct hats and headdresses, some explicitly intended to recall the physiognomy of Ottoman rulers. Heads are presented in a variety of views: profiles, three-quarter views, and some from rather unorthodox angles. Vogtherr's audiences were less interested in the precise moral qualities of these faces' identities than in the quiddity of their variety. Nevertheless, their pictures were clearly in dialogue with physiognomic abundance. Vogtherr's precedents and the contemporary valence of *copia*, as well as the artist's role in producing it, have been explored by Jaya Remond.[183] Vogtherr's publications that sourced images in Netherlandish paintings, prints, and ancient coins attempted to turn a profit during a particularly parched season for artists in a market of diminishing resources. During the Reformation, the art market was not only imperiled by evaporating commissions but also threatened by iconoclastic firebrands. Fear of a disappearing artistic legacy may also have animated the need for a book that could claim not only to produce ersatz observations, but also to collect objects that captured past achievements in art's history.

Also important was the role of the physiognomy in establishing facial aptitude of a general kind for artists and facial literacy for observers. The idea of many of these publications was to expand facial literacy, rather than aiming for precise diagnosis or positive identification – an echo of what Maria Loh has concretized as the pursuit of *faciality* in much Renaissance portrait production.[184] The printing of physiognomies dovetailed with a tradition of picturing faces such as those in Vogtherr's *Kunstbüchlin* and the repertoire of types that developed around it. Variety and human diversity were becoming ever more apparent from the many genres of circulating books: travel, costumes, and books about the customs and habits of nations.[185] Such books, in addition to the many physiognomies whose character busts derive from the Indagine and Cocles editions, essentially establish a collection of recognizable heads. The pictured heads that Vogtherr adds to this repertoire introduces to a wider audience visual material sourced from a range of media. Vogtherr's practical collecting of "sourced" visual material could also be a driving force behind the visual programs of physiognomic literature of the late sixteenth century, such as Giambattista Della Porta's *Of Human Physiognomy*, for example, whose purposes begin to shift away from diagnostics of moral character and toward the accumulation of images.

The pedagogical direction of early modern physiognomy was ultimately determined by the tradition of picturing that developed around it. By the 1550s, images of faces had thoroughly rewired their text's content away from the character diagnosis that had underwritten the classical tradition of *Secrets*. The illustrative program of physiognomies printed between the 1520s and 1540s in Strasbourg seems indeed frenetic – often to the point of jeopardizing the texts' coherence. The "complexion" part of the text of the 1540 *Phisionomi und Chiromanci*, as well as the title and closing pages, seems now to be arbitrarily, and perhaps even gratuitously, illustrated with faces.[186] Adorning the last page of the volume (Figure 3.24) are sets of faces excerpted from the text's interior. These later physiognomies assembled visual images in arrangements similar to those of a *Kunstbuch*.

Meanwhile, the "compare and contrast" mechanism set up by the German mid-century physiognomies spurred new cognitive experiments and visual shorthand that would obtain in later physiognomies. The late sixteenth-century physiognomic texts signal the devolution of the genre's once diagnostic origins into a mere visual game. New directions in illustrating texts of predictive astrology occurred in the laboratory of the sharp-eyed assembly of Roman aristocrats and polymaths organized around Federico Cesi. Cesi christened this society after the visual prowess of the lynx; indeed, the goal of the so-called Lincean Academy was to apply their heightened powers in observation to the natural word. With the emergence of *Of Human Physiognomy* c. 1586, a book by Lincean member Giambattista Della Porta, physiognomies became a venue for a visually contrastive exercise. Della Porta's researches parallel those of his fellow Linceans in his consideration of the continuities of art and nature. Della Porta's *modus operandi* in classifying things of the visual world, per David Freedberg, was a manifestation of an even larger impulse to master the "science of surfaces."[187] The Linceans obsessively documented the world through the pictorial description of its parts, and Della Porta followed in this vein. Della Porta's arresting comparisons of the physiognomies of humans and animals have captured the attention of scholars excavating the remnants of a doctrine of signs. Della Porta's passion for comparatism stretched from faces to the phytography of plants. A fairly recent scholarly tradition of natural philosophy had investigated the world through resemblances that connected astral and lunar influences to signs visible on the face and forehead, explored by Michel Foucault as a doctrine of signatures in *The Order of Things*.[188] From this perspective, Della Porta's physiognomy can be seen as a throwback to the early *Secreti* tradition that forged those resemblances.[189] This text's rhetorical directive, I would argue, was focused on unpacking the meaning of images, even at the mercy of the signs that stood behind them.

IMAGES AS DATA

Although the book purported to be a digest of humoral philosophy, most of the images in *Of Human Physiognomy* have their origin in prototypes from the sculpture and numismatic collection of Della Porta's brother, the portrait collection of Paolo Giovio, and the repertoire of printed literature.[190] In this respect, the images in *On Human Physiognomy* resemble the borrowings from other media that animated the production of Vogtherr's *Kunstbüchlin*. However, Della Porta redeployed that borrowed content in a way that was

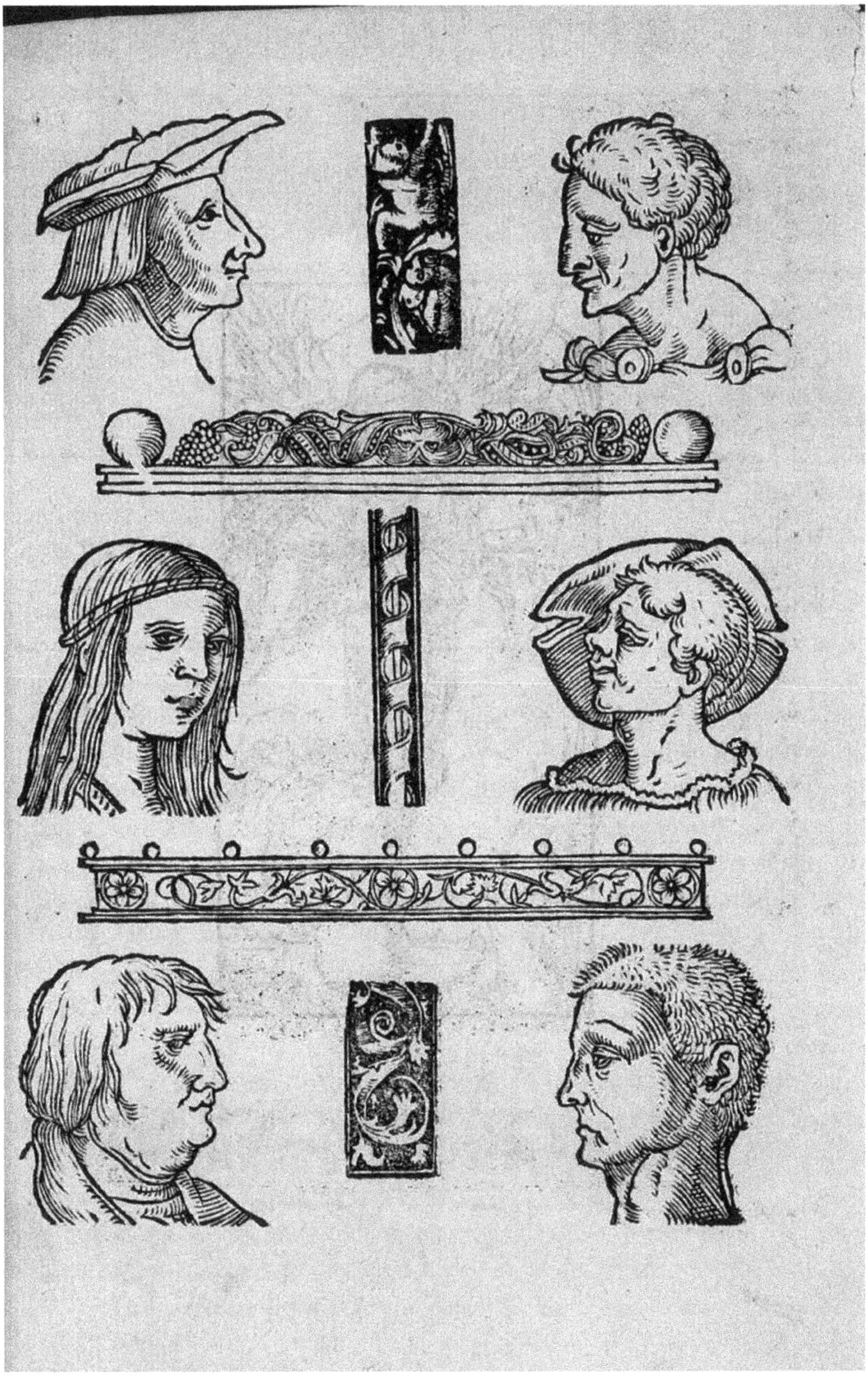

3.24. "Assorted heads," woodcut, in Bartolomeo Cocles, *Phisionomi und Chiromanci. Eyn newß Complexion Büchlein* (Strasbourg: Jacob Cammerlander, 1540), 76r. *Source:* HAB N97.4 Helmst. 7. Courtesy of Herzog August Bibliothek, Wolfenbüttel.

novel to printmaking. By staging physiognomic comparisons of heads derived from antique sculpture or contemporary portraiture with images of animal faces, the page becomes a place to forge new knowledge about old pictures in the tradition of common-placing.[191] The preeminence assumed by Della Porta's images, as argued by Francis Haskell, was a first for the active role of images in driving the text.[192] Data gathering underwrote the visual directive of Della Porta's text. Della Porta sought not just to add new knowledge to the old repertoire, but to awaken new epistemic processes with it. His physiognomy sought to exercise the comparative skills that Indagine and Cocles had established with their visual strategy of pairing faces. Bronwen Wilson has suggested that the recursive nature of the pairing strategy found in physiognomies and portrait books engineered new cognitive pathways in viewers' minds.[193] Recognition and discernment were also the cognitive objectives of certain antiquarian books that collected artifacts and visual materials, books whose collections aimed to establish the lineage of biography through portraiture, as we can see in Fulvio Orsini's *Elogia Virorum Ilustrium*, which was published in Rome in 1570.[194] In a book that sought to organize Orsini's vast resources of engraved gems, portrait busts, and coins into a narrative of famous men, the exercise became a *de facto* comparative search for resemblances. This search is similar to Della Porta's objectives. Physiognomic analysis became a self-conscious game for both amateur physiognomists and art appreciators alike – readers grew skilled at comparing identities and objects over temporal and visual distances. The goal of Della Porta's physiognomy was to synthesize visual knowledge by recognizing pictorial analogies.

In the book's chapter on noses, for example, the profiles of a poet and a rhinoceros were borrowed from recognizable visual sources (Figure 3.25). The likeness of the Florentine poet Angelo Poliziano first appeared in a painting that hung in a renowned collection belonging to Paolo Giovio in Como.[195] The impression of the poet in Della Porta's print came by way of a printed book illustrating illustrious men, along with the recorded deeds of their sitters. The *Musaei iovani imagines*, published in Basel in 1577, with woodcuts by Tobias Stimmer, was a project related to Paolo Giovio's earlier compendium, *Elogia Virorum bellica virtute illustrium*, whose first edition appeared in 1575 (a later printing, from Petri, dates from 1577).[196] The books' printer, Pietro Perna, sent Stimmer to copy the Como portraits, and Stimmer's woodcuts of those rulers and writers had the effect of standardizing these representations in the printed repertoire.[197]

The objective of Della Porta's text was to compare human faces to those of animals. In this particular pairing, Della Porta settled his critique on Poliziano's nose. His task was to find a suitable beast that could sustain the character assassination he proposed for Poliziano's nefarious character. A woodcut of a rhinoceros by Albrecht Dürer, originally printed in 1515, assumed the identity of Poliziano's animal avatar (Figure 3.26). The image of the sharp-nosed

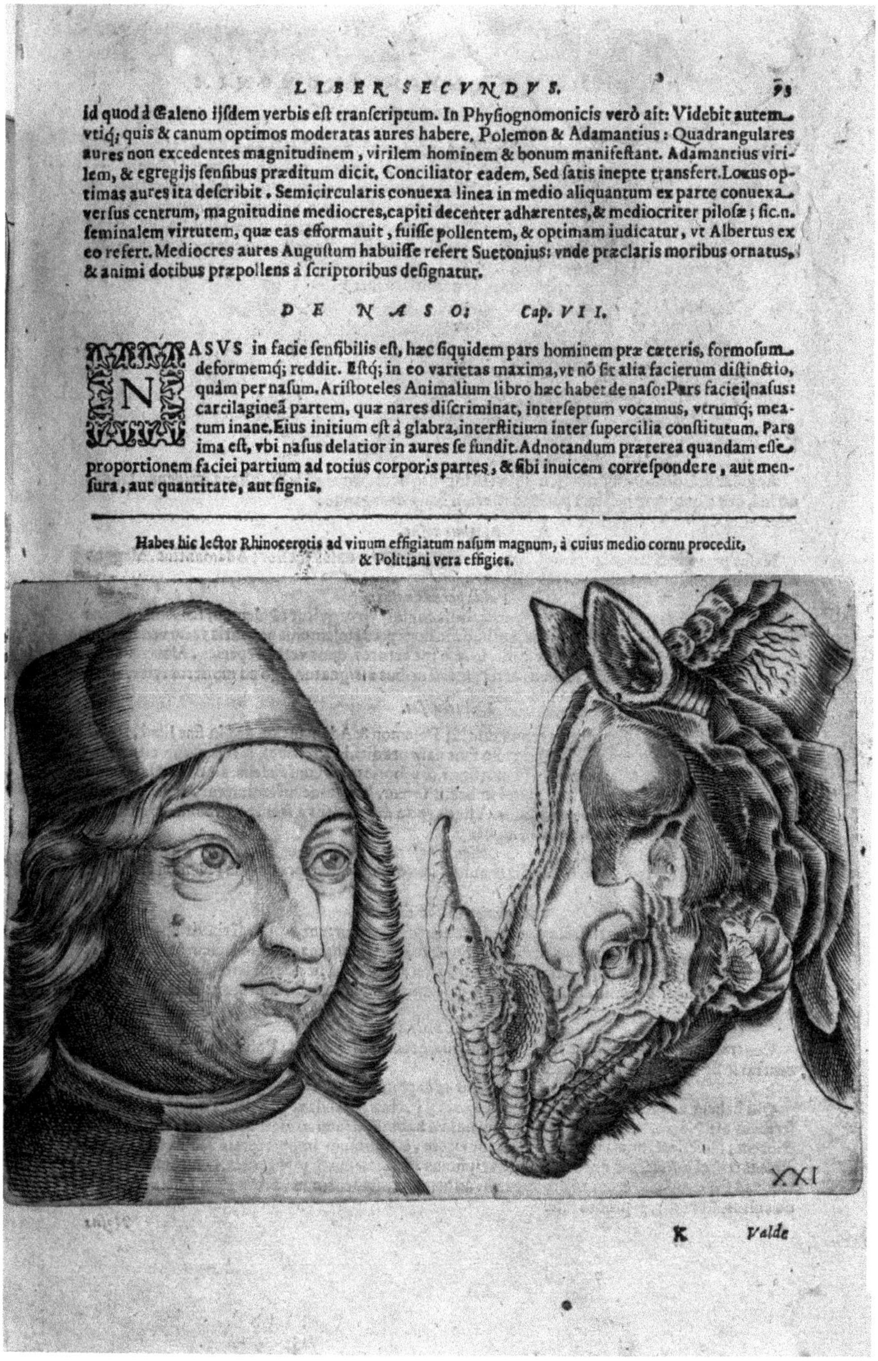

LIBER SECVNDVS. 93

id quod à Galeno iiſdem verbis eſt tranſcriptum. In Phyſiognomonicis verò ait: Videbit autem vtiq; quis & canum optimos moderatas aures habere. Polemon & Adamantius: Quadrangulares aures non excedentes magnitudinem, virilem hominem & bonum manifeſtant. Adamantius virilem, & egregijs ſenſibus præditum dicit. Conciliator eadem. Sed ſatis inepte transfert. Locus optimas aures ita deſcribit. Semicircularis conuexa linea in medio aliquantum ex parte conuexa verſus centrum, magnitudine mediocres, capiti decenter adhærentes, & mediocriter piloſæ; ſic.n. ſeminalem virtutem, quæ eas efformauit, fuiſſe pollentem, & optimam iudicatur, vt Albertus ex eo refert. Mediocres aures Auguſtum habuiſſe refert Suetonius: vnde præclaris moribus ornatus, & animi dotibus præpollens à ſcriptoribus deſignatur.

DE NASO: Cap. VII.

NASVS in facie ſenſibilis eſt, hæc ſiquidem pars hominem præ cæteris, formoſum deformemq; reddit. Eſtq; in eo varietas maxima, vt nõ ſit alia facierum diſtinctio, quàm per naſum. Ariſtoteles Animalium libro hæc habet de naſo: Pars faciei naſus: cartilagineã partem, quæ nares diſcriminat, interſeptum vocamus, vtrumq; meatum inane. Eius initium eſt à glabra, interſtitium inter ſupercilia conſtitutum. Pars ima eſt, vbi naſus delatior in aures ſe fundit. Adnotandum præterea quandam eſſe proportionem faciei partium ad totius corporis partes, & ſibi inuicem correſpondere, aut menſura, aut quantitate, aut ſignis.

Habes hic lector Rhinocerotis ad viuum effigiatum naſum magnum, à cuius medio cornu procedit, & Politiani vera effigies.

XXI

K Valde

3.25. Giambattista Della Porta, *De Humana Physiognomonia* (Naples: Tarquinium Longum, 1602), sig. 2, phil. 73, fol. 73. *Source:* Courtesy of Augsburg, Staats- und Stadtbibliothek.

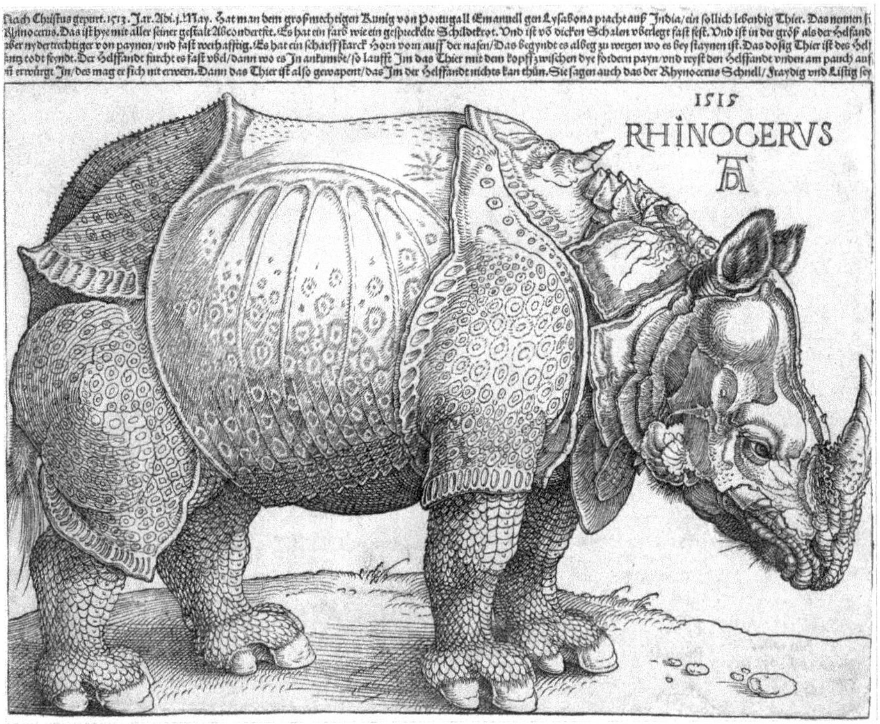

3.26. Albrecht Dürer, *Rhinoceros*, 1515, woodcut, 21.3 cm × 29.5 cm. Gift of Junius Spencer Morgan, 1919. *Source:* Courtesy of Metropolitan Museum of Art, New York.

rhinoceros sent by the sultan of Gujarat to Portuguese King Manuel I had already charged through literature on zoology and other related genres.[198] The fact that it was ferocious, according to its caption in Dürer's print, surely made it tempting material for Della Porta to borrow, but perhaps the fact that it was also familiar made an equal impression on the rhinoceros's copier.

Viewers' ability to decode images in this text was aided by their familiarity with the repertoire of images established by prints. Such familiarity was built through copies of portraits, often found in portrait books, which, according to Cecil Clough, gave them a "patina of authenticity."[199] Della Porta's comparisons depended on his readers' conversance with both Poliziano's portrait and the rhinoceros through the circulation of prints. Scholars have pointed to a variety of non-physiognomic genres that likely influenced Della Porta's text: printed biographies and courtier manuals were among the most compelling precedents for his work.[200] Drawing parallels between these surviving monuments and known portrait likenesses, Della Porta guides readers through the repertoire of existing images to find a compelling match. Sometimes the pendant to a portrait was supplied by the head of an animal, but Della Porta also included side by side views of antique portrait busts and other specimens from local art collections with which he was familiar.

Entirely novel in Della Porta's approach to physiognomy was the potential that he saw in examples from the repertoire of sculpture, painting, and print to serve as subjects of analysis. He gave his audience leave to interrogate visually works they probably never before considered on these merits. Indeed, Della Porta seems to have been the first to detect in the profile of Dürer's rhinoceros an unambiguous physiognomic message. He certainly was unique in registering the debt of Dürer's description of the rhinoceros's character to the physiognomic literature and shoring up that visual connection – a connection, as far as I know, unnoted by earlier readers. As we have seen, Dürer himself was both sketching human physiognomy *c.* 1513 and staging the form of the human body between poles of opposites; he might well have had such physiognomic precepts in mind as he was constructing the rhinoceros. Dürer diagnosed the rhinoceros's nature with the language of physiognomy; the words that he carved into the xylograph block were "*Freydig, listig*" (wild, crafty, cunning).[201] It might have been Dürer's "physiognomic" description of character mapped onto an already ignominious profile that inspired Della Porta to subject the rhinoceros to physiognomic analysis in the first place.

Della Porta's Italian edition of the physiognomy, *Della Fisonomia dell'huomo*, printed in Padua in 1613, included not just the animal and human comparisons but also gridded graphs of facial ratios familiar from artists' manuals. In that context, graphs would have served the purpose of reducing large noses to medium and small ones (Figure 3.27).[202] The common grid shared by the three noses facilitated comparisons of their sizes by the reader/viewer in the manner in which an artist might have. Including studies like these from practical artists' manuals (of the order of Dürer's *Vier Bücher* and Erhard Schön's *Unterweisung*) show the common visual vocabulary that linked the traditions of *Practica* to "physiognomic texts" in the *Secrets* traditions and to those of *Kunstbücher*.

The extent to which Della Porta's visual programming was contested by his colleagues can be tracked by later redactions of the work. While Della Porta might have been preoccupied with the "science of surfaces," fellow Linceans had other objectives in mind for the data processed in their think-tank.[203] As part of the academy's pursuit of collecting knowledge, Della Porta's colleague Francesco Stelluti offered a different view of the physiognomic images: he bemoaned the capacity of images to derail the project of divination and thought that the description of likeness was a job best left to the text. Stelluti's redaction of Della Porta's work, *Della Fisonomia di Tvtto il Corpo Hvmano del S. Gio. Batta della Porta* (1637), supplied a physiognomy of the entire body.[204] While Della Porta's volume had been visually driven, Stelluti converted the data from the illustrations of the original edition into synoptic tables. Stelluti ranked these tables superior to illustrations for the purpose of searching for non-visible essences.[205] Stelluti's volume, per its subtitle, which advertises the synoptic tables, would feature physiognomic information in

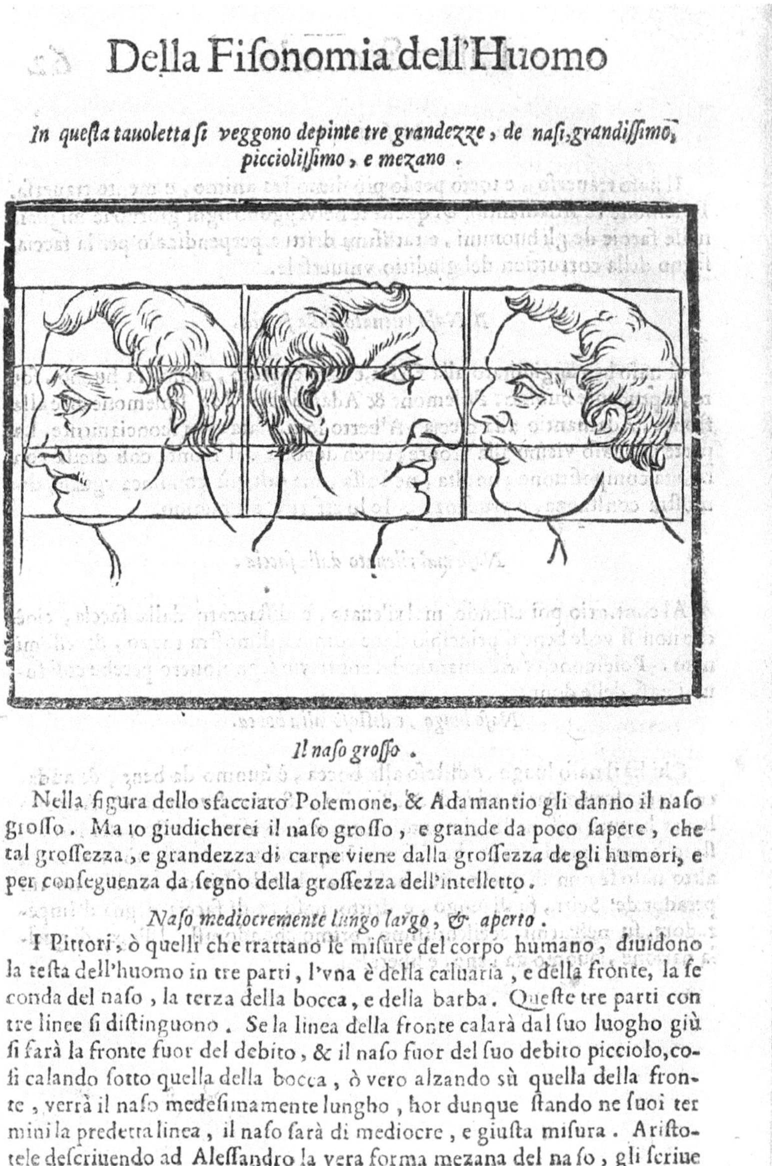

Della Fisonomia dell'Huomo

In questa tauoletta si veggono depinte tre grandezze, de nasi, grandissimo, picciolissimo, e mezano.

Il naso grosso.

Nella figura dello sfacciato Polemone, & Adamantio gli danno il naso grosso. Ma io giudicherei il naso grosso, e grande da poco sapere, che tal grossezza, e grandezza di carne viene dalla grossezza de gli humori, e per conseguenza da segno della grossezza dell'intelletto.

Naso mediocremente lungo largo, & aperto.

I Pittori, ò quelli che trattano le misure del corpo humano, diuidono la testa dell'huomo in tre parti, l'vna è della caluaria, e della fronte, la seconda del naso, la terza della bocca, e della barba. Queste tre parti con tre linee si distinguono. Se la linea della fronte calarà dal suo luogho giù si farà la fronte fuor del debito, & il naso fuor del suo debito picciolo, così calando sotto quella della bocca, ò vero alzando sù quella della fronte, verrà il naso medesimamente lungho, hor dunque stando ne suoi termini la predetta linea, il naso sarà di mediocre, e giusta misura. Aristotele descriuendo ad Alessandro la vera forma mezana del naso, gli scriue cosi

3.27. Giambattista Della Porta, *Della fisonomia dell'huomo (De humana physiognomonia)* (Padua: Pietro Paolo Tozzi, 1613), fol. 62v. *Source:* Courtesy of Hathi Trust, Duke University. Image in the public domain.

clearly legible flow charts that were also easy to search and were more reliable than pictures.[206] This is especially striking given Stelluti's sustained engagement with the visual pursuits of the Linceans, which include his panegyric about observations obtained with instruments such as the microscope and telescope.[207] Stelluti's fear about images' superficial connection to diagnoses demonstrates to what extent the entire genre had been colonized by images.

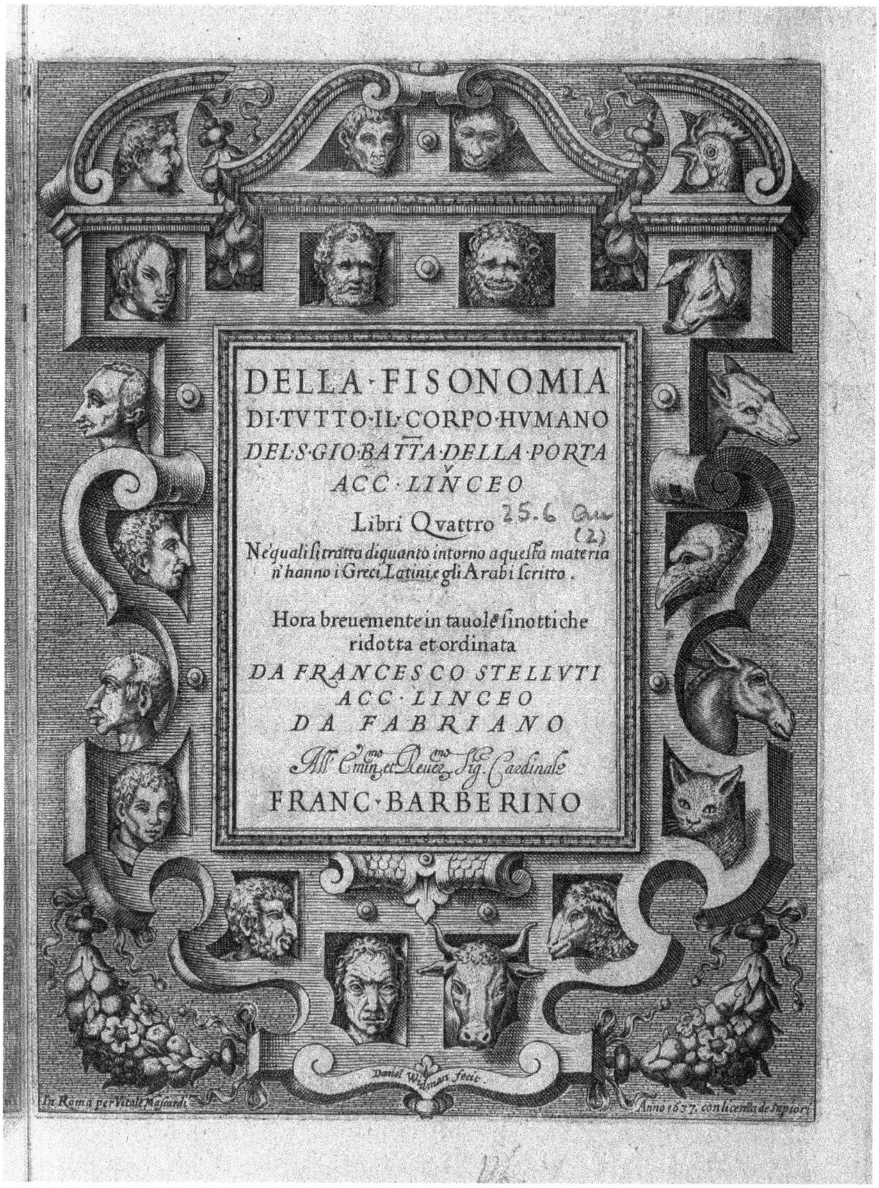

3.28. Francesco Stelluti, *Della Fisonomia di Tvtto il Corpo Hvmano del S. Gio. Batta della Porta* (Rome: Mascardi,1637). *Source:* HAB A25.6 Quod. 2. Courtesy of Herzog August Bibliothek, Wolfenbüttel.

Despite Stelluti's deep skepticism about the ability of pictures to carry these essences, his volume's organization depended on a preceding generation of pictures. Even the title page revives and compresses the most popular physiognomic illustrations of Della Porta's earlier editions (Figure 3.28). In his dedication to Cardinal Francesco Barberini, Stelluti indicates that his version of the physiognomic material represents a return to content typical of the *Mirror for*

Princes: character divination.[208] While Stelluti's faith in images as the basis of diagnoses fades, their most potent effects remain: Stelluti stresses the importance of choice (*elezzione*) as a procedure for interpreting signs. Choosing is here constituted as an important epistemic process. One had to be good at visual recognition and choosing. In his privileging of choice, Stelluti seems to have recognized in Della Porta's work a visual compendium about how to read pictures versus a targeted diagnostic manual. Della Porta's volume privileged the searchability of features, and the idea of the intrinsic nature of either humans or animals as something that could be called up by striking images.

Della Porta's efforts here have also been connected to other epistemic pursuits of illustrated books to collect already circulating information. Della Porta's interest in physiognomy could also be interpreted, as Katherine MacDonald has done, as a vehicle that could produce and reinforce individual celebrity and notoriety as they were shaped by contemporary biographies.[209] In contemporary portrait books that emerged in the Veneto, profiles were also an integral element of sitters' biographies, as Bronwen Wilson has shown.[210] In a similar way, Della Porta's comparisons were staged for the benefit of biography, which physiognomic particularities helped enliven and make memorable. The reader is asked to compare Socrates with a deer, Zeus with a lion, Plato with a hound, and Poliziano with a rhinoceros. In some cases, the character assessments of these personalities were driven by the pictures themselves and by the qualities viewers had been primed to associate with them. Viewers' associations with images were built up through the repertoire of printed facial images distributed in a host of media.

These generalized associations traveled with their specimens and their copies. Physiognomic profiles proliferated and became familiar. In an illuminating tale of how the reading public of early modern London was exposed to a variety of character heads, Taylor Clement has dubbed these recycled profiles a series of "moveable types."[211] Profiles with origins in continental physiognomies were liberally repurposed in broadside ballads, for instance, or used interchangeably in printed editions of plays such as Christopher Marlowe's *Tamburlaine* (printed in London by Richard Jones in 1590). It is important to remember that, regardless of the purpose of the texts articulated by the printers, in their afterlives in their new contexts, these images could change their meaning. The fact of the facial image's iterability was more tenacious than an image's fixity to a specific diagnostic reading. English printers distilled physiognomies to their visual images – in their journey from the continent to England, the light hand luggage of moral character had shifted into character assassinations of sketchy personality types. After several reprintings, woodcut portraits that originated in a 1533 Strasbourg edition of Cocles's *Physiognomiae & Chiromantiae* emerge in a series of physiognomic texts compiled by Thomas Hill and printed in London, such as *A Brief and Most Pleasaunt Epitomye of the*

Whole Art of Phisiognomie (Waylande, 1556) and his *Contemplation of Mankind* (William Seres, 1571). By the 1580s, these images appearing in Hill's physiognomic manuals had in turn been reused in several different texts to represent the human nature of both honorable *and* treacherous types.[212] We might reasonably suspect that these discussions of diverse natures would employ images of polar opposites, but this was not the case.

From here, these stock character heads easily volunteered themselves into new propaganda that required faces to incriminate. These images from physiognomies were marshaled into the broadside ballad of Thomas Deloney, *A Most Joyfull Songe [of] ... the great joy, which was made in London* (Figure 3.29). Inserted into the broadsheet, the physiognomy heads were now enlisted to represent the suspects of Anthony Babington's plot to overthrow the Crown, as a type of police lineup (or identity parade) into which images from other related sources also elbowed their way. In its original source in a continental metoscopy manual that coached how to read lines in the brow, the head marked with forehead lines was a mere instructional image whose purposefully generic head cued incised brow lines to planetary influence. What suggested its cameo appearance in the broadside was surely its connection to the diagnostic arts. The other images were cherrypicked from both continental and English complexion books.

Despite the sometimes arbitrary repurposing of images by printers, according to Clement, others strategically read between the lines to identify examples that might substitute for portrait likenesses of individuals.[213] The deeds of criminals implicated in the Babington plot were indicted by their images. These heads came to represent the diagnostic art of reading faces and shored up the conviction that inner character could also be read from surfaces. What remains in these publications are little more than visual analogies. Although physiognomies were ostensibly outlawed on the continent by papal edict in 1559 and in England by Elizabethan decree in 1598, the arbitrary nature of the images associated with the practice might have disqualified them long before.[214] Their uselessness for character divination, their cautionary notes about aids to self-improvement, and the frenetic reuse of copies of heads had already prompted the kind of skepticism about the art of physiognomy that provoked their dismissal by the essayist Michel de Montaigne.[215] Montaigne disputed that human nature could remain stable for even brief periods of time. With this idea about human inconstancy, he essentially undermined the diagnostic utility of physiognomy.[216] Despite the skepticism we see rehearsed in the rhetorical literature, at least part of those aspersions might have been cast by readers confused by, or perhaps even cognizant of, how thoroughly dilute physiognomy's images had become.

In the twilight of the utility of physiognomic diagnosis in the late sixteenth century, we see the complexion books' textual struts dissolve into a repertoire

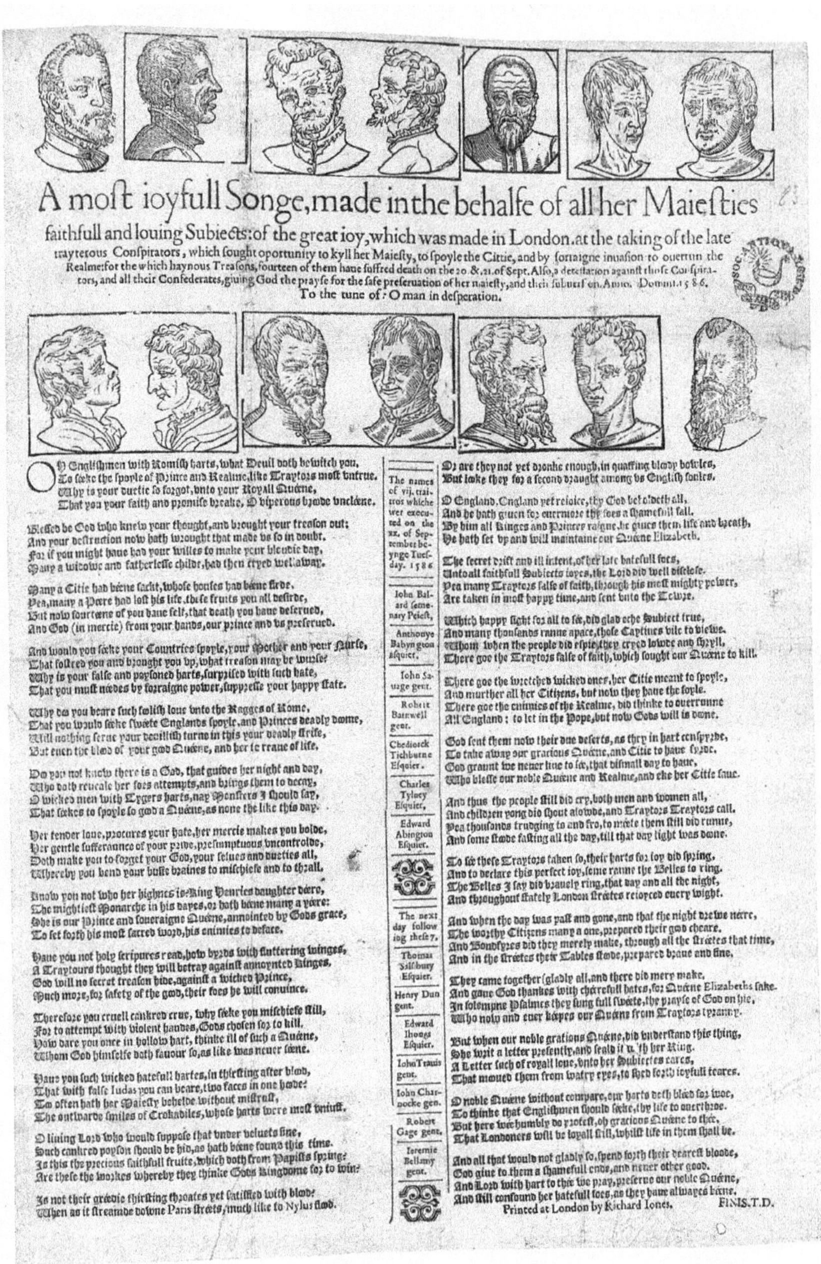

3.29. "Criminal heads" in Thomas Deloney, *A Most Joyfull Songe* (London: Richard Jones, 1586). *Source:* EBBA 36315. © The Society of Antiquaries of London.

of images that could be mined for illustrating criminal anthropology, dramatic works, or portrait collections, and for decorating the cover pages of chiromancies. These purposes were very far from the original intent of the first pictorialized volumes that aimed to deliver character from the arch of the eyebrow to the nose's tip. But even with this dilution of diagnoses, we see a strengthening of the image to guarantee the claims made in the text. Physiognomies readied their readers for visual interface with both their environment and the world delivered by books. In the ecology of printed books, facial images assumed a sovereignty that was reified by their repetition in a variety of genres. The texts of some of these books became little more than narrative prompts that encouraged viewers' interactions with their accompanying images. Venetian portrait books profusely collected physiognomic likenesses and developed their texts to support the facts already supplied by the image: reading such books became an exercise in memorizing the facts of the text by way of the image. According to Bronwen Wilson's reading of Turkish portraits that appeared in a series of Venetian portrait books, both portrait and biography mutually confirmed the historical facts of nearby passages.[217] The portrait book was the matrix in which the connection between deeds and likeness was forged. Later books that collected types – costume books, for example, such as Bertelli's *Diversarum nationum* (printed in Padua in 1594–6), Jost Amman and Hans Weigel's *Habitus praecipuorum populorum* (Nuremberg, 1577), and Jean-Jacques Boissard's *Recueil de costumes étrangers* (Paris, 1581) – were furnished with precious little text to carry their messages. Many such costume, portrait, and numismatic books were marketed as compilations in their titles, such as collections of costumes of strangers, or collections of portraits.

Not since the early block books had images performed the heavy lifting of the page. While some of these later volumes retained text as dressing, in many cases the images did most of the work. The image collections became desiderata in themselves. Collections of pictures provided the target of reading messages into images. Via the journey of faces, we arrived at a state of image sovereignty that was now guiding the visual program of books of all types. Dürer posited faces as a canvas for technical instruction and exploring difference. Vogtherr decided that collecting faces for a databank could capture some level of experience for his reader/viewers. English broadsides provoked a use for the faces of physiognomy that depended on them as elements of a repertoire. The collections of faces on view in portrait books and numismatic manuals, and the facial experiments active in the Lincean Academy, suggest that faces formed image environments that were mutually reinforcing. The ipseity of faces was more important than any particular context.

Once venerable members of the chambers of *Secrets*, by the end of the sixteenth century physiognomies had become dusty closets of collections. But it was the insertion of their images into neat drawers that permitted comparative and new cognitive horizons to be breached. Armed with these images of faciality, the vernacular viewer essentially shut the door on the old physiognomic diagnoses of the 1530s and 1540s. Physiognomic images could be featured to show bad attitudes, but they could just as easily reflect valiant behavior by a printer's mercurial substitution. Even after they outlasted their diagnostic usefulness, physiognomic images had afterlives of their own, as visual collections would begin to reify them as important features of the portrait landscape. The pedagogical strategies of these books taught a generation of viewers to read messages into the images, but they also organized those images as carriers of meaning across the genres. Physiognomic images appeared on playbills that announced noble characters, they comprised collections of sourced images, and books that were nominally studies of human physiognomy primarily functioned as anthologies of images. Physiognomies equipped reader/viewers with agency and cognitive potential to make informed decisions about the world by teaching them to read representative options in a world distilled by images. Images of heads from portrait, sculpture, coin, and print collections quizzed viewers on their skills in faciality. These images struck new deals with their captions, and arguably sidelined them, as they assumed the burden of the texts' didactics.

NOTES

1 Maria Loh, "Renaissance Faciality," *Oxford Art Journal* 32, no. 3 (2009), 346. According to Loh, Guerre's case reminds us that remembering and recognition also need to be historicized. The classic study of Martin Guerre's trial is Natalie Zemon Davis, *The Return of Martin Guerre* (Cambridge, MA: Harvard University Press, 1981).

2 Bartolommeo della Rocca, known as Cocles, *Complexion/ Natur || vnd eigenschafft eines yeden menschen || zu erfaren/ auch seiner geburt stund vnnd zeychen/|| dardurch jm all sein glück vnnd vnfal/ so jm in || der zeyt seyns lebens begegnen wirt/ er-||öffnet mag werden/ . . . || Der sieben Planeten sampt den zwölff heimli=||schen zeichen wirckung in des menschen geburt/|| clerlich beschrieben.|| . . . ||* (Mainz: Peter Jordan, 1534), HAB N97.4 Helmst. 3. Images of amateur astronomers found in such complexion books are related to illustrations of stargazers seen in contemporary manuals devoted to celestial instruments (astrolabes, quadrants, cross-staffs), such as Peter Apian's *Instrument-Buch* (Ingolstadt: Apian, 1533). In the Wolfenbüttel Sammelband HAB N97.4 Helmst., this edition of Cocles's *Complexion* is also bound with one of these: Sebastian Münster, *Erklerung des newen Instruments* (Worms: Schoeffer, 1529), HAB N97.4 Helmst. 4. The appearance of stargazers in these distinct genres signals the empirical processes by which celestial bodies were tracked.

3 Robin Bruce Barnes, *Astrology and Reformation* (New York: Oxford University Press, 2016), 25. Barnes agrees that astrology's appearance as mass media helped determine the larger shift from oral and communal culture to one that was visualized and individualized by the print industry.

4 Pamela H. Smith, "Making as Knowing: Craft as Natural Philosophy," in Smith et al., *Ways of Making and Knowing: The Material Culture of Empirical Knowledge* (New York: Bard Graduate Center, 2017), 19.

5 Barnes, *Astrology and Reformation*. For the relationship between the calendar tradition and the books of planets, the so-called *Planetenbücher*, see "From Alexandria to Augsburg," in Barnes, *Astrology and Reformation*, 16–47, especially 17–18.

6 Cocles, *Barptolomaei Coclitis Bononiensis, Naturalis Philosophiæ ac Medicinæ Doctoris, Physiognomiæ et Chiromantiæ Compendium* (Argentorati: Albertus, 1536).

7 Christoph Metzger, "'Wie man den Menschen erkennen soll': Neue Überlegungen zu den Charakterstudien Hans Schäufelins, mit einem Technologischen Anhang von Monika Strolz," *Jahrbuch des Kunsthistorischen Museums Wien* 12 (2010), 8–39. Metzger argues that Wechtlin might have had access to designs of character studies that were being developed in Augsburg in the circle of Hans Burgkmair and Albrecht Dürer, as well as the painted panels of a cycle of temperaments by Hans Schäufelin. For the attribution of the illustrations to Wechtlin, see Heinrich Röttinger, "Hans Wechtlin," *Jahrbuch der Kunsthistorischen Sammlung der Allerhöchsten Kaiserhauses* 27 (1907–9), 1f., note 1, nr. 5, p. 51. See also Ulrich Reisser, *Physiognomik und Ausdruckstheorie der Renaissance: der Einfluss charakterologischer Lehren auf Kunst und Kunsttheorie des 15. und 16. Jahrhunderts* (Munich: Scaneg, 1997), 67–73. For Wechtlin, see also Heinrich Röttinger, "Die Holzschnitte der Druckerei des Jakob Cammerlander in Straßburg," *Gutenberg-Jahrbuch* 11 (1936), 125–40, especially 128, note 2. Metzger argues for the possibility of a common source for the Strasbourg editions and for the appearance of these heads in the pages of the *Liber Quodlibetarius*. Since this publication, another edition of Cocles has surfaced: Cocles, *Ein kurtzer bericht der gantzen Phisionomey* (Strasbourg: Johann Grüninger, 1524). And perhaps there is yet another intervening edition or another source translation between the 1511 Schäufelin paintings and the 1524 printing. Metzger speculates that this could have been an Augsburg printing prior to 1524, perhaps one involving the collaboration of Schäufelin and Hans Burgkmair. Weiditz may have been introduced to these prototypes during his travels to Augsburg in 1518; see Metzger, "'Wie man den Menschen erkennen soll,'" 26–7. Some scholars have attributed these same designs to the Basel artist Conrad Schnitt. See notes for the book in the New York Public Library Spencer Collection (Ger. 1533), per Edward Rosen, *Copernicus and His Successors* (London: Hambledon Press, 1995), 173–81.

8 For the Schnitt copies, see Taylor Clement, "Moveable Types: The De-individuated Portrait in the Age of Mechanical Reproduction," *Renaissance Studies* 31, no. 3 (2016), 7 and note 22. Schnitt is mostly known for his work on Sebastian Münster's *Cosmographia*, for which he did produce several independent heads.

9 Joan K. Stemmler, "The Physiognomical Portraits of Johann Caspar Lavater," *Art Bulletin* 75 (1993), 151–68.

10 Cocles, *Phisonomei: Eins jeden menschen Art, Natur und Complexion* (Strasbourg: Egenolf, 1530). See the last page's caveat: "*Phisonomeibeschluß ... Es seind auch vil zufell/ dadurch die urtheyl ungewiß gmacht/ Als alter/ verwandlung des luffts/ krankheit ic/ Die ding enderen natürliche Complexion/ unnd machen die urtheyl und zeychen offt ungewiß.*"

11 According to Pliny, Apion the grammarian reports on metoscopers and physiognomers who could read events from portraits; my thanks to Allison Smith for pointing this out. See chapter 36 of the *Natural History* for instance, in which Apelles was compelled into physiognomic exercises. See note 53 at www.perseus.tufts.edu/hopper/text?doc=Perseus:abo:phi,0978,001:35:36.

12 For the history of the *Secretum Secretorum*, see William Eamon, *Science and the Secrets of Nature: Books of Secrets in Medieval and Early Modern Culture* (Princeton, NJ: Princeton University Press, 1994), 45–53, 134; see also W. F. Ryan and Charles B. Schmitt, *Pseudo-Aristotle, the Secret of Secrets: Sources and Influences* (London: Warburg Institute, University of London, 1982); Steven J. Williams, *The Secret of Secrets: The Scholarly Career of a Pseudo-Aristotelian Text in the Late Middle Ages* (Ann Arbor: University of Michigan Press, 2003), especially chapter 6.

13 See Joseph Ziegeler, "Philosophers and Physicians on the Scientific Validity of Latin Physiognomy, 1200–1500," *Early Science and Medicine* 12, no. 3 (2007), 297; Eamon, *Science and the Secrets of Nature*, 49. For medieval glossing by Magnus and Scotus, see Martin Porter, *Windows of the Soul: Physiognomy in European Culture 1470–1780* (Oxford: Clarendon Press and Oxford University Press, 2005), 69ff.

14 See Valentin Groebner, "Complexio/Complexion: Categorizing Individual Natures, 1250–1600," in Lorraine Daston and Fernando Vidal, *The Moral Authority of Nature* (Chicago: University of Chicago Press, 2010), especially 372ff.

15 Indagine's introduction recommends dates for the meeting of the electoral college. See Barbara Bauer, "Die Rolle des Hofastrologen und Hofmathematicus als fürstlicher Berater," in August Buck, ed., *Höfischer Humanismus* (Weinheim: Acta Humaniora, 1989), 93–117, especially 95. Bauer's supposition is that the geocentrism was difficult to overcome in part because so many courtly horoscopes depended on relationships of stars to planets.

16 Reisser, *Physiognomik und Ausdruckstheorie*, 53ff.

17 Alessandro Achillini, *Chyromantiae principiis et Physionomiae* (Bologna: Benedetti, 1503), HAB A95.2 Quod. 2.

18 Cocles, *Chyromantie ac physionomie Anastasis: cum Approbatione Magistri Alexandri de Achillinis* (Bologna: Per Joannem Antonium Platonidem Benedictorum, 1504), NLM 240 C666c 1504.

19 For Achillini, see Lynn Thorndike, *A History of Magic and Experimental Science* (New York: Columbia University Press, 1941), vol. 5, 37–49.

20 The book carries a lengthy dedication to the city of Bologna from Bichardus Fanensis (a student of Philippus Beroaldus) and Alexander Bentivolio. See Herbert Jaumann, *Handbuch Gelehrtenkultur der frühen Neuzeit* (Berlin: Walter de Gruyter, 2004), vol. 1, 93.

21 For Cocles, see Thorndike, *A History of Magic and Experimental Science*, vol. 5, 50–68. See Reisser, *Physiognomik und Ausdruckstheorie*, 52ff; Porter, *Windows of the Soul*; Claire Sherman and Brian Copenhaver, *Writing on Hands: Memory and Knowledge in Early Modern Europe* (Seattle: University of Washington Press, 2001), 52.

22 For a comprehensive breakdown of the various editions and the source material from which they were derived, see Reisser, *Physiognomik und Ausdruckstheorie*, 56–61.

23 See Reisser, *Physiognomik und Ausdruckstheorie*, 61.

24 Lorraine Daston and Elizabeth Lunbeck, *Histories of Scientific Observation* (Chicago: University of Chicago Press, 2011), 18; see also Steven J. Williams, "Roger Bacon and the *Secret of Secrets*," in Jeremiah Hackett, ed., *Roger Bacon and the Sciences* (Leiden: Brill, 1997), 375ff.

25 In a particular Strasbourg edition of a pseudo-Cocles complexion book attributed to Aristotle and Michael Scotus, the sole image that furnished both title page and colophon showed two robed philosophers pointing at three stars. See Aristotle and Michael Scotus, eds., *In disem Biechlin wirt erfunden von Complexion der Menschen: zuerlernen leibliche unnd menschliche Natur ir Siten, Geberden und Nayglichayt zuerkennen und urtaylen* (Strasbourg: Mathis Hüpfuff, 1511); see NLM WZ 240 I355 1511.

26 Reisser, *Physiognomik und Ausdruckstheorie*, 57ff. The early Strasbourg and Augsburg editions of Cocles and pseudo-Cocles actually go back to the medieval physiognomic tradition of Michael Scotus, which also relies on pseudo-Aristotle and Albert Magnus.

27 See Susan Dackerman, *Prints and the Pursuit of Knowledge in Early Modern Europe* (Cambridge, MA: Harvard Art Museums, 2011), 126–7; see also Lorraine Daston, "On Scientific Observation," *Isis* 99, no. 1 (2008), 97–110.

28 See Thorndike, *A History of Magic and Experimental Science*, vol. 5, 58: "No one can be a good physiognomist who has not some knowledge of astronomy and medicine, because a great and most important part of that science depends on these," in Cocles, *Chyromantie ac physionomie Anastasis*, book IV.

29 Barnes, *Astrology and Reformation*, 22–3. Calendars based on Regiomontanus's observations were printed beginning in 1474 and presented astronomical data for lunar cycles from 1475 to 1532.

30 Johannes Regiomontanus, *Kalendarius Johannis Künigspergers: News und Volmon ... Eyn schön Vergleichung der Astronomi mit der Artznei* (Strasbourg: Cammerlander, 1532), HAB N97.4 Helmst. 2.

31 Regiomontanus, *Kalendarius Johannis Künigspergers*, HAB N97.4 Helmst. 2.

32 For a succinct discussion of astral influence on the body, see Mitchell B. Merback, *Perfection's Therapy: An Essay on Albrecht Dürer's Melencolia I* (New York: Zone Books, 2017), 150.

33 For a zodiac man whose organs are not shown, see the blockbook calendar *c.* 1457 included in HAB Cod. Guelf.1189 Helmst., in Christian Heitzmann, *Die Sterne Lügen Nicht: Astrologie und Astronomie im Mittelalter und in der Frühen Neuzeit*, Ausstellungskataloge der Herzog-August-Bibliothek 1972–90 (Wiesbaden: Harrassowitz, 2008), 39–45, especially 37f.

34 Planetary influence could be mapped onto the zodiac man by region or by particular organs. For a representation of the former, see the *Iatromathematisches Hausbuch* (Augsburg: Blaubirer, 1481), preserved in the Bayerische Staatsbibliothek, 4Inc.c.a.190 at www.digitale-sammlungen.de/view/bsb00029544?page=41.

35 Data from Avicenna's *Canon* is interspersed with more empirically derived knowledge updated for sixteenth-century readers. Information about complexion appears as *Complexions of Man* in a few short pages cinched in at 27r between the *Seasons of the Year* (chapter 5) and *Regimens of Mankind* (from the book of Avicenna, chapter 7), *Bathing*, and then the *Canons of Venesection* (also from Avicenna).

36 *Des wassers der Menschen Judicia und urteyl einem jeglichen seine kranckeyt nach des Harns gestalt* . . .

37 Urine charts broken down into descriptions of a sample's appearance also set the stage for rudimentary practices of observation.

38 "*Wer artznei sich gebrauchen dar/ und nit der zeychen wol nimbt war/ und sein sach nicht richtet darnach/ Der leyd gern ob er schad empfach. Hüt dich mit laß das glid an air/ So das zeychen die ader rürt. Wie dir außweißt diß figure güt/ So bleibst du schon in guter hüt*," HAB HN97 Helmst. 4, 26r. The note here cautions one to observe the stars carefully and perform venesection during times designated by zodiac sign.

39 The zodiac man explicates information about the planets on the previous page: "the seven planets and the twelve zodiac signs (for the purposes of venesection): Jupiter rules the liver; Mars . . . the stomach, the sun. Aries rules the interior of the head; during Aries, one can let blood in the head region. Taurus governs the throat, therefore blood letting during that time is not advised" (30v). Regiomontanus, *Kalendarius* (Strasbourg, Cammerlander, 1532).

40 Cocles, *Complexion/ Natur | | vnd eigenschafft eines yeden menschen* . . ., fol. 1v. To determine a subject's nature and complexion from numerology, these volumes provide charts that assign numbers to both the alphabet and the planets. In this exercise, a reader is instructed to write out the name of the person under analysis, together with the father's name, and assign numbers to these letters in order to compute their sum. From this sum, subtract nine. This final figure determines which planet holds influence over that person.

41 Cocles, *Complexion/ Natur | | vnd eigenschafft eines yeden menschen* . . . For example, the children born under Saturn are described thus: "melancholics, have thinning beards and rounded heads . . . are idle and unreliable in their activities, are not happy in the company of others, don't socialize with women . . . frequently talk to themselves, are unfriendly and seldom come to an agreeable fate" (3r). Children born under Mars, by contrast, are "angry, have harsh faces, brown in color or red as if burned by the sun, long face, long noses . . . don't sleep well and are therefore prone to headaches" (4r). Venus's child is "exceedingly romantic, well-groomed, unchaste by nature, and has a preference for white clothes" (5r). Men born under Mercury's influence are "talented in Astronomy and natural arts, and gravitate toward the ladies" (5v).

42 These were likely generated from designs prepared for earlier books, such as Hartmann Schedel's *Weltchronik* (1493).

43 "*Des Lewenkind ist von der Sonnen natür/ ein Cholericus heyß und drucken*" (13v). This is followed by the explanation of the complexion: "*Des fewers natür hatt er am meysten/ ist heyß und trucken/ gleicht dem fewer unnd Sommer/ ist ein mittel Complex. Der mensch ist bleycher farb/ er drinckt mehr dan er isset/ kleyner glider/ mager/ eines schnellen grimmigen zorns/ der ist bald widerhin/ kün und in allen dingen schnel. Redt viel/ ist unforchtsam/ hatt viewl harts hares. Das obertheyl seines leibs ist im grösser dann das underteil. Ist milt/ unstet/ begert vil zu unkeüschen/ und mag wenig. Er hüt sich vor hitzigen truckenen speisen/ Alles was kalt und feücht/ ist im gesundt*" (14v).

44 Here, observation is expressed via prolonged daily experience, or "*langwerige erfarung von tag zu tag.*" See *Geomantia.|| Kuenstlicher und rechtschaffner gebrauch || der alten kleynen Geomancey/ mit welcher durch hilff der || Rechnung vnd des menschen Tauffnamens/ Sampt der || Planeten wirckung/ in jren stunden/ allen Adams || Kindern/ Künfftiger zůfall ges gůtten vnd || bœsen glücks erœffnet wirt.|| Zů sampt andern fünff . . . || Tafeln . . . || Mit beygesetztem Kuenstlichen Jnstrument vñ regeln/|| . . . ||* (Mainz: Peter Jordan, 1534), fol. 1v.

45 Representations of the planets here are personifications derived from Hans Burgkmair's *c.* 1510–14 woodcut series of the *Seven Planets*; see Jupiter, for example, at http://diglib.hab.de/drucke/n-97-4f-helmst-3s/start.htm?image=00006. Compare with Hans Burgkmair's planets at https://library.artstor.org/#/asset/BARTSCH_17000043; Tilman Falk, Isolde Lübbeke, and Rolf Biedermann, *Hans Burgkmair: 1473–1973: Das Graphische Werk* (Augsburg: Städtische Kunstsammlungen, 1973); for the seven planets, see cat. 64–5, plates 81–2. The first copies of this series appeared in Antwerp in 1514 and popularized Burgkmair's influence in the Netherlands. The designs that accompany Jordan's edition are from recut blocks smaller in size and less elaborate in design.

46 Burgkmair et al., *Hans Burgkmair*, cat. 77, plate 95; see also Ashley West, "Conrad Peutinger and the Visual Arts: Collaborating with Hans Burgkmair the Elder," in Reinhard Laube and Helmut Zäh, eds., *Gesammeltes Gedächtnis: Konrad Peutinger und die kulturelle Überlieferung im 16. Jahrhundert* (Lucerne: Quaternio Verlag, 2016), 52–73.

47 The text advises one to "avoid purchasing weapons during the best hours of Jupiter," fol. 23r.

48 For the new emphasis on external signs in sixteenth-century complexion literature, see Groebner, "Complexio/Complexion," especially 372ff.

49 See Wolfgang Kuhoff, "Markus Welser als Erforscher des römischen Augsburg," in Johannes Burkhardt and Mark Häberlein, eds., *Die Welser: Neue Forschungen zur Geschichte und Kultur des oberdeutschen Handelshauses* (Berlin: Akademie, 2002), 587–617; Stephanie Leitch, *Mapping Ethnography in Early Modern Germany: New Worlds in Print Culture* (Basingstoke: Palgrave Macmillan, 2010), 92–3; West, "Conrad Peutinger and the Visual Arts," 62–73, 118–22.

50 Stephen Perkinson, "From an 'Art de Memoire' to the Art of Portraiture: Printed Effigy Books of the Sixteenth Century," *Sixteenth Century Journal* 33, no. 3 (2002), 687–723; Stephen Perkinson, "Likeness," *Studies in Iconography* 33 (2012), 15–28.

51 Cocles, *In Disem Büechlin Wirt Erfunden von Complexion der Menschen* (Augsburg: Hans Schönsperger, 1515), 1v.

52 Stephen Perkinson, *The Likeness of the King: A Prehistory of Portraiture in Late Medieval France* (Chicago: University of Chicago Press, 2009), 72ff.

53 Cocles, *In Disem Büechlin*, 2v.

54 "[H]*ochgelerten weisen natürlich maister Ypocras abkunterfayt und gemalt worden.*"

55 Cocles, *In Disem Büechlin*, 4v: "*es soll auch kayner auß diser geschrifft unnd kunst niemand böß noch uneerlich schelten/ sonder allain ain naygung der natur und des gebluts der menschen/ darauß anzaigen unnd urtailen wellich naigung mit vernufft unnd liebhabung warer phylosophey und eere behaltung fürkomen/ gewent und abgestelt werden mag.*"

56 "*Beschlußred der Phisonomey: Wiltt du ain Phisonomist sein/ so must du wyssen und weißlich betrachten alles das in allen hievor getruckten capiteln gesagt ist/ auff das du dadurch deiner urtailen gewis werdest/ unnd nitt falest. Die weil kain urtail der Phisonomey allain auff ain Capitel zu setzen oder auszusprechen ist. Sonnder soll ain yeder in ym selbst betrachten unnd zusamen samlen die gezeügknuss aller glider des ganntzen leibs (die nitt durch zufall verwanndelt sein.*"

57 Hans von Gersdorff and Johannes Indagine, *Feldtbůch der Wund-Artzney: sampt vilen Instrumenten der Chirurgey; vß dem Albucasi contrafayt. Chiromantia Jo. Jndagine. das Ist, die Kunst der Handtbesehung. Natürliche Astrologey, . . . Physiognomey, . . . Complexion Buch. . . . Canones, oder Regelen eins Yeden Kranckheyt Warlich zu Erkündigen . . .* (Strasbourg: Schott, 1540), HAB HQuH 20.4.

58 I am very grateful to Ulrich Kopp for examining the annotations with me in the summer of 2018. Kopp believes that the manuscript hand can be dated between 1540 and 1594, when

Heinrich Brandes, a member of Helmstedt Ratsherren (*prefecti*), inscribed it with his autograph. This is likely an unskilled hand, as traces of handwriting practice can be seen here, and a later hand likely blotted out some of the annotations and in some cases added paper to cover them.

59 Porter, *Windows of the Soul*, 14. Thomas Browne advocates for physiognomy thus: "for there are mystically in our faces certain characters which carry in them the motto of our Soules, wherein he that cannot read A.B.C. may read our natures," in Sir Thomas Browne, *Religio medici*, ed. Jean-Jacques Denonian (Cambridge: Cambridge University Press, 1953), 90–1.

60 Porter, *Windows of the Soul*, 17.

61 See Katherine Park, "Observation in the Margins, 500–1500," 15–44 and Gianna Pomata, "Observation Rising: Birth of an Epistemic Genre, 1500–1650," 45–80, both in Daston and Lunbeck, *Histories of Scientific Observation*; see also Alisha Rankin, "How to Cure the Golden Vein: Medical Remedies as *Wissenschaft* in Early Modern Germany," in Smith et al., *Ways of Making and Knowing*, 113–37.

62 Lorraine Daston and Peter Galison, *Objectivity* (New York: Zone Books, 2007); Sietske Fransen, "Antoni van Leeuwenhoek, His Images and Draughtsmen," *Perspectives on Science* 27, no. 3 (2019), 485–544.

63 Christian Egenolff or Egenolph (1502–55), born in Hadamar, studied humanities in Mainz, and worked first for the printer Wolfgang Küpfel in Strasbourg. Around 1530, he departed for Frankfurt, where he became the first publisher of note, printing, publishing, and type-casting. He often collaborated with Hans Sebald Beham and Virgil Solis.

64 Cocles, *Phisonomei: Complexio und Art eins jeden Menschen ausz Gestalt und Form des Angesichts, Glider unnd allen geberden zu erlernen* (Strasbourg: Egenolff, 1529). There is no date in the colophon, but the online catalogue of the Bayerische Staatsbibliothek supplies the date of 1529 (see BSB Rar.1502#Beidb.7).

65 Cf. for example, Reisser, *Physiognomik und Ausdruckstheorie*, fig. 34; *Kalender, Iatromathematisches Hausbuch* (Augsburg: Blaubirer, 1481), BSB-Ink K-4 – GW M16008.

66 See the digital edition in Munich at https://mdz-nbn-resolving.de/details:bsb00027286.

67 Eucharius Rößlin, d.J., *Kalender mit allen As=||stronomischen haltungen. Von natürlichem Jnfluß der Gestirn/|| Planeten vnd Zeychen … || ASTROLABIVM TETRAGONON.|| Ein gar kunstlich Astrolabium/ Alle wirck||ungen des Firmaments … zefindenn. Durch … || D.Eucharium Rößlin/ Statartzt zů Franck||furt am Meyn/ New añ tag geben.|| Register … zů end des Kalenders*, ed. Johannes Stöffler (Frankfurt: Egenolff, 1533); Eucharius Rößlin and Johannes Stöffler, *Kalendar mit allen Astronomischen haltungen* (Frankfurt: Egenolff, 1533), HAB HN94.4 Helmst. 4.

68 Cocles, *Phisonomei: Eins jeden menschen Art*, NLM WZ 240 C666 pg 1530. For the numismatic inscriptions of Marchio Montisferrati Casale Monferrato, see www.coingallery.de/KarlV/Monferrato_E.htm. I'm very grateful to my anonymous reviewers for help in the identification of this medal.

69 West, "Conrad Peutinger and the Visual Arts," 62–73, see also 117–22. A full set of these are in vellum. Peutinger saw his primary contribution to antiquarianism as presenting historical sources in an orderly format (see p. 108). A digitized version of the volume can be seen here: https://mdz-nbn-resolving.de/details:bsb00105880.

70 For Peutinger's and Burgkmair's understanding of the term *imagines* and the veristic guarantees embedded in references to portraits as *vera effigies*, see West, "Conrad Peutinger and the Visual Arts," 120. For Burgkmair's involvement in the *Kaiserbuch* project, see Campbell Dodgson, "Die Cäsarenköpfe, eine unbeschriebene Folge von Holzschnitten Hans Burgkmair d.Ä.," in *Beiträge zur Geschichte der deutschen Kunst, Bd. II* (Augsburg: Benno Filser, 1928).

71 Cocles, *In Disem Büechlin*.

72 Among those represented were the merchant banker Jakob Fugger, the humanist Konrad Peutinger, the artists Albrecht Dürer and Hans Burgkmair, and Maximilian I's court jester Kunz von der Rosen. Werner Hofmann, *Köpfe der Lutherzeit: Hamburger Kunsthalle, 4. März bis 24. April 1983* (Munich: Prestel, 1983), 254; see also Hanna Gagel, ed., *Der Mensch um*

1500: Werke aus Kirchen und Kunstkammern (Berlin: Staatliche Museen Preussischer Kulturbesitz, 1977), 101–2. On portrait medals in general, see also Stephen K. Scher, *The Currency of Fame: Portrait Medals of the Renaissance* (New York: Abrams, 1994), 24.

73 See Larry Silver, "The Face is Familiar: German Renaissance Portrait Multiples in Print and Medals," *Word & Image* 19, no. 1 (2003), 17. For instance, Melanchthon's printed portrait carries this text.

74 Silver, "The Face is Familiar," 13; see also Scher, *The Currency of Fame*, 24. In contrast to their Italian counterparts, Scher characterizes German medallions by the uncompromising realism of their portraits, which showed the influence of the meticulous linear style of woodcuts. Medallion producers employed techniques familiar from the type-casting process. Another aspect linking them to the print trade was a material similarity: many of the northern examples were first carved in stone or wood before the casting process.

75 Francis Haskell, *History and Its Images: Art and the Interpretation of the Past* (New Haven, CT: Yale University Press, 1995).

76 Porter, *Windows of the Soul*, 14. Of physiognomic work, Thomas Browne says, "for there are mystically in our faces certain characters which carry in them the motto of our Soules, wherein he that cannot read A.B.C. may read our natures"; Browne, *Religio medici*, ed. Denonian, 90–1.

77 Perkinson, *The Likeness of the King*.

78 See John Cunnally, *Images of the Illustrious: The Numismatic Presence in the Renaissance* (Princeton, NJ: Princeton University Press, 1999). This is per Pliny the Younger's panegyric to Trajan as Optimus Princeps. The inscription combines a common obverse of Trajan's name and titles (IMP TRAIANO AVG GER DAC P M TR P COS V P P) with the most common reverse legend on the coins of this emperor (SPQR OPTIMO PRINCIPI). Many warm thanks to John Cunnally for his help deciphering this.

79 Perkinson, "From an 'Art de Memoire,'" 687–723, especially 720–3.

80 Cocles, *Phisonomei: Eins jeden menschen art*.

81 Although the name of the author is frequently omitted in the early modern physiognomies, here Egenolff includes the name Cocles, rendered here as *Coclitus*.

82 Peter Parshall, "The Art of Memory and the Passion," *Art Bulletin* 81 (1999), 456–72.

83 Kathryn M. Rudy, *Rubrics, Images and Indulgences in Late Medieval Netherlandish Manuscripts* (Leiden: Brill: 2017), 8.

84 See the predella of the Ecce Homo triptych attributed to Bosch's workshop in the Museum of Fine Arts, Boston. Luuk Hoogstede et al., *Hieronymus Bosch, Painter and Draughtsman: Technical Studies* (New Haven, CT: Yale University Press, 2016), 337.

85 Image reproduced in Rudy, *Rubrics, Images and Indulgences*, 19; for the devotional type of the mass of St. Gregory, see pp. 101–36.

86 On the topic of types in relation to portraits, see Robert Scheller, *A Survey of Medieval Model Books* (Haarlem: De Erven F. Bohn, 1963). On the idea of usefulness in illustration, see Brian W. Ogilvie, *The Science of Describing: Natural History in Renaissance Europe* (Chicago: University of Chicago Press, 2006), 192–8.

87 David Landau and Peter W. Parshall, *The Renaissance Print, 1470–1550* (New Haven, CT: Yale University Press, 1994), 247ff., especially 252–3. The collaboration between Brunfels and Weiditz may have been mediated by the printer Johannes Schott in Strasbourg, whom Peter Parshall credits with the inspiration for the book.

88 Sachiko Kusukawa, *Picturing the Book of Nature: Image, Text, and Argument in Sixteenth-Century Human Anatomy and Medical Botany* (Chicago: University of Chicago Press, 2011), 87–90 and note 31. Among the editions published by Egenolff were the *Kreuterbuch* attributed to Rösslin and Johannes von Cube, later followed by *Herbarum Imagines Vitae/ Der kreuter Lebliche Contrafaytung* (1535). For further sources, see Eamon, *Science and the Secrets of Nature*, 387, note 67.

89 Schott's defense at the imperial cameral tribunal in Speyer on October 17, 1533 claimed that he was protected by an imperial privilege granted by Charles V. See Joseph Leo

Koerner, *The Moment of Self-Portraiture in German Renaissance Art* (Chicago: University of Chicago Press, 1996), 215ff. The classic work on the conferring of printing privileges in the sixteenth-century German lands is Karl Schottenloher, "Die Druckprivilegien des 16. Jahrhunderts," *Gutenberg Jahrbuch* (1933), 89–110.

90 Landau and Parshall, *The Renaissance Print*, 247.

91 Landau and Parshall, *The Renaissance Print*, 253ff.; *De historia stirpium commentarii insignes* (Basel: Michael Isengrin, 1542).

92 Kusukawa, *Picturing the Book of Nature*; Sachiko Kusukawa, "Leonhart Fuchs on the Importance of Pictures," *Journal of the History of Ideas* 58, no. 3 (1997), 403–27; Ogilvie, *The Science of Describing*, 34–46, 203–8.

93 For examples of Indagine's unique contributions, see Reisser, *Physiognomik und Ausdruckstheorie*, 62–3.

94 The crest and the author portrait, however, are attributed to Hans Baldung Grien. Reisser, *Physiognomik und Ausdruckstheorie*, 62; see also Alice Klein, "Hans Wechtlin, peintre à Strasbourg à la veille de la Réforme," PhD dissertation, Université Paris-Sorbonne, 2014.

95 Reisser, *Physiognomik und Ausdruckstheorie*, 62.

96 Joannes ab Indagine and Jan Berntsz, *Chyromantia ... Enn Dit Boec Leert van Drie Naturlike Consten Als Phisiognomia, Astrologia Naturalis, Chiromantia* (Utrecht: Jan Berntsz, 1536), NLM ID 2255015R.

97 Brabant, *Van Brabant die excellente Cronike ... totten iare M. CCCCC. ende XXX in Junio* (Antwerp: J. van Doesborch, 1530). Many thanks to Hans van der Mark for his assistance navigating the Brabant Chronicle.

98 F. Herrmann, "Der Astrolog Johannes Indagine, Pfarrer zu Steinheim a.M., und die Frankfurter Kaiserwahl des Jahres 1519," *Archiv für Hessische Geschichte und Alterthumskunde* 18 (n.d.), 274–91.

99 Porter, *Windows of the Soul*, 11.

100 Maria C. Oldenbourg, *Die Buchholzschnitte des Hans Baldung Grien: Ein Bibliographisches Verzeichnis ihrer Verwendungen*, Studien zur Deutschen Kunstgeschichte 335 (Baden-Baden: Verlag Heitz, 1962), 140, fig. 199. Baldung also produced a portrait of Brunfels for Schott and Theodor De Bry produced an engraving of Indagine inspired by Baldung's (see Wellcome Collection 4668i).

101 Philip Schaff, *History of the Christian Church. Volume 7: Modern Christianity – The German Reformation* (Grand Rapids, MI: Eerdmans, 1980), 126. Albrecht was largely indebted to the rich banking house of Fugger in Augsburg, from whom he had borrowed 30,000 florins in gold to pay for the papal pallium. By an agreement with the pope, he had permission to keep half of the proceeds arising from the sale of indulgences. The agents of that commercial house stood behind the preachers of indulgence and collected their share for the repayment of the loan. I'm grateful to Rachel Carlisle for this lead.

102 Ioannes ab Indagine and Johannes Schott, *Introdvctiones Apoteles||maticæ elegantes, in Chyromantiam, Physiognomiam, || Astrologiam naturalem, Complexiones hominum, || Naturas planetarum. Cum periaxiomatibus de|| faciebus Signorum, & canonib. de ægritu-||dinibus, nusqua [m] fere simili tractata|| compendio* (Strasbourg: Schott, 1522). See Reisser, *Physiognomik und Ausdruckstheorie*, 61–5.

103 Alexander Jones, ed., *Ptolemy in Perspective: Use and Criticism of His Work from Antiquity to the Nineteenth Century*, Archimedes: New Studies in the History of Science and Technology 23 (Dordrecht: Springer, 2010). See Stephan Heilen, "Ptolemy's Doctrine of the Terms and Its Reception," in Jones, ed., *Ptolemy in Perspective*, 45.

104 Johannes ab Indagine et al., *Die Kunst der Chiromantzey: vsz Besehung der Hend. Physiognomey / vsz Anblick des Menschens ...* (Strasbourg: Schott, 1523).

105 Aspects are the angular relationships between planets in a horoscope, measured as angles within the ecliptic circle. Indagine's text proposes to give information about the effects of the sun on the planets in each house.

106 Alice Klein, "Hans Wechtlin and the Production of German Colour Woodcuts," in Ad Stijnman and Elizabeth Savage, eds., *Printing Colour 1400–1700: History, Techniques, Functions and Receptions* (Leiden and Boston, MA: Brill, 2015), 103–15. Wechtlin has recently received attention for his potential role in the early development of the chiaroscuro woodcut and might be a key player in establishing this technique in Strasbourg in the first two decades of the sixteenth century. From 1506–7, Wechtlin was court painter to Duke René II de Lorraine; later he became a burgher in Strasbourg, a status he inherited from his father in 1514 and one compulsory for opening a workshop in the city (p. 107).

107 Reisser, *Physiognomik und Ausdruckstheorie*, 62. Indagine says that few good judgments can proceed from the chin or the nose (see note 126).

108 Reisser, *Physiognomik und Ausdruckstheorie*, 66.

109 Stephanie Leitch, "Visual Acuity and the Physiognomer's Art of Observation," *Oxford Art Journal* 38, no. 2 (2015), 189–208.

110 Barnes, *Astrology and Reformation*, 21, note 64; see also Jonathan Green, *Printing and Prophecy: Prognostication and Media Change 1450–1550* (Ann Arbor: University of Michigan Press, 2012), 79–84.

111 Indagine et al., *Die Kunst der Chiromantzey*. The 1523 edition begins with Indagine and doesn't include the volume by Hans von Gersdorff.

112 I am very grateful to Daniel Kaune for helping me parse "*augenschein*" and "*anblick*."

113 Gersdorff and Indagine, *Feldtbůch der Wund-Artzney*. "*Dagegen sehen wir augenschynlich/ das die cholerischen menschen/ von wegen ir hitze und verbrante[n] feüchtigkeit/ dickha[e]rig und gantz rauh von haren seind*," in *Kunst der Chiromanzey* (1523); the discussion of hair appears on p. 33r.

114 Daniel Kaune explores this term *Augenschein* in relation to a cartographic form that appears in documents presented to the imperial court; see Daniel Kaune, "Vom Grenzstein zum Augenschein: von der Essenz und Relevanz eines Kartentypus," BA/MA thesis, Gottfried Wilhelm Leibniz Universität, Hannover, n.d., especially 10ff.

115 *Die Kunst der Chiromanzey* (1523), 31v–32r.

116 These two skills were simultaneously being vetted in *Vexierbilder* (see Chapter 5).

117 Gersdorff and Indagine, *Feldtbůch der Wund-Artzney*, lxv. "[F]urther *experience* [*experientz*] and *knowledge* [*erfarunüß*] can be derived from [investigation of] the nose. That nose which divides in the front at the septum [as if touched by a finger] is a sign that same person is a maiden or youth who has become unchaste. There would be more to say here on the topic of noses, but since none of it would especially serve this skill [of reading noses], it is omitted, not unreasonably." Thanks to Elio Brancaforte and Charlotte Lang Brancaforte for assistance with the translation.

118 For artisanal epistemology (experimental knowledge as certain as deductive knowledge), see Pamela H. Smith, *The Body of the Artisan: Art and Experience in the Scientific Revolution* (Chicago: University of Chicago Press, 2012), 59; see also Rankin, "How to Cure the Golden Vein," note 36.

119 "*Das ist aber auch erfaren/ das die menschen so dyne leffzen haben/ gemeyne-tlich viler wort/ geschwätzig/ und darbey wol beredt seind/ fürsychtig/ weiß/ schafpffsynnig/ unnd geschwinder anschleg*" (1540, lxv).

120 "Von der Physiognomey und urteyl des Munds/ wie der mensch dar bey erkandt werd" (1540, lxv).

121 Fol. lxv.

122 Melanie Panse, *Hans von Gersdorffs "Feldbuch der Wundarznei": Produktion, Präsentation und Rezeption von Wissen* (Wiesbaden: Reichert, 2012), 221–7. Copies of Gersdorff's manual circulated in Augsburg and Frankfurt until *c.* 1606.

123 Schott boasts that it is "*bequem und handtsam . . . anfenglich vor augen sycht, damit er geschwynd vervassen und auch bald finden moeg das so er sucht und zu wissen begert.*"

124 Indeed, the quarto edition was a good deal handier but it was probably no small effort to produce. In order to recycle his original woodblocks developed for a folio edition, Schott likely had to cut away part of the block to trim it down to print on quarto-sized paper. Indeed, the quarto's layout seems hasty and the images' scale appears outsized for the

smaller volume. Schott correctly guessed that the more handy-sized volume invited more interactive readership: the quarto editions of the *Feldbuch* are the ones that show the most consistent signs of wear.

125 The woodblocks were apparently stripped of their borders around 1528 to resize them for the quarto editions. When the later folio edition is printed, those images are also missing their borders.

126 M. Klein, "Les Physiognomistes haut-rhénans du XVIe siècle," in *Atti del XIV Congresso internazionale di storia della medicina sotto l'Alto Patronato del Presidente della Repubblica, Roma – Salerno, 13–20 settembre 1954* (Rome: Guerra & Belli, 1960), 3–16.

127 Sabine Söll-Tauchert, *Hans Baldung Grien (1484/85–1545): Selbstbildnis und Selbstinszenierung* (Cologne: Böhlau, 2010), 78ff.; Panse, *Hans von Gersdorffs "Feldbuch der Wundarznei,"* 166. In fact, Schott might have introduced Indagine to the physician and naturalist Otto Brunfels, whose herbal Schott printed. In his correspondence with Brunfels, Indagine endorses some of the early dictates of Martin Luther. Indagine probably supported Brunfels's reforms of pharmacology.

128 Publius Ovidius Naso, *P. Ouidii Nasonis Metamorphoseon Libri XV. Index Repertorius, Omniu [m] Fabularum, Ad Numerum Chartarum, & Seriem Alphabeti, Illis [a]Ppositus Est* (Strasbourg: Schott, 1515). For Schott's chiaroscuro woodcuts, see Oldenbourg, *Die Buchholzschnitte des Hans Baldung Grien*, 153.

129 Alice Klein, "Hans Wechtlin and the Production of German Colour Woodcuts," 103–15; see also Oldenbourg, *Die Buchholzschnitte des Hans Baldung Grien*, 74, no. 309, L59.

130 The title page lists the contents as follows: "*Feldtbůch der Wund/ Arzney/ sampt vilen Instrumenten der Chirurgey (uß dem Albucasi contrafayt); Chiromantia Jo. Indagine (das ist die Kunst der Handtbesehung); Natürliche Astrologey (nach warem Lauff der Sonnen); Physiognomey (uß des Menschens Anblick und Glyderen sein angeborne neygung zu erlernen); Complexion Buch (eins yeden Natur zu erkennen/ durch der Planeten/ und xii. Uffsteigenden Zeychen Geburtstund); Canones/ oder Regelen (eins yeden Kranckheyt warlich zu erkündigen/ wie auch und wenn sich der Artzney zugebrauchen).*"

131 "*uß dem Albucasi contrafayt.*"

132 Martin Clayton et al., *Leonardo da Vinci: The Divine and the Grotesque* (London: Royal Collection, 2002), 79.

133 For physiognomic studies circulating in Italy, see Piers D. G. Britton, "The Signs of Faces: Leonardo on Physiognomic Science and the 'Four Universal States of Man,'" *Renaissance Studies* 16, no. 2 (2002), 148.

134 Royal Collection Trust, RCIN 12495. Clayton et al., *Leonardo da Vinci*; see also Martin Clayton, "Leonardo's Gypsies and the Wolf and the Eagle," *Apollo* 155, no. 486 (2002), 27–33, especially 29. Clayton suggests a narrative meaning premised on a cropped drawing, while Piers Britton sees, from left to right, personifications of the four humoral types: sanguine, choleric, melancholic, and phlegmatic. Britton, "The Signs of Faces," 143–62.

135 Chriscinda Henry argues that we might be viewing a type of Florentine *beffa*, a set piece of popular comic mockery, but she argues that the narrative is seemingly incidental to the real physiognomic focus. See Chriscinda Henry, "Leonardo da Vinci, Parody, and Pictorial Magic," in Allison M. Levy, ed., *Playthings in Early Modernity: Party Games, Word Games, Mind Games* (Kalamazoo: Western Michigan University, 2017), 87–9, notes 49 and 50.

136 Clayton, "Leonardo's Gypsies," 29.

137 For speculation about Leonardo's own planned physiognomic tracts, see Reisser, *Physiognomik und Ausdruckstheorie*, 276–7.

138 Michael W. Kwakkelstein, *Leonardo da Vinci as a Physiognomist: Theory and Drawing Practice* (Leiden: Primavers Pers, 2014), 50.

139 Kwakkelstein, *Leonardo da Vinci*, 50. Gaurico's text, an artists' manual inflected by physiognomic literature, was added to Indagine's *Introductiones Apotelesmaticae* (Strasbourg: Lazarus Zetzneri, 1603). In this book, the physiognomic tract beginning on p. 346 is organized by the eyes, brow, lashes, nose, and forehead, and progresses to the feet.

140 Pomponio Gaurico and Guglielmo Gratarolo, *Introductiones apotelesmaticae in physiognomiam, astrologiam naturalem, complexiones hominum, naturas planetarum. Cum periaxiomatibus de faciebus signorum . . . Quibus . . . accessit Gulielmi Gratatoli . . . opuscula De memoria reparanda, augenda, conservanda; De praedictione morum naturarumque hominum; De mutatione temporum . . . et Pomponii Gaurici . . . tractatus De symmetriis, lineamentis & physiognomia, ejusque speciebus, etc.* (Ursellis: Apud Cornelium Sutorium, impensis Lazari Zetzneri, 1603).

141 Clayton, "Leonardo's Gypsies," 27–34, especially 29. Leonardo's first physiognomy is dated to the 1490s; by the 1510s, he also owned a chiromantic volume, and he dedicated a portion of his budget to fortune telling. Leonardo makes notes about physiognomy and chiromancy in the *Codex Urbanis*; his book list can be found in the *Codex Atlanticus* and the Madrid manuscript. Clayton speculates on the texts Leonardo might have been familiar with (see note 16). See also Henry, "Leonardo da Vinci, Parody, and Pictorial Magic," 89, note 50; see also Reisser, *Physiognomik und Ausdruckstheorie*, 151ff., 276ff.

142 Clayton et al., *Leonardo da Vinci*, 73–99.

143 Claire J. Farago et al., *The Fabrication of Leonardo Da Vinci's Trattato della Pittura, with a Scholarly Edition of the Editio Princeps (1651) and an Annotated English Translation* (Leiden and Boston, MA: Brill, 2018), vol. 1, 166; for the passages that pertain to profiles, noses, and physiognomies (chapters 188–90 in the *Trattato della Pittura*), see vol. 2, 741–3. Farago offers correspondence in the *Libro da Pittura*, f. 108v, note 289. The *Trattato* was to include small-scale physiognomic drawings with character studies of heads and full figures, likely removed from their parent sheets. See Michael Kwakkelstein, "The Lost Book on 'Moti Mentali,'" in Claire J. Farago, *Leonardo's Writings and Theory of Art* (New York: Garland, 1999), 223.

144 Kwakkelstein, *Leonardo da Vinci as a Physiognomist*, 73; see also 63–78 for the variety of facial expressions as a result of emotion – the so-called motions of the mind.

145 Kwakkelstein, *Leonardo da Vinci as a Physiognomist*, 73.

146 Kwakkelstein, *Leonardo da Vinci as a Physiognomist*, 57–8.

147 Michael W. Kwakkelstein, "Leonardo da Vinci's Recurrent Use of Patterns of Individual Limbs, Stock Poses and Facial Stereotypes," in I. Ciulisova, ed., *Artistic Innovations and Cultural Zones*, Spectrum Slovakia 7 (Berlin: Peter Lang, 2015), 45–6.

148 See the drawing at https://art.nelson-atkins.org/objects/7030/four-heads.

149 Friedrich Winkler, *Die Zeichnungen Albrecht Dürers* (Berlin: Deutscher Verein für Kunstwissenschaft, 1938), vol. 3, 70–7; Walter L. Strauss, *The Complete Drawings of Albrecht Dürer. Volume 3: 1510–1519* (New York: Abaris, 1974), 1342–51.

150 Strauss, *The Complete Drawings of Albrecht Dürer*, 1344; see also Clayton et al., *Leonardo da Vinci*, 16. While the draftsman typically constructs the profile with the hand "inside" the face, Dürer must have engineered these profiles from right to left. Many thanks to Thomas Schauerte for sharing his insights about this drawing with me.

151 Michael Roth et al., *Dürers Mutter: Schönheit, Alter und Tod im Bild der Renaissance* (Berlin: Staatliche Museen zu Berlin and Nicolai, 2006), 88. Although these faces can be seen as examples deviating from a norm, Roth cautions against reading in these cascading faces a comment on character or sensibility.

152 Stephanie Porras explores the variety of functions that drawing had for Dürer, including autonomous drawings. See Stephanie Porras, "'Ein freie hant': Autonomy, Drawing and the Young Dürer," in Albrecht Dürer, Daniel Hess, and Thomas Eser, *Der frühe Dürer* (Nuremberg: Verlag des Germanischen Nationalmuseums, 2012), 245–59, especially 247–8.

153 Hans Rupprich and Albrecht Dürer, *Schriftlicher Nachlass* (Berlin: Deutscher Verein für Kunstwissenschaft, 1956), vol. 1; for the plan for this text, see Albrecht Dürer and Hans Rupprich, *Schriftlicher Nachlaß* (Berlin: Deutscher Verein für Kunstwissenschaft, 1966), vol. 2, 395ff.

154 For Albrecht Dürer's postscript to the third of *Four Books on Human Proportion*, known as the "Aesthetic Excursus," composed between 1513 and 1515, see Peter Parshall, "Graphic Knowledge: Albrecht Dürer and the Imagination," *Art Bulletin* 95, no. 3 (2013), 395–410.

155 See Fedja Anzelewsky, "Albrecht Dürers Suche nach dem Schönen und die Definition des Hässlichen in seinem theoretischen Werk," in Michael Roth et al., *Dürers Mutter*, 69ff.

156 Winkler, *Die Zeichnungen Albrecht Dürers*, 72.
157 Theon Alexandrinus et al., *Euclidis Megaresis Philosophi Platonici Mathematicaru Disciplinaru Janitoris* ... (Venice: Tacuini, 1505). Dürer noted on the title page of the edition preserved at the Herzog August Bibliothek in Wolfenbüttel that he purchased the volume for a single ducat: "*Daz puch hab ich zw Venedich vm ein Dugatn kawft im 1507 jor. Albrecht Dürer.*"
158 Dürer and Rupprich, *Schriftlicher Nachlaß*, vol. 2, 12; Reisser, *Physiognomik und Ausdruckstheorie*, 193. For Dürer and the library of Regiomontanus and Bernhard Walter, see Noam Andrews, "Albrecht Dürer's Personal *Underweysung der Messung*," *Word & Image* 32, no. 4 (2016), 409–29, especially 410–11.
159 Roth et al., *Dürers Mutter*, 88.
160 Roth et al., *Dürers Mutter*, 88.
161 Raymond Klibansky, Erwin Panofsky, and Fritz Saxl, *Saturn and Melancholy: Studies in the History of Natural Philosophy, Religion, and Art* (New York: Basic Books, 1964); see also Erwin Panofsky, *Life and Art of Albrecht Dürer* (Princeton, NJ: Princeton University Press, 1995 [1943]), 159–62. Dürer's figure, according to Panofsky, engages more with the "Typus Geometriae" of philosophical treatises such as Gregor Reisch's *Margarita Philosophica* than with the representations of miserly and sluggish male melancholics memorialized in the Calendar tradition.
162 Cocles, *Der schapherders || Kalender. Eyn sere schone vnde nutthe || boek/ myt velen fruchtbaren mate=||rien ... || Jtem tho ende dusses bokes vyndeth || men de Kleyne Physonomye/ vth welkere/ || des mynschen Complexie vnde tone=||gynghe der natuer klärlyck to || erkennen werth. ||* (Rostock: Dietz, 1523), fol. 69r.
163 The more direct influence for the figure on the title page of the *Shepherd's Calendar* seems to be a woodcut of an astronomer made, possibly by Dürer, for an edition of Messahalah's *De scientia motus orbis* (Nuremberg: Weissenburger, 1504). Resonances with the Messahalah astronomer can also be seen in Dürer's *Melencolia*.
164 Information about bathing according to humoral type is synthesized in a volvelle discussed in Chapter 4.
165 For the rich nature of Dürer's response to human physiology, see Merback, *Perfection's Therapy*, especially 29–30.
166 *Underweysung der Messung, mit dem Zirkel und Richtscheyt, in linien eben und gantzen Corporen* (Nuremberg: [H. Andreae], 1525).
167 Thomas Schauerte, "Hitler's Dürer?: The Nuremberg Painter between Self-Portrait and National Appropriation," in Debra Taylor Cashion, Henry Luttikhuizen, and Ashley D. West, eds., *The Primacy of the Image in Northern European Art, 1400–1700: Essays in Honor of Larry Silver* (Leiden: Brill, 2017), 318; see also Ulrich Pfisterer, "Apelles im Norden: Ausnahme Künstler, Selbstbildnisse und die Gunst der Mächtigen um 1500," in Matthias Müller, ed., *Apelles am Fürstenhof* (Berlin: Coburger Landesstiftung, 2010), 8–21.
168 Jeffrey Ashcroft, "Black Arts: Renaissance and Printing Press in Nuremberg, 1493–1528," *Forum for Modern Language Studies* 45, no. 1 (2008), 3–18, see especially notes 38–40.
169 Jaya Remond, "Bodies of Knowledge: Movement, Variety and Imagination in a German Renaissance Art Primer," in Andreas Beyer and Guillaume Cassegrain, eds., *Mouvement. Bewegung* (Berlin: Deutscher Kunstverlag, 2015), 54, see also 45–60.
170 Joseph Leo Koerner, *The Moment of Self-Portraiture in German Renaissance Art* (Chicago: University of Chicago Press, 1996).
171 Roth et al., *Dürers Mutter*, 88. Roth notes that the *Ten Heads* have an almost internal integrity in which the last head peers back at the first. Hans Baldung also produces such a study of five cascading heads *c.* 1519–20.
172 Albrecht Dürer, Franz Louis Fuhse, and Konrad Lange, *Dürers schriftlicher Nachlass auf Grund der Originalhandschriften und theilweise neu entdeckter alter Abschriften* (Halle an der Saale: Niemeyer, 1893), 298–9. "*Ich hab oft Schmerzen, da(ß) ich der vorbestimmten Meister Kunstbücher beraubt mu(ß) sein.*"

173 Jutta Funke, "Beiträge zum graphischen Werk Heinrich Vogtherrs d.Ä.," dissertation, Freie Universität, Berlin, 1967, 48.

174 Alexander Marr, "Walther Ryff, Plagiarism and Imitation in Sixteenth Century Germany," *Print Quarterly* 31, no. 2 (2014), 142.

175 Vogtherr's book can be seen as a response to entreaties such as Dürer's for contemporary artists to share their technical knowledge with others. Funke, "Beiträge zum graphischen Werk," 49.

176 Frank Muller, *Heinrich Vogtherr l'Ancien: un artiste entre Renaissance et Réforme* (Wiesbaden: Harrassowitz, 1997); Funke, "Beiträge zum graphischen Werk," 50ff. According to Funke, both Dürer and Sebald Beham also bemoan this in *Kunst und Ler Büchlein/ Malen und Reissen zu Lernen* (Frankfurt: Egenolff's Heirs, 1546).

177 *Ein Wolgegrindtes Kunstreichs Sumari Büchlin Aller Sonnen Uur Uff Acht Oder Viereckette Stecklen, Innbuchsen, Zylinder u. Guldine Ring, Auch Uff Glaß, Alle Mauren Schreg Oder Unschreg Zu Machen* ... (Strasbourg: Vogtherr, 1539).

178 Heinrich Vogtherr, *Ein newes hochnutzlichs Büchlin von Erkantnüs der Kranckeyten der Augen sampt einer Figur oder Anothomia eines Augs: wie es innwendig gestaltet, volget in der andern Colum: auch Erklärung der selbigen mit Anzeigung viler nutzlicher undbewerter Hülff als Purgation, Pflaster, Collirien, Sieff, Pulver, Salben und Augenwassern wie mans machen und gebrauchen soll, einem jeden Hausshalt nutzlich* (Strasbourg: Vogtherr, 1538). The portrait of the printer also appears on the verso of the last leaf. Other practical publications from Vogtherr include booklets on ringworm, the cure of hernias, and properties of urine. For Vogtherr's ophthalmology publication *Büchlin*, loosely based on Leonhart Fuch's *Alle Krackheyt der Augen* (Strasbourg: Vogtherr, 1539), see Donald L. Blanchard, "Vogtherr's *Büchlin*," *Documenta Ophthalmologica* 93 (1997), 73. The design for the diagram *Anatomia Oculi* was taken from Gregor Reisch's *Margarita Philosophica*.

179 The book's usefulness as a how-to manual is staged in its title: "A new and extremely useful pamphlet about the *Erkantnus* [knowledge] of ailments of the eye, together with an image of the interior of the eye ... also with the explanation of the same with a demonstration of the more useful and valuable cures ... how to perform them and how to use them ... which will be useful in every household."

180 Rhenanus's copy is preserved in the Bibliothèque Humaniste de Sélestat.

181 Reisser, *Physiognomik und Ausdruckstheorie*, 193.

182 Jaya Remond, "Artful Instruction: Pictorializing and Printing Artistic Knowledge in Early Modern Germany," *Word & Image* 36, no. 2 (2020), 114.

183 Remond, "Bodies of Knowledge," 45–60.

184 Loh, "Renaissance Faciality," 341–63.

185 Giorgio Riello, "The World in a Book: The Creation of the Global in Sixteenth-Century European Costume Books," *Past & Present* 242, no. 14 (2019), 281–317; Bronwen Wilson, "Reflecting on the Turk in Late Sixteenth-Century Venetian Portrait Books," *Word & Image* 19, no. 1(2003), 38; Bronwen Wilson, *The World in Venice: Print, the City and Early Modern Identity* (Toronto: University of Toronto Press, 2005); Charlotte Colding Smith, *Images of Islam, 1453–1600: Turks in Germany and Central Europe* (London: Pickering & Chatto, 2014).

186 Cocles, *Phisionomi vnd || Chiromanci. || Eyn newß Complexion Büch=||lein/ Der Menschen Geburt/ Sitten/ Geberden vnd Neyg=||ligkeyten/ Außder Phisionomi/ Chiromanci/ Den Siben || Planeten/ Zwölff Zeichen/ Vnnd den XXXvj. Bildern || Deß Himels/ Auch Nach den Zwölff Monaten/ Leichtlich || Vnd Grundtlich Zulernen/ Auß Platone/ Aristotele/ Pto||lomeo/ Hali/ Albumasar/ vnnd Johanne Künigsper=||ger #c. in Fünff Büchlin Kurtzlich Gezogen/ Vnd im Sech||sten Werden Erzelt Wunder Gestalt Lewt Mit Jren Siten* (Strasbourg: Jakob Cammerlander, 1540), http://diglib.hab.de/drucke/n-97-4f-helmst-7s/start.htm; see HAB HN97.4 Helmst. 7.

187 David Freedberg, *The Eye of the Lynx: Galileo, His Friends, and the Beginnings of Modern Natural History* (Chicago: University of Chicago Press, 2002), 402.

188 Michel Foucault, *The Order of Things: An Archaeology of the Human Sciences* (New York: Vintage Books, 1994).

189 For example, in Indagine we read: "On the judgment of the chest and the ribs: just as we can identify a lion's strength and wisdom by his chest, as the natural philosophers write. In the same manner, we can identify peoples [*thirst/thürstig*] and boldness [*keck*] from those who have a pronounced [*erhabene*] chest." See Indagine, *Die Kunst der Chiromantzey* (Strasbourg: Schott, 1523), fol. XXXVIr.

190 For a discussion of early modern portrait collections, see Haskell, *History and Its Images*, 26–79; Wilson, *The World in Venice*, 206 and note 52.

191 Alexander Marr, "Copying, Commonplaces and Technical Knowledge: The Architect-Engineer as Reader," in Heiko Damm et al., eds., *The Artist as Reader: On Education and Non-Education of Early Modern Artists* (Leiden and Boston, MA: Brill, 2013), 421–46.

192 Haskell, *History and Its Images*, 64. For strategies of comparison of works of antiquity, see Fulvio Orsini, *Elogia virorum illustrium* (Rome: Lafreri, 1570). Reflecting his activity as an antiquarian in Cardinal Farnese's employ, Orsini combined sculpture, bust, and gems to form a semi-systematic study of ancient portraiture.

193 Bronwen Wilson, "Learning How to Read: Giovanni Battista Della Porta, Physiognomy, and Printed Portrait-Books," paper delivered at Visual Knowledges Conference, University of Edinburgh, 17–20 September 2003. "New formats for printed images prompted encounters with human faces in ways never seen before, and new uses for images of faces would have encouraged viewers to compare faces. In so doing, these new forms and uses of print contributed to a shift in the ways in which identities accrued to individuals."

194 Haskell, *History and Its Images*, 39–40.

195 Wilson, *The World in Venice*, 201; see also Haskell, *History and Its Images*, 63.

196 Linda Susan Klinger, *The Portrait Collection of Paolo Giovio* (Ann Arbor: UMI Dissertation Services, 2003); Linda Klinger Aleci, "Images of Identity: Italian Portrait Collections of the Fifteenth and Sixteenth Centuries," in Nicholas Mann and Luke Syson, eds., *The Image of the Individual: Portraits in the Renaissance* (London: British Museum Press, 1998), 67–80. Perna was a Protestant exile from Lucca who actively printed classical texts in Basel.

197 See Cecil Clough, "Italian Renaissance Portraits and Printed Portrait Books," in Denis V. Reidy, ed., *The Italian Book: 1465–1800. Studies Presented to Dennis E. Rhodes on His 70th Birthday* (London: British Library, 1993), 183–223.

198 For the itinerary of Dürer's rhinoceros through related literature in the sixteenth century, see Stephanie Leitch, "Dürer's Rhinoceros Underway: The Epistemology of the Copy in the Early Modern Print," in Cashion et al., *The Primacy of the Image*, 241–55.

199 Clough, "Italian Renaissance Portraiture and Printed Portrait Books," 183–223, especially 194; Wilson, "Reflecting on the Turk," 68.

200 Katherine MacDonald, "Humanistic Self-Representation in Giovan Battista Della Porta's 'Della Fisonomia dell'Uomo': Antecedents and Innovation," *Sixteenth Century Journal* 36, no. 2 (2005), 397–414.

201 "*Nach Christus geburt. 1513. Jar. Adi.1. May. Hat man dem großmechitgen Kunig von Portugall Emanuell gen Lysabona pract ausz India/ ein sollich lebendig Thier. Das nennen sie Rhinocerus. Das ist hye mit aller seiner gestalt Abconderfet. Es hat ein farb wie ein gespreckelte Schildtkrot. Und ist von dicken Schalen uberlegt fast fest. Und ist in der größ als der helfand Aber nydertrechtiger von paynen/ und fast werhafftig. Es hat ein scharff starck Horn vorn auff der nasen/ Das begyndt es albeg zu wetzen wo es bey staynen ist. Das dosig Thier ist des helffantz todt feyndt. Der helffandt furcht es fast ubel/ dann wo es In ankumbt/ so laufft Im das Thier mit dem kopff zwischen dye fordern payn/ und reyst den helffandt unden am pauch auff und erwürgt In/ des mag er sich nit erwern. Dann das Thier ist also gewapent/ das Im der helffandt nichts kan thun. Sie sagen auch das der Rhynocerus Schnell/ Fraydig und Listig sey.*" For a translation, see Dackerman, *Prints and the Pursuit of Knowledge*, 167–8. See image at www.metmuseum.org/art/collection/search/356497.

202 This might have been inspired by the Italian version of Dürer's *Four Books on Human Proportion* that was printed in Venice: Giovanni Paolo Gallucci, *Della simmetria dei corpi humani* (Venice: Meietti, 1594); see also Reisser, *Physiognomik und Ausdruckstheorie*, 277.

203 Freedberg, *The Eye of the Lynx*, 402. Among the texts produced were treatises on phytognomics, chirognomics, cryptography, and celestial physiognomy.
204 Francesco Stelluti, *Della Fisonomia di Tvtto il Corpo Hvmano del S. Gio. Batta Della Porta. Acc. Linceo Libri Quattro Ne' Quali Si Tratta di Quanto Intorno a Questa Materia n' Hanno i Greci, Latini, e gli Arabi Schritto: Hora Bruemente in Tauole Sinottiche Ridotta et Ordinata* (Rome: Mascardi, 1637), HAB A25.6 Quod. 2. See title page engraving, attributed to Daniel Widman, in which heads of people and corresponding animals peer out of strapwork volutes.
205 Freedberg, *The Eye of the Lynx*, 401–4.
206 "*Hora brevemente in tavole sinottiche ridotta et ordinate.*"
207 These projects include poems to Galileo in treatises on sunspots of 1613, as well as in the *Assayer* of 1623. See Freedberg, *The Eye of the Lynx*, 160–3, 179–94.
208 Freedberg, *The Eye of the Lynx*, 414. Cassiano dal Pozzo was Barbarini's secretary. A former supporter of Galileo, Barbarini eventually abandoned him.
209 MacDonald, "Humanistic Self-Representation in Giovan Battista Della Porta's 'Della Fisonomia dell'Uomo,'" 413.
210 Wilson, *The World in Venice*, 245–7.
211 Clement, "Moveable Types," 1–24.
212 As Clement notes, the same images appeared in *The honorable reputation of a soldier* (London: Richard Jones, 1585), as well as in *A short admonition or warning, vpon the detestable treason* (London: Richard Jones, 1587). Clement, "Moveable Types," 4.
213 Clement, "Moveable Types," 17–22.
214 Clement, "Moveable Types," 16.
215 Adriana Bontea, "Montaigne's On Physiognomy," *Renaissance Studies* 22, no. 1 (2008), 41–62; Joshua Scodel, "The Affirmation of Paradox: A Reading of Montaigne's 'De La Phisionomie' (III:12)," *Yale French Studies* 64 (1983), 209–37.
216 "Anyone who turns his prime attention on to himself will hardly ever find himself in the same state twice. I give my soul this face or that, depending upon which side I lay it down on. I speak about myself in diverse ways: that is because I look at myself in diverse ways. Every sort of contradiction can be found in me, depending upon some twist or attribute: timid, insolent, chaste, lecherous; talkative, taciturn; tough, sickly; clever, dull, brooding, affable; lying, truthful; learned, ignorant; generous, miserly and then prodigal – I can see something of all that in myself, depending on how I gyrate; and anyone who studies himself attentively finds in himself and in his very judgement this whirring about and this discordancy. There is nothing I can say about myself as a whole simply and completely, without intermingling and admixture." Montaigne, *The Essays of Michel de Montaigne*, translated and edited by M. A. Screech (London: Allen Lane, 1991), II:1, "On the inconstancy of our actions," 373–7.
217 Wilson, *The World in Venice*, 231–40.

PART II

COLLECTING AND COGNITIVE CHALLENGES

FOUR

VISUALIZED DATA AND SEARCHABLE SCIENCE

The *Liber Quodlibetarius* (*c.* 1524)

Books with ancient pedigrees, such as cosmographies and physiognomies, became newly visualized once they reached print. Although both genres had emerged from unillustrated manuscript iterations that had languished as arcane pursuits of the *Mirror of Princes*, publishers updated them in the early sixteenth century and repackaged them in new vernacular languages geared toward practitioners. This chapter considers two manuscripts with related aims that reflect the prerogatives of these printers/publishers to situate their content in environments of pictorial data. The manuscripts' images reflected the way in which prints prompted empirical interventions in the field and how the images themselves brokered a shift toward visual sovereignty. The graphic design of one of these manuscripts, the *Liber Quodlibetarius*, sharpened the emphasis on visual knowledge in the scribe's printed source material. The manuscripts translated this information into transcripts of empirical activity. These data displays activated new cognitive potential in the reader; chief among these expectations was empowering observation as a mode of gathering and remembering knowledge.

The newfound sovereignty that images attained in printed texts can be seen in the way they negotiated both knowledge and audience. How printed images could help readers pick up the pace of knowledge acquisition emerges here, perhaps unexpectedly, in a pair of sixteenth-century miscellany manuscripts. Two related pictorial codices were produced during the first three decades of the sixteenth century, both written in the vernacular of the local area, a dialect of *Baierisch.*[1] The *Liber Quodlibetarius*, a manuscript illuminated *c.* 1524, is preserved today in the university library in Erlangen, and it has only recently sparked scholarly analysis.[2] The so-called sister manuscript, produced around the same time, resides today in the Jagiellonian Library in Cracow. The codex preserved today at the Biblioteka Jagiellońska, hereafter referred to as the Jagiellonian manuscript, has been treated in the secondary literature as a "Housebook" of medieval knowledge, and bears the name Bavarian Housebook.[3]

Both codices presented many images that were circulating in printed practical how-to texts – manuals devoted to astronomy, surgery, distillation, cosmography, and physiognomy, to name just a few (Plate I).[4] These images were copied from vernacular printed publications by amateur practitioners who had access to printed texts. Indeed, such educated non-specialists had already been placed in the crosshairs as a new target audience by savvy publishers who organized older textual material into pictorialized units of knowledge.

Short vernacular pamphlets tried unlike any other contemporary publications to convey their information visually. The new sovereignty claimed by images in the era of print is key to figuring out the function of the illustrations in the manuscripts. The codices retain manuscript illuminations' ability to embed information independent of narrative, but they also flag transformations in patterns of knowledge-making that were primarily an intervention of printmaking. The manuscript in the Jagiellonian Library is likely the earlier of the two manuscripts; while I will refer occasionally to this codex in this chapter for purposes of comparison, I will largely center my discussion on the codex in Erlangen, the *Liber Quodlibetarius*, because of its more explicit connections to printed literature. The *Liber Quodlibetarius* juxtaposed images from a variety of printed sources on the strength of their kindred epistemic aims and the commonality of their visual programs. The book's aims can be expressed in two broad categories: first, it approximates encyclopedic genres in its capacity to organize emergent disciplinary knowledge. Second, it mobilized that knowledge from the point of view of useful aims. I will argue that the presentation of images in the *Liber Quodlibetarius* as visualized knowledge sharpened practical and epistemic skills already active in the printed source material on which it relied. In some cases, the codex's formulaic reformatting of images even surpassed those printers' strategies to clarify information via images. Reflecting on the book as a repository of knowledge, this chapter proposes an epistemology for the secondhand printed images that comprise the *Liber Quodlibetarius*'s visual program. Functioning as technical shorthand for knowledge-based pursuits, those images spurred the reader's investigations of the vernacular world. They both activated the reader's cognition of a variety of knowledge fields and forged novel epistemic commerce among themselves. Central to the compiler's project was the idea that collected knowledge could be experienced visually. To the extent to which viewing is the operative mode of knowledge acquisition, this manuscript suggests that the "observations" gathered in this book could constitute an analogue to experience in the field.

CUSTOMIZED BOOKS

While the related codices have been identified in the secondary literature as miscellanies, *Bildenzyklopädien*, or Housebooks, this chapter examines them as customized or composite books, entities with sovereign and independent epistemological concerns.[5] Methodological approaches by book historians of the customized, or composite, book permits a broader consideration of not only its content but also its structure. While the term "miscellany" can sometimes usefully embrace the random content of a scribal collection, these two codices are self-consciously organized to represent distinct forms of knowledge. How that knowledge was represented betrays the compiler's close engagement with the printed tradition. Printed books that inform the *Liber Quodlibetarius* were slender volumes studiously engaged in organizing disciplinary fields. Printers of illustrated books in the sixteenth century repackaged information from the scribal tradition into images that gave easier access to the knowable world. One of the ways in which knowledge was packaged for prompt delivery was the circular format that is the book's organizing graphic layout and into which a variety of diverse material is embedded. The roundel format made it easy to compare the relationship between differing knowledge groups – such forms were employed to organize elements of the creation narratives in manuscripts and early printed books.[6] Another critical component of the book's design was the pithy vernacular captions that alluded to the images' content. Despite the varied source material that informed the book's content, its regular presentation in homogeneous formulas linked these sources together. The compilers extracted from printed books precisely that data that could be imported into roundels and rows, display spreads familiar from books like *Kunstbücher*, such as recipe books, how-to pamphlets, and artists' manuals.

This chapter also aims to explore prints' proprietary role in organizing visual information. Printed genres at the time provided novel empirical and cognitive approaches to the world that encouraged the viewer to observe, cue, and test visual hypotheses.[7] Material was now deployed to serve as an interface between the object and the user. Part of what drove these cognitive approaches was the confidence that images could distill sovereign information from the accompanying text. The scribe of the *Liber Quodlibetarius* consigned the textual accompaniments to brief commentary in canons at the end of the volume. These canons explain what knowledge can be gained from the images, or what knowledge-making practices they signal.

Issues relating to the reproduction, transmission, and "transformission" in these codices will *de facto* consider the drift from the original; these modes of transferring knowledge raise concerns with the epistemology of the copy. The technical reproducibility of print, according to Christopher S. Wood, merely amplified modes of repetition that already inhered in manuscript culture. An exploration of images derived from print lets us consider approaches to the types of transformation that took place between scribal knowledge and knowledge mediated by print. In examining the shift from the scribal tradition, Wood explores the repertoire of gelled iconography and what represented drift from the point of origin.[8] He notes that an uncanny and "exceptional and not always warranted" authority adhered to the medium of print in the early sixteenth century.[9] Instead of weighing which medium took the job of copy more seriously, however, I posit that the sovereignty developed by printed images positioned the print as an important wellspring around which other knowledge-based pursuits would accrue.

Lastly, these manuscripts can illuminate the reception of images through the printed texts' readers, the vernacular practitioners to whom these image collections were self-consciously addressed. Scholarship has constituted the reception of books and prints in this period as one mediated by users: for example, Margaret Gaida claims that cosmographic texts were increasingly designed for readers who conceived of themselves as mathematical amateurs.[10] The host of prints that gave the viewer active and somatic things to do impressed novel cognitive impulses on a new class of "interactive" users.[11]

INFORMATION IN SEARCH OF SEEKERS

The practical knowledge collected in the codices was sourced from a generation of manuscripts and *Kunstbücher* whose themes often overlapped with those of more practical how-to books. At their most fundamental level as a category of text, *Kunstbücher* and *Hausbücher* presumed their readers to be in need of their advice. The thematic focus of these books varied, but it was the practical nature of recommendations made by them that united the diverse material that traded under these titles. Once the initial impulse to issue printed versions of older genres had passed, a marketing push by printers who appealed to known humanist audiences as likely buyers of familiar genres, only then did printing books "on demand" by publishers begin in earnest. The invocations of lofty aristocratic patrons in the introductions to technical manuals frequently served as a pretext for another type of reader entirely: primarily humanists, physicians, aristocrats, lawyers, and intellectuals.[12]

The move to capture larger audiences coincided roughly with open market forces that took over the production of single-leaf prints as well.[13] Publishers tried to assess the needs of new audiences, and thus established a market. The targeted demographic of readers was often articulated in the front matter of some of these volumes themselves. In his prefaces, the printer/publisher Walther Ryff cultivated *der gemeine Mann*, a type of "common man" more frequently referred to as a *Hausvater*, a head of household who was in search of useful information. These readers, according to William Eamon, were industrious urban citizens established in the middle ranks of society, and a group that increasingly included women.[14] These readers were literate in local vernaculars but not necessarily learned in Latin. Ryff was particularly canny in uniting diverse audiences under an initiative to publish Housebooks for heads of households.[15] The *Haus* in *Hausbücher* and *Hausvater* indicated the domestic setting in which the practical knowledge could be mobilized.

The interest of such buyers in the content of these books might have led to a prioritization of content over its authorship. Indeed, the idea of authorship as intellectual property in the way that modern readers conceive of it was hardly on the horizon. In fact, Ryff's key role as a popularizer, even as some contemporaries condemned him for his piracy, provides a foil to the notion that sixteenth-century scientific authority should rest on the shoulders of an author: almost all of the books he published were existing texts repackaged to streamline that knowledge for wide availability. In the age of print before recycled intellectual property became suspect, Ryff also did not shy away from trying to conceal the authorship of the sources on which he relied; his intent was primarily to convert older material into updated forms for consumers of useful knowledge.[16] Ryff was hopeful that audiences would buy his books on the strength of the practical knowledge they presented. Important agents in spreading that practical knowledge were vernacular printings of pithy volumes in quarto and octavo formats that were richly illustrated to assist in the interpretation of key concepts in the text. The image environment that characterizes those publications could substantially shorten the textual explanations – and, correspondingly, the length of the texts. In an indirect but substantial way, the prospective user, the *Hausvater*, might have provided the impetus for succinct and visually packaged knowledge of the type that Ryff delivered.

The compiler of the *Liber Quodlibetarius* was also a consumer of such practical texts, since the codex takes such publications as its source material. In fact, our compiler was first and foremost a close reader who distilled the information that the printed volumes put on view. From a library he must have had on hand, the compiler reduced the tangled data of the text into its pictorial substrate. It is almost as though he saw the pages of those texts before they were printed: as woodblocks locked into the printer's forme, along with printing furniture and movable type. Our compiler only had eyes for the images. The manuscript abridges knowledge already existing in printed volumes, deleting most of the text that embedded the images, collapsing the vital information into the residual images. The brief captions are the only remnant of the text. Entire domains of knowledge were represented by their pictures. The sovereignty that printed images exercised over the textual accompaniment in which they were previously embedded allowed them to forge connections among similar images from unrelated genres.

For instance, images from chronicles and natural histories did not necessarily have an obvious relationship to images of vats and beakers from distillation manuals, or to ornately shaped headdresses from model books. Certain manuscript genres (such as the *Liber Floridus* or the *Image du Monde*) had united diverse content via similar display objectives, creating a homogeneous look to some of their images. The compiler took over these formulas for the *Liber Quodlibetarius*. As a result, unrelated content such as lunar tables, musical instruments, and horse bits could bump against each other; this proximity forged new synergies between discrete domains of knowledge. The *Liber Quodlibetarius* thus networked its various visual units in ways that publishers who printed the genres separately had not attempted. Such new juxtapositions were akin to how scientific instruments generated new formulations of knowledge. Hailing their new neighbors across the pages, these independent images suggested new groupings of data. This manuscript provides a telling example of how transformations can be embedded in the process of translation, per a formulation of textual transformission that Randall McLeod proposes.[17] Thus, novel and unique data was generated from lessons learned from familiar images.

Many of these images also had a particular relationship to knowledge-making. The idea of "knowing" or epistemic images has underwritten some recent scholarship in the history of both art and science that encompasses a broad range of knowledge-based pictorial genres, including organization, collecting, demonstrating theories, scientific tools, and direct reference to natural objects.[18] It can also refer to technical images or ones specifically deployed in the acquisition of new skills, per Horst Bredekamp.[19] The practical goals of recipe books, or *Kunstbücher*, have begged their consideration under the rubric of epistemic aims. So have other volumes like Walther Ryff's *Vitruvius teutsch*, which conveyed architectural principles for the layman. Images of cosmographies that instructed readers how to observe and measure the heavens belong in this category, as do images from instrument books that taught the fundamentals of surveying or keeping time. Some scholars debate whether the term "epistemic" should delimit only images that can replicate a natural process, or ones that serve as functioning tools, per Lorraine Daston.[20] These categories give us a good place to begin to parse the various functions of knowledge-generating images, such as theoretical, indexical, and purely practical.[21] However, this chapter queries instead if sovereignty itself can adjudicate an image's epistemic potential. The evidence provided by hand-produced books in the age of print tests the functional properties of epistemic images, especially when detached from the matrix of the text believed to be critical to those images' didactic potency. It is no accident that scholarship on epistemic images has recently collected around published images: that is, those active in print that birthed practical concerns and adopted diverse strategies to speak to audiences in need of technical information. They are characterized by a dialogue between publisher and reader/viewers, who both sought to gain from information emerging from the corner press and the new open publishing market. The scribe's consensus that these images can serve as freestanding data, as this chapter argues, is as important as the images' rhetorical didactics or actual functionality. The sovereignty of these images as crystalized knowledge, I argue, is an element whose importance rivaled whether or not images could serve as functioning tools or diagrams, or ones that instructed a process. Images in these books do all of those things.

Items featured in the codices belonged to the repertoire of knowledge-based pursuits as they were enunciated and organized by contemporary prints.[22] Among the books pirated for these codices' source material were Hartman Schedel's *Liber Chronicarum* (Nuremberg, 1493), Peter Apian's *Cosmographicus Liber* (Landshut, 1524), Bartolomeo Cocles's *Physiognomie* (Strasbourg, 1533), and Hans von Gersdorff's *Feldbuch der Wundarzenei* (Strasbourg, 1517). The compilers clearly had access to extensive libraries in which these printed texts were kept, and the manuscripts present that knowledge for ready reference.[23] The printed genres represented in these manuscripts are similar in the attention they granted to images and featured visual accompaniment as an apparatus critical to their argumentation.

The *Liber Quodlibetarius* was probably produced with knowledge of the earlier codex now at the Jagiellonian Library. Codicological analysis indicates that the books are of roughly the same dimensions: the *Liber Quodlibetarius* measures 21 cm × 29 cm[24] while the Jagiellonian codex measures 22.5 cm × 30 cm.[25] Past scholarship has assigned an earlier date for the completion of the sister manuscript, but recent research suggests that the production of the two books was much closer in date, around the mid-1520s.[26] The *Liber Quodlibetarius* has been given a *terminus ante quem* around 1524; the date inscribed on the back cover, perhaps by a later owner, is 1543.[27] Both manuscripts are comprised mostly of illuminated pages, with brief captions penned in a *Baierisch* dialect that sometimes refer to longer explanations in the form of *Canons* at the back of the book. The inscriptions in both codices are rendered in a gothic cursive script, a rounded humanistic *Fraktur* hand active in the south German–Austrian context, popularized by typefaces that appeared in editions printed in Nuremberg and Augsburg.[28]

Providing clues about the identity of illuminists active in the *Liber Quodlibetarius* is the recurrence of the initial "W" in several places. The name that appears in the Erlangen manuscript, Benedictus Rughalm, has been proposed as the patron.[29] We see the monogram WR along with the year 1524 on folio 86v of the *Liber Quodlibetarius* (see Plate I). The initial W appears in a hand resembling typography in the sister codex in Cracow on folio 57r.[30] Codicologists have detected five hands active in the Jagiellonian manuscript.[31] The two hands at work in the *Liber Quodlibetarius* are both Franconian, from the region around Passau. The contents of both manuscripts are scavenged from earlier manuscript and print sources to which the illustrators had ready access. I will refer to the primary agent driving the production of this book as the compiler, although scribes were also involved, since choosing and organizing images already in circulation seems to have been the primary task in creating this vessel of knowable knowledge.

VISUAL DISPLAY AS COLLECTED KNOWLEDGE

The compilers of these codices were self-conscious about the collecting efforts that they were undertaking. While the compiler of the Jagiellonian codex did not give his book a title page, the Erlangen manuscript takes the title *Liber Quodlibetarius*, or "whatever pleases," alluding to the miscellaneous information collected there. Quodlibetal debates, or *ensenhamen*, were rhetorical practices that were simultaneously pedagogical and performative: they showed off the participants' wit and skill in rhetoric.[32] Early modern bibliophiles also used this term to refer to books whose content combined several categories or lay outside recognizable genres.[33] Indeed, the title "whatever pleases" seems not so much an expedient here as a deliberate choice for the display of wide-ranging units of knowledge.[34]

While the term "miscellany" can refer to a book's plurality of content, new studies on the sociology of the book prefer the monikers customized, composite, or multi-text book as a way to enunciate the material structure of the book.[35] This approach to the book as a "whole book" goes beyond simply content to also consider practices of compilation and book binding, as well as print collecting within books. The entire book can also be mined in the context of materialist philology, which attempts to expand outward from mere textual analysis to unpack the book as an artifact conceived by its owner.[36] The composite book considers the elements that comprise a codicological unit.[37] The term "composite book" can also perhaps better capture the quality of an illustrated manuscript, the materiality and production of the printed book, as well as the physical operations of textual transmission, or radical "transformission," a theory predicated on the belief that texts were transformed from the moment they were transmitted.[38] Current studies on manuscripts increasingly treat them as objects evolving over time.[39] The approach to the book as a composite book allows us to look at the interstices between manuscript and prints. It also permits investigations into the formation of genres. Such an approach could be productive, for instance, for mining the line between astrology and astronomy, two pursuits that were related to judicial astrology in this period but would soon go their separate ways. It might also illuminate the shared concerns of texts that simultaneously treat the cosmology of creation and proto-scientific cosmography. Another relationship that such an approach could unpack is the kinship between Books of Secrets (or *Secreti*) and technical manuals. *Secreti* and technical manuals share a common concern in the practice of revealing secrets, but because Books of Secrets were unillustrated, and technical manuals were essentially collections of pictures with brief captions, their aims are not often considered together.

On one level, the morphology of the *Liber Quodlibetarius* and the sister manuscript in the Jagiellonian Library reflects organizational operations that may have derived from a variety of structural models of knowledge collecting, methods of common-placing from the manuscript miscellany tradition, and displays active in the *Wunderkammer*. What qualified content for admission into these manuscripts was the capacity of that knowledge to be represented by pictures. If gathering pictorialized knowledge was the first priority of the compilers, it makes sense that both of these books rely on systems of knowledge as they were codified by earlier textual transmission. Books were the vessels wherein knowledge was stored and their visual programs presented readymade systems of knowledge. These manuscripts relied on textual traditions reaching back to the order of scripture; the practice of chronicling historical events; the encyclopedic impulse of manuscripts in the tradition of *Materia Medica* of Dioscorides, *Image du Monde*, or the *Liber Floridus*; Ptolemaic geography; Aristotelian natural philosophy; and the pseudo-Aristotelian *Secretum Secretorum*.[40] In the era of print, these older genres became systematically visualized. In a few cases, some of these textual traditions, such as cosmography and physiognomy (the subjects of Chapters 2 and 3 respectively), received their very first visual treatments in their sixteenth-century printed iterations. These two sixteenth-century codices brought pictorial traditions from chronicles and cosmography into dialogue, as well as opening a visual commerce among images from more contemporary genres, such as books advertising designs for horse bits, books of field surgery, and manuals for fencing.

Sixteenth-century printers did capitalize on the visual apparatus of a variety of traditions. Some manuscripts were furnished with ample illustrations and the mandate to tell stories visually, such as we see in the Apocalypse tradition, or in collections such as bestiaries and natural histories. Technical manuals were historically well illustrated; in some cases, they were mostly made of images with textual commentary.[41] So dedicated to pictorial rhetoric were their programs that their dense illustration would have put them beyond the budget of publishers wanting to print expediently and economically.[42] Astrological material found itself in a range of different manuscript genres and frequently packed usable data reserves into volvelles; such dials served as an early form of artificial intelligence.[43] The various visual supports of the manuscript tradition thus informed the printing of repackaged genres in early modernity.

Some of the early organizational principles of visual data in these codices might even resemble the format of plans later developed for the *Wunderkammer*.[44] The blending of man-made knowledge and knowledge of the natural world evident in their arrangement of objects and images, as well as the shift of their presentations toward the visual, suggest the encyclopedic display of the collecting of curiosities, as well as the idea that the book could function as an "ark" of information.

Furthermore, these manuscripts reflect practices of collating printed texts that their compilers may have already encountered as editions collected into a single bound volume, or *Sammelband*.[45] The bringing together of printed literature with similar objectives was already the *modus operandi* of book collectors who bound diverse, but frequently related, texts together in a single volume. Concurrent with the production of these sixteenth-century manuscripts is the appearance of printed commonplace books.[46] Adages, emblems, and proverbs were assembled along the lines of medieval modes of organizing knowledge via common-placing, but these were also beginning to be printed and organized via paratextual finding aids such as tables of content and indices.[47] Such books really start to resemble our vernacular manuscripts when they take on the additional burden of preserving common cultural knowledge. Jaya Remond has linked the appearance of commonplace books to the pictorial strategies of *Kunstbücher*, which simultaneously fielded a variety of sources for visual inspiration before organizing them into artfully designed pages.[48] They also share an objective in their efforts to preserve vernacular German knowledge for posterity. Thus, these two manuscripts can shed light on both early modern collecting practices and the reception of printed books.

COLLECTING IN A VIRTUAL ARK

The orderly division of the primordial chaos into elements and organic matter with which the book of Genesis opens furnished a logical starting point for many types of books, including etymologies and secular chronicles. It was not uncommon for such chronicles to begin with the history of creation, so readers would not have been surprised to find illustrations of the creation narrative at the beginning of these customized books. Both codices begin with a series of images devoted to the creation described in Genesis and the world's wonders. Images of chaos are followed by the separation of the elements, the division of night and day, earth from water, the creation of Eve and Adam, and many creatures of the earth (featuring marvels of the East, marked by cyclops, cynocephali, and seafarers). Noah's ark is presented at the threshold of world wonders. Both codices rely on common visual sources for the organization of the creation narrative; a strong candidate for this original source is Hartmann Schedel's *Weltchronik* or *Nuremberg Chronicle* of 1492, whose format both the Erlangen and Jagiellonian codices follow for their creation sequences.[49] The respective compilers culled data from the "ages of the world" from books including the printed *Weltchronik*, only to reorganize that information into a stricter, more searchable format. One compositional choice from that section of the *Weltchronik* was the roundel format, which unified the treatment of the diverse content presented. For example, while the marvels of the East stacked themselves around the edges of a Ptolemaic map of the world in the *Weltchronik*, both codices reintegrate the standard repertoire of marvels as elements of the creation narrative in episodes devoted to the animals of the earth. The accompanying caption, "various animals of the earth" (*manigerlay thier auf der erdreich*), points to the images' informational value (Figure 4.1). These monsters were stock images of wonders that the *Weltchronik* had already imported from less orderly groupings in books containing similar data, such as Konrad von Megenberg's *Buch der Natur*.[50] In the *Liber Quodlibetarius*, the griffon and cynocephali share a visual field with elephants and mountain goats. But here, the strict organizing formula made them easier to search.

The compiler capitalized on scripture's own organizing structure. When told pictorially in chronicles, scriptural narrative was broken down into its data content. This move toward pictorial sequencing likely suggested the next section's focus on wonders outside of the scriptural tradition. Immediately following the creation story in both codices is a sequence of images representing marvelous occurrences whose wondrous nature rivaled the events of the creation narrative. Presented in similar layout, with the same *mise-en-page*, the wonders conformed to the "collected" aspect of the information therein. However, they were more easy to search here: whereas contemporary chronicles packaged the tumbling of the Colossus of Rhodes within other events occurring during the fifth world age, the illuminist of the *Liber Quodlibetarius* presents it as an intact pillar 70 *ellenpogen* high with an image of the sun in the middle and the other planets represented above and below it (fol. 12v).[51] Billed as world wonders, this section added to the canonical marvels of the ancient world (originally transmitted via Herodotus and Callimachus of Cyrene) contemporary ones remarkable for their miraculous or improbable foundations. Among them are a bath that was heated with a single candle, a building made from a single stone, and a bronze horse and rider, likely Bellerophon and Pegasus, held in place by magnets floating over the city of Smyrna (Figure 4.2).[52] The inclusion of more contemporary marvels along with recorded knowledge about ancient wonders demonstrates that this book's approach to wonders expanded beyond the classical set of marvels of the ancient world. This certainly had resonance in the realm of sixteenth-century

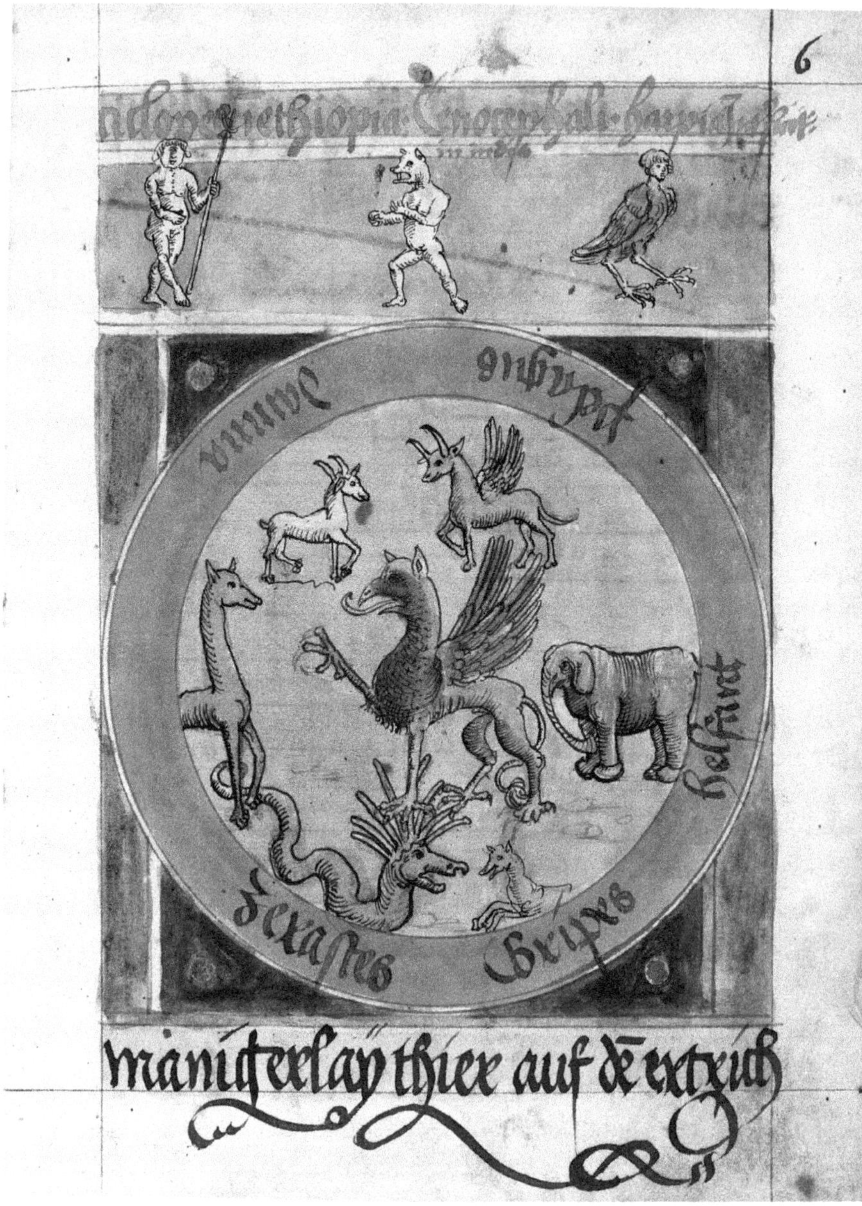

4.1. Master WR, Benedictus Rughalm, *Liber Quodlibetarius*, fol. 6r. *Source:* MS.B 200. Courtesy of Universitätsbibliothek Erlangen-Nürnberg.

German prints in which unscheduled astronomic events and monstrous births coexisted with reported canonical wonders. These depicted wonders draw attention to their construction, such as a building made of a single stone, or a weather vane supported only by magnets. Whereas compilers and scribes might have interrogated the plausibility or logic of these miraculous qualities, they nonetheless had full confidence in the ability of images to translate the data of those recorded wonders.

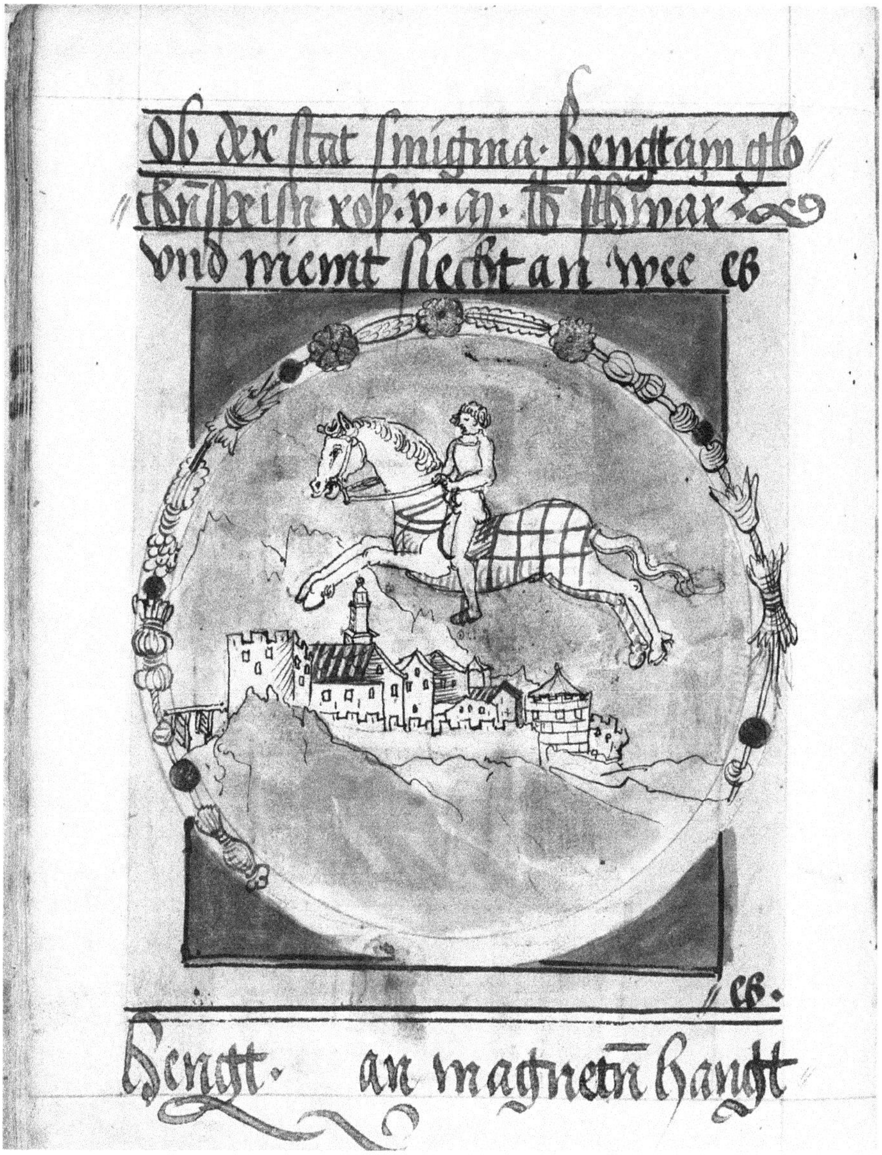

4.2. Master WR, Benedictus Rughalm, *Liber Quodlibetarius*, fol. 11v. *Source:* MS.B 200. Courtesy of Universitätsbibliothek Erlangen-Nürnberg.

An image of Noah's ark divides the creation narrative from the wonders of the world in the *Liber Quodlibetarius* (Figure 4.3). This use of the ark at the threshold of wonders differs from its use as a chronological boundary between world ages in the *Weltchronik*. In the chronicle literature, the ark marks the temporal threshold of spiritual redemption and therefore a significant moment in the chronology of world events.[53] In its placement within the codices, the ark signals itself as a vessel for organizing data: a two-page spread of the vast and unadorned exterior left its interior structure up to the imagination of the

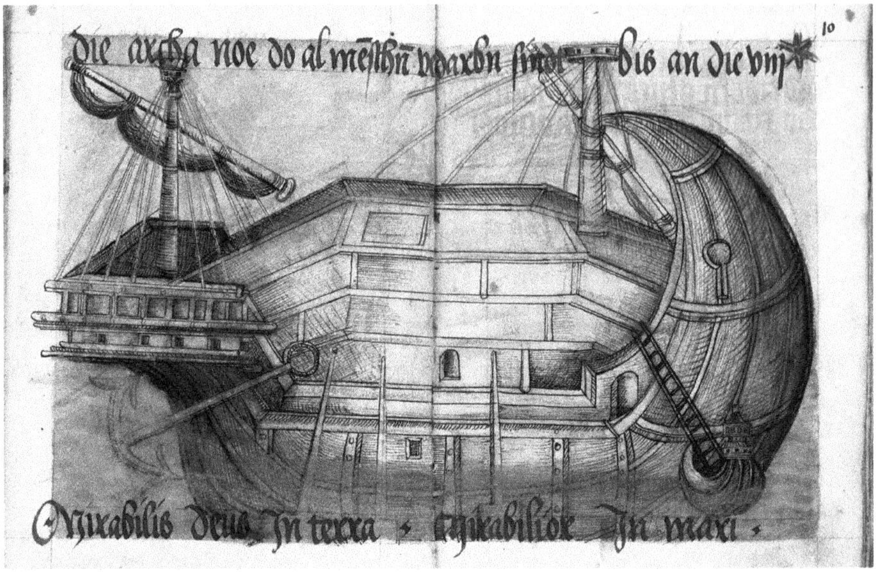

4.3. Master WR, Benedictus Rughalm, *Liber Quodlibetarius*, fols. 9v–10r. *Source:* MS.B 200. Courtesy of Universitätsbibliothek Erlangen-Nürnberg.

reader.[54] In this way, the Erlangen codex anticipates later collections of curiosities that forged references to the ark as an example of the earliest curiosity cabinet. The sixteenth-century English botanist and avid collector of natural specimens John Tradescant, for instance, drew self-conscious allusions to Noah's ark in the christening of his own collection of *naturalia* in Lambeth as "The Ark," because it aimed to encompass what could be found on the earth, sea, and air.[55] The ark's looming presence at the juncture of biblical narrative and secular collectibles signals that a similar assemblage of data follows. While the ark amassed organized specimens from the natural world, this codex gathered its collection from the world of manuscripts and printed motifs.

As virtual arks themselves, these codices organized groups of pictorialized things. Displays of animals presented in the codices assume their visual formats from their own summarizing or visual epitomizing of printed late medieval bestiaries and travel accounts. For instance, the camel, crocodile, monkeys, and goats that appear in the Erlangen manuscript (Figure 4.4) were cribbed from Erhard Reuwich's designs for Bernard von Breydenbach's *Peregrinatio in Terram Sanctam* (Figure 4.5). Overall, the arrangements of natural specimens appearing in *Liber Quodlibetarius* (fols. 87–91) can be usefully compared to printed editions that already attempted to visually organize that material.[56] The demands of creating printed editions from earlier manuscript iterations that interleaved pictures of specimens with the narrative discussions of animals gave rise to creative display and reorganizations of the urtexts. For instance, printed editions of Bartholomaeus Anglicus's *De Proprietatibus Rerum* and Megenberg's

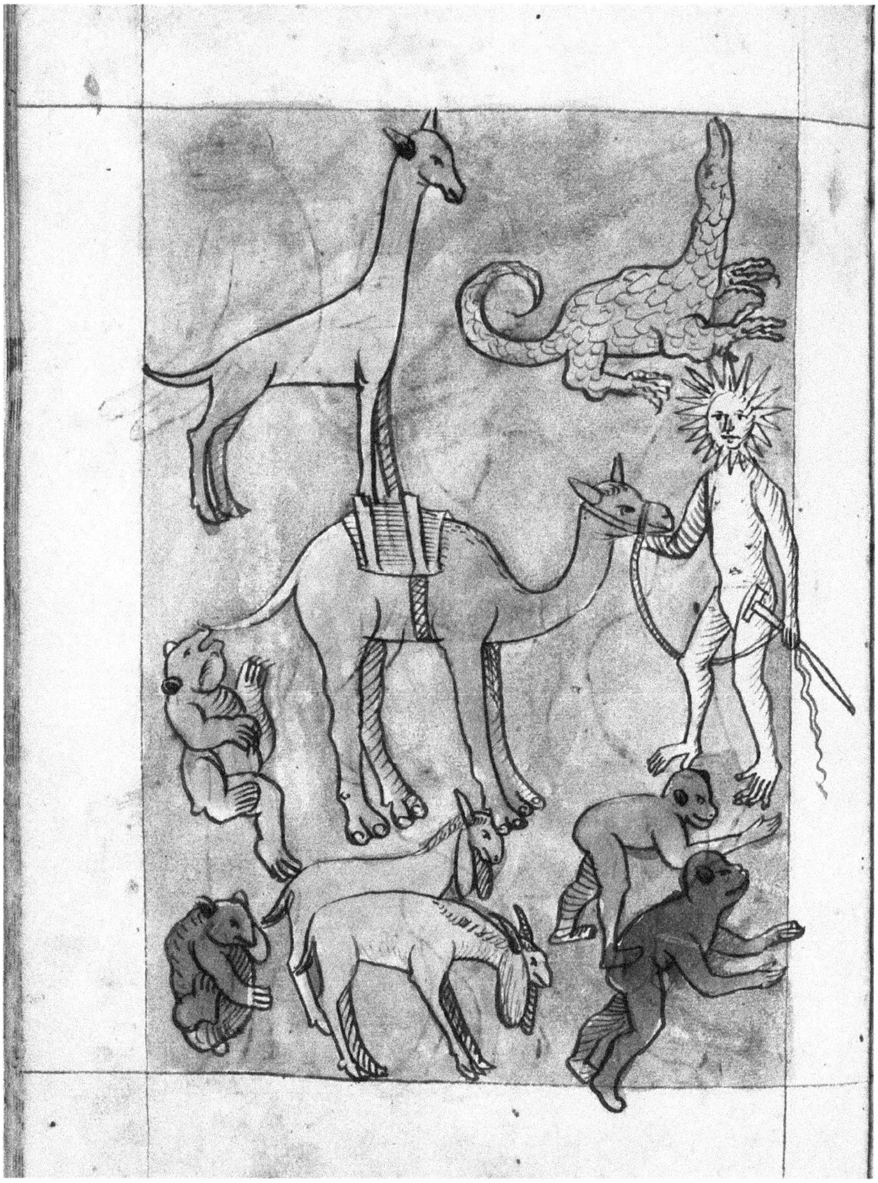

4.4. Master WR, Benedictus Rughalm, *Liber Quodlibetarius*, 89r. *Source:* MS.B 200. Courtesy of Universitätsbibliothek Erlangen-Nürnberg.

Buch der Natur are sparingly illustrated – only a handful of illustrations were supplied by the printers, mostly at section breaks. The pressures of expedient printing rearranged the graphic design of books: letterpress printing incorporating woodblocks encouraged the printer to group animals discussed throughout the text at convenient visual junctures, referring the reader to a single page on which many specimens were collected.[57] Anglicus's bestiary aimed for encyclopedic knowledge and print editions illustrated with woodcuts were

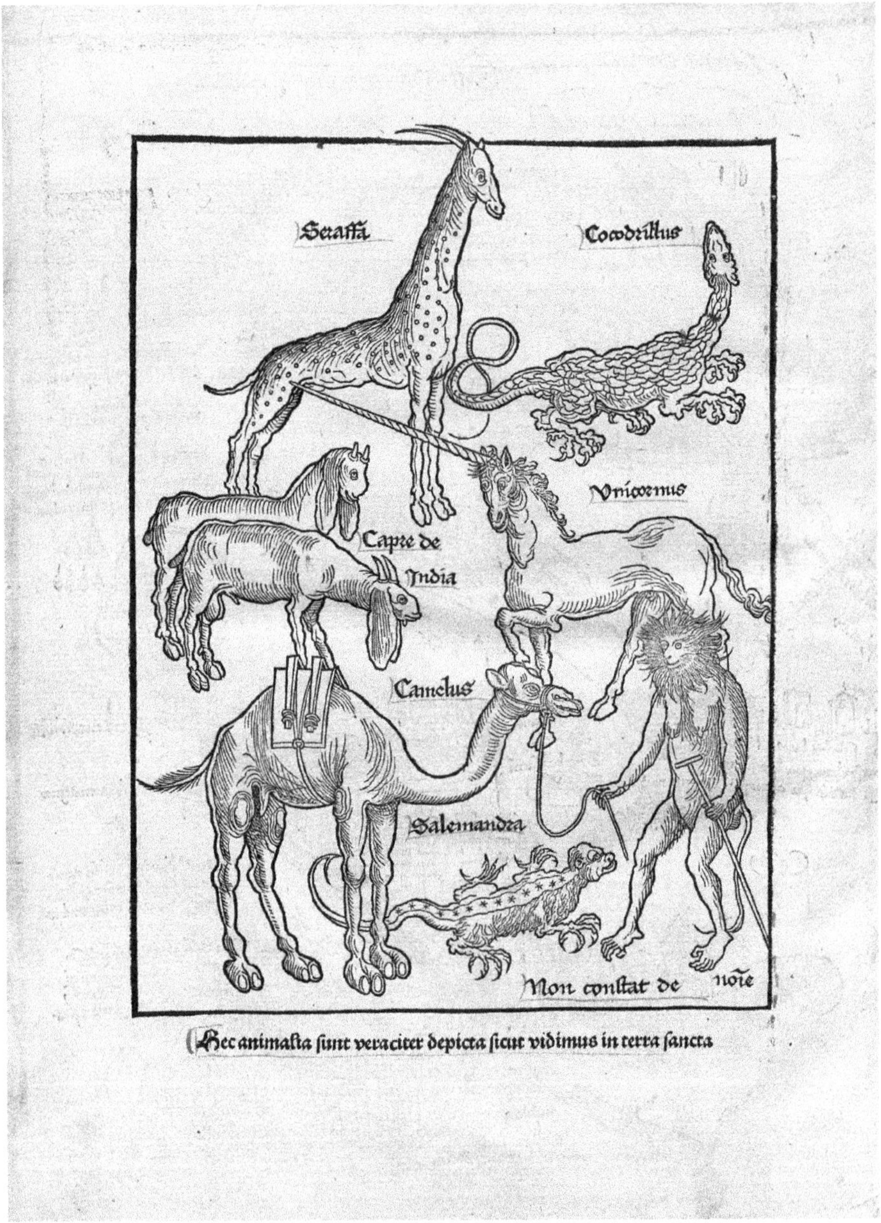

4.5. Erhard Reuwich, for Bernard von Breydenbach, *Peregrinatio in Terram Sanctam* (Mainz: Schöffer, 1486), 131v. *Source:* 2 Inc.c.a1725. Courtesy of Bayerische Staatsbibliothek, Munich. CC BY-NC-SA 4.0.

produced in Lyon, Nuremberg, and Haarlem. Konrad von Megenberg's *Buch der Natur*, a vernacular update of Thomas of Cantimpré's *Liber de Natura rerum*, similarly arranged creatures in crowded display formats. The full title of a vernacular edition of Megenberg printed in Augsburg in 1475 claims that its mandate was to present a comprehensive array of information.[58] The animals' cramped presentations represent the illustrator's attempt to compress the data provided by the text into a visual synopsis on a single page. This space also permitted the cohabitation of creatures sourced from radically different genres of collected information.

Collecting such randomly presented specimens had a history in the printing of sheets of playing cards, or model sheets, often bound into books. Familiar animals gathered from printed sources followed formulas of textual commonplacing, as well as the visual conceits of artists' model books.[59] These pages of collections anchored images of other species that might have come from heraldry or other types of model books, characterized by animals presented from unusual angles, such as cows turning their heads away from the viewer or climbing bears, for example. Model books already exemplified the practice of collecting images: images were sovereign in these genres, often appearing without text and mostly intended for artists to copy. While these natural histories unpacked the etymologies and moral profiles of the beasts in their pages, the *Liber Quodlibetarius* presents them as a record of what could be found in an array of printed books including bestiaries, etymologies, natural histories, travel accounts, and even life studies from model books. In short, this was an array of secular data following the collectible pattern of model books.

The rubric of composite texts compels book historians to consider the unifying structural format of the book, in addition to the diverse content typical of customized miscellanies and commonplace books. Both manuscripts and early printed illustrated books prompted visual collecting practices that were modified as a result of observations. These two sister codices, although informed by both the manuscript and the printed tradition, reveal an organization of knowledge perhaps more radically pictorialized than what we find in either tradition considered separately. In these two manuscripts, text functions as an accessory to the images; it appears in the form of captions, sometimes expanded as canons at the rear of the book. The images of the manuscript were formatted into roundels that housed the critical data: compressed and abbreviated forms of information that was typically found in more embedded contexts, but here no longer supported by text. The regularity of that formatting reinforced the standalone nature of images that was simultaneously developing in the printed literature. The compiler was cognizant of how those developments facilitated organization and searchability, which were also the mandate of printed genres that encouraged the explicit observation of their pictures.

FINDING AIDS FOR CONSULTABLE IMAGES

Emerging printed genres of the sixteenth century attempted to give readers a contemporary purchase on their environments, especially by sharpening the skills of those readers to become observers in their local settings. While biblical narratives and chronicles presented knowledge about God's endowments to the natural world, the new didactic (or knowledge-based) literature of the contemporary press deployed those gifts as things to be used and consumed. The circulation of repackaged versions of older manuscript genres – such as cosmography, physiognomy, and chiromancy – in vernacular tongues familiarized audiences with nascent bodies of disciplinary knowledge. Fundamentally, this was knowledge in the process of being shaped by books, or, more specifically, shaped by pictures. Arguably just as critical as vernacular printings for the book's address to a broad sixteenth-century audience, however, were the choices made by printers to craft an accompanying visual apparatus designed to facilitate the book's use. Explanatory pictures were confected for the purpose of making texts more handy and user-friendly. Systematic visual programs served publishers' aims to build consumers of do-it-yourself knowledge.

We can track the ways in which books exercised control over the natural world by looking at the specific types of pictures that aimed to organize it and help establish agency over it. Instead of exclusively privileging the nature of prints' use in this capacity, we might look at how information in books proposed to be found. Among the reasons that data suggests itself as a term to describe the images in this book is the extent to which they are largely independent of their textual supports, but also the way that they function. Those images can be redeployed in a variety of settings, they can be repeated without damage to the original information, and they lend themselves to searches. They are images collected for reference purposes, and, as such, they are able to be located via finding aids. Searchable user interfaces became important. The new functionality of these images for everyday observers – specifically in helping them measure, gauge, and assess things in the world around them – can support our description of them as epistemic images for the vernacular viewer. Searchability by knowledge domains as a proprietary feature of images underwrote the grouping of prints articulated by Susan Dackerman's exhibition and catalogue *Prints and the Pursuit of Knowledge*.[60] A large range of sensory and cognitive exercises were inspired by these prints and their designs became critical for a user who would privilege easy retrieval, condensed information, and visual tools that would store and generate new information.[61] The manuscript images reflect this ontology of the print's visual program. The way in which this codex attempted to keep images handy and searchable suggests their function as data reserves.

Many images in the *Liber Quodlibetarius* came from books whose objectives were to foster lay and vernacular knowledge. Replicating that objective from images in its printed ancestors, the *Liber Quodlibetarius* is remarkable for its efforts to organize useful information and to present that in a digestible and relevant manner for the layman. Presentation strategies often took the shape of informing the reader about the natural world. The kind of useful knowledge developed here came in the form of nascent pedagogies that introduced new cognitive engagement, such as mnemonics, how to use body parts in navigating the world (via embodied measurements, chiromancy, and physiognomy), and how to scan the heavens for useful information (cosmography). Not least in relationship to these new pedagogies, print processes were arising as an adept technology to capture and store information about the world, to make it memorable, and, perhaps most importantly, to make it searchable.

Discerning character and predicting outcomes from body parts was largely the domain of complexion books, but prescriptions also circulated about how to use body parts for knowledge practices. Bodily epistemology in early modernity has been studied through the lens of the tacit knowledge of the artisan and craftsman, explored by Pamela Smith, and perception tied to specific place, explored by Tom Conley. Both scholars have centered the body and its limbs as agents of measuring and gauging in early modernity and endowed them as epistemic instruments by which to navigate the world.[62]

One place where bodily calibration was knit into the fabric of empirical investigation was in the cosmographic literature, sections of which the *Liber Quodlibetarius* reproduces. Like physiognomy, cosmography also had its origins in antique material that had slumbered for centuries in dense Greek and Latin manuscripts, whose offerings were consulted by learned scholars primarily interested in theoretical models of the universe. One of the first packings of cosmographic material for practical use was published by the Ingolstadt mathematician and printer Peter Apian, who updated models of Ptolemaic geography in the *editio princeps* of *Cosmographicus Liber* printed in Landshut in 1524.[63] (See Chapter 2) In contrast to geography's representation by a whole head, chorography, or the art of local topographic description, is represented by images of an eye and the ear derived from Apian's text (Plate II). Critical to the scribe's understanding of topographic description was the agency of the creator, or the artist, who makes a chorographic image. The pertinent passage in the canons, one copied from the marginal gloss in Apian's printed edition, is about the creator: "*Chorography is a perfected and wrought form of representation made by an artist.*"[64] Here the reader is taught that the chorographer scans the world visually just as an artist would approach the representation of the bodily units of an eye or an ear. The images headline a folio that reminds the reader that chorography is a graphic pursuit generated by an artist.

The *Liber Quodlibetarius*'s project of synopsizing practical knowledge through images made Apian's *Cosmographicus Liber* an ideal source of visualized and searchable data. The frequent recurrence of images from Apian's printed edition of that same year makes 1524 a plausible *terminus post quem* for the *Liber Quodlibetarius*. Indeed, the presentation of material from Apian's text in a large gathering at the beginning of the codex makes it plausible that the

Cosmographicus Liber was the book that determined the trajectory of the *Liber Quodlibetarius*. Apian's volume of cosmographic tools played a significant role in investing images with authoritative and fact-finding properties. Apian was an enthusiast and advocate for images. The visual program that he developed for the *Cosmographicus Liber* substantially updated available cosmographic content while most publishers were still rehearsing thirteenth-century cosmographic models of Sacrobosco's astronomy textbook, *De Sphaera*, in new printed editions.[65] While also illustrated, Sacrobosco's text was aimed at university students interested in theory. Apian recognized a lacuna for useful illustrated cosmographic texts for lay readers that could expand a market that had previously served primarily university audiences. For Apian's business plan, the existing theoretical literature had little to impart to the lay readers for whom useful cosmographic data was increasingly in demand for activities such as the planning of seasonal labor, including planting and harvesting, and for predicting eclipses and planetary conjunctions, or for drawing up horoscopes or nativities. In this way, the *Cosmographicus Liber* was an outgrowth of the *Kalendaria* tradition.

Sensing a demand for more digestible cosmographic information, Apian presented his work as a quarto-sized abridgment of Ptolemy translated into useful principles. He packaged astronomical and geographic knowledge in ways that could help the reader navigate the local landscape firsthand. Apian's prompts to empirical interaction with the world met a book market in which instrument prints and interactive books were becoming popular, and one in which, according to Suzanne Karr Schmidt, the reader was increasingly addressed as a user.[66] Indeed, the growing usefulness of Apian's text can be measured by the profusion of vernacular editions published post 1529; the images that eased the text's transition to a lay readership may well have helped shape a popular market. Apian's first offering was in Latin, but it was the later vernaculars, which first appeared in Antwerp in 1537 (in Dutch, Spanish, and French), that caused demand to skyrocket. While Apian still couched his book in terms of Ptolemaic cosmology, data from Apian's book in the *Liber Quodlibetarius* was broken down into only the useful component parts. The *Quodlibetarius* simplified the Apian material into diagrams and roundels and came with brief explanations in the local dialect – incidentally, this is the only recension of Apian's that attempted to explain those principles in German. In this capacity, our compiler anticipated the vernacularization and distillation of the Apian material that scholars typically associate with its circulation through the Antwerp press.

HANDY TOOLS

The *Liber Quodlibetarius*'s presentation of Apian in explanatory diagrams framed by inscriptions in vernacular German represents a unique attempt to increase the user-friendliness of the material. While Apian had converted academic astronomy into practical lessons for making visual judgments, the abridgments of the text and distillation of information into images that appear in the *Liber Quodlibetarius* intensify the efforts that were already underway in shaping the visual horizon for a vernacular viewer. These efforts featured Apian's visual demonstrations that animated and explained the celestial sphere; in some cases important diagrams were expanded to show new data. Instructions for empowering body parts as technical tools abound in the manuscript in illustrations in which hands and feet are exploited for their sensorial epistemic agency (see 30v, for example) and, in some cases, new cognitive practices. The agency of hands and feet as critical common denominators of early modern man's empirical experience of the world would be reprised in the manuscript's display of palms and feet (to be discussed later) as surfaces to be read.

An elaborate dial (Plate III) brings together a few illustrations originating in Apian's text into a central movable wheel of measurements calibrated to body parts. Reprising Apian's own use of volvelles as data generators, this sectioned dial provides a platform for multiplying this dataset into a group of other measuring units. This wheel converts smaller bodily units, penned in red on the interior dial, into larger common measurements, found in black on the circle's exterior. In some cases, the units translated Latin units into vernacular expressions. This dial is not a functioning tool per se but a visual chart, a clearing house of data that embeds it in a legible and searchable format. The dial aims to store the copious visual data borrowed from Apian's text into a form that is easily searchable. Smaller units are expressed in German, but they switch to Latin as the size increases as a means of relating vernacular expressions to the surveying terms and units used by the cosmographer.

This volvelle expanded exponentially information gathered from a tabular list of parts found in the text preceding the demonstration of the *passus geometricus* (geometric step) on folio 34 of the *Cosmographicus Liber.*[67] Embedded in a visual schema that reminded viewers that their own palms and strides were the common denominators of somatic experience, this complex dial simultaneously taught that common units had more technical equivalents. This folio's compression of several of Apian's devices to obtain measurements expanded the reader's range of empirical and cognitive practices already articulated by the printed volume. For example, the volvelle itself simulates the shape of another tool made to facilitate empirical engagement with the environment: a nocturnal dial. A pop-out model of this device by which time could be told at night could be found at the end of the *Cosmographicus Liber.*[68] Pamela Smith's work on the embodied experience that drove early modern artisanal pursuits can be usefully brought to bear on Apian's suggestions of empirical methods and the ways in which the reader's cognition and experience of the world could be extended by emerging parameters defined by tools.[69] Such new data encouraged weighing and comparison of units that extended outward from bodily experience. As an notional volvelle, the *Liber Quodlibetarius*'s measurement dial merely organizes the data. Reference to the nocturnal dial by its shape was probably meant to remind the reader that somatically mediated surveying could render practical information such as telling the time at night. It presented data in a conceptual manner similar to those searches inspired by the other dials in the manuscript. According to Margaret Gaida, these new combinations of measurement, calculation, and squaring astronomical to terrestrial parameters became the central occupation of a new class of data-loving dilettantes, whom she calls mathematical amateurs.[70] This "how-to" format proved to be a winning formula; Apian familiarized a generation of readers with the principles of dialing up to discover new data, turning the volvelles themselves into informational images.

DATA OF THE EARTH'S SHAPE

The scavenging of discrete pictorial fragments by the *Liber Quodlibetarius*'s compiler testifies to the sovereign rigor that already inhered in Apian's presentation of data in the *Cosmographicus Liber*. A visual vignette at the base of folio 27v (see Plate III) shows the earth's reflection on the surface of the moon during an eclipse as one that is explicitly round. This fragment from the *Cosmographicus Liber* recapitulated to the reader that inferences from sightings of lunar phenomena could substantiate theoretical proofs about larger concepts, such as the shape of the earth (Figure 4.6). The reminder that systematic elimination of phenomena *not observed* (scattered over the next few pages where we see that the earth's shape cannot be a square, hexagon, or triangle) demonstrated the value of do-it-yourself scanning of the heavens. Thus, the compiler placed the observation of celestial phenomena on the same footing as other empirical processes of measuring and gauging by strides and hand measurements.

Presented independently, each image exhibits a fragment of Apian's proof of the earth's shape, an observation that can be substantiated from the geometric shape cast on the moon's surface during an eclipse. The inscription at the base of folio 28v incorporates the Latin of Apian's original text – *Schema demonstrat terram esse Globusam* – but it ends with the compiler's vernacular abridgment. This caption campaigns for the role of the image in a hypothetical proposition that can be empirically confirmed: "if the earth were triangular, it would look like this."[71] The image's rhetorical function, one that adheres to the outline of a logical proposition (if x, then y), seems to suggest that it can stand on its own as a sovereign concept. Its fragmentary appearance in the *Liber Quodlibetarius* tests the image's structural integrity as an independent proof. The compiler saw in its quasi-sovereignty its potential for repackaging.

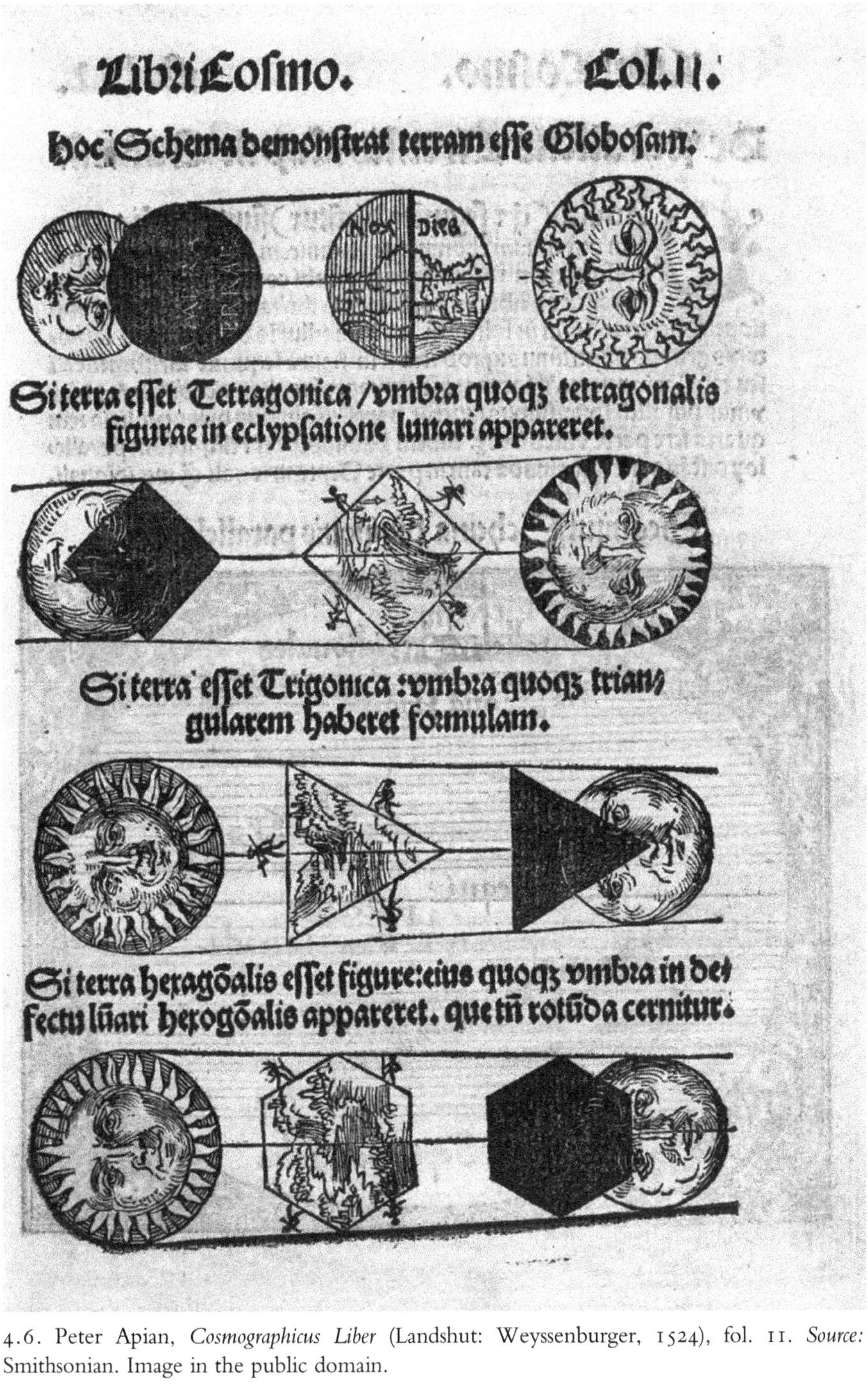

4.6. Peter Apian, *Cosmographicus Liber* (Landshut: Weyssenburger, 1524), fol. 11. *Source:* Smithsonian. Image in the public domain.

Such diagrammatic images supported epistemic operations such as seeing, proving, eliminating, and discovering. Functioning less at the level of representation, these images were proofs of visual logic. The didactic point of the exercise was for the reader/viewer to select the image that matched a visual process. The image is neither purely diagrammatic, nor naturalistic, nor a representation of an instrument or a device. It belongs to a category of technical images that served, per Gabriele Werner, as "active and operative entities that organize and regulate a knowledge process."[72] In the *Liber Quodlibetarius*, this process is made clear on a nearby page where the "schema demonstrates that the earth is a globe." This image served as counterproof produced by the triangular-shaped earth. This process of elimination was presented in the form of a dialectical pop quiz that helped recall the original proof, possibly from the printed edition.

Apian's many interactive volvelles attracted both attention and pirates for their portrayal of dense cosmographic principles in pithy, memorable, and engaging ways. A simple volvelle that was frequently copied, for example, shows horizon and zenith in relation to each other, and thus expressed the relativism of man's placement on a rotating earth. No matter what his terrestrial position would be, his zenith was always directly overhead. Another volvelle required familiarity with the phases of the moon. This bit of basic empirically derived input would help set the dials of a device that could render the time at night. This operation was similar to that of another lunar dial designed by Apian that appeared in the appendix of the *Cosmographicus Liber.*[73] Entering an observed value (the moon's phase) into the window of the inner dial of Apian's lunar volvelle permitted the viewer to extrapolate related principles. With the additional input of calendrical data, the user could determine the position of the sun with respect to the moon, and thus understand the phase of the moon as a measurement of the angle between them. Once users could track the position of the sun with respect to the moon at any time of day or night, it was possible to schedule lunar phases and also to predict the position of the sun beneath the horizon at night.[74] Apian's dial enabled methods of timekeeping and seasonal tracking of the moon from which other astrological data could be derived. Various dials following folio 38v in the *Liber Quodlibetarius* demonstrate such extrapolations.

Apian's innovations fortified the natural endowments of vision, but they also presupposed the visual acuity of the beholder. The process of observation, the call to experience, and the mandate to look accurately unite the diverse range of visual material in the book. We see sights, and we see people seeing. Even when eyes are just meant to be conceptual representations, in the *Liber Quodlibetarius* they seem to see actively. The engagement with sight is apparent in the codex's rendition of the cosmographic eye: using an eye to explain the schema of cosmography writ large (Plate IV). This eye cannot mimic the process of sight because the illustration takes on an impossible point of view for a mortal eye. Significantly, a mortal eye is chosen as a conceptual metaphor for the process by which the heavens are observed – one that takes in the celestial sphere as seen through the terrestrial sphere. Likewise, the pictured eye in the analogy of chorography (see Plate II) seems also to be engaged in the process of animated sight. Typically, in Apian's formula, the eye and ear are merely analogues for an explanation of the act of portraiture, but a stronger mimicry of the process of sight seems to be at work here.

In some of its unorthodox presentations of images from the *Cosmographicus Liber*, the *Liber Quodlibetarius* shook up some of the older formulae from the printed editions. Even Ptolemy's classic simile of the relationship between geography and chorography gave way to new interpretations in the manuscript. In the manuscript recensions of Ptolemy's *Geographia*, the text compares the purview of geography to the work of the portraitist entrusted with making a face. To show this visually, Apian paired a representation of the earth's surface with a head in profile (see Fig. 1.2). In order to distinguish between the descriptive projects of geography and chorography, Apian's analogy relied on the evocation of a profile view of a hill town compared to the particularities (such as an eye or an ear) that attended the production of a portrait; Apian was the first to turn that analogy into a visual image.

Missing entirely from the *Liber Quodlibetarius*'s Ptolemaic analogy is the portrait head that represents the pendant to geography in the *Cosmographicus Liber*. In its place, the reader encounters an abstract diagram – perhaps a map, perhaps a ground plan, or an island seen from above (see Plate II).[75] This geometric shape is surrounded by a series of concentric lines. Portions of these encircling lines have been formed with a compass, but those circles have been broken to make the outer rings closely follow the outlines of the geometric shape. Those sections have been completed with a straightedge. Clearly, painstaking effort with tools has been expended to precisely shape this image.

This schematic, geometric model has frustrated attempts to decipher it – as well as attempts to find its source in printed books, a logical place to look for precedents in a manuscript whose images derive largely from such books. In the absence of a source, we might suppose it to be a schematic model of the exercise of cartography itself, or perhaps even a diagram of the act of vision.[76] Could this strange shape chart the wave patterns of what the eye in the first pair of images is actually seeing? After all, the idea of observation was already enshrined in Apian's presentation of the Ptolemaic formula. As observation was a warrant used to verify information in the Renaissance cultural landscape, Apian exploited this visual mode of authentication.[77] In addition, Apian had already invoked the "monocular eye," per Tom Conley, to anchor the cosmographic mode of description: he posited an eye looking through the earth into the celestial spheres.[78] This was a metaphor for geographic seeing, but it was presented in perspectival projection. The act of viewing along perspectival lines is suggested again in the following two modes of description: a profile head looking at the earth for geography; and, to explain chorography, a disembodied eye peering at a topographically rendered hill town. Apian uses the images of the profile head and floating eye to explain Ptolemy's distinction between levels of graphic description of the earth in terms of description relevant to a portraitist. Conley reminds us that the early modern reader may have also read these images as embodiments of the act of looking.[79] The act of printing as the engine of somatic stimulus was invoked by Martin Luther to describe the centrality of Nuremberg in Germany's media network in his letter to Eobanus Hessus of 1528 in which Luther dubs the city the eyes and ears of Germany: "*das Aug und Ohr Deutschlands.*" [80] At this date, Nuremberg's prominence in generating topographic images of the world, which might have qualified it for this praise, was unsurpassed due to the volume of views made for Hartmann Schedel's *Weltchronik*.

As a mode of picturing, the chorographic view relied on both optical and conceptual models. Chorography, according to Lucia Nuti, negotiated these two strands of epistemological modes of verification in early modernity. The optical model pinned its guarantees of direct observation on mimetic renderings. On the other hand, a conceptual model was favored by geographers and architects; this was a form of knowledge-making that employed measurement and mathematics without relying on mimesis.[81] But the chorographer/topographer, however, needed to toggle between these two modes of representation when his eye was trained on the quantitative and pictorial demands of practical chorography. These included making images that accompanied land disputes, battle plans, and military operations. Chorography was simultaneously employed by professionals in subfields such as surveying and ballistics.[82] Creating a chorographic view simulated the act of representation; as Nuti would have it, the professional chorographer could easily accommodate this bivalent form of cognition.[83] It is not unlikely that the image's creator would have reached for a model that might have been partly instrumental and partly theoretical in nature.

New cognitive approaches were awakened by the instrumentation introduced by books in the form of printed tools; these also presented alternative possibilities and options for visual projections for the professional and amateur alike. Apain's *Cosmographicus Liber*, per Margaret Gaida, was itself perched on the threshold of book and instrument; she calls it a book/instrument hybrid.[84] Apian's printed instruments suggested multiple conceptual angles of representation. The diverse visual modes of instrumentation/data/knowledge that Apian's text brought together expanded the range of possible pictorial models that a reader might have referenced here. The strange shape at the base of folio 29v might represent a mode of projection that a reader of Apian's text was inspired to consider – perhaps, for example, wave patterns bouncing off a landmass could alert mariners to the presence of islands. The "waves" could also indicate the gentle contouring of a hillside in ichnographic plans reflecting subtle rises in altitude that the profile view of the town could not capture.[85]

A remote possibility is that this shape could be the floorplan for the bottom plate of a volvelle on top of which another one might be layered. While this image has stumped most modern viewers whom I have consulted, that doesn't dampen its usefulness as data for the compiler. Its very inscrutability reminds us that the compiler found in the image a sovereignty compelling enough not to need to pad it with explanatory text.

In what follows, I propose that this image might represent a graphic projection of sight. Such a model is thinkable in relation to the surrounding images with their start in Apian's *Cosmographicus Liber*. A reference to vision might have been instigated by the free-floating eye above; this could be a visualization of extramissive vision. Such entities were routinely paired in constructions of the eye. It might be a cross-section of the eye, as was introduced in print in Gregor Reisch's *Margarita Philosophica* (printed in Strasbourg by Schott in 1504), or as it was reprised in Vogtherr's ophthalmology booklet, *Ein newes hochnutzlichs Büchlin von Erkantnüs der Kranckeyten der Augen sampt einer Figur oder Anothomia eines Augs* (1538). Alternatively, these waves might serve as a representation of the visual cone of the monocular eye of the cosmographic diagram at folio 29r (see Plate IV).[86] This particular eye, as discussed earlier, appears at the vertex of a visual cone used to explain cosmography as the mode of inquiry that infers earthly coordinates from celestial ones: a type of perspective that involves a seeing through the world to the celestial realm. Apian's theoretical model is endorsed in the *Liber Quodlibetarius* by images on each of the three preceding folios. Empirical observation is also suggested (and reiterated) by the shape of the earth proof in which triangular, hexagonal, and square shapes are systematically eliminated by empirical observation. These practical mnemonics remind the viewer to channel their knowledge of the world through empirical observation.

If we assume that this geometric shape represents a form of projection, it might have derived from manuals of practical geometry and perspective drawing. Peter Apian himself took over the printing of one such manual, Witelo's *Vitellionis Mathematici doctissimi Peri optikes, id est de natura, ratione & proiectione radiorum visus* ... (1535), for which Georg Tannstetter designed the woodblocks.[87] The diagram on 55r resembles what we see in the *Liber Quodlibetarius*'s design on folio 29v. Witelo's *Perspectiva* revived Alhazen's arguments against Greek theories of extramission (offered by Ptolemy and in Euclid's *Optica*) in favor of an intramissive model that proposes light entering the eye.[88] This reversed the directional logic of extramission, which explained vision as a result of rays issuing from the observer's eye. Alhazan and his medieval European followers such as Grosseteste, Pecham, and Witelo presented a tenacious overhaul to this model, arguing instead that vision was the manifestation of rays emerging from seen objects that fell perpendicularly onto the eye's glacial humor, where they were both reflected and partially refracted.[89] But, as Sven Dupré has argued, extramission died hard as a theory of vision because practical mathematics presented optics in geometric terms, a science that was explained by lines and angles, and rarely with reference to the physics of light. Thus, the diagrams of practical mathematicians seemed to endorse extramission as the workable theory of sight.[90] After all, the light waves were harder to convey in illustration, but geometry of perspective and angles enjoyed a contemporary popularity in the printing of practical manuals.

The image's ambivalence is understandable in light of the fact that it followed the fundamental tweaking of the manuscript's presentation of the Ptolemaic formula. The compiler's omission of Apian's portrait head is telling. Because the material presented here centers on chorography as a description of observed particulars, the portrait head that was critical to Apian's analogy would be an extraneous detail. Knowledge was shuffled around in the codex; new associations could amplify the old formulae. The profile image was central to Apian's analogy – and it remained critical to a succession of printers of copies of Apian's text. For one printer of several Paris editions, for example, that head soon adopted the physiognomy of Christ, per the so-called Lentulus letter that described his face in detail, from circulating broadsides about Christ's appearance.[91] But the profile that appeared in every printed edition of Apian lost its relevance in the *Liber Quodlibetarius*'s formulation of the analogy. Instead, the compiler restricted the data of portrait heads to a section that was more explicitly devoted to knowledge that could obtain from the reading of faces. Discussion of portraits would occur in a section on deciphering planetary residues left on body parts in a special section devoted to physiognomy.

DATA ENVIRONMENTS OF VISUALIZED FACTS

The manuscripts' sections on physiognomy (books on complexion and face-reading) and chiromancy (palm reading) exemplify how new epistemic functions accrued to independent images and articulated new fields of knowledge-making. Printed physiognomies had rewired the idea of complexion that was presented in the manuscript tradition as a list catalogued from head to foot.[92] This collection of features was streamlined as the information moved from manuscript recensions into the printed physiognomies.[93] Circulating guidebooks for the study of complexion reduced this catalogue to facilitate inquiry into the lines on palms and facial features, and, importantly, visualized the texts as data reserves of features that could serve as visual aids. Soon images of these body parts, profiles, and palms came to dominate the books' structures. Printers of vernacular abridgments of those murky ancient physiognomies distilled their data into visual formats conducive to searches for practical information, as can be seen in the physiognomies attributed to Bartolomeo Cocles and Johannes ab Indagine circulating in northern Europe beginning in the 1520s (Figure 4.7).

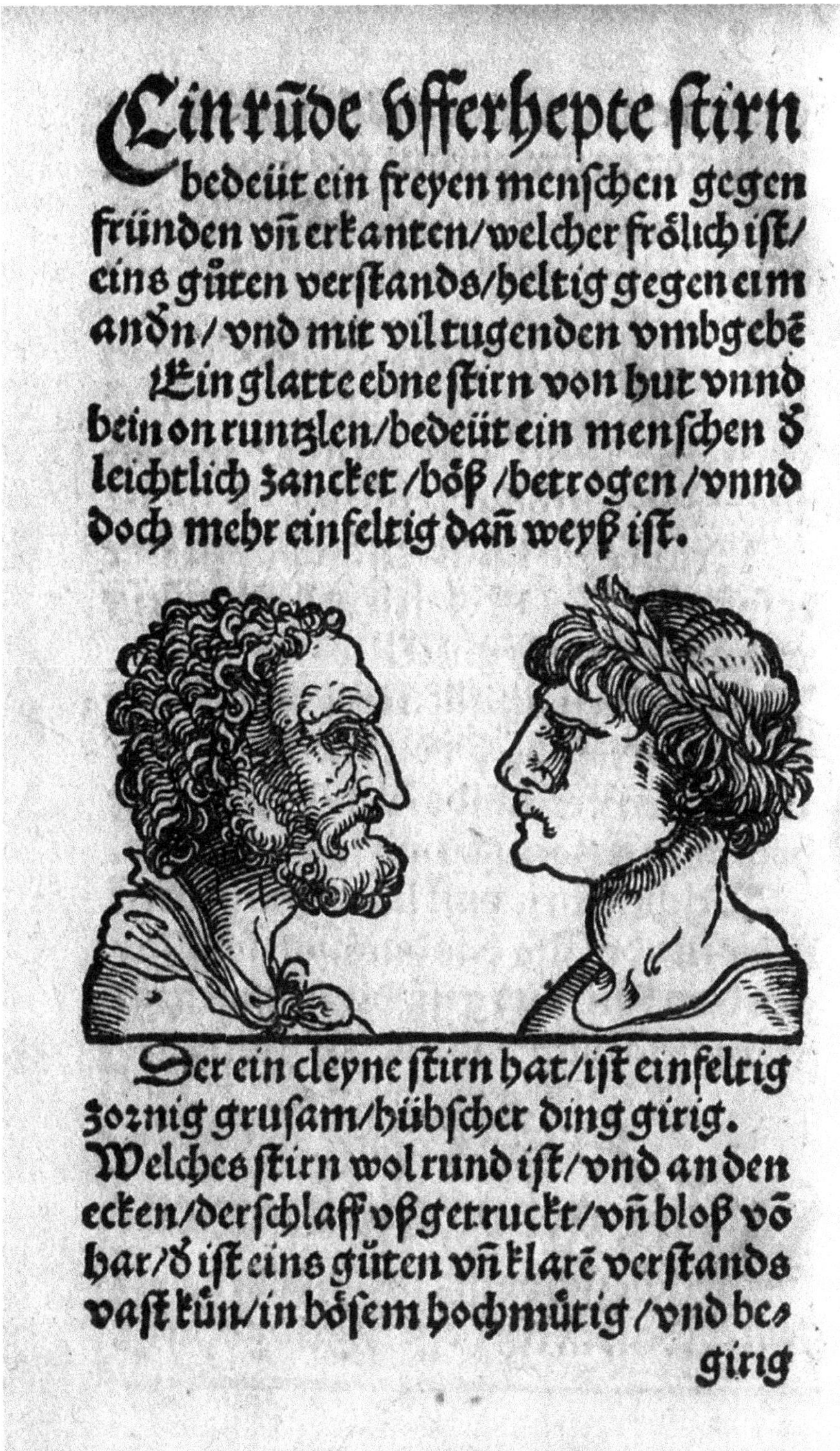

Ein rūde vsserhepte stirn
bedeüt ein freyen menschen gegen
fründen vñ erkanten/welcher frölich ist/
eins gůten verstands/heltig gegen eim
andn/vnd mit vil tugenden vmbgebē
Ein glatte ebne stirn von hut vnnd
bein on runtzlen/bedeüt ein menschen d
leichtlich zancket/böß/betrogen/vnnd
doch mehr einfeltig dañ weyß ist.

Der ein cleyne stirn hat/ist einfeltig
zornig grusam/hübscher ding girig.
Welches stirn wol rund ist/vnd an den
ecken/der schlaff vßgetruckt/vñ bloß võ
har/d ist eins gůten vñ klarē verstands
vast kün/in bösem hochmůtig/vnd be-
girig

4.7. Character heads in Cocles, *Ein kurtzer bericht der gantzen Phisionomey vnd Ciromancy* (Strasbourg: Johannes Albertus, 1534). *Source:* BSB Res/Anthr. 259p#Beibd.1. Courtesy of Staatsbibliothek Munich.

Released from the instructional narratives in which they were previously embedded, these images assumed a sovereignty that expanded their role in empirical activity and demanded new cognitive exercises from their readers.

Because of the way chiromancies and physiognomies began to guide their readers through searches for external signs on the body, they can be considered diagnostic, and thus as contributing to a class of knowledge-based analysis of the body. In early modernity, this type of investigative approach to diagnosis was intimately connected to astrology and anatomy, but it was more directly visualized as an investigation of the body as a grouping of signs. The data of this epistemic pursuit presented hands, feet, and faces as loci for visual decision-making. According to these highly illustrated books, such external features increasingly served as a map that spurred viewers to decipher it.

The idea that the surface of the body could serve as a topography of signs that could reveal human nature was popular in the epistemic literature. The shift in focus of a person's complexion in early modernity from an internal balance of humors to externally observable traits accompanied the development of pictorialized chiromancies and physiognomies.[94] These perceptible and visible traits, increasingly presented as visual data in books, certainly also stimulated the reading public's desire to both recognize and search for them.

The intense pictorialization of sixteenth-century editions printed in German-speaking regions turned the physiognomic literature into *de facto* field guides for distinguishing among lines on hands and features of faces.[95] Their new visual emphasis effectively repackaged the genre's historic presentation of long descriptive passages into technical tools that assisted the viewer in making visual assessments. The practical result of this robust visualization redirected these books' emphasis to the types of judgments that could be made on the basis of observable features (See Chapter 3).

While the printed prototypes organized their textual explanations around paired sets of images, copies of the same images surface in the *Liber Quodlibetarius* with little narrative context save brief vernacular captions that explain their significance, typically in terms of how the objects represented were to be used. The compiler's distillation of profuse information from printed books into these epitomized formats partly reflects how the images themselves were rewired as independent units in the early decades of printing; their reception as movable data reserves can be seen in attempts to generate new contexts for the images lifted from printed books.[96] But this radical sovereignty of the image in the codices reimagines their functions as free agents representing cognitive practices.

This is especially apparent in chiromancy, or the art of reading marks on the palm. The practice's popularity in the sixteenth century can be inferred from the multiple editions that coached readers in how to do it.[97] Like physiognomies, the chiromantic literature likewise came out of the tradition of *Secreti* and was updated into components of the popular *Complexionbücher* circulating by the mid-1530s in Germany. The *Liber Quodlibetarius* reduces forty-four pages of a popular contemporary printed edition into just ten pages of images, omitting the diagnoses that were spelled out by the text in the printed edition, stressing instead how those images could visually cue the reading. Many printed chiromancy compendiums separate the palm- and face-reading chapters by interspersing sections on the zodiac symbols and personifications of the planets. Those zodiac and narrative images are purposefully omitted from the codex; the compiler skips these digressions and features only the images that could be deployed as epistemic tools.

Instead of including the diagnostic text in which images of hands were embedded in the printed versions, the captions of the *Liber Quodlibetarius* announce the utility of the data in a pithy format. On folio 82v, the inscription provides a synopsis of the logic that pulled together this data grouping of chiromantic hands – in this case, the divided line that sections these palms: "scattered lines indicate strength, weakness, or length of life, happiness or bad luck, riches or poverty" (Figure 4.8).[98] In the images, the compiler also abridges the text's recommendations about which lines to follow, directing the reader's attention to the image's lines that could best distill character. These captions on the lines of the illuminated hands thus have a tricky job to perform. They endeavor to connect the particular variation in the divided line to the most potent of character traits. Thus, the unbroken pair of lines that leads to the ring finger on 82v indicates someone who would excel in aristocratic employment, could be trusted, would be valued for his duties, and rewarded for his service: "*Dient fürst/ herrenn hant in lieb (or sint i(h)m lieb)/ begabenn i(h)n.*" This caption is abridged from the first paragraph of folio xlix in the printed text (Figure 4.9). Some featured lines could be used to predict an employee's reliability; others weighed the employee's longevity against their propensity for travel. Solid lines extending to the little finger indicate someone who is "*Hofartig/ schwätzig/ knecht/ landfahrer,*" or suited for courtly settings, but they can also diagnose garrulousness, menial nature, or vagrancy. A set of lines that are broken into two segments that extend from the wrist to the middle finger indicate someone who will live for a long time abroad but who will die in his own country: "*Wohnen in der frembt lange/ wird doch in sein Vaterland sterben.*" Solid lines extending only to the middle of the palm indicate a remorseless chatterbox: "*Ein schwatze/ klaeffer.*" Broken lines extending only to the middle of the palm signal a cretin and a fool: "*Ein grob mensch/ narr/ thor.*" These brief descriptors try to compress into brief data points the longer glosses in the printed text. These palms facilitate the search for information as visual aids; they obviate the need to wade through the contradictory readings sometimes precipitated by the text and instead the viewer could browse through information stored as pictorialized data. The image becomes the accessory to the search.

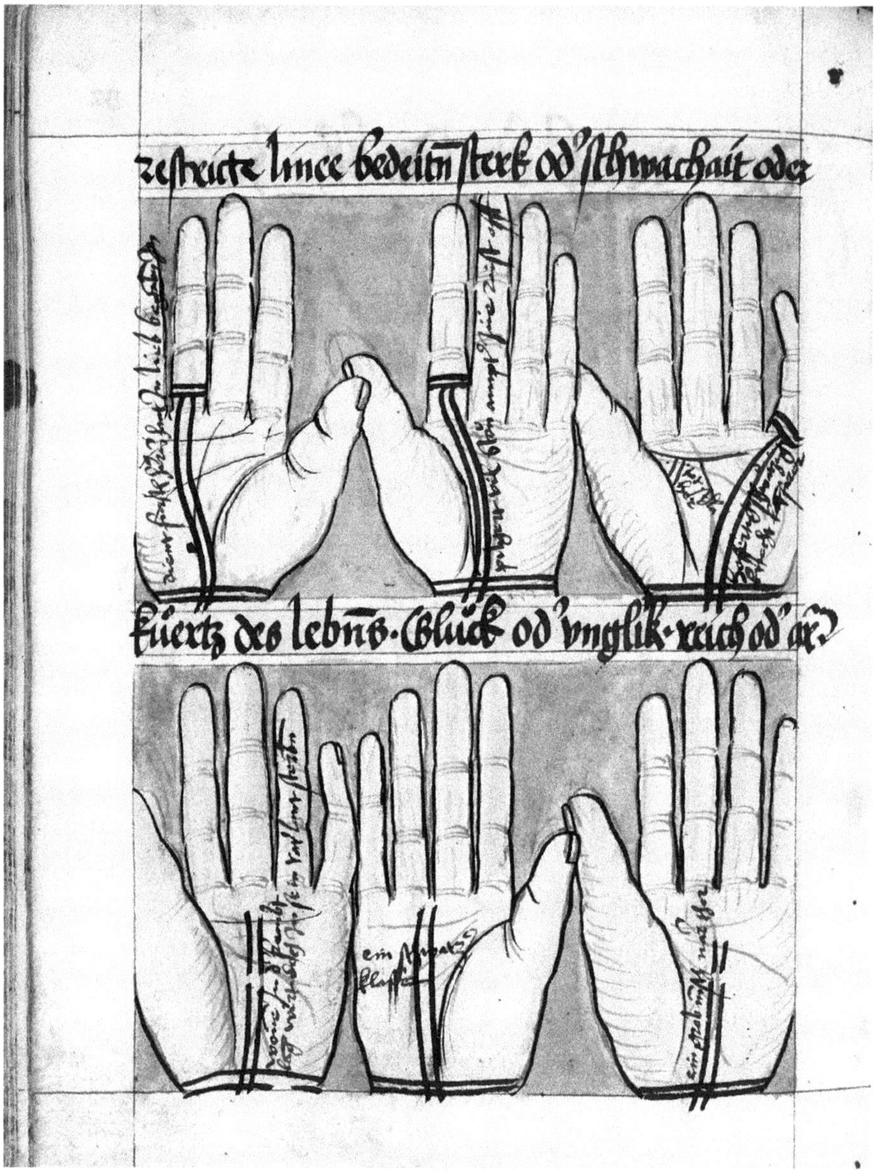

4.8. Master WR, Benedictus Rughalm, *Liber Quodlibetarius*, fol. 82v. *Source:* MS.B 200. Courtesy of Universitätsbibliothek Erlangen-Nürnberg.

This distillation of critical data into sovereign images is perhaps even more pronounced in the physiognomic section that shows how data can be represented by the images themselves. The format of paired profiles of sixteenth-century vernacular physiognomies prompted the cognitive activity of comparing and contrasting specimens in the field. The images accompanying Johannes ab Indagine's *Introductiones Apotelesmaticae* show the stark profiling at work in the editions printed in the German-speaking lands: the book's visual

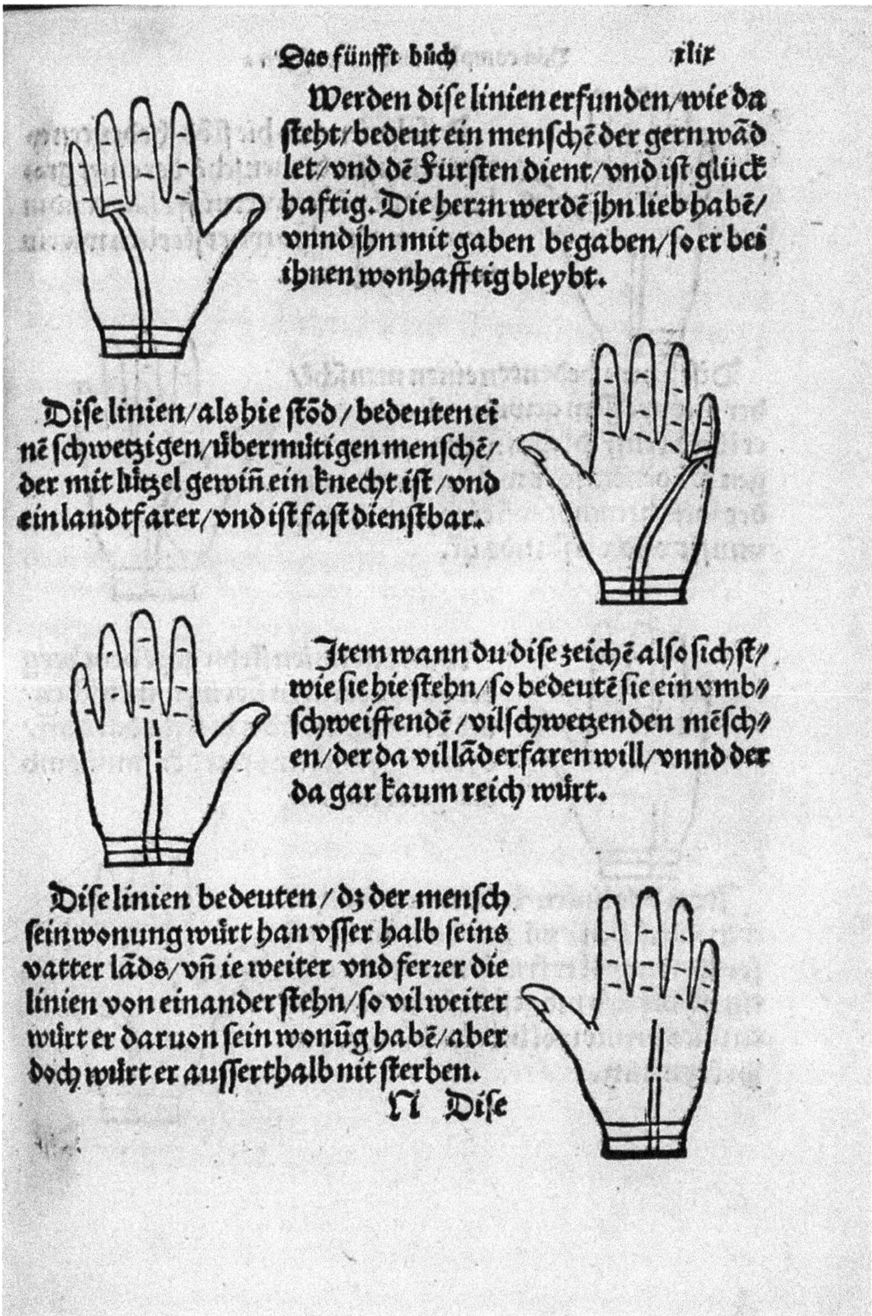

Das fünfft büch xlix

Werden dise linien erfunden/ wie da steht/ bedeut ein menschē der gern wād let/ vnd dē Fürsten dient/ vnd ist glück hafftig. Die herrn werdē jhn lieb habē/ vnnd jhn mit gaben begaben/ so er bei jhnen wonhafftig bleybt.

Dise linien/ als hie stōd/ bedeuten ei nē schwetzigen/ übermütigen menschē/ der mit lützel gewiñ ein knecht ist/ vnd ein landtfarer/ vnd ist fast dienstbar.

Jtem wann du dise zeichē also sichst/ wie sie hie stehn/ so bedeutē sie ein vmb schweiffendē/ vilschwetzenden mēsch en/ der da vil lāder faren will/ vnnd der da gar kaum reich würt.

Dise linien bedeuten/ dz der mensch sein wonung würt han vsser halb seins vatter lāds/ vñ ie weiter vnd ferrer die linien von einander stehn/ so vil weiter würt er daruon sein wonūg habē/ aber doch würt er ausserthalb nit sterben.

N i Dise

4.9. Cocles, *Phisionomi und Chiromanci* ... (Strasbourg: Cammerlander, 1540), xlix. *Source:* HAB N97.4f Helmst. 7s. Courtesy of Herzog August Bibliothek, Wolfenbüttel.

apparatus was organized by paired character heads. The pictured heads of the Indagine and Cocles editions came to characterize the operation of a physiognomist in the field as someone who considered features between poles that marked differences.

The twenty-two heads collected in the *Liber Quodlibetarius* (Plates V and VI) would have reminded a reader of heads in the complexion compendiums popular in the German lands from the 1520 to the 1540s. The compiler cribbed this particular set of heads showing types of hair texture from Cocles's *Ein kurtzer bericht der gantzen Phisionomey unnd Ciromancy* (Figure 4.10), retaining the paired structure established by this edition.[99] In their original contexts in the printed books, the heads marked rough oppositions of traits. The first pair we see, for example, contrasts types of foreheads; the second juxtaposes hot and cold complexions; the next pair displays a set of cold complexions. The man in a fancy hat next to a woman with downcast eyes contrasts a well-tempered body type with an unhealthy one. But instead of precise diagnosis as their aim, the brief captions woven throughout these pages of the Erlangen codex give pointers about how to use a physiognomy and how to judge character from the texture of hair and the size of the teeth.

> This section is devoted to physiognomy, or how to read character from the face. Long straight hair signals timidity, as does soft and dry hair, which can also point to docility. Very frizzy hair indicates ignorance and naïveté. Thin and small teeth portend a short life, whereas thick and strong teeth predict a long one. A quick tongue exhibits naiveté, while broad teeth indicate phoniness.[100]

Such a caption unpacks the compiler's recording of these images as instrumental data that could be implemented in generating knowledge.

What, then, is the function of these images if their accompanying texts are so cursory that their original contexts can hardly be discerned? As Ewa Chojecka has shown, print unmoored images from the texts in which they were previously embedded, discussing the particularities of their production, and also showing how elements of their design depended on decisions about formatting and placement.[101] Some of these formulae were carried over into the *Liber Quodlibetarius*, which coopted the autonomy cultivated by printed texts, and, in some cases, the images' sovereignty in the manuscript went so far as to estrange the text that had harbored them in printed editions. Sometimes, text was removed entirely, or reassigned to captions that do not reflect the original context. The explanatory text that accompanies the physiognomic images, for instance, only summarizes the epistemic skill of face-reading instead of providing relevant details about how to do it. The synopsis here epitomizes the complexion book's themes but provides only the images by which to reference them. Their succinct presentation here suggests that the images serve to refresh skills whose in-depth explanations reside elsewhere. The images argue for themselves as useful data. Whether or not a contemporary viewer would have been familiar with the printed urtexts, the necessary graphic layout and scaffolding were preserved in the Erlangen codex as a type of facial collection that could be referenced, a guide to images.

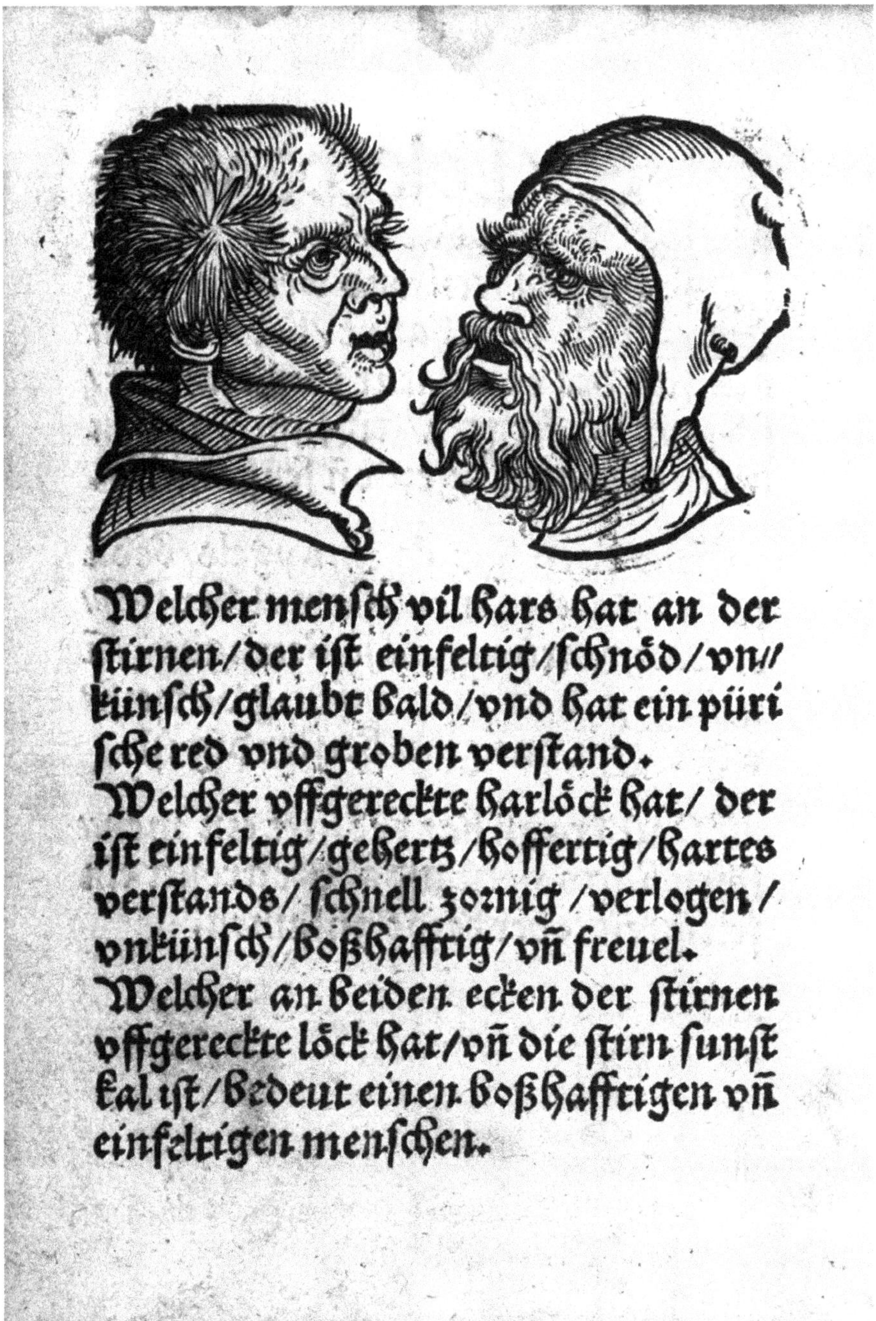
Welcher mensch vil hars hat an der
stirnen/der ist einfeltig/schnöd/vn//
künsch/glaubt bald/vnd hat ein püri
sche red vnd groben verstand.
Welcher vffgereckte harlöck hat/ der
ist einfeltig/gehertz/hoffertig/hartes
verstands/ schnell zornig /verlogen /
vnküнsch/boßhafftig/vñ freuel.
Welcher an beiden ecken der stirnen
vffgereckte löck hat/vñ die stirn sunst
kal ist/bedeut einen boßhafftigen vñ
einfeltigen menschen.

4.10. Bartolomeo Cocles, *Ein kurtzer bericht der gantzen Phisionomey unnd Ciromancy* (Strasbourg: Johann Grüninger, 1524). *Source:* Siegel 19, W 8 Philos. 959. Courtesy of Universitätsbibliothek der LMU München.

The growing sovereignty of printed images is evidenced not just in how well pictures distilled prescriptions embedded in texts and encouraged empirical processes, but also in the degree to which images could signal related fields of empirical inquiry. That the manuscript's images were developing a representational sovereignty that could stand in for epistemic procedures is supported by an image added to the repertoire of physiognomic heads that cross-references a related field of empirical inquiry. A drawing of a head with an articulated brow appears at the bottom left of the introductory page of the physiognomy section (Plate VII). This forehead marked with lines and symbols is of the type that we see in manuals relating to metoscopy, or the art of reading lines in the forehead, on which planetary symbols are marked in order to show astrological influence over the individual subject. This drawing, likely inserted by a later hand, linked the practices of chiromancy and physiognomy to metoscopy, a genre of judicial astrology overlooked by the earlier illustrator of *Liber Quodlibetarius*; this edit inscribes an omitted genre that similarly advocated the use of images to navigate the empirical world. The compiler's placement of the brow-reading citation with the physiognomic images completes a set of epistemic gestures related to deciphering marks on the human face. With this gesture, our compiler takes the existing images as a place from which to launch connections to related practices.

The growing significance of images as sites of data analysis seems to also be what suggests the foot's sole as a diagnostic tool in the *Liber Quodlibetarius*. In the book's presentation of feet whose meridians could also be subjected to visual analysis, we see an expansion of body surfaces that could be exploited for chiromantic analysis (fol. 85r). To date, I have not found references to the foot as a locus for physiognomic diagnoses in any of the pamphlets I have consulted. Possibly it was a field of encryption invented by the compiler, perhaps one precipitated by the manuscript's surrounding images of palms, whose lines also lent themselves to diagnoses. At the very least, this inclusion of feet reflects the book's visual organization to implement new surfaces for line reading.

The practice of character divination using foreheads, palms, profiles, and feet was served by images that provided analogues for comparison with real-world examples. The ossification of the precepts of complexion literature into the manuscript's collection of chiromantic, physiognomic, and metoscopic images parallels the use of body parts for knowledge retrieval active in printed chiromancies and physiognomies. The image collection of the *Liber Quodlibetarius* could be used as a database for cuing diagnoses of actual subjects, providing rough guidelines to follow in the analyses. Such analyses would come to rest on empirical scrutiny that could be compared with images presented in the manuscript's easily searchable rows. The compiler's weeding out of allegorical representations and zodiac signs from the source literature to which these heads also belonged suggests that the aim was to preserve and feature the user-friendly data presented as a tool for analysis in the real world.

SHAPING KNOWLEDGE DISCIPLINES WITH TOOLS

Tools and the skill sets they enunciated helped to shape emergent knowledge disciplines. The type of observations that the above images prompted were among these; to them we might add gauging and measuring – but it was an important link to empirical experience generally. As tools taught viewers how to observe and thus arguably democratized knowledge derived from firsthand experience, printed images were critical visual technology that built knowledge acquisition. The extent to which printed illustrations promoted empirical investigation and shaped disciplinary fields of study has been the subject of recent sustained inquiry.[102] These prints helped their readers perform and hone skill such as gauging, sighting, and measuring, but also skills like remembering protocols and what kinds of situations to avoid, such as games of chance.

Tools and objects, such as paraphernalia for juggling and games of chance, are presented with a kind of clarity that features their palpable qualities, or their ipseity (Plate VIII). How better to remember the warnings about gambling than by viewing the playing cards and dice in these images. Making music required knowledge, as well as technique, for both the practitioner and the laypersons who heard the music – perhaps even the parent of a student who might need supervision when a teacher could not provide it, or an amateur listener who required background information.[103] Images of musical instruments (Plate IX), likely sourced from printed manuals of instruments – such as Sebastian Virdung's handbook *Musica getutscht*, published in Basel in 1511 – display material whose source lies in the exploration of the liberal arts, but they are deployed for practical ends: the image features the fingering of a recorder to show the reader how to use it – "left hand above, the right hand goes below." Our codices attempt to instruct readers in practices that could be learned through instruments. Activities about which a reader might seek procedural knowledge, in topics as wide ranging as distillation, urinalysis, and fencing, can be learned through the manuscript's image interface. The similar functionality of images in instructional texts as seemingly disparate as these provided the mortar between diverse modes of empirical investigation. The *Liber Quodlibetarius* shows how their principles could be synthesized by images.

As vernacular knowledge gained traction among audiences in the German press via cosmography, chiromancy, and physiognomy, new genres jumped on the bandwagon in their desire to help visually unpack the experience of empirical practitioners. Often, we find a kinship in the illustrated desiderata of texts that similarly engaged the empirical experience of practitioners (implied or actual), especially as we see the new formatting developing in tandem and often from common printshops. For example, Indagine's physiognomy and chiromancy emerged from the same press in Strasbourg five years after the appearance of an important book on field surgery with woodcuts by the same illustrator, Hans Wechtlin. Vernacular publications such as Hans von Gersdorff's *Feldbuch der Wundarzenei* of 1517 was one such reference book for field surgeons, likely also intended to present the work and tools of medics in combat zones to an audience of householders and humanists. The organization of these books took into consideration the urgency of professionals providing emergency care on the battlefield and presented that information as easily searchable views of collections of tools for those procedures; laymen would now also learn the trade by way of its images.

Such tools appear in both manuscripts in novel display formats. Tools that were in the employ of a personal physician (Plate X) are presented in the Jagiellonian codex in a roundel schema that displays them almost decoratively, as "all the tools of the personal physician [*Leibarzt*]."[104] In the *Liber Quodlibetarius*, other tools from the *Wundarznei* (Figure 4.11) are presented in a manner that alludes to the procedures for using certain surgical instruments. The pictured head brace, similar to a device used for trepanation, retrieved bits of skull impacted in cranial injuries; the image references it specific function.[105] These vivid images illustrate the extent to which the practicalities of battlefield surgery were becoming organized along the lines of tools used to treat the injury. Wechtlin's woodcuts seek to bolster the guarantees of eyewitness present in the text. These guarantees are made visually, according to Melanie Panse, first by having images reinforce the idea that sensory perception, especially visual processes, could confirm experience and confer knowledge.[106] Several page spreads devoted to the display of surgical instruments shore up this emphasis on praxis.[107] But there are other images, such as the one that serves as the model for the venesection man, that posed as the product of eyewitness investigation. Gersdorff's image labeled *Augenschinliche Anatomy* and *Contrafacter Laßman* (fol. XIII) was made at the dissection of a hanged man that was attended by local medical specialists. Gersdorff attempts to guarantee the image as the product of eyewitness testimony with labels such as this; these guarantees perform the act of double eyewitnessing, according to Panse, with the act of viewing reconfirming the authenticity of the representation.[108]

In addition to the information about the tool itself, the version of this instrument that appears in the *Liber Quodlibetarius* produces auxiliary knowledge about the procedure (Figure 4.12). While borrowing the general design from Hans Wechtlin's print, the artist of the *Liber Quodlibetarius* placed this device in the roundel format that standardized the depictions of tools within the codex. To this image, the illuminist also added tears streaming down the face of the patient. This patient's emotional response added to the information about the procedure: it not only shows the range of practices that occur on the battlefield but also attempts to show the suffering of the patient. The compiler was quite possibly interested as much here in the information for the benefit of

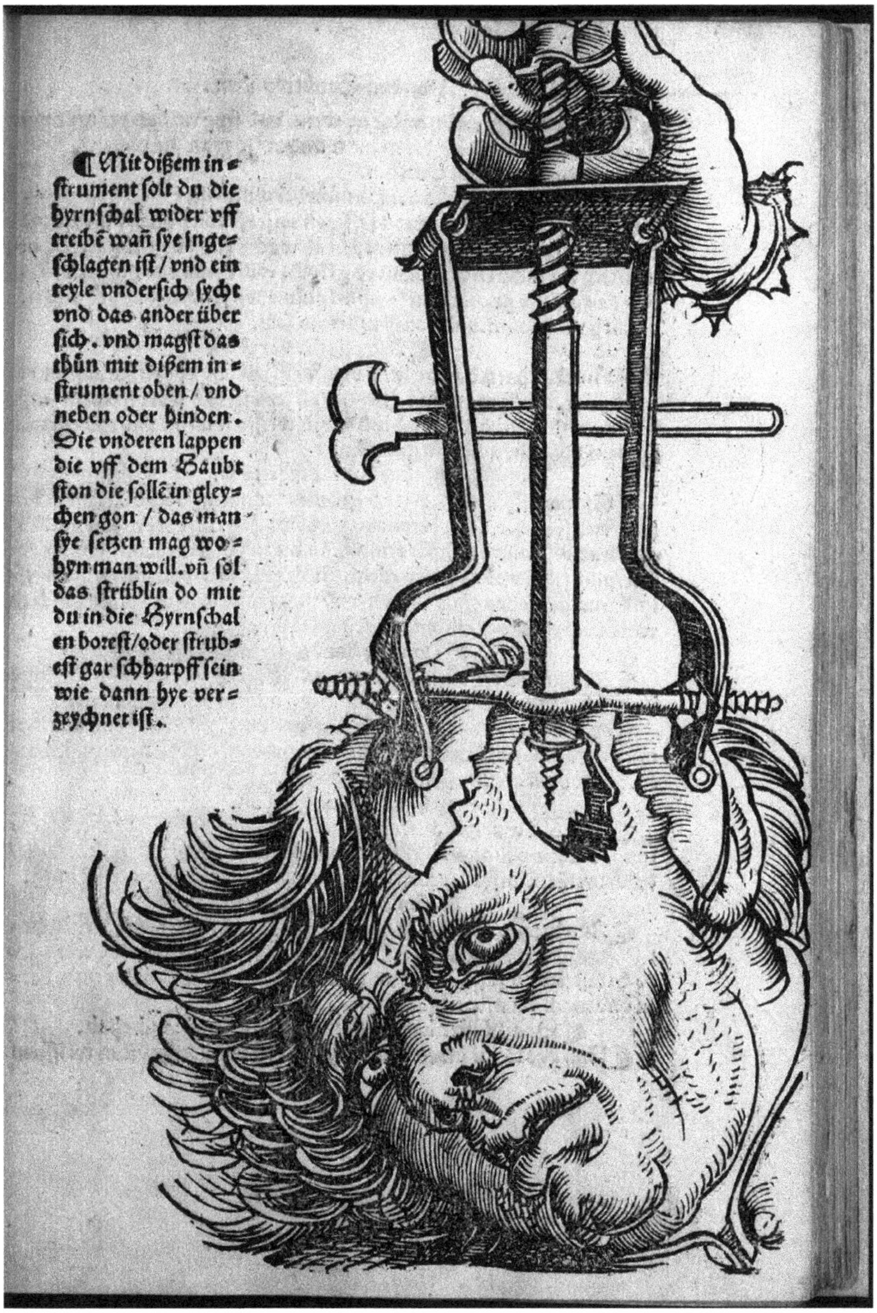

4.11. Hans Wechtlin and Hans von Gersdorff, *Feldtbuch der Wundartznei* (Strasbourg: Schott, 1530). *Source:* Shelfmark EPB/B/2761. Courtesy of Wellcome Collection. Image in the public domain.

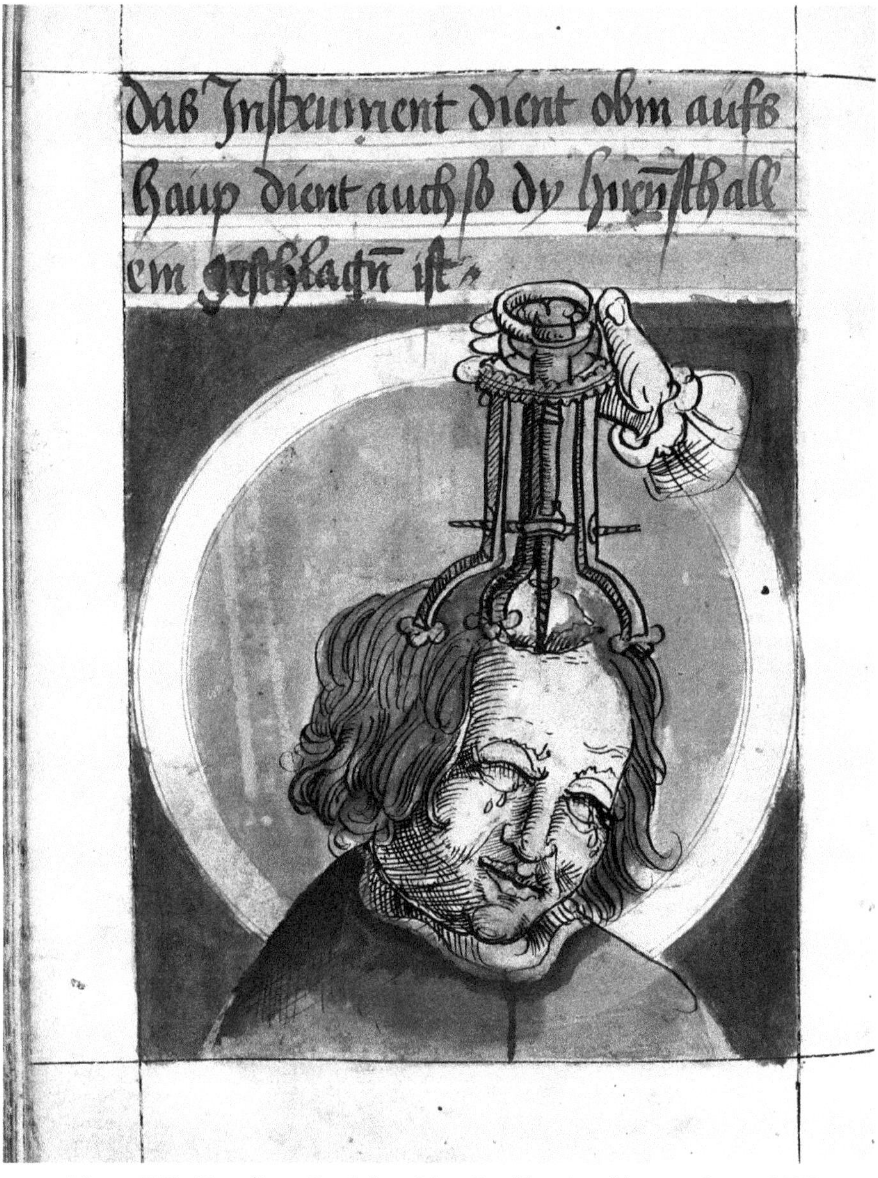

4.12. Master WR, Benedictus Rughalm, *Liber Quodlibetarius*, fol. 68v. *Source:* MS.B 200. Courtesy of Universitätsbibliothek Erlangen-Nürnberg.

the patient, or the reader as potential patient, as much as he might have been in the information that Gersdorff prepared for field surgeons. In this case, we see the compiler's interest in documenting not only the tool, but also the practice, and also the experience. By including the tears, the illuminist is setting the stage for showing emergency treatments from the point of view of the patient and provoking reflections on the strategy of pain management.

Vernacular illustrated manuals rewired genres into a focus on tools and how to use them; this was the intent of short, pithy *Kunstbücher*, or practical manuals. The codices reiterate this focus, and sometimes even surpass the intentions of the printed books, in their presentation of embedded but searchable images.

Just how much the manuscripts distilled the tools and procedures from their sources can be seen in the compiler's deliberate omissions from the printed manuals they sourced. The compiler of the *Liber Quodlibetarius* copied images selectively from Gersdorff's text, discarding the material that would not fit well into rows and roundels and didn't point to an ostensible purpose, such as St. Anthony in a section that discusses ergotism (St. Anthony's fire) and Job in discussions of the plague. The images from Wechtlin that make it into the Erlangen manuscript are also the more "practical" images that feature tools at their center.[109]

Some of the compiler's amendments to the printed sources are also telling for the kind of knowledge inscription that these scribal efforts represent. Take for instance, Wechtlin's image of the procedure for setting an arm in a winch. In an accompanying caption, Gersdorff's text suggests a how-to strategy for pain management: "I am called the Fool with courtly customs; he who needs me does not ridicule me."[110] While this fool is mentioned in the printed text's caption, only a civilian bonesetter is depicted in Wechtlin's image. This omission is corrected by the *Liber Quodlibetarius*'s illuminist. Into the scene of setting an arm in a winch, this bonesetter has been transformed into a fool (Plate XI). Behind a patient about to undergo the procedure, we now see a figure in striped tights and a cap with long ears who seems to voice the accompanying caption.

This fool adds epistemic range to what might have been a humorless presentation of instruments: he serves as commentary on a painful surgical procedure that would profit from the distraction supplied by a jester. This type of peripheral knowledge would slowly drop out of the printed books of field surgery, as they increasingly come to feature mostly the tools used by the surgeon, but surely it was a useful preview of ad hoc anesthesia for practitioners who may have had a funny person at their disposal to help distract a suffering patient. While these narratives and perhaps extraneous additions did amplify surgical knowledge, they would be among the images that were later eliminated, along with pictorial references to St. Anthony and Job. The content of the next generation of printed literature on field surgery would increasingly coalesce around the tools of the trade.

This trend toward practical imagery anticipated by the *Liber* Quodlibetarius would dominate in the mid-century popular press. For example, the distressed heads undergoing surgery in Gersdorff's *Feldbuch* bow out of Walter Ryff's handy edition of the *Stat und Feldbuch Bewerter Wundarzney*, which appeared in 1551.[111] In this edition, only the tools remain – gone are the expressive heads and gone is the allusion to the jester as anesthesia. Where there are winches, only the arms and legs appear; the narrative scenes are gone. The compiler of the *Liber Quodlibetarius* clearly saw the fool as part of the technical apparatus for the procedure of bone setting versus anecdotal narrative, because he served a function related to the operation. Consumers of such knowledge were no longer restricted to personal physicians (*Leibärzte*); they now included armchair physicians, or readers who may or may not have actually practiced trades with these instruments but made it their business to engage in knowledge realms once reserved for specialists.[112]

To be sure, image groups in both the *Liber Quodlibetarius* and its sister codex in the Jagiellonian Library in Cracow reflect the privileging of informational images already operative in many of the printed books from which the images come. Images in the codices also borrowed from printed texts some of their metadata, such as captioning and formatting. Certainly, the full-page layout chosen by the compiler and the organizational logic of reining the relevant information into taut roundels or rows with minimal text lent themselves to this kind of expedient visual encryption. This model of formatting is also operative in the Jagiellonian codex, but the compiler of the *Liber Quodlibetarius* seems to have filtered it through graphic packaging familiar from printed media.[113]

FAKE TOOLS AND SOVEREIGN IMAGES

The extent to which images gained sovereignty in these codices reflects the degree to which the status of the tool (or machine) rose in the hierarchy of knowledge production. A class of amateur users came into being in the sixteenth century's first half; Suzanne Karr Schmidt calls them users, while Margaret Gaida invokes the persona of a book-buying and instrument-consuming mathematical amateur.[114] But perhaps we can also speak of a class of image learners, such as the students who gave scholarly discourses on the topic of emblems; such pedagogy was active at Altdorf Academy in the late sixteenth century.[115] Among the owners of the Erlangen codex was Johann Jacob Baier (d. 1735), a physician connected to this academy whose graduates performed orations whose topics were prompted by emblems.[116] The roundels of the *Liber Quodlibetarius* might have had a formal kinship with the emblem format – could such a manuscript have been used for the orations, or did the round images serve to spur mnemonic meditation in a similar fashion?

Just as the epistemic emphasis of developing disciplinary fields was beginning to accrue around the use of tools, technical images were gaining traction. Images were being selected and commissioned for their use value or epistemic potential. Technical images, or images functioning like tools, were independent agents. Even if they weren't particularly self-explanatory, and perhaps especially when they were not, images in the pursuit of knowledge increasingly passed themselves off as ones with epistemic functions.

The images in the codices inhabit a representational space between tools and images of tools.[117] Images in the liminal zone between functional tools and images of functionality require the rhetorical and argumentative program of *Bildwissenschaft* to unpack.[118] This German subdiscipline of visual culture can treat the books' agency in the evolution of these cognitive models. As books remapped their focus on disciplinary organization onto pictures of tools themselves, the pressure of utility bore down on the images. Buckling under the growing formalization of certain bodies of knowledge around tools, it is no accident that even images that were not explicitly instruments saw the advantages of looking like them. Indeed, a well-organized set of tools could obscure the distinction between real and actual objects or machines. In their epistemic guises, such tools could also herald a field of disciplinary inquiry, per the visualizations of reading the sole of the foot or early modern anesthesia discussed above, where none had previously existed.

A series of decorative horse bits occupies an ample section of both the Erlangen and Cracow codices (Figure 4.13). Ten pages of the Erlangen manuscript (fols. 58r–62v) and the concluding thirteen pages of the Jagiellonian manuscript (fols. 458–70) display designs of the elaborate ways in which the compilers fantasized about imprisoning the tongues of horses to make them tractable.[119] Each bridle bit sports slightly different furnishings, and it seems that the compiler wanted to feature their individuality within the multiplicity. This particularity exhibits well the highly differentiated forms of knowledge that, according to Marcus Popplow, we also see in images of machines.[120] Indeed, the bits begged to be treated as differentiated examples: the short inscriptions that justified their *copia* attempt to distinguish among them and the different types of behavior they were meant to condition. The designs could possibly have functioned as a model book for a blacksmith or a spur maker – as they do later in the century, when Mang Seuter, stable master to Marx Fugger, printed luxury editions of large-format and decorative books of highly wrought bits beginning in 1584. The authors of these bit books were spur makers or farriers themselves and they asserted their authorial presence by boasting that they had artisanal knowledge to bring customized bits to fruition.[121]

The bridle bits collected in the two manuscripts can illuminate the way in which hardware helped shape the care and training of horses. While the text of printed horse manuals would digress into treatments and exercise for horses, the bits offered precise corrections to their behavior. In the collection of bits, ordering the flow of data and metadata about horses resonates with Foucault's anxiety about control exercised by social governance. Discrete data units become hardware for structuring order, writ large.[122]

Technology was the means by which owners could dominate the horse, according to Pia Cuneo; after equestrians assessed the horse's behavior, a proper tool to fix the deviance was assigned.[123] For books pertaining to the

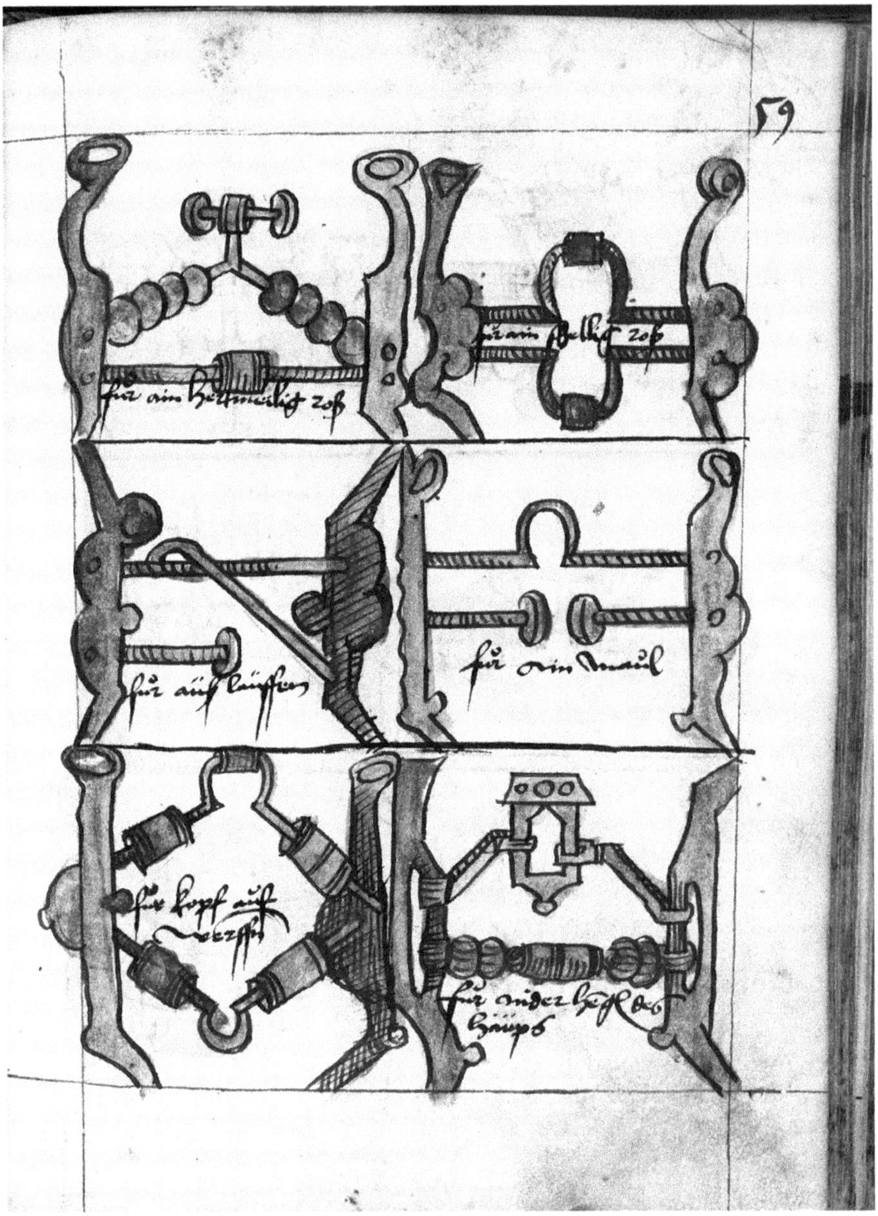

4.13. Master WR, Benedictus Rughalm, *Liber Quodlibetarius*, fol. 59r. *Source:* MS.B 200. Courtesy of Universitätsbibliothek Erlangen-Nürnberg.

domestication of the horse, the instruments themselves stage the process by which the horse comes under man's control. The extent to which these representations of tools take over pedagogy relating to horses is reflected in the multiplicity of the designs. Such images catapulted instrumentation into the foreground of these trades, occupations, and training processes, leaving the text to back up warrants made by the pictures themselves.[124]

Images standing in for processes was already a function of technical manuals of different sorts. This type of spare design on the page with minimal captioning was already present in battlefield manuals and manuscripts on the art of war, such as *Bellifortis*, Konrad Kyeser's manuscript on siege warfare that was frequently copied through the sixteenth century, and the *Eyb Kriegsbuch* of Ludwig von Eybe zum Hartenstein, *c.* 1500.[125] Dedicating this work to Philip the Upright (1448–1508), the elector of the Rhineland Palatinate, the aristocratic compiler Ludwig von Eybe likely did not have much involvement in the practice of war, but aimed to summarize its aims through visualization of weapons and war machinery. Like some of the items in these manuscripts, the horse bits were imaginative variations on the "idea" of technical devices. The license taken in the plurality of these designs indicates that they might just be fantastic riffs on designs deemed strictly essential – they show the creative spirit mimicking the divine act of creation.[126]

The vast trove of bit designs in the codices seems to predate the printed bit books. The published volumes begin to be printed in Augsburg around 1530.[127] They are printed throughout Bavaria in that decade, with an edition appearing in Regensburg in 1539.[128] Designs in these printed texts are more modest and spare than the examples in the codices. In fact, the collections of horse bits in both the Erlangen and Jagiellonian codices exceed in number and complexity the designs of horse bits in any printed bit book of the next decade. The *fantasia* of the bits likely amplified designs already in circulation as tools or ones found in manuscripts, but their presentation seems inspired by prints' ordering capacity, seriality, and repeatability. The bit collections seem to be a meditation on the kinds of tools that might be developed for emotionally charged horses – variations on a theme that the art historian Christopher Wood characterizes as style. Repetition amplifies an image's iconic present; departures from this present, according to Wood, translate into style. As information drifts from the iconic, style differentiates itself. In the horse bits of the *Liber Quodlibetarius*, this drift could buoy the epistemic image, as well as its implementation. In the display of tools intended to tackle the epistemic pursuit of horse training, new tools (and, *ipso facto*, new conditions) were invented. In this case, tools would be the *fantasia* that precedes the knowledge discipline. Images could generate new related images, even *copia* for their own sake.[129] In the *Liber Quodlibetarius*, these highly intricate designs follow folios devoted to images of herbs and a pilgrim map without introduction and without reference to any outside text found in the canons. Their primary relevance to the foregoing material seems to be that they, too, embed data and follow similar design principles. Visual overload guides the presentation of the bits, and sensory overload describes the emotion one has viewing them. The primary reason for the excess seems to be that they are seen as embedding noniterative data.

The presentation of horse bits betrays the inspiration they took from other early modern knowledge regimes treated by contemporary books, such as physiognomy and chiromancy. After the character profiling of the horses had been assessed, these tools aimed to correct their flaws. Desire to meet the need for character diagnoses possibly spurred the fabrication of tools to investigate a horse's character. Horse bits are tools used to encourage certain behavior in horses (to encourage trotting in an enclosure, for example, to direct a head upward, or to orient it downward instead), and many of these actions are conceived with the intent to redirect a horse's natural proclivities. Diagnosing one's horse properly is to read its nature, just as a chiromancer could predict character by distinguishing among lines on palms. In a printed volume, the need for a multitude of examples prompted one Augsburg printer to stamp portions of the bits' hardware in order to reduce the parts of new blocks that needed carving. This practice produced somewhat sloppy and unregistered images simply in order to generate variety.[130] The images that appear in the codices multiply the models on offer with many designs challenging the idea that these are plausible instruments. Alternatively, they might be designs for custom fabrication; certainly, no blacksmith or spur maker would have prefabricated such tools that appear to be designed for an individual horse. Like many images in other technical literature, these are speculative tools.[131] They seem to be the product of an image fetishist who speculates on the myriad ways in which horses' functionality could be improved by finely engineered instrumentation. Literally putting the hardware before the horse, these images reflected theoretical positions that might invite new cognitive pathways about ordering behavior, or even taxonomies of types of horses.

Is "epistemic" a fitting term for such diverse tools that communicate knowledge-making claims? It is a fraught term in the scholarship, one whose capaciousness causes it to snag between an image that demonstrates a theory or a method of obtaining knowledge on the one hand, and a "working object of science" on the other. Most of the images in the manuscript tread a tightrope between these. Some show the compiler's intention to locate images of epistemic inquiry in a communal storehouse; others express the functionality of existing tools known in part from the repertoire of data established by prints.

PRACTICES OF ANNOTATION

Epistemic, or technical, images could also describe the range of uses exhibited by nature prints, or inked impressions of botanical specimens, *Naturselbstdrücke*, that appear throughout the two codices.[132] These impressions left by leaves printed when wet with ink serve as mnemonic reminders of the natural world; they sometimes function decoratively, and at other times they function indexically. They belong to a set of artisanal practices that produced new knowledge themselves. Ann Blair has shown how similar acts of knowledge collecting, such as Jean Bodin's commonplace book *Universae naturae theatrum* (1596), built a repertoire of facts that comprised reference material for subsequent generations of natural philosophers.[133] The cognitive dissonance that Blair proposes as an important tolerance of common-placing can perhaps be seen in the range of operations touched on by nature prints in these manuscripts.

The variety of informational backdrops in the codices on which impressions of leaves and herbs left their mark gives us pause about how the act of common-placing can generate new knowledge structures. Impressions of herbs sometimes appear as printed afterthoughts placed on top of other images, such as atop the dial on folio 19v of the Jagiellonian manuscript. Here, they seem to function decoratively – the impressions are poor and the relationship to the volvelle is unclear. In the context of manuscripts whose images address modes of knowing about the natural world rather than its content, the random placement of many nature impressions might recall the practice of pressing leaves or flowers into books, an act with epistemic agency that breathed inspiration into marginalia mimicking the look of pressed flowers in Flemish manuscript illumination.[134] While prints of leaves appear scattered throughout both the Erlangen and Jagiellonian manuscripts, one page of the Erlangen codex devoted solely to nature prints shows deliberately placed and carefully inked herbs (Plate XII). An inscription announces them as "various herbs and spices" and refers the reader back to a lengthier explanation at the end of the book.[135] Suggesting empirical investigations such as measuring and comparing, the unit markings at the bottom of the page invite the reader to consider these impressed leaves indexically by providing a knowledge-based framework for the image. The ability to gauge the scale of a specimen by way of unit markers provides an example of how new knowledge schemas cropped up around natural impressions.

Among the nature prints in the *Liber Quodlibetarius*, however, we see new cognitive bridges being built by the images. On folio 117v of the manuscript (Figure 4.14), leaf prints surround several fishes. The captioned text promises to show "which fish are healthy or useful, and how to catch them ... also how to preserve them." The reader is referred to the canons on folio 157r; there we find descriptions of different methods of capturing fish. Sage, an herb recalled by the shape of the leaf depicted, is also mentioned for use in fishing. This same type of linking of an image to a method appears on a page devoted to birds (fol. 87r), where we find an inscription that relates to their trapping: "You will find how to catch birds on folio 157."[136] Nothing in the image seems to suggest the act of catching birds; indeed, the birds come from a variety of manuscript and printed sources unrelated to trapping. But the inscription suggests that the knowledge structures tipped off by the pictorial collection of birds will be expanded in the canons at the rear of the book. The captions that attach themselves to the images do so in a manner of common-placing in

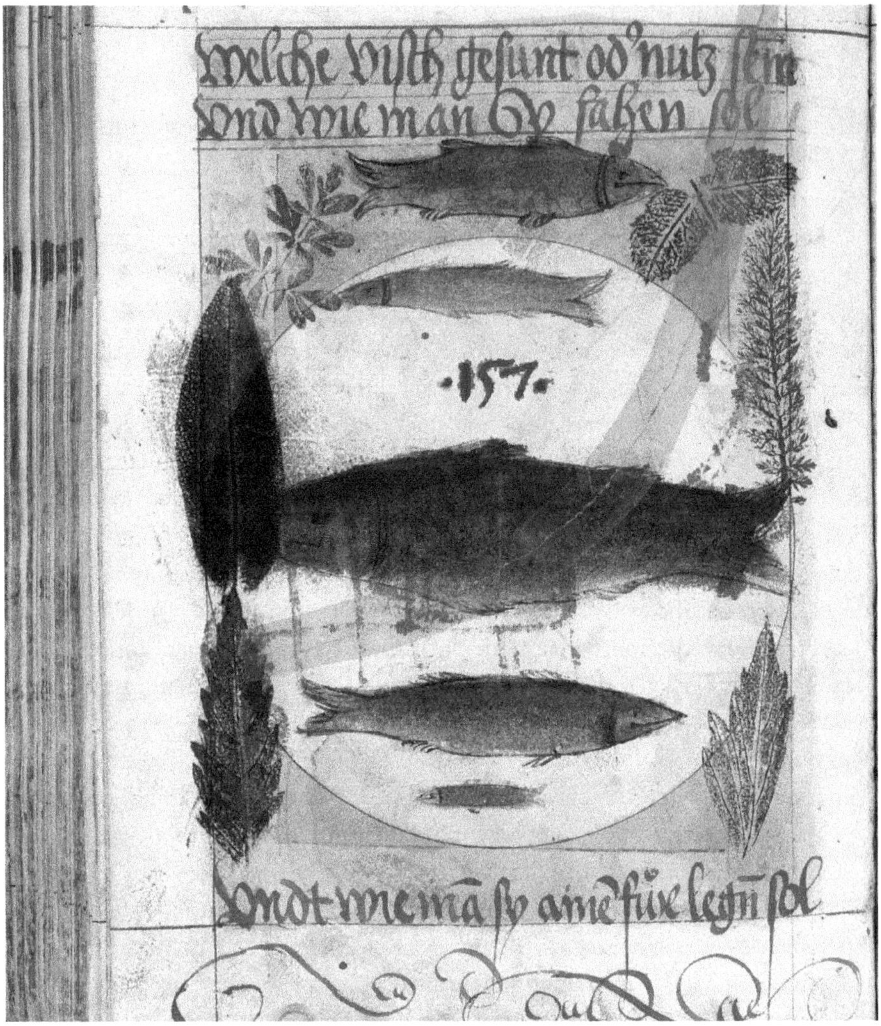

4.14. Master WR, Benedictus Rughalm, *Liber Quodlibetarius*, fol. 117v. *Source:* MS.B 200. Courtesy of Universitätsbibliothek Erlangen-Nürnberg.

which the image points to a different kind of know-how than what the image itself overtly asserts. The inscription almost reads as a type of disingenuous apology for unequivocal variety presented for its own sake, and not so much for the purpose of catching birds. Relating free-floating images to text that recommended more useful ends was the way in which the compiler marshaled not unambiguously useful images into more self-consciously epistemic paradigms. Even images that were not tools, but rather were useful representations insofar as they pulled together a multiplicity of genres all in one place, developed ostensibly useful purposes. Their placement within the book was the context that christened these images as tools; they earned their invitation to the text by announcing their function in useful terms.

ARTISTS AS INVENTORS

These codices accord an important role to the artist in the creation of usable knowledge. Self-conscious references to creators of images was a trope gaining traction in the printed literature: Apian invokes the artist in the beginning of his volume, likening his act of portraiture to the description of the world, and a printed gloss in the margins suggests that "no one but an artist can [make such representations]." The compilers of both manuscripts, if also the scribes who were *de facto* artists in their own right, pay a subtle debt to visual collecting practices that sustained their own efforts in these books.[137] Many pages are devoted to studies of geometrical and architectural motifs, and designs that likely originated in circulating artists' manuals, among the many types of practical volumes sometimes also called *Kunstbücher*. Such images remind us of the new epistemic agency that attended ambitious and artistically inclined heads of households (*Hausväter*). Such artists' manuals, like their anatomical, optical, and physiognomic counterparts in the *Kunstbuch* literature, endowed the reader/user with the capacity to generate knowledge well beyond the scope of the published and circulating literature. A wide array of subjects are treated under the rubric *Kunstbuch/Kunstbücher*, but these books are perhaps best united by the way in which they hail a reader. William Eamon dates the widespread appearance of recipe books that feature *Kunstbuch* in their titles to around 1531–3.[138] The variety of topics treated by books carrying this title suggests that what unites them is the way they empowered the reader to learn skills and solve problems.

Readers desiring to implement their own autodidactically sourced knowledge became an important target of book marketing. Editors such as Ryff, along with publishers like Schott and Egenolff, were rushing to meet the demand of readers needing to scour surfaces, distill grains, collect botanical specimens, or sketch designs for furniture. Printers of *Kunstbücher* were rarely concerned with endowing books with unique content or authorship; instead, they recycled and repackaged texts with impunity, and frequently privileged illustrations as the most important apparatus for conveying information. Perhaps this is also why images were made the actionable element of litigation around copies.[139] Artists' manuals that were issued in the period also adopted the title *Kunstbücher*. This was mostly because of their practical value: they were developed expressly to recirculate images with the goal of sending more copies of these images into circulation.[140] These images were tools of a self-conscious sort, sometimes sidelining the text that accompanied them.

One such contemporary manual for artistic instruction was almost entirely comprised of images. Heinrich Vogtherr's *Ein frembds und wunderbars Kunstbüchlin* unapologetically advertised itself as a collection of designs for artists to freely lift for new compositions. It has received recent attention from

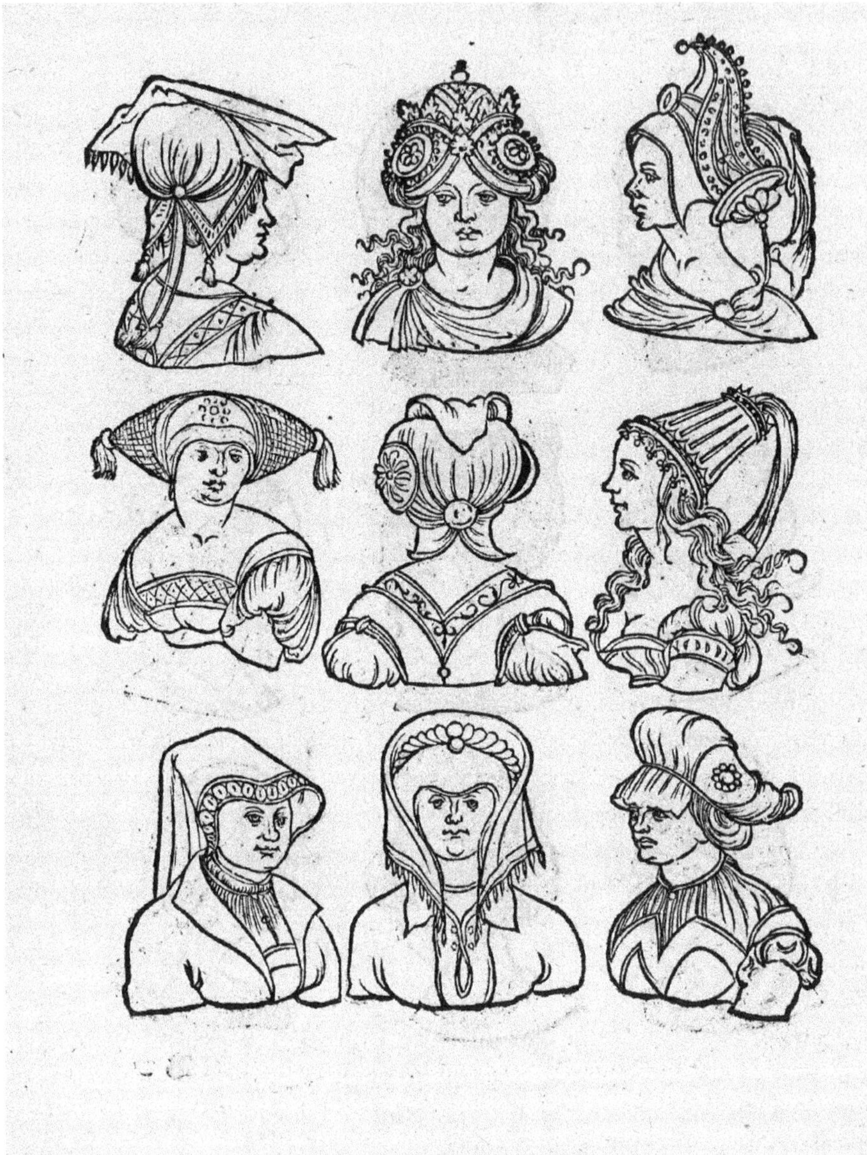

4.15. Head coverings for women in Heinrich Vogtherr, *Ein frembds und wunderbars Kunstbüchlein allen Malern, Bild/ schnitzern, Goldschmieden, Steinmetzen, Schreinern/ Platnern, Waffen und Messerschmiden hochnutzlich/ zu gebrauchen* ... (Strasbourg: H. Vogtherr, 1538), Sig. 15/157. *Source:* Courtesy of Universitätsbibliothek Johann Christian Senckenberg, Frankfurt.

scholars interested in artisanal knowledge.[141] Vogtherr both designed and printed this popular title with a preface in German in 1538 and reissued the book with a Latin preface the following year.[142] The pages featured arrays of heads, assorted body parts, sartorial accessories, and architectural features designed to be used as boilerplate by other artists (Figure 4.15). Vogtherr's

Kunstbuch represents an image reservoir of designs that he himself pirated from a variety of sources, including Netherlandish painting, Roman coins, Italian prints, and German model sheets.[143] The book's purpose, according to the preface, was to collect data that would be a storehouse that artists and artisans could crib from to inspire new designs: the logic of his appeal to a lineage of *Kunstbücher* in his title was to reinforce the usefulness of his book, in the way that a recipe or alchemical manual might serve the needs of its readers.[144] Vogtherr himself was unapologetic about his own liberal borrowings, none of which are credited in his book. All of these designs were unprotected from copyists and fair game in a climate of artistic transmission via emulation, or *aemulatio*, of earlier models. While Vogtherr was a print designer in his own right, his legacy rests on his acts of pictorial compilation as a publisher. He advertised heavily in the title page about the *Kunstbüchlin*'s usefulness, coaxing his readers to buy the book for the expedience it offered in the form of time and cost savings.[145] The data he presented, Vogtherr argued, could substitute for eyewitness experience gleaned during the journeyman's *Wanderjahre*, with the expectation that these ersatz "observations" would establish the groundwork for a skillful assembly of atomized parts necessary to build new visual narratives. Vogtherr worked in an environment where motifs floated freely between artists, many of whom invented designs and ornaments as "easily retrievable rubrics" that lent themselves to a variety of purposes.[146]

While artists were quick to capitalize on Vogtherr's collection by cribbing such motifs for their altarpiece and furniture design, our codices suggest that compilers found such *Kunstbücher* fertile sources from which to borrow and generate new knowledge. Clearly, they copied data heavily from such model manuals. Vogtherr announced that his primary goal was to present designs for artists unable to broaden their experiential horizons through empirical study. The recommendations of publishers of *Kunstbücher* were taken to heart by illuminists like ours in need of material to copy: the compilers took motifs from a variety of model books and recombined them in new ways. The page of projecting capitals and cornices in the manuscript in the Jagiellonian Library (Plate XIII) also features in its center the seemingly unrelated material of three types of headdresses. Although seemingly disruptive to a unified visual field, this juxtaposition was standard fare in artists' manuals. The image contained various motifs that an artist might be called upon to produce: garlands, headdresses, cornices, and pedestals.[147] This unusual arrangement was the attempt of the Jagiellonian codex's illustrator to synthesize material from different pages of model books. Similar items are presented separately in the *Liber Quodlibetarius*: one folio (Figure 4.16) is devoted to designs for stonework and salt containers; another page (Plate XIV) features designs for headdresses that likely originated in an artists' manual like Vogtherr's *Kunstbüchlein*. The

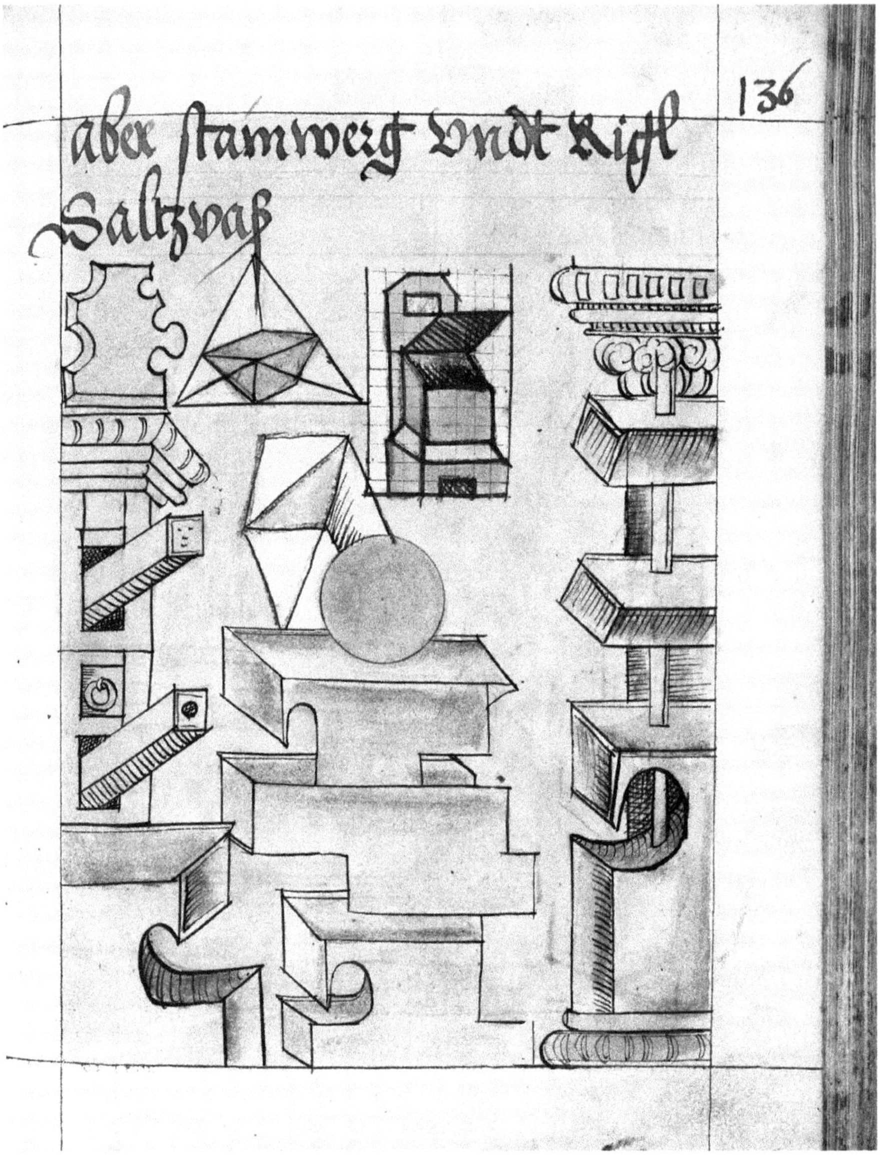

4.16. Master WR, Benedictus Rughalm, *Liber Quodlibetarius*, fol. 136r. *Source:* MS.B 200. Courtesy of Universitätsbibliothek Erlangen-Nürnberg.

Jagiellonian manuscript also featured geometric designs for knots, architectural features, spheres and parabolas, pedestals with receding steps, and motifs that would later become familiar from perspective manuals composed by Wenzel Jamnitzer and Walter Ryff.

Collected motifs from artists' manuals spontaneously generated new knowledge in the manuscripts. The generative premise of such design manuals mimic the epistemologically rich trajectory of nature prints. Both kinds of images (headdresses and pressed leaves) exemplify the tension that Horst

Bredekamp identifies between two related impulses toward imitation: *natura naturata* (the urge to imitate existing creation) and *natura naturans* (the desire to imitate the creativity of nature).[148] The liminal space between artifice and nature also underwrote the epistemology of the *Kunstkammer*: nature as a starting point from which to expand into other rubrics of knowledge. On the level of morphology, the *Liber Quodlibetarius* and its sister manuscript both reflect organizational operations that may have derived from a variety of structural models, including florilegia in the manuscript tradition, the practice of collating printed texts in collected volumes like *Sammelbände*, and the displays active in the *Wunderkammern*. Images and objects in the *Kunstkammer* stood in for analogues of nature and could themselves generate new knowledge. In a similar way, new knowledge could obtain from the surrounding visual prompts in the codices, and in ways not necessarily present in the printed sources from which they came. The advantages of presenting those prompts in a handmade book format that could evolve over time meant that this knowledge could be cross-referenced with other information. Such images provided the foundation for ever more elaborate and abstract *fantasia*, such as we have seen in the designs for horse bits. As with highly pictorialized technical manuals of the early fifteenth century, those whose conceptualization presupposed a level of artistic ability on the part of the inventor, Bert S. Hall proposes that the artistic modes of representing technical knowledge very likely influenced the process of invention itself.[149] And the speculative part, the urge to fantasy, often occurred in the act of drawing itself. In the technical realm, drawings became major contributors to the theatre of knowledge, and, thus, to the theatre of the world. In the hands of a capable inventor or draftsman, items added to the theatre of knowledge were secularized acts of creation. Drawings were *de facto* inventions.

THE GENERATIVE KNOWLEDGE OF GEOMETRY

A significant epistemic gesture among the codices' other references to knowledge-building campaigns resides in the materialized act of representation as a site of invention. Many of their designs show invention to be the operative inspiration for design. Techniques for representing objects in space can be seen in images that treat gauging or stereometry and show how to render figures in spatial grids. For instance, an image of a mannequin's head with orthogonal lines emerging from its side appears in the Jagiellonian codex (Figure 4.17). These lines should help a practitioner understand how to render a head from an oblique angle, made easier by reducing the head into stereometric components from which such lines could be drawn. The caption uses the term "*austailung der angesicht*" (the portioning of the face); the word *Austailung/Austeilung* is used in technical manuals for the gridding of objects into sections that can be measured.

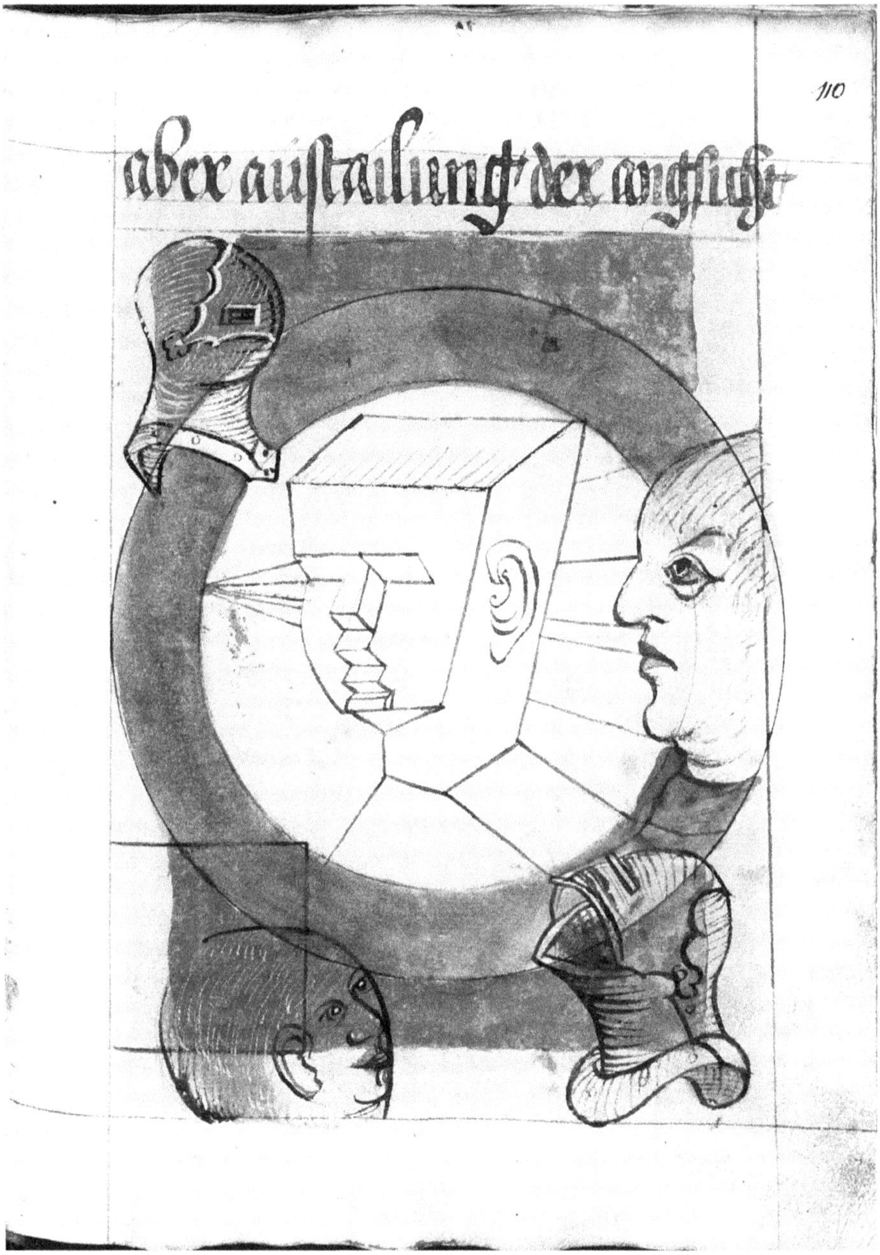

4.17. Manuscript Rkp. Przyb. 35/64. Jagiellonian Library, Cracow, fol. 110r. *Source:* Courtesy of Jagiellonian Library. Work in the public domain.

Some *Kunstbücher* were more self-conscious than others in advertising their generative potential – and the codices take on these printed images in a variety of ways. The compiler of the *Liber Quodlibetarius* drew on several circulating manuals on measurements and proportions to generate new designs and endeavored to show how new designs could be generated. The stereometric figure that converts the body into volumes may have been derived from familiarity with either Erhard Schön's technical publications or possibly Albrecht Dürer's proportion manuals – perhaps designs kept now in the so-called *Dresden Sketchbook*.[150] In a folio of the *Liber Quodlibetarius*, the head of such a mannequin shares the page with other geometric designs, such as a cradle and a sphere, and variations on Platonic solids such as those found in Wenzel Jamnitzer's *Perspectiva Corporum Regularium* (Nuremberg, 1568). The caption "*abgestollen wiegen und angesicht*" refers to a method used by artists to transfer bodies in the real world into representations via a method of measurement of observed objects (as in foreshortening) – this replicates the language from perspective and measurement manuals, such as Dürer's *Underweysung der Messung, mit dem Zirckel und Richtscheydt, in Linien, Ebenen unnd gantzen corporen*, which was printed by the woodblock cutter Hieronymus Andreae in Nuremberg in 1525.[151] The related page in the Jagiellonian manuscript (fol. 110r) forges new cognitive links from the same common motif of the geometric head by actually drawing those lines, taking the schematic image and showing how an artist might derive (*abstehlen*: loosely, to transfer via perspective) from that form other heads and helmets encountered from different angles. Although the illuminator did not draw the skewed head in convincing perspective, he managed to extrapolate from it the purpose of a proportioned perspectival rendering of the head, to show from different angles based on a roving point of view. In the model book of Villard of Honnecourt, the artist first drew a set of faces and then layered on top of those the simplified geometric shapes that might be used to generate them. While Stephen Perkinson notes that this method surprisingly inverts the logic of the "model" book – which typically proceeds from the abstract shape to the finished form – the possibility remains open that the designer intended to show the method in action, as proof of a theory. As in the Honnecourt model book, the image in the Jagiellonian codex announces itself as the model from which the surrounding designs can be generated.

These studies of gridded facial elements seem to be related to Albrecht Dürer's study of stereometric projections in which he lays out rules for the division of the face. Such grids were also used by Albrecht Dürer in the *Dresden Sketchbook* to present different aspects of the human figure, including side views and ground plans. Walter Strauss connects the Dresden studies to illustrations Dürer sets out in the *Four Books on Human Proportion*, illustrations that served to assist a sculptor who must cut away either wood or stone, and who must first render geometric surfaces before organically shaped forms. Such methods can be seen in Dürer's construction of faceted heads, on the same page as physiognomic heads, in the *Dresden Sketchbook* (fol. 101v), or in the "ground plan" for his stereometric man (fol. 141r).[152] The images of the mannequin's heads in both codices show what can be gleaned through measurement of geometric solids in order to draw projections. This common instructional theme united the seemingly unrelated data presented on these pages. Indeed, this data was derived from sources as diverse as Erhard Schön's *Underweisung der Proportion und Stellung der Possen*, for the stereometrically gridded faces and horses, and Jean Pelerin's *Kunst der Perspectiva*, for some of this section's figures composed as volumetric solids, barrels and wagons shown in perspective, and architectural fragments, such as a cross-topped shrine projected at an angle.[153]

Immanent in such idealized "model" images were new ones that could be generated from them. The geometric mannequin in the Jagiellonian codex shows its potential as a model for new designs for heads rendered in profile, in angles, and for renderings of the same for a helmeted head, some of which are derived from orthogonal lines drawn from the mannequin. In this, the compiler showcases the formal properties of the mannequin that could be constitutive of new knowledge – its use as a tool for the construction of a variety of new forms. This head models in microcosm how images in the manuscript function as a whole: images throughout the codices enable the accretion of new knowledge around them. Borrowed images were recontextualized to build knowledge-based bridges to other types of empirical acts, artisanal practices, and new cognitive connections.

The geometric mannequin, when transferred to the *Liber Quodlibetarius*, shares the space with other forms whose fashioning depends on a knowledge of geometry (Figure 4.18). Forms here are announced as "*ab[ge]stolen*," or rendered from a system of measurements that makes them appear to recede in space.[154] The images on this page point back to the epistemic practice of rendering according to a system of rules. A system of projection, this folio tries to say, underwrites the drafting of three-dimensional forms, such as a sectioned sphere, an intarsia sphere, a mannequin sectioned according to ratios of facial proportions, or a cradle at an angle to the picture plane. This mannequin's face adrift in a sea of other non-representational images (diagrammatic or expressive of the epistemic process of construction) seems a fitting place to end this preliminary review of the *Liber Quodlibetarius*'s content because it presents a face in its net of rhetorical, practical, and epistemic gestures – all of which were highly constructed.[155] In staging the face as a data platform that can absorb the competing paradigms of geography and chorography (see Figure 1.2), Apian's primary point was to articulate the skill of the artist to differentiate between the levels of the episteme of picturing. It was the artist's ability to picture that underwrote Apian's entire campaign to pictorialize the premise of cosmography. As we have explored in our discussions of facial knowledge, such meaning-filled gestures supplied a net for the other heads of physiognomy, metoscopy, and cosmography – and now as one that points back to the epistemic inflection of the practice of rendering with a foundation in geometry. Toward the close of the volume, the *Liber Quodlibetarius* introduces designs that can be extrapolated from

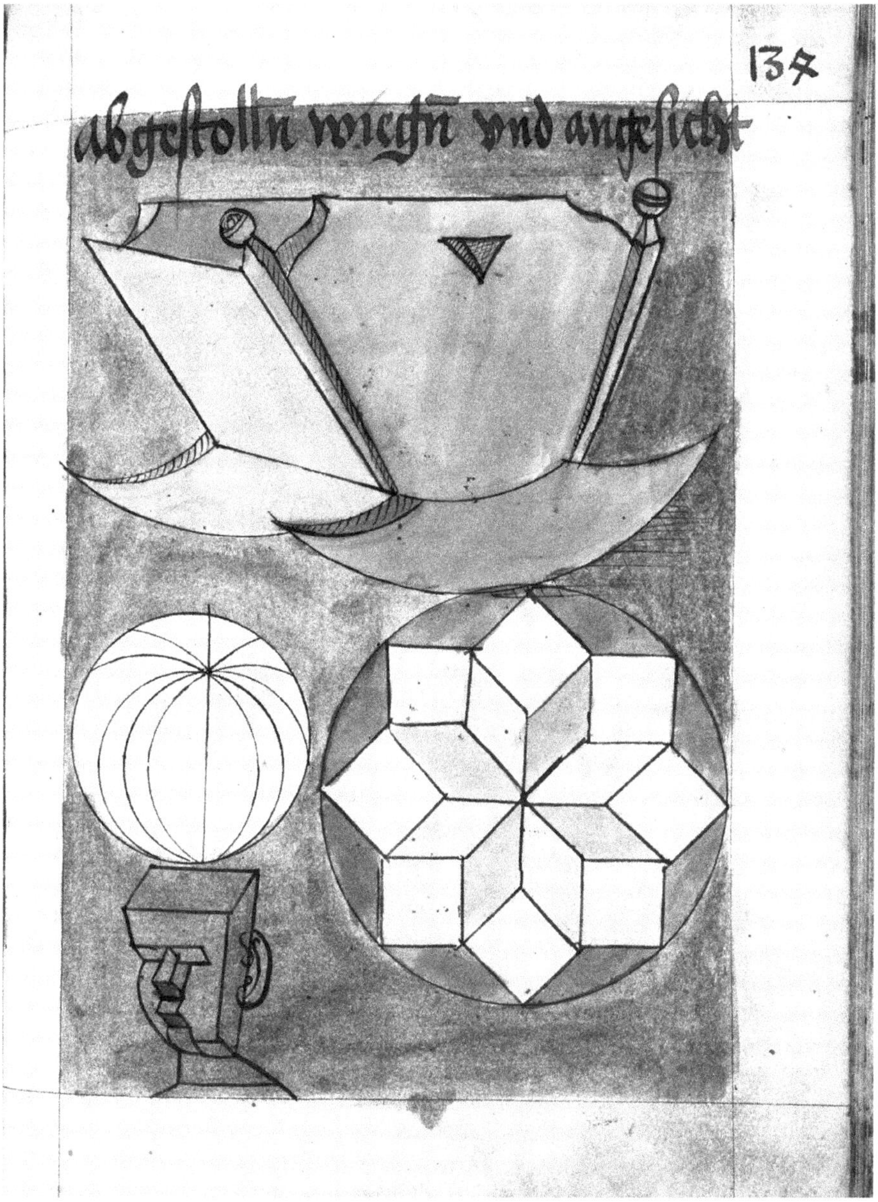

4.18. Master WR, Benedictus Rughalm, *Liber Quodlibetarius*, fol. 134r. *Source:* MS.B 200. Courtesy of Universitätsbibliothek Erlangen-Nürnberg.

geometry with images of surveyors measuring distances via dividers and a Jacob's staff; but in these images (likely also from Apian's publication on astronomical and surveying instruments, the *Instrument-Buch*), the compiler of the manuscript shows them as lay geometers. The title to this page announces the exercises that follow to be a subset of endeavors in geometry (and, understood, in art): *sections (or divisions) made with compasses and quadrants.* This language echoes the titles of Dürer's technical manuals as well.

These images from circulating model books tacitly lobby for the power of the artist. They show the skills over which mastery was expected and the new combinations enabled by artistic practice. Apian's invocation of the artist's generative capacity echoes throughout the *Liber Quodlibetarius*. On folio 155, the canons reprises this reference to the role of the artist in the creation of chorographic rendering, borrowing from Apian's text the statement that "only an artist can do it" – that is, produce a topographic scene. Geometry, on the macrocosmic scale, and art, on the level of the microcosm, both articulated practices of representation. The understanding of geometry in the creative process by technically gifted artisans models the way in which the content of the *Liber Quodlibetarius* provides a resource for the *Hausvater*: the manuscript collected principles of recorded data for the purpose of deriving the next generation of knowledge from them. Both manuscripts characterize artistic practice as an exercise in repurposing, recreating novel, unanticipated, and sometimes surprising new meanings. If the astonished reactions of modern readers to the material are revelatory of its sixteenth-century audience, then these new meanings will continue to evolve.

The *Liber Quodlibetarius* concludes with images from artists' model books; the Jagiellonian codex concludes with a sensational display of bridle bits. Both suggest a multiplicity of design possibilities generated by the artisan with the mastery of such knowledge; but the manuscripts also reveal the steady undercurrent of the power of printed images to summarize knowledge, spur empirical engagement, and generate new epistemologies – which in this context could very well be synonymous with new images.

In conclusion, the *Liber Quodlibetarius* provides the reader with an encyclopedic view of the information that was circulating in printed sources in early modernity. In printed texts, increased need for useful knowledge gave rise to publications that featured dense and searchable images. Insofar as it borrowed some of its morphology from the printed texts whose visual data it stored, the *Liber Quodlibetarius* can serve as a reference tool that the milieu of profuse images in print might have helped suggest. The *Liber Quodlibetarius* synthesized data from printed images, integrated that data with related information, outfitted it with finding aids, and made it searchable. Textual references relegated to the manuscript's canons prove that images still invited narrative explanations, but the compilers of both codices under review in this chapter embedded the most critical component of the knowledge presented in the images themselves. Within the vessels of data presented here, the codices collect knowledge from circulating books and chronicle common vernacular practice. Released from their original moorings in diverse and varied texts whose pictorial programs were far from homogeneous, the uprooted images withstood this transfer with a surprising integrity that suggests something kindred about their independent function.

The extent to which the images operate semi-independently in the codices as standalone or sovereign knowledge gives credence to the idea that their operations and agency were authoritative. Indeed, their sovereignty was already vetted by the printed editions from which many of them were transferred. The creation of these manuscript compilations coincided with the intense visualization of most early modern instructional genres. The manuscripts' concentration on the ways in which these printed books structured information through illustrations highlights the commonality among diverse genres including cosmography, physiognomy, astrology, astronomy, field surgery, and artists' manuals. All of these genres sought to verify knowledge through visual models.

The seeds of knowledge-based pursuits were sewn into the orderly rows and patterns of the *Liber Quodlibetarius*. Through passages of visually arresting color backgrounds, the compiler led the reader down cognitive pathways groomed by visual experience. Among the diverse lessons learned in this garden were remembering, memorizing, distinguishing, and forging connections between knowledge fields. Such skills were shaped by a visual program orchestrated for a subject constituted as a viewer. The eye hovering over this pictorial landscape was held in place by mandates for mid-sixteenth-century readers already developed by printed books. Such bookworms were nourished on a diet of visual learning and were being trained as active observers of the world through images.

NOTES

1 *Baierisch* refers to the early modern language spoken in a large area of present-day Bavaria.

2 Michele C. Ferrari, *Le monde en images: Deux encyclopédies manuscrites à Erlangen et à Cracovie*, Art de l'enluminure 76 (Dijon: Éditions Faton, 2021). The manuscript is the topic of a research team (Michele C. Ferrari, Manuel Teget-Welz, and Stefan Weber) at the Friedrich-Alexander Universität Erlangen-Nürnberg that investigates early modern illustrated encyclopedias, *Bildenzyklopädien des frühen 16. Jahrhunderts*: www.mittellatein.phil.fau.de/forschung/#collapse_4.

3 The manuscript preserved in Cracow's Biblioteka Jagiellońska, Rkp. Przyb. 35/64, is catalogued as "a Housebook of medieval knowledge" at this link: https://jbc.bj.uj.edu.pl/dlibra/publication/283753/edition/271106#info.

4 For an overview of the content and partial identification of a selection of printed templates, see Pia Rudolph, "Hausbücher. Bayerische Bild-Enzyklopädien," No. 49a.5.1, in Ulrike Bodemann et al. (eds.), *Katalog der deutschsprachigen illustrierten Handschriften des Mittelalters (KdiH)* (Munich: C. H. Beck, 2015), vol. 6, 466–73, https://kdih.badw.de/datenbank/handschrift/49a/5/1; https://kdih.badw.de/datenbank/handschrift/49a/5/2; see also https://handschriftencensus.de/24571.

5 Lynn Thorndike, "The Problem of the Composite Manuscript," in *Giovanni Mercati: Miscellanea Giovanni Mercati 6* (Vatican City: Biblioteca Apostolica Vaticana, 1946), 93–104. Thorndike's magisterial *A History of Magic and Experimental Science* poises him well to speculate on the collection and packaging of miscellaneous knowledge. Lynn Thorndike, *History of Magic and Experimental Science* (New York: Columbia University Press, 1923–58).

6 For the round image generated by a compass, see Jean-Claude Schmitt, *Penser par figure: du compas divin aux diagrammes magiques* (Paris: Arkhê, 2019), especially 53–99; for the history of this formatting, especially in the *Liber Floridus*, see Jean-Claude Schmitt, *L'Histoire en lignes et en rondelles: les figures du temps chretien au Moyen Age* (Wiesbaden: Reichert Verlag, 2015). For how the circular format resonated in maps, see Lucia Nuti, "Mapping Places: Chorography and Vision in the Renaissance," in Denis E. Cosgrove, ed., *Mappings* (London: Reaktion Books, 1999), 92.

7 Susan Dackerman, *Prints and the Pursuit of Knowledge in Early Modern Europe* (Cambridge, MA and New Haven, CT: Harvard Art Museums, 2011); Suzanne Kathleen Karr Schmidt and Edward H. Wouk, *Prints in Translation, 1450–1750: Image, Materiality, Space* (Abingdon: Routledge, 2017), 7.

8 Christopher S. Wood, *Forgery, Replica, Fiction: Temporalities of German Renaissance Art* (Chicago: University of Chicago Press, 2008), for discussions of style and iconographic drift, see 236ff, and chapter 3.

9 Wood, *Forgery, Replica, Fiction*, 236. Christopher Wood examines the authenticating function of replication in other media generated before the era of print: for example, methods of citation active in architectural motifs, the minting of medals, as well as the production of alphabets.

10 Margaret Gaida, "Reading Cosmographia: Peter Apian's Book-Instrument Hybrid and the Rise of the Mathematical Amateur in the Sixteenth Century," *Early Science and Medicine* 21, no. 4 (2016), 277–302.

11 Suzanne Karr Schmidt, *Interactive and Sculptural Printmaking in the Renaissance* (Leiden and Boston, MA: Brill, 2018). Many such books were designed for lay users generally despite the frequent dedications to aristocrats such as Matthias Lang, prince-bishop of Salzburg.

12 Denise Schmandt-Besserat, *Early Technologies* (Malibu, CA: Undena Publications, 1979), 48.

13 Peter Parshall, "Prints as Objects of Consumption in Early Modern Europe," *Journal of Medieval and Early Modern Studies* 28, no. 1 (1998), 19.

14 William Eamon, *Science and the Secrets of Nature: Books of Secrets in Medieval and Early Modern Culture* (Princeton, NJ: Princeton University Press, 1996), 100–1. For Eamon, the essential condition of being *gemein* was having legal rights in a *Gemeinde*, a municipality or village.

15 Alexander Marr, "Walther Ryff, Plagiarism and Imitation in Sixteenth Century Germany," *Print Quarterly* 31, no. 2 (2014), 131–43, especially 139–40.

16 Marr, "Walther Ryff," 135, see also Ryff bibliography at note 17.

17 Random Clod [Randall McLeod], "Information on Information," *Text* 5 (1991), 246.

18 The history, relevance, and limitations of this term are vetted in Alexander Marr's essay: "Knowing Images: A Review Essay," *Renaissance Quarterly* 69, no. 3 (2016), 1000–13. See also Christoph Lüthy and Alexis Smets, "Words, Lines, Diagrams, Images: Towards a History of Scientific Imagery," *Early Science and Medicine* 14 (2009), 398–439.

19 Horst Bredekamp et al., *Das Technische Bild: Kompendium zu einer Stilgeschichte wissenschaftlicher Bilder* (Berlin: Akademie Verlag, 2012).

20 Lorraine Daston, "Epistemic Images," in Alina Payne, ed., *Vision and Its Instruments: Art, Science, and Technology in Early Modern Europe* (University Park: Penn State University Press, 2015), 13–35.

21 Ruth S. Noyes, ed., *Reassessing Epistemic Images in the Early Modern World* (Amsterdam: Amsterdam University Press, 2022).

22 An early bibliographer of the Erlangen manuscript announced any attempt to catalogue its source material to be a pyrrhic undertaking: "*die Vorlagen sämtlich nachweisen zu wollen, wäre natürlich ein ebenso unnützes, wie jedenfalls vergebliches Unternehmen.*" See Christian Ferckel, "Eine Bilderhandschrift v. J. 1524," *Mittheilungen zur Geschichte Medizin und der Naturwissenschaften* 12 (Leipzig and Hamburg: Leopold Voss Verlag, 1913), 279.

23 François Dupuigrenet Desroussilles links the type of common-placing in Rughalm to medieval *loci communes* such as Bartholomaeus Angelicus's *De proprietatibus rerum*, whose

printed editions span from 1492 to 1609. Based on email conversations with Desroussilles, March 24, 2016.

24 UER Ms. B 200, with 124 picture folios.

25 Biblioteka Jagiellońska, Rkp. Przyb. 35/64 (49a.5.2.); 1–150 picture folios; 151–92 text; 192v–199r geometric designs.

26 Ewa Chojecka, *Bayerische Bild-Enzyklopädie: das Weltbild eines wissenschaftlich-magischen Hausbuches aus dem frühen 16. Jahrhundert*, Studien zur Deutschen Kunstgeschichte, vol. 358 (Baden-Baden: Verlag Valentin Koerner, 1982), 15.

27 The date appears in these sections: 86v; 164r (both 1524); inside of rear cover (1524, 1543).

28 Chojecka, *Bayerische Bild-Enzyklopädie*, 8. Chojecka gives the examples of the Schönsperger editions of Maximilian's *Gebetbuch* (1513) and *Theuerdank* (1517).

29 We don't know much about the manuscript's likely compiler, Benedictus Rughalm, except that he is noted as a cleric within the book. The bibliographer of Erlangen's illustrated manuscripts, Eberhard Lutze, notes the designation of Rughalm throughout the manuscript, and specifically as a priest – "Benedictus Rughalm *patavius pfaff*" or "Rughalm, cleric from Passau" – at the base of the canons on fol. 164r. Rughalm's name appears on the back cover with the words "*Allerley Sach*" and 1524. A second hand inscribes the date 1543 next to the name G. Scheck. Lutze identifies two hands at work in the manuscript; the primary draftsman WR (86v), Lutze claims as Franconian, probably from around Nuremberg.

30 Chojecka, *Bayerische Bild-Enzyklopädie*, 13.

31 Chojecka, *Bayerische Bild-Enzyklopädie*, 13–14.

32 Stephen G. Nichols and Siegfried Wenzel, *The Whole Book: Cultural Perspectives on the Medieval Miscellany* (Ann Arbor: University of Michigan Press, 1996), 99. For William of Ockham's role in Quodlibetal disputations, see Michael J. Sauter, *The Spatial Reformation: Euclid between Man, Cosmos, and God* (Ann Arbor: University of Michigan Press, 2019), 11–12.

33 A section of the library inventory of Herzog August in Wolfenbüttel carries this moniker; it also refers to pedagogical exercises in the university setting and to open debate on learned topics.

34 Carla Yanni, *Nature's Museums* (Princeton, NJ: Princeton Architectural Press, 2005).

35 Sabrina Corbellini, Giovanna Murano, and Giacomo Signore, *Collecting, Organizing and Transmitting Knowledge: Miscellanies in Late Medieval Europe* (Turnhout: Brepols, 2018), 11. See especially Marilena Maniaci, "Miscellaneous Reflections on the Complexity of the Medieval Manuscripts," 11–22; Kimberly Rivers, "Composition and Career: The Composite Manuscripts of Johannes Sintram, OFM," 149–50, which considers the composition of codicological units, as well as a "Unité de Production."

36 Nichols and Wenzel, *The Whole Book*, 1–6.

37 See J. P. Gumbert, "Codicological Units: Toward a Terminology for the Stratigraphy of the Non-Homogenous Codex," in Edoardo Crisci and Oronzo Pecere, eds., *Il codice miscellaneo: tipologie e funzioni: atti del convegno internazionale, Cassino 14–17 maggio 2003* (Cassino: University of Cassino, 2004), 17–42; see also Patrick Andrist et al., eds., *La Syntaxe du codex: essai de codicologie structural* (Turnhout: Brepols, 2013).

38 A. E. B. Coldiron, "Translation and Transformission; Or, Early Modernity in Motion," *Canadian Review of Comparative Literature* 46, no. 2 (2019), 205–16; Clod, "Information on Information," 246, 248–81.

39 Michael Friedrich and Cosima Schwarke, *One-Volume Libraries: Composite and Multiple-Text Manuscripts* (Berlin and Boston, MA: De Gruyter, 2016).

40 Hanna Vorholt, *Shaping Knowledge: The Transmission of the Liber Floridus* (London: Warburg Institute, 2017). On the medieval encyclopedic tradition, see also the upcoming essay by Jean-Claude Schmitt, "Enzyklopädismus und Bild-Enzyklopädien im Mittelalter," in the proceedings of *Die Welt im Bild. Bildenzykopädien um 1500*, conference at Friedrich-Alexander Universität Erlangen, July 13–15, 2022.

41 Bert Hall claims that technical manuals are groupings of "pictures with running commentary ... [essentially] 'picture books' of technology with verbal comments." Bert S. Hall, "*Der Meister sol auch kennen schreiben und lesen*: Writings about Technology ca. 1400–ca. 1600 AD and Their Cultural Implication," in Schmandt-Besserat, *Early Technologies*, 47–58, especially 53.

42 This is the case in manuscripts of the military engineer Konrad Kyeser in his *Bellifortis*, *c.* 1405 and the popular *Feuerwerkbücher*, for example. See Schmandt-Besserat, *Early Technologies*, 49. The shipbuilding books of Michael of Rhodes were also restricted to presentation copies; see Pamela O. Long, David McGee, and Alan M. Stahl, eds., *The Book of Michael of Rhodes: A Fifteenth-Century Maritime Manuscript* (Cambridge, MA: MIT Press, 2009).

43 Gaida, "Reading Cosmographia," 288. Gaida cites Raymond Llull's *Ars generalis* and *Ars brevis*, both in the collection of Regiomontanus; cf. Ernst Zinner, *Regiomontanus: His Life and Work* (Amsterdam: North-Holland, 1990), 227, n. 92; see also Karr Schmidt, *Interactive and Sculptural Printmaking*, 210.

44 See Mark Meadow's graphic arrangement of Quiccheberg's system of the *Kunstkammer* and related workshops in Samuel Quiccheberg, Mark A. Meadow, and Bruce Robertson, eds., *The First Treatise on Museums: Samuel Quiccheberg's Inscriptiones, 1565* (Los Angeles: Getty Research Institute, 2013), 23–7. Creation and enacted knowledge mutually inform each other in Quiccheberg's treatise *Inscriptiones Vel Tituli Theatri Amplissimi* (1565). The Kunstkammer and the *Liber Quodlibetarius* also share a cosmological interface. I thank Emily Gattuso for sharing her insights here. A similar encyclopedic grouping of tools can be seen on the title page of Giovanni Battista Della Porta's manual on distillation, *De distillatione* (Rome, 1608). Many of these items are also collected by the *Liber Quodlibetarius*. On Della Porta, see Paula Findlen, *Possessing Nature: Museums, Collecting, and Scientific Culture in Early Modern Italy* (Berkeley: University of California Press, 1994), 322–5.

45 See Jürgen Wolf, "Sammelhandschriften – mehr als die Summe der Einzelteile," in Horst Brunner et al., eds., *Überlieferungsgeschichte transdisziplinär: neue Perspektiven auf ein germanistisches Forschungsparadigma* (Wiesbaden: Dr. Ludwig Reichert Verlag, 2016), 69–82. For miscellany versus *Sammelband*, see Friedrich and Schwarke, *One-Volume Libraries*, 2.

46 Ann Moss, *Printed Commonplace-Books and the Structuring of Renaissance Thought* (Oxford: Clarendon Press, 2000), see especially 186–214.

47 One such book was Johann Agricola and Johann Friedrich, *Drey hundert gemeyner Sprichwörtter: der wir Deutschen uns gebrauchen, un̄ doch nicht wyssen wo her sie kommen* (Nuremberg: F. Peypûs, 1529). This collection of 300 German proverbs, also printed in Hagenau and Zwickau that same year, was billed by its authors as a way to investigate and preserve vernacular culture.

48 Jaya Remond, "Bodies of Knowledge: Movement, Variety and Imagination in a German Renaissance Art Primer," in Andreas Beyer and Guillaume Cassegrain, eds., *Mouvement. Bewegung* (Berlin: Deutscher Kunstverlag, 2015), 53.

49 Albeit with slightly different ordering.

50 Megenberg's *Das puch der natur* (Augsburg: Bämler, 1475), with six reprints in Augsburg before 1500, was the first incunabulum to consider the illustration of plants independent of their ornamental function. See Dominic Olariu, *The Misfortune of Philippus de Lignamine's Herbal or New Research Perspectives in Herbal Illustrations from an Iconological Point of View* (Berlin: Max-Planck-Institut für Wissenschaftsgeschichte, 2015), 10.

51 An *ellenbogen* spans roughly the length of a forearm from the tip of the middle finger to the elbow. The Nuremberg Chronicle (*Liber chronicarum*) attributes this information to Eusebius at fol. LXXXIIv and gives the height at 170 *ellenbogen*.

52 Chojecka, *Bayerische Bild-Enzyklopädie*, 25. Chojecka suggests that this image invokes Bellerophon and compares it to Dürer's print of this subject (B. 134). For the evolution of this motif from a sculpture into a world wonder, see Dunstan Lowe, "Suspending Disbelief Magnetic and Miraculous Levitation from Antiquity to the Middle Ages," *Classical Antiquity* 35, no. 2 (2016), 247–78, especially 259. Medieval treatments of world

wonders included Isidore of Seville, Venerable Bede, Gregor Anglicus, and Agrippa von Nettesheim. For systematic reproduction of world wonders in early modernity, see Philip Galle, after Maarten van Heemskerck, *The Eight Wonders of the Ancient World* (1572).

53 Cara Bishop, "Prophecy, Position, and Predetermination: The World of the Nuremberg Chronicle," n.d., http://arthistory.us/display.php?eid=42.

54 Anke te Heesen, *The World in a Box: The Story of an Eighteenth-Century Picture Encyclopedia* (Chicago: University of Chicago Press, 2002), see 166, n. 1 for historical comparisons of the Kunstkammer to Noah's ark.

55 Yanni, *Nature's Museums*, 20.

56 For the woodcut of animals, see Larry Silver, "World of Wonders: Exotic Animals in European Imagery, 1515–1650," in Pia F. Cuneo and Alison G. Stewart, eds., *Animals and Early Modern Identity* (London: Routledge, 2014), 291–327.

57 The entire repertoire of beasts discussed in Anglicus's *Van der proprieteyten der dinghen* is represented by approximately twelve illustrations in total. Bartholomaeus Anglicus, *Van den Proprieteyten der Dinghen* (Haarlem: Jacobus Bellaert, 1485), http://daten.digitale-sammlungen.de/~db/0007/bsb00079541/images; for animals, cf. http://daten.digitale-sammlungen.de/bsb00079541/image_738.

58 Conradus Megenberg, *Hye Nach Volget das Puch der Natur das Innhaltet zu dem Ersten von Eygenschafft und Natur des Menschen, Darnach von der Natur und Eygenschafft des Himels, der Tier des Gefügels[!], der Kreuter, der Steyn und von Vil Ander Natürlichen Dingen* (Augsburg: Baemler, 1475), https://opacplus.bsb-muenchen.de/metaopac/search?id=10524470&db=100; see also https://nbn-resolving.org/urn:nbn:de:bvb:29-bv008994279–3.

59 The images of the bears follow motifs known from a playing card, *Nine of the Beasts of Prey*, from the Playing Card Master, whose widely copied engraved prototypes for playing cards are found today in the Bibliothèque Nationale in Paris. See Anne H. van Buren and Sheila Edmunds, "Playing Cards and Manuscripts: Some Widely Disseminated Fifteenth-Century Model Sheets," *Art Bulletin* 56, no. 1 (1974), 12–30, especially 14. For this reference, I am grateful to Anna Dlabacova, who is preparing a study of manuscripts with printed prototypes. For model books, see Stephen Perkinson, "Portraits and Counterfeits: Villard de Honnecourt and Thirteenth-Century Theories of Representation," in David S. Areford and Nina A. Rowe, eds., *Excavating the Medieval Image* (Aldershot: Ashgate, 2004), 13–35.

60 Dackerman, *Prints and the Pursuit of Knowledge*.

61 Karr Schmidt and Wouk, *Prints in Translation*, 6–7.

62 Pamela H. Smith, *The Body of the Artisan: Art and Experience in the Scientific Revolution* (Chicago: University of Chicago Press, 2012); Pamela H. Smith, Amy R. W. Meyers, and Harold J. Cook, *Ways of Making and Knowing: The Material Culture of Empirical Knowledge* (New York: Bard Graduate Center, 2017); Tom Conley, *The Self-Made Map: Cartographic Writing in Early Modern France* (Minneapolis: University of Minnesota Press, 1996); Tom Conley, *An Errant Eye: Poetry and Topography in Early Modern France* (Minneapolis: University of Minnesota Press, 2011).

63 Peter Apian, *Cosmographicus Liber* (Landshut: Weyssenburger, 1524). For Apian's text, see Chapter 2.

64 This passage appears in *Liber Quodlibetarius* at fol. 155v: "*corographia est consumata (et) perfecta pictura et nulla nisi homo pictor ripotest exerce eam*" (chorography is a perfected and used/wrought image; no one but an artist is able to do it). Warm thanks to Barbara Tramelli for assistance with the translation.

65 Kathleen Crowther et al., "The Book Everybody Read: Vernacular Translations of Sacrobosco's Sphere in the Sixteenth Century," *Journal for the History of Astronomy* 46, no. 1 (2015), 4–28; Kathleen M. Crowther and Peter Barker, "Training the Intelligent Eye: Understanding Illustrations in Early Modern Astronomy Texts," *Isis* 104, no. 3 (2013), 429–70.

66 Suzanne Kathleen Karr Schmidt, "Art – A User's Guide: Interactive and Sculptural Printmaking in the Renaissance," PhD dissertation, Yale University, 2006, see especially chapters 3 and 4; see also Karr Schmidt, *Interactive and Sculptural Printmaking*.

67 See "De Partibus mensurae seu Speciebus geometriae practicae," in *Cosmographicus Liber*, fol. 32–3.
68 See http://daten.digitale-sammlungen.de/~db/ausgaben/zweiseitenansicht.html?fip=193.174.98.30&id=00064968&seite=119.
69 Smith, Meyers, and Cook, *Ways of Making and Knowing*, 6–8.
70 Gaida, "Reading Cosmographia," 285.
71 "*sodas ertricht trieckt war so waer es also*" (28v).
72 Per Gabriele Werner in Horst Bredekamp, Vera Dünkel, and Birgit Schneider, eds., *The Technical Image: A History of Styles in Scientific Imagery* (Chicago: University of Chicago Press, 2015), 11.
73 Gaida, "Reading Cosmographia," 298–9.
74 I am indebted to DeWayne Carver for his unflagging enthusiasm in helping me decode Apian's instruments.
75 Many thanks to Zoltàn Biedermann, Jim Ackerman, Tom Conley, and Tony Campbell for their ingenuity and creativity in helping me think through this image.
76 On the entanglements of vision, surveying, and cartography, see Tom Conley's post "The Engineer's Art: Surveying the Origins of the French Cartographic Imagination" at www.americanacademy.de/the-engineers-art.
77 Cosgrove, *Mappings*, 93.
78 Conley, *An Errant Eye*, 65.
79 Conley, *An Errant Eye*, 66.
80 Thomas Ulrich Schauerte, ed., *Deutschlands Auge & Ohr: Nürnberg als Medienzentrum der Reformationszeit* (Nuremberg: Tümmel Verlag, 2015); Martin Luther and Wilhelm Martin Leberecht de Wette, *Dr. Martin Luthers Briefe, Sendschreiben und Bedenken ... Gesammelt, Kritisch und Historisch Bearbeitet von Dr. W. M. L. de Wette* (Berlin: Reimer, 1825), 6–7. See the letter from Luther to Eobanus Hess from April/May of 1528 that mentions an elegiac poem for Dürer (d. April 6, 1528) sent to him by Hess. "There is nothing new here that we can send to your emporium, with Nuremberg being the eye and ear of Germany, which sees and hears everything which will never make it to us [in Wittenberg]."
81 Lucia Nuti, "Mapping Places: Chorography and Vision in the Renaissance," in Cosgrove, *Mappings*, 90–108.
82 Gaida, "Reading Cosmographia," 282.
83 Nuti, "Mapping Places," 93.
84 Gaida, "Reading Cosmographia," 277.
85 John A. Pinto, "Origins and Development of the Ichnographic City Plan," *Journal of the Society of Architectural Historians* 35, no. 1 (1976), 44. Although the practice of using such lines to indicate contour was uncommon in the sixteenth century, Leonardo's Imola plan shows the emergence of this. We might consider the roundel organized from above to be such a method for representing either a city (orthographic view) or a tool. If the image in the *Liber Quodlibetarius* means to synthesize different points of view, this attempt at contouring would anticipate the first use of this practice associated with Leonardo Bufalini's plan of Rome from 1551. The unique combination of "spatial measurability with topographical relief" of the Rome plan would ultimately give rise to contour lines in ichnographic plans. This kind of abstraction might be an attempt to convey concepts stereometrically, as Gemma Frisius does with maps in his treatise on triangulation, *Libellus de locorum describendorum ratione* (1533), and as Albrecht Dürer does with forms and shapes in *Underweysung der Messung* (1525).
86 Tom Conley wonders if the projection refers to the extramission model of vision. See Conley, "The Engineer's Art."
87 Georg Tannstetter, Petrus Apian, and Witelo, *Vitellionis Mathematici Doctissimi Peri optikes* (Nuremberg: Petreius, 1535), see 55v, HAB A25.1 Geom. 2. For the digital edition, see http://digital.slub-dresden.de/id274466821.
88 *Perspectiva* is closely linked to the Latin version of Ibn al-Haytham's Arabic opus, the *Book of Optics* (*Kitab al-Manazir*, also known in Latin as *De aspectibus* or *Perspectiva*).

89 David Charles Lindberg, "Alhazen's Theory of Vision and Its Reception in the West," *Isis* 58, no. 3 (1967), 331.

90 See Sven Dupré, "Printing Practical Mathematics: Oronce Fine's *De speculo ustorio* between Paper and Craft," in Alexander Marr, ed., *The Worlds of Oronce Fine: Mathematics, Instruments, and Print in Renaissance France* (Donington: Shaun Tyas, 2009), 67.

91 For the *Imago Christi* in the Paris editions, see Conley, "The Engineer's Art."

92 Most sixteenth-century vernacular editions of the *Phisonomei* or *Complexionbuch*, under which rubrics portions of the *Secretum Secretorum* were published, began with fragments from treatises by Galen on humors. The distribution of these humors in humans comprised their complexion. See Valentin Groebner, "Complexio/Complexion: Categorizing Individual Natures, 1250–1600," in Lorraine Daston and Fernando Vidal, *The Moral Authority of Nature* (Chicago: University of Chicago Press, 2010), especially 372ff.

93 For the printing history of the Latin *Secreti*, see Steven J. Williams, *The Secret of Secrets: The Scholarly Career of a Pseudo-Aristotelian Text in the Late Middle Ages* (Ann Arbor: University of Michigan Press, 2003), 294–7, n. 465. While print editions of the *Secreti* had largely run their course by 1550, the physiognomic section of this work had a longer active career in print.

94 For the new emphasis on external signs in sixteenth-century complexion literature, see Daston and Vidal, *The Moral Authority of Nature*, 361–83, especially 372ff.

95 Stephanie Leitch, "Visual Acuity and the Physiognomer's Art of Observation," *Oxford Art Journal* 38, no. 2 (2015), 187–206, https://doi.org/10.1093/oxartj/kcv010.

96 For the creative reuse of prints, see Michael Gaudio, *The Bible and the Printed Image in Early Modern England: Little Gidding and the Pursuit of Scriptural Harmony* (New York: Routledge, 2017); Joyce Zelen, *Blinded by Curiosity: The Collector-Dealer Hadriaan Beverland (1650–1716)* (Leiden: Primavera Pers, 2022); see also Anna Dlabačková's upcoming work on the Kattendijke Chronicle.

97 Claire Richter Sherman et al., *Writing on Hands: Memory and Knowledge in Early Modern Europe* (Seattle: University of Washington Press, 2001).

98 "*Zerstreute linee bedeiten sterk oder schwachait oder Kuertz des lebens. Glueck oder unglik reich oder ar(m).*" This particular diagnosis can be found in Cocles, *Phisionomi vnd || Chiromanci.|| Eyn newß Complexion Büch=||lein* (Strasbourg: Jakob Cammerlander, 1540), http://diglib.hab.de/drucke/n-97-4f-helmst-7s/start.htm.

99 Cocles, *Ein kurtzer bericht der gantzen phisionomey vnd Ciromancy* (Strasbourg: Grüninger, 1524) LMU (Siegel 19), VD16 ZV30228. Many thanks to Johanna Wittstatt for calling my attention to this source.

100 "*Da hebt sich an die phisonomey. Zu seh[e]n am angesicht was aigenschaft ainer sey. Lang schlecht har sint forchtsam auch die lint vn[d] feucht sin. aber gelurnig/ vast Kraüs har ist vnv[er]stendig. ai[n]faltig/ welch zent dunn vn[d] klai[n] sint bedeit/ ein kuertz leb[e]n. aber dick stark la[n]g leb[en].*"

101 See Ewa Chojecka, "Zur Stellung des gedruckten Bildes im 15. und 16. Jahrhundert: Zwischen Kunstwerk und 'Massenmedium,'" in *Reform, Reformation, Revolution: Ausgewählte Beiträge einer wissenschaftlichen Konferenz in Leipzig am 10. und 11. Oktober 1977* (Leipzig: Karl Marx Universität, 1980), 123–7.

102 Important studies by Susan Dackerman, Suzanne Karr Schmidt, Sachiko Kusukawa, Brian Ogilvie, Lorraine Daston, Katherine Park, Alexander Marr, Volker Remmert, Gianna Pomata, and William Eamon have scrutinized how prints fixed the approach and parameters of the emergent disciplines of botany, anatomy, medicine, and astronomy, highlighting their central role in cuing firsthand engagement with the world.

103 I thank one of my anonymous reviewers for sharing this insight.

104 "*Allen werckzeug eines leib artz.*"

105 "This instrument is to be used for wounds to the top of the head and also serves to extract pieces of the skull that have caved in."

106 Frequently, these entreaties to the eyewitness are made in the captions that accompany the images. Melanie Panse, "Hans von Gersdorffs 'Feldbuch der Wundarznei': Produktion,

Präsentation und Rezeption von Wissen" (Wiesbaden: Reichert, 2012), 108–9. For the mediality of evidence through the rhetoric of the eyewitness, also note Jan-Dirk Müller, "Evidentia und Medialität. Zur Ausdifferenzierung von Evidenz in der Frühen-Neuzeit," in Gabriele Wimböck et al., eds., *Evidentia. Reichweiten visueller Wahrnehmung in der Frühen Neuzeit* (Berlin: Lit Verlag, 2007), 57–81, especially 61–7.

107 Dackerman, *Prints and the Pursuit of Knowledge*, 60. Gersdorff's emphasis on the invasive treatments of battle wounds, especially ones inflicted by gunshot, show his appeal to knowledge that could be gathered firsthand or confirmed by sight.

108 Panse, "Hans von Gersdorffs 'Feldbuch der Wundarznei,'" 108.

109 This has been noted by both Lacy Gillette and Emily White – I am grateful for their observations.

110 "*Ich haiß der narr höflich mit sit/ Der mein bedarf der lacht mein nit.*" Alternatively, *heiszen* can also mean to summon, or command.

111 Hans von Gersdorff, *Stat vnd Feldtbůch || Bewerter Wundtartznei. New || Widerumb Ersehen. Zusampt dem Antidotari/|| Fürsorg vnd Vorrath der Chirurgei. Beschriben || von Herrn Vualthero Riuio, Medico.||, Zů Franckenfurt. Bei Christian Egenolff.||(M.D.LI.||)* (Frankfurt: Christian Egenolff d.Ä., 1551).

112 See Rudolf Schenda, "Der 'gemeine Mann' und sein medikales Verhalten im 16. und 17. Jahrhundert," in Joachim Telle, ed., *Pharmazie und der gemeine Mann: Hausarznei und Apotheke in der frühen Neuzeit: erläutert anhand deutscher Fachschriften der Herzog-August-Bibliothek Wolfenbüttel und pharmazeutischer Geräte des Deutschen Apotheken-Museums Heidelberg* (Weinheim: VCH, Acta Humaniora, 1988), 9–20; see also Lyndal Roper, "'The Common Man', 'The Common Good', 'Common Women': Gender and Meaning in the German Reformation Commune," in Merry E. Wiesner, *Women and Gender in the Early Modern World: Critical Concepts in Women's History* (London: Routledge, 2016), vol. 4, 227–49.

113 Andrea Van Leerdam, "Talking Heads. The Visual Rhetoric of Recurring Scholar Woodcuts in a Sixteenth-Century Handbook on Chiromancy," *Jaarboek Voor Nederlandse Boekgeschiedenis* 26 (2019), 11–29. See this article and the upcoming book by Andrea Van Leerdam for discussions of the role of images in text flow and page flow.

114 Karr Schmidt, *Interactive and Sculptural Printmaking*; Gaida, "Reading Cosmographia," 2016.

115 Mara Wade, "The Emblems of the Altdorf Academy: Emblematic Pedagogy and Nuremberg Civic Culture," in *Histories of Universities* XXXIV, no. 2 (2021), 137–70; Frederick J. Stopp, *The Emblems of the Altdorf Academy: Medals and Medal Orations, 1577–1626* (London: Modern Humanities Research Association, 1974), vol. 6.

116 Eberhard Lutze, *Die Bilderhandschriften der Universitätsbibliothek Erlangen* (Wiesbaden: Otto Harrassowitz, 1971), 58.

117 See Popplow for the role of models in early modern technology, as well as for the relationship between object and prints. Marcus Popplow, "Why Draw Pictures of Machines?: The Social Contexts of Early Modern Machine Drawings," in Wolfgang Lefèvre, ed., *Picturing Machines, 1400–1700* (Cambridge, MA: MIT Press, 2004).

118 Horst Bredekamp, "A Neglected Tradition? Art History as Bildwissenschaft," *Critical Inquiry* 29, no. 3 (2003), 418; Bredekamp, Dünkel, and Schneider, *The Technical Image*.

119 Lutze attributes the horse bits in the Erlangen manuscript to the hand of the later illuminist. Lutze, *Die Bilderhandschriften*, 59.

120 Popplow, "Why Draw Pictures of Machines?," 48.

121 For these, see Pia F. Cuneo, "Just a Bit of Control: The Historical Significance of Sixteenth- and Seventeenth-Century German Bit-Books," in Karen Raber et al., *The Culture of the Horse: Status, Discipline, and Identity in the Early Modern World* (New York: Palgrave Macmillan, 2005), 141–73, especially 149ff.

122 See Michel Foucault et al., *The Birth of Biopolitics: Lectures at the Collège de France 1978–79* (Basingstoke: Palgrave Macmillan, 2008); see also Gilles Deleuze, "Postscript on the Societies of Control," *October* (1992), 3–7.

123 Cuneo located seventeen editions of such texts printed between 1532 and 1639 in the collections of Wolfenbüttel's Herzog August Bibliothek and in the Bayerische Staatsbibliothek in Munich. See Karen Raber et al., *The Culture of the Horse*, 144.

124 See Bert S. Hall, "The Didactic and the Elegant: Some Thoughts on Scientific and Technological Illustrations in the Middle Ages and the Renaissance," in Brian Scott Baigrie, ed., *Picturing Knowledge: Historical and Philosophical Problems Concerning the Use of Art in Science* (Toronto: University of Toronto Press, 1996), 36.

125 See MS.B 26 in the Universitätsbibliothek Erlangen-Nürnberg.

126 Schmandt-Besserat, *Early Technologies*, 57.

127 Illustrated bit books that featured designs for metal mouthpieces for domesticating horses began to appear in Augsburg around 1530: for example, *Hier Inn Begriffne Pis, Zaigen Clärlich an, Wie Ain Yedess Roß, Iüng und Alt Soll Gezämbt, Dadurch Ime, Angenomene Pöse Gewonhait Ubelstandt, ... Benomen ... Werden Mag*, VD 16 G 592 ([Augsburg?], 1530). See the edition in the Staats-und Stadbibliothek Augsburg (and Wolfenbüttel) for a patinated palette similar to that used for the bits in the *Liber Quodlibetarius*.

128 Hans Brolesse, *Hierin Begriffne Pis/ Zaygen Klaær=| |lich an/ Wie Ain Yedes Roß/ Jung vñ Alt Sol Gezämbt ...* (Regensburg: Hans Kohl, 1539); see also illustrations by Sebald Beham in Laurentius Rusius, *Hippiatria, sive, Marescalia Laurentii Rusii* (Basel: Chrestien Wechel, 1532), https://archive.org/details/bub_gb_EXEkRgSMHXwC/page/n11/mode/thumb.

129 For the relationship of rhetorical *copia* to images, see Remond, "Bodies of Knowledge," especially 54–6.

130 *Hier Inn Begriffne Pis, Zaigen Clärlich an, Wie Ain Yedess Roß, Iüng und Alt Soll Gezämbt, Dadurch Ime, Angenomene Pöse Gewonhait Ubelstandt, ... Benomen ... Werden Mag*, VD 16 G 592 ([Augsburg?], 1530). See the edition in the Herzog August Bibliothek in Wolfenbüttel, A108.14 Quod. 3, fol. 58r, for an example. I am grateful to Abigail Youngblood for discovering this and pointing out the stamping of the printed images' portion.

131 Popplow, "Why Draw Pictures of Machines?," 43.

132 Olariu, *The Misfortune of Philippus de Lignamine's Herbal*, 1–28. On the relationship between nature printing and naturalism, see Dominic Olariu, "Herbs under Pressure: Plant Illustrations and Nature Printing in the First Half of the Fifteenth Century," in Robert Felfe and Maurice Saß, *Naturalismen* (Berlin: De Gruyter, 2019), 9–31.

133 Ann Blair, "Humanist Methods in Natural Philosophy: The Commonplace Book," *Journal of the History of Ideas* 53, no. 4 (1992), 541–51; Ann Blair, *Too Much to Know: Managing Scholarly Information before the Modern Age* (New Haven, CT and London: Yale University Press, 2011); see also Ann Moss, "Locating Knowledge," in K. A. E. Enenkel and Wolfgang Neuber, eds., *Cognition and the Book: Typologies of Formal Organisation of Knowledge in the Printed Book of the Early Modern Period* (Leiden and Boston, MA: Brill, 2005).

134 Thomas DaCosta Kaufmann and Virginia Roehrig Kaufmann, "The Sanctification of Nature: Observations on the Origins of *Trompe l'Oeil* in Netherlandish Book Painting of the Fifteenth and Sixteenth Centuries" *J. Paul Getty Museum Journal* (1991), 43–64.

135 This page number is missing from the illustration.

136 UER, fol. 117v; "*Wie man vogl sol vahen vindest am 157 blat.*"

137 UER, fols. 131v–144r; JAG 453–7.

138 Eamon, *Science and the Secrets of Nature*, 113.

139 Karl Schottenloher, "Die druckprivilegien des 16. Jahrhunderts," *Gutenberg Jahrbuch* (1933), 89–110; David Landau and Peter W. Parshall, *The Renaissance Print, 1470–1550* (New Haven, CT: Yale University Press, 1994); see also H. Grotefend, *Christian Egenolff der erste ständige Buchdrucker zu Frankfurt a. M.* (Frankfurt: K. T. Völcker's Verlag, 1881), 26.

140 Translated into English as "art book," the *Kunstbuch* only later came to refer to books about art. Throughout the sixteenth century, the term is more commonly used for recipe and how-to books.

141 Heinrich Vogtherr, "Heinrich Vogtherr: Ein frembds und wunderbars Kunstbüchlin allen Molern/ Bildschnitzern/ Goldschmiden/ Steinmetzen/ Schreinern/ Platnern/ Waffen un Messerschmiden hochnutzlich zu gebrauchen (Straßburg 1538/1572) herausgegeben und

kommentiert von Maria Heilmann," ed. Maria Heilmann, *FONTES* 61 (2011); see also Jaya Remond, "The *Kunstbüchlein*: Printed Artists' Manuals and the Transmission of Craft in Renaissance Germany," PhD dissertation, Harvard University, 2014.

142 Heinrich Vogtherr, *Ein frembds und wunderbars Kunstbüchlein allen Malern, Bild/ schnitzern, Goldschmieden, Steinmetzen, Schreinern/ Platnern, Waffen und Messerschmiden hochnutzlich/ zu gebrauchen* ... (Strasbourg: H. Vogtherr, 1538). For a monograph on Vogtherr, see Frank Muller, *Heinrich Vogtherr l'ancien: un artiste entre Renaissance et Réforme*, Wolfenbütteler Forschungen vol. 72 (Wiesbaden: Harrassowitz, 1997), 296ff. For Vogtherr's activity as a printer, see also François Ritter, *Histoire de l'imprimerie alsacienne aux 15e et 16e siècles* (Strasbourg: Institut des Hautes Études Alsaciennes, 1955), 281–8.

143 Jutta Funke, "Beiträge zum graphischen Werk Heinrich Vogtherrs d.Ä.," PhD dissertation, Freie Universität, Berlin, 1967, 52ff.

144 Funke, "Beiträge zum graphischen Werk," 48.

145 In his preface, Vogtherr appealed to overworked and homebound artists "burdened with wife and child ... and also those unaccustomed to frequent travel."

146 See Ashley West, *Hans Burgkmair and the Visual Translation of Knowledge in the German Renaissance*, forthcoming. Thanks to Ashley for sharing a chapter of this unpublished material with me.

147 Some of these elements resemble Dürer's ornamental cornices in the *Dresden Sketchbook*.

148 Horst Bredekamp, Vera Dünkel, and Birgit Schneider, *Das Technische Bild: Kompendium zu einer Stilgeschichte wissenschaftlicher Bilder* (Berlin: Akademie Verlag, 2012), 27.

149 Hall, "*Der Meister sol auch kennen schreiben und lesen*," 53.

150 See, for example, Schön, *Unterweisung der Proportion und Stellung der Possen* (Nuremberg: 1542) at https://doi.org/10.1524/9783050062198.

151 *Abgestolen* is used, for example, in Dürer's explanation of how he proceeds to render in a painting a cube that he sees via an empirical process that involves mimicking sightlines with three threads. We can loosely translate this as "snatch, transfer, move to." In explaining this concept over the next few pages, Dürer announces his intention in diagram 62 by use of a free-floating eye that "sees" the cube and means to transfer it. See the *Underweysung der Messung*, diagram 62, at https://digital.slub-dresden.de/werkansicht/dlf/17139/178/0/. Erhard Schön's own *Unterweisung* uses this term to designate a method for transferring proportions of horses and mannequins: "*possen auch abgestolen auff einem plaster wie vor augenn ist*." The mannequins are also derived from measurements taken from a grid (rendered in perspective or foreshortened), "as you can see before your eyes." The editor of the facsimile of Schön's *Unterweisung*, Leo Baer, renders *abstehlen* as foreshorten. See https://digi.ub.uni-heidelberg.de/diglit/schoen1920/0013.

Many thanks to Thomas Schauerte and Tilly Laaser for their willingness to help in deciphering some of these specialized terms. A translation of Dürer's *Underweysung* was edited by Walter Strauss: Albrecht Dürer and Walter L. Strauss, *The Painter's Manual: A Manual of Measurement of Lines, Areas, and Solids by Means of Compass and Ruler Assembled by Albrecht Dürer for the Use of All Lovers of Art with Appropriate Illustrations Arranged to be Printed in the Year MDXXV* (New York: Abaris Books, 1977).

152 Walter L. Strauss, *The Human Figure by Albrecht Dürer: The Complete "Dresden Sketchbook"* (New York: Dover Publications, 1972), see fols. 101v and 141r, at pp. 232, 208–9.

153 Erhard Schön, *Underweisung der Proportion und Stellung der Possen* (Nuremberg: Zell, 1524 (?), 1538, 1543); Erhard Schön, Leo Baer, and Christoph Zell, *Unterweisung der Proportion und Stellung der Possen, Nürnberg 1542* (Frankfurt: J. Baer & Co., 1920); Jean Pelerin, *Von der Kunst Perspectiva* (Nuremberg: Georg Glockendon, 1509).

154 Walter Strauss translates *abstehlen* variously as "perspective" (cf. p. 427) or the idea of transferring a design from a viewed object (as in p. 371); see Dürer and Strauss, *The Painter's Manual*.

155 On the mediality of the face, see Jeanette Kohl and Dominic Olariu, "En face: seven essays on the human face," in *Kritische Berichte: Zeitschrift für Kunst- und Kulturwissenschaften* 40 (Marburg: Jonas Verlag, 2012).

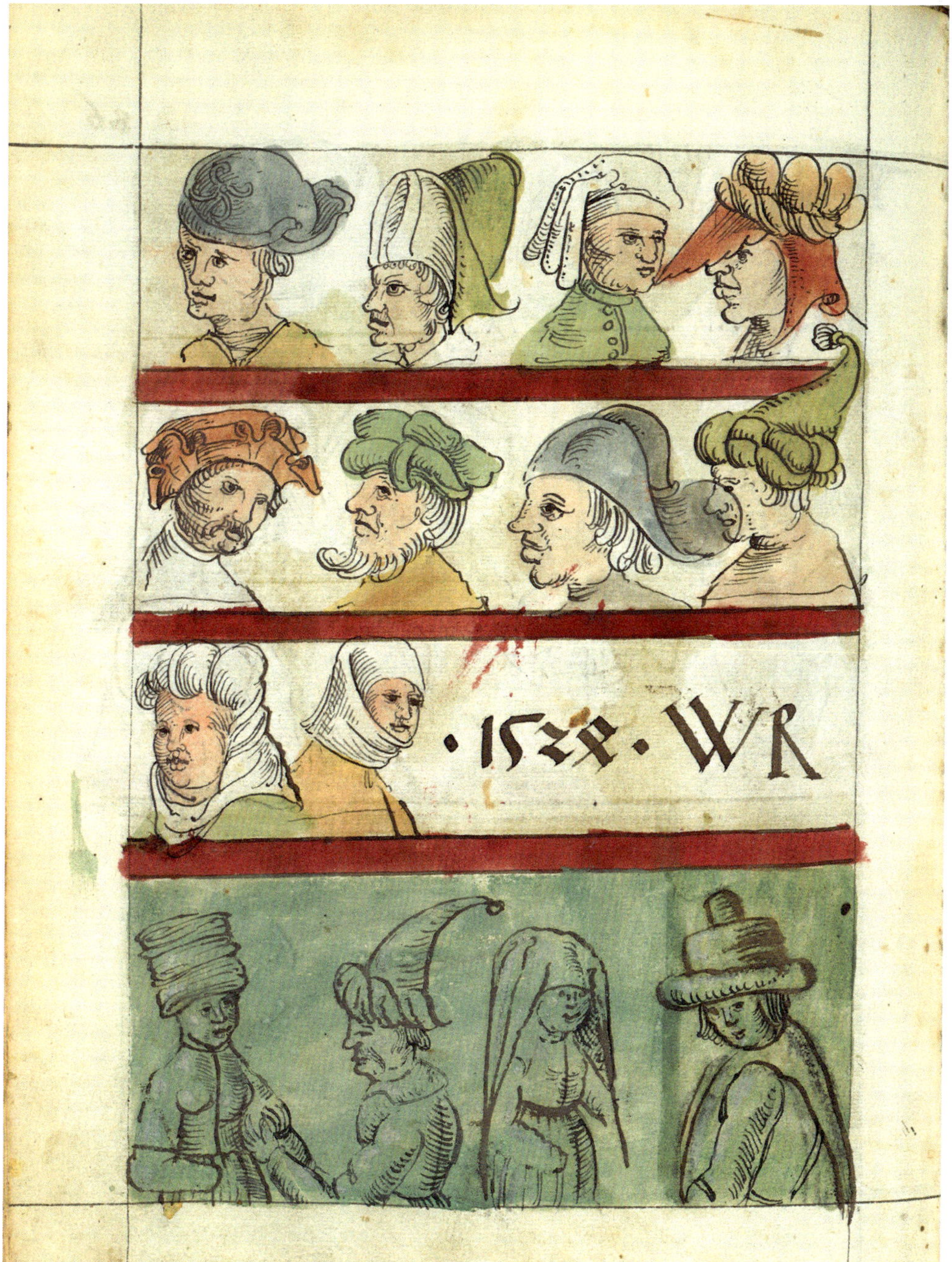

PLATE 1. Master WR, Benedictus Rughalm, *Liber Quodlibetarius*, fol. 86v. *Source:* MS.B 200. Courtesy of Universitätsbibliothek Erlangen-Nürnberg.

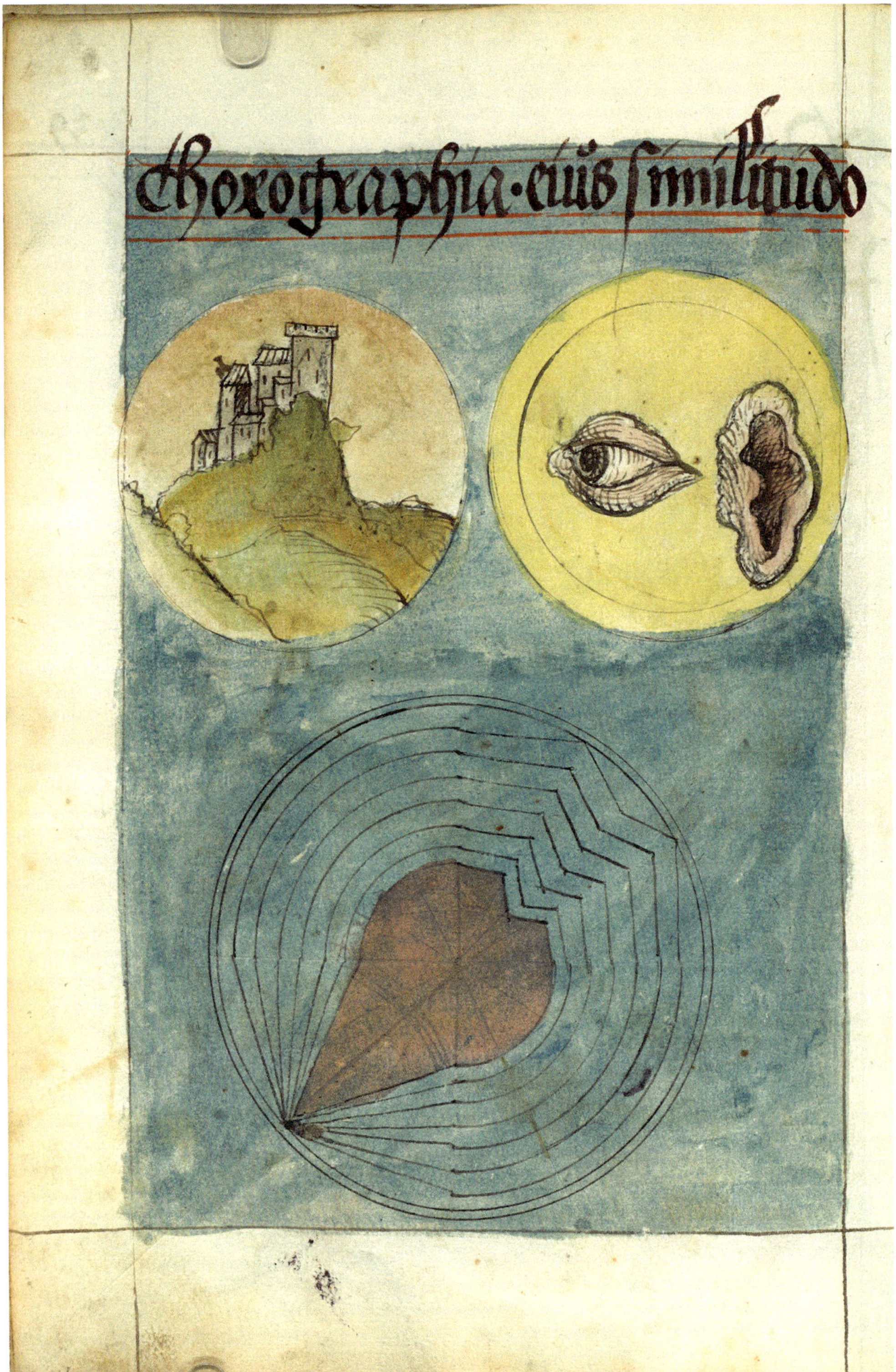

PLATE 11. Master WR, Benedictus Rughalm, *Liber Quodlibetarius*, fol. 29v. *Source:* MS.B 200. Courtesy of Universitätsbibliothek Erlangen-Nürnberg.

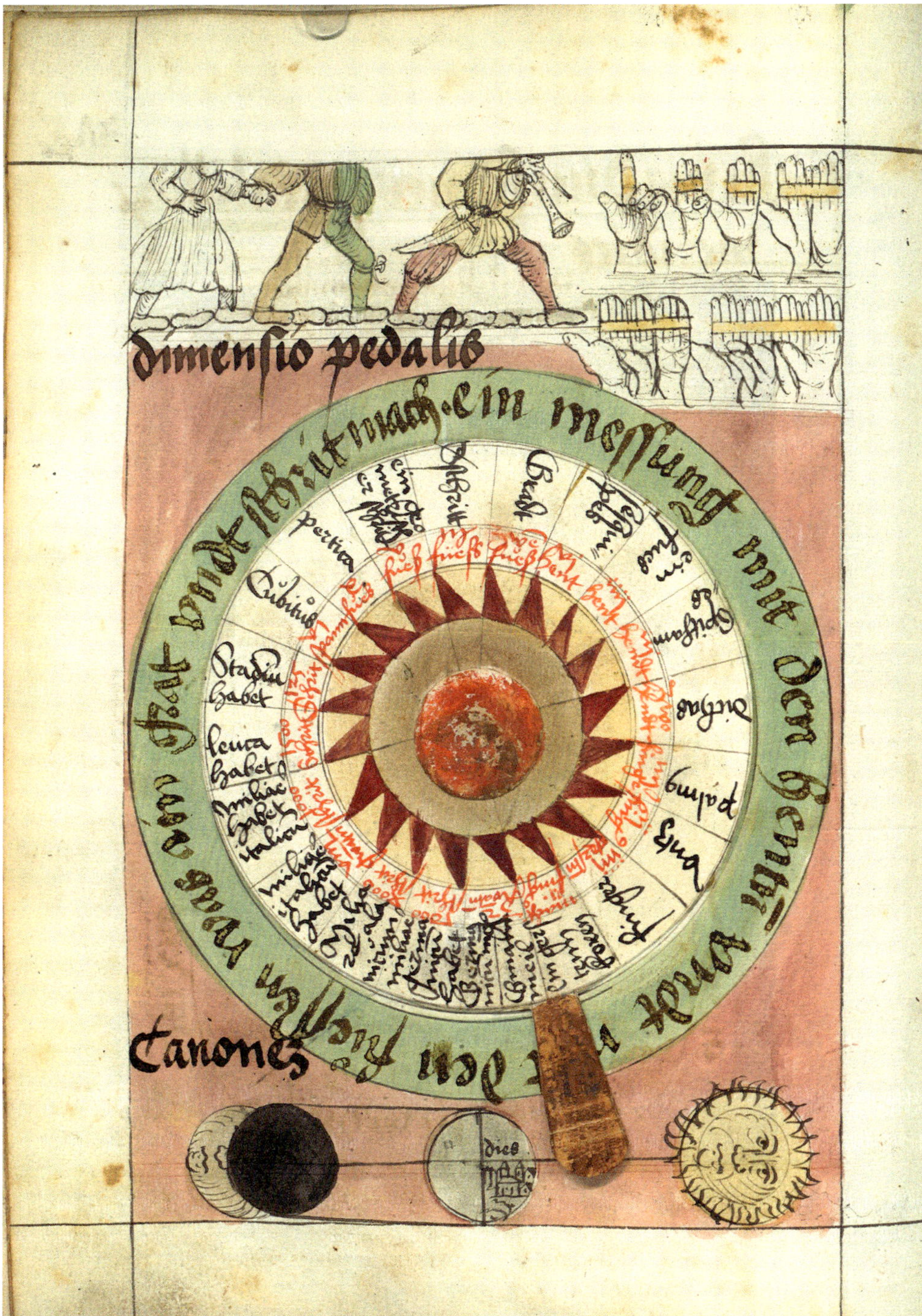

PLATE III. Master WR, Benedictus Rughalm, *Liber Quodlibetarius*, fol. 27v. *Source:* MS.B 200. Courtesy of Universitätsbibliothek Erlangen-Nürnberg.

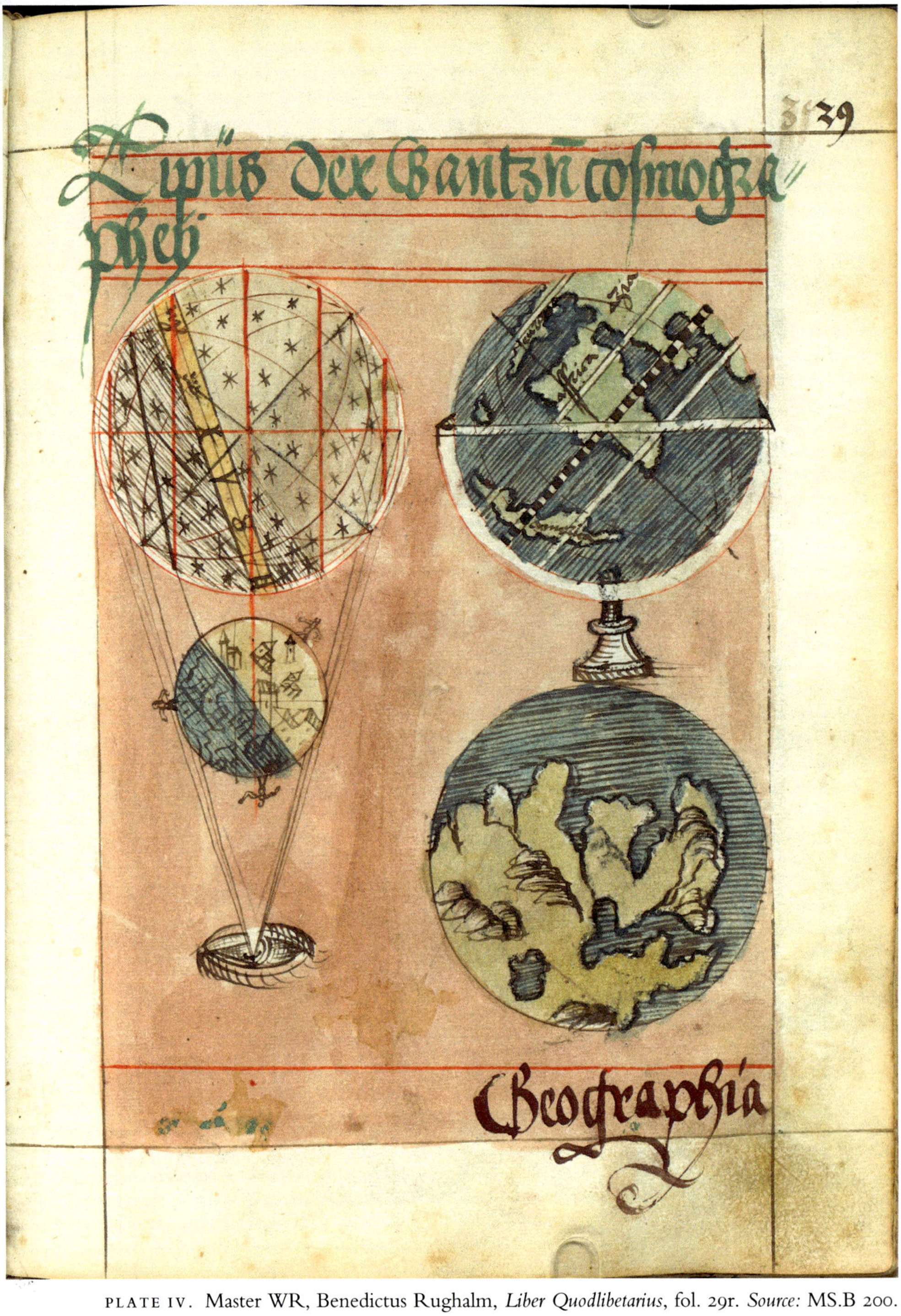

PLATE IV. Master WR, Benedictus Rughalm, *Liber Quodlibetarius*, fol. 29r. *Source:* MS.B 200. Courtesy of Universitätsbibliothek Erlangen-Nürnberg.

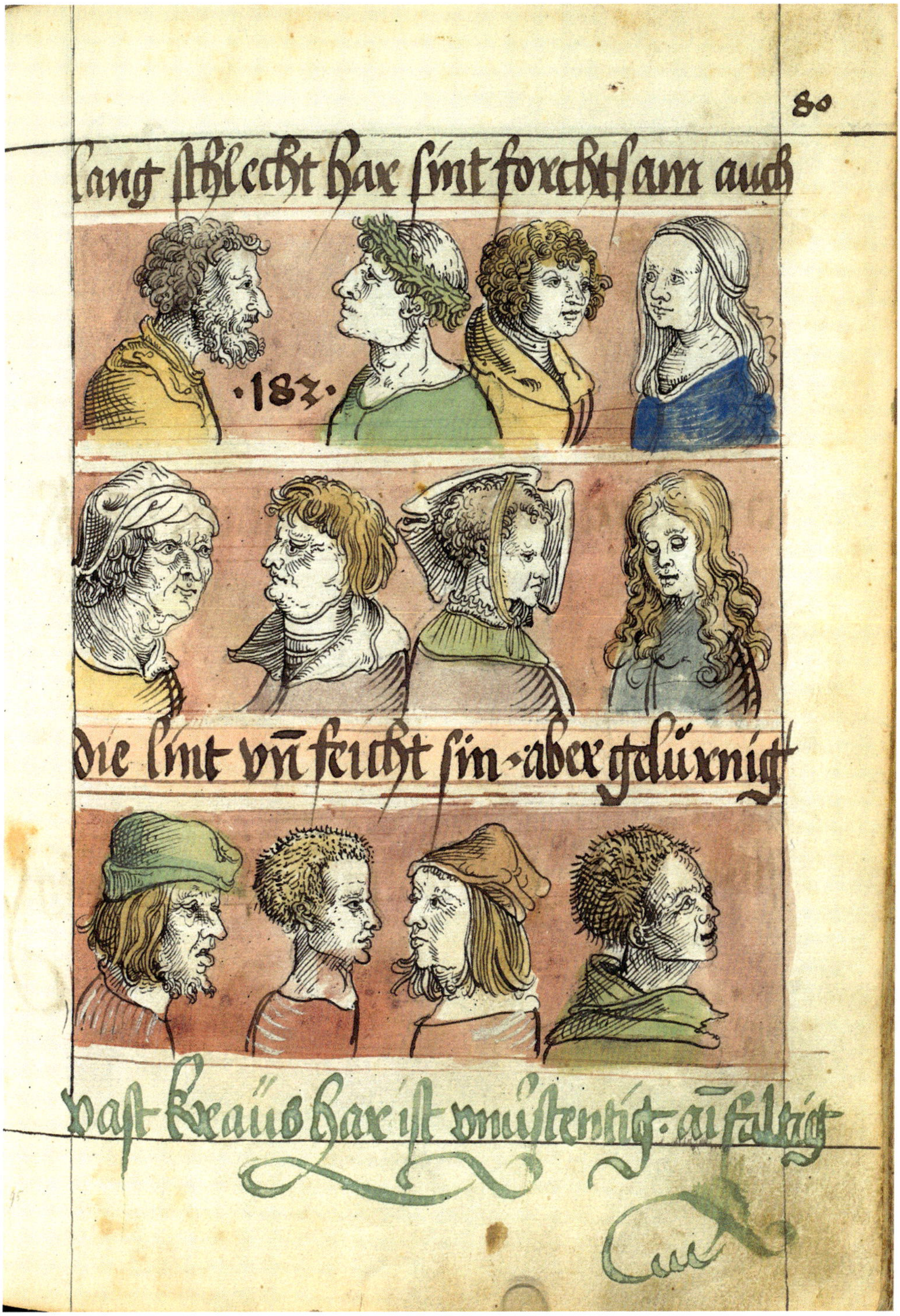

PLATE V. Master WR, Benedictus Rughalm, *Liber Quodlibetarius*, fol. 80r. *Source:* MS.B 200. Courtesy of Universitätsbibliothek Erlangen-Nürnberg.

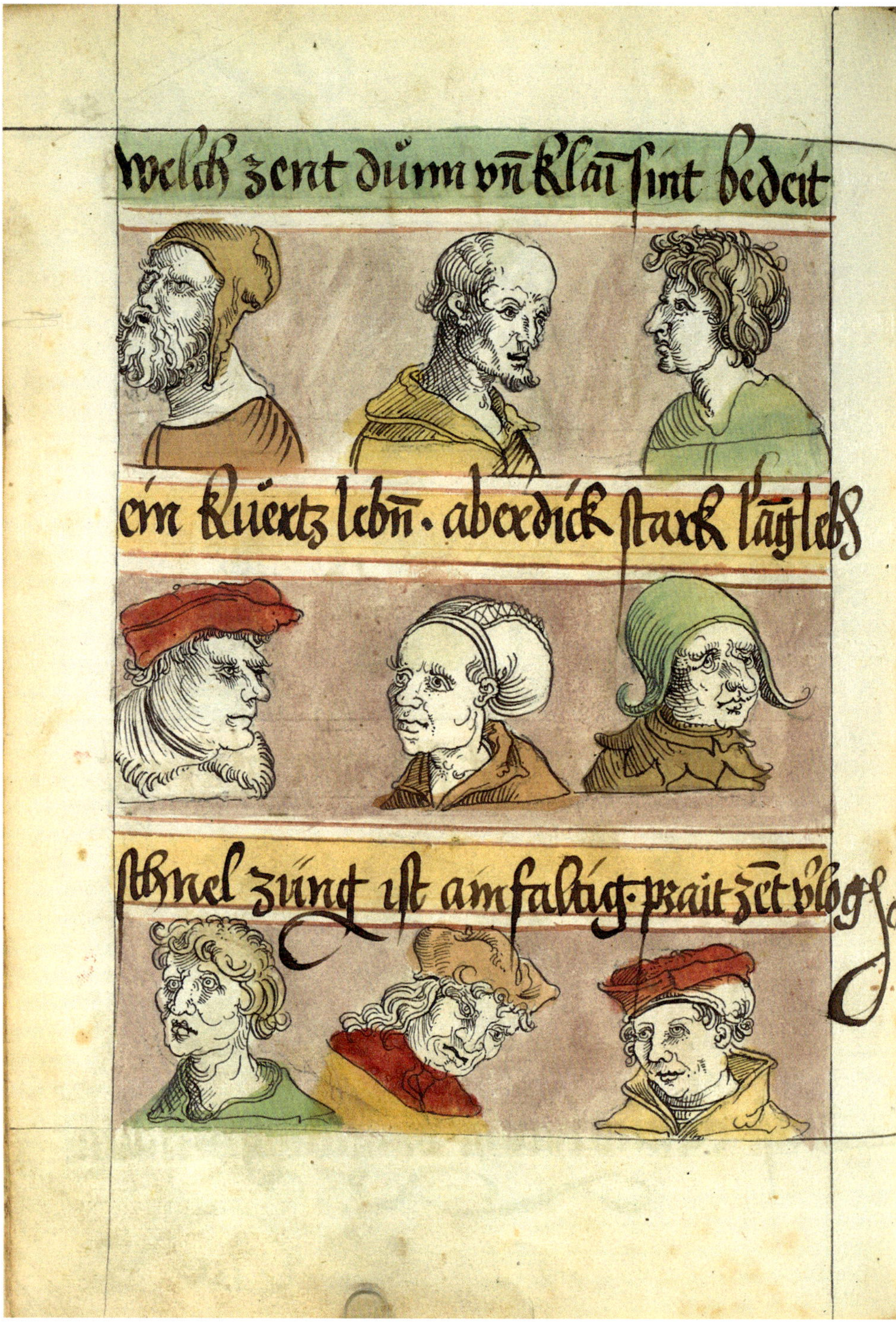

PLATE VI. Master WR, Benedictus Rughalm, *Liber Quodlibetarius*, fol. 80v. *Source:* MS.B 200. Courtesy of Universitätsbibliothek Erlangen-Nürnberg.

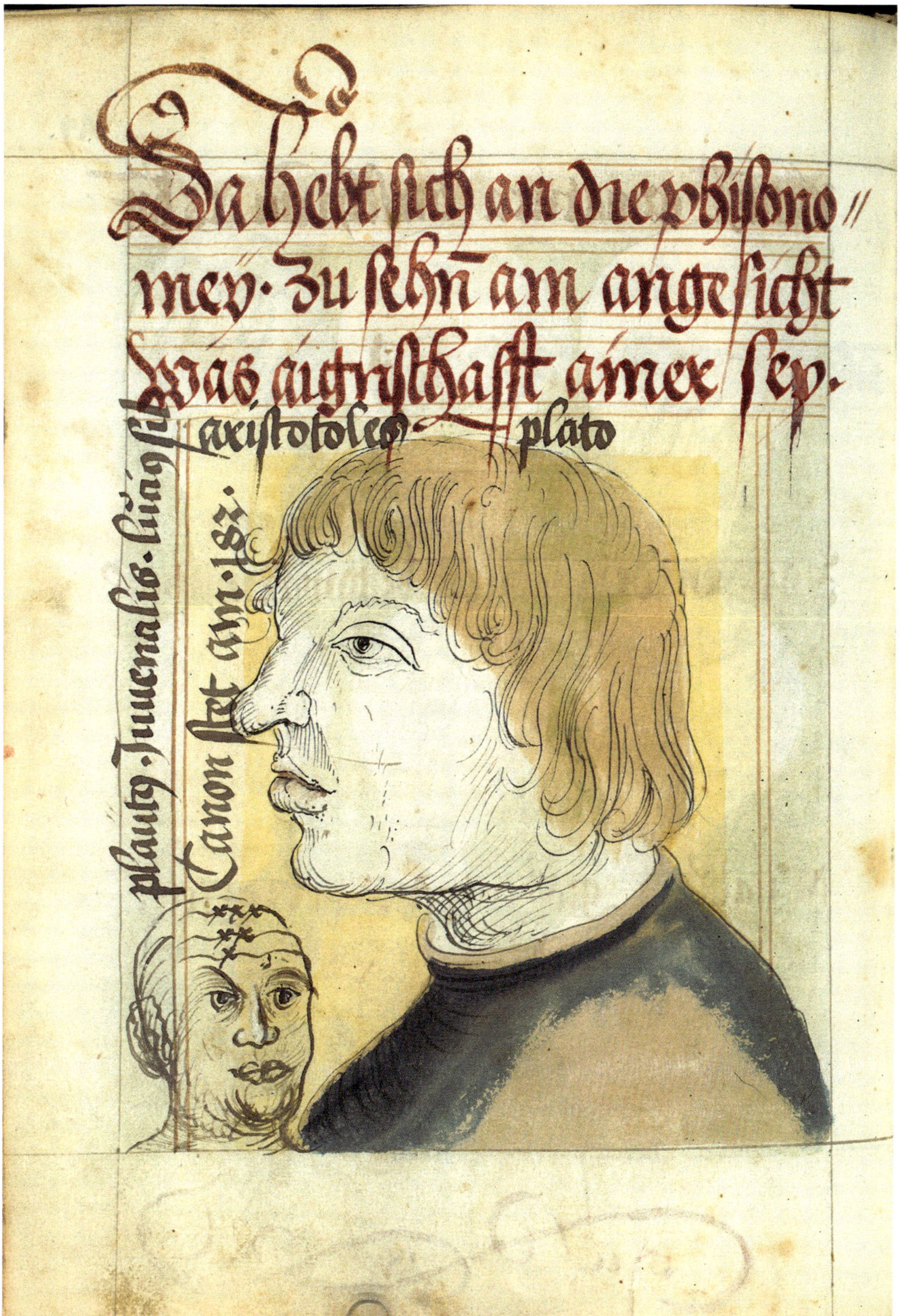

PLATE VII. Master WR, Benedictus Rughalm, *Liber Quodlibetarius*, fol. 79v. *Source:* MS.B 200. Courtesy of Universitätsbibliothek Erlangen-Nürnberg.

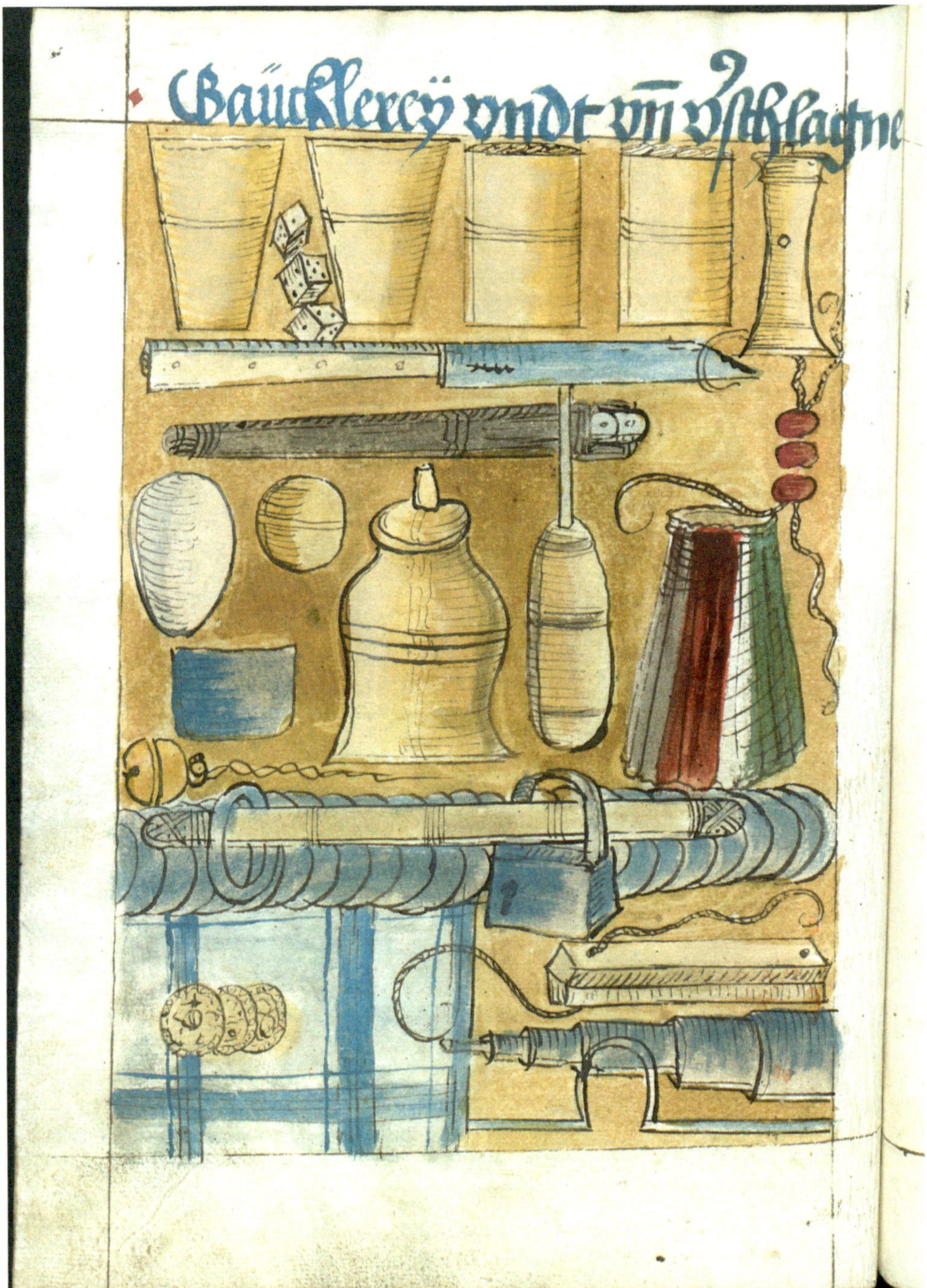

PLATE VIII. Manuscript Rkp. Przyb. 35/64. Jagiellonian Library, Cracow, fol. 55v. *Source:* Courtesy of Jagiellonian Library. Work in the public domain.

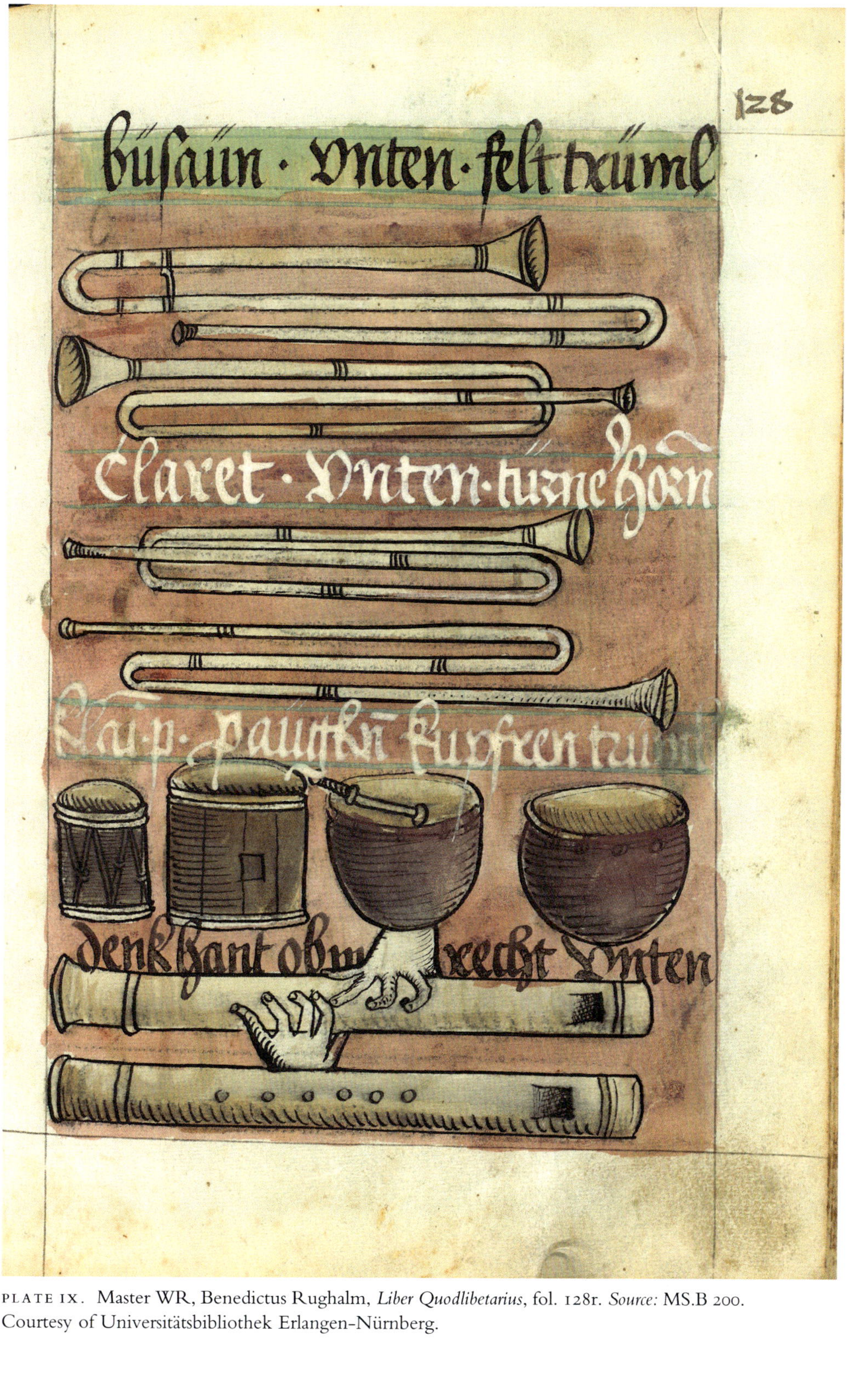

PLATE IX. Master WR, Benedictus Rughalm, *Liber Quodlibetarius*, fol. 128r. *Source:* MS.B 200. Courtesy of Universitätsbibliothek Erlangen-Nürnberg.

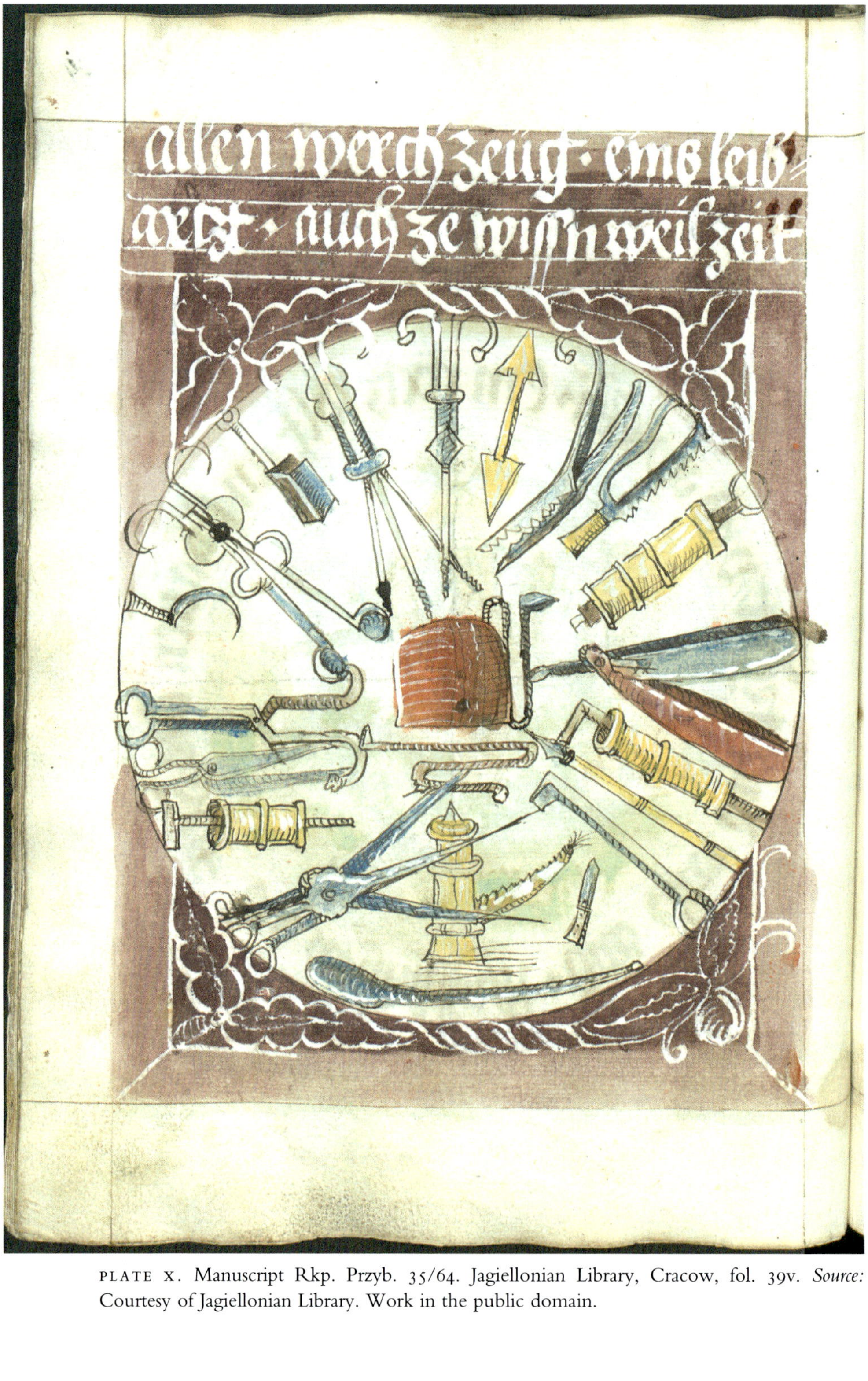

PLATE X. Manuscript Rkp. Przyb. 35/64. Jagiellonian Library, Cracow, fol. 39v. *Source:* Courtesy of Jagiellonian Library. Work in the public domain.

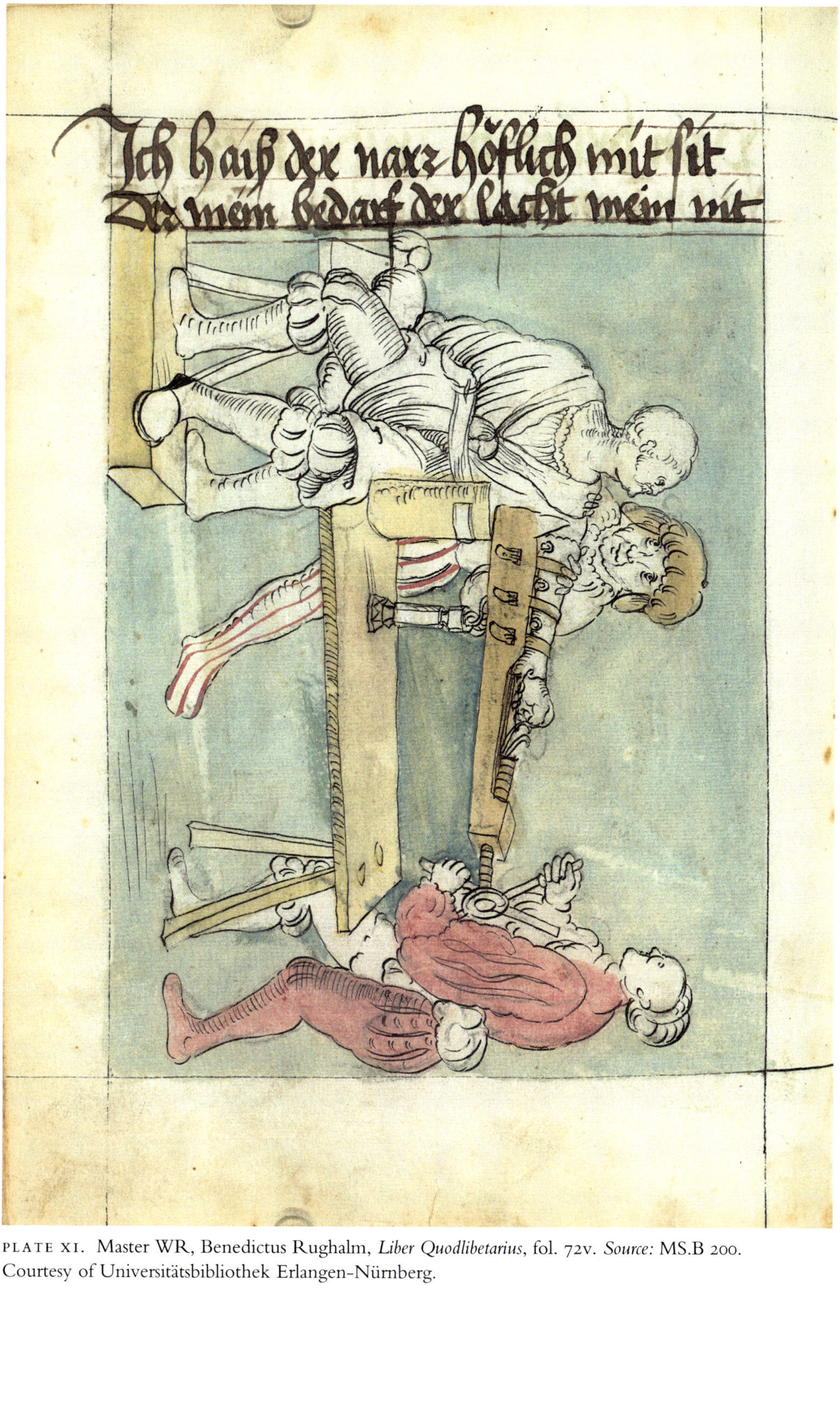

PLATE XI. Master WR, Benedictus Rughalm, *Liber Quodlibetarius*, fol. 72v. *Source:* MS.B 200. Courtesy of Universitätsbibliothek Erlangen-Nürnberg.

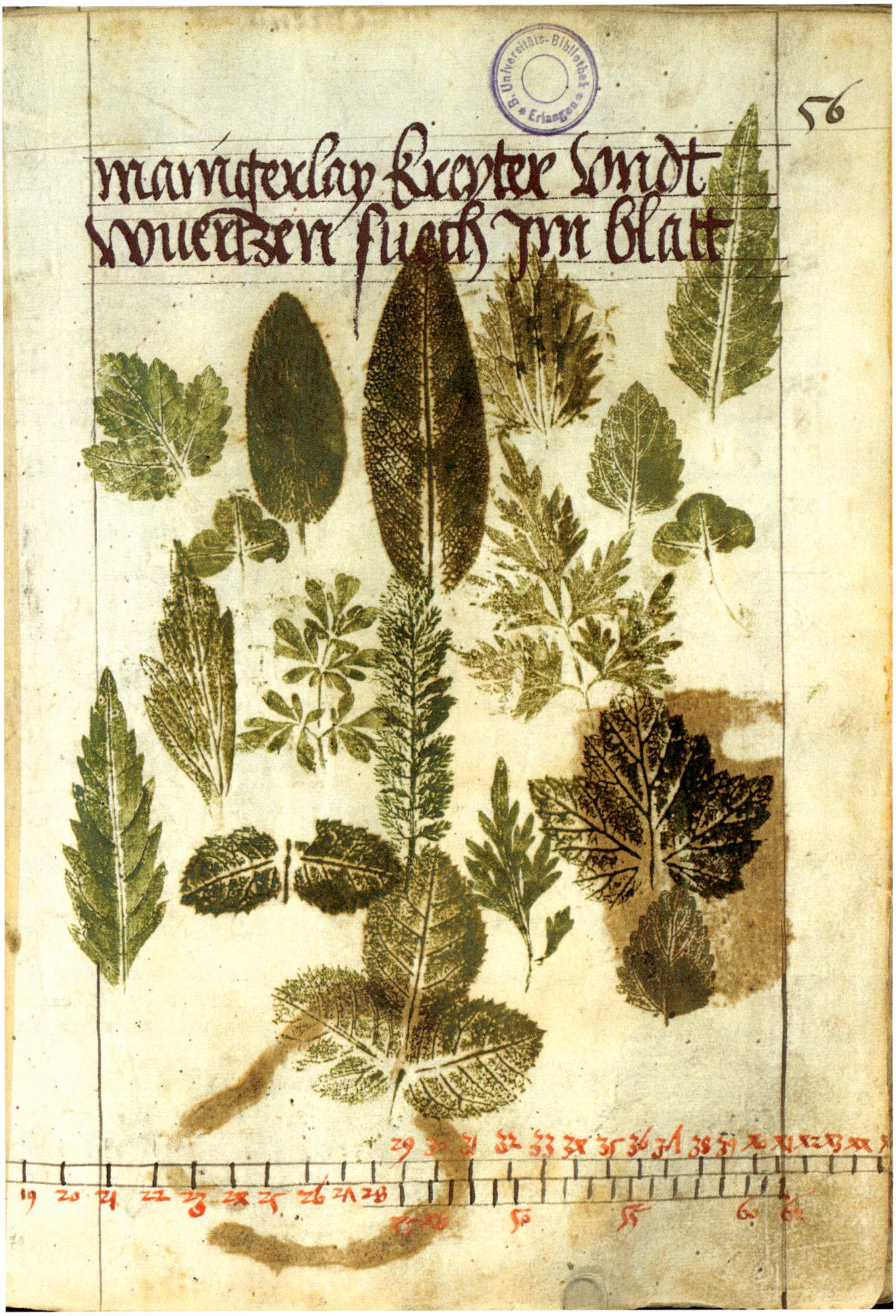

PLATE XII. Master WR, Benedictus Rughalm, *Liber Quodlibetarius*, fol. 56r. *Source:* MS.B 200. Courtesy of Universitätsbibliothek Erlangen-Nürnberg.

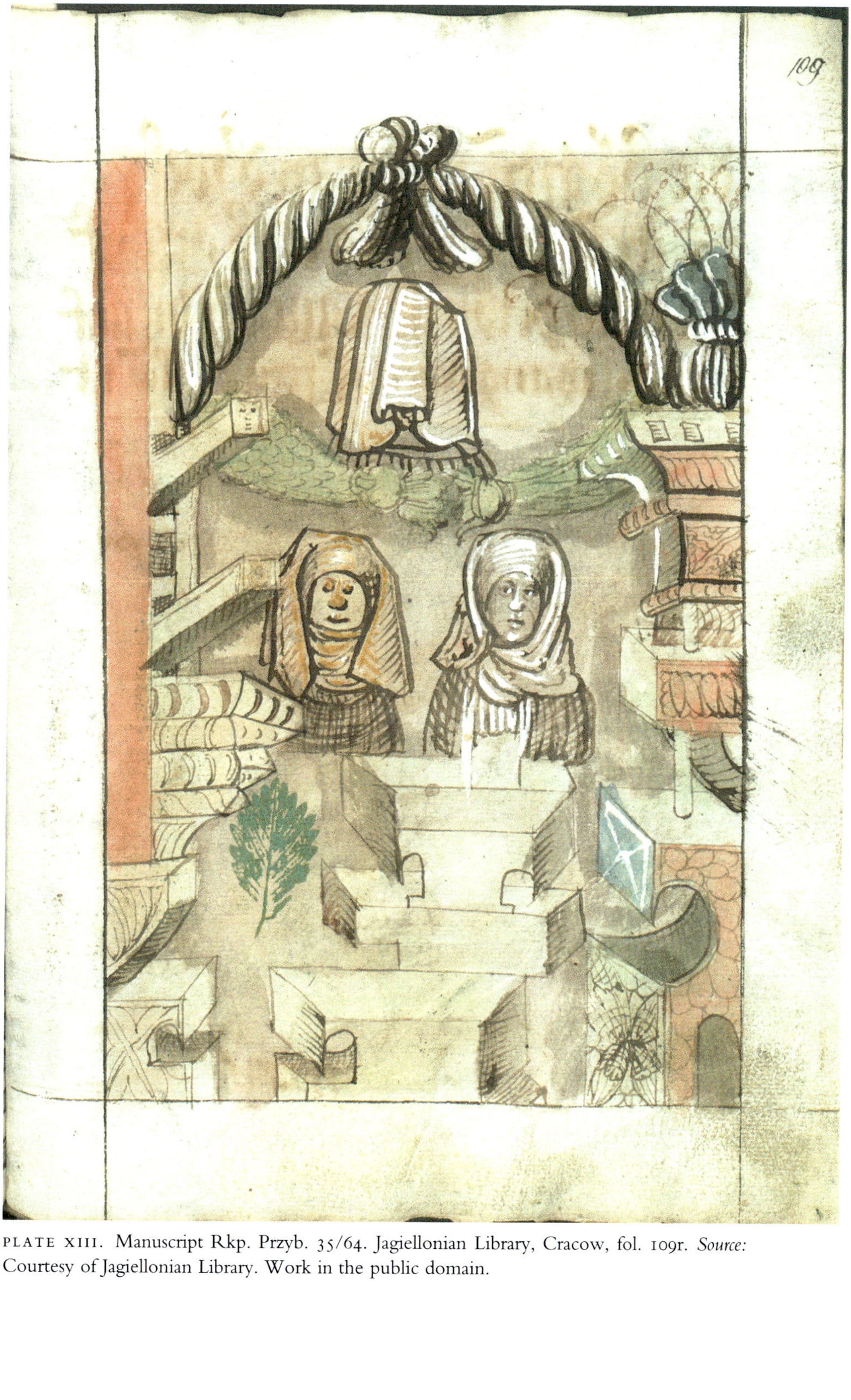

PLATE XIII. Manuscript Rkp. Przyb. 35/64. Jagiellonian Library, Cracow, fol. 109r. *Source:* Courtesy of Jagiellonian Library. Work in the public domain.

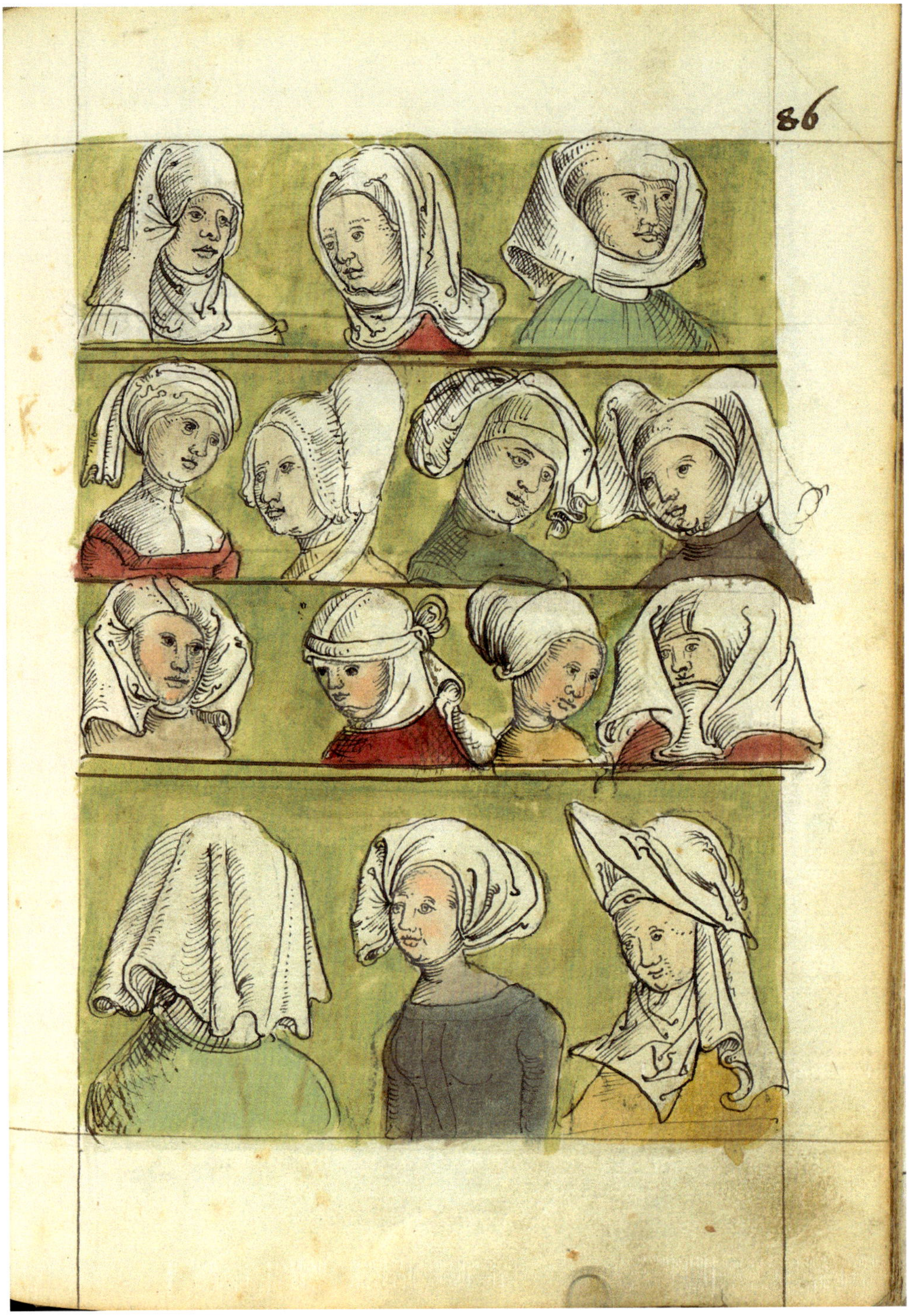

PLATE XIV. Master WR, Benedictus Rughalm, *Liber Quodlibetarius*, fol. 86r. *Source:* MS.B 200. Courtesy of Universitätsbibliothek Erlangen-Nürnberg.

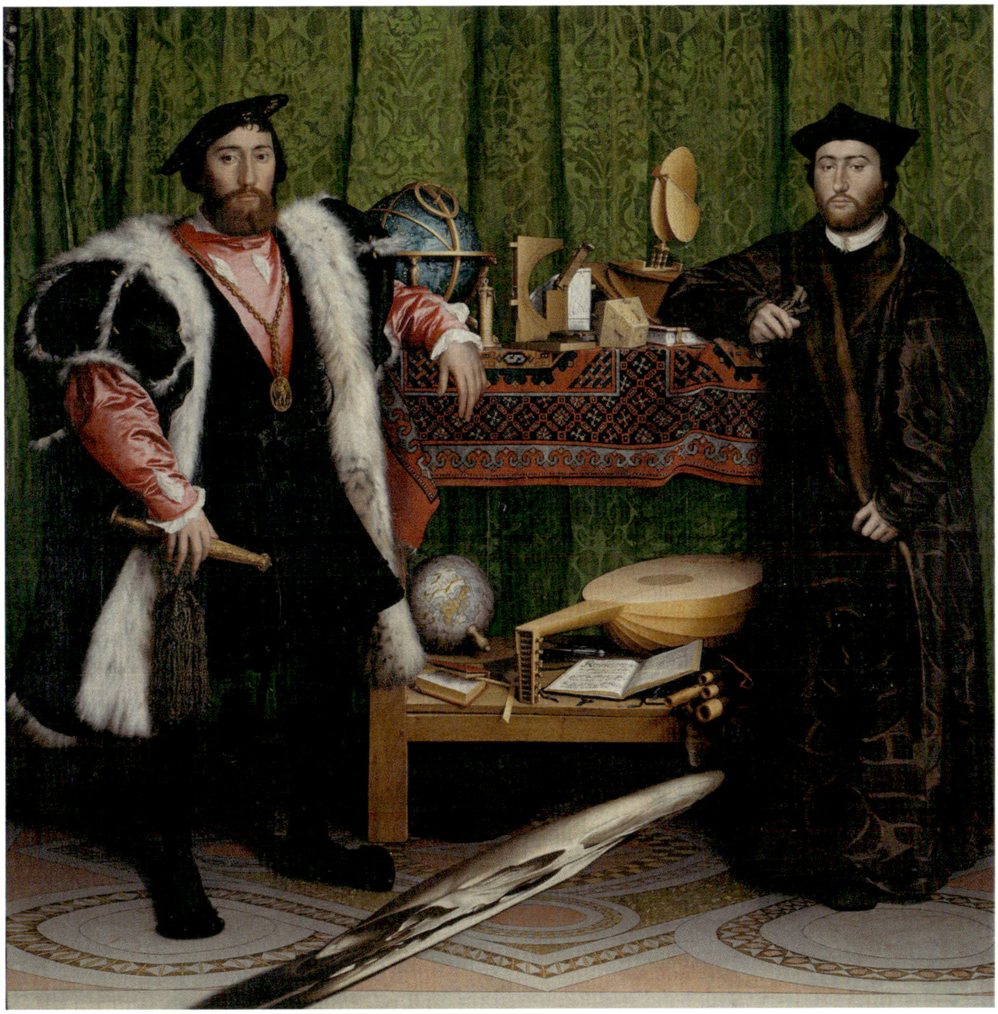

PLATE XV. Holbein the Younger, *The Ambassadors*, 1533, oil on oak, 207 cm × 209.5 cm. *Source:* Courtesy of National Gallery, London.

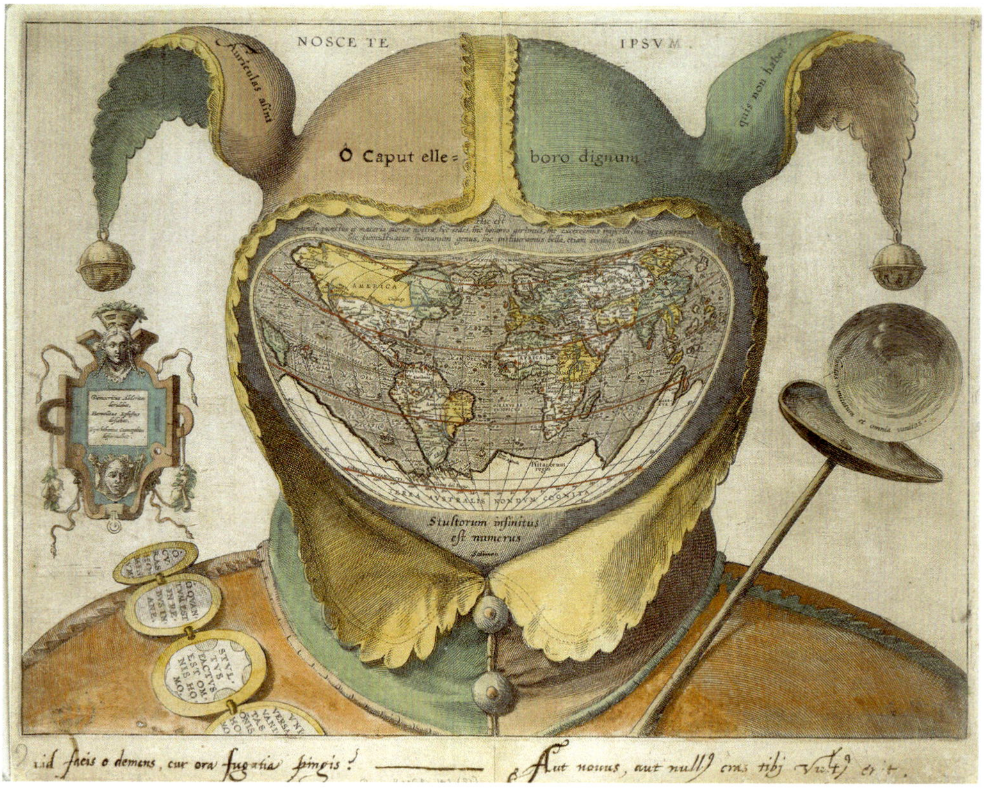

PLATE XVI. Anonymous Antwerp artist, *Fool's Cap Map of the World*, 1580–90, hand-colored engraving on off-white paper, 49.7 cm × 38.8 cm. *Source:* Courtesy of Ashmolean Museum, University of Oxford/Bridgeman Images.

FIVE

VEXED VIEWING

Anamorphosis and the Visual Argumentation of Labored Looking

Was Siehst Du? (Figure 5.1), a curiously shaped woodcut from 1538, issues a viewing advisory: "What do you see?" This is the same question that publishers of cosmographies and physiognomies had already been putting to vernacular audiences for some time. A spate of such how-to publications in the preceding decade had made strong pitches for sustained and critical looking. The printmaker Erhard Schön assumed that such visually astute audiences were ready for new tricks in the shape of printed puzzle pictures. Anamorphic, or deformed, images like these were not in focus head-on and required both a positioned point of view and a special kind of cognition. Only when viewers approached the print askew did the true subject come into view. The innocent question "What do you see?" seemed less innocuous when that close scrutiny revealed a pile of excrement. Schön satirizes close looking and the possible perils associated with it. This type of scrutiny afforded novel prospects and perceptions that brought along with them new perspectives about the subject matter and the ends of observation itself.

Could prints interrogating the fixity of traditional perspectives have emerged from the new observational skills associated with cosmography and physiognomy? We know that the viewer's visual skills were sharpened by prints associated with those genres. The evolution of faces from physiognomic ciphers into anamorphic projections – a visual technique of distortion by which some of these images, known as *Vexierbilder*, were made – suggests a preoccupation with related subject matter and skill sets. This chapter inspects why skills developing

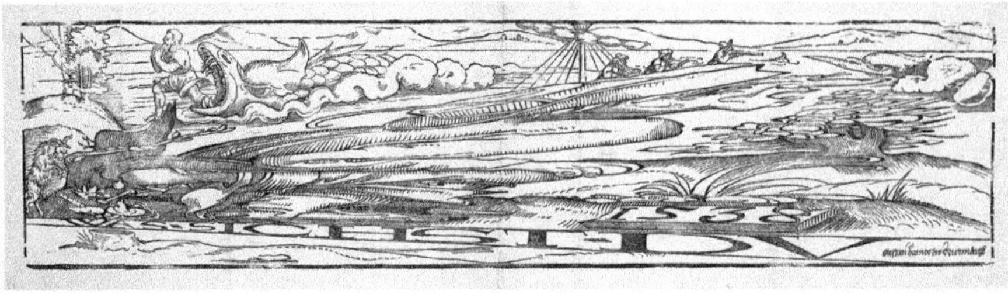

5.1. Erhard Schön, *Was Siehst Du(?)*, 1538, woodcut, 21.2 cm × 85.1 cm. *Source:* © The Trustees of the British Museum.

from these genres were now marshaled to push visual acuity to new limits. Trick images developed alongside anamorphosis and challenged the visual premises cultivated by these genres, demanding the viewer's visual attention and then sending ominous messages through the medium. This chapter inspects the value of embedding contradictions into pictures and queries why this ambivalence seemed especially suited to the subject matter tracked by this book, physiognomy and cosmography. How did the anamorphic image challenge the eye as a sensory conduit for knowledge?

New subjects emerged at the intersection of textual and visual literacy. The relative affordability of woodcuts made them accessible to swaths of the population as perhaps no other artistic medium had been before. Handheld objects such as prints literally collapsed the spatial distance between viewer and object.[1] As a result, new themes evolved that groomed audiences for subjectivity, as printmakers took on more intimate topics.[2] Jürgen Müller and Bertram Kasheck have argued for a new liberation and self-reflexivity of pictures in the age of print. Novel responses were required to printed provocations that were pornographic, satirical, or irritating pictures that vexed both the eye and the emotions. New modes of picturing in the form of puzzle pictures, per Jennifer Nelson, ushered in social critique as a result of relativistic thinking about the stability of social structures.[3] Unconventional perspectives on class and gender status were also topics tossed into debate by print media. Such content suitably accompanied the flux in visual positions that the potential for social fluidity brought.

Observational tools that developed during the sixteenth century commanded vernacular viewers to attention, and indeed hailed them as self-conscious observers. Abandoning strategies used to capture the unblinking stare of the medieval worshipper, prints now incentivized sharp seeing and encouraged a critical and judgmental eye. Genres including physiognomy and cosmography with a venerable tradition in manuscripts since late antiquity were retooled in the printshop by printers who simplified their visual formats to prepare viewers for new interactive experience with the world. Printed trick images, or *Vexierbilder*, developed alongside these genres and shared some of

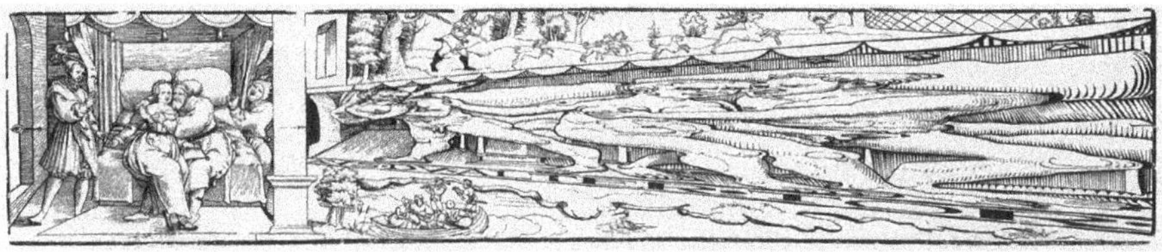

5.2. Erhard Schön, *Aus du alter Tor*, 1530s, woodcut, 15.6 cm × 17.5 cm. Modern imprint. *Source:* Inv. Derschau 297. Bpk Bildagentur/Kupferstichkabinett/Staatliche Museen Berlin. Photograph: Volker-H. Schneider/Art Resource, NY.

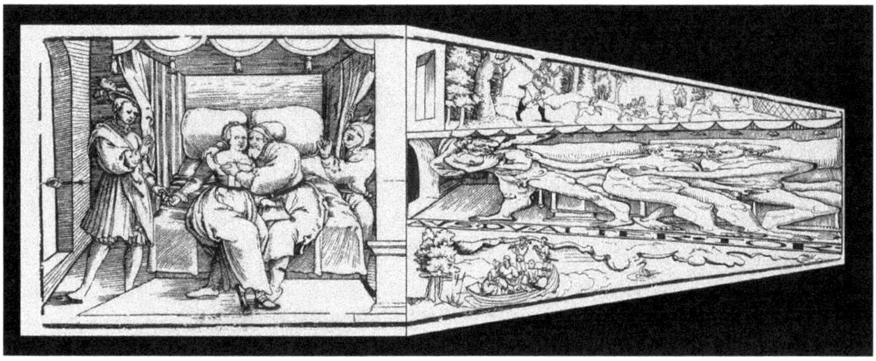

5.3. Erhard Schön, *Aus du alter Tor*, 1530s, woodcut, 15.6 cm × 17.5 cm. *Source:* Chase A. Van Tilburg.

their concerns about viewing practices. Another anamorphic image by Erhard Schön extends new agency to the viewer first by calling him out, and then by admonishing him with a virtual slap down (Figure 5.2). Head-on, we see an image of a young woman permitting an older man to grab her breasts as she passes his purse to another suitor closer to her own age. The gateway to the viewer's access to the true image is the fool who parts the curtain.

But the subjects invoked in the image's admonitory address are the viewers themselves. Rearranging oneself at an oblique angle to the image, aligning one's eye with the pictured one, the viewer now encounters the young lovers groping each other, naked, while the old man is cast out (Figure 5.3). *Aus du alter Tor*, an inscription in distorted letters, reads "Get out, you old fool." The addressee of the inscription could refer to three potential agents: the pictured fool, the old man, and perhaps most importantly, the alarmed viewer. After being invited into the composition via the free-floating eye at the far left, innocent viewers now find themselves the butt of the joke.[4]

This chapter argues that such visual tricks appear as the outgrowth of empirical practices taught by prints. These early anamorphic prints winked at the viewer as they revealed hidden truths.[5] Pictorial discourses on the act of vision, they thematize and in some cases literally construct the act of viewing. Given the claims of observational authority of prints of this period, it is not surprising that they also became the locus of optical tricks that questioned that same authority. This view was both prescriptive and proscriptive; pictured agents showed viewers how to see, and some even tried to reprimand them through their own visual perception.

This chapter considers images that placed the practice of sustained viewing in the crosshairs; they add to the repertoire of visual practices such as scanning for visual knowledge, in addition to *Anblick* and *Augenschein* prompted by the images of earlier chapters (see Chapters 3 and 4). Anamorphic images often directed the viewer to shift registers in order to see the image, requiring multiple points of view and some degree of patience. Observations prompted by these images were transactional and suspended the resolution of the ostensible subject matter. Observation itself became a rhetorical position, tricky, and frequently left viewers scratching their heads. Some of the images were uncomfortable and itchy.

Anamorphic or "deformed" images commented on strategies of viewing by deconstructing representation. Once the province of artists' studio experimentation and humanist curiosity, anamorphic art that became popular in print reflects concerns particular to the medium's own exigencies, especially those developed in the circulating how-to literature. Illustrated publications that emerged from Reformation-era presses presented lay audiences with new information. These texts, such as physiognomy and cosmography, updated old knowledge in vernacular tongues and new visual languages. Via these illustrations, prints and printed books coached the lay viewer to engage with the world firsthand. With origins in older traditions of geography and *Books of Secrets* respectively, sixteenth-century cosmographies and physiognomies began to take the shape of tight and profusely illustrated vernacular editions that advertised themselves as sharpening the eye of the literate layperson. Both of these genres of cosmography and physiognomy newly coalesced around the precepts of close observations and the practical applications of tight inspections.

Among subjects for printed *Vexierbilder* are portraits that capitalized on visual skills generated by physiognomic texts during the first few decades of the sixteenth century. These accompanied the rise of facial literacy as an optical skill, something we see in the proliferation of contemporary printed portraits. The profile portrait received an infusion at the meeting of the imperial diet in Augsburg in 1518, called to decide the candidacy of Emperor Maximilian's successor. This was an auspicious venue for portraitists who produced likenesses of the assembled civil servants, humanists, and artists.[6] Artists including Albrecht Dürer used the occasion to produce likenesses of the attendees in medallions and prints. The portraits generated during this inaugural event of self-publishing constituted a major public relations initiative and established a formative moment in the development of individual identities in German Renaissance circles. Jeffrey Chipps Smith has argued for the importance of these likenesses in establishing a new benchmark for one-to-one

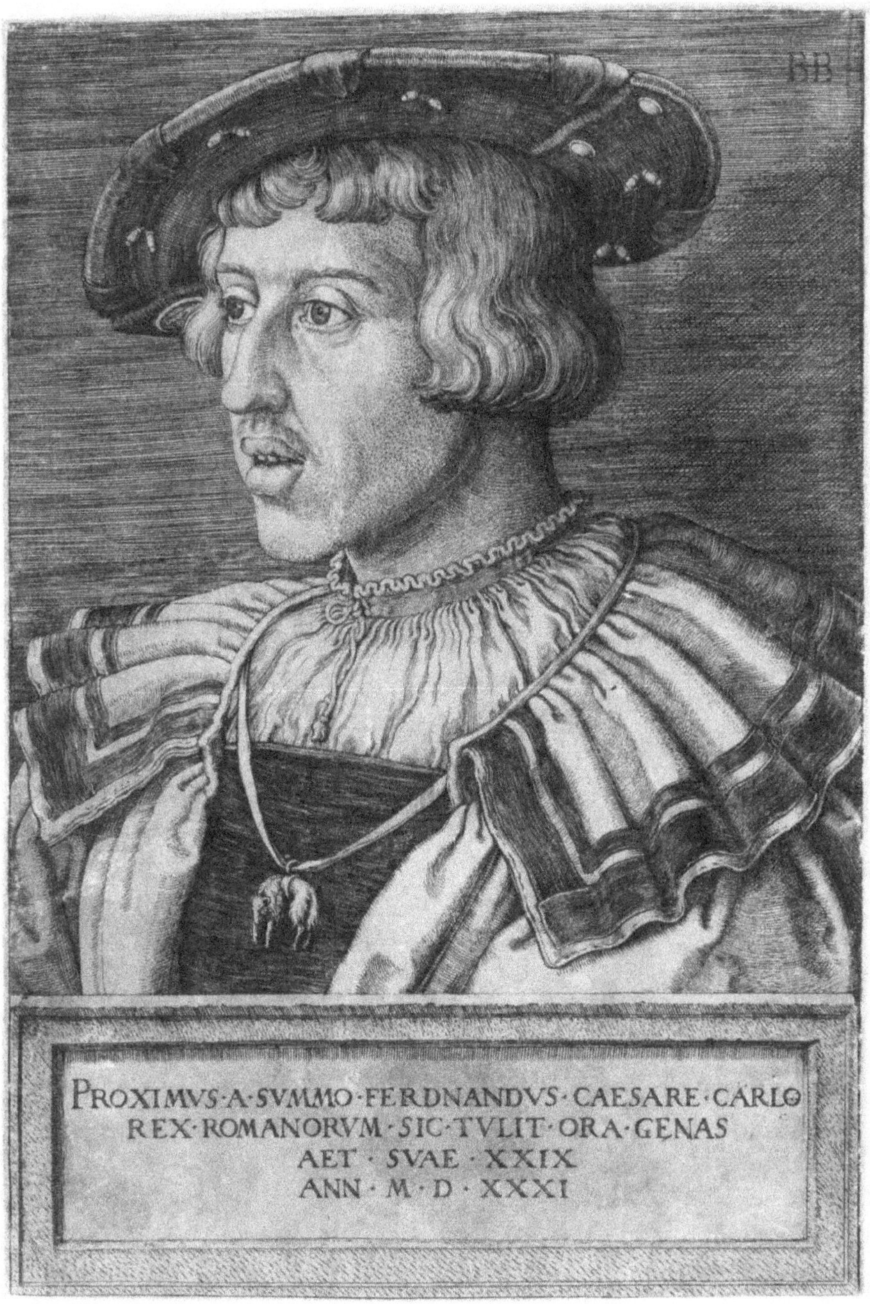

5.4. Barthel Beham, *Emperor Ferdinand I*, c. 1531, engraving, 19.5 cm × 13.5 cm. *Source:* Metropolitan Museum of Art. Image in the public domain.

correspondences between images and their sitters, as well as in shaping the contours of positive identification.[7]

The familiarity of such visages from their proliferation in print, such as the likeness of Ferdinand I engraved by Barthel Beham (Figure 5.4), made portraits

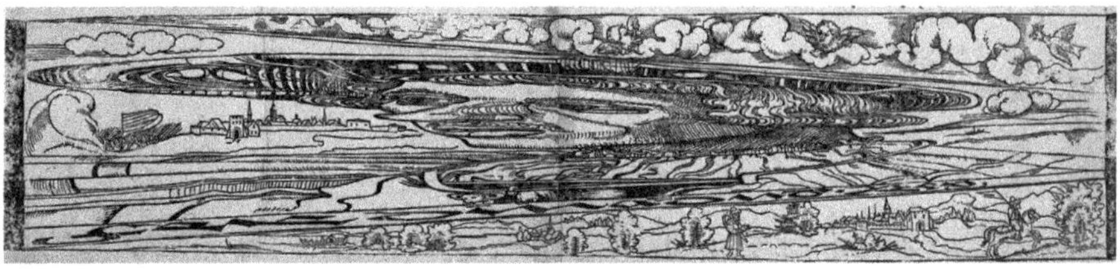

5.5. Erhard Schön (after Beham), *Ferdinand I*, anamorphic woodcut. *Source:* © The Trustees of the British Museum.

good baselines for distortions.[8] Erhard Schön's anamorphic woodcut shows Ferdinand I's face as a series of abstract lines that only resolve after the image has been turned at an acute angle and viewed from the side (Figure 5.5). Familiar faces became the site of calibrated deconstructions that require the viewer's interaction and intense visual scrutiny. The profile was also popularized in medallion production, whose format was taken over by prints and small limestone reliefs between 1520 and 1530 when medals proliferated in Augsburg and Nuremberg, after models created by Hans Schwarz and Matthes Gebel.[9]

Especially popular were the likenesses of regents, such as the Hapsburg siblings Charles V and Ferdinand I, whose faces also circulated widely in medallion form.[10] In curiosity cabinets, such medallions sized for portability mingled with prints of the same likenesses, as well as other types of natural and visual jokes.[11] Dynastic likenesses formed a visual collection whose repertoire was reinforced by frequent citations. Among the gaming pieces preserved today in the Kunsthistorisches Museum in Vienna and the Kunstmuseum in Stuttgart are boxwood and walnut roundels that feature portraits of the Hapsburgs.[12] Another type of gaming skill, perhaps developed in dialogue with such decorative and applied arts, was to be found in *Vexierbilder*, such as Erhard Schön's *Anamorphic Woodcut with Four Heads* (Figure 5.6). In this woodcut, Schön has stacked four skewed portraits of contemporary political figureheads: Charles V, Ferdinand I, Pope Paul III, and Francis I.[13] The circulation of such visages in print, medal, and wood helped to popularize these likenesses. The size and proliferation of these objects made them portable and accessible. As such, portraits of rulers spurred familiarity with the identity of these sitters. It should not surprise us that familiar profiles became preferred content for anamorphic innovation; distorted portraits made little sense unless the viewer had a pretty good grasp of what the sitter actually looked like.

COMPARATIVE SCRUTINY

Contemporary physiognomic literature also honed new visual skills through exercises in facial literacy. Physiognomies, books that purported to guide character assessments based on profiles, were among the earliest genres to

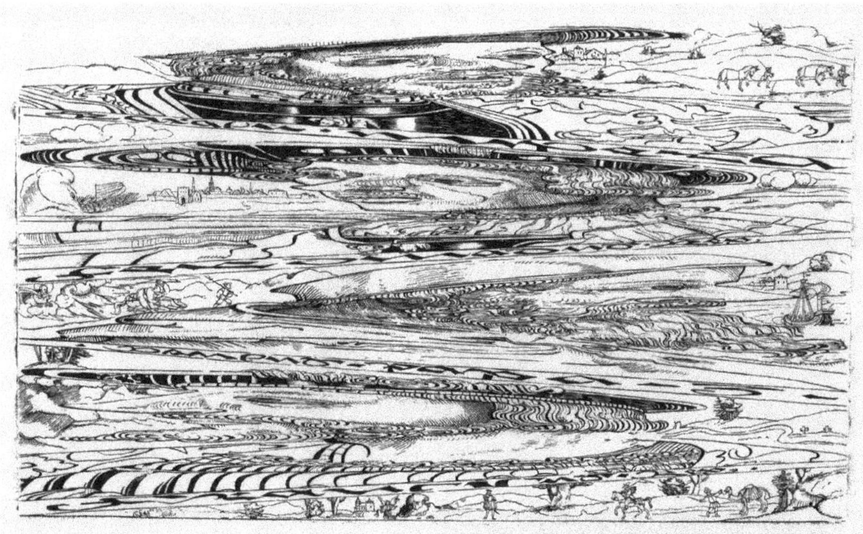

5.6. Erhard Schön, *Anamorphic Portraits of Charles V, Ferdinand I, Pope Paul III, and Francis I*, c. 1530–5, anamorphic woodcut. *Source:* Bpk Bildagentur/Kupferstichkabinett/Staatliche Museen Berlin. Photograph: Jörg Anders/Art Resource, NY.

recommend visual searches, and among the first to market themselves as especially helpful in sharpening the reader's scrutiny.[14] The graphic set-up of these physiognomies invoked a specific strategy premised on a new interactive cognitive exercise structured by prints: compare and contrast (Figure 5.7). Physiognomies asked the viewer to consider a subject in the field between the two poles provided by the image, structuring a physical and mental comparison. The reader's experience of these books was rewired by such pictorial prompts. Indeed, the visual program developed in these early illustrated physiognomies was tenacious. After the first generation of unillustrated physiognomies, paired profiles such as these became the standard format for most later editions. Comparisons were also at the heart of both Leonardo's and Albrecht Dürer's physiognomic studies.

Modalities of viewing suggested by printed physiognomies became part of the cognitive infrastructure for facial analysis. Not only did their pictorial content provide the primer for the development of visual acuity, these books also tried to parse forms of visual attention. A physiognomy printed in Strasbourg posited two distinct modes of visual inquiry that its text could help cultivate: a quick glance (*Anblick*) and detailed scrutiny (*Augenschein*).[15] Two further registers of epistemic practice – experience (*Experientz*) and knowledge (*Erfarnüß*) – were cited as byproducts of nose reading.[16] The experiential knowledge cultivated by such manuals was a multi-step process that described seeing as an operation comprised of both sensory and judgmental stages. An image of the sensing brain by Leonardo reflects his understanding of visual judgment to be a procedural step in knowledge acquisition; Lorenzo Pericolo shows this as Leonardo's

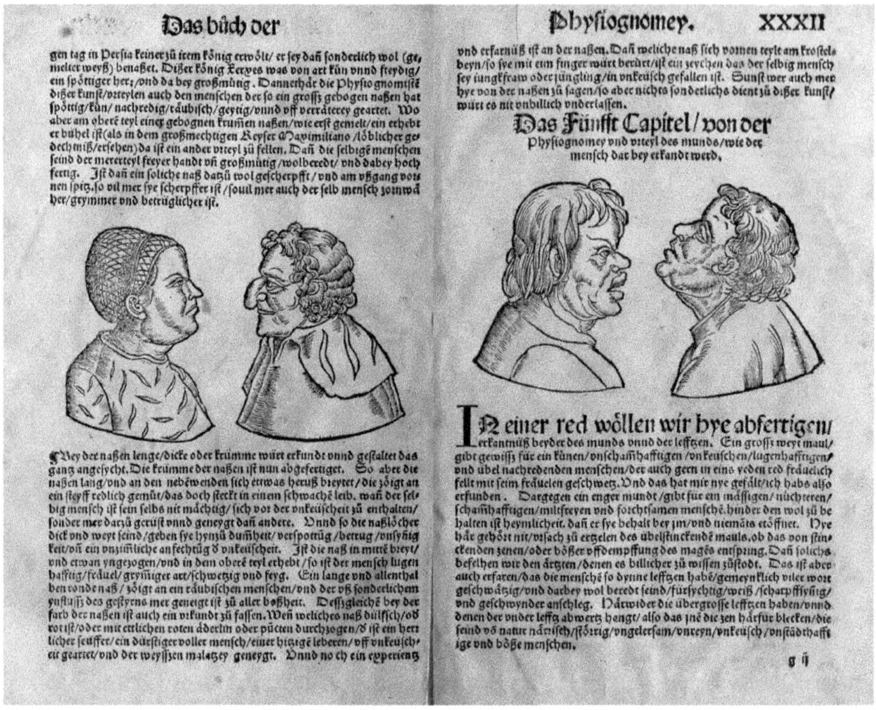
Das büch der

Physiognomey. XXXII

Das Fünfft Capitel/von der physiognomey und urteyl des munds/wie der mensch dar bey erkandt werd.

5.7. Hans Wechtlin, pairs of noses and mouths, in Johannes Indagine, *Die Kunst der Chiromantzey … Physiognomey … Natürlichen Astrologey … Complexion eines yegklichen menschens …* (Strasbourg: Johannes Schott, 1523), fols. XXXIv–XXXIIr. *Source:* NLM WZ 240 I38G 152. Courtesy of US National Library of Medicine.

adaptation of Alhazen's *intuitio*.[17] These two modes of inquiry, experience and knowledge, were skills simultaneously being vetted in the *Vexierbilder*. Puzzle pictures, like physiognomic analysis, commandeered perception and then steered those resulting insights into the service of more reasoned knowledge.[18]

A particular index of visual discrimination was located in facial comparisons. We have seen how facial recognition as a register for knowledge developed around the practice of scanning profiles. As we can see in this drawing of the Emperor Charles V and King Ferdinand I that carries the label *Keiser Konig* (Figure 5.8),[19] such scrutiny was the building block of comparative visual analysis.[20] It is no accident that this anamorphic image also invited the same strategy of facial comparison that was required to navigate physiognomies. This drawing of *Keiser Konig* essentially asked the viewer to distinguish between them, borrowing physiognomy's formal set-up of facing profiles for its comparative potential, where the subjects are presented *vis à vis*, or, literally, face to face.[21] Paired profiles such as this one, likely based on a double portrait of the two brothers made at the diet of Augsburg in 1530, I would argue, recalled formulas for comparison established by illustrated physiognomies and invited similar cognitive acts of pictorial scanning. These formulas demanded close

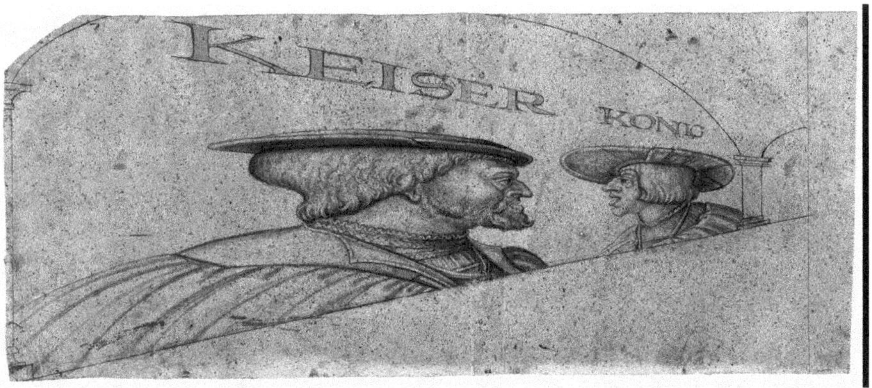

5.8. Artist unknown (likely Augsburg, Master CB?), *Keiser Konig* (Charles V and King Ferdinand I), *c.* 1530–40, pen and ink, heightened in gray on gray paper, 25.1 cm × 60.5 cm. *Source:* Inv. nr. 1975-44. Hamburger Kunsthalle. Photograph: Christoph Irrgang.

observation for the purposes of parceling people into groups, or types, or separate identities. In these visual searches, the nose frequently became a productive locus for meaning.

While features such as the distended bellies and tonsures of Catholic monks were favored sites of parody in Reformation polemic, misshapen noses were unequivocal indices of bad habits.[22] Noses increasingly bore the burden as the locus of character assassination in physiognomic diagnoses. In the *Devil's Bagpipe* (Figure 5.9), the monk's nose has morphed into the peasant's shawm. The monk is transformed into a diabolical instrument through the devil's manipulation of his proboscis. A distended nose whose profile was linked to deceptive character traits was also previewed for audiences in the complexion literature. For this visual and rhetorical joke, Schön relies on the viewer's visual acuity. Through a flickering of visual switchbacks, Schön unsteadies the observer in front of the image – asking viewers if they see a monk or a devil. The experience of such images also paired the epistemological approaches of two separate viewing habits described in printed physiognomies: *Anblick* and *Augenschein*. A demonic glance from the belly of the devil dissolves the fourth wall between image and viewer, summoning the viewer to attention, as if to signal that from these cognitive steps will come understanding.[23]

The transformation of the monk into an appendage of the devil happens only with a shift in perspective. But the joke's payoff resides in the viewer's recognition of the monk's exposure as the devil. This resolution is checked by the demonic head peering out at the viewer. With this direct address, viewers are hailed to search for the folly inside themselves, and also to be vigilant in scanning the field for (in this case Catholic) manipulators. This call to self-knowledge through the act of viewing reminds us that visual judgment can lead from experience to knowledge, thus positing viewing as a self-conscious epistemic act.

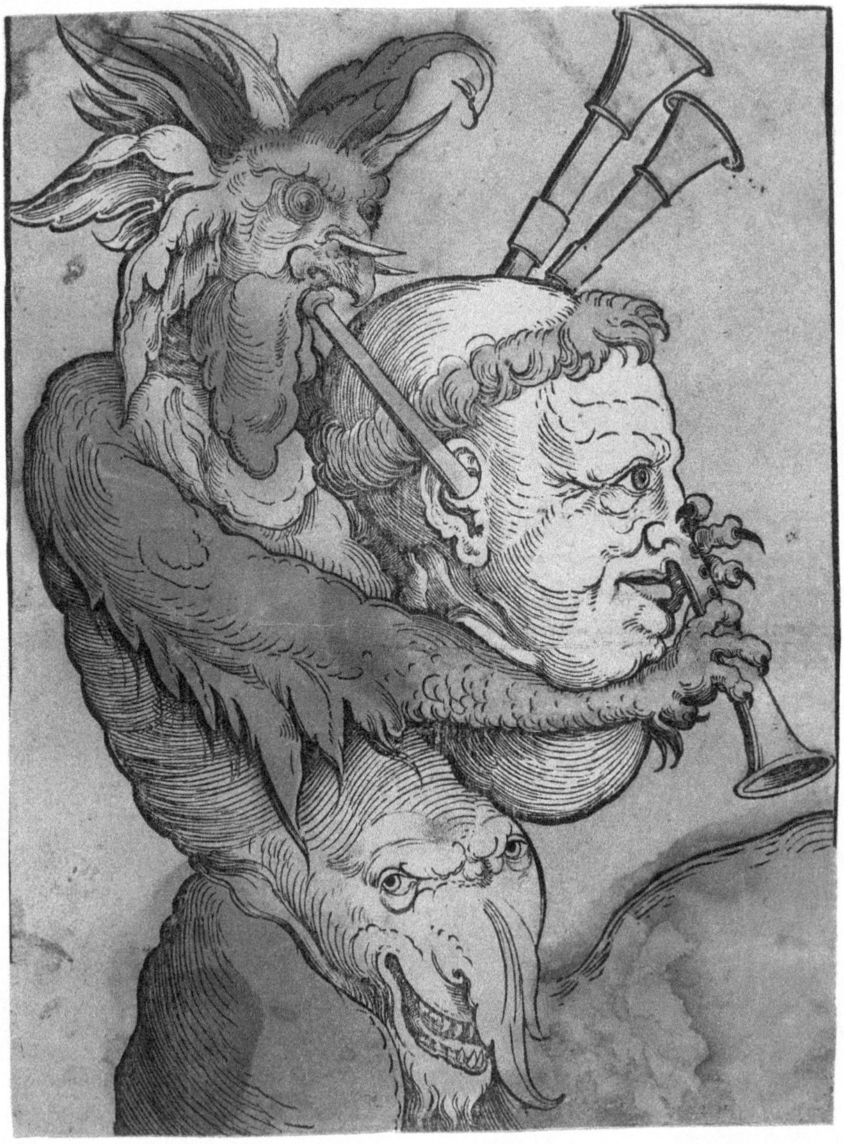

5.9. Erhard Schön, *Devil's Bagpipe*, *c.* 1530, woodcut. *Source:* © The Trustees of the British Museum.

Picturing bivalence was also the aim of the by now well-known images in Apian's *Cosmographicus Liber* that likewise introduced two competing modes of picturing and processing visual information. In an example from an Antwerp reprint of 1584 that featured both parts of the analogy on a single page (Figure 5.10), the image differentiates between macroscopic geography and the microcosm of topographic detail, which are presented as two *distinct* modes of knowledge production. They likewise embed two modalities of projection: geography and chorography. Geography described the world from a broad

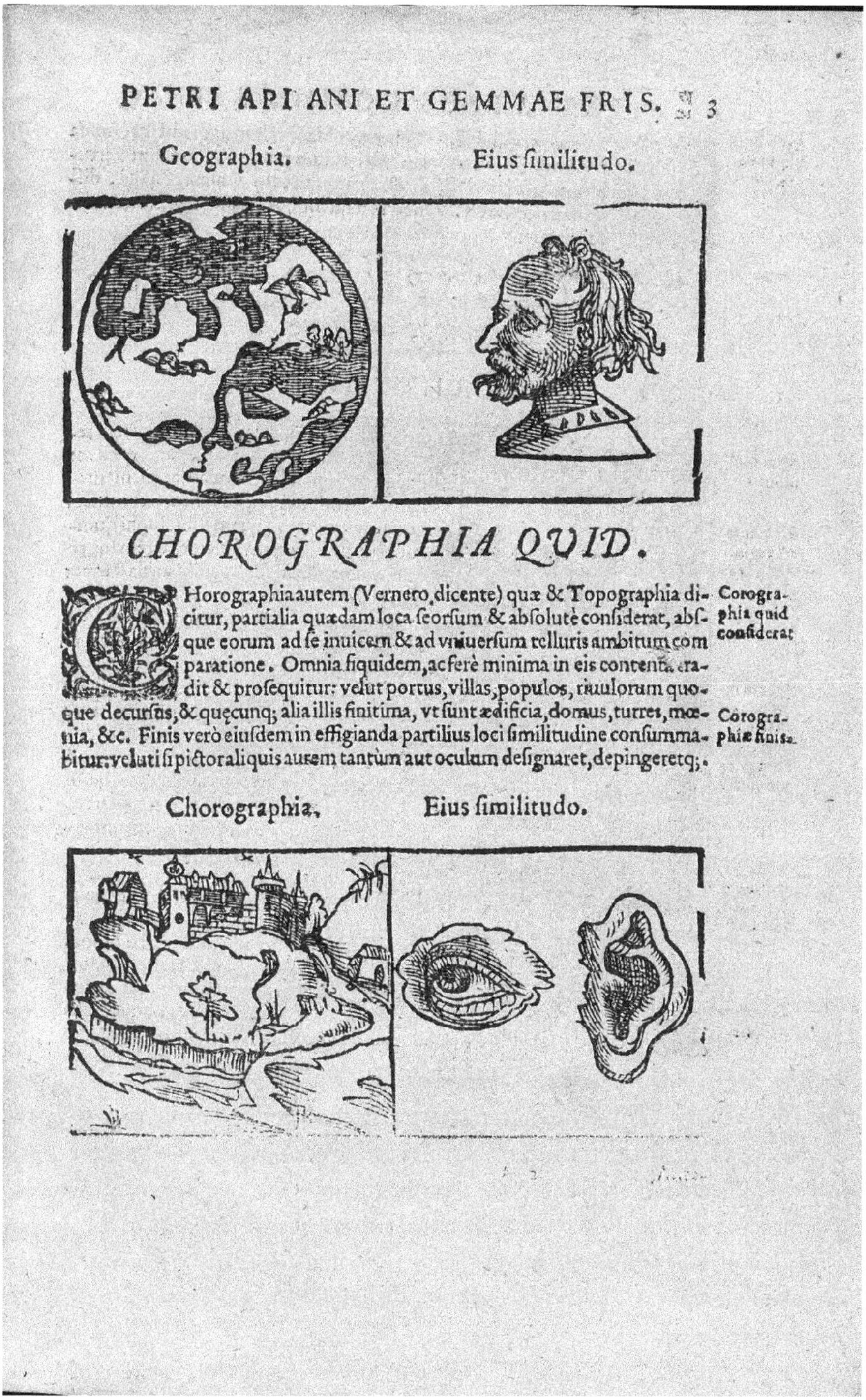
PETRI APIANI ET GEMMAE FRIS. 3

Geographia. Eius ſimilitudo.

CHOROGRAPHIA QVID.

CHorographia autem (Vernero dicente) quæ & Topographia dicitur, partialia quædam loca ſeorſum & abſolutè conſiderat, abſque eorum ad ſe inuicem & ad vniuerſum telluris ambitum comparatione. Omnia ſiquidem, ac ferè minima in eis contenta tradit & proſequitur: velut portus, villas, populos, riuulorum quoque decurſus, & quęcunq; alia illis finitima, vt ſunt ædificia, domus, turres, mœnia, &c. Finis verò eiuſdem in effigianda partilius loci ſimilitudine conſummabitur: veluti ſi pictor aliquis aurem tantùm aut oculum deſignaret, depingeretq;.

Corographia quid conſiderat

Corographiæ finis.

Chorographia. Eius ſimilitudo.

5.10. Peter Apian and Rainer Gemma Frisius, *Cosmographia, siue Descriptio vniuersi orbis* (Antwerp: Withagen, 1584). *Source:* Vault GA6.A55. Florida State University Special Collections & Archives.

perspective: landmasses, mountains, plains, and rivers. The fundamental task of the geographer was to render more than what the eye could see; intuition was key to filling in what could not be perceived. Apian calls upon this formulation by Ptolemy in the *Cosmographicus Liber*. To be understood, geography also had to be projected and understood by the sensing brain.[24] Chorography, by contrast, was the topographic rendering of local features such as the hill town taken in by the eye. Apian's marginal gloss tells us that chorography is a perfected and "used" representation, and no one but a painter can achieve it.[25] Apian likens this description of chorography to the portraitist's task of rendering the individual features of faces, such as eyes and ears. Topographic features can be seen in a single take and are critical building blocks of chorographic description. Cosmography oscillates between these two modes of information gathering and projection. But the main point here is that Apian reprises the Ptolemaic geographic tradition to acknowledge that the art of cosmography involves a dual process of cognition. It is both a mental state and an image, a diagram and an icon; according to Strabo, the geographer performs an act of intellectual synthesis at which two strands of epistemic inquiry meet. The geographer takes in impressions from the senses and assembles these into a concept that is distinct from those sensory impressions: the *diagramma*. The map, like the anatomical diagram, results from the synthesis of intellectual processes residing in the graphic sign: it is both an idea *and also* an image. Perhaps the best proof of this is that the geographer must consistently render territories "whose size exceeds individual sense perception."[26] The cartographic image, two things at once, required mental gymnastics to process what one sees and what one can intuit from that.

Critical for our discussion of puzzle pictures premised on shifting perspectives, this oscillation between two modes of visual knowledge also recognizes a dichotomy of perception. In order to pursue one, the viewer must exclude the other: the observer must consider the individual features of a face while holding the head in abeyance, for example; and then vice versa. This was precisely the cognitive strategy that activated anamorphic images: one perspective had to be held in visual suspension if the other perspective was to resolve properly. Puzzle pictures posited insight as the prize of visual scrutiny. The rise of representation in early modern scopic regimes was forecasted by images of visual complexity, some of which made themselves ardently self-aware. They provoked viewers as interpreters, often bringing them to the brink of embattled visual positions.[27]

As a genre of conceptual and representational complexity, cartography was reimagined in the sixteenth century as an intensive visualization of the earth's surface. This coincided with a shift in geography's emphasis away from simply filling in the blanks left by Ptolemy to explaining how to derive local data firsthand.[28] Apian's *Cosmographicus Liber* cultivated a readership able to apply those skills in charting their local coordinates. One of Apian's images demonstrated how coordinates on a globe could be understood and simulated by two sets of hands holding string between them, identifying the town in the crosshairs.[29] Ultimately, the cosmographer's job to unite astronomy and geography required facility with a third skill: the geometry needed to produce projections. Cosmographers and map and atlas makers in the era of Mercator created projections that would enable the translation of the three-dimensional globe on a two-dimensional surface via geometric triangulation.[30] This skill was required to reproduce geographic knowledge as it was served up via many different kinds of cartographic projections. Globes, maps, and atlases alike were all visual distortions that angularly transformed flat grids into multidimensional models of the world.

SEEING DOUBLE

A symphonic meditation on Apian's analogy between cosmography and portraiture can be found in Hans Holbein's panel of two Catholic statesmen painted at the English court in 1533, *The Ambassadors* (Plate XV). The two kinds of epistemic images that this book has explored in popular media – physiognomic and geographic representation – surface in Holbein's painting on the ontological level of art. Among their parallels domains of concern are their commentary on visual knowledge, common directives for close looking, and where to locate oneself while doing it.

On the table between the two sitters, we see instrumentation and maps that characterized the period's height of cosmographic learning through empirical study. Scholars have argued that these objects unlock the painting, whose "meaning" interrogates the pursuit of knowledge via contemporary exploits in empirical activity. The exactitude with which some of this scientific activity was undertaken has inspired scholars to pinpoint in the painting specific coordinates and an angular value for the height of the sun at the Crucifixion.[31] No doubt these feats of intellectual inquiry were ideals with which the two pictured sitters desired identification, as indeed did Holbein himself. But I would argue that another epistemic pursuit, a major intellectual cornerstone of Holbein's own artistic preoccupation with faciality, is also being vetted here: that of portraiture.

Holbein's composition is devoted to two major focus areas of empirical study in the sixteenth century as they were defined in printed books: portraiture and cosmography mediated by instruments. To be sure, Holbein's famous "double portrait" of Jean de Dinteville and the Bishop Georges de Selve is *actually* a triple portrait, with the third visage hidden in the picture. Using this painting as a touchstone for Renaissance man's desire to fashion his individuality, Stephen Greenblatt calls attention to worldly pursuits like portraiture.

Indeed, the skill set that summoned Holbein to the Tudor court was his penchant to staunch the ephemerality of time with flattering and bombastic likenesses. Less frequently observed are the common techniques that Holbein used to produce both faces and skull. Holbein's rendering of both portraits and skull were preceded by his visually acute observation of visages. We can argue that Holbein's composition is a sustained meditation on the pursuit of observational knowledge, a conceit that the artist bolstered with his painterly striving for faces reflected in mirror-like surfaces. Holbein's skull is also a portrait, but one of a different order: a study worked up from close attention of geometrical principles applied to physiognomy.

That Holbein intended to parallel portraiture with cosmography can be seen in the many references to the instruments involved in producing that science. The scientific instruments on the table between the sitters show Holbein's facility with the principles of celestial and terrestrial geometry – they include a polyhedral and cylindrical sundial, a quadrant and a torquetum (used for determining positions via angular altitudes), many of which Holbein seems to have imported from his earlier portrait of Henry VIII's astronomer Nicholas Kratzer in 1528.[32] Not purely secular, some instruments of this ilk were designed to be auto-critical of worldly pursuits and came with posted warnings. Evidence for the double action of instruments as both agents for meditation on mortality and instruments of knowledge can be found in a cruciform ivory sundial designed by Georg Hartmann inscribed with cautionary reliefs of the Crucifixion and the Bronze Serpent.[33] Such tools that interfaced with worldly knowledge also persistently cautioned the viewer not to be misled by it.

Holbein's engagement with scientific knowledge is clear from his own collaborations and from the array of data-gathering instruments that fill out the backdrop of this composition. These objects form the cultural capital of mathematical learning that was part of the sitters' program of self-fashioning, as well as Holbein's devising of his own reputation. Holbein's content here, as well as his technique, were guided by practical geometry. Jennifer Nelson shows that Holbein rendered these objects in virtuoso turns of foreshortening that sometimes obeyed and at other times defied strict rules of perspective.[34] All of these instruments – and, indeed, the programs of the many volumes that circulated about their use – pertained to the practice of "practical geometry," including navigation, surveying, engineering, and warfare.[35] In addition to tools for the larger universal project of measuring, quantifying, and mapping European expansion active in cosmographic texts of the period, practical geometry was also a critical building block of the artist's technique.[36] Holbein provided the design elements for several cosmographic projects, including a book on planetary motion and an astronomical wall chart that was a collaboration with the cosmographer Sebastian Münster on the *Organum*

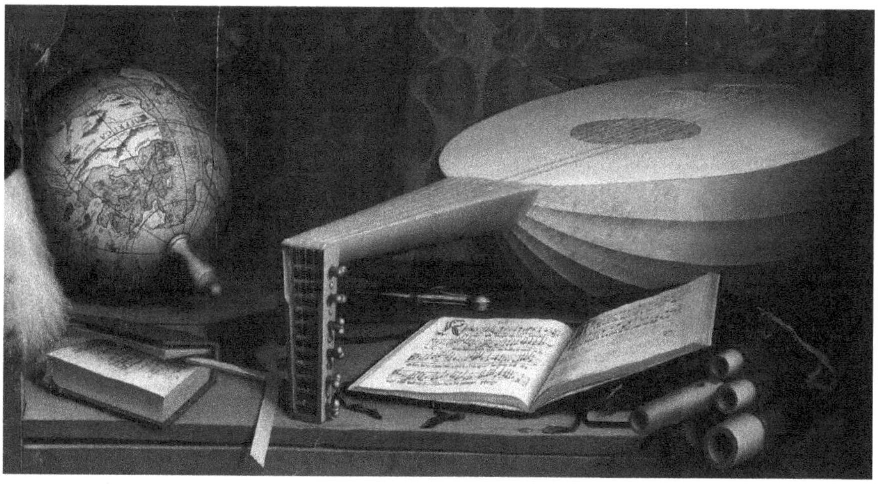

5.11. Detail of globe from Holbein the Younger, *The Ambassadors*, 1533, oil on oak, 207 cm × 209.5 cm. *Source:* Courtesy of National Gallery, London.

Uranicum (printed in Basel in 1536). The design of the celestial globe on the upper shelf derives from gores that the Nuremberg geographer Johannes Schöner produced *c.* 1515.[37] The instruments on the table are ones used to chart the motion of the planets and trace their trajectories on the spherical earth. On the credenza's lower level, we see a terrestrial globe likely inspired by an engraved set of gores that followed the model of the earth imagined by Maximilianus Transylvanus, who authored the first published account of the circumnavigation of Ferdinand Magellan and Juan Sebastián Elcano.[38] This model included the line of demarcation, *Linea Divisonis Castellanoru(m) et Portugallen(ium)*, the division of the earth into hemispheres belonging to Spain and Portugal respectively as determined by the Treaty of Tordesillas (1494) (Figure 5.11). The relevance of the portioning of the globe via longitude lines that ceded the spices of the Moluccan Islands to Spain was an emphasis that could also be tracked in the first published edition of *De Moluccis insulis* (which appeared in 1523 in both Rome and Cologne), Transylvanus's report that interviewed the few returning members of Magellan's voyage.[39] Such a globe that demarcated Habsburg possessions showed the cosmographic perspective subtended by the geopolitical lines that cartographers inscribed on the earth. Terrestrial lines of latitude and longitude, as well as the shapes of the continents that lay beneath them, diminished along lines of projection that required Holbein's skill as a geometer to envision. The geometry of perspectival rendering must have evolved in tandem with the cosmographic advancements that he pictured. Clearly, Holbein was familiar with Apian's material and the instrument manuals that developed in his circle. It was also very likely Apian's cosmographic work that inspired Holbein's participation in Münster's *Organum Uranicum*.[40] Holbein's familiarity with instruments might have been mediated by some of Apian's publications that were responsible for knowledge about scientific instruments circulating in his pamphlet about the comet and the related *Practica* of 1532, whose title page featured a torquetum.[41] Another publication by Apian designed for crossover audiences of learned and practical readers is the mathematics manual that Holbein pictured on the lower credenza.

Mastery in geometry was also required to conjure the semi-spherical shape of an "unresolved" skull, which had to be first rationalized before it was distorted. The skull, in some respects, is a critical item in the inventory of "knowing images," or epistemic devices, on display here. The torquetum and dial were tools necessary to capture data points from which other cosmographic calculations were made – these data points were necessary to produce the geographic projections that we see on the globe.[42] Representations of the continents on globes are essentially geometric distortions. The instruments are not only marshaled to evoke empirically derived data, but with them Holbein also raises curiosity about their use, as well as about how they were made – in terms of textures, materials, and lines. Anamorphosis requires knowledge of perspectival recession in order to reverse engineer it. To render the skull required deconstructing the principles of perspective by relocating the distance point to the head of the visual cone, reversing the projection of the perspectival cone into the viewer's space. To create an anamorphic distortion, the viewing point must merge with the distance point, the value that determined the rate of diminution of forms in a typical perspectival projection.[43]

Holbein had to both generate the skull and then stretch it. Artists typically stretched their subjects by way of a trapezoidal grid.[44] Perspective manuals such as Giacomo Barozzi da Vignola's *Le due regole della prospettiva practica* showed how to distort likenesses, specifically faces (Figure 5.12). Faces seem to be the content of choice for anamorphic distortion from its earliest experiments by Leonardo to manuals by Daniele Barbaro, Egnazio Danti, Salomon de Caus, and Jean-François Niceron.[45] Perhaps the distortion that occurs in Holbein's anamorphosis can best be seen in a volume in which Egnazio Danti replicates a face stretched by a viewing instrument in an illustration attributed to Tommaso Laureti. In this peep box, an image can be observed obliquely through a viewfinder, by first stretching a square grid into a rectangle twice its length.[46]

Anamorphic rendering was an epistemic inquiry into the optics of vision that posited how the viewer's visual cone could be moved around. The technique used to distort the skull required the transformation of a square grid into a trapezoid. Distortion was then performed via an angular approach in order to orient spatial depth toward the eye of the viewer. This trapezoidal distortion was similar to that employed by cosmographers to depict the heavens and by geographers to render the shape of the earth. This was a

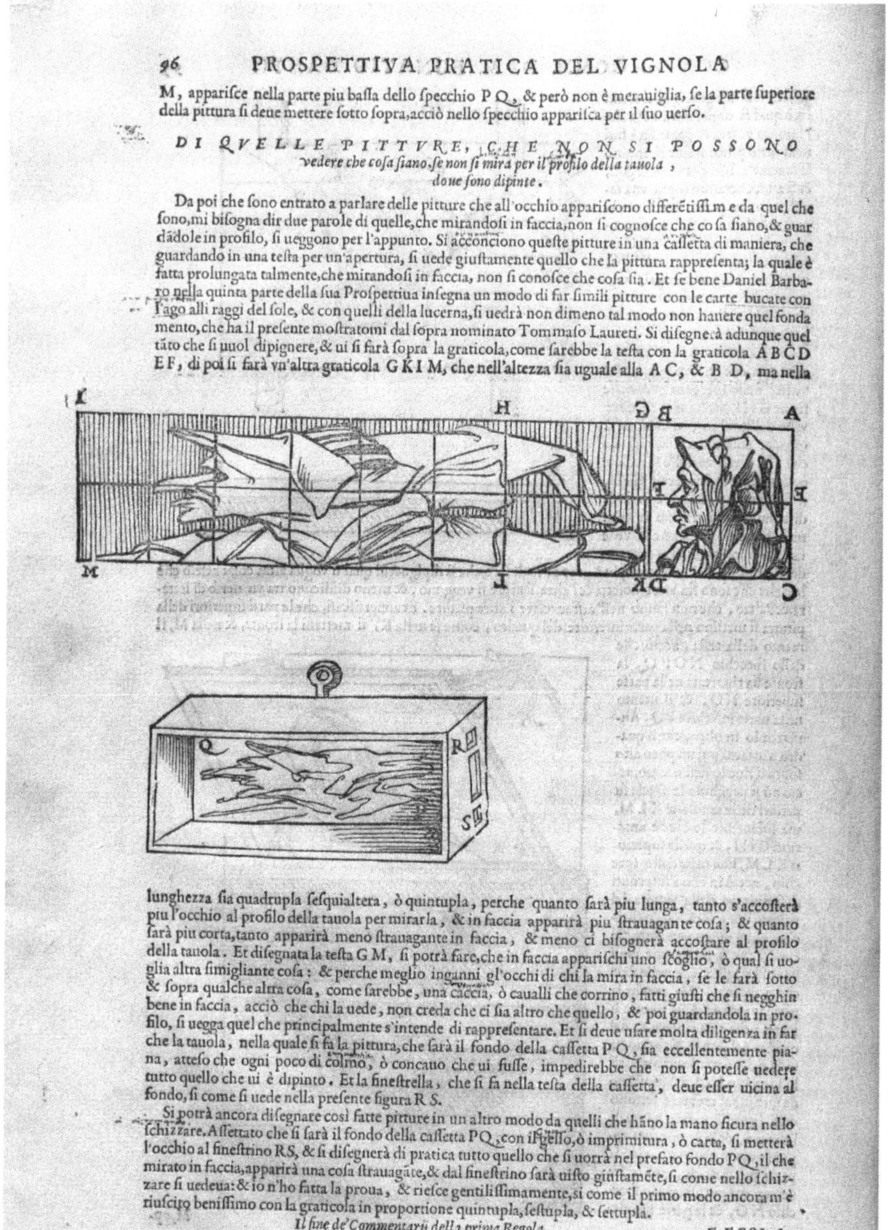

96 PROSPETTIVA PRATICA DEL VIGNOLA

M, appariſce nella parte piu baſſa dello ſpecchio P Q, & però non è merauiglia, ſe la parte ſuperiore della pittura ſi deue mettere ſotto ſopra, acciò nello ſpecchio appariſca per il ſuo uerſo.

DI QVELLE PITTVRE, CHE NON SI POSSONO vedere che coſa ſiano, ſe non ſi mira per il profilo della tauola, doue ſono dipinte.

Da poi che ſono entrato a parlare delle pitture che all'occhio appariſcono differētiſſim e da quel che ſono, mi biſogna dir due parole di quelle, che mirandoſi in faccia, non ſi cognoſce che coſa ſiano, & guardādole in profilo, ſi ueggono per l'appunto. Si acconciono queſte pitture in una caſſetta di maniera, che guardando in una teſta per un'apertura, ſi uede giuſtamente quello che la pittura rappreſenta; la quale è fatta prolungata talmente, che mirandoſi in faccia, non ſi conoſce che coſa ſia. Et ſe bene Daniel Barbaro nella quinta parte della ſua Proſpettiua inſegna un modo di far ſimili pitture con le carte bucate con l'ago alli raggi del ſole, & con quelli della lucerna, ſi uedrà non dimeno tal modo non hauere quel fondamento, che ha il preſente moſtratomi dal ſopra nominato Tommaſo Laureti. Si diſegnerà adunque quel tāto che ſi uuol dipignere, & ui ſi farà ſopra la graticola, come ſarebbe la teſta con la graticola A B C D E F, di poi ſi farà vn'altra graticola G K I M, che nell'altezza ſia uguale alla A C, & B D, ma nella lunghezza ſia quadrupla ſeſquialtera, ò quintupla, perche quanto ſarà piu lunga, tanto s'accoſterà piu l'occhio al profilo della tauola per mirarla, & in faccia apparirà piu ſtrauagante coſa; & quanto ſarà piu corta, tanto apparirà meno ſtrauagante in faccia, & meno ci biſognerà accoſtare al profilo della tauola. Et diſegnata la teſta G M, ſi potrà fare, che in faccia appariſchi uno ſcoglio, ò qual ſi uoglia altra ſimigliante coſa: & perche meglio inganni gl'occhi di chi la mira in faccia, ſe le farà ſotto & ſopra qualche altra coſa, come ſarebbe, una caccia, ò caualli che corrino, fatti giuſti che ſi ueggħin bene in faccia, acciò che chi la uede, non creda che ci ſia altro che quello, & poi guardandola in profilo, ſi uegga quel che principalmente s'intende di rappreſentare. Et ſi deue uſare molta diligenza in far che la tauola, nella quale ſi fa la pittura, che ſarà il fondo della caſſetta P Q, ſia eccellentemente piana, atteſo che ogni poco di colmo, ò concauo che ui fuſſe, impedirebbe che non ſi poteſſe uedere tutto quello che ui è dipinto. Et la fineſtrella, che ſi fa nella teſta della caſſetta, deue eſſer uicina al fondo, ſi come ſi uede nella preſente figura R S.

Si potrà ancora diſegnare così fatte pitture in un altro modo da quelli che hāno la mano ſicura nello ſchizzare. Aſſettato che ſi ſarà il fondo della caſſetta P Q, con il geſſo, ò imprimitura, ò carta, ſi metterà l'occhio al fineſtrino R S, & ſi diſegnerà di pratica tutto quello che ſi uorrà nel prefato fondo P Q, il che mirato in faccia, apparirà una coſa ſtrauagāte, & dal fineſtrino ſarà uiſto giuſtamēte, ſi come nello ſchizzare ſi uedeua: & io n'ho fatta la proua, & rieſce gentiliſſimamente, ſi come il primo modo ancora m'è riuſcito beniſſimo con la graticola in proportione quintupla, ſeſtupla, & ſettupla.

Il fine de' Commentarij della prima Regola.

F. EGNA

5.12. Giacomo Barozzi da Vignola, *Le due regole della prospettiva practica* (Rome: Francesco Zannetti, 1583). *Source:* Courtesy of Hathi Trust.

method very similar to the one that Holbein must have used to stretch the pictured continents over the graticule of Schöner's globe. The dividers for doing so lay nearby.

Perspective techniques employed by instrument makers to fashion tools such as astrolabes, according to Samuel Gessner, were the *sine qua non* required to project the celestial spheres onto the planisphere. Indeed, art history's understanding of perspective models as a crutch used by painters to map the coordinates of illusionistic space vastly underrepresents the use and sophistication of projection models employed by instrument makers. The torchbearers of these formulae were mathematically adept producers of astrolabes, quadrants, and maps, who, like artists, believed that they inherited Vitruvian principles that were transmitted by painters' manuals including Albrecht Dürer's.[47] These professionals understood perspective as optical theory.

Geometry was long hailed as one of the most powerful tools of the artist. Dürer's skill in geometry, for example, was considered by contemporaries to rival his artistic technique.[48] Holbein shared an interest with astronomers and instrument makers such as Nicolaus Kratzer, the math tutor to Thomas More's children at the English court, whose portrait he painted in 1528. The two would also produce maps together. Holbein's portrait depicts Kratzer with a polyhedral dial in his hands, as well as a pair of dividers. Such compasses were implements of astronomers, artists, and mapmakers (and feature as attributes in their portraits) – but, indeed, the dividers were critical to any art of mensuration and thus, as a tool, they anchored the mercurial nature of invention onto the more solid footing of technical mastery.[49]

We can assume that Holbein was familiar with how the pictured instruments abetted the task of art but was also curious about how these instruments mediated the act and recording of observations. Such technical skills also fed Holbein's own interest in the related empirical pursuit of portraiture. Indeed, the artist must have seen the rendering of instruments as a skill comparable to portraiture to have given them kindred emphasis and the almost identical depths of field that bring all of these objects into focus. Holbein focused the viewer's visual and mental engagement on the mirror-like reflection of the sitters with an enthusiasm equal to his detailed exploration of scientific tools.

Any beholder of Holbein's sitters versed in contemporary physiognomic and cosmographic publications would have been reminded of their epistemic lessons. In these publications, both faces and instruments paraded as tools of visual knowledge. The genres of physiognomy and cosmography, as we have seen, were ones for which the fruits of optical knowing had already been established by printed books that broke down the principles for the literate eye. Holbein's portraits reflect geometric gymnastics similar to those required to produce cosmography and physiognomy. It also instructs viewers how to switch between them (on the level of face as well as feature) – he thus brought

Apian's analogy of geography and chorography full circle. It is not a stretch to think that Holbein might have had Apian's analogies from the *Cosmographicus Liber* in mind. Holbein's inclusion of Apian's accounting textbook for merchants printed in 1527, a page of which is held open here with a T-square, suggests his familiarity with Apian's oeuvre, which included an array of publications on instruments, ones that were required reading for anyone who wanted to understand these tools.[50] This tactical display of instruments and publications on the two shelves between the sitters suggests that knowledge is hard-won and moderated by heuristic models for measuring and gauging.

PLOTTED PORTRAITS

While *The Ambassadors*' presentation of scientific instruments alone should be an insistent reminder of the mediated nature of viewing practices, observers typically forget this mediation when confronted by a portrait. Since the Renaissance, and perhaps largely through the intervention of Holbein's skill, portraits appear to Western viewers as something approaching mirror reflections of their sitters. Many of Holbein's portraits seem to us naturalized representations of their subjects. Many personalities of the Tudor court and celebrities of the Republic of Letters sat for Holbein; if the modern reader conjures any mental image of Thomas More, Anne of Cleves, Henry VIII, or Erasmus, that picture is likely an image of Holbein's. The smooth surfaces of Holbein's brushwork suggest an immediacy of the encounter between subject and viewer. Holbein's high-resolution reflection of the sitter is consonant with the possibility of direct address that his compositions promise. Viewers exposed to the library of likenesses of Holbein's clientele might have very well been misled by the idea that objective picturing guides the hand of the portraitist, but anyone who has ever sat for a portrait intuitively challenges this idea of truth in the image. Holbein also problematized and prodded at the idea of naturalized viewing in portraiture by visually interrogating the truth of the painted subjects through anamorphosis.

The data points of facial features were as precise and particular as empirical data recorded by the scientific instruments. Holbein, had, in fact, built his career around the supposition of truth in portraiture. Holbein knew how visages changed over time; as a portraitist, he produced multiple likenesses for some longstanding clients, some of whom became obstreperous when their appearance was poorly reflected by their painters.[51] Precisely because portraits were the bread and butter of Holbein's trade, the deathly footnote supplied by the skull might well signal his skepticism about the fixity of physiognomic knowledge. He had already factored the nose, the focus of so much physiognomic analysis, out of the skull. Indeed, what seems to be vetted here is the epistemic potential of faces. Faces, whether specific or general, could be the locus of knowledge.[52] The skull deconstructs the painting's overt nod to worldly knowledge by providing perspective from the world beyond the grave. Instead of commanding the sitters, the skull beseeches viewers to recognize themselves in the image.

The skull shows Holbein's approach to facial metamorphosis as both a function of time and a skill in perspectival projection. In some sense, the skull represents the self's truer portrait. Its anamorphic adjustments are pictorial expressions of the change that can occur through time, and, for Holbein, that change was expressed through his mastery of perspective. In addition to the portraits of the sitters Dinteville and Selve, Holbein's other important message about metamorphosis wreaked by time was sent through an anamorphic interlocutor. This messenger was conceived through the virtuoso deployment of mathematical skills. Holbein shows off the technical skills needed to create the picture, but he also chooses to thematize the way in which such skills could also bring the world crashing down. Anamorphic transformation of faces works only if the face is conceived as a tight collection of coordinates that can be rearranged when subjected to metamorphosis. Such adjustments to faces presume that a rigorous grammar of representation underlie them.

To the painter, the face is a series of carefully plotted data points, as it also is to the physiognomer. We can still see traces of plotting in some of Holbein's preparatory sketches. In a pen and ink sketch from approximately 1535, Holbein shows his engagement with perspectival techniques, rendering a number of heads seen from many different angles (Figure 5.13).[53] Their proportions are preserved by Holbein's sketching in the main axes of the face: center lines and the axis on which the eyes align. The lines of the eyes, mouth, and nose of a figure in the lower left-hand corner of the sketch demonstrate recession to a vanishing point. The potential for a geometric model to facilitate the recession of planes represented by the various joints of the fingers is demonstrated by a schematic hand in Holbein's sketch. Holbein might have indeed commanded the use of geometric models from which to derive these examples.[54] One of the critical functions of performing such studies in proportion and perspective was to permit the image to resolve from a variety of viewpoints. Demonstrations of proportions and perspective performed by geometrically schematized mannequins appear in Erhard Schön's *Unterweisung der Proportionen und Stellung der Possen* (*c.* 1542), a manual that Schön pitched as an abridgment of the publications of Dürer and Vitruvius.[55] Holbein's sketch seems like a summation of geometric tricks employed by the painter when he approached the two important loci that Holbein foregrounded in many of his preparatory studies: the head and the hands.

Certain prominent marks on the surface of some of Holbein's sketches may indicate his use of a drawing device with which he rapidly marked key

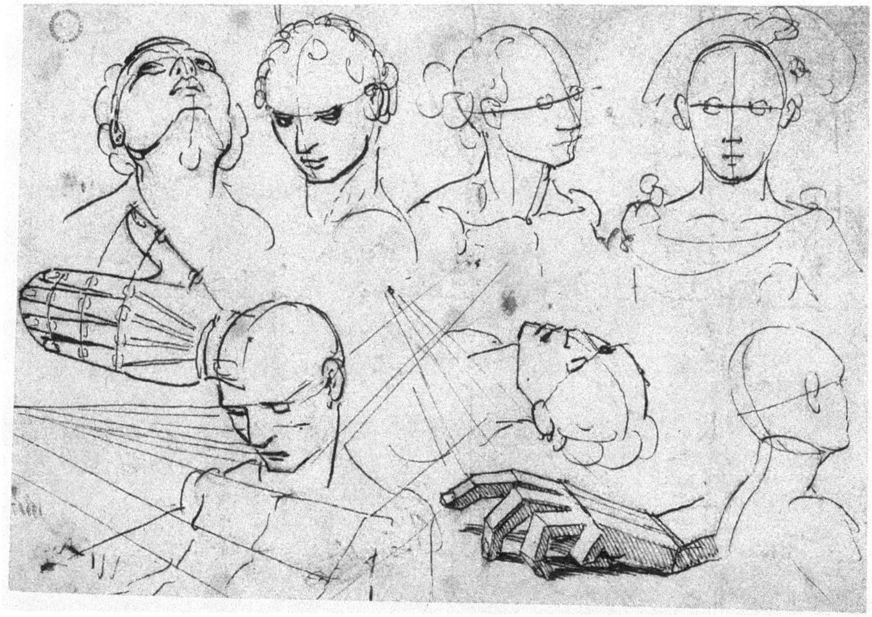

5.13. Hans Holbein the Younger, *Studies of Heads and Hands*, 1535, pen and ink over chalk, sheet 13.2 cm × 19.2 cm. *Source:* Inv. 1662.165.16. Kunstmuseum Basel, Kupferstichkabinett.

coordinates that he could fill in later.[56] The use of such a contraption to trace elements of a sitter's physiognomy was explained as a working practice in technical manuals such as Albrecht Dürer's *Underweysung der Messung* (Figure 5.14).[57] Devices like these were used to mark angles, to determine relative distances between compositional elements, and also to render objects otherwise difficult to foreshorten. Using a translucent screen, or velo, with a string for reference, Dürer's manual for painters shows how to render a lute in perspective. The lute that appears on Dürer's velo takes the same angle as the one that appears on the lower shelf of Holbein's credenza.

Such rigor in plotting was also a feature of puzzle pictures that functioned as multivalent images that could be viewed in two registers. In images of Turks produced in Venice, we see stereotypes created by collective data points, rather than individual likenesses, like the reversible image of a Turk that morphs into a devil when turned upside down (Figure 5.15).[58] This is a double image, but it is also packaged as one face disguised as another. To the dissimulation at work among crypto-worshippers of all confessions during the years of religious tumult as explored by Perez Zagorin, anamorphosis would have been a fitting chaperone. Anamorphosis was the visual conceit of disguises and a perfect tool to conceal "that which one was, and to reveal that which one was not."[59] Faces became fields of discursive units. A high-water mark of facial discursivity occurred in the printing scene in sixteenth-century Venice, according to Bronwen Wilson, in which the pernicious profiling of the character of the Turk that played out in

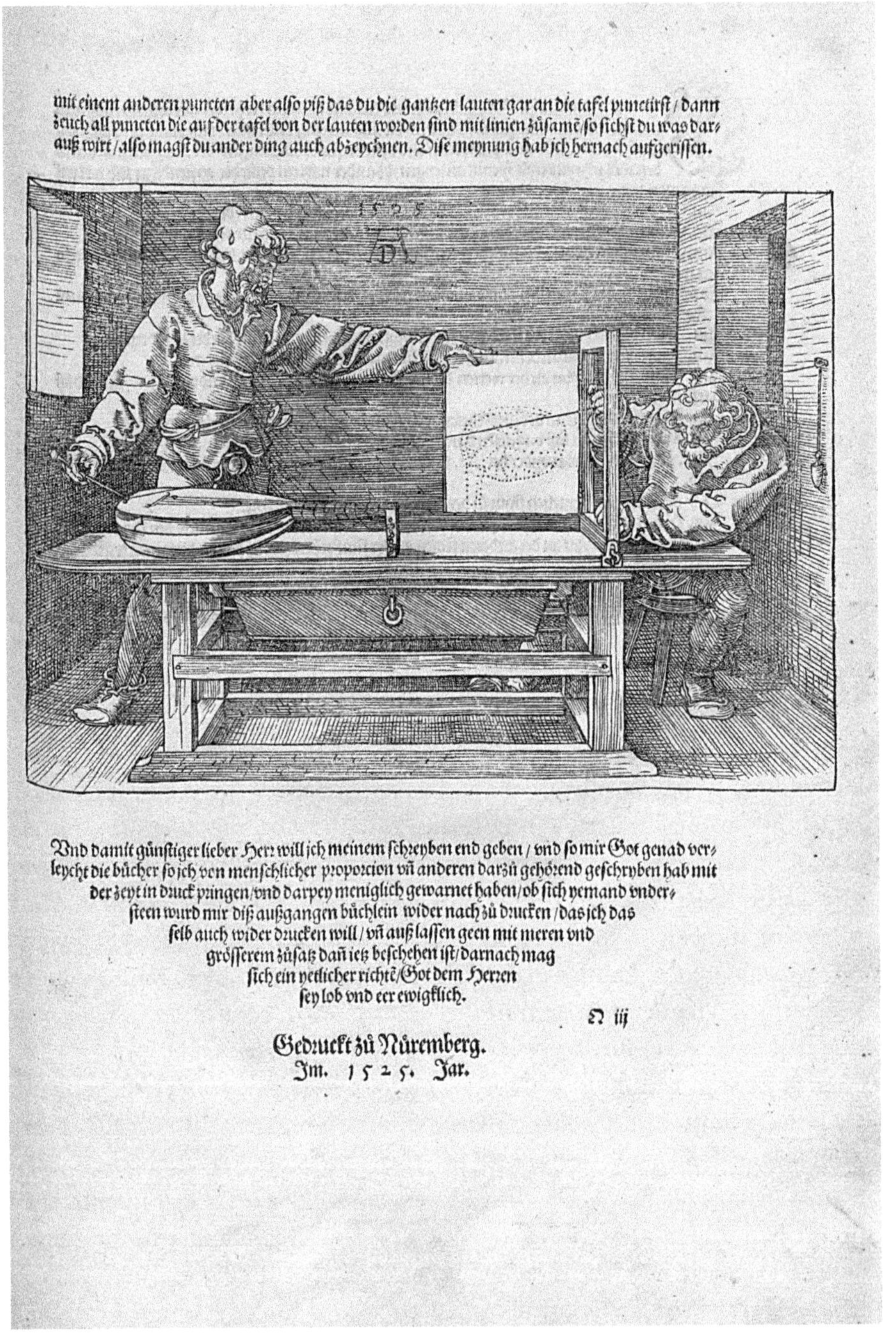

mit einem anderen puncten aber also piß das du die gantzen lauten gar an die tafel punctirst / dann zeuch all puncten die auf der tafel von der lauten worden sind mit linien zůsamē / so sichst du was darauß wirt / also magst du ander ding auch abzeychnen. Dise meynung hab jch hernach aufgerissen.

Vnd damit günstiger lieber Herr will jch meinem schreyben end geben / vnd so mir Got genad verleycht die bücher so jch von menschlicher proporcion vñ anderen darzů gehörend geschryben hab mit der zeyt in druck pringen / vnd darpey meniglich gewarnet haben / ob sich yemand vndersteen wurd mir diß außgangen büchlein wider nach zů drucken / das jch das selb auch wider drucken will / vñ auß lassen geen mit meren vnd grösserem zůsatz dañ ietz beschehen ist / darnach mag sich ein yetlicher richtē / Got dem Herren sey lob vnd eer ewigklich.

N iij

Gedruckt zů Nůremberg.
Im. 1525. Jar.

5.14. Albrecht Dürer, *Underweysung der Messung* (Nuremberg: Hieronymus Andreae Formschneider, 1525), 91r. *Source:* National Gallery of Art, Washington, DC.

costume and portrait books came to roost in the syntax of the face.[60] Nicolò Nelli's engraving incorporates these discrete data points into a single profile – which had to be scrupulously plotted in order to be successfully interpreted in two registers. Physiognomic pamphlets (such as those explored in Chapter 3) likewise

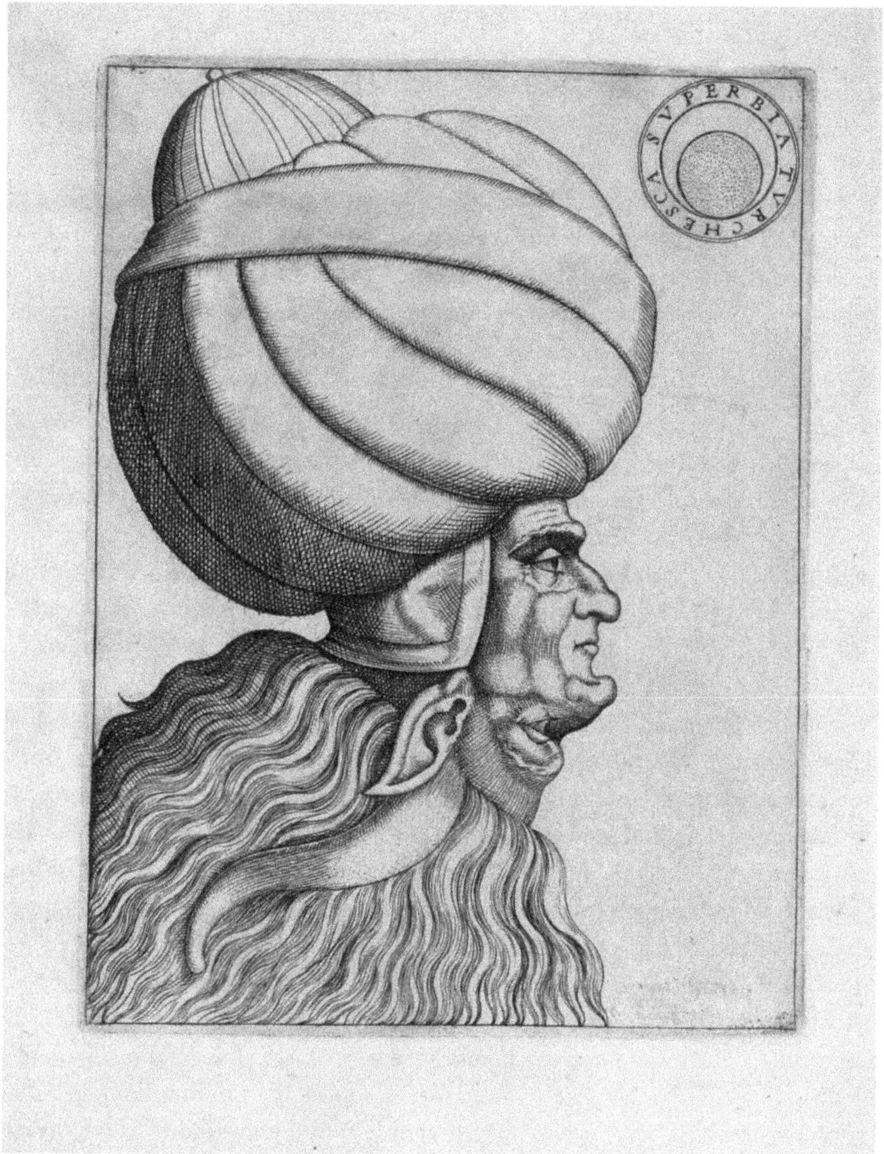

5.15. Nicolò Nelli, *Turkish Pride*, engraving, *c.* 1565. *Source:* A25.3 Geom. Courtesy of Herzog August Bibliothek.

parsed the grammar of the face, breaking it down into atomized data points – and even cautioned astute observers to preserve the independence of one feature from another and to weigh these separately.

INVITATION TO VISUAL SCRUTINY

Holbein's composition, like Nelli's, doubles back on the viewer in order to problematize the act of viewing. After asking observers to closely examine the painting, he then proceeded to unsettle their ideas about perception. Holbein enticed the viewer to observe the mirror-like surfaces with a focus seemingly conditioned by instruments such as lenses. The faces reflected on the painting's surface are the types we observe when our own reflections are mirrored. The skull that reminded the viewer of the folly that lurked behind such transitory pursuits of scientific knowledge also warned against scrutiny, or the fetishized looking that this panel's mirror-like surface encouraged. Holbein's skull stares back at the viewer; it hails both us and the process of recognition. The image observes us observing it. The skull inhabits both representational and phenomenological space; as Lyle Massey notes, this is a constant of anamorphic images.[61]

Holbein's anamorphosis interrogates the space between representation and the embodied practice of vision. One aspect of the historical phenomenology of sight has been recently treated in the context of recognition. Recognition was a pedagogical strategy employed by reflections in polished surfaces in which the viewer's acknowledgment of self leads to knowledge; narrative and pictorial recognition can be tracked in the gradual shift from ignorance to knowledge.[62] The idea of reflections revealing the self follows a tradition of self-help guides that advertised themselves under the title of *Speculum*, or mirror. Many of these were manuals of spiritual exercises that showed paths to self-improvement, such as the *Ars Moriendi*, *Ars memorativa*, *Apocalypse*, and *Dance of Death*.[63] Related books provided itineraries to salvation; other *Specula* functioned as books of advice on how to rule, or helped to pave paths to revelation or self-knowledge.[64] These books emphasized that teaching and reflection could lead readers to a better picture of themselves. A vernacular, secular, and popular offshoot of such moralizing was the *Narrenschiff*, in which the author Sebastian Brant entreats: "with caution everyone should look to see if he's in this my book."[65] Mirrors began to show the path to self-knowledge, to how to recognize oneself in the puzzle, and, ultimately, in the mid-sixteenth century, to how to thematize that relationship visually. Holbein's skull is not just a touchstone to acknowledge mortality or complicity in futile pursuits; it is also a self-aware instrument of epistemic inquiry. Part of the strategy of showing this in the mirror-like surface created by oil paint on oak panel was that painting could literally reflect the result of self-knowledge in a way that was impossible in print.[66]

THE DARKER SIDE OF VISUAL KNOWING

Holbein's anamorphic skull problematized the authority of the eye by activating the awareness of divisions within the viewing subject. Insofar as optical theory was a subject for interrogation, we see the ambition of anamorphosis to both embrace and disrupt the visual fictions negotiated by contemporary metapictures.[67] Holbein's use of anamorphosis compels the viewing subject to introspection, among the contemplations his panel destabilized was the authority of the idea of portraiture itself. The separation of the viewer from the subject, or the divided subject that Lyle Massey posits at the heart of anamorphic theoretical strategies, coerces viewers to see themselves as the object of the joke when they perceive themselves as the viewing subject.[68] Thus, the viewer becomes a critical part of the triangulation of the picture. Viewers both see the portraits depicted differently and are also encouraged to reflect on their own sense of self and the capacity of the self to be depicted at all.

A notable agent of self-reflection invoked by Holbein's props was St. Jerome. By reviving the epistemological furnishings of St. Jerome's studio, such as the curtain, the crucifix, and the cosmographic tools, Holbein also conjures the skull that mediated Jerome's own introspection. With it, Holbein queries the very nature of the self.[69] Holbein's grandiloquent anamorphic skull, the double of Jerome's *memento mori*, likewise asks us to contemplate other boundaries. One of these was the liminal space of the picture plane, whose very purpose is to vet the idea of selfhood.

Here, the skull instigates the introspection. Part of the epistemic functionality of anamorphosis resides in the subject's ability to halt the attention of the viewer before an epiphany. Hans Holbein's distorted skull subverted the values more clearly resolved in the portraits and in the scientific instrumentation that are the painting's actual subject. The time-honored instrument of self-reflection in the saint's narratives, the skull, had a counterpart in the other agent who popularly arrested man's attention before a revelation: the fool. This agent was also linked to cartographic knowledge in early modernity because reports of newly discovered territories brought readers to the brink of stark reflections on the European self.

Meditations on shifts subtended by new geographic, facial, and moral knowledge come to a skeletal head in Holbein's *Ambassadors*. Contemporary literary texts also shaped both geographic and theoretical new worlds through a variety of genres and moralizing by way of perspectival shifts; frequently their writers also activated the cognitive pathways required to process those shifts. Cartographic knowledge in the early sixteenth century was both plotted on a coordinate plane and weighed on a moral scale. Travel accounts reporting new peoples and habits also stretched over new geographic coordinates. Some of the narratives describing customs in the Americas had the effect of distorting them, via authors whose aim was to hold a mirror up to the moral and social perspectives of the European reader. The moral relativism of customs in the Americas, to certain analysts, provided material ripe for anamorphic distortions. Sir Thomas More, Jean de Léry, Shakespeare, and Michel de Montaigne all used data collected in the Americas to propose correctives to Europe, and then presented this new data by way of innovative perspectival adjustments. Such literary inversions accompanied contemporary shifts in cartographic perspective.

Holbein's skull was the twin of another character frequently conjured by publications of the period to make interventions of behalf of the reader. The fool, as a sentient counterpart of the skull, guided the reader through both content and method. The fool's agency was celebrated in the sophisticated pun Erasmus provided in the Latin title of *Praise of Folly*, or *Encomium Moriae* (1511), referring to his friend Thomas More, who would contribute his own critique of folly in his *Utopia* (1516). On the surface, the content of More's text was indebted to maps made from circulating reports about the discoveries of new lands.[70] While More intended to take account of these in his text, *Utopia*'s more strident objective was to reveal Europe as a dystopia. More's moralizing hinged on seeing England's follies via the overhaul provided by information returning from the Americas. As such, More's moralizing in *Utopia* relied on perspectival inversions that we can call literary anamorphosis: his view of England was presented as it might have appeared seen through the wrong end of the telescope.

To subvert the information he acquired, More took geographic data gathered by other travelers and cosmographers, but he fed it to his readers through the report of Raphael Hythlodaeus, literally a dispenser of nonsense. More's overhaul was premised on a cartographic "over there," and was one that slanted the truth. Not surprisingly, More had composed the text in Antwerp, the site of a flurry of cartographic activity, where he would have been privy to both returning travel accounts and the visual presentations of travelers' findings in the shape of images and maps. The image from the first edition of *Utopia* kept to this cartographic tradition by featuring the island as a crescent-shaped landmass (Figure 5.16).[71]

Two years later, a woodcut from the Basel printing of 1518 replaced this image with one by Hans Holbein's brother, Ambrosius Holbein (1495–1519) (Figure 5.17). This modified print of the island was accompanied by a group of foreground viewers spying it from a distant perch. Holbein's image presented Utopia's geographic bearings as a landmass disposed in relation to a group of observers – namely, Hythlodaeus pointing it out to Thomas More and Peter Gillis. Holbein's image focused on the data's delivery by a group of firsthand observers sighting the island. It was other firsthand observers, such as Columbus and Vespucci, after all, who had disrupted the status quo of the Ptolemaic worldview in their shipboard sightings of never before reported lands.

The selection of Ambrosius Holbein's image probably fell to Erasmus, who oversaw the printing and layout of *Utopia*'s second edition, printed in Basel in 1518. Erasmus recognized the potential of liminal images that might have matched the inversions embedded in More's anamorphic text. Zeal for satire in his own texts was a preoccupation Erasmus shared with the humanist circle connected by Johannes Froben's press, a circle that included Thomas More and both Holbein brothers.[72] Hans Holbein produced many border designs that

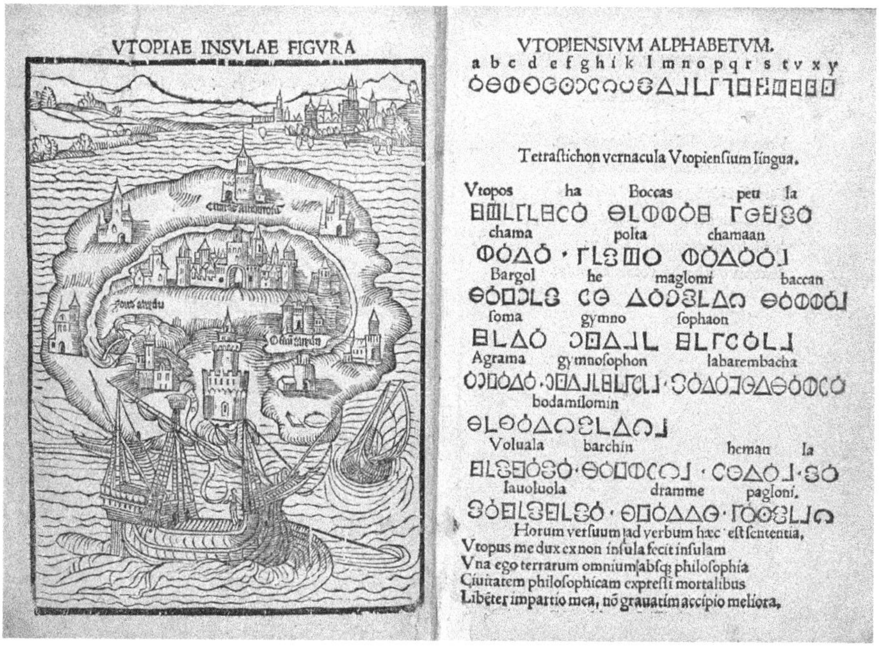

5.16. Map of Utopia, in Thomas More, *Libellus vere aureus nec Minvus Salvartis Quam Fesitiuus* (Louvain: Martens, 1516). *Source:* Courtesy of British Library. Image in the public domain.

deployed themes of inversions and the *verkehrte Welt*, or the world turned upside down, for books printed by the Froben shop.[73]

So it is not surprising that such a rhetorical strategy would dictate the bivalent image on Froben's edition of *Utopia*. Seen one way, Utopia took the shape of a map, but from another point of view, it also had the potential to double as a skull (Figure 5.18).[74] Holbein's shaping of the island's geography into a cranium and the harbor into a jawbone effectively forges a skull, according to a short brief by the British dentist Malcolm Bishop, whose professional association with this group of bones sharpened his own visual acuity.[75] When viewed obliquely, the island morphs into an anamorphic *memento mori* as the brightly lit hollows of the ship's hull transform themselves into teeth.[76] The aspect of the skull in this print is almost identical to a *memento mori* print produced in the Netherlands between 1500 and 1525, housed today in the British Museum.[77]

A significant squint is required to unlock the map as a skull, similar to the perspectival shift required to decode *Vexierbilder*. This distortion also mimics the oblique perspective on which the intellectual puzzle of the text of *Utopia* depends. Perhaps the reference to *vanitas* previews for the reader the inversions on which *Utopia*'s self-knowledge is predicated – it adumbrates that a journey is embedded here, that the viewer needs to probe deeper into the meaning. *Vanitas* would become popular content for visual anamorphosis. Does the skull portend, via a contemplation of death, an unmooring from the orientation of

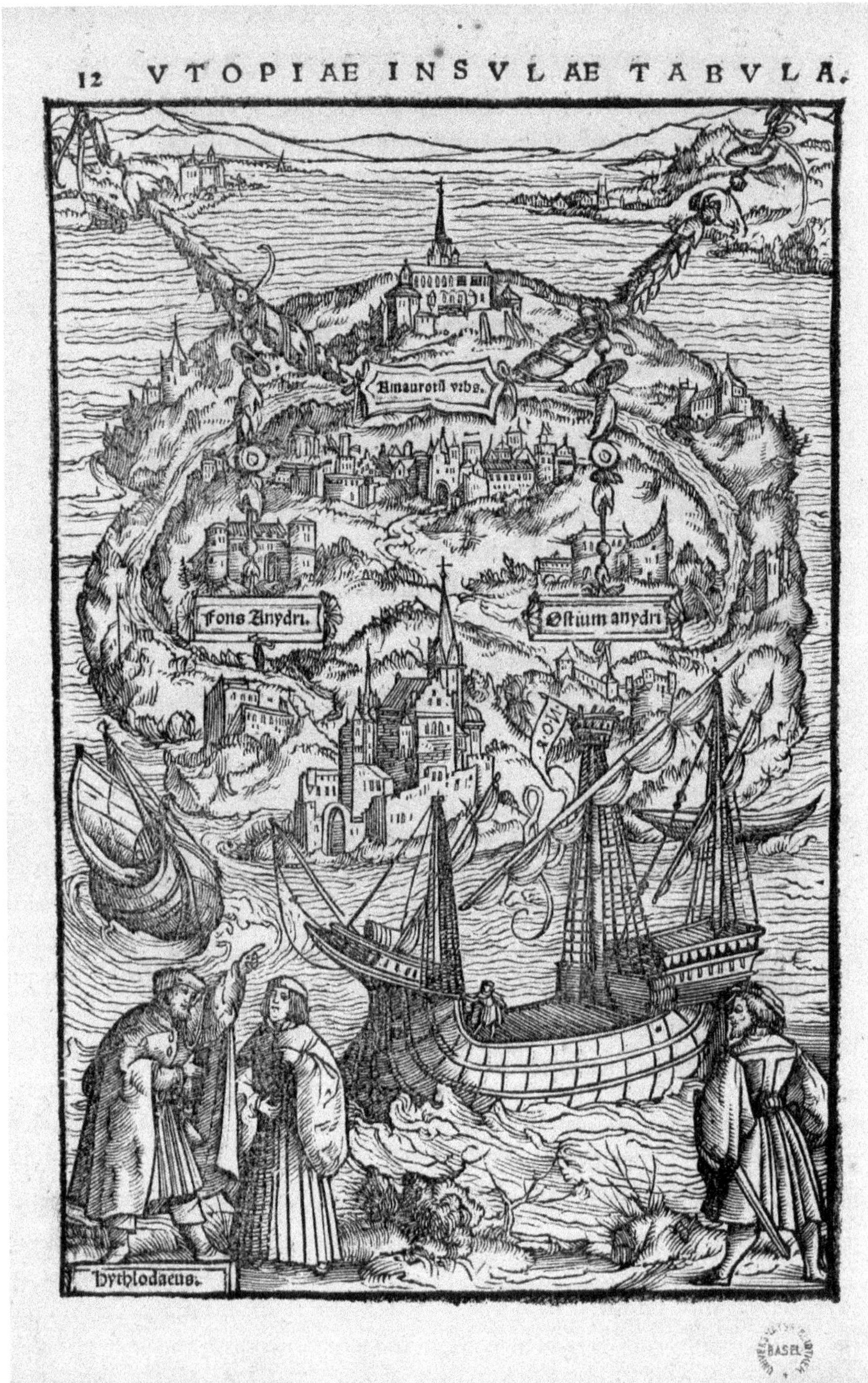

5.17. Ambrosius Holbein, *Utopiae insulae tabula*, for Thomas More, *De optimo reip. statu deque nova insula Utopia* (Basel: Froben, 1518). *Source:* UBH Rb80. Courtesy of Universitätsbibliothek Basel.

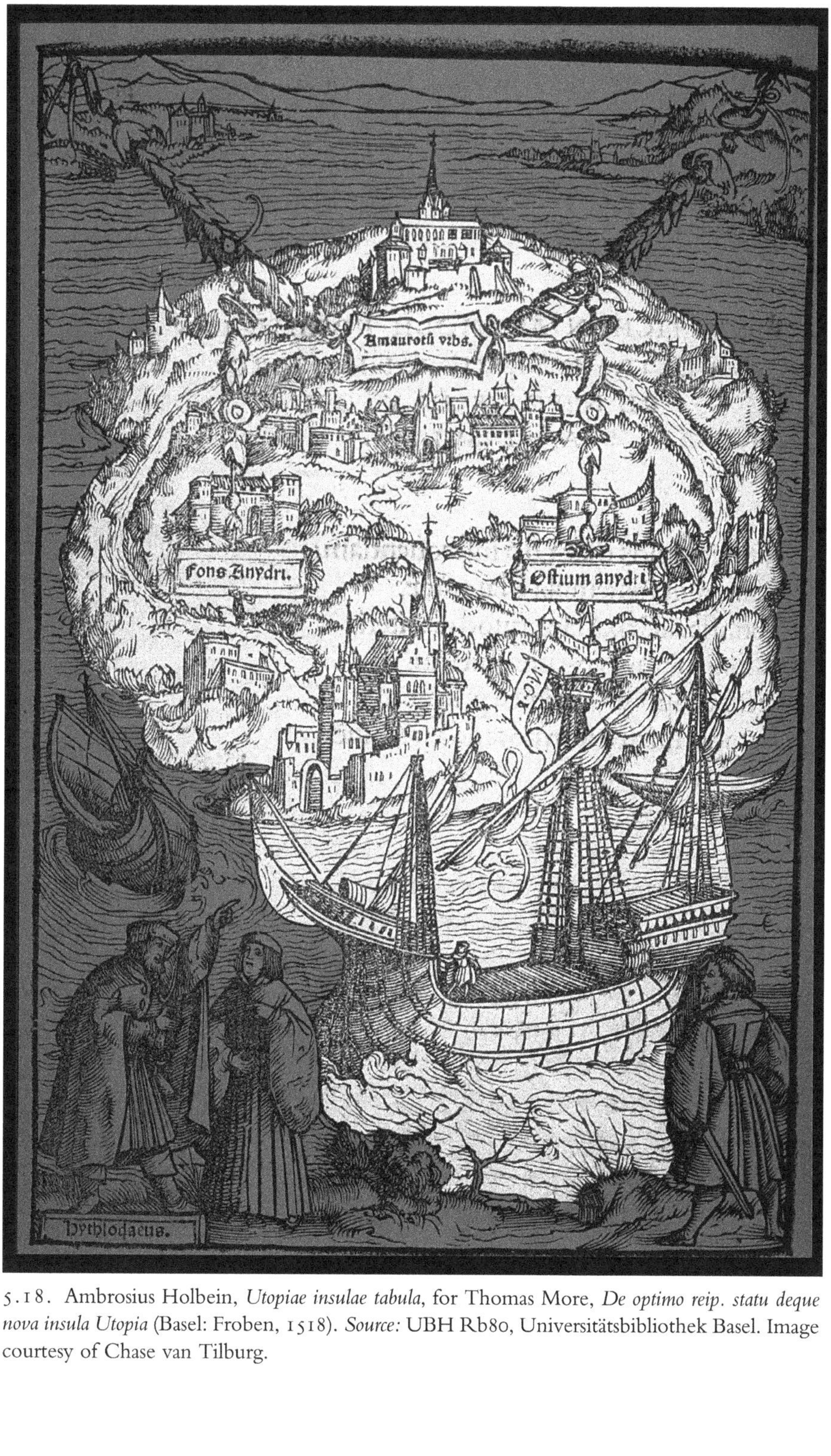

5.18. Ambrosius Holbein, *Utopiae insulae tabula*, for Thomas More, *De optimo reip. statu deque nova insula Utopia* (Basel: Froben, 1518). *Source:* UBH Rb80, Universitätsbibliothek Basel. Image courtesy of Chase van Tilburg.

the world as the reader knew it, a departure required to understand the impact of these new truths? Did it require the radical abandonment of "normal" vision, as Stephen Greenblatt characterizes the interpretive gesture required to read the more famous skull fashioned by Ambrosius's brother Hans in *The Ambassadors*?[78] If *Utopia*'s cartographic image could indeed double as a skull, what justifies it as a *memento mori* is its link to the epistemology of self-reflection. The theme of *vanitas* was well suited to anamorphic inversions as it matched the visual conceit about the gradual nature of recognition's arrival, as its point was to encounter wisdom through a protracted moral journey. We need only to think of St. Jerome's meditations on the skull that ultimately brought him wisdom. Jerome meditated on one worldly object to see through to an invisible truth; this "seeing through" is the original meaning of *perspicere*, a word at the etymological root of our term perspective. The skull itself can be considered a spiritual anamorphic device: a tool used as a gateway to another world.

When the skull was on holiday, worldly concerns might instead summon the iconography of the fool as a similar moral interlocutor for self-critique. The printed woodcut *Lunar Phase Instrument* of 1529 also presented the fool as a commentary on viewing practices – in this case, the observation of lunar phases.[79] In collaboration with the cosmographer Sebastian Münster, Hans Holbein designed this dial-shaped lunar instrument, which was originally accompanied by a booklet (Figure 5.19). This chart of lunar phases simultaneously advertises the minutiae of secular and sacred data that can be derived from tracking lunar phases, even as the character of the fool raises the specter of the futility of doing so. While Atlas bears the burden of carrying the earth on the right side of the composition, the fool spins the moon as an ever-metamorphizing plaything.[80] A warning similar to that delivered by *The Ambassadors*' skull is also at play here: too much attention to earthly and heavenly coordinates could be fool's work. The proscriptive nature of this reprimand, however, is outweighed by the prescriptive work of the wall chart itself. The fool aimlessly juggles the lunar phases without a calendar and, as we are to read it, finds himself surprised by each new phase. In order to avoid such capricious juggling of time, this sheet puts the owner of the almanac in charge of scheduling events cued to lunar observations. The instrument itself was intended to impose predictability on the calendar scheduled by the lunar cycle; such a chart provides the crib sheet for marking the data points correctly. With this knowledge, it is possible to plan events such as blood lettings, planting, and harvests, and making predictions about fortunes; these events are all pictured in a later iteration of a similar wall chart.[81] Holbein and Münster seem to imply that only way to avoid the path of the fool is to control knowledge about the heavens. The fool's simultaneous embodiment of help and hinderance exposed a dual nature that became the site of a feedback loop between subject and viewer, ultimately putting the onus on viewers to decide if they were aided by

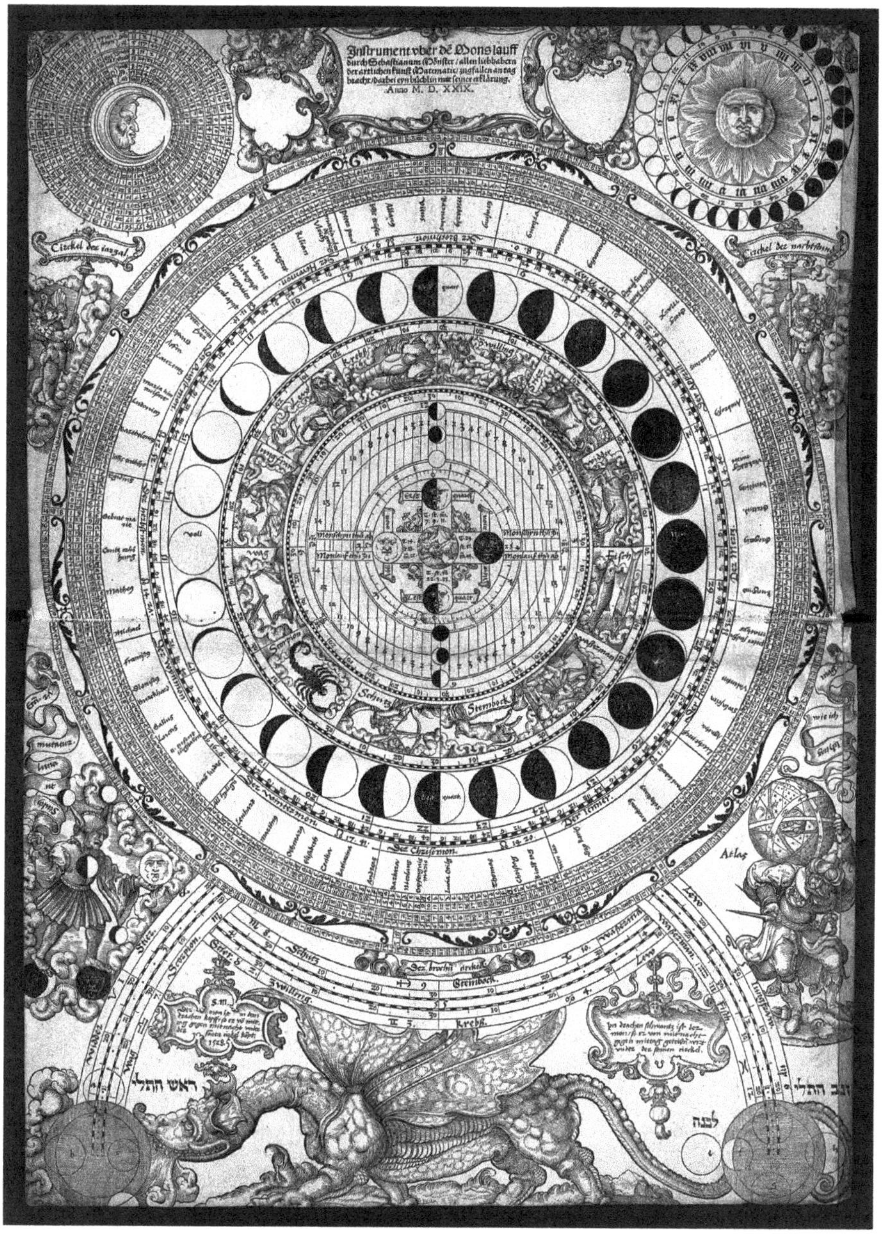

5.19. Hans Holbein and Sebastian Münster, *Instrument des Monslauf* (1529). *Source:* W 2 Math.336(1). Courtesy of Universitätsbibliothek der LMU, Munich.

the knowledge provided. Thus, the printed sheet provided assurances from within to convince viewers of its usefulness.

A similar feedback loop materialized in another instrument that warned against worldly pursuits. In a map/fool's cap combination, cartography's fruits were delivered doubled up with a simultaneous reminder of its futility (Plate XVI). The so-called *Fool's Cap Map of the World*, printed in Antwerp sometime after 1587, placed the end goal of both physiognomy and cosmography directly in the crosshairs, where the folly of these pursuits met the viewer head-on.[82] The engraving's projection of the earth is of a type derived from Martin Waldseemüller,[83] but one that was organized into a fool's head in a similar map made by the French mapmaker Jean de Gourmont in the 1570s.[84] The post-1587 dating proposed for the map follows the printing of Ortelius's third "Typus Orbis Terrarum," whose coordinates it follows.[85] Other contemporary maps demonstrated the capacity of the cartographic impulse to feature symbolic valences over precise geographic coordinates, such as the map of *Utopia* that the mapmaker and antiquarian Abraham Ortelius designed around 1596 in Antwerp.[86] This type of hermeneutic reflexivity, on the level of conception and also of picturing, has accorded a special place to maps in the staging of metapictures.[87] In the *Fool's Cap Map*, the Americas shift into bilateral symmetry with Europe and Africa; centered in the map, the continents give the appearance of sockets in a skull. If a common strain of utopian thinking connected these two cartographic productions (they both hail the viewer with grotesques and inscriptions), perhaps they were even inflected by the commemorative *memento mori* emblem of Ambrosius Holbein's *Utopia* map.

Both the *Fool's Cap Map* and the skull-shaped island of *Utopia* are virtuoso products of triangulated knowledge that the printmakers created from earlier models, but they present these only to shoot down the marvel of their technological production. This strategy should be familiar now from anamorphosis's epistemology; it embeds the critique of man's folly in the vanity of scientific pursuits, alluding here to cartography and geometry's complicity in designing the authoritative image. Also attempting to discredit the authority of the *Fool's Cap Map* is the weight of the literary tradition made manifest in Latin epigrams surrounding the fool in inscriptions and medallions.[88] Inscriptions from both biblical and classical sources critique worldly knowledge at the expense of empirical knowledge (or knowing oneself).[89] Such warnings that reflect contemplatively on mortality and the unknown hour of the second coming are also present in contemporary prints in the *memento mori* tradition, such as Mattheus Greuter's engraving of a head-on skull printed in Cologne *c.* 1588.[90] The similar rhetorical framing shows how both cartography and the skull that the map here simulates are fashioned from kindred anamorphic pursuits.

Both the skull in the fool's cap and the map address the viewer in a similar way: in the map, the continents float like eyes and the longitude markings atop the white of Antarctica's grin reprise the "teeth" of the ship's hull in Ambrosius Holbein's view of *Utopia*. Connecting this map with the *Utopia* skull not least is the idea of "terra incognita," enunciated on the fool's jaw. Such textual reflections on mortality and uncertainty threaten to discredit what seems to be a precise, painstaking, and up-to-date rendering of world cartography. Perhaps such doubt is less about the vanity of man's pursuits, the interpretation most often delivered in the secondary literature, but instead is commentary on the distortions that guided new cartographic picturing techniques.

Cosmography as a mode of knowing oscillated between two related approaches: astronomy and geography.[91] The geographic pursuits of the mathematician Oronce Fine attempted to knit together these discrete modes of projection in a scientific manual devoted to an instrument he calls the *quadrans universalis*, whose construction he explores in two closely related treatises published around 1527–32. This tool, which permitted timekeeping by day and by night, depended on a geometric presentation of the celestial circles with terrestrial circles and latitude lines superimposed upon them.[92] Fine's work with such tricky geometric map projections might have singled him out for comment in the *Fool's Cap Map*.[93] The figure of Ptolemy brokers a similar relationship between celestial and terrestrial coordinates, as he triangulates between them with a gesture that points simultaneously down and upward in a few important period maps.

Ptolemy presents these as competing "mental orientations," according to Jean-Marc Besse, on the title page for Mercator's *Tabulae Geographicae* (Cologne, 1578). Reprised in *Nouveau Theatre du Monde* (printed by Henricus Hondius in 1639 in Amsterdam), the image now appears along with a preface to the reader that characterizes cosmography's oscillation between heavenly and earthly viewpoints as one that is mediated by angular shifts of the eyes: "in cosmography, [the viewer] must alternately raise his eyes to the heavens and [then] shift them downward to contemplate the earth."[94] Anamorphosis requires precisely the same bifocal vision and geometric adjustments that underwrote cosmography. Tom Conley shows that toggling between the topographic local description and the astronomically determined description of the world was also the effect Apian cultivated with his deconstruction of the face's physiognomy (see Figure 5.10).[95] Both the local and universal are implied in Apian's analogy, which stands in as a metaphor for seeing. Cartographic projection itself required triangulation between stellar and earthly coordinates manifested in geometry – the same technical skills whose mastery the artist needed in order to create anamorphoses. The *Fool's Cap Map* vets that task, the description of geography through geometry, precisely where the face is found. The face seems to query if distortion was not a necessary component to any projection.

Under the hood of the fool's cap, the epistemic modes of portraiture and cosmography, as they were outlined by Apian, meet again. Did the fool's cap mapmaker engage with the Ptolemaic precepts of explaining geography via the portraitist's presentation of the face? In swapping out the face for cosmography, does the image critique the vanity of projection and anamorphosis on which both the art of physiognomy and cosmography depended? Thomas More has already projected society's failings against the pristine backdrop of a largely imagined New World. But now, a generation later, the epistemology of world creation itself has been brought to account. The fool's cap suggests that even this detailed cartographic projection embeds a significant critical blind spot – and quite possibly shows us that our image of the world is largely in our own heads.

The fool's props provided the viewer with reflections that revealed self-knowledge; typically, that came by shedding light on human character, insofar as it could be distinguished from its outward manifestations. But the marotte of the *Fool's Cap Map* resists our gaze (see Plate XVI). We see no reflection; instead, we are cautioned about the pursuit of empirical and perhaps also optical knowledge: "Vanity of vanities, all is vanity" (Ecclesiastes 1.2). The fool's marotte usually provided the locus for the encounter with self and self-knowledge, but here we don't come away the wiser. If we consult the fool's face for advice, we are equally confounded. Does the head's resistance to our gaze mirror that of the skull whose message about vanity reminds us of what we will become? The skull's power, according to Mitchell Merback, was not in its representational legibility, but precisely in its illegibility. The promise of clarity about the future in the way that crystal balls resolve ambiguity is what makes the skull, for Merback, an "instrument par excellence of penitential optics" – it gestures to truths beyond itself.[96] To this I would add that the skull shows human metamorphosis, but also mimesis. Skulls scare viewers on precisely these two ontological levels. Through mimesis, skulls force the viewer to reflect on mortality's metamorphic effects on the body. This decay of the body is different and absent from the heuristic established by portraiture, which halts temporality and freezes time. From the introspective St. Jerome of the early sixteenth century to the outward-facing St. Jerome of Joos van Cleve of the 1520s, the skull was a devotional instrument that would mediate reflections on revelation and mortality. In both the cranium of Holbein's *Ambassadors* and the empty sockets of the *Fool's Cap Map* face, skulls resolve into the *loci* of a sight-based recognition process. The skull is perhaps the anamorphic device par excellence in the way it accompanies the viewer's journey to enlightenment: the viewer's comprehension dawns just as the image comes into sharp focus.

The Antwerp map confronts the viewer with a projection that invites precisely the visual scrutiny that the fool's mirror cautions against. Inundated with cartographic images, audiences in Antwerp were no doubt beginning to associate maps of the world with empirical authority, but which view was authoritative? Perhaps the *Fool's Cap Map* ponders the confusion produced by a local embarrassment of cartographic riches. As the cap and bells close in on the projection, forgetful viewers are reminded again that they are confronting the face of the fool. This double image of map and fool reorders the view through the rationalizing force of geometry.[97] Geometry is the shared technique on which both anamorphosis and cartography depended. The technical virtuosity that produced the skull of Holbein's *The Ambassadors* and the map wedged into the fool's cap have guided readings of the images as metapictures. The artists both created and then threatened to annul the meaning of their own stunts, pointing out the overall futility and vanity of the pursuits of knowledge embedded in their compositions. In such recursive loops, these metapictures would seem to cancel themselves out. But the heuristic leap the viewer must make to unlock them is precisely *not* that knowledge is meaningless. The viewer is instead asked to weigh the ontology of what appears here on the plane of another visual reality, that of representation. The map in the fool's cap representation is quite literally a *Weltanschauung* – a merging of the concept of the world with the act of viewing it.[98] The representation cancels out the fool and puts the viewing subject in his place. After all, the fool hasn't made the map appear; the viewer has. At its root, this conjuring of the world is a calamity of the viewer's own creation. It was a fool's errand to put all of the data into a meaningful framework.[99] Recognition of this reality was also the epistemological thrust of the skull of *The Ambassadors*. Assuming both representational and phenomenological space, anamorphic images inhabit a threshold between directing the process of observation and representation itself.[100] Insofar as they draw our attention to this dichotomy, the skulls found in *Utopia*, *The Ambassadors*, and the *Fool's Cap Map* are all metapictures whose visual complexity threatens to cancel out the pictured. They borrow from the conceit of anamorphosis: they use representation to comment on concerns about the embodied practice of vision that are more phenomenological in nature.

Confronting the viewer beneath the fool's cap is a prospect of the world that could never meet the observer's eye – a notional diagram that is the project of geography.[101] How to create models of the world that superseded what a viewer could see or absorb sensorily was the lesson that cosmography taught. Maps would precipitate from this pedagogy. Is it more than a coincidence that the pragmatic result of cosmographic learning, cartography, resolves in the fool's face – another entity under review by contemporary physiognomies?[102] This image placed both cosmography and physiognomy in the crosshairs of scrutiny – perhaps because they were among the most persistent genres that promised self-knowledge, and thus they lent themselves to anamorphic critique. But the dissonance caused by these competing knowledge domains, the "itchiness" of the fool's cap, alerts the viewer to the different order of picturing that distinguishes the fool from the map. The map does not inhabit the realm of verisimilitude; instead, it is a self-conscious representation achieved by geometric angling.[103] Knowledge of the world was pre-digested by the mediation of mapping: cartography was its own form of anamorphosis achieved by careful observation of the cosmos.

Equipped with growing visual skills honed by encounters with physiognomic, cosmographic, and anamorphic images, viewers increasingly found their own visual acuity unpacked in the punchline of sixteenth-century polemic. By foregrounding the spatial conflict produced by perspective, anamorphic images thematized the visual and cognitive attention embraced by physiognomy and cosmography. In this particular journey through anamorphic portraiture, we detect an epistemology that elbowed sensational subject matter out of the way in order to investigate its own methodology. Instead of the scatological and prurient subjects of Schön's early printed anamorphoses, the viewers' payload for their visual labors in deciphering puzzle pictures would become noses and faces. These features were further distorted into facial extremes of long-nosed fools or hollowed-out skulls. As the fool's long nose was sacrificed for what the viewer could see beyond it, moralization and self-critique materialized in the shape of a skull. Uneasy pictures and vexed viewers braced themselves for an extended staring match. With visual attention and insight replacing and now filling the shoes of the traditional subjects of parody, such interactive images pushed the envelope of optical exercises that prints could handle.

NOTES

1 For the phenomenon of something proximate, akin to holding in the hand, see Korner's notion of "*handlichkeit*" and "*zuhandenheit.*" Hans Korner, *Der früheste deutsche Einblattholzschnitt* (Munich: Mäander Kunstverlag, 1979), 81–3.

2 Patricia A. Emison, "Prolegomenon to the Study of Italian Renaissance Prints," *Word & Image* 11, no. 1 (1995), 1–15.

3 Jennifer Nelson, "Directed Leering: Social Perspective in Erhard Schön's Anamorphic Woodcuts," *Source: Notes in the History of Art* 34, no. 4 (2015), 20.

4 Lyle Massey, *Picturing Space, Displacing Bodies: Anamorphosis in Early Modern Theories of Perspective* (University Park: Pennsylvania State University Press, 2007), 69. The separation of the viewer from the subject that Massey posits at the heart of anamorphic theoretical strategies permits viewers to see themselves as the object of this joke because they can perceive themselves implicated as the self-aware viewing subjects. This reaffirms the viewer as a divided subject. I interpret this to mean that they can see themselves seeing, versus impersonating an embodied viewer.

5 Nelson, "Directed Leering," 17–22.

6 The Augsburg stonecutter and sculptor Hans Schwarz issued twenty-five medals that year, including medals of members of the patriciate and merchant community, as well as court fixtures. See Werner Hofmann, *Köpfe der Lutherzeit: Hamburger Kunsthalle, 4. März bis 24. April 1983* (Munich: Prestel, 1983), 254; Hanna Gagel, ed., *Der Mensch um 1500: Werke aus Kirchen und Kunstkammern* (Berlin: Staatliche Museen Preussischer Kulturbesitz, 1977), 101–2; see also Stephen K. Scher, *The Currency of Fame: Portrait Medals in the Renaissance* (New York: Abrams, 1994), 215ff., cat. 84. Schwarz's medals include: *Medal of Jakob Fugger*, bronze, 1518 (Kunsthistorisches Museum, Vienna); *Medal of Konrad Peutinger*, bronze (Skulpturengalerie, Münzkabinett, Staatliche Museen zu Berlin); a medal of the court jester Kunz von der Rosen (1518); *Medal of Albrecht Dürer, c.* 1520?; and a pearwood model (Herzog Anton-Ulrich Museum, Braunschweig/Kunsthistorisches Museum, Münzkabinett, Vienna) and *Medal of Hans Burgkmair*, bronze, 1518 (Staatliche Münzsammlung, Munich).

7 Jeffrey Chipps Smith, "A Creative Moment: Thoughts on the Genesis of the German Portrait Medal," in Stephen Scher, ed., *Perspectives on the Renaissance Medal* (New York:

Garland Press, 2000), 177–99. These medallion effigies were designed to be held in the hand and experienced as reliefs; they had tactile qualities, as well as visual ones. They appeared before many humanists collected coins or medals and before many had portrait likenesses of themselves. Smith suggests that Peutinger's itinerary in Padua and Bologna might have instigated much of the interest, especially in the creation of the Kaiserbuch portraits, seventeen of which were used for commentary of Suetonius's *Twelve Caesars* (Paris, 1512).

8 See www.metmuseum.org/art/collection/search/392906.

9 Also by Hans Daucher and Joachim Forster. See Gagel, ed., *Der Mensch um 1500*, 70.

10 Of the so-called presentation medals, or *Schaumünzen*, over 250 of Charles V are known. Gagel, ed., *Der Mensch um 1500*, 70.

11 Gagel, ed., *Der Mensch um 1500*, 68–70. These were precisely the kinds of art that Galileo disliked: *pietre dure*, intarsia, and the painted works of the Arcimboldisti. See Eileen Reeves, *Painting the Heavens: Art and Science in the Age of Galileo* (Princeton, NJ: Princeton University Press, 1999), 18.

12 Kunsthistorisches Museum Vienna, Kunstkammer, inv. no. KK3858, in the style of Hans Kels d.Ä. von Kaufbeueren. See also Hans Kels der Ältere von Kaufbeueren, "Brettspiel für den 'Langen Puff'," www.khm.at/objektdb/detail/89425/. This backgammon board for Ferdinand I was a collaboration between Hans Kels and Jörg Breu, produced *c.* 1537 in Kaufbeuern near Augsburg: www.chess-museum.com/rudolf-ii-and-the-history-of-games-by-barbara-hollaumlnder.html/. See references in the exhibition catalogues Wilfried Seipel and Hans Holländer, eds., *Spielwelten der Kunst – Kunstkammerspiele* (Vienna: Kunsthistorisches Museum, 1998), 201–7; Sabine Haag et al., eds., *Die Kunstkammer: die Schätze der Habsburger* (Vienna: Brandstätter Verlag, 2012), 119–21.

13 Thomas Eser, *Schiefe Bilder – die Zimmernsche Anamorphose und andere Augenspiele aus den Sammlungen des Germanischen Nationalmuseums* (Nuremberg: Verlag des Germanischen Nationalmuseums, 1998), 98.

14 Stephanie Leitch, "Visual Acuity and the Physiognomer's Art of Observation," *Oxford Art Journal* 38, no. 2 (2015), 189–208.

15 Physiognomic literature included in a compendium of how-to literature searchable under Hans von Gersdorff, *Feldtbuch der Wund-Artzney Sampt Vilen Jnstrumenten der Chirurgey vß dem Albucasi Contrafayt. Chiromantia Jo. Jndagine. das Ist, die Kunst der Handtbesehung. Natürliche Astrologey ... Physiognomey ... Complexion Buch ... Canones, Oder Regelen eins Yeden Kranckheyt Warlich zu Erkündigen ...* (Strasbourg: Schott, 1540), front matter. I am very grateful to Daniel Kaune for assistance in parsing the distinctions between "*Augenschein*" and "*Anblick*."

16 With its Latin root in *experientia*, and given its association with the genre *practica*, the word *experienctz* here recalls the practice of artisans.

17 For Leonardo's understanding of the physiology of vision as a two-staged process of perception, see the *Paragone*. For Leonardo, the eye is not just an agent of perception, but a sensory organ capable of knowledge and judgment. See Lorenzo Pericolo, "Knowing through the Eye: Leonardo da Vinci's *Imprensiva* and Alhazen's *Intuitio*," *Römisches Jahrbuch der Bibliotheca Hertziana* 44 (2019–20), 237–8.

18 In a posthumous printing of his sermon in 1517, the Strasbourg reformer and Franciscan preacher Johann Geiler von Kaisersberg implored audiences to observe themselves in order to know themselves: "[focus] on your own complexion ... to take utmost care to decipher the signs of one's own nature on one's own body." Valentin Groebner, "Complexio/Complexion: Categorizing Individual Natures, 1250–1600," in Lorraine Daston and Fernando Vidal, *The Moral Authority of Nature* (Chicago: University of Chicago Press, 2010), 373.

19 Pen and ink, heightened in gray on gray paper, 25.0 cm × 60.6 cm, Kupferstichkabinett, Hamburg Kunsthalle.

20 Werner Hofmann, *Köpfe der Lutherzeit* (Munich: Prestel, 1983), 206; see also Wolf Stubbe, "Unbekannte Zeichnungen altdeutscher Meister," in Wolf Stubbe et al., eds., *Museum und*

Kunst: Beiträge für Alfred Hentzen (Hamburg: Christians, 1970), 254, also see figure 115. Hofmann notes that Stubbe misidentifies Friedrich III as Kaiser and Maximilian as König. On the website for the Hamburg Kunsthalle, Peter Prange argues for its similarity to a double portrait of Charles V and Ferdinand I produced at the 1531 Augsburg Diet by Master CB (Christoph Bockstorffer?). Cf. https://online-sammlung.hamburger-kunsthalle.de/de/objekt/1975-44. The drawing seems to be related to the etching style of CB, as well as that of the Augsburg Hopfer family of etchers. Prange speculates that this study may have served as a preparatory sketch for an anamorphic print.

21 This pictorial conceit of the French idiom *vis-à-vis* would later refer in English to a carriage in which two passengers sit opposite each other. Perhaps the carriage was named for the point of view of an exterior observer.

22 Alison G. Stewart, *Before Bruegel: Sebald Beham and the Origins of Peasant Festival Imaginery* (Hampshire: Ashgate, 2008), 168–9. Already popular items on the physiognomer's checklist, the shapes of noses were also parodied in satirical literature where they were the protagonists of the so-called nose dances, as we see in Sebald Beham's *Nose Dance* of 1534. The nose dance celebrated distorted shapes and sizes of noses, and some fake noses were even tried on for size. Prizes were distributed accordingly: The nose with the most glorious profile took the garland; the second-place finisher won a nose mask; the third-place winner received a pair of underpants. How could a panel of judges rank such features had they not been alert to facial comparisons, perhaps prompted by physiognomic texts?

23 Mitchell Merback explored a similar revelatory profile belonging to a Jew who looks back at himself in horror through a reflective piece of armor in a south German altar panel of the Crucifixion. See Mitchell B. Merback, "Recognitions: Theme and Metatheme in Hans Burgkmair the Elder's Santa Croce in Gerusalemme of 1504," *Art Bulletin* 96, no. 3 (2014), 300. Merback also traces the fool's trajectory through works by Holbein. Erasmus's praise of folly drawing shows a fool examining himself in the bauble as if in a mirror. See also Elisabeth Drago Berry, "Surface and Substance: Physiognomy and Hans Holbein's Pictures of Death," *Montage* 6 (2012), 1–12.

24 "*Geographia non est pictura (e) sed picture imitation seu inchoation.*"

25 I'm grateful to Barbara Tramelli for help with the translation.

26 Jean-Marc Besse, "Mapping, Constructing, Inventing: On the Notion of Project and Its Epistemology," (n.d.), 7. Article first published in *Le Gout du monde: Exercises de paysage* (Arles: Actes Sud/ENSP, 2009).

27 For a succinct discussion of images that demanded from new audiences that they be seen as representation, see Todd Olson, "Markers: Le Moyne de Morgues in Sixteenth-Century Florida," in Dana Leibsohn and Jeanette Favrot Peterson, eds., *Seeing across Cultures in the Early Modern World* (Burlington, VT: Ashgate, 2012), 195–9.

28 Many maps marked unknown territories as "*extra Ptolemeum*," or the world unknown to Ptolemy.

29 Peter Apian, *Cosmographicus Liber* (Landshut: Weyssenburger, 1524), fol. 60.

30 See Jean-Marc Besse, "Cosmography and Geography in the Sixteenth Century: The Position of Oronce Fine between Mathematics and History," in Alexander Marr, ed., *The Worlds of Oronce Fine: Mathematics, Instruments and Print in Renaissance France* (Donington: Shaun Tyas, 2009), 100ff. For a discussion of the relationship between cartography and perspective, see Samuel Y. Edgerton, *The Renaissance Rediscovery of Linear Perspective* (New York: Basic Books, 1975), 91–123.

31 John David North, *The Ambassadors' Secret: Holbein and the World of the Renaissance* (London: Phoenix, 2004).

32 The globe hints at America with the toponym *Brasilici*. The other printed texts here include a mathematical text and a hymnal of Luther's choral compositions (Wittenberg, 1524).

33 Suzanne Kathleen Karr Schmidt and Edward H. Wouk, *Prints in Translation, 1450–1750: Image, Materiality, Space* (Abingdon: Routledge, 2017), 274–6. This belonged to Anna of Bohemia and Hungary (1503–47), wife of Emperor Ferdinand I (1503–64).

34 Jennifer Nelson, *Disharmony of the Spheres: The Europe of Holbein's Ambassadors* (University Park: Pennsylvania State University, 2019), 16–17.

35 Jim Bennett, "Practical Geometry and Operative Knowledge," *Configurations: A Journal of Literature, Science and Technology* 6 (1998), 195–222.

36 See Alexandra Challenger, *Printing the Cosmos: Images, Readers, and Mathematics in Peter Apian's Instrumental Texts*, PhD dissertation, Florida State University, 2022, see especially chapter 2: "Learning by Doing: the *Instrument Buch* and Mathematical Practice." See also Noam Andrews, *The Polyhedrists: Art and Geometry in the Long Sixteenth Century* (Cambridge, MA: MIT Press, 2022).

37 Elly Dekker and Rudolf Schmidt, "The Globes in Holbein's Painting *The Ambassadors*," in *Der Globusfreund: Bericht Über das IX. Symposium der Internationalen Coronelli-Gesellschaft, Berlin, 3.–7. Oktober 1998* (Vienna: Internationale Coronelli-Gesellschaft für Globen- und Instrumentenkunde, 1999), 19–52, especially 20–1, 24. On the Schöner globe, see Chet Van Duzer, "Johann Schöner's Globe of 1515: Transcription and Study," *Transactions of the American Philosophical Society* 100, no. 5 (2010), 1–217.

38 See Samuel Gessner, "The Perspective of the Instrument Maker: The Planispheric Projection with Gemma Frisius and the Arsenius Workshop at Louvain," in Sven Dupré, ed., *Perspective as Practice: Renaissance Cultures of Optics* (Turnhout: Brepols, 2019), 105.

39 Dekker and Schmidt, "The Globes in Holbein's Painting," 31–5. Elly Dekker and Rudolf Schmidt have connected the representation shown here to a copy of a globe that Maximilianus Transylvanus, Charles V's private secretary at Valladolid, had sent to a Spaniard of note. Evidence for the "Transylvanus" globe, Dekker points out, is provided by Gemma Frisius's dedication in 1537 to Transylvanus on his own terrestrial globe that reflects America and Asia separated by an ocean (p. 35).

40 Sebastian Münster, *Organum Uranicum: Habes in hoc Libro Amice Lector, Explicatas Theoricas Omnium planetaru[m], atq[ue] eorunde[m] varios, singulos & quotidianos ad annos usq[ue] & ultra expressos motus, Lunæ quoq[ue] in lumine crescentis, senesce[n]tis & per eclipsim deficientis, & item Solis deliquiu[m] patientis, omne[s] varietate[s] quibus omnibus comodi adiecti sunt canones* (Basel: Petri, 1536).

41 Apian's horoscope for Charles V, the *Astronomicum Caesarum* (Ingolstadt: Apian, 1540), also featured the torquetum as well as an explanation of the path of the comet of 1532. See Sonja Draxler and Max E. Lippitsch, "Peter Apian and His Astronomicum Caesareum," in *Proceedings of the 2nd European History of Physics (EHoP) Conference* (Pöllauberg: Living Edition, 2012), 31–46.

42 This room's resonance with St. Jerome's study is evoked by the profusion of instrumentation, which we also see in Ghirlandaio's frescoes of Jerome and Botticelli's of St. Augustine in the Vespucci chapel in the Chiesa di San Salvatore in Ognissanti, Florence.

43 Massey, *Picturing Space, Displacing Bodies*, 56.

44 For a handy summary of speculation about Holbein's techniques in the secondary literature, see Nelson, *Disharmony of the Spheres*, 4–71.

45 Massey, *Picturing Space, Displacing Bodies*, 37–69. Such treatises discussed the fundamentals of geometric projection and were contributions to practical geometry similar to techniques employed by instrument makers to achieve planispheric projections. See Gessner, "Perspective of the Instrument Maker," in Dupré, *Perspective as Practice*, 109.

46 Massey, *Picturing Space, Displacing Bodies*, 63.

47 Dupré, ed., *Perspective as Practice*, 103.

48 Evelin Wetter, Frits Scholten, and Jeffrey Chipps Smith, *Prayer-Nuts, Private Devotion and Early Modern Art Collecting* (Riggisberg: Abegg-Stiftung, 2017), 141. Jeffrey Smith says that Paoletti considered Dürer equal parts astronomer and geometer.

49 Michael Gaudio, *Engraving the Savage: The New World and Techniques of Civilization* (Minneapolis: University of Minnesota Press, 2008), 33–43. See Gaudio's discussion of De Bry's 1597 self-portrait with a skull and dividers in the context of artists' productions from Dürer's *Melencholia* (1515) to Ripa's *Iconologia* (1618).

50 Nelson, *Disharmony of the Spheres*, 112. See Peter Apian, *Eyn newe unnd wolgegründte underweysung aller Kauffmanß Rechnung in dreyen Büchern, mit schönen Regeln und fragstucken begriffen. Sunderlich was fortl unnd behendigkait in der Welschen Practica unnd Tolletn gebraucht wirdt, des gleychen fürmalß wider in Teützscher noch in Welscher sprach nie gedrückt* (Ingolstadt: Georg Apian, 1527). Nelson believes that this is either the 1527 edition printed by Georg Apian or the 1532 Frankfurt edition.

51 Erasmus's complaints about Dürer's rendering of him in the 1526 engraving were deeply informed by Holbein's skill in capturing temporal veracity.

52 Maria Loh calls this signifying aspect of facial representation *faciality*. Maria H. Loh, "Renaissance Faciality," *Oxford Art Journal* 32, no. 3 (2009), 341–63.

53 Christian Müller et al., *Dürer, Holbein, Grünewald: Meisterzeichnungen der Deutschen Renaissance aus Berlin und Basel* (Basel: Offentliche Kunstsammlung, 1997), 408–11.

54 Joris van Gastel, Tannis Hadjinicolaou, and Markus Rath, eds., *Paragone als Mitstreit* (Berlin: Akademie Verlag, 2014), 99–108. For the use of puppets, models, and geometric figures as an intermediary stage in the creative process, see Markus Rath, "Manipulation: Modellformung, Bildrelief und kubische Denkfigur als Moment des Mitstreits," in Gastel, Hadjinicolaou, and Rath, eds., *Paragone als Mitstreit*, 99–118.

55 Gastel, Hadjinicolaou, and Rath, eds., *Paragone als Mitstreit*, 114.

56 Jane Roberts et al., *Drawings by Holbein from the Court of Henry VIII: Fifty Drawings from the Collection of Her Majesty the Queen, Windsor Castle* (New York: Harcourt Brace Jovanovich, 1988), 24–5.

57 K. T. Parker, *The Drawings of Hans Holbein in the Collection of His Majesty the King at Windsor Castle* (Oxford: Phaidon Press, 1945), 29–30.

58 Preserved in a print album at the Herzog August Bibliothek. This album, A25.3 Geom. 2, includes prints by Ferdinando Bertelli, Martinus Rota, and Nicolò Nelli, Venice, *c.* 1565. For literature on this print, see Bronwen Wilson, *The World in Venice: Print, the City and Early Modern Identity* (Toronto: University of Toronto Press, 2005), 252–3; see also Francesco Sorce, "Metafore in bianco e nero: Propaganda antiturca nelle stampe di Nicolò Nelli," in Francesco Sorce, ed., *En Blanc et Noir: Studi in onore di Silvana Macchioni* (Rome: Campisano Editore, 2007), 47–60. I'm grateful to Bronwen Wilson for drawing my attention to this source. Nelli's anamorphosis operates on two levels: in one, the Turk morphs into a devil; on the second level, it was meant to be held up as a mirror to the Venetian self. Most images of Turks circulating in a range of media were stereotypical demonizations of the political threat they posed to contemporary Venetians.

59 Perez Zagorin, *Ways of Lying* (Cambridge, MA: Harvard University Press, 2014), 12.

60 Wilson, *The World in Venice*, 252–3.

61 Massey, *Picturing Space, Displacing Bodies*, 66–9.

62 Merback, "Recognitions," 301.

63 Sabine Mertens et al., *Blockbücher des Mittelalters: Bilderfolgen als Lektüre: Gutenberg-Museum, Mainz, 22. Juni 1991 bis 1. September 1991* (Mainz am Rhein: von Zabern, 1991).

64 Examples include the *Speculum humanae salvationis* printed in the Netherlands in the second half of the fifteenth century and the many editions of *Specula* that emerged from Koberger's Nuremberg press in the late fifteenth century.

65 Sebastian Brant and Edwin Hermann Zeydel, *The Ship of Fools "Das Narrenschiff": Translated into Rhyming Couplets with Introduction and Commentary* (New York: Dover Publications, 1944), 60.

66 The mirror was by no means thought of as an unambivalent reflective device: obscured vision and the inability to see one's true self were frequently thematized, as can be seen in a broadside printed by Konrad Kachelofen in Leipzig *c.* 1498. Here, the ability to properly see the reflection depended on the agent brandishing the mirror: In the devil's mirror, the pictured couple sees only beauty and pride. The same surface presented to them by an angel reveals the skull in the mirror. In this didactic print, representational unity is sacrificed here for the main commentary on vision. These pendant images vet the type of vision employed for successful results.

67 For the self-aware image, see Victor Stoichita, Anne-Marie Glasheen, and Lorenzo Pericolo, *The Self-Aware Image: An Insight into Early Modern Metapainting* (London: Harvey Miller, 2015), 12. See the cogent introduction provided by Lorenzo Pericolo, "What is Metapainting? *The Self-Aware Image* Twenty Years Later," 11–31. For cultures of play generally and the hermeneutics of visual difficulty, see Brett Rothstein, "Visual Difficulty as a Cultural System," *Res* 65–6 (2014), 332–47.

68 Massey, *Picturing Space, Displacing Bodies*, 69.

69 In the skull, we also hear echoes of Erasmus's chosen device, the Roman god Terminus, also pictured frequently by Holbein, whose motto intones "I am the boundary of all things."

70 Toby Lester, *The Fourth Part of the World: An Astonishing Epic of Global Discovery, Imperial Ambition and the Birth of America* (New York: Free Press, 2010), 377–8. Toby Lester also reminds us that Columbus's reports emphasized the new islands and didn't allude to Cathay.

71 Thomas More, *Libellus vere aureus nec Minvs Salvtaris Qvam Festiuus de optimo reip. statu, deq [ue] noua Insula Vtopia authore clarissimo viro Thoma Moro* ... (Louvain: Martini, 1516).

72 Stephanie Buck et al., *Holbein, 1497–1543* (Cologne: Könemann, 1999), 10; Christian Müller et al., *Hans Holbein the Younger: The Basel Years, 1515–1532* (Munich: Prestel, 2006), 146–57. Erasmus himself was aware of, if he did not actually contribute to, the satirical images that at least one owner of the *Encomium Moriae*, the Swiss classicist and theologian Oswald Myconius, hoped would amplify the satire of the published text. Myconius had solicited satirical textual commentary from the Holbein brothers with their production of eighty-two marginal drawings for his own Folly edition, including one of a fool peering out of his mirror.

73 Stephanie Leitch, *Mapping Ethnography in Early Modern Germany: New Worlds in Print Culture* (Basingstoke: Palgrave Macmillan, 2010), 159–68.

74 Jan Van der Stock, *In Search of Utopia: Art and Science in the Era of Thomas More* (Leuven: Davidsfonds Uitgeverij, 2016), 104–7.

75 Malcolm Bishop, "Ambrosius Holbein's Memento Mori Map for Sir Thomas More's *Utopia*: The Meanings of a Masterpiece of Early Sixteenth Century Graphic Art," *British Dental Journal* 199, no. 2 (2005), 107–12. Malcolm Bishop asserts that Erasmus's verbal punning on More's name for *Encomium moriae* devised in 1509–10 was carried over here in the second edition in which the colophon caries a reference to More or death: MORI DE R. P. (of More, or concerning the *Rei Publicae*) (p. 109). The territory of Utopia featured in the first edition, noted as *Figura* (Louvain: Thierry Martens, 1516), has by a later edition (Basel: Froben, 1518) transformed itself into both a map labeled *Tabula* and a skull, the emblematic *memento mori*, reprising a pun from Erasmus's *Encomium Moriae* (Basel: Froben, 1509–10) on which both Holbein brothers worked.

76 Indeed, Hythlodaeus refers to the entrances of the strait as "jaws." See Clarence Miller et al., *Utopia* (New Haven, CT: Yale University Press, 2001), 51. Hythlodaeus also points out "no place" to Peter Gillis and Thomas More; see Riccardo Padron, "Mapping Imaginary Worlds," in James Ackerman et al., eds., *Maps: Finding Our Place in the World* (Chicago: University of Chicago Press, 2007), 255–87, especially 267–9.

77 Suzanne Karr Schmidt, "Memento Mori: The Deadly Art of Interaction," in Laura Deborah Gelfand and Sarah Blick, eds., *Push Me, Pull You: Physical and Spatial Interaction in Late Medieval and Renaissance Art* (Leiden and Boston, MA: Brill, 2011), 264.

78 Stephen Jay Greenblatt, *Renaissance Self-Fashioning from More to Shakespeare* (Chicago: University of Chicago Press, 2005), 19.

79 The *Instrument des Monslauf* is pasted onto the cover of Johannes Schöner, *Aequatorium Astronomicum* (1521); Universitätsbibliothek München, Inv. W 2 Math. 336(1). Many thanks to Alexandra Challenger for alerting me to this image.

80 For the Christian fool, see Robert Starr Kinsman, "Folly, Melancholy, and Madness: A Study in the Shifting Styles of Medical Analysis and Treatment, 1450–1675," in

Robert Starr Kinsman, *The Darker Vision of the Renaissance: Beyond the Fields of Reason* (Berkeley and Los Angeles: University of California Press, 1974), 276.

81 Susan Dackerman, *Prints and the Pursuit of Knowledge in Early Modern Europe* (Cambridge, MA: Harvard Art Museums, 2011), 306.

82 For a succession of related fool's cap maps, see Larry Silver, *Art and Dis-Illusion in the Long Sixteenth Century* (Leiden: Brill, 2023), 239–41.

83 Besse, "Cosmography and Geography," 103. Oronce Fine's name is inscribed on the upper left corner of the map, but as his death predates the date of the projection, Fine cannot be directly associated with the production of the map itself. The origin of the motif of a fool's cap encasing a map is believed to reside with the French mapmaker Jean de Gourmont (1570).

84 Andrew Gordon and Bernhard Klein, *Literature, Mapping, and the Politics of Space in Early Modern Britain* (Cambridge: Cambridge University Press, 2010), 234.

85 Royal Museums Greenwich, https://collections.rmg.co.uk/collections/objects/206385.html.

86 In the guise of a region inspired by Thomas More's *Utopia*, this engraved map plotted geographic features named after several of Ortelius's associates in Silesia, Jakob Monau (Monavius), and Johannes Matthaeus Wacker von Wackenfels, whose friendship it simultaneously commemorates. See Joost Depuydt, "The Utopia Map by Abraham Ortelius: New Home – New Research," *De Gulden Passer: Tijdschrift Voor Boek Wetenschap* 97, no. 2 (2019), 242–6; Cécile Kruyfhooft, "A Recent Discovery: Utopia by Abraham Ortelius," *Map Collector* (September 1981), 10–14; Dirk Sacré et al., *Utopia & More: Thomas More, de Nederlanden en de utopische traditie: catalogus bij de tentoonstelling in de Leuvense Universiteitsbibliotheek, 20 Oktober 2016–17 Januari 2017* (Louvain: Leuven University Press, 2016).

87 Stoichita, Glasheen, and Pericolo, *The Self-Aware Image*, 183–227.

88 Even the typically reflective and mirror-like quality of the fool's marotte seems here to be clouded by doubts about the certainty of perception and the knowability of the world.

89 This is underlined by the mottoes of biblical and classical origin (mostly in Latin, addressed therefore to a learned, if not pedantic, audience) dotted across the map. These include mottoes that comment on the world as a spring of poison, a source of deception, or a well of self-reflection. In these, the idea of physiognomy and knowledge go in and out of focus. Certainly implicated here are both the map and the face as loci of knowing. For a summary and translation of these inscriptions, see a link to the map at the Royal Museums Greenwich: www.rmg.co.uk/collections/objects/rmgc-object-206385.

90 See Karr Schmidt, "Memento Mori," 282. Greuter's engraving provides the inscription "Be vigilant and pray, for you know neither the day nor the hour," adapted from the prediction of the second coming in Matthew 25.13.

91 Jean-Marc Besse calls astronomy and geography two distinct "mental orientations." See Besse, "Cosmography and Geography," 106.

92 According to Samuel Gessner, folding the planisphere twice about the pole enabled the presentation of celestial circles as a sphere and allowed the stars to be tracked across the entire vault of the heavens. See Dupré, ed., *Perspective as Practice*, 116–17.

93 Historians assume that this reference to Fine serves to number his cosmographic pursuits among the list of vanities, rather than acting as an attribution for the map, which was produced many years after his death. See Besse, "Cosmography and Geography," 103ff.

94 Jean-Marc Besse quotes from the preface of Hondius, *Nouveau Theatre du Monde* (Amsterdam, 1639); Besse, "Cosmography and Geography," 106.

95 Tom Conley, "A Topographer's Eye: From Gilles Corrozet to Pieter Apian," in Walter S. Melion and Lee Palmer Wandel, eds., *Early Modern Eyes* (Leiden: Brill, 2010), 62–7.

96 Merback, "Recognitions," 301.

97 Massey, *Picturing Space, Displacing Bodies*, 42.

98 For an reflection on the map's address to the individual in the project of worldmaking situated between the local and the global, see Ayesha Ramachandran, *The Worldmakers: Global Imagining in Early Modern Europe* (Chicago: University of Chicago Press, 2015), 221–7.

99 Perhaps the frenetic pace of travel publications had something to do with this pessimism. Many of these publications were data in search of authors; the pamphlet's authors were increasingly billed as anonymous members of nations. See, for instance, the publications of Pieter van der Aa and Levinus Hulsius.

100 Massey, *Picturing Space, Displacing Bodies*, 66–9.

101 For how a map produces a reality, see Jean-Marc Besse, "Mapping, Constructing, Inventing," 1–26, especially 4–6.

102 See the image of a fool appearing in the nose section of Cocles, *Phisionomei und Chiromanci* (Strasbourg: Cammerlander, 1540), Herzog August Bibliothek, Wolfenbüttel, Sig. HN97.4 Helmst. 7, http://diglib.hab.de/drucke/n-97-4f-helmst-7s/start.htm.

103 See the discussion of the shifting vantages of the viewer's positions that this map provokes in Rose Marie San Juan, *Vertiginous Mirrors: The Animation of the Visual Image and Early Modern Travel* (Manchester: Manchester University Press, 2011), 1–5, 59–61.

SIX

CONCLUSION

Observational Thinking

This book has considered the wealth of practical knowledge that emerged from vernacular and pictorialized sixteenth-century texts. These visualized texts gave rise to a class of amateur weather watchers, astrologers, bloodletters, field surgeons, cosmographers, and physiognomers. Such practitioners armed with new visual skills formed mass readership for the presses whose printed material encouraged them to undertake empirical examinations difficult to imagine without these books. Some of this observational attention aggregated around celestial bodies and faces; books that directed such pursuits have formed the focus of this study.

As visual acuity was sharpened by these books, artists developed technical systems to convey those data points of observation. Was the subject matter of faces and the heavens really so far apart? One reader of Apian's text inscribed lunar phases onto a visual field that was also inhabited by a portrait. On a blank page of the *La Cosmographie de Pierre Apian* (printed by Gaultherot in Paris in 1553), preserved in the Bibliothèque Ceccano in Avignon, this reader constructed a face atop a drawing session originally dedicated to reproducing the phases of the moon, a doodle whose layers Tom Conley surmises might respond to the similitudes constructed by Apian throughout this book (Figure. 6.1).[1] The content of cosmography, as Apian asserted, was analogous to physiognomy: both the moon and faces were surfaces whose signs could be read. Apian alluded to as much in his images of moons and suns sporting different facial expressions. To amateur astrologers whose art was being professionalized by the printing

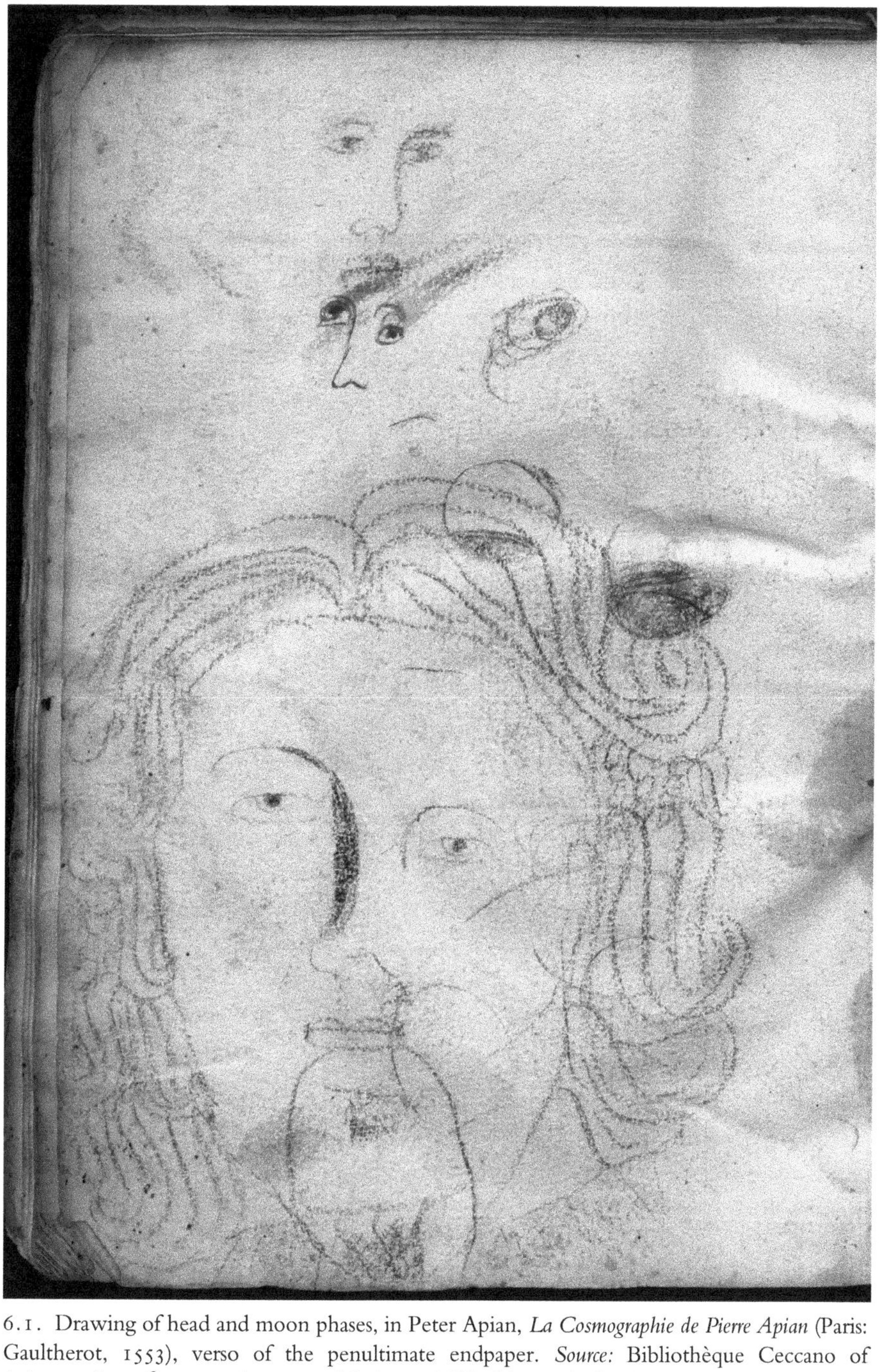

6.1. Drawing of head and moon phases, in Peter Apian, *La Cosmographie de Pierre Apian* (Paris: Gaultherot, 1553), verso of the penultimate endpaper. *Source:* Bibliothèque Ceccano of Avignon, Inv. 8° 15624. Courtesy of Avignon Bibliothèques (Ville d'Avignon), state deposit.

press, the face's surface could also be determined by the data points of a horoscope. If the night sky commanded a field of knowledge that was universal in scope, nativities recorded the personal information encoded in the stars. Likewise, physiognomy was an art that necessitated the study of generalities in order to visually assess individual subjects between poles. The pictorial program of the *Liber Quodlibetarius*, which included cosmography and physiognomy among the genres it synthesized, lays bare the throughline of many printed books: it shows us how such universal and particular knowledge was mediated by pictures, and how sovereign images themselves began to constitute forms of disciplinary knowledge. This manuscript condensed available know-how into pictorialized formats that guided visualized thinking about a surprising variety of knowledge-based pursuits.

Each chapter of this book has explored how pictures in service of a knowledge domain contributed to visual literacy. Cosmography trained the eye on the heavens and recommended viewing practices that were designed to focus celestial observations. Chapter 2, "Don't Forget Your Apian: A DIY Guide to the Cosmos," argued that Peter Apian's *Cosmographicus Liber* was one of the first substantial printed volumes that enunciated visual processes at the center of understanding and knowledge-making about the heavens, such as celestial geometry and astronomy. Diagrams and moving pictures invented by Apian provided memorable tips for the amateur stargazer about how to read the sky. These visual demonstrations took the form of a mix of conceptualizations that organized an array of observational practices, such as tracking the stars overhead. Visual discrimination of the moon's phases and eclipse cycles could provide clues to other propositions about the shape and movement of heavenly bodies. In addition, such visual judgments might provide clues about one's temporal and geographical positioning. Apian's use of portraiture as a metaphor for conveying the principles of cosmography assumes that interest in deciphering facial features was already partially in place. Indeed, a mutual reinforcement between decoding the heavens and reading faces ensured that both would continue to hold visual interest for readers of texts eager to learn how to make judgments themselves. Perhaps this elision of subject matter accounts for the eye in the moon of the Avignon *Cosmographie*. The sketch has been produced by an artist practicing both eyes and moons before finally settling on an eye cavity comprised of a moon phase.[2] My consultation of many editions of these cosmographic texts suggests that readers were eager to try their own hand at summarizing some of these texts' principles, notating them in visual formats. The reader of our *Cosmographie* preserved in Avignon annotated their copy with an attempt to produce knowledge about the rendering of faces. The most complete of these efforts quite literally commandeers a waning gibbous to define the cavity formed by the brow and nose of the figure's right eye. After viewing the faces of Apian's many moons, this reader supplied a moon for a face. For this doodler, the idea of a man in the moon could reflexively produce analogies of celestial bodies hidden in the face.

Chapter 3, "Facial Profiling: Physiognomy and the Art of Inspection," argued that an exercise of visual comparisons on the printed page developed into a science of studying faces. Only once physiognomy became fully constituted by paired groups of faces derived from printed editions did it become a how-to skill packaged for transfer to the field. Physiognomy was a specious science, to be sure. Practiced in the field, it probably amounted to little more than impolite staring. But the genre's importance resides in how those images increased visual acuity; from these acutely honed observers, new acts of visual cognition emerged. Physiognomy typified a trend in the visualization of experimental sciences. The move of images in a host of genres toward visual sovereignty reflects how popular science was being shaped by them. Chapter 4, "Visualized Data and Searchable Science: the *Liber Quodlibetarius* (*c.* 1524)," offered the evidence of this sovereignty reflected against the backdrop of a manuscript that organized such independent images. The practical application of most of these source publications was aimed to sharpen the reader's/viewer's ability to extrapolate new data from the results of eyewitness observations. In this collection of images cribbed from printed books, practitioners were encouraged to interface with a world increasingly constituted as visually knowable and searchable. Reconciling an array of dissimilar material to a common format, the *Liber Quodlibetarius* collects images together for their ability to articulate similar kinds of experiential approaches. The *Liber Quodlibetarius* presents images of instruments that embedded practical information – all derived from how-to guides with which to empirically investigate the terrestrial and celestial world. The way in which these prints were appropriated and cataloged suggests that practical skills gained from observation were the methodology that united them. In the form of a user-friendly interface, we can detect a new functionality that condensed that data as visual tools and privileged ease in searchability.

Rounding out the importance of eyewitness claims that ultimately certified early modern knowledge, this book also investigated the physical act of eyewitnessing as it was embedded in art. Compelling documents for showing how vision was conceptualized on a phenomenological level were modeled by puzzle pictures that froze the process of viewing. Chapter 5, "Vexed Viewing: Anamorphosis and the Visual Argumentation of Labored Looking," demonstrated how trick pictures that tried to confound observers (or, in some cases, to show how they could confound observers) did so by having their focus resolve from different points of view, forcing viewers to adjust their sightlines by physically rearranging their positions. As some images formed, others were deformed. Acts of visual choice raised the viewers' suspicions about the ambivalence of images in general. Such visual decision-making was previewed by didactic images, such as those found in the previous three chapters that coached vernacular viewing. Having been taught observational practices by vernacularized how-to genres, the viewer was visually prepared to be admonished by pictures that puzzled over observation and its discontents. Interestingly, these cautionary notes frequently took as their subject matter topography and portraiture, content familiar from the printed genres of cosmography and physiognomy.

NEW AVENUES FOR RESEARCH: TOPOGRAPHIC PORTRAITURE

While this study has argued for the commonality of the visual approach embedded in cosmography and physiognomy, future studies of this material might aim to test whether the content of types of images that issued from them was also related. As iconoclasm and shifting ideas about art's role in the liturgy and devotional practices sidelined the production of subject matter enshrined by the Catholic Church, portraits and landscapes remained secure content around which artists in Reformation Germany would rally. The ostensibly neutral subject matter of portraits and landscapes more easily evaded the firebrands of confessional struggles. This seemingly non-partisan content had also been invested with documentary guarantees for which there was a presumption of objectivity. Another similarity was that both genres could serve the needs of both the particular (topography and portraits) and non-particular (generic views and character heads).[3]

Renaissance cosmography, which had implications for future pursuits in topography, united two sciences of discrete epistemological heritage: mathematical geography and descriptive chorography. These were two modes of description that were inherited from Ptolemy and Strabo.[4] This distinction became untenable by the end of the sixteenth century, at which point they parted ways as a useful union. Frank Lestringant describes the crossroads that met the later cosmographic literature and the increasingly encyclopedic activity that it needed to tackle as a "crisis" moment.[5] Later cosmographies (such as those by Sebastian Münster and André Thevet) changed course and "wrote themselves back into medieval, encyclopedic tradition, bestiary, universal history, adding to these recent geographic usurpations."[6] From that point, mathematical geography became the province of atlas makers, and descriptive geography was a concern increasingly handled by travel literature. The commercial success of travel literature over traditional cosmography was a victory for the particularity and individuality of these accounts – a rhetorical approach that won out over the idea of synthetic universal knowledge historically managed by compilers of chronicles or cosmographies, such as Hartmann Schedel or Sebastian Münster respectively. Taking the place of increasingly retrograde cosmography, travel literature was a victory for the subjectivity of data.[7] To travel literature, we can also add the particularity of topographic views, which had once lurked in the background of paintings, but whose popularity came to the fore in the independent prints of Matthäus Merian, who published serial views of famous cities beginning in 1640. These albums of the *Topographia Germaniae* collected single sheets that lacked the context given by the written descriptions that had framed earlier such views. Such topographic views formed the desiderata of contemporary print collections, such as those of the Antwerp collector Geerard Grameye and Archduke Ferdinand of Tyrol.[8]

We see similar impulses to collect in the other genre that this study has treated: physiognomy. Representations of faces in the early modern press populated different genres with varying evidentiary assurances, from specific names attached to generalized faces (as in the Nuremberg *Weltchronik*), to new types of genres such as numismatic books (*Bildnisvitienbücher*) that reproduced specific likenesses gathered from the guarantees of coins. For these, we can consider the generic character heads in physiognomy, which were not meant to invoke specific individuals, and portrait books in which named faces presented in succession could be read as a catalog of data points. As we have seen in Erhard Schön's and Hans Holbein's puzzle pictures, portrait likenesses had to be converted precisely into such data points of mouths, noses, and eyes in order to create anamorphic views. In later periods, we see portraiture becoming subjective again. Such arcs might have been carved out through the intervention of collecting.

The albums of Archduke Ferdinand and Ferdinand Columbus show that collecting accrued around subject matter. Other albums, such as those of Cassiano dal Pozzo, a member of the society named for their visual acuity, the *Accademia dei Lincei*, organized faces as items around which new cognitive activity could be structured. Why were portraits collected? Some of these albums suggest that portraits were a readymade genre for collection: perhaps it only made sense to own portraits in the context of other faces with which to compare them.[9] Genre formation, of the sort that this study has treated through the intervention of printed images, can also be investigated in the collecting efforts of several important early modern print collectors, including Ferdinand Columbus and Cassiano dal Pozzo, as Mark McDonald has done. The print albums of Cassiano dal Pozzo, for instance, exemplify the organizing impulses that were afoot among enthusiasts of visual images. The glut of images unleashed by the printing press required such overarching structures – we might call them algorithms in the case of Columbus – in order to keep them organized (and their owners sane: in Columbus's case, for example, so that he wouldn't purchase the same print twice). But surely they also required an interface to facilitate print viewing.[10]

Some of these print-collecting efforts can be likened to impulses that governed the cabinets of curiosity. Many collectors started to expect the same cognitive payload from prints that keepers of such cabinets sought from the heterogeneous collection of *naturalia* and *artificialia* in the *Kunstkammer*. Mark McDonald refers to the organizing impulse native to both as "miniaturization and domestication" – in short, a form of possessing and shrinkage.[11] In Cassiano's albums, prints were first grouped by type, hierarchically, and geographically; portraits were organized by hierarchy and chronology. Cassiano's heterodox organization might have been intended to prompt new cognitive exercises.[12] Thus, the inventories of early modern print collectors can provide a unique view into the organization of visual observations that would advance diverse pursuits of knowledge. Such encyclopedic collecting efforts from members of the Lincean Academy to document and organize form the apogee of compendiums and reflect the state of science before the formation of the Royal Society.

Collecting interests in topography also came to shape the topographic eye, an agent, per Tom Conley, whose literacy was binocular: assessing the world on both the local and the universal level, and increasingly cognizant that knowledge of one presumes an understanding of the other. This was a skill that later editors of Peter Apian and Gemma Frisius's *Cosmographia* were quick to promote and to capitalize on.[13] Perhaps we can also see this skill at the heart of the confluence of portraiture and topography that we might call facial topography. A portrait morphs into both terrain and an oculus in a minute engraving by Frans Crabbe van Espleghem (Figure 6.2).[14] The content of this face of an African man, inspired by a figure in Albrecht Dürer's *Adoration of the Magi*, is refocused by the process of engraving.[15] Crabbe sends the viewer's attention into orbit around concentric circles that surround the subject's eye. The circles present the eye as a sensory agent that returns the gaze of the viewer. This probing eye interrogates the viewer, inviting speculation on how the sitter saw his European viewers. This endows the sitter with a type of agency we rarely see in African subjects of the period. While the subject's quickened eye provokes curiosity about the physiological process of viewing, equally pronounced are the graphic effects of the engraving that holds the viewer's eye in its thrall. The eye, with its contested focus, commands the viewer's attention before releasing our own eyes to explore the rest of the composition in an outward spiral. The eye slowly releases its grip to allow the viewer to emerge from this point of entry to circle around the engraving's syntax of concentric lines. While the engraving is not a puzzle picture per se, Crabbe engages a type of seeing that challenged naturalistic presentation by setting the bar of optical difficulty very high. Such perceptual complexity was also the subject of Claude Mellan's engraving of the *Sudarium* (Figure 6.3) from 1649, whose lines call the viewer's attention back to the surface of the print to

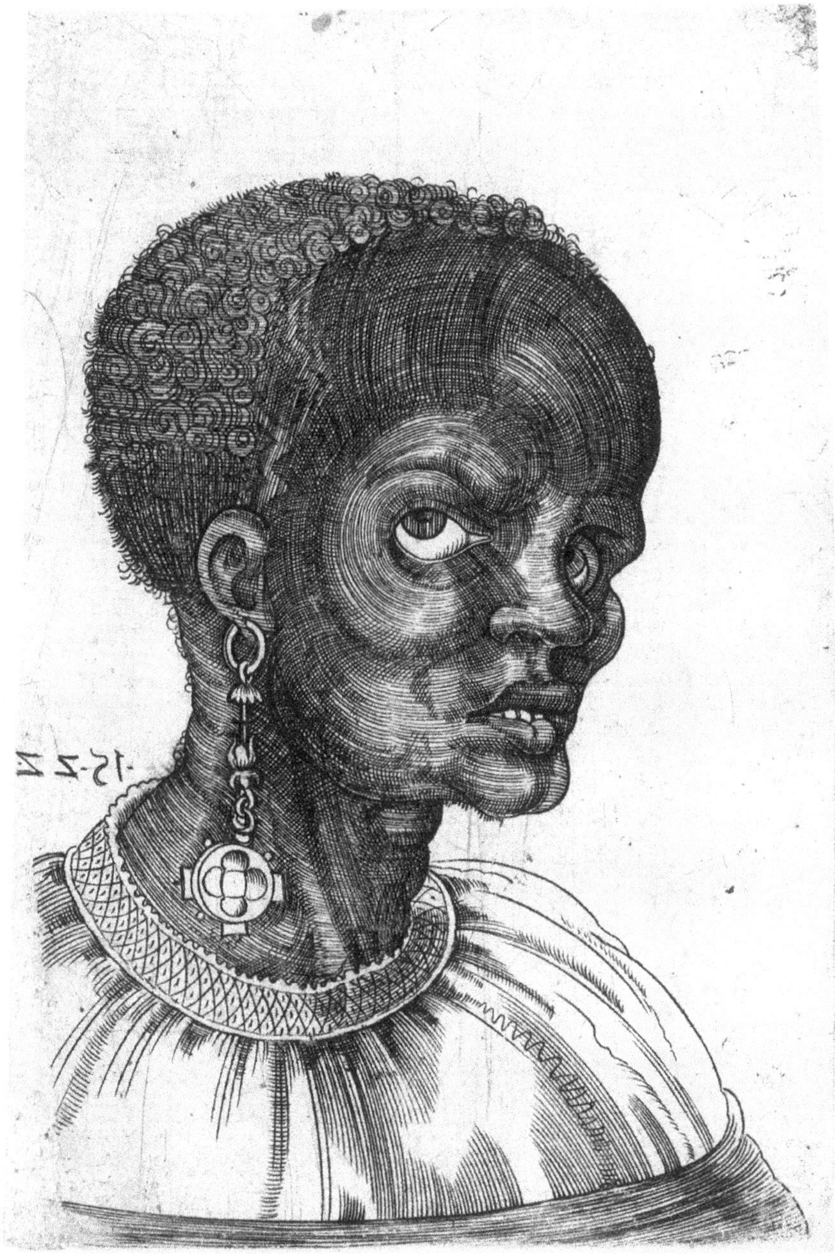

6.2. Frans Crabbe (van Espleghem), *Man in Three-Quarter Profile*, 1522, engraving, 10.4 cm × 7.1 cm. *Source:* Purchase, Louis V. Bell Fund and Joseph Pulitzer Bequest, 1998, Acc. Nr. 1998.415. Metropolitan Museum of Art.

explore the nostril of Jesus as the center of a graphic system of concentric orbits.[16] This graphic topography becomes a means of describing contour and would become the standardized form of inscription in contour mapping. In these prints, the face and topography vie with each other for the dominant

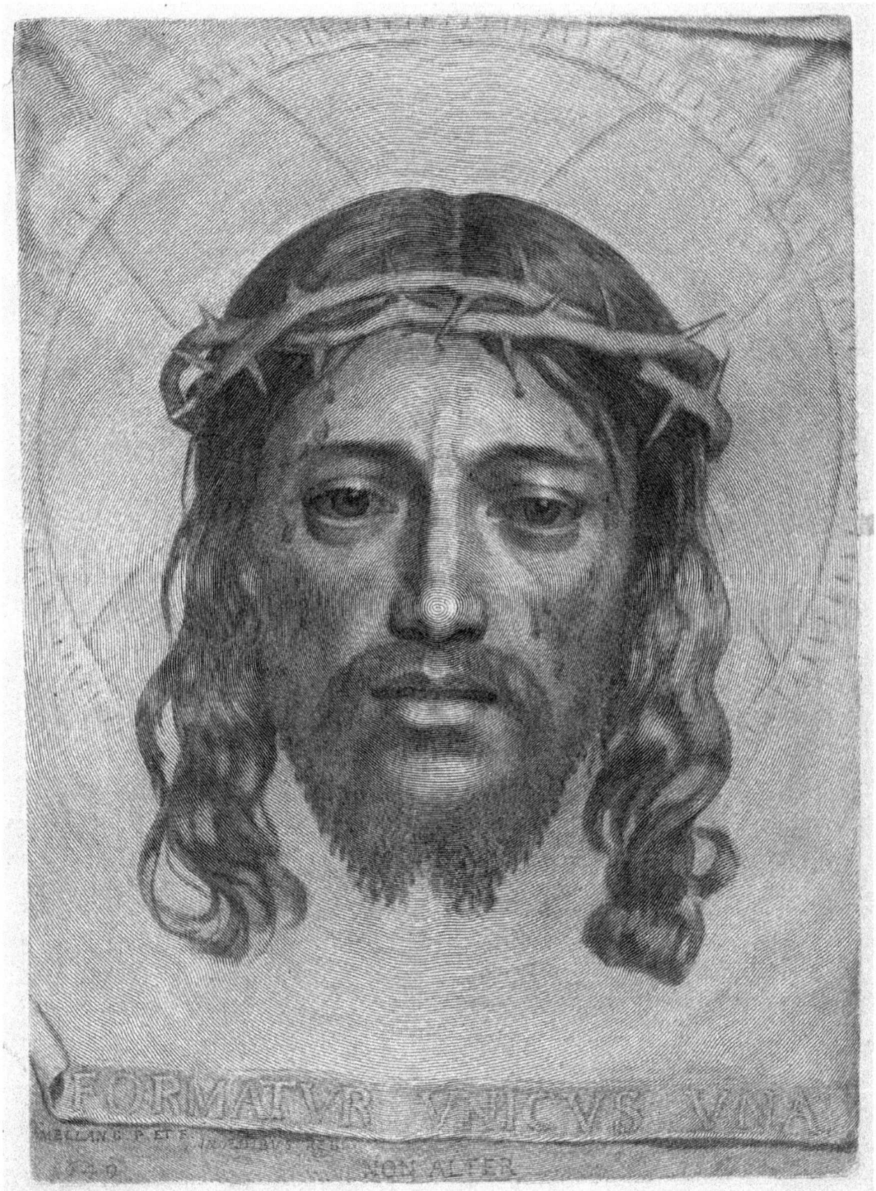

6.3. Claude Mellan, *Sudarium*, 1649, engraving, 43 cm × 31.5 cm. *Source:* Purchase, Elisha Whittelsey Collection, Elisha Whittelsey Fund, 1969, Acc. Nr. 69.581.5. Metropolitan Museum of Art.

or privileged view, a rhetorical tension that also drove the programs of *Vexierbilder*. This tension also dominates anthropomorphic landscapes, which Rosemary San Juan explores in the context of Jesuit devotional practice.[17] Thus, the tension between the two elements of Ptolemy's analogy that Apian pictorialized are here finally united. Such double seeing drives home Apian's marginal note fixed to his citation of Ptolemy on the relationship between art and chorography in the early pages of the *Cosmographicus Liber*. Apian's claim that "only an artist can do it" was not an idle one, especially in the virtuoso production of anamorphic puzzle pictures. In these facial landscapes we see artists challenging themselves to combine portraiture and topography, content recently under the scrutiny of a rhetoric of close observation. These landscaped portraits represent a showdown between topography and portraiture in a graphic and cognitive match. The central tenets of both genres rested on observational practices honed by cosmographic and physiognomic texts.

Only by way of the entreaties of publishers of cosmography and physiognomy to compare and contrast what they saw could viewers be expected to parse visual conundrums by exercising their observational skills. Tracking the slow movement of storms across the surface of the sun could serve as an example of imaging that set store by visual acuity. Only equipped with such powers of cognitive discernment coached by cosmography and physiognomy would a viewer have had the visual acuity to parse differences among the thirty-eight etched plates of Galileo's *Macchie Solari* (1613). The ipseity of sunspots that Mattheus Greuter referenced in his etchings of Galileo's observations matched the indexical reflexivity that prints of the *Vera Icon* assumed to have with the relic of the Holy Face.[18] Insofar as they did this, they mirrored Galileo's own drawn "observations," themselves an index of a proto-mechanical process of recording.[19] Galileo's sunspots, published in 1613, as well as the engraved reproductions of his views of the moon (1611), can be said to mark a turning point in the idea of the printing of observations. Images generated by tools became records of observed material; these photomechanically recorded impressions of wandering spots of the sun can be thought of as types of nature impressions.[20] Repetition in drawing and copied and collected prints fed new subjectivities. This collecting, ordering, and serial viewing reflected the state of pre-Baconian science, and it also helped to build consensus among observers. Thus, this is rich material that can inform the better organized collecting campaigns that shaped the working methods of the Royal Society.

Such new qualities of perception and cognition invited by seventeenth-century experimental printmaking intersected with efforts to reveal vernacular knowledge in the sixteenth-century woodcuts under review in this book. The impulse to collect that knowledge in print albums and other types of encyclopedic compendiums such as customized books reveals a taxonomic impulse akin to that active in the printed how-to books of the early to mid-sixteenth century. Cosmography and physiognomy brokered the visual acuity by which viewers became sensitized to optical phenomena and began to recognize qualitative differences. On the strength of such cognitive decision-making coached by printed images, active lay viewership developed the visual literacy that would guide the autodidact through subjective experiences of the world.

NOTES

1 Per email correspondence with the author on August 29, 2015. For Conley's work on the edition of Apian's *La Cosmographie de Pierre Apian* (Paris: Gaultherot, 1553) in which the drawing appears and that is housed in the Bibliothèque Ceccano of Avignon (15624), see Tom Conley, "A Topographer's Eye: From Gilles Corrozet to Pieter Apian," in Walter S. Melion and Lee Palmer Wandel, eds., *Early Modern Eyes* (Leiden: Brill, 2010), 55–79. Warmest thanks to Tom Conley for sharing this image and so many other insights with me over the years.

2 The other phases on the page may have been generated by spinning the text's lunar volvelle.

3 For landscape's toggle between the particular and the general, as well as between the view and the representation, see Charles Talbot, "Topography as Landscape in Early Printed Books," in Sandra Hindman, *The Early Illustrated Book: Essays in Honor of Lessing Julius Rosenwald* (Washington, DC: Library of Congress, 1982), 112–13.

4 See Frank Lestringant, "The Crisis of Cosmography at the End of the Renaissance," in Philippe Desan, ed., *Humanism in Crisis: The Decline of the French Renaissance* (Ann Arbor: University of Michigan Press, 1991), 153–79, especially 154.

5 See Lestringant, "The Crisis of Cosmography," 153–79.

6 Denis E. Cosgrove, *Apollo's Eye: A Cartographic Genealogy of the Earth in the Western Imagination* (Baltimore: Johns Hopkins University Press, 2001), 96–9. Cosgrove argues that by the mid-sixteenth century, the job of the cosmographer was to organize information coming in from many avenues. With court cosmographers processing the data that came into the realm, cosmography necessarily became a collective enterprise of explorers, navigators, writers, and engravers – a "center of calculation."

7 Desan, *Humanism in Crisis*, 174.

8 Geerard Grameye's inventory of 1580 lists his prints according to subject matter: perspective views, architectural elements, landscape, ships, and classical and biblical scenes. According to Peter Parshall, the dedication of a category to landscape and topographic views can be answered, at least in part, by the proliferation of images whose content was driven by large publishing firms such as those of Hieronymus Cock and Philips Galle, whose capital could bring previously insecure subject matter for prints to fruition and to the market. Likewise, the 1596 inventory of Ferdinand Archduke of Tyrol identifies "topography" as an operative category that includes engravings of renowned biblical and historical significance, fortifications, and buildings. See Peter W. Parshall, "The Print Collection of Ferdinand, Archduke of Tyrol," *Jahrbuch der Kunsthistorischen Sammlungen in Wien* (Vienna: Kunsthistorisches Museum, 1982), 141–6, 163–9. For the inventory of Geerard Grameye, see Jean Denucé, *De Antwerpsche "Konstkamers": Inventarissen van Kunstverzamelingen te Antwerpen in de 16e en 17e Eeuwen* (Antwerp: De Sikkel, 1932), 7–10.

9 See, for example, the portrait album containing Roman emperors in the Herzog August Bibliothek in Wolfenbüttel (HAB AE1.1 Geom. 2(2)); thanks to Zoe Langer and Britta-Juliane Kruse for their help. Additionally, we might consider books of famous men, such as Paolo Giovio's *Elogia Virorum literis illustrium* (Basel: Perna, 1577), *Emblemata Nobilitati* (Frankfurt: De Bry, 1593), or Hendrick Hondius's *Pictorum aliquot celebrium praecipuae Germaniae Inferioris effigies* (The Hague: Hondius, 1610). Less orthodox collections of heads, such as Simon Frisius's *Saints and Sibyls* (1548–56), also fall under this category.

10 Mark P. McDonald, *The Print Collection of Ferdinand Columbus: 1488–1539: A Renaissance Collector in Seville* (London: British Museum Press, 2004), 53–78.

11 McDonald quotes Daston here: "representing such an array of objects and organizing the images into sequences is an act of 'miniaturization' and 'domestication.'" Mark P. McDonald, *The Paper Museum of Cassiano dal Pozzo: A Catalogue Raisonné: Drawings and Prints in the Royal Library at Windsor Castle, the British Museum, the Institut de France and Others Collections. Series C – Prints Part One: Ceremonies, Costumes, Portraits and Genre* (London: Harvey Miller, 2017), 3.

12 Mark McDonald argues as much: Cassiano's organization was not always driven by didactic or documentary impulses but to "capture different examples of subjects, and through recognition to prompt cognitive extrapolation." See McDonald, *The Paper Museum of Cassiano dal Pozzo*, 6.

13 Conley, "A Topographer's Eye," 62–72.

14 Frans Crabbe van Espleghem (Flemish, *c.* 1480–1552), *Man in Three-Quarter Profile*, 1522, engraving, 10.2 cm × 6.7 cm, Metropolitan Museum of Art.

15 See www.metmuseum.org/art/collection/search/336982. For literature on Crabbe, see Karel G. Boon, "Frans Crabbe en de Monogrammist A.C.," in *De Gulden Passer 52* (Antwerp: Nederlandse Boekhandel, 1974), 44–52; M. Friedländer, "Nicolas Hogenberg und Frans Crabbe die Maler von Mechelen," *Jahrbuch der Preuszischen Kunstsammlungen* 42, no. 4 (1921), 161–8. Crabbe was said to have explored printmaking after Dürer's visit to Brussels and Antwerp in 1521.

16 Mellan, *Sudarium*, 1649, engraving, 42.8 cm × 31.3 cm, image from the Rijksmuseum, http://hdl.handle.net/10934/RM0001.collect.152641.

17 Rose Marie San Juan, *Vertiginous Mirrors: The Animation of the Visual Image and Early Modern Travel* (New York: Palgrave Macmillan, 2011), 56–85.

18 Or indeed, we might say, with Greuter's own *memento mori*, a skull that addressed the viewer. See Suzanne Karr Schmidt, "Memento Mori: The Deadly Art of Interaction," in Laura Deborah Gelfand and Sarah Blick, eds., *Push Me, Pull You: Imaginative and Emotional Interaction in Late Medieval and Renaissance Art* (Leiden and Boston, MA: Brill, 2011), 282–4.

19 Ruth S. Noyes, "Mattheus Greuter's Sunspot Etchings for Galileo Galilei's *Macchie Solari* (1613)," *Art Bulletin* 98, no. 4 (2016), 473. Because he could not look through the scope at the sun, Galileo describes exposing the lens to a sheet of paper which would capture the impression of the spots.

20 Insofar as the paper was prepared to accept these impressions, these can be thought of as similar to nature prints. Thomas Eser, "Ordnende Dinge in unordentlichen Zeiten die 'kulturelle Gelegenheit' des 16. Jahrhunderts," in Thomas Eser and Stephanie Armer, eds., *Luther, Kolumbus und die Folgen: Welt im Wandel 1500–1600* (Nuremberg: Germanisches Nationalmuseum, 2017), 67.

BIBLIOGRAPHY

PRIMARY SOURCES

Agricola, Johann and Johann Friedrich. *Drey hundert gemeyner Sprichwörtter: der wir Deutschen uns gebrauchen, und doch nicht wyssen wo her sie kommen.* Nuremberg: F. Peypůs, 1529.

Anglicus, Bartholomaeus. *Van den Proprieteyten der Dinghen.* Haarlem: Jacobus Bellaert, 1485.

Apian, Peter. *Cosmographia, Additis de Eadem Re Libelllis, ut Sequens Pagina Docet.* Ed. Rainer Gemma Frisius. Antwerp: Birckman, 1539.

Cosmographiae Introductio: Cum Quibusdam Geo-Metriae ac Astronomiae Prin=||cipijs ad eam Rem Necessarijs.||. Ingolstadt: Peter and Georg Apian, 1529.

Cosmographie, Oft Beschrijvinghe der Geheelder Werelt van Petrus Apianus. 3. Werk, Nu Ghecorrigeert van Gemma Frisio. Metten Zeecompasse Ende Anderen Boecxkens Byden Selven Gemma Daer Toegedaen. Ed. Rainer Gemma Frisius. Antwerp: de Bonte, 1553.

Instrument-Buch Durch Petrum Apianum erst von new beschriben. Zum Ersten ist darinne begriffen ein newer Quadrant, dardurch Tag vnd Nacht, bey der Sonnen, Mon vnnd andern Planeten, auch durch ettliche Gestirn die Stunden vnd ander nutzung Gefunden werden. Zum Andern, wie man die höch der Thuern vnd anderer gebew ... messen soll. Zum Dritten wie man das wasser absehen oder abwegen soll ... vnd wie man die Bruenne suchen soll. ... Ingolstadt: Apian, 1533.

Practica Auff Das 1532 Jar Zu Eeren den Durchleutchtigen Hochgebornen Fürsten und HH Hern Wilhelmen und Hernn Ludwigen Pfalz Bei Rehyn Herzogen in Obern und Nider Bayern ... Durch Petrum Apianum der Loblichen Hohennschul zu Ingelstat Mathematicum nach Rechter Kunst und Art der Astronomei Practiciert. Auch Wird Nachvolgenden von dem naeschst Erschinen Cometen/ Wie unnd in was Gestalt in Gemelter Apianus Observiert hat und Welhe Biß Her Dero Vil Sindt in Irem Schreiben Irrig Gefunden Bewerlich Angezaygt. Landshut: Georg Apian, 1532.

Aristotle and Michael Scotus, eds. *In disem Biechlin wirt erfunden von Complexion der Menschen: zuerlernen leibliche unnd menschliche Natur ir Siten, Geberden und Nayglichayt zuerkennen und urtaylen.* Strasbourg: Mathis Hüpfuff, 1511.

Brabant. *Van Brabant die excellente Cronike ... totten iare M. CCCCC. ende XXX in Junio.* Antwerp: J. van Doesborch, 1530.

Brolesse, Hans. *Hierin Begriffne Pis/ Zaygen Klaœr=||lich an/ Wie Ain Yedes Roß/ Jung vñ Alt Sol Gezämbt/|| Dadurch Jme/ Angenomene Pœse Gewonheit/ Vbelstandt/ Vnd Vntugent/|| Benomen/ Vnd Abgewent Werden Mag||.* Regensburg: Hans Kohl, 1539.

Cocles [Bartolommeo della Rocca]. *Barptolomaei Coclitis Bononiensis, Naturalis Philosophiæ ac Medicinæ Doctoris, Physiognomiæ et Chiromantiæ Compendium.* Argentorati: Albertus, 1536.

Complexion/ Natur || vnd eigenschafft eines yeden menschen || zu erfaren/ auch seiner geburt stund vnnd zeychen/|| dardurch jm all sein glück vnnd vnfal/ so jm in || der zeyt seyns lebens begegnen wirt/ er-||öffnet mag werden/ ... || Der sieben Planeten sampt den zwölff heimli=||schen zeichen wirckung in des menschen geburt/|| clerlich beschrieben.||. Mainz: Peter Jordan, 1534.

Der schapherders || Kalender. Eyn sere schone vnde nutthe || boek/ myt velen fruchtbaren mate=||rien ... || Jtem tho ende dusses bokes vyndeth || men de Kleyne Physonomye/ vth welkere/|| des mynschen Complexie vnde tone=||gynghe der natuer klärlyck to || erkennen werth. Rostock: Ludwig Dietz, 1523.

In Disem Büechlin Wirt Erfunden von Complexion der Menschen. Augsburg: Hans Schönsperger, 1515.

Phisonomei: Complexio und Art eins ieden Menschen, ausz Gestalt und Form des Angesichts, Glider unnd allen geberden zu erlernen. Strasbourg: Egenolff, 1529.

Phisonomei: Eins jeden menschen Art, Natur und Complexion. Strasbourg: Egenolff, 1530.

Phisionomi vnd || Chiromanci.|| Eyn newß Complexion Büch=||lein/ Der Menschen Geburt/ Sitten/ Geberden vnd Neyg=||ligkeyten/ Auß der Phisionomi/ Chiromanci/ Den Siben || Planeten/ Zwölff Zeichen/ Vnnd den XXXvj. Bildern || Deß Himels/ ... Quarto. Strasbourg: Jakob Cammerlander, 1540.

Copp, Johann. *Erklärung unnd grüntliche Underweysung, alles nutzes, so in dem edlen Instrument, Astrolabium genannt, begriffen, und erfunden würt/ denen so der lateinischen Sprach unverstendig/ doch liebhaber der Kunst/ erkannt trewlich verteütscht/ unnd durch den Truck außgegangen.* Augsburg: Otmar, 1525.

Dryander, Johann. *SPHERAE MATERIALIS.|| Siue globi coelestis. <Das ist> || Des Hymels lauff gründtliche außle=||gung/ so vil zur anleytung der Astro||nomie dienet/ mit vilen nützlichen regeln verfast/|| durch IOHAN DRYANDERN/ genent || Eychman/ ordinarien Medicum, der löblichen Vni=||uersiteten Marpurg/ von newem ver=||deütscht vnnd ann tag bracht.||.* Marburg: Johannis Dryander and Christian Egenolff d. Ä., 1539.

Fabri, Johannes and Wenceslaus Fabri. *Opus sphericum Johannis de sacro busto: figuris et p [er]utili co[m]mento illustratu[m].* Agrippine: Per Henricum Quentell, 1501.

Gersdorff, Hans von. *Stat vnd Feldtbůch || Bewerter Wundtartznei. New || Widerumb Ersehen. Zusampt dem Antidotari/|| Fürsorg vnd Vorrath der Chirurgei. Beschriben || von Herrn Vualthero Riuio, Medico.||. Zů Franckenfurt. Bei Christian Egenolff.||(M.D.LI.||).* Frankfurt: Christian Egenolff d.Ä., 1551.

Gersdorff, Hans von and Johannes Indagine. *Feldtbůch der Wund-Artzney: sampt vilen Instrumenten der Chirurgey; vß dem Albucasi contrafayt. Chiromantia Jo. Jndagine. das Ist, die Kunst der Handtbesehung. Natürliche Astrologey, ... Physiognomey, ... Complexion Buch. ... Canones, oder Regelen eins Yeden Kranckheyt Warlich zu Erkündigen ...* Strasbourg: Schott, 1540.

Gratarolo, Pomponio and Guglielmo Gratarolo. *Introductiones apotelesmaticae in physiognomiam, astrologiam naturalem, complexiones hominum, naturas planetarum. Cum periaxiomatibus de faciebus signorum ... Quibus ... accessit Gulielmi Grataroli ... opuscula De memoria reparanda, augenda, conservanda; De praedictione morum naturarumque hominum; De mutatione temporum ... et Pomponii Gaurici ... tractatus De symmetriis, lineamentis & physiognomia, ejusque speciebus, etc.* Ursellis: Apud Cornelium Sutorium, impensis Lazari Zetzneri, 1603.

Hier Inn Begriffne Pis, Zaigen Clärlich an, Wie Ain Yedess Roß, Iüng und Alt Soll Gezämbt, Dadurch Ime, Angenomene Pöse Gewonhait Ubelstandt, ... Benomen ... Werden Mag. VD 16 G 592. Augsburg[?], 1530.

Indagine, Joannes ab and Jan Berntsz. *Chyromantia ... Enn Dit Boec Leert van Drie Naturlike Consten Als Phisiognomia, Astrologia Naturalis, Chiromantia.* Utrecht: Jan Berntsz, 1536.

Indagine, Ioannes ab and Johannes Schott. *Introdvctiones Apoteles||maticæ elegantes, in Chyromantiam, Physiognomiam, || Astrologiam naturalem, Complexiones hominum, || Naturas planetarum. Cum periaxiomatibus de|| faciebus Signorum, & canonib. de ægritu-||dinibus, nusqua[m] fere simili tractata|| compendio.* Strasbourg: Schott, 1522.

Indagine, Johannes ab et al. *Die Kunst der Chiromantzey: vsz Besehung der Hend. Physiognomey / vsz Anblick des Menschens. Natürlichen Astrologey noch dem Lauff der*

Soñen. Complexion eins yegklichen Menschens. Natürlichen Ynflüssz der Planeten. der zwolff Zeichen Angesychten. Ettliche Canones / zu Erkantnüsz der Menschen Kranckheiten / solicher weisz vormals nye beschriben oder gedruckt. Zusamen verordnet / vnd verteütscht durch ... Strasbourg: Schott, 1523.

Jordan, Peter. *Geomantia.|| Kuenstlicher vnd rechtschaffner gebrauch || der alten kleynen Geomancey/ mit welcher durch hilff der || Rechnung vnd des menschen Tauffnamens/ sampt der || Planeten wirckung/ in jren stunden/ allen Adams || Kindern/ künfftiger zůfall des gůtten vnd || bœsen glücks erœffnet wirt.|| Zů sampt andern fünff ... || Tafeln ... || Mit beygesetztem kuenstlichen Jnstrument vñ regeln/|| ... ||.* Mainz: Peter Jordan, 1534.

Megenberg, Conradus. *Hye Nach Volget das Puch der Natur das Innhaltet zu dem Ersten von Eygenschafft und Natur des Menschen, Darnach von der Natur und Eygenschafft des Himels, der Tier des Gefügels[!], der Kreuter, der Steyn und von Vil Ander Natürlichen Dingen.* Augsburg: Baemler, 1475.

More, Thomas. *Libellus vere aureus nec Minvs Salvtaris Qvam Festiuus de optimo reip. statu, deq[ue] noua Insula Vtopia authore clarissimo viro Thoma Moro inclytæ ciuitatis Londinensis ciue & vicecomite cura M. Petri Aegidii Antuerpie[n]sis, & arte Theodorici Martini Alustensis, Typographi almæ Louaniensium Academiæ nunc primum accuratissime editus.* Louvain: Martini, 1516.

Münster, Sebastian. *Organum Uranicum: Habes in hoc Libro Amice Lector, Explicatas Theoricas Omnium planetaru[m], atq[ue] eorunde[m] varios, singulos & quotidianos ad annos usq[ue] & ultra expressos motus, Lunæ quoq[ue] in lumine crescentis, senesce[n]tis & per eclipsim deficientis, & item Solis deliquiu[m] patientis, omne[s] varietate[s] quibus omnibus comodi adiecti sunt canones.* Basel: Petri, 1536.

Ovidius Naso, Publius. *P. Ouidii Nasonis Metamorphoseon Libri XV. Index Repertorius, Omniu[m] Fabularum, Ad Numerum Chartarum, & Seriem Alphabeti, Illis [a]Ppositus Est.* Strasbourg: Schott, 1515.

Pelerin, Jean. *Von der Kunst Perspectiva.* Nuremberg: Georg Glockendon, 1509.

Regiomontanus, Johannes. *Calendarium... Dvctv Ioannis De Monteregio.* Nuremberg: Johannes Regiomontanus, 1474.

Kalendarius Johannis Künigspergers: News und Volmon ... Eyn schön Vergleichung der Astronomi mit der Artznei. Strasbourg: Cammerlander, 1532.

Regiomontanus, Johannes and Johannes Schöner. *Scripta clarissimi mathematici M. Ioannis Regiomontani, de torqueto, astrolabio armillari, regula magna ptolemaica, baculo [que] astronomico, & observationibus cometarum, aucta necessariis, Ioannis Schoneri ... additionibus. Item observationes motuum solis, ac stellarum tam fixarum [qua ...] erraticarum. Item libellus M. Georgii Purbachii de quadrato geometrico.* Nuremberg: Joannis Montanus and Ulricus Neuber, 1544.

Reisch, Gregorius. *Margarita Philosophica.* Strasbourg: Johannes Schott, 1504.

Rößlin, d.J., Eucharius. *Kalender mit allen As=||stronomischen haltungen. Von natürlichem Jnfluß der Gestirn/|| Planeten vnd Zeychen ... || ASTROLABIVM TETRAGONON.|| Ein gar kunstlich Astrolabium/ Alle wirck||ungen des Firmaments ... zefindenn. Durch ... || D.Eucharium Rößlin/ Statartzt zů Franck||furt am Meyn/ New añ tag geben.|| Register ... zů end des Kalenders.* Ed. Johannes Stöffler. Frankfurt: Christian Egenolff d.Ä., 1533.

Sacrobosco, Johannes de. *Ioannis De Sacrobusto Libellus, De Sphaera: Eiusdem Autoris Libellus, Cuius Titulus Est Computus, Eruditißimam Anni & Mensium Descriptionem Continens.* Ed. Philipp Melanchthon. Wittenberg: Jospeh Clug, 1538.

Sphaera Mundi: Eyn Anfang und Fundament der Astronomi/ Aus den Alten Astronomis dur Johannem de Sacro Busto ins Latin Zusamen Gesetzt und Nachmals Durch M. Cunrad Heynfogel von Nuremberg Verteutscht/ Unnd in Vier Teyl Getylt/ Deß Himmels Lauff Sampt Allem Gestirn/ Leichtlicher auß den bei Gesatzten Figuren Zuerlernen. Ed. Conrad Heinfogel. Strasbourg: Cammerlander, 1539.

Sphera Materialis: Eyn Anfang und Fundanment der Astronomi. Ed. Jakob Cammerlander and Conrad Heinfogel. Strasbourg: Cammerlander, 1533.

Sacrobosco, Johannes de and Peter Apian. *Sphaera Iani de Sacrobusto astronomiae ac cosmographiae candidatis scitu apprime necessaria.* Ingoldstadt: Peter and Georg Apian, 1526.

Sacrobosco, Johannes Regiomontanus and Georg von Peuerbach. *Spaerae Mvndi Co [m]pendiu[m] Foeliciter Inchoat.: Daran: Regiomontanus, Johannes: Disputationes contra Cremonensia in planetarum theoricas deliramenta. Mit Widmungsvorrede des Autors an die Gelehrten. – Peuerbach, Georg: Theoricae novae planetarum. Mit Gedicht auf die Drucker'Uranie quantum quantum* ... Venice: Johannes Lucilius Santritter and Hieronymus de Sanctis, 1488.

Solinus, Caius Julius, Joannes Camers, and Johann Singriener. *Joannis Camertis ... in C Julii Solini Polyistora Enarrationes. Additus Eiusdem Camertis Index.* Vienna: Alantse, 1520.

Stelluti, Francesco. *Della Fisonomia di Tvtto il Corpo Hvmano del S. Gio. Batta Della Porta. Acc. Linceo Libri Quattro Ne' Quali Si Tratta di Quanto Intorno a Questa Materia n' Hanno i Greci, Latini,e gli Arabi Schritto: Hora Bruemente in Tauole Sinottiche Ridotta et Ordinata.* Rome: Mascardi, 1637.

Tannstetter, Georg, Petrus Apian, and Witelo. *Vitellionis Ma/||thematici Doctissimi Peri Optikēs,|| Id Est de Natura, Ratione, & Proiectione Radiorum Uisus, Lu=||minum, Colorum At# Formarum, Quam Uul=||go Perspectiuam Uocant,|| LIBRI X.|| ... Omnia Ab Hoc Autore ... || Diligentissime Tradita ... || Nunc Primum Opera Mathematico# Praestantiss.Dd.Ge-||orgij Tanstetter & Petri Apiani in Lucem Aedita.||.* Nuremberg: Johann Petreius, 1535.

Vogtherr, Heinrich. *Ein Frembds und wunderbars Kunstbüchlin allen Molern, Bildschnitzern, Goldschmiden, Steinmetzen, Schreinern, Platnern, Waffen und Messerschmiden hochnutzlich zu gebrauchen.* Strasbourg: Vogtherr, 1537.

Ein newes hochnutzlichs Büchlin von Erkantnüs der Kranckeyten der Augen sampt einer Figur oder Anothomia eines Augs: wie es innwendig gestaltet, volget in der andern Colum: auch Erklärung der selbigen mit Anzeigung viler nutzlicher undbewerter Hülff als Purgation, Pflaster, Collirien, Sieff, Pulver, Salben und Augenwassern wie mans machen und gebrauchen soll, einem jeden Hausshalt nutzlich. Strasbourg: Heinrichen Vogtherr, 1538.

Ein Wolgegrindtes Kunstreichs Sumari Büchlin Aller Sonnen Uur Uff Acht Oder Viereckette Stecklen, Innbuchsen, Zylinder u. Guldine Ring, Auch Uff Glaß, Alle Mauren Schreg Oder Unschreg Zu Machen ... Strasbourg: Vogtherr, 1539.

SECONDARY SOURCES

Alpers, Svetlana. *The Art of Describing: Dutch Art in the Seventeenth Century.* Chicago: University of Chicago Press, 1983.

Andrews, Noam. "Albrecht Dürer's Personal *Underweysung der Messung.*" *Word & Image* 32, no. 4 (2016): 409–29.

The Polyhedrists: Art and Geometry in the Long Sixteenth Century. Cambridge, MA: MIT Press, 2022.

Areford, David S. *The Viewer and the Printed Image in Late Medieval Europe.* Farnham and Burlington, VT: Ashgate, 2010.

Areford, David S. and Nina A. Rowe, eds. *Excavating the Medieval Image.* Aldershot: Ashgate, 2004.

Ashcroft, Jeffrey. "Black Arts: Renaissance and Printing Press in Nuremberg, 1493–1528." *Forum for Modern Language Studies* 45, no. 1 (2008): 3–18.

Baigrie, Brian Scott, ed. *Picturing Knowledge: Historical and Philosophical Problems Concerning the Use of Art in Science.* Toronto: University of Toronto Press, 1996.

Baldasso, Renzo. "Illustrating the Book of Nature in the Renaissance: Drawing, Painting, and Printing Geometric Diagrams and Scientific Figures." PhD dissertation, Columbia University, 2007.

"The Role of Visual Representation in the Scientific Revolution: A Historiographic Inquiry." *Centaurus* 48 (2006): 69–88.

Balfe, Thomas, Joanna Woodall, and Claus Zittel. *Ad Vivum?: Visual Materials and the Vocabulary of Life-Likeness in Europe before 1800*. Leiden: Brill, 2019.

Barnes, Robin Bruce. *Astrology and Reformation*. New York: Oxford University Press, 2016.

Bauer, Barbara. "Die Rolle des Hofastrologen und Hofmathematicus als fürstlicher Berater." In August Buck, ed., *Höfischer Humanismus*. Weinheim: Acta Humaniora, 1989.

Baxandall, Michael. *The Limewood Sculptors of Renaissance Germany*. New Haven, CT: Yale University Press, 1980.

Painting and Experience in Fifteenth Century Italy: A Primer in the Social History of Pictorial Style. 2nd edition. New York: Oxford University Press, 1988.

Bennett, Jim. "Practical Geometry and Operative Knowledge." *Configurations: A Journal of Literature, Science and Technology* 6 (1998): 195–222.

Besse, Jean-Marc. "Cosmography and Geography in the Sixteenth Century: The Position of Oronce Fine between Mathematics and History." In Alexander Marr, ed., *The Worlds of Oronce Fine: Mathematics, Instruments and Print in Renaissance France*. Donington: Shaun Tyas, 2009.

"Mapping, Constructing, Inventing: On the Notion of Project and Its Epistemology." First published in *Le Gout du monde: Exercises de paysage*. Arles: Actes Sud/ ENSP, 2009.

Bishop, Malcom. "Ambrosius Holbein's Memento Mori Map for Sir Thomas More's Utopia: The Meanings of a Masterpiece of Early Sixteenth Century Graphic Art." *British Dental Journal* 199, no. 2 (2005): 107–12.

Blair, Ann. "Humanist Methods in Natural Philosophy: The Commonplace Book." *Journal of the History of Ideas* 53, no. 4 (1992): 541–51.

Too Much to Know: Managing Scholarly Information before the Modern Age. New Haven, CT and London: Yale University Press, 2011.

Blanchard, Donald L. "Vogtherr's *Büchlin*." *Documenta Ophthalmologica* 93 (1997): 73–9.

Bleichmar, Daniela. *Visible Empire: Botanical Expeditions and Visual Culture in the Hispanic Enlightenment*. Chicago: University of Chicago Press, 2012.

Boas, Marie. *The Scientific Renaissance 1450–1630*. New York: Harper and Row, 1962.

Bontea, Adriana. "Montaigne's *On Physiognomy*." *Renaissance Studies*, 22, no. 1 (2008): 41–62.

Boon, Karel G. "Frans Crabbe en de Monogrammist A.C." In *De Gulden Passer 52*. Antwerp: Nederlandse Boekhandel, 1974.

Bredekamp, Horst. "A Neglected Tradition? Art History as *Bildwissenschaft*." *Critical Inquiry* 29, no. 3 (2003): 418–28.

The Technical Image: A History of Styles in Scientific Imagery. Chicago: University of Chicago Press, 2015.

Bredekamp, Horst and Pablo Schneider. *Visuelle Argumentationen: die Mysterien der Reprasentation und die Berechenbarkeit der Welt*. Munich: Wilhelm Fink, 2006.

Bredekamp, Horst, Vera Dünkel, and Birgit Schneider. *Das Technische Bild: Kompendium zu einer Stilgeschichte wissenschaftlicher Bilder*. Berlin: Akademie Verlag, 2012.

Britton, Piers D. G. "The Signs of Faces: Leonardo on Physiognomic Science and the 'Four Universal States of Man.'" *Renaissance Studies* 16, no. 2 (2002): 143–62.

Brosseder, Claudia. *Im Bann der Sterne: Caspar Peucer, Philipp Melanchthon und andere Wittenberger Astrologen*. Berlin: Akademie Verlag, 2004.

"The Writing in the Wittenberg Sky: Astrology in Sixteenth-Century Germany." *Journal of the History of Ideas* 66 (2005): 557–76.

Browne, Thomas. *Religio medici*. Ed. Jean-Jacques Denonian. Cambridge: Cambridge University Press, 1953.

Brunner, Horst, Freimut Löser, and Dorothea Klein, eds. *Überlieferungsgeschichte transdisziplinär: neue Perspektiven auf ein germanistisches Forschungsparadigma*. Wiesbaden: Dr. Ludwig Reichert Verlag, 2016.

Buck, Stephanie et al. *Holbein, 1497–1543*. Cologne: Könemann, 1999.

Buren, Anne H. van and Sheila Edmunds. "Playing Cards and Manuscripts: Some Widely Disseminated Fifteenth-Century Model Sheets." *Art Bulletin* 56, no. 1 (1974): 12–30.

Burke, Peter. *Eyewitnessing: The Uses of Images as Historical Evidence*. Ithaca, NY: Cornell Paperbacks, 2008.

Burkhardt, Johannes and Mark Häberlein, eds. *Die Welser: Neue Forschungen zur Geschichte und Kultur des oberdeutschen Handelshauses*. Berlin: Akademie, 2002.

Cashion, Debra Taylor, Henry Luttikhuizen, and Ashley D. West, eds. *The Primacy of the Image in Northern European Art, 1400–1700: Essays in Honor of Larry Silver*. Leiden: Brill, 2017.

Catteneo, Angelo. "Map Projections and Perspective in the Renaissance." In Zur Shalev and Charles Burnett, eds., *Ptolemy's Geography in the Renaissance*. Warburg Institute Colloquia. London: Warburg Institute, 2011.

Challenger, Alexandra. "Printing the Cosmos: Images, Readers, and Mathematics in Peter Apian's Instrumental Texts." PhD dissertation, Florida State University, 2022.

Chojecka, Ewa. *Bayerische Bild-Enzyklopädie: das Weltbild eines wissenschaftlich-magischen Hausbuches aus dem frühen 16. Jahrhundert*. Studien zur Deutschen Kunstgeschichte, vol. 358. Baden-Baden: Verlag Valentin Koerner, 1982.

"Zur Stellung des gedruckten Bildes im 15. und 16. Jahrhundert: Zwischen Kunstwerk und 'Massenmedium.'" In *Reform, Reformation, Revolution: Ausgewählte Beiträge einer wissenschaftlichen Konferenz in Leipzig am 10. und 11. Oktober 1977*. Leipzig: Karl Marx Universität, 1980.

Chrisman, Miriam Usher. *Lay Culture, Learned Culture: Books and Social Change in Strasbourg, 1480–1599*. New Haven, CT: Yale University Press, 1982.

Clark, Stuart. *Vanities of the Eye: Vision in Early Modern European Culture*. Oxford: Oxford University Press, 2007.

Clayton, Martin. *Leonardo da Vinci: The Divine and the Grotesque*. London: Royal Collection, 2002.

"Leonardo's Gypsies, and the Wolf and the Eagle." *Apollo* 155, no. 486 (2002): 27–33.

Clement, Taylor. "Moveable Types: The De-individuated Portrait in the Age of Mechanical Reproduction." *Renaissance Studies* 31, no. 3 (2017): 383–406.

Clod, Random. "Information on Information." *Text* 5 (1991): 241–78.

Clough, Cecil. "Italian Renaissance Portraits and Printed Portrait Books." In Dennis V. Reidy, ed., *The Italian Book 1465–1800: Studies Presented to Dennis E. Rhodes on His 70th Birthday*. London: British Library, 1993.

Colding Smith, Charlotte. *Images of Islam, 1453–1600: Turks in Germany and Central Europe*. London: Pickering and Chatto, 2014.

Coldiron, A. E. B. *Printers Without Borders: Translation and Textuality in the Renaissance*. Cambridge: Cambridge University Press, 2015.

"Translation and Transformission; Or, Early Modernity in Motion." *Canadian Review of Comparative Literature / Revue Canadienne de Littérature Comparée* 46, no. 2 (2019): 205–16.

Comisso, Giovanni, ed. *Gli ambasciatori veneti, 1525–1792. Relazion di viaggio e di missione*. Milan: Longanesi, 1985.

Conley, Tom. *An Errant Eye: Poetry and Topography in Early Modern France*. Minneapolis: University of Minnesota Press, 2011.

The Self-Made Map: Cartographic Writing in Early Modern France. Minneapolis: University of Minnesota Press, 1996.

"A Topographer's Eye: From Gilles Corrozet to Pieter Apian." In Walter S. Melion and Lee Palmer Wandel, eds., *Early Modern Eyes*. Leiden: Brill, 2010.

Corbellini, Sabrina, Giovanna Murano, and Giacomo Signore. *Collecting, Organizing and Transmitting Knowledge: Miscellanies in Late Medieval Europe*. Turnhout: Brepols, 2018.

Cosgrove, Denis E. *Apollo's Eye: A Cartographic Genealogy of the Earth in the Western Imagination*. Baltimore: Johns Hopkins University Press, 2001.

"Images of Renaissance Cosmography." In David Woodward, ed., *The History of Cartography. Volume 3: Cartography in the European Renaissance*. Chicago and London: University of Chicago Press, 2007.

ed. *Mappings*. London: Reaktion Books, 1999.

Crisci, Edoardo and Oronzo Pecere. *Il codice miscellaneo: tipologie e funzioni: atti del convegno internazionale, Cassino 14–17 maggio 2003*. Cassino: University of Cassino, 2004.

Crowther, Kathleen M. and Peter Barker. "Training the Intelligent Eye: Understanding Illustrations in Early Modern Astronomy Texts." *Isis* 104, no. 3 (2013): 429–70.

Crowther, Kathleen M., Ashley Nicole McCray, Leila McNeill, Amy Rodgers, and Blair Stein. "The Book Everybody Read: Vernacular Translations of Sacrobosco's *Sphere* in the Sixteenth Century." *Journal for the History of Astronomy* 46, no. 1 (2015): 4–28.

Cuneo, Pia F. "Just a Bit of Control: The Historical Significance of Sixteenth- and Seventeenth-Century German Bit-Books." In Karen Raber, Treva J. Tucker, and Pia F. Cuneo, *The Culture of the Horse: Status, Discipline, and Identity in the Early Modern World*. New York: Palgrave Macmillan, 2005.

Cuneo, Pia F. and Alison G. Stewart, eds. *Animals and Early Modern Identity*. London: Routledge, 2014.

Cunningham, Andrew and Sachiko Kusukawa. *Natural Philosophy Epitomised: A Translation of Books 8–11 of Gregor Reisch's Philosophical Pearl (1503)*. Farnham: Ashgate, 2010.

Dackerman, Susan. *Prints and the Pursuit of Knowledge in Early Modern Europe*. Cambridge, MA and New Haven, CT: Harvard Art Museums, 2011.

Damm, Heiko, Michael Thimann, and Claus Zittel, eds. *The Artist as Reader: On Education and Non-Education of Early Modern Artists*. Leiden and Boston, MA: Brill, 2013.

Daston, Lorraine. "Epistemic Images." In Alina Alexandra Payne, *Vision and Its Instruments: Art, Science, and Technology in Early Modern Europe*. University Park: Pennsylvania State University Press, 2015.

"On Scientific Observation." *Isis* 99, no. 1 (2008): 97–110.

Daston, Lorraine and Elizabeth Lunbeck. *Histories of Scientific Observation*. Chicago: University of Chicago Press, 2011.

Daston, Lorraine and Fernando Vidal. *The Moral Authority of Nature*. Chicago: University of Chicago Press, 2010.

Daston, Lorraine and Peter Galison. *Objectivity*. New York: Zone Books, 2007.

Davis, Natalie Zemon. *The Return of Martin Guerre*. Cambridge, MA: Harvard University Press, 1981.

Dear, Peter Robert. *Revolutionizing the Sciences: European Knowledge in Transition, 1500–1700*. Oxford and London: Macmillan International Higher Education and Red Globe Press, 2019.

Dekker, Elly and Rudolf Schmidt. "The Globes in Holbein's Painting 'The Ambassadors.'" *Der Globusfreund: Bericht über das IX. Symposium der Internationalen Coronelli-Gesellschaft, Berlin, 3.–7. Oktober 1998* 47–8 (1999): 19–52.

Deleuze, Gilles. "Postscript on the Societies of Control." *October* (1992): 3–7.

Denucé, Jean. *De Antwerpsche "Konstkamers": Inventarissen van Kunstverzamelingen te Antwerpen in de 16e en 17e Eeuwen*. Antwerp: De Sikkel, 1932.

Depuydt, Joost. "The Utopia Map by Abraham Ortelius: New Home – New Research." *De Gulden Passer: Tijdschrift voor Boek Wetenschap* 97, no. 2 (2019): 242–6.

Desan, Philippe, ed. *Humanism in Crisis: The Decline of the French Renaissance*. Ann Arbor: University of Michigan Press, 1991.

Dodgson, Campbell. "Die Cäsarenköpfe, eine unbeschriebene Folge von Holzschnitten Hans Burgkmair d. Ä." In *Beiträge zur*

Geschichte der deutschen Kunst, Bd. II. Augsburg: Benno Filser, 1928.

Draxler, Sonja and Max E. Lippitsch. "Peter Apian and His Astronomicum Caesareum." In *Proceedings of the 2nd European History of Physics (EHoP) Conference*. Pöllauberg: Living Edition, 2012.

Dupré, Sven, ed. *Perspective as Practice: Renaissance Cultures of Optics*. Turnhout: Brepols, 2019.

"Printing Practical Mathematics: Oronce Fine's *De speculo ustorio* between Paper and Craft." In Alexander Marr, ed., *The Worlds of Oronce Fine: Mathematics, Instruments, and Print in Renaissance France*. Donington: Shaun Tyas, 2009.

"Trading Luxury Glass, Picturing Collections and Consuming Objects of Knowledge in Early Seventeenth-Century Antwerp." *Intellectual History Review* 20, no. 1 (2010): 53–78.

Dupré, Sven and Christopher Lüthy, eds. *Silent Messengers: The Circulation of Material Objects of Knowledge in the Early Modern Low Countries*. Berlin: Lit Verlag, 2012.

Dürer, Albrecht. *The Painter's Manual: A Manual of Measurement of Lines, Areas, and Solids by Means of Compass and Ruler Assembled by Albrecht Dürer for the Use of All Lovers of Art with Appropriate Illustrations Arranged to Be Printed in the Year MDXXV. The Literary Remains of Albrecht Dürer.* New York: Abaris Books, 1977.

Dürer, Albrecht and Hans Rupprich. *Schriftlicher Nachlaß*, vol. 2. Berlin: Deutscher Verein für Kunstwissenschaft, 1966.

Dürer, Albrecht, Daniel Hess, and Thomas Eser. *Der frühe Dürer*. Nuremberg: Verlag des Germanischen Nationalmuseums, 2012.

Dürer, Albrecht, Franz Louis Fuhse, and Konrad Lange. *Dürers schriftlicher Nachlass auf Grund der Originalhandschriften und theilweise neu entdeckter alter Abschriften*. Halle an der Saale: Niemeyer, 1893.

Eamon, William. *Science and the Secrets of Nature: Books of Secrets in Medieval and Early Modern Culture*. Princeton, NJ: Princeton University Press, 1996.

Edgerton, Samuel Y. *The Renaissance Rediscovery of Linear Perspective*. New York: Basic Books, 1975.

Eisenstein, Elizabeth L. *The Printing Press as an Agent of Change: Communications and Cultural Transformations in Early-Modern Europe*. Cambridge and New York: Cambridge University Press, 1979.

Elkins, Jim. *Visual Literacy*. New York: Routledge, 2008.

Ellenbogen, Josh and Adam Jolles. "Visual Literacy and 1960s Photography." *Critical Inquiry Critical Inquiry* 47, no. 3 (2021): 565–91.

Emison, Patricia A. "Prolegomenon to the Study of Italian Renaissance Prints." *Word & Image* 11, no. 1 (1995): 1–15.

Enenkel, K. A. E. and Wolfgang Neuber, eds. *Cognition and the Book: Typologies of Formal Organisation of Knowledge in the Printed Book of the Early Modern Period*. Leiden and Boston, MA: Brill, 2005.

Engammare, Max. *Calendrier des bergers*. Paris: Presses Universitaires de France, 2008.

Eser, Thomas. "Ordnende Dinge in unordentlichen Zeiten die 'kulturelle Gelegenheit' des 16. Jahrhunderts." In Thomas Eser and Stephanie Armer, eds., *Luther, Kolumbus und die Folgen: Welt im Wandel 1500–1600*. Nuremberg: Germanisches Nationalmuseum, 2017.

Schiefe Bilder – die Zimmernsche Anamorphose und andere Augenspiele aus den Sammlungen des Germanischen Nationalmuseums. Nuremberg: Verlag des Germanischen Nationalmuseums, 1998.

Falk, Tilman, Isolde Lübbeke, and Rolf Biedermann. *Hans Burgkmair: 1473–1973: Das Graphische Werk*. Augsburg: Städtische Kunstsammlungen, 1973.

Farago, Claire J. *Reframing the Renaissance: Visual Culture in Europe and Latin America, 1450–1650*. New Haven, CT: Yale University Press, 1995.

Farago, Claire J., Janis Callen Bell, Carlo Vecce, and Martin Kemp. *The Fabrication of Leonardo da Vinci's Trattato della Pittura, with a Scholarly Edition of the Editio Princeps (1651) and an Annotated English Translation*. Leiden and Boston, MA: Brill, 2018.

Ferckel, Christian. "Eine Bilderhandschrift v. J. 1524." *Mitteilungen zur Geschichte der Medizin und der Naturwissenschaften* 12. Leipzig and Hamburg: Leopold Voss Verlag, 1913.

Ferrari, Michele C. *Le monde en images: Deux encyclopédies manuscrites à Erlangen et à Cracovie*. Art de l'enluminure 76. Dijon: Éditions Faton, 2021.

Findlen, Paula. *Possessing Nature: Museums, Collecting, and Scientific Culture in Early Modern Italy*. Berkeley: University of California Press, 1994.

Foucault, Michel et al. *The Birth of Biopolitics: Lectures at the Collège de France 1978–79*. Basingstoke: Palgrave Macmillan, 2008.

The Order of Things: An Archaeology of the Human Sciences. New York: Vintage Books, 1994.

Fransen, Sietske. "Antoni van Leeuwenhoek, His Images and Draughtsmen." *Perspectives on Science* 27, no. 3 (2019): 485–544.

Freedberg, David. *The Eye of the Lynx: Galileo, His Friends, and the Beginnings of Modern Natural History*. Chicago: University of Chicago Press, 2002.

Friedländer, M. "Nicolas Hogenberg und Frans Crabbe die Maler von Mechelen." *Jahrbuch der Preuszischen Kunstsammlungen* 42, no. 4 (1921): 161–8.

Friedrich, Michael and Cosima Schwarke. *One-Volume Libraries: Composite and Multiple-Text Manuscripts*. Berlin and Boston, MA: De Gruyter, 2016.

Funke, Jutta. "Beiträge zum graphischen Werk Heinrich Vogtherrs d.Ä." Dissertation, Freie Universität, Berlin, 1967.

Gagel, Hanna, ed., *Der Mensch um 1500: Werke aus Kirchen und Kunstkammern*, 2nd edition. Berlin: Felgentreff & Goebel, 1977.

Gaida, Margaret. "Reading Cosmographia: Peter Apian's Book-Instrument Hybrid and the Rise of the Mathematical Amateur in the Sixteenth Century." *Early Science and Medicine* 21, no. 4 (2016): 277–302.

Gastel, Joris van, Tannis Hadjinicolaou, and Markus Rath, eds. *Paragone als Mitstreit*. Berlin: Akademie Verlag, 2014.

Gaudio, Michael. *The Bible and the Printed Image in Early Modern England: Little Gidding and the Pursuit of Scriptural Harmony*. New York: Routledge, 2017.

Engraving the Savage: The New World and Techniques of Civilization. Minneapolis: University of Minnesota Press, 2008.

Gelfand, Laura Deborah and Sarah Blick, eds. *Push Me, Pull You: Physical and Spatial Interaction in Late Medieval and Renaissance Art*. Leiden and Boston, MA: Brill, 2011.

Gessner, Samuel. "The Perspective of the Instrument Maker: The Planispheric Projection with Gemma Frisius and the Arsenius Workshop at Louvain." In Sven Dupré, ed., *Perspective as Practice: Renaissance Cultures of Optics*. Turnhout: Brepols, 2019.

"The Use of Printed Images for Instrument-Making at the Arsenius Workshop." In Nicholas Jardine and Isla Fay, *Observing the World through Images: Diagrams and Figures in the Early-Modern Arts and Sciences*. Leiden and Boston, MA: Brill, 2014.

Gingerich, Owen. "Astronomical Paper Instruments with Moving Parts." In Robert Anderson, Jim Bennett, and W. F. Ryan, eds., *Making Instruments Count: Essays on Historical Scientific Instruments Presented to Gerard L'Estrange Turner*. Aldershot: Variorum, 1993.

"Sacrobosco as a Textbook." *Journal for the History of Astronomy* 19, no. 4 (1988): 269–73.

Gordon, Andrew and Bernhard Klein. *Literature, Mapping, and the Politics of Space in Early Modern Britain*. Cambridge: Cambridge University Press, 2010.

Grafton, Anthony. *Commerce with the Classics: Ancient Books and Renaissance Readers*. Ann Arbor: University of Michigan Press, 1997.

"Some Uses of Eclipses in Early Modern Chronology." *Journal of the History of Ideas* 64, no. 2 (2003): 213–29.

Green, Jonathan. *Printing and Prophecy: Prognostication and Media Change 1450–1550*.

Ann Arbor: University of Michigan Press, 2012.

Greenblatt, Stephen Jay. *Renaissance Self-Fashioning from More to Shakespeare.* Chicago: University of Chicago Press, 2005.

Grimm, Melanie, Claudia Kleine-Tebbe, and Ad Stijnman. *Lichtspiel und Farbenpracht: Entwicklungen des Farbdrucks 1500–1800: aus den Beständen der Herzog-August-Bibliothek.* Wiesbaden: Harrassowitz, 2011.

Groebner, Valentin. "Complexio/Complexion: Categorizing Individual Natures, 1250–1600." In Lorraine Daston and Fernando Vidal, *The Moral Authority of Nature.* Chicago: University of Chicago Press, 2010.

Grotefend, H. *Christian Egenolff der erste ständige Buchdrucker zu Frankfurt a. M.* Frankfurt: K. T. Völcker's Verlag, 1881.

Haag, Sabine et al., eds. *Die Kunstkammer: die Schätze der Habsburger.* Vienna: Brandstätter Verlag, 2012.

Hall, Bert S. "*Der Meister sol auch kennen schreiben und lesen*: Writings about Technology ca. 1400–ca. 1600 AD and Their Cultural Implication." In Denise Schmandt-Besserat, *Early Technologies.* Malibu, CA: Undena Publications, 1979.

Hamel, Jürgen. *Studien zur "Sphaera" des Johannes de Sacrobosco.* Leipzig: Akademische Verlagsanstalt, 2014.

Hardman, Phillipa and Nicola Bradbury. *Medieval and Early Modern Miscellanies and Anthologies. The Yearbook of English Studies*, vol. 33. Leeds: Maney Publishing for the Modern Humanities Research Association, 2003.

Haskell, Francis. *History and Its Images: Art and the Interpretation of the Past.* New Haven, CT: Yale University Press, 1993.

Hayton, Darin. *The Crown and the Cosmos. Astrology and the Politics of Maximilian I.* Pittsburgh: University of Pittsburgh Press, 2015.

Heesen, Anke te. *The World in a Box: The Story of an Eighteenth-Century Picture Encyclopedia.* Chicago: University of Chicago Press, 2002.

Heitzmann, Christian. *Die Sterne Lügen Nicht: Astrologie und Astronomie im Mittelalter und in der Frühen Neuzeit.* Wiesbaden: Harrassowitz, 2008.

Henry, Chriscinda. "Leonardo da Vinci, Parody, and Pictorial Magic." In Allison M. Levy, ed., *Playthings in Early Modernity: Party Games, Word Games, Mind Games.* Kalamazoo: Medieval Institute Publications, Western Michigan University, 2017.

Herrmann, F. "Der Astrolog Johannes Indagine, Pfarrer zu Steinheim a.M., und die Frankfurter Kaiserwahl des Jahres 1519." *Archiv für Hessische Geschichte und Alterthumskunde* 18 (1934): 274–91.

Hindman, Sandra. *The Early Illustrated Book Essays in Honor of Lessing Julius Rosenwald.* Washington, DC: Library of Congress, 1982.

Hofmann, Werner. *Köpfe der Lutherzeit.* Munich: Prestel, 1983.

Holländer, Hans, ed. *Erkenntnis, Erfindung, Konstruktion: Studien zur Bildgeschichte von Naturwissenschaften und Technik von 16. bis zum 19. Jahrhundert.* Berlin: Gebr. Mann, 2000.

Hollstein, F. W. H. et al. *Hollstein's German Engravings Etchings and Woodcuts 1400–1700*, vol. 30. Amsterdam: M. Hertzberger, 1991.

Hoogstede, Luuk et al. *Hieronymus Bosch, Painter and Draughtsman: Technical Studies.* New Haven, CT: Yale University Press, 2016.

Hoskin, Michael, ed. *The Cambridge Concise History of Astronomy.* Cambridge: Cambridge University Press, 1999.

Ivins, William Mills. *Prints and Visual Communication.* New York: Da Capo Press, 1969.

Jardine, Nicholas and Isla Fay. *Observing the World through Images: Diagrams and Figures in the Early-Modern Arts and Sciences.* Leiden and Boston, MA: Brill, 2014.

Jaumann, Herbert. *Handbuch Gelehrtenkultur der frühen Neuzeit.* Berlin: Walter de Gruyter, 2004.

Johns, Adrian. *The Nature of the Book: Print and Knowledge in the Making.* Chicago: University of Chicago Press, 2009.

"The Uses of Print in the History of Science." *Papers of the Bibliographical Society of America* 107, no. 4 (2013): 393–420.

Johnson, Christine R. *The German Discovery of the World: Renaissance Encounters with the Strange and Marvelous*. Charlottesville: University of Virginia Press, 2008.

Johnston, Sky Michael. "Printing the Weather: Knowledge, Nature, and Popular Culture in Two Sixteenth-Century German Weather Books." *Renaissance Quarterly* 73, no. 2 (2020): 391–440.

Jones, Alexander. *Ptolemy in Perspective: Use and Criticism of His Work from Antiquity to the Nineteenth Century*. Dordrecht: Springer, 2010.

Karr Schmidt, Suzanne Kathleen. "Art – A User's Guide: Interactive and Sculptural Printmaking in the Renaissance." PhD dissertation, Yale University, 2006.

Interactive and Sculptural Printmaking in the Renaissance. Leiden and Boston, MA: Brill, 2018.

"Memento Mori: The Deadly Art of Interaction." In Laura Deborah Gelfand and Sarah Blick, eds., *Push Me, Pull You: Imaginative and Emotional Interaction in Late Medieval and Renaissance Art*. Leiden and Boston, MA: Brill, 2011.

Karr Schmidt, Suzanne and Kimberly Nichols. *Altered and Adorned: Using Renaissance Prints in Daily Life*. Chicago and New Haven, CT: Art Institute of Chicago, distributed by Yale University Press, 2011.

Karr Schmidt, Suzanne Kathleen and Edward H. Wouk. *Prints in Translation, 1450–1750: Image, Materiality, Space*. Abingdon: Routledge, 2017.

Kaune, Daniel. "Vom Grenzstein zum Augenschein: von der Essenz und Relevanz eines Kartentypus." BA/MA thesis, Gottfried Wilhelm Leibniz Universität, Hannover, n.d.

Kemp, Martin. "Temples of the Body and Temples of the Cosmos: Vision and Visualization in the Vesalian and Copernican Revolutions." In Brian Scott Baigrie, ed., *Picturing Knowledge: Historical and Philosophical Problems Concerning the Use of Art in Science*. Toronto: University of Toronto Press, 1996.

Kinsman, Robert Starr. *The Darker Vision of the Renaissance: Beyond the Fields of Reason*. Berkeley and Los Angeles: University of California Press, 1974.

"Folly, Melancholy, and Madness: A Study in the Shifting Styles of Medical Analysis and Treatment, 1450–1675." In Robert Starr Kinsman, *The Darker Vision of the Renaissance: Beyond the Fields of Reason*. Berkeley and Los Angeles: University of California Press, 1974.

Klein, Alice. "Hans Wechtlin and the Production of German Colour Woodcuts." In Ad Stijnman and Elizabeth Savage, eds., *Printing Colour 1400–1700: History, Techniques, Functions and Receptions*. Leiden: Brill, 2015.

"Hans Wechtlin, peintre à Strasbourg à la veille de la Réforme." PhD dissertation, Université Paris-Sorbonne, 2014.

Klein, M. "Les Physiognomistes haut-rhénans du XVIe siècle." In *Atti del XIV Congresso internazionale di storia della medicina sotto l'Alto Patronato del Presidente della Repubblica, Roma – Salerno, 13–20 settembre 1954*. Rome: Guerra & Belli, 1960.

Klibansky, Raymond, Erwin Panofsky, and Fritz Saxl. *Saturn and Melancholy: Studies in the History of Natural Philosophy, Religion, and Art*. New York: Basic Books, 1964.

Klinger Aleci, Linda. "Images of Identity: Italian Portrait Collections of the Fifteenth and Sixteenth Centuries." In Nicholas Mann and Luke Syson, eds., *The Image of the Individual: Portraits in the Renaissance*. London: British Museum Press, 1998.

Klinger, Linda Susan. *The Portrait Collection of Paolo Giovio*. Ann Arbor: UMI Dissertation Services, 2003.

Koerner, Joseph Leo. *The Moment of Self-Portraiture in German Renaissance Art*. Chicago: University of Chicago Press, 1996.

Kohl, Jeanette and Dominic Olariu. "En face: seven essays on the human face." In *Kritische Berichte: Zeitschrift für Kunst-*

und Kulturwissenschaften 40. Marburg: Jonas Verlag, 2012.

Korner, Hans. *Der früheste deutsche Einblattholzschnitt.* Munich: Mäander Kunstverlag, 1979.

Kremer, Richard L. "Incunable Almanacs and *Practica* as Practical Knowledge Produced in Trading Zones." In Matteo Valleriani, ed., *The Structures of Practical Knowledge.* Cham: Springer, 2017.

"Playing with Geometrical Tools: Johannes Stabius's Astrolabium Imperatorium (1515) and Its Successors." *CNT Centaurus* 58, nos. 1–2 (2016): 104–34.

Kruyfhooft, Cécile. "A Recent Discovery: Utopia by Abraham Ortelius." *Map Collector* 16 (1981): 10–14.

Küchler, Susanne and Walter S. Melion. *Images of Memory: On Remembering and Representation.* Washington, DC: Smithsonian Institution Press, 1991.

Kuhoff, Wolfgang. "Markus Welser als Erforscher des römischen Augsburg." In Johannes Burkhardt and Mark Häberlein, eds., *Die Welser: Neue Forschungen zur Geschichte und Kultur des oberdeutschen Handelshauses.* Berlin: Akademie, 2002.

Kusukawa, Sachiko. "Leonhart Fuchs on the Importance of Pictures." *Journal of the History of Ideas* 58, no. 3 (1997): 403–27.

Picturing the Book of Nature: Image, Text, and Argument in Sixteenth-Century Human Anatomy and Medical Botany. Chicago: University of Chicago Press, 2011.

The Transformation of Natural Philosophy: The Case of Philip Melanchthon. Cambridge and New York: Cambridge University Press, 1995.

Kusukawa, Sachiko and Ian Maclean. *Transmitting Knowledge: Words, Images, and Instruments in Early Modern Europe.* Oxford and New York: Oxford University Press, 2006.

Kwakkelstein, Michael W. *Leonardo da Vinci as a Physiognomist: Theory and Drawing Practice.* Leiden: Primavers Pers, 2014.

"Leonardo da Vinci's Recurrent Use of Patterns of Individual Limbs, Stock Poses and Facial Stereotypes." In I. Ciulisova, ed., *Artistic Innovations and Cultural Zones.* Spectrum Slovakia 7. Berlin: Peter Lang, 2015.

"The Lost Book on 'Moti Mentali.'" In Claire J. Farago, *Leonardo's Writings and Theory of Art.* New York: Garland, 1999.

Landau, David and Peter W. Parshall. *The Renaissance Print, 1470–1550.* New Haven, CT: Yale University Press, 1994.

Lattis, James M. "Christopher Clavius and the 'Sphere' of Sacrobosco: The Roots of Jesuit Astronomy on the Eve of the Copernican Revolution." PhD dissertation, University of Wisconsin-Madison, 1989.

Laube, Reinhard and Helmut Zäh, eds. *Gesammeltes Gedächtnis: Konrad Peutinger und die kulturelle Überlieferung im 16. Jahrhundert.* Lucerne: Quaternio Verlag, 2016.

Lefèvre, Wolfgang, ed. *Picturing Machines, 1400–1700.* Cambridge, MA: MIT Press, 2004.

Leibsohn, Dana and Jeanette Favrot Peterson, eds. *Seeing across Cultures in the Early Modern World.* Burlington, VT: Ashgate, 2012.

Leitch, Stephanie. "Dürer's Rhinoceros Underway: The Epistemology of the Copy in the Early Modern Print." In Debra Taylor Cashion, Henry Luttikhuizen, and Ashley D. West, eds., *The Primacy of the Image in Northern European Art, 1400–1700: Essays in Honor of Larry Silver.* Leiden: Brill, 2017.

Mapping Ethnography in Early Modern Germany: New Worlds in Print Culture. Basingstoke: Palgrave Macmillan, 2010.

"Visual Acuity and the Physiognomer's Art of Observation." *Oxford Art Journal* 38, no. 2 (2015): 187–206.

Lester, Toby. *The Fourth Part of the World: An Astonishing Epic of Global Discovery, Imperial Ambition and the Birth of America.* New York: Free Press, 2010.

Lestringant, Frank. "The Crisis of Cosmography at the End of the Renaissance." In Philippe Desan, ed., *Humanism in Crisis: The Decline*

of the French Renaissance. Ann Arbor: University of Michigan Press, 1991.
Levy, Allison M., ed. *Playthings in Early Modernity: Party Games, Word Games, Mind Games*. Kalamazoo: Medieval Institute Publications, Western Michigan University, 2017.
Lindberg, David Charles. "Alhazen's Theory of Vision and Its Reception in the West." *Isis* 58, no. 3 (1967): 321–41.
Loh, Maria H. "Renaissance Faciality." *Oxford Art Journal* 32, no. 3 (2009): 341–63.
Long, Pamela O., David McGee, and Alan M. Stahl, eds. *The Book of Michael of Rhodes: A Fifteenth-Century Maritime Manuscript*. Cambridge, MA: MIT Press, 2009.
Lowe, Dunstan. "Suspending Disbelief Magnetic and Miraculous Levitation from Antiquity to the Middle Ages." *Classical Antiquity* 35, no. 2 (2016): 247–78.
Luther, Martin and Wilhelm Martin Leberecht de Wette. *Dr. Martin Luthers Briefe, Sendschreiben und Bedenken ... Gesammelt, Kritisch und Historisch Bearbeitet von Dr W. M. L. de Wette*. Berlin: Reimer, 1825.
Lüthy, Christoph and Alexis Smets. "Words, Lines, Diagrams, Images: Towards a History of Scientific Imagery." *Early Science and Medicine* 14 (2009): 398–439.
Lutze, Eberhard. *Die Bilderhandschriften der Universitätsbibliothek Erlangen*. Wiesbaden: Otto Harrassowitz, 1971.
MacDonald, Katherine. "Humanistic Self-Representation in Giovan Battista Della Porta's 'Della Fisonomia dell'Uomo': Antecedents and Innovation." *Sixteenth Century Journal* 36, no. 2 (2005): 397–414.
Machilek, Franz. "Astronomie und Astrologie: Sternforschung und Sternglaube im Verständnis von Johannes Regiomontanus und Benedikt Ellwanger." *Astronomie und Astrologie in der Frühen Neuzeit: Akten des Interdisziplinären Symposions* 21, no. 22 (1990): 11–32.
Maier, Jessica. *Rome Measured and Imagined: Early Modern Maps of the Eternal City*. Chicago: University of Chicago Press, 2015.
Maniaci, Marilena. "Miscellaneous Reflections on the Complexity of the Medieval Manuscripts." In Sabrina Corbellini, Giovanna Murano, and Giacomo Signore, *Collecting, Organizing and Transmitting Knowledge: Miscellanies in Late Medieval Europe*. Turnhout: Brepols, 2018.
Mann, Heinz Herbert. "Optische Instrumente." In Hans Holländer, ed., *Erkenntnis, Erfindung, Konstruktion: Studien zur Bildgeschichte von Naturwissenschaften und Technik von 16. bis zum 19. Jahrhundert*. Berlin: Gebr. Mann, 2000.
Marr, Alexander. "Copying, Commonplaces and Technical Knowledge: The Architect-Engineer as Reader." In Heiko Damm, Michael Thimann, and Claus Zittel, eds., *The Artist as Reader: On Education and Non-Education of Early Modern Artists*. Leiden and Boston, MA: Brill, 2013.
"Ingenuity in Nuremberg: Dürer and Stabius's Instrument Prints." *Art Bulletin* 100, no. 3 (2018): 48–79.
"Knowing Images: A Review Essay." *Renaissance Quarterly* 69, no. 3 (2016): 1000–13.
"Walther Ryff, Plagiarism and Imitation in Sixteenth Century Germany." *Print Quarterly* 31, no. 2 (2014): 131–43.
ed. *The Worlds of Oronce Fine: Mathematics, Instruments, and Print in Renaissance France*. Donington: Shaun Tyas, 2009.
Marr, Alexander and Christopher P. Heuer "Introduction: The Uncertainty of Epistemic Images." *21: Inquiries into Art, History, and the Visual* 1, no. 2 (2020): 251–5.
Massey, Lyle. *Picturing Space, Displacing Bodies: Anamorphosis in Early Modern Theories of Perspective*. University Park: Pennsylvania State University Press, 2007.
McDonald, Mark P. *The Paper Museum of Cassiano dal Pozzo: A Catalogue Raisonné: Drawings and Prints in the Royal Library at Windsor Castle, the British Museum, the Institut de France and Others Collections. Series C – Prints Part One: Ceremonies, Costumes, Portraits and Genre*. London: Harvey Miller, 2017.

The Print Collection of Ferdinand Columbus: 1488–1539: A Renaissance Collector in Seville. London: British Museum Press, 2004.

Melion, Walter and Lee Palmer Wandel, eds. *Early Modern Eyes.* Leiden: Brill, 2010.

Merback, Mitchell B. *Perfection's Therapy: An Essay on Albrecht Dürer's Melencolia I.* New York: Zone Books, 2017.

"Recognitions: Theme and Metatheme in Hans Burgkmair the Elder's Santa Croce in Gerusalemme of 1504." *Art Bulletin* 96, no. 3 (2014): 288–318.

Mertens, Sabine, Elke Purpus, and Cornelia Schneider. *Blockbücher des Mittelalters: Bilderfolgen als Lektüre: Gutenberg-Museum, Mainz, 22. Juni 1991 bis 1. September 1991.* Mainz am Rhein: von Zabern, 1991.

Metzger, Christoph. "'Wie man den Menschen erkennen soll': Neue Überlegungen zu den Charakterstudien Hans Schäufelins, mit einem Technologischen Anhang von Monika Strolz." *Jahrbuch des Kunsthistorischen Museums Wien* 12 (2010): 8–39.

Meurer, Peter. "Cartography in the German Lands, 1450–1650." In David Woodward, ed., *The History of Cartography. Volume 3: Cartography in the European Renaissance.* Chicago and London: University of Chicago Press, 2007.

Miller, Clarence et al. *Utopia.* New Haven, CT: Yale University Press, 2001.

Mitchell, W. J. Thomas. *Picture Theory: Essays on Verbal and Visual Representation.* Chicago: University of Chicago Press, 2014.

Montaigne. *The Essays of Michel de Montaigne.* Trans. and ed. M. A. Screech. London: Allen Lane, 1991.

Morrison, James E. *The Astrolabe.* Rehoboth Beach, DE: Janus, 2007.

Mosley, Adam. "The Cosmographer's Role in the Sixteenth Century: A Preliminary Study." *Archives Internationales d'Histoire des Sciences* 59 (2009): 424–39.

"Early Modern Cosmography: Fine's *Sphaera Mundi* in Content and Context." In Alexander Marr, ed., *The Worlds of Oronce Fine: Mathematics, Instruments, and Print in Renaissance France.* Donington: Shaun Tyas, 2009.

Moss, Ann. "Locating Knowledge." In K. A. E. Enenkel and Wolfgang Neuber, eds., *Cognition and the Book: Typologies of Formal Organisation of Knowledge in the Printed Book of the Early Modern Period.* Leiden and Boston, MA: Brill, 2005.

Printed Commonplace-Books and the Structuring of Renaissance Thought. Oxford: Clarendon Press, 2000.

Müller, Christian et al. *Dürer, Holbein, Grünewald: Meisterzeichnungen der Deutschen Renaissance aus Berlin und Basel.* Basel and Berlin: Öffentliche Kunstsammlung, Staatlichen Museen, and Preussischer Kulturbesitz, 1997.

Hans Holbein the Younger: The Basel Years, 1515–1532. Munich: Prestel, 2006.

Muller, Frank. *Heinrich Vogtherr l'Ancien: un artiste entre Renaissance et Réforme.* Wiesbaden: Harrassowitz, 1997.

Müller, Jan-Dirk. "Evidentia und Medialität. Zur Ausdifferenzierung von Evidenz in der Frühen-Neuzeit." In Gabriele Wimböck et al., eds., *Evidentia. Reichweiten visueller Wahrnehmung in der Frühen Neuzeit.* Berlin: Lit Verlag, 2007.

Müller-Jahncke, Wolf Dieter. "Melanchton und die Astrologie: Theoretisches und Mantisches." In Frank Günter and Stefan Rhein, eds., *Melanchthon und die Naturwissenschaften Seiner Zeit.* Sigmaringen: Jan Thorbecke, 1998.

Mundy, Barbara E. *The Mapping of New Spain: Indigenous Cartography and the Maps of the Relaciones Geográficas.* Chicago: University of Chicago Press, 1996.

Münkner, Jörn. *Eingreifen und Begreifen: Handhabungen und Visualisierungen in Flugblättern der Frühen Neuzeit.* Berlin: Erich Schmidt, 2008.

Nelson, Jennifer. "Directed Leering: Social Perspective in Erhard Schön's Anamorphic Woodcuts." *Source: Notes in the History of Art* 34, no. 4 (2015): 17–22.

Disharmony of the Spheres: The Europe of Holbein's Ambassadors. University Park: Pennsylvania State University, 2019.

Nichols, Stephen G. and Siegfried Wenzel. *The Whole Book: Cultural Perspectives on the Medieval Miscellany*. Ann Arbor: University of Michigan Press, 1996.

North, John David. *The Ambassadors' Secret: Holbein and the World of the Renaissance*. London: Phoenix, 2004.

Noyes, Ruth S. "Mattheus Greuter's Sunspot Etchings for Galileo Galilei's Macchie Solari (1613)." *Art Bulletin* 98, no. 4 (2016): 466–87.

ed. *Reassessing Epistemic Images in the Early Modern World*. Amsterdam: Amsterdam University Press, 2022.

Nuti, Lucia. "Mapping Places: Chorography and Vision in the Renaissance." In Denis E. Cosgrove, ed., *Mappings*. London: Reaktion Books, 1999.

Ogilvie, Brian W. *The Science of Describing: Natural History in Renaissance Europe*. Chicago: University of Chicago Press, 2006.

Olariu, Dominic. "Herbs under Pressure: Plant Illustrations and Nature Printing in the First Half of the Fifteenth Century." In Robert Felfe and Maurice Saß, *Naturalismen*. Berlin: De Gruyter, 2019.

The Misfortune of Philippus de Lignamine's Herbal or New Research Perspectives in Herbal Illustrations from an Iconological Point of View. Berlin: Max-Planck-Institut für Wissenschaftsgeschichte, 2015.

Oldenbourg, Maria C. *Die Buchholzschnitte des Hans Baldung Grien: Ein Bibliographisches Verzeichnis ihrer Verwendungen*. Baden-Baden: Verlag Heitz, 1962.

Olson, Todd. "Markers: *Le Moyne de Morgues* in Sixteenth-Century Florida." In Dana Leibsohn and Jeanette Favrot Peterson, eds., *Seeing across Cultures in the Early Modern World*. Burlington, VT: Ashgate, 2012.

Oosterhoff, Richard J. "A Book, a Pen, and the Sphere: Reading Sacrobosco in the Renaissance." *History of Universities* 28, no. 2 (2015): 1–54.

Ortroy, Fernand van. *Bibliographie de l'oeuvre de Pierre Apian*. Amsterdam: Meridian, 1963.

Padron, Riccardo. "Mapping Imaginary Worlds." In James Ackerman et al., eds., *Maps: Finding Our Place in the World*. Chicago: University of Chicago Press, 2007.

Panofsky, Erwin. *Life and Art of Albrecht Dürer*. Princeton, NJ: Princeton University Press, 1995 [1943].

Perspective as Symbolic Form. Trans. Christopher S. Wood. New York: Zone Books, 1991.

Panse, Melanie. *Hans von Gersdorffs "Feldbuch der Wundarznei": Produktion, Präsentation und Rezeption von Wissen*. Wiesbaden: Reichert, 2012.

Park, Katherine. "Observation in the Margins, 500–1500." In Lorraine Daston and Elizabeth Lunbeck, *Histories of Scientific Observation*. Chicago: University of Chicago Press, 2011.

Parker, K. T. *The Drawings of Hans Holbein in the Collection of His Majesty the King at Windsor Castle*. Oxford: Phaidon Press, 1945.

Parshall, Peter. "The Art of Memory and the Passion." *Art Bulletin* 81 (1999): 456–72.

"Graphic Knowledge: Albrecht Dürer and the Imagination." *Art Bulletin* 95, no. 3 (2013): 395–410.

"*Imago Contrafacta*: Images and Facts in the Northern Renaissance." *Art History* 16, no. 4 (1993): 554–79.

"Prints as Objects of Consumption in Early Modern Europe." *Journal of Medieval and Early Modern Studies* 28, no. 1 (1998): 19–36.

"The Print Collection of Ferdinand, Archduke of Tyrol." *Jahrbuch der Kunsthistorischen Sammlungen in Wien* (1982): 139–90.

Parshall, Peter and David Landau. *The Renaissance Print 1470–1550*. New Haven, CT: Yale University Press, 1994.

Parshall, Peter and Rainer Schoch. *Origins of European Printmaking: Fifteenth-Century Woodcuts and Their Public*. New Haven, CT: Yale University Press, 2005.

Payne, Alina Alexandra. *Vision and Its Instruments: Art, Science, and Technology in*

Early Modern Europe. University Park: Pennsylvania State University Press, 2015.

Pericolo, Lorenzo. "Knowing through the Eye: Leonardo da Vinci's *Imprensiva* and Alhazen's *Intuitio*." *Römisches Jahrbuch der Bibliotheca Hertziana* 44 (2019–20): 205–61.

Perkinson, Stephen. "From an 'Art de Memoire' to the Art of Portraiture: Printed Effigy Books of the Sixteenth Century." *Sixteenth Century Journal* 33, no. 3 (2002): 687–723.

"Likeness." *Studies in Iconography* 33 (2012): 15–28.

The Likeness of the King: A Prehistory of Portraiture in Late Medieval France. Chicago: University of Chicago Press, 2009.

"Portraits and Counterfeits: Villard de Honnecourt and Thirteenth-Century Theories of Representation." In David S. Areford and Nina A. Rowe, eds., *Excavating the Medieval Image*. Aldershot: Ashgate, 2004.

Pfisterer, Ulrich. "Apelles im Norden: Ausnahme Künstler, Selbstbildnisse und die Gunst der Mächtigen um 1500." In Matthias Müller, ed., *Apelles am Fürstenhof*. Berlin: Coburger Landesstiftung, 2010.

Pinto, John A. "Origins and Development of the Ichnographic City Plan." *Journal of the Society of Architectural Historians* 35, no. 1 (1976): 35–50.

Pomata, Gianna. "Observation Rising: Birth of an Epistemic Genre, 1500–1650." In Lorraine Daston and Elizabeth Lunbeck, *Histories of Scientific Observation*. Chicago: University of Chicago Press, 2011.

Pon, Lisa. *A Printed Icon: Forlì's Madonna of the Fire*. New York: Cambridge University Press, 2015.

Popplow, Marcus. "Why Draw Pictures of Machines?: The Social Contexts of Early Modern Machine Drawings." In Wolfgang Lefèvre, ed., *Picturing Machines, 1400–1700*. Cambridge, MA: MIT Press, 2004.

Porras, Stephanie. "'Ein freie hant': Autonomy, Drawing and the Young Dürer." In Albrecht Dürer, Daniel Hess, and Thomas Eser, *Der frühe Dürer*. Nuremberg: Verlag des Germanischen Nationalmuseums, 2012.

Porter, Martin. *Windows of the Soul Physiognomy in European Culture 1470–1780*. Oxford: Clarendon Press and Oxford University Press, 2005.

Price, David. *In the Beginning Was the Image: Art and the Reformation Bible*. New York: Oxford University Press, 2021.

Ptolemaeus, Claudius. *Ptolemy's Geography: An Annotated Translation of the Theoretical Chapters*. Ed. John L. Berggren and Alexander Jones. Princeton, NJ: Princeton University Press, 2000.

Quicchelberg, Samuel, Mark A. Meadow, and Bruce Robertson. *The First Treatise on Museums: Samuel Quiccheberg's Inscriptiones, 1565*. Los Angeles: Getty Research Institute, 2013.

Raber, Karen, Treva J. Tucker, and Pia F. Cuneo. *The Culture of the Horse: Status, Discipline, and Identity in the Early Modern World*. New York: Palgrave Macmillan, 2005.

Ramachandran, Ayesha. *The Worldmakers: Global Imagining in Early Modern Europe*. Chicago: University of Chicago Press, 2015.

Rath, Markus. "Manipulation: Modellformung, Bildrelief und kubische Denkfigur als Moment des Mitstreits." In Joris van Gastel, Tannis Hadjinicolaou, and Markus Rath, eds., *Paragone als Mitstreit*. Berlin: Akademie Verlag, 2014.

Reeves, Eileen. *Painting the Heavens: Art and Science in the Age of Galileo*. Princeton, NJ: Princeton University Press, 1999.

Reidy, Dennis V., ed. *The Italian Book 1465–1800: Studies Presented to Dennis E. Rhodes on His 70th Birthday*. London: British Library, 1993.

Reisser, Ulrich. "Physiognomik und Ausdruckstheorie der Renaissance: der Einfluss charakterologischer Lehren auf Kunst und Kunsttheorie des 15. und 16. Jahrhunderts." Munich: Scaneg, 1997.

Remmert, Volker R. *Picturing the Scientific Revolution*. Philadelphia: Saint Joseph's University Press, 2011.

Remond, Jaya. "Artful Instruction: Pictorializing and Printing Artistic Knowledge in Early Modern Germany." *Word & Image* 36, no. 2 (2020): 101–34.

"Bodies of Knowledge: Movement, Variety and Imagination in a German Renaissance Art Primer." In Andreas Beyer and Guillaume Cassegrain, eds., *Mouvement. Bewegung.* Berlin: Deutscher Kunstverlag, 2015.

"The Kunstbüchlein: Printed Artists' Manuals and the Transmission of Craft in Renaissance Germany." PhD dissertation, Harvard University, 2014.

Rhodes, Neil and Jonathan Sawday. *The Renaissance Computer: Knowledge Technology in the First Age of Print.* London and New York: Routledge, 2000.

Richter Sherman, Claire et al. *Writing on Hands: Memory and Knowledge in Early Modern Europe.* Seattle: University of Washington Press, 2001.

Riello, Giorgio. "The World in a Book: The Creation of the Global in Sixteenth-Century European Costume Books." *Past & Present* 242, no. 14 (2019): 281–317.

Ritter, François. *Histoire de l'imprimerie alsacienne aux 15e et 16e siècles.* Strasbourg: Institut des Hautes Études Alsaciennes, 1955.

Roberts, Jane et al. *Drawings by Holbein from the Court of Henry VIII: Fifty Drawings from the Collection of Her Majesty the Queen, Windsor Castle.* New York: Harcourt Brace Jovanovich, 1988.

Ronsin, Albert, Pierre Monat, and Amerigo Vespucci. *La fortune d'un nom: America: le baptême du Nouveau Monde à Saint-Dié-des-Vosges.* Grenoble: J. Millon, 1991.

Roper, Lyndal. "'The Common Man', 'The Common Good', 'Common Women': Gender and Meaning in the German Reformation Commune." In Merry E. Wiesner, *Women and Gender in the Early Modern World: Critical Concepts in Women's History.* London: Routledge, 2016.

Rosen, Edward. *Copernicus and His Successors.* London: Hambledon Press, 1995.

Roth, Michael et al. *Dürers Mutter: Schönheit, Alter und Tod im Bild der Renaissance.* Berlin: Staatliche Museen zu Berlin and Nicolai, 2006.

Röttel, Karl. *Peter Apian: Astronomie, Kosmographie und Mathematik am Beginn der Neuzeit: Mit Ausstellungskatalog.* Buxheim: Polygon-Verlag, 1995.

Röttinger, Heinrich. "Hans Wechtlin." *Jahrbuch der Kunsthistorischen Sammlung der Allerhöchsten Kaiserhauses* 27 (1907–9).

"Die Holzschnitte der Druckerei des Jakob Cammerlander in Straßburg." *Gutenberg-Jahrbuch* 11 (1936): 125–40.

Rubiés, Joan-Pau. "Instructions for Travellers: Teaching the Eye to See." In Joan-Pau Rubiés, *Travellers and Cosmographers: Studies in the History of Early Modern Travel and Ethnology.* Aldershot: Ashgate, 2007.

Rudolph, Pia. "Hausbücher. Bayerische Bild-Enzyklopädien." In Ulrike Bodemann et al. (eds.), *Katalog der deutschsprachigen illustrierten Handschriften des Mittelalters (KdiH).* Munich: C. H. Beck, 2015.

Rudy, Kathryn M. *Rubrics, Images and Indulgences in Late Medieval Netherlandish Manuscripts.* Leiden: Brill, 2017.

Rupprich, Hans and Albrecht Dürer. *Schriftlicher Nachlass*, vol. 1. Berlin: Deutscher Verein für Kunstwissenschaft, 1956.

Ryan, W. F. and Charles B. Schmitt. *Pseudo-Aristotle, the Secret of Secrets: Sources and Influences.* London: Warburg Institute, University of London, 1982.

Sacré, Dirk, Erik de Bom, Demmy Verbeke, and Gilbert Tournoy. *Utopia & More: Thomas More, de Nederlanden en de utopische traditie: catalogus bij de tentoonstelling in de Leuvense Universiteitsbibliotheek, 20 oktober 2016–17 januari 2017.* Louvain: Leuven University Press, 2016.

San Juan, Rose Marie. *Vertiginous Mirrors: The Animation of the Visual Image and Early Modern Travel.* Manchester: Manchester University Press, 2011.

Sarton, George. *The Appreciation of Ancient and Medieval Science during the Renaissance (1450–1600).* Philadelphia: University of Pennsylvania Press, 1955.

Sauter, Michael J. *The Spatial Reformation: Euclid between Man, Cosmos, and God*. Ann Arbor: University of Michigan Press, 2019.

Sawday, Jonathan. *The Machine Mind: Technology and Culture in the European Renaissance*. London: Routledge, 2007.

Schauerte, Thomas Ulrich, ed. *Deutschlands Auge & Ohr: Nürnberg als Medienzentrum der Reformationszeit*. Nuremberg: Tümmel Verlag, 2015.

Scheller, Robert. *A Survey of Medieval Model Books*. Haarlem: De Erven F. Bohn, 1963.

Schenda, Rudolf. "Der 'gemeine Mann' und sein medikales Verhalten im 16. und 17. Jahrhundert." In Joachim Telle, ed., *Pharmazie und der gemeine Mann: Hausarznei und Apotheke in der frühen Neuzeit: erläutert anhand deutscher Fachschriften der Herzog-August-Bibliothek Wolfenbüttel und pharmazeutischer Geräte des Deutschen Apotheken-Museums Heidelberg*. Weinheim: VCH, Acta Humaniora, 1988.

Scher, Stephen K. *The Currency of Fame: Portrait Medals of the Renaissance*. New York: Abrams, 1994.

ed. *Perspectives on the Renaissance Medal*. New York: Garland Publishing and American Numismatic Society, 2000.

Schmandt-Besserat, Denise. *Early Technologies*. Malibu, CA: Undena Publications, 1979.

Schmitt, Jean-Claude. "Enzyklopädismus und Bild-Enzyklopädien im Mittelalter." In the proceedings of *Die Welt im Bild. Bildenzykopädien um 1500*. Conference at Friedrich-Alexander Universität Erlangen, July 13–15, 2022.

L'Histoire en lignes et en rondelles: les figures du temps chretien au Moyen Age. Wiesbaden: Reichert Verlag, 2015.

Penser par figure: du compas divin aux diagrammes magiques. Paris: Arkhê, 2019.

Schön, Erhard, Leo Baer, and Christoph Zell. *Unterweisung der Proportion und Stellung der Possen, Nürnberg 1542*. Frankfurt: J. Baer & Co., 1920.

Schöner, Christoph. *Mathematik und Astronomie an der Universität Ingolstadt im 15. und 16. Jahrhundert*. Berlin: Duncker & Humblot, 1994.

Schottenloher, Karl. "Die Druckprivilegien des 16. jahrhunderts." *Gutenberg Jahrbuch* (1933): 89–110.

Die Landshuter Buchdrucker des 16. Jahrhunderts. Nieuwkoop: B. de Graaf, 1967.

Scodel, Joshua. "The Affirmation of Paradox: A Reading of Montaigne's 'De La Phisionomie' (III:12)." *Yale French Studies* 64 (1983): 209–37.

Shalev, Zur and Charles Burnett, eds. *Ptolemy's Geography in the Renaissance*. Warburg Institute Colloquia. London: Warburg Institute, 2011.

Shapin, Steven. *Scientific Revolution*. Chicago: University of Chicago Press, 2019.

Sherman, Claire Richter and Brian P. Copenhaver. *Writing on Hands: Memory and Knowledge in Early Modern Europe*. Seattle: University of Washington Press, 2001.

Shirley, John W. and F. David Hoeniger, eds. *Science and the Arts in the Renaissance*. Washington, DC and London: Folger Shakespeare Library and Associated University Presses, 1985.

Shirley, Rodney W. *The Mapping of the World: Early Printed World Maps, 1472–1700*. Riverside, CT: Early World Press, 2001.

Silver, Larry. *Art and Dis-Illusion in the Long Sixteenth Century*. Leiden: Brill, 2023.

"The Face Is Familiar: German Renaissance Portrait Multiples in Print and Medals." *Word & Image* 19, no. 1 (2003): 6–21.

"World of Wonders: Exotic Animals in European Imagery, 1515–1650." In Pia F. Cuneo and Alison G. Stewart, eds., *Animals and Early Modern Identity*. London: Routledge, 2014.

Smith, Bruce R. *The Key of Green: Passion and Perception in Renaissance Culture*. Chicago: University of Chicago Press, 2009.

Smith, Jeffrey Chipps. "A Creative Moment: Thoughts on the Genesis of the German Portrait Medal." In Stephen Scher, ed.,

Perspectives on the Renaissance Medal. New York: Garland Press, 2000.

ed. *Visual Acuity and the Arts of Communication in Early Modern Germany*. Abingdon: Routledge, 2018.

Smith, Pamela H. *The Body of the Artisan: Art and Experience in the Scientific Revolution*. Chicago: University of Chicago Press, 2012.

"Making as Knowing: Craft as Natural Philosophy." In Pamela H. Smith, Amy R. W. Meyers, and Harold J. Cook, *Ways of Making and Knowing: The Material Culture of Empirical Knowledge*. New York: Bard Graduate Center, 2017.

Smith, Pamela H., Amy R. W. Meyers, and Harold J. Cook. *Ways of Making and Knowing: The Material Culture of Empirical Knowledge*. New York: Bard Graduate Center, 2017.

Snyder, John P. "Map Projections in the Renaissance." In David Woodward, ed., *The History of Cartography. Volume 3: Cartography in the European Renaissance*. Chicago and London: University of Chicago Press, 2007.

Söll-Tauchert, Sabine. *Hans Baldung Grien (1484/85–1545): Selbstbildnis und Selbstinszenierung*. Cologne: Böhlau, 2010.

Sorce, Francesco. "Metafore in bianco e nero: Propaganda antiturca nelle stampe di Nicolò Nelli." In Francesco Sorce, ed., *En Blanc et Noir: Studi in onore di Silvana Macchioni*. Rome: Campisano Editore, 2007.

Spiller, Elizabeth. *Science, Reading, and Renaissance Literature: The Art of Making Knowledge, 1580–1670*. Cambridge: Cambridge University Press, 2007.

Stafford, Barbara Maria. *Artful Science: Enlightenment, Entertainment, and the Eclipse of Visual Education*. Cambridge, MA: MIT Press, 1994.

Body Criticism: Imaging the Unseen in Enlightenment Art and Medicine. Cambridge, MA and London: MIT Press, 1997.

Stemmler, Joan K. "The Physiognomical Portraits of Johann Caspar Lavater." *Art Bulletin* 75 (1993): 151–68.

Stephenson, Bruce, Marvin Bolt, and Anna Felicity Friedman. *The Universe Unveiled: Instruments and Images through History*. New York: Cambridge University Press, 2000.

Stewart, Alison G. *Before Bruegel: Sebald Beham and the Origins of Peasant Festival Imaginery*. Hampshire: Ashgate, 2008.

Stijnman, Ad and Elizabeth Savage. *Printing Colour 1400–1700: History, Techniques, Functions and Receptions*. Boston, MA: Brill, 2015.

Stock, Jan Van der, ed. *In Search of Utopia: Art and Science in the Era of Thomas More*. Leuven and Amsterdam: Davidsfonds Uitgeverij and Amsterdam University Press, 2016.

Stoichita, Victor, Anne-Marie Glasheen, and Lorenzo Pericolo. *The Self-Aware Image: An Insight into Early Modern Metapainting*. London: Harvey Miller, 2015.

Stopp, Frederick J. *The Emblems of the Altdorf Academy: Medals and Medal Orations, 1577–1626*. London: Modern Humanities Research Association, 1974.

Strauss, Walter L. *The Complete Drawings of Albrecht Dürer. Volume 3: 1510–1519*. New York: Abaris, 1974.

The Human Figure by Albrecht Dürer: The Complete "Dresden Sketchbook." New York: Dover Publications, 1972.

Stubbe, Wolf. "Unbekannte Zeichnungen altdeutscher Meister." In Wolf Stubbe et al., eds., *Museum und Kunst: Beiträge für Alfred Hentzen*. Hamburg: Christians, 1970.

Taape, Tillmann. "Common Medicine for the Common Man: Picturing the 'Striped Layman' in Early Vernacular Print." *Renaissance Quarterly* 74 (2021): 1–58.

Talbot, Charles. "Topography as Landscape in Early Printed Books." In Sandra Hindman, *The Early Illustrated Book Essays in Honor of Lessing Julius Rosenwald*. Washington, DC: Library of Congress, 1982.

Telle, Joachim, ed. *Pharmazie und der gemeine Mann: Hausarznei und Apotheke in der frühen Neuzeit: erläutert anhand deutscher Fachschriften der Herzog-August-Bibliothek Wolfenbüttel und pharmazeutischer Geräte des Deutschen Apotheken-Museums Heidelberg.* Weinheim: VCH, Acta Humaniora, 1988.

Tessicini, Dario. "Definitions of 'Cosmography' and 'Geography' in the Wake of 15th and 16th Century Translations and Editions of Ptolemy's Geography." In Zur Shalev and Charles Burnett, eds., *Ptolemy's Geography in the Renaissance.* Warburg Institute Colloquia. London: Warburg Institute, 2011.

Thorndike, Lynn. *A History of Magic and Experimental Science.* New York: Columbia University Press, 1941.

"The Problem of the Composite Manuscript." In *Giovanni Mercati: Miscellanea Giovanni Mercati.* Vatican City: Biblioteca Apostolica Vaticana, 1946.

Thorndike, Lynn and Joannes de Sacro Bosco, eds. *The Sphere of Sacrobosco and Its Commentators. Corpus of Mediaeval Scientific Texts: Volume 2.* Chicago: University of Chicago Press, 1949.

Turner, Anthony John. *Early Scientific Instruments: Europe 1400–1800.* London: Sotheby's Publications, 1987.

Valleriani, Matteo, ed. *De Sphaera of Johannes de Sacrobosco in the Early Modern Period: The Authors of the Commentaries.* Cham: Springer, 2020.

The Structures of Practical Knowledge. Cham: Springer, 2017.

van Buren, Anne H. and Sheila Edmunds. "Playing Cards and Manuscripts: Some Widely Disseminated Fifteenth-Century Model Sheets." *Art Bulletin* 56, no. 1 (1974): 12–30.

vanden Broecke, Steven. *The Limits of Influence: Pico, Louvain and the Crisis of Renaissance Astrology.* Leiden and Boston, MA: Brill, 2003.

"The Use of Visual Media in Renaissance Cosmography: The Cosmography of Peter Apian and Gemma Frisius." *Paedagogica Historica* 36, no. 1 (2000): 130–50.

Van der Stock, Jan. *In Search of Utopia: Art and Science in the Era of Thomas More.* Leuven: Davidsfonds Uitgeverij, 2016.

Van Duzer, Chet. "Johann Schöner's Globe of 1515: Transcription and Study." *Transactions of the American Philosophical Society* 100, no. 5 (2010): 1–217.

van Gastel, Joris, Tannis Hadjinicolaou, and Markus Rath, eds. *Paragone als Mitstreit.* Berlin: Akademie Verlag, 2014.

Van Leerdam, Andrea. "Talking Heads. The Visual Rhetoric of Recurring Scholar Woodcuts in a Sixteenth-Century Handbook on Chiromancy." *Jaarboek voor Nederlandse Boekgeschiedenis* 26 (2019): 11–29.

van Ortroy, Fernand. *Bibliographie de l'oeuvre de Pierre Apian.* Amsterdam: Meridian, 1963.

Van Putten, Jasper. *Networked Nation: Mapping German Cities in Sebastian Münster's "Cosmographia."* Leiden: Brill, 2018.

Veltman, Kim H. "Ptolemy and the Origins of Linear Perspective." In *Atti del Convegno Internazionale di Studi Tenutosi al Castello Sforzesco, Civiche Raccolte d'Arte di Milano, dall'11 al 15 Ottobre del 1977.* Florence: Centro Di, 1980.

Vogtherr, Heinrich. "Heinrich Vogtherr: Ein frembds und wunderbars Kunstbüchlin allen Molern/ Bildschnitzern/ Goldschmiden/ Steinmetzen/ Schreinern/ Platnern/ Waffen und Messerschmiden hochnutzlich zu gebrauchen (Straßburg 1538/1572) herausgegeben und kommentiert von Maria Heilmann." Ed. Maria Heilmann, *FONTES* 61 (2011).

Voigt, Lisa and Elio Brancaforte. "The Traveling Illustrations of Sixteenth-Century Travel Narratives." *PMLA* 129, no. 3 (2014): 365–98.

Vorholt, Hanna. *Shaping Knowledge: The Transmission of the Liber Floridus.* London: Warburg Institute, 2017.

Wade, Mara. "The Emblems of the Altdorf Academy: Emblematic Pedagogy and Nuremberg Civic Culture." *Histories of Universities* XXXIV, no. 2 (2021): 137–70.

Walsby, Malcolm and Graeme Kemp. *The Book Triumphant: Print in Transition in the Sixteenth and Seventeenth Centuries.* Leiden and Boston, MA: Brill, 2011.

West, Ashley. "Conrad Peutinger and the Visual Arts: Collaborating with Hans Burgkmair the Elder." In Reinhard Laube and Helmut Zäh, eds., *Gesammeltes Gedächtnis: Konrad Peutinger und die kulturelle Überlieferung im 16. Jahrhundert*. Lucerne: Quaternio Verlag, 2016.

Westman, Robert S. "The Astronomer's Role in the Sixteenth Century: A Preliminary Study." *History of Science* 18 (1980): 105–47.

Wetter, Evelin, Frits Scholten, and Jeffrey Chipps Smith. *Prayer-Nuts, Private Devotion and Early Modern Art Collecting*. Riggisberg: Abegg-Stiftung, 2017.

Williams, Steven J. "Roger Bacon and the *Secret of Secrets*." In Jeremiah Hackett, ed., *Roger Bacon and the Sciences*. Leiden: Brill, 1997.

The Secret of Secrets: The Scholarly Career of a Pseudo-Aristotelian Text in the Late Middle Ages. Ann Arbor: University of Michigan Press, 2003.

Wilson, Bronwen. "Learning How to Read: Giovanni Battista Della Porta, Physiognomy, and Printed Portrait-Books." Paper delivered at Visual Knowledges Conference, University of Edinburgh, 17–20 September 2003.

"Reflecting on the Turk in Late Sixteenth-Century Venetian Portrait Books." *Word & Image* 19, no. 1 (2003): 38–58.

The World in Venice: Print, the City and Early Modern Identity. Toronto: University of Toronto Press, 2005.

Winkler, Friedrich. *Die Zeichnungen Albrecht Dürers*. Berlin: Deutscher Verein für Kunstwissenschaft, 1938.

Wood, Christopher S. *Forgery, Replica, Fiction: Temporalities of German Renaissance Art*. Chicago: University of Chicago Press, 2008.

Woodward, David, ed. *The History of Cartography. Volume 3: Cartography in the European Renaissance*. Chicago and London: University of Chicago Press, 2007.

Yanni, Carla. *Nature's Museums*. Princeton, NJ: Princeton Architectural Press, 2005.

Zagorin, Perez. *Ways of Lying*. Cambridge, MA: Harvard University Press, 2014.

Zelen, Joyce. *Blinded by Curiosity: The Collector-Dealer Hadriaan Beverland (1650–1716)*. Leiden: Primavera Pers, 2022.

Ziegeler, Joseph, "Philosophers and Physicians on the Scientific Validity of Latin Physiognomy, 1200–1500." *Early Science and Medicine* 12, no. 3 (2007): 285–312.

Zinner, Ernst. *Deutsche und niederländische astronomische Instrumente des 11.–18. Jahrhunderts*. 2nd ed. Munich: Beck, 1967.

Regiomontanus: His Life and Work. Amsterdam: North-Holland, 1990.

INDEX